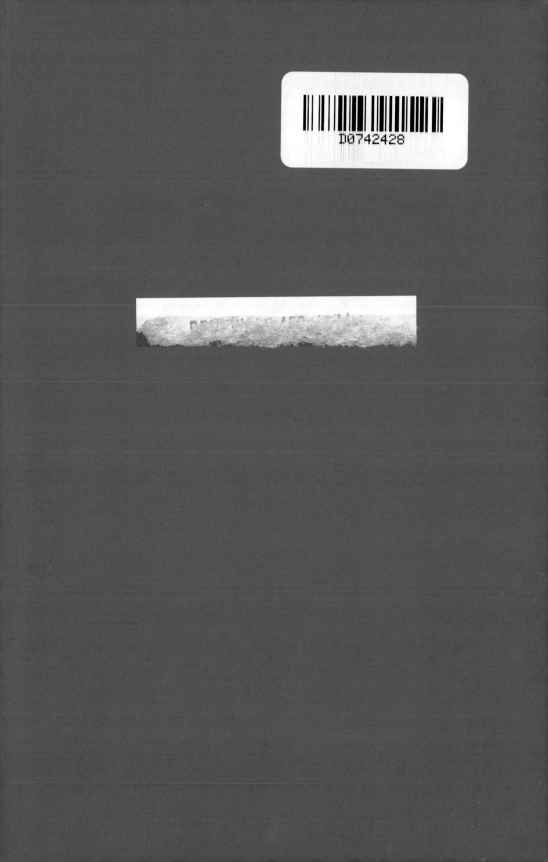

**Education, Culture, and Identity
in Twentieth-Century China**

Education, Culture, and Identity in Twentieth-Century China

Edited by
GLEN PETERSON, RUTH HAYHOE,
and YONGLING LU

Ann Arbor
THE UNIVERSITY OF MICHIGAN PRESS

2004   2003   2002   2001   4   3   2   1

A CIP catalog record for this book is available from the British Library.

Library of Congress Cataloging-in-Publication Data

Education, culture, and identity in twentieth-century China / edited by
    Glen Peterson, Ruth Hayhoe, and Yongling Lu.
        p.   cm.
    Includes bibliographical references and index.
    ISBN 0-472-11151-5 (alk. paper)
        1. Education—China—History—20th century.   I. Peterson, Glen.
    II. Hayhoe, Ruth.   III. Lu, Yongling, 1962–

LA1131.81 .E38   2001
370'.951—dc21   2001027376

Contents

Introduction

Glen Peterson and Ruth Hayhoe

Educational pursuits run like a rich thread through the social, cultural, and political fabric of China's turbulent twentieth century. The century opened with educational reform as the cornerstone of an ailing effort by the last imperial dynasty to save itself and the country from collapse. In 1902 the Qing government decreed the creation of a modern public school system for the first time in China's history. The Qing dynasty fell in 1911, but "saving the country through education" (*jiaoyu jiuguo*) became the rallying cry of several subsequent generations of Chinese social and political reformers. Critics of this embrace assailed what they considered to be a naively optimistic faith in the "omnipotence of education" (*jiaoyu wanneng*) to solve China's myriad problems, and they seem to have had history on their side. China could only be "saved" through the fires of political and social revolution, at least as far as its ability finally to stand up and establish itself as an independent socialist nation. Still, when one looks back to the period of the 1920s and 1930s, it is hard to escape the conclusion that many of the most innovative developments, in terms of new ideas and institution building, occurred within the world of education. Liberal and conservative educators like Tao Xingzhi, Liang Shuming, and Yan Yangchu (James Yen), who led the great mass education experiments of the 1920s and 1930s, are prime examples of such creativity. Communist revolutionaries also embraced education. As Suzanne Pepper has recently shown, the link between education and political radicalism spanned the century, culminating in the Cultural Revolution vision of education as the "training of revolutionary successors" (*peiyang wuchan jieji jieban ren*).[1] In recent years China's post-Mao leaders have accorded education a central role in their quest for rapid modernization, from Deng Xiaoping's call for education to "face modernization, the world and the future" in the early 1980s to Jiang Zemin's slogan of "science and education to revitalize the nation" (*kejiao xingguo*) in the late 1990s. Long regarded as a civilization that placed a high value on education, China in the twentieth century has continued to uphold the primacy of education in economic, political, social, and cultural life.

This study seeks to build upon the foundations created by several existing works on the history of Chinese education in the periods preceding the twentieth century. Especially noteworthy are two recent major studies, one on the formation of the Neo-Confucian educational tradition in the Song period (960–1280) and the other on the role of education in late imperial China. Wm. T. De Bary and John Chaffee's aptly titled compilation, *Neo-Confucian Education: The Formative Stage,* underscored the wide-ranging influence that Song Neo-Confucian educators such as Zhu Xi (1130–1200) had upon Chinese cultural life, influences that were to last through the Yuan, Ming, and Qing dynasties.[2] Ever since the era of Confucius (551–479 B.C.E.) Chinese thinkers had stressed the importance of education as a means for self-cultivation and recruiting "men of talent" to administer the affairs of the state. The value that Chinese culture traditionally placed on education, both for self-enlightenment and the service of the state, was greatly strengthened following the appearance in the Song dynasty of a revived metaphysical strand of Confucian moral philosophy incorporating elements of Daoism and Buddhism, known as *Daoxue* (Studies of the Way) and today as Neo-Confucianism. Within a century the influence of this new brand of philosophy grew well beyond the realm of Confucian academicians. Elevated to state orthodoxy during the succeeding Yuan dynasty (1280–1368), it was eventually internalized by tens of thousands of civil service candidates. In combination with the Ming (1368–1644) institutionalization of the civil service examination system, Neo-Confucian education affected cultural attitudes toward literacy and learning at all levels of society. Its universalistic claims also exerted a profound normative influence on the construction of the family, of gender roles, and of social attitudes toward female education. Historians have only just begun to investigate the significance of these latter aspects of the Neo-Confucian legacy.

The question of what sorts of Neo-Confucian education actually emerged after the Song period is taken up by Benjamin Elman and Alexander Woodside's splendidly conceived volume, *Education and Society in Late Imperial China.* The volume seeks, in the editors' words, "to probe beneath the educational ideals enunciated by Neo-Confucian philosophers and get a more precise historical glimpse of how education actually was practiced in China from 1600 until 1900."[3] Accordingly, the contributors to this volume were concerned not only with the detailed workings of classical education but also with identifying the multiple forms of education that were available beyond the elite competition for examination success and literati prestige, for commoners, women, and non-Han minority peoples.

Our understanding of the history of Chinese education before the twentieth century is heavily indebted to these two major complementary studies. Thus far, however, there have been no studies that attempt to do something similar for the history of education in China's tumultuous twentieth century.

This book seeks to fill that gap with a multidisciplinary study of the history of education in China from 1900 to the closing years of the century. Our decision to take the twentieth century as the focus of inquiry is based on the major transformations in educational thought and practice that occurred at the turn of the century. The 1902 and 1904 school regulations formally dethroned the Neo-Confucian orthodoxy in education that had prevailed since the Song period.[4] The abolition of the centuries-old civil service examination system in 1905 destroyed the structure of the old education system. Thus, within the space of a few years following 1900 the Neo-Confucian orthodoxy that had been the foundation of Chinese education for more than seven centuries was swept away. In its place rose a complex new pedagogy that stressed universal literacy and education's role in the creation of the modern Chinese nation.[5] Since then every national government in China has looked to modern education to perform the essential tasks of nation building: the creation of a unified, loyal, and economically productive citizenry.

If the existence of an optimistic faith in education's power to forge the modern nation has been a permanent feature of the twentieth-century Chinese view of education, it is also true that there has been an equally pervasive, more or less permanent sense of dissatisfaction with the actual state of education in each succeeding period. This dissatisfaction has often been based on a trenchant critique of the alleged inherent failings of modern schooling, ranging from allegations of its imported nature, urban bias, and elitist character to charges of chronic underfunding and even deliberate official neglect. Indeed, this critique fueled a steady stream of educational reform thought and action that began almost from the moment modern schools were introduced at the turn of the century and continues down to the present. The year 1900 thus marks a logical starting point for this study, as the point in time at which Neo-Confucian education was discarded for a modern model that has ever since served to enchant and disillusion in roughly equal measure. We leave it up to future historians to decide whether the close of the twentieth century also represents a turning point in the history of Chinese education.

Turning from general definitions to more specific questions concerning the meanings of education, we have found it fruitful to conceive of education in terms of its constituent activities. The best way to grasp the significance of these activities in the changing contexts of the twentieth century is to begin by locating them on the broader historical canvas of Chinese educational thought and practice. In their introduction to *Education and Society in Late Imperial China* Woodside and Elman refer to the "three inexhaustible categories of 'teaching' (*jiao*), 'learning' (*xue*) and 'culture/literature' (*wen*)" that made up the corpus of educational pursuits in the late imperial period.[6] Teaching, in the late imperial context, referred to the production of a classically educated elite and to the socialization, through exhortation and ritual, of commoners. Learning, as Tu Wei-ming had earlier pointed out, encompassed a complex set of "interrelated visions" involving poetic, political, social, historical, as well as metaphysical forms of knowledge.[7] Social distinctions also pervaded late imperial conceptions of learning. Thus, this vision applied mainly to the classically educated elite, while elite-prescribed definitions of commoner learning emphasized the acquisition of essential notions of moral order and ritual obligation. Written culture in the late imperial context encompassed all aspects of elite literary behavior, ranging from the literary and stylistic standards of bureaucratic communication and the proper use of examination prose to elite anxiety over the corrupting influence of popular novels and the infiltration of Daoist and Buddhist vocabulary. To what extent did educational activities in China after 1900 resemble these categories?

Teaching remained a category of central concern to twentieth-century educators as well as to political leaders and revolutionaries. Indeed, teaching was invested with a new and even greater significance in the context of twentieth-century pedagogy and its association of universal education with the goals of national wealth and power. The officially understood premise of teaching was transformed from the former Confucian one of producing and reproducing a classically educated elite and of socializing commoners to one of creating a disciplined and economically productive citizenry for the modern nation. At first glance, the association of universal education with national power—including the requirements of state building and of revolutionary politics—would seem to have lent renewed impetus to the Confucian pedagogical notion of the "unity of teaching and politics" (*zhengjiao heyi*). As the essays by Nina Borevskaya and Ningsha Zhong and Ruth Hayhoe in this volume clearly show, however, the history of Chinese education in the twentieth century is also replete with repeated demands and strivings for educational autonomy and for the separation of education and politics.

Learning was also cut loose from its Neo-Confucian moorings after 1900. Neo-Confucian theories of learning, with their emphases upon rote memorization, group discussion, gradual accumulation and digestion of ancient textual knowledge over years, and the internalization of moral truths were gradually displaced by the appearance and growing popularity among educators and academics of modern theories of learning psychology, introduced from the West and later from the Soviet Union. In addition, there also took place what may be described as the disenchantment of learning, as Neo-Confucian understandings of the nature and accumulation of knowledge were gradually displaced by the twentieth century's growing emphasis on secular learning, utilitarian knowledge, and vocational study. Finally, education as a process involving the acquisition and transmission of written culture was subject to sustained attempts to change and destabilize its received meanings since 1900. The social and cultural prestige of classical learning—not to mention its usefulness as the means to an official career—was fatally undermined by the abolition of the civil service examination system in 1905. The residual status of classical learning was further eroded, at least among China's more educated urban citizens, by the root and branch condemnation of an undifferentiated Chinese "tradition" espoused by Chinese intellectuals during the May Fourth period.

Finally, serious analysis of the twentieth-century fate of traditional written culture must also take into account the varying cultural projects of the diverse political regimes that have ruled China this century. It is well-known that traditional written culture was denigrated in socialist China and that its academic study, greatly diminished after 1949, could occur only within the limited confines of a strictly Marxist framework. What may be less well-known, however, is the extent to which, as shown by Zheng Yuan in this volume, successive political regimes in the first half of the century continued, despite otherwise widely varying ideologies, to uphold the cultural claims of Confucianism, as expressed in their respective school curricula. And yet, taken together, the essays that make up this book make it abundantly clear that the twentieth century in China has been marked above all by the absence of cultural consensus. Seen from a historical perspective, the creative tensions in Chinese education over the past one hundred years have been firmly rooted in the century's profound and continuous sense of cultural uncertainty, questioning, and contestation on the part of individuals, social groups, and states.

The idea for the present volume originated in early 1995 as a result of a lecture that one of us, Ruth Hayhoe, gave at the University of British Columbia. In the discussion that followed she suggested the need for a comprehensive volume on twentieth-century Chinese education that would complement the recently published study of *Education and Society in Late Imperial China* edited by Elman and Woodside. There was immediate agreement on the need for a study that would illuminate the complex relation between "educational theory and actual processes of education, learning, and socialization" as well as providing a historical portrait of the role that education has played in twentieth-century China, in a way that aspired to achieve what Elman and Woodside had done for the imperial period.[8]

Too often, the role of education in twentieth-century Chinese history has been seen mainly as a derivative of politics and studied mainly by political scientists. This may be understandable, given the importance that Chinese political leaders have attached to education throughout the twentieth century and the strength of the belief that educational revolution must accompany political revolution. Nonetheless, it has served to obscure the dynamic aspects of education as a social and cultural force in its own right. This book tries to avoid a reductionist tendency that regards education as a mere reflection of politics and societal conditions or which treats education simply as socialization. Our approach to the study of education is closer to the one advocated by the American historian Bernard Bailyn in his classic study of the formative role of education in early American society. Bailyn described education as constituting "the entire process by which a culture transmits itself across generations" and called for an approach that recognized education's "elaborate, intricate involvements with the rest of society."[9] Accordingly, this book locates education firmly within the context of the broad issues that have enlivened China studies in recent years: issues of gender representation and identification, Sino-foreign cultural interactions, dichotomies of state/society and of public/private, and the question of "inside" versus "outside" voices in the writing of history.

Our treatment of these themes has been guided by two considerations. One is the need for a genuinely multidisciplinary approach. It is simply not possible to explore the richness of a society's educational experience without involving a range of disciplines, each of which is capable of illuminating a different aspect of that experience. It is a curious artifact of the institutional development of educational studies as the academic adjunct of professional institutions for teacher education that has led to a situation in which specialists in Chinese education tend to interact among themselves or with other comparative education specialists. By contrast, political scientists, anthropologists, sociologists, and historians of modern China tend to interact with one another within the institutional frameworks of area studies, since this has been the institutional basis for modern China studies. This volume seeks to transcend those boundaries by fostering a cross-fertilization among scholars in a range of disciplines. It presents the perspectives of seven education specialists, seven historians, three sinologists, two sociologists, and one political scientist drawn from three continents and eight countries, thus representing a whole range of intellectual traditions. Furthermore, we have endeavored to include a mix of senior academics and younger scholars who are just establishing their reputations in the field.

The question of voice has increasingly come to the fore in recent years, and this volume encompasses many facets of it—the differences between approaches to scholarship in capitalist and socialist societies, among European, North American, and Chinese academic traditions, between mainstream and feminist approaches to inquiry. The group of authors who worked together on this volume represent a rich eclecticism of perspective, with many overlapping threads: three Chinese Canadians and three Anglo-Canadians; three Europeans from Denmark, Norway, and Scotland; two Chinese from the Mainland and two from Hong Kong; three Americans; one Japanese; and one Russian; and eight women among the eighteen contributors. A further distinction might be drawn between outsiders studying modern China and insiders who grew up within socialist China or the Soviet Union. One unforgettable moment in the deliberations that took place at the second of the two conferences held to develop the chapters in this volume may illuminate the difference in perspective between insider and outsider. Glen Peterson was in the process of presenting a detached analysis of the character of some of China's literacy campaigns of the 1950s, distinguishing with gentle irony between socialist rhetoric and the actual achievements of the events. At that point Nina Borevskaya, a distinguished Sinologist from the Russian Academy of Sciences, whose essay appears in part 1 of this volume, burst forth with the comment that it was not easy for outsiders to reconstruct the social and political atmosphere of literacy campaigns. People were deeply enthusiastic and idealistic over literacy activities in both the Soviet Union and China, she insisted.

Our effort to integrate educational problems with broader themes in twentieth-century Chinese social, cultural, and political history also informs a conscious commitment on the part of the volume's contributors to transcend the "1949 barrier" that continues to bisect the study of modern Chinese history. While the communist revolution of 1949 constitutes a major watershed in modern Chinese history in crucial respects, especially in the realms of state building, economic development, and China's relations with the world, it is our view that recent research has shifted the focus toward previously unnoticed continuities between the pre- and postrevolutionary periods in areas such as popular culture and beliefs, political culture, and patterns of reform.[10] Ironically, however, this recent line of inquiry continues to reflect conventional historiography in certain key respects. There is a tendency, in particular, to compare late imperial China with the communist period while largely ignoring the republican era, the latter having been relegated either implicitly or explicitly to the status of "interregnum" between the fall of one centralized bureaucratic state and the rise of another, even more powerful one. By contrast, this book takes the view that the republican era is of crucial importance for understanding the history of education in post-1949 China, as well as for the twentieth century as a whole. Thus, each of its three sections seek to traverse the century in terms of themes and issues raised. In addition, many individual essays, including those by Borevskaya, Ding, Hayhoe and Zhong, Peterson, Ross and Thøgersen, are explicitly concerned with bridging the 1949 divide.

We have not attempted to offer a comprehensive view of all aspects of education's role in Chinese society during the twentieth century. Such an undertaking would be difficult, if not impossible, within the confines of a single volume. Rather than seeking an exhaustive treatment of the subject, we have restricted ourselves to three themes that reveal the significance of education for the construction of social, cultural, and political identities in twentieth-century China: Sino-foreign interactions, state-society relations, and gender representation and identification. Each of these themes is the focus of a separate section within the volume. Each section begins with a brief introduction that discusses the theme and ties together its constituent chapters.

Part 1, "Sino-Foreign Interactions in Education," offers a variety of fresh and innovative approaches to a theme that has long been recognized as being of central importance in the history of modern Chinese education. As Douglas Reynolds observes in his introduction to part 1, the twentieth century has been singularly an age of internationalization for China, when the country has had to reinvent itself for the first time in its history according to outside rules, whether European, American, Japanese, or Soviet. Nowhere has this search for an appropriate identity and development model been more urgently felt—and more fiercely contested—than in the realm of education. And yet, if the six essays that make up this section make one thing perfectly clear, it is that the process of cultural borrowing is one of selective change and adaptation, in which foreign ideas and institutions not only changed China but also became Chinese. The subtle nuances of this process are brilliantly captured in Nina Borevskaya's opening essay on the "search for individuality" in Chinese and Russian pedagogy during two critical periods in the twentieth-century history of both countries: the 1920s and the 1980-90s. The comparative approach proves to be highly illuminating in Borevskaya's detailed depiction of the efforts of Chinese democratic educators to develop alternatives to Confucian pedagogy. She begins with a delicate comparative analysis of state Confucianism and the Russian Orthodox tradition of Christianity. While she finds Confucian orthodoxy basically unfriendly to the concepts of individual, subject, personality, and individuality that underlay liberal progressivism, Russian orthodoxy had already been softened by elements of European Renaissance thought long before the October Revolution. By contrast, Chinese liberals introduced the humanistic individualism of Rousseau and Kant only as a part of the campaign to discredit state Confucianism in the late Qing and early Republican periods.

Borevskaya explores fascinating parallels between the progressive movements that arose in Russia and China in the 1920s. She makes the point that, while the revolutionaries claimed a concern with the liberation of individuals and the development of personality, it was the progressive educators in both societies who created alternative pedagogies that could realize this goal. In Russia they gained considerable state support in the first decade after the revolution, losing it soon thereafter, while in China they blossomed in the anarchic period of warlord rule. Both were sympathetic to social and collectivist concerns but were undermined by traditions that only too easily led to the cementing of collectivism and totalitarianism.

In the second half of her essay Borevskaya uses this backdrop to examine the experience of China and Russia in the 1980s and 1990s, as educators grappled with new opportunities and social demands in very different sets of circumstances. The greater freedom for social and educational experimentation in the Russian context has made possible an alternative source of pedagogical ideas to Chinese educators, which they have debated alongside the European and American theories introduced in recent years. The concepts of personality, subject, and individual and individualization are thus revisited in the context of an evolving pedagogy in both China and Russia through a wide-ranging discussion of recent Chinese- and Russian-language writings on education in both societies. The ways in which differences in cultural heritage and social conditions have affected the educational expression of these concepts constitutes an intriguing set of conclusions to Borevskaya's essay.

If Western students of Chinese education do not often have the opportunity to hear Russian voices, the same may be said of Japanese voices on the subject. In his essay Yutaka Otsuka provides a rare glimpse into Japanese and Soviet Russian involvement in Chinese higher education. Complementing Borevskaya's chapter without duplicating her philosophical focus on the "search for individuality," Otsuka's essay sets out to examine institutions inherited by Japan after the creation of the Japanese puppet state of Manchukuo in 1932. His primary focus is a richly documented case study of the Harbin Polytechnical University (HPU), now known as the Harbin Institute of Technology. HPU was founded by the Soviets in 1920 to provide personnel for the Chinese Eastern Railway, which connected Manchuria to Russia under an agreement originally signed between the czarist Russian and Qing governments. The school was run along Soviet administrative and curricular lines, used Russian as the language of instruction, and had a predominantly Russian study body. HPU fell under Japanese influence in 1932 and was under direct Japanese control for a period of eight years, from 1937 to 1945. During this time the language of instruction changed to Japanese, and the proportion of Japanese instructors and students increased significantly. Following the end of World War II, the school reverted to joint Sino-Soviet management for five years, from 1945–50. When the Soviet educational model was formally adopted by China in the early 1950s, HPU was designated a national model because of its long experience as a Soviet-style technical institution.

Despite its status, in Otsuka's words, as an "imposed form of educational cooperation," HPU's period of Japanese tutelage reveals some interesting contrasts with the earlier period of Soviet control. For one thing, the proportion of Chinese graduates rose from 19 percent during the initial Soviet period to nearly 47 percent during the period of "Japanization" from 1932 to 1945. Whether this reflected a greater sense of educational responsibility toward its colonial subjects on Japan's part or simply a difference in strategies of dominance or of Japan's tighter control over Manchuria is, of course, an open question. But it does caution us against accepting at face value HPU's subsequent root and branch condemnation (made in 1952, at the height of official enthusiasm for the Soviet model of education) of the Japanese period as one of wanton destruction and deterioration.

Douglas Reynolds's comparative study of Christian mission schools and Japan's Tō-A Dōbun Shoin (East Asia Common Culture Academy) in Shanghai complements Otsuka's essay by illuminating another example of Sino-Japanese educational cooperation and at the same time widens our lens of inquiry into Sino-foreign educational interaction by bringing into focus the role of Christian missions. As the son of American educational missionaries in China and the author of a major study of Japanese influences, educational and otherwise, on the late Qing reforms to state and society, Reynolds offers a deeply personal assessment of the origins, development, and long-term legacies of these two examples of foreign educational influence. Tō-A Dōbun Shoin was founded by Japan's Prince Konoe in Shanghai in 1899–1900 with the intention that it provide joint education for Chinese and Japanese students, centered around the Japanese language, in Chinese classics and Western subjects. The school was a manifestation of Konoe's conviction that Chinese and Japanese were fated to become the sworn enemies of whites as the world marched toward an inevitable struggle for supremacy between "the white and yellow races." The ideal for a joint education for Chinese and Japanese was abandoned within a year, however, and a subsequent effort to reintroduce the ideal in the late 1910s and early 1920s also failed, for reasons that Reynolds discusses. He details the process by which Tō-A Dōbun Shoin, as a foreign educational institution on Chinese soil, gradually became more and more *foreign* while simultaneously distancing and insulating itself from the revolutionary currents and struggles swirling in China from the early 1920s.

As a consequence of these developments, Tō-A Dōbun Shoin Daigaku (the school was elevated to university status in 1939 in anticipation of Japan's wartime and postwar needs) did not leave behind a core group of Chinese students, staff, or "converts" because Chinese were almost nonexistent in its operations. Its legacy thus ended up not in China but outside of China, in Japan, among its Japanese students and staff, for whom the school remains an object of affection and remembrance. By contrast, Reynolds argues, the legacy of Christian mission schools is alive and well *inside* China, although still largely subterranean. Ironically, as Tō-A Dōbun Shoin was becoming more foreign and more insulated from its Chinese environment in the 1920s through the 1940s, Christian mission schools were becoming more indigenized and more Chinese during this same period. Chinese attacks on foreign mission schools prior to 1949 served to accelerate an indigenization process already under way, which led to Chinese leaders assuming positions of greater authority and influence, which in turn gave them a greater stake in the future fortunes of mission schools. The resurgence of "Christianity fever" in China in recent years owes much, in Reynolds's view, to the indigenization of mission schools before 1949.

The theme of indigenization is also taken up by Ryan Dunch in his pioneering study of the Anglo-Chinese College (ACC) in Fuzhou. Founded by American Methodist missionaries in 1881 with a gift from a wealthy Chinese merchant and recent convert, Zhang Heling (whose contribution was reflected in the school's Chinese name, Heling yinghua shuyuan), the ACC grew into the largest mission school in China and the largest school of any kind in Fujian province by the early 1900s. The school became a target of the anti-Christian and nationalization movements of the mid-1920s, was forced to close in 1927, but reopened in 1928 with its administrative structure and teachers and staff overwhelmingly Chinese. Within a few years the ACC regained its status as one of the largest and wealthiest schools in the province and continued to flourish for the next two decades, attracting numerous sons (the school began to admit girls for the first time in 1940) of the political and commercial elite as well as those of prominent Protestant families. The school was absorbed into China's new educational system after 1949 and in recent years has been generously revived with the financial support of alumni at home and abroad. Dunch suggests that the history of the ACC relates closely to our broader understanding of the relationship between education and social and political change in modern China. He argues that the ACC and mission schools in general were "harbingers of modernity" on many levels. The ACC produced a disproportionate number of republican China's growing urban professional elite of educators, civil servants, managers, Western-style physicians, and church workers. Most important, the ACC embraced a modern concept of the nation in which students were educated to play a role in the transformation of China and therefore to locate the meaning of their lives in relation to the nation. This ethos of patriotism, with its emphasis on service and self-sacrifice, was a value that missionaries, Chinese Christians, liberal modernizers, and Communists alike could all agree upon, while at the same time the appeal was sufficiently general for it to be translated into multiple and radically different frameworks for action.

Whereas Dunch focuses his attention on a single American mission school, Dan Cui examines the full range of British Protestant educational activities in China against the background of the turbulent politics of the 1920s. Cui sees the 1920s as marking the turning point in what she calls the "nationalization" of Christian mission education. While commitment to eventual Chinese control had long been affirmed by many foreign missionaries, the principle of Chinese leadership was realized when mission schools became swept up by the consuming fires and passions of Chinese nationalism in the 1920s. The fact that this occurred at the same time as the entire British Protestant mission enterprise itself was changing from within, as evangelism receded and was replaced by a social gospel commitment to developing education as a means of reforming and improving society, made it possible for mission schools to identify themselves as legitimate and loyal partners in the pursuit of national progress. Interestingly, Cui also uncovers a whole realm of informal British Protestant educational pursuits that remained all but untouched by Chinese nationalism during this period, which included such activities as public hygiene campaigns, public lectures, amateur societies, and the establishment of China's earliest modern museums. Such activities were immensely popular among both elite and illiterate audiences who flocked to consume British religious and cultural influence on subjects as diverse as modern Western labor-saving inventions, Scottish orphanages, and Shakespeare's England.

The twin forces of nationalization and internationalization are taken up by Gang Ding in the final chapter in part 1. Ding takes the same two time periods as Borevskaya does—the 1920s and the 1980s—but approaches them in a different way. His central question revolves around the process of educational borrowing. Under what conditions were foreign influences able to be integrated within China's evolving educational reforms and have a genuine impact on the process of change? His answer is that it was only when Chinese educators drew upon and transformed positive elements in their own heritage, such as the patterns and pedagogy of the Neo-Confucian *shuyuan,* that they were able to graft progressive elements drawn from American, European, or Russian experience into their own practices. Nationalization, or the conscious building of national identity through education, was therefore an essential precondition to successful internationalization. Conscious efforts to preserve or revive Confucian tenets were not, in Ding's view, merely a political device to bolster the legitimacy of successive post-imperial regimes (as Zheng Yuan suggests in his essay) but a genuine cultural effort to adapt the past to the needs and challenges of a China whose future was necessarily and inextricably intertwined with international influences.

Part 2, "State and Society in Chinese Education," examines the diverse interactions between China's modern state structure and various societal forces in the realm of education. Zheng Yuan's essay traces the evolution of curricular patterns, from the time of the first modern education system, legislated in 1902, up to the beginning of the Communist era in 1949. His careful and detailed account elaborates a concept of "conservative reform" or "authoritarian modernization," illustrating how Confucian values and the texts that communicated them repeatedly found their way back into the curriculum, in spite of an avowed republicanism after 1911. On the surface this was a matter of national pride and cultural loyalty, yet underneath the surface it could also be explained as a calculated strategy of beleaguered rulers to make use of a Confucian orthodoxy that had succeeded over centuries in ensuring a compliant and subservient populace. This point was as true of Chiang Kai-shek's (Jiang Jieshi) Nationalist regime as of the Manchu rulers, the Beijing warlords, and even the Japanese imperialists.

In illustrating this position, Yuan carries forward an intellectual perspective that probably found its fullest expression in the May Fourth Movement and which has been widely held to by intellectuals on the Chinese Mainland since 1949. Possibly one of the reasons for the tenacity of this perspective lies in the fact that it also explains a great deal of what took place in education under Chinese socialism. While Confucianism may have been openly repudiated and attacked, the classics of Marxism-Leninism were given a parallel position in the curriculum at key junctures. No mention is made of the post-1949 period in this essay, yet a passionate sense of critique running through the chapter hints at this kind of interpretation. Yuan's interpretation of the uses of tradition contrasts sharply with Gang Ding's argument that it was precisely the willingness to draw upon and transform positive elements in the

Confucian heritage that enabled Chinese educators to integrate foreign experience into their own practices successfully. Meanwhile, Borevskaya provides a
different but equally compelling counterfoil to Yuan's theme of conservative
reform, with her detailed depiction of the efforts of Chinese democratic
educators to develop alternatives to Confucian pedagogy. The historical problem of "Confucian tradition" and its modern fate is a genuine one that
continues to fascinate and confound scholars.

The power of the Chinese state to shape educational patterns and practice is approached from another perspective in Glen Peterson's essay on
"peasant education" (*nongmin jiaoyu*). Focusing on the rural literacy campaigns of the 1950s, he examines the nature and results of the state-led effort
to transform the economic and social structures of China's villages through
education. Viewing literacy campaigns through the lens of state-society relations allows Peterson to discuss the ways in which official conceptions of the
uses and significance of literary clashed with popular expectations. Whereas
official goals for spreading literacy in the countryside were closely related to
the perceived educational requirements for the successful implementation of
collectivized agriculture, villagers often tended to value literacy for different
and contending reasons: as a means of escaping agricultural labor and as a
skill for evading and challenging state authority. In the long run, Peterson
argues, the genuinely empowering effects of literacy may have resided in these
unintended uses and consequences as much as in the economically and politically restricted uses envisioned by state educational planners.

The disjunction between the official aims of schooling and the actual
processes by which communities and individuals learn and apply skills is also
the focus of Stig Thøgersen's detailed examination of career patterns in a
single Shandong village over the course of the twentieth century. Using a
wealth of personal interviews and documentary evidence, he makes a strong
case that formal schooling has played only a marginal role in the transmission
of economically relevant skills in the village for most of the twentieth century.
Instead, traditional modes of learning through participation and apprenticeship, though ignored or despised by successive generations of educational
reformers, remained an essential means by which teachers, medical practitioners, artisans, and managers acquired their knowledge and skills. Interestingly, however, most families have nonetheless continued to value their children's participation in general academic schooling. Why should this be so?
Chinese educational reformers have tended to label the academic aspirations
of rural youth and their families as irrational or "feudal." But Thøgersen sees
this apparent contradiction as the manifestation of a historically rooted cultural consensus that talented persons (*rencai*) are best identified through

academic tests, even when the job concerned demands little or no academic preparation. Strong school performance is viewed by villagers as a prerequisite to being selected for skilled jobs within the village as well as for higher education.

The sweeping reforms initiated by Deng Xiaoping in 1978 have had a sizable impact upon educational developments in China during the past two decades. One reason for this is that the reforms view educational institutions in many ways as enterprises, and many of the decision-making powers and fiscal responsibilities that have been handed over by the central state to individual enterprises have been similarly devolved to educational institutions. The final two essays in part 2 are concerned with the opening up of private spaces that are not under the immediate or direct control of the Party-state as a result of this process of devolution. In their examination of university autonomy in modern China, Ningsha Zhong and Ruth Hayhoe explore the significance of the concept of "university autonomy" that emerged in China since the 1980s. They draw an important distinction between *zizhiquan* (autonomy as independence, or self-governance) and *zizhuquan* (autonomy as self-mastery, or the authority to take initiatives). They argue that the former term most closely resembles the Western ideal of university autonomy, which evolved in the medieval period from the conception of separate spheres of state versus religious and civil authority. Protracted conflicts over the boundaries between the spheres led, in the West, to an emphasis on negative freedom defined in terms of constitutional or legal guarantees against state interference. By contrast, the latter term, which Zhong and Hayhoe say occurs more frequently in the Chinese literature, derives from Chinese epistemological traditions and is related to a longstanding Chinese concern over the autonomous person, and their ability and responsibility to take action within the larger whole of society and state, for the good of that whole. The distinction between the two conceptions forms the basis for the authors' understanding of the emergence of university autonomy in contemporary China.

In the twentieth century, university autonomy as *zizhuquan* (self-mastery) has acquired three levels of meaning. At the outermost level, self-mastery is defined in terms of national sovereignty in the face of Western and Japanese imperialism; the second level concerns relations between universities and the central state; while the third concerns practical expressions of autonomy by individual institutions in areas such as recruitment, fees, external consultancies, and other initiatives. Whereas the issue of national sovereignty of educational institutions was resolved by the revolution of 1949, Zhong and Hayhoe argue that developments during the reform period since 1978, especially the 1995 Education Law, which granted universities the status of "legal

persons" (*faren*), have resulted in considerable increases in university autonomy in the second and third spheres. Concrete examples of this trend are
provided by way of case studies of three universities in Sichuan province.

Relative autonomy is also the focus of David Chan and Ka-Ho Mok's
study of the recent resurgence of private education in post-Mao China. They
begin by tracing the policy of educational decentralization from its beginnings
in the 1980s to the Education Law of 1995, which affirmed the need for local
authorities and individual institutions to create "multiple channels" of educational funding outside the state sector. This legitimated the reappearance of
private education in the People's Republic of China for the first time since the
early communist government abolished private schooling in 1952. While there
has been a rapid and steady growth in the number of private schools at all
levels—primary, secondary, as well as tertiary—such schools vary tremendously in terms of their quality and ability to attract students. They include
highly elitist schools that charge exorbitant fees and provide the most modern
equipment as well as shoddily run and poorly equipped operations out to
make a quick profit. Significantly, the authors argue that, while "privatization" and "marketization" are clearly observable trends in recent years, a
genuine "internal market" for educational services does not yet exist in China.
For various reasons the private sector remains very much on the periphery of
the educational system. The state, meanwhile, continues to wield enormous
influence and power over the extent and pace of privatization through its
crucial ability either to extend or to withhold certification of private schools.

Part 3, "Gender Representation and Identification," takes as its focus a
theme that has attracted a great deal of scholarly attention in recent years.
The role of education and schooling in the construction, representation, and
transmission of gender identities remains surprisingly understudied despite
the obvious centrality of the school as a primary socializing agent in modern
societies. Readers will find much that is new in these essays that embrace the
entire sweep of the twentieth century, from Paul Bailey's and Sarah Coles
McElroy's efforts to probe the early 1900s debate over women's education to
Mette Halskov Hansen's analysis of the gendered effects of Chinese state
schooling on minority girls in Yunnan in the 1990s; Heidi Ross's illuminating
account of how a tradition of social activism has defined the students and
alumni of a Shanghai girls' school for more than a century; and Ping-Chun
Hsiung's wide-ranging analysis of the women's studies movement in post-
Mao China.

Despite a growing effort in recent years to "bring women in" to the social
and cultural history of modern China, surprisingly little attention has been
focused on the subject of women's education and its relationship to nation

building and the construction of modern identities. Educational reform, specifically the creation of a national school system, was hailed by the ailing Qing dynasty and its officials as a means to consolidate dynastic rule and by educators and gentry reformers as the means of overcoming the backwardness of China's peasant cultures and building a cohesive and economically productive modern Chinese nation. Yet the 1904 regulations for a national school system contained no provision for the education of girls; indeed, its leading architect argued that establishment of formal education for girls outside the home would be a national disaster. In 1907 the Qing government cautiously sanctioned separate female education at the primary level and lower normal schools (secondary education for females was officially introduced in 1912, while female tertiary education was not sanctioned until 1919).

Focusing on elite discourses, Paul Bailey makes clear that the "project" of women's education during the late Qing and early Republic was not at all clear; on the contrary, there was spirited, freewheeling debate and a plethora of contending and contradictory images and notions. Arguments for and against women's education were limited and delimited by received notions of innate gender difference, while at the same time shifting notions of femininity were constantly being challenged and reconfigured. While Bailey dissects the anxieties expressed by elite (mostly male) commentators in the debate over the nature, purpose, and extent of women's education in the early twentieth century, Sarah Coles McElroy approaches the growth of women's education during this period from the perspective of women as active subjects. McElroy looks at the origins and development of one of the earliest products of the elite discourse on women's education, the Zhili First Women's Normal School founded in Tianjin in 1906. Despite the reformers' ambivalent attitude toward female education and the extremely small proportion of girls who actually received formal education during this period (less than 5 percent of the school-age population in 1912), the new educational opportunities for women did contribute, in McElroy's view, to a gradual but significant transformation of Chinese society. Through their attendance at institutions such as the Zhili First Women's Normal School, elite women gained not only academic knowledge and professional training but also a new understanding of their role in Chinese society. The promoters of female education, including the founder of Zhili First Women's Normal, may have sought to train better mothers and more efficient housewives to nurture the Chinese nation while preserving traditional female virtues. But many women who studied at the new schools came to reject the traditional moral and social code and enlisted themselves instead in the struggle for greater social equality—in the name of revitalizing the Chinese nation.

Heidi Ross approaches the conjunction of women's education, personal transformation, and national rejuvenation from a somewhat different perspective. Like McElroy, Ross is also interested in understanding how women have appropriated nationalist discourses on female education for their own purposes. But, whereas McElroy views this process through the lens of an early-twentieth-century women's school sponsored by a member of the gentry elite, Ross examines the collective spirit of social purpose that infuses the history of a leading former mission school, the Shanghai McTyeire School for Girls. Founded by American Methodist missionaries in 1892 to provide a liberal education to young women of "well-to-do" Chinese families, the school's development as well as the lives of its several generations of graduates have been shaped by missionary, republican, and socialist goals for the education of young women. Ross traces the multiple interpretations of social service and cultural identity that have emerged from this history as expressed in the reminiscences of overseas alumni and interviews with the school's present leaders, both of whom are involved in an effort to preserve the school's ethic of community service by providing funding and teaching staff for a project to enhance educational opportunities for young girls in the poorest areas of Jiangxi province. The ways in which the school's institutional and financial goals and the personal search for self-definition and community of alumni living in China and abroad conjoin to define the relationship between education and social responsibility has a close resonance with the school spirit described in Ryan Dunch's essay on the history of the Anglo-Chinese College.

A unique feature of the section on gender representation and identification in education is our decision to place the discussion of minority issues alongside that of gender, in order to highlight how minority issues often parallel those of gender relations and women's position. Mette Halskov Hansen's case study of minority education policies in China's southwest shows the ways in which state schooling for minority girls works to reproduce conflated notions of gender identity and minority stereotypes. Minority girls' encounter with a state education system that emphasizes Chinese language, atheism, modernization, and nationalism and which also transmits an "eroticized, exoticized, and feminized image" of non-Han peoples is, Hansen argues, a profoundly alienating experience. While participation in the state education system is a key means of achieving social mobility and gaining higher status in Chinese society, state schools also instill feelings of cultural inadequacy and inferiority. Not only are non-Han ethnic groups associated with cultural and economic "backwardness," but such backwardness is often presented in school texts as being directly connected to female practices and behavior, including female shamans and sorcerers, traditional costumes, illiteracy, and early marriage. The increasing commodification of minority cultures in the reform period is also having an effect on minority education, as schools increasingly educate minority girls for jobs as exoticized "folk" entertainers, hostesses, and other types of service provider in the burgeoning tourism industry whose consumers are mainly Han Chinese. Hansen's essay is a powerful reminder that educational opportunities for women cannot be understood apart from the larger cultural, political, and economic contexts in which they are embedded.

The power of the state education system to construct social and political meaning looks much different in Ping-Chun Hsiung's analysis of the women's studies movement that has emerged in Chinese universities in recent years. Hsiung follows other scholars in suggesting that, while the CCP-led Party-state possesses immense "iron-fisted power" to defeat any overt challenges to its authority, its giant bureaucratic system is highly fragmented and inefficient in most of its routine operations. Advocates of women's studies programs accordingly have sought to avoid open confrontations with state authorities while at the same time striving to "take advantage of cracks in the existing system and make their way into new territory." The taking of new territory involves, in the first place, garnering institutional resources and funds to support the development of women's studies programs in universities. But, more important, it also entails using such resources to construct autonomous institutional spaces in which the official definitions of gender equality and women's liberation—a permanent feature of the official ideology—can be questioned and challenged and alternative routes to women's emancipation set forth. This includes, for example, highlighting female subjectivity over the official emphasis on "objective" conditions for women's liberation and the assertion of "femaleness" against the dominant discourse in which "becoming men's equals" in practice meant denying and suppressing one's femaleness and becoming identical to men. Hsiung's focus upon the interplay of agency and structure underscores, as do the other essays in this section, the complex and unpredictable ways in which schools have contributed to and reflected gender identification and representation in twentieth-century China.

The preparation of this book has been greatly aided by two international conferences, which brought the contributors together for several intensive days of debate and planning. An initial conference was held at the University of British Columbia in September 1996. Eleven participants gathered over three days to debate the volume's principal themes and objectives and to present preliminary versions of their respective contributions. A second conference convened exactly one year later, in September 1997, at the University of Toronto. A total of thirty participants met for three days to present final versions of their essays and discuss the major issues and themes arising from the meeting. A special tribute is due to Yongling Lu for her work in organizing the Toronto conference and for her painstaking efforts in editing the present volume.

The Toronto conference benefited immeasurably from the enthusiastic participation of faculty and graduate students from the Ontario Institute for Studies in Education of the University of Toronto (OISE/UT) and the departments of East Asian Studies, History, and Political Science at the University of Toronto and York University, who served as paper commentators and session chairs. We would especially like to express our appreciation to Pik-chun Liu, Chris Munn, Maire O'Brien, Qingzhi Zhao, Huiping Wu, and Feng Xu for their excellent work as conference commentators. We also wish to thank Jinghuan Shi, Timothy Brook, Daniel Culp, B. Michael Frolic, Joan Judge, Bernard Luk, Graham Sanders, and Jeffrey Wasserstrom for their insightful participation and comments throughout the Toronto conference and to Yu Li, Joanne Poon, and Norman Smith for logistical support during the Vancouver conference. At the University of Michigan Press, Ingrid Erickson and Marcia LaBrenz ensured meticulous editing and a smooth and humane publication process.

Finally, we wish to acknowledge the generous support provided by the Social Sciences and Humanities Research Council of Canada, the Connaught Committee of the University of Toronto, OISE/UT, the University of Toronto–York University Joint Centre for Asia Pacific Studies, and the Centre for Chinese Research and Institute of Asian Research at the University of British Columbia, which has made this volume possible.

NOTES

1. Suzanne Pepper, *Radicalism and Education Reform in 20th Century China* (Cambridge and New York: Cambridge University Press, 1996). Among historians, Paul Bailey was one of the first to locate the intellectual origins of the Maoist educational experiments of the 1960s in various strands of late Qing and early republican educational reform thought. See Paul Bailey, *Reform the People: Changing Attitudes towards Popular Education in Early Twentieth Century China* (Vancouver: University of British Columbia Press, 1990).

2. Wm. T. De Bary and John Chaffee, eds., *Neo-Confucian Education: The Formative Stage* (Berkeley: University of California Press, 1989).

3. Alexander Woodside and Benjamin Elman, "Introduction," in Elman and Woodside, eds., *Education and Society in Late Imperial China, 1600–1900* (Berkeley: University of California Press, 1994), 2.

4. For a detailed discussion of the 1902 and 1904 school regulations, see Hiroshi Abe, "Borrowing from Japan: China's First Modern Educational System," in Ruth Hayhoe and Marianne Bastid, eds., *China's Education and the Industrialized World: Studies in Cultural Transfer* (Armonk, N.Y.: M. E. Sharpe, 1987), 57–88. See also Douglas R. Reynolds, *China, 1898–1912: The Xinzheng Revolution and Japan* (Cambridge, Mass.: Council on East Asian Studies, Harvard University, 1993).

5. Sally Borthwick, *Education and Social Change in China: The Beginnings of the Modern Era* (Stanford: Hoover Institution Press, 1983); Bailey, *Reform the People*.

6. Woodside and Elman, "Introduction," 3.

7. Tu Wei-ming, "The Sung Confucian Idea of Education," 142, cited in Woodside and Elman, "Introduction," 4.

8. Woodside and Elman, "Introduction," 3.

9. Bernard Bailyn, *Education in the Forming of American Society: Needs and Opportunities for Study* (Cambridge, Mass.: Harvard University Press, 1960), 14.

10. For a thoughtful critique of the "1949 barrier" in Western scholarship on modern China, see Paul A. Cohen, "The Post-Mao Reforms in Historical Perspective," *Journal of Asian Studies* 43, no. 3 (1988): 519–41.

Part 1
Sino-Foreign Interactions in Education

Douglas R. Reynolds

China entered the twentieth century rethinking its educational policies at the highest levels. Directing this effort were government officials guided by Empress Dowager Cixi's Reform Edict of January 1901, which authorized a sweeping review of China's administrative affairs. Over much of the next decade the court instituted fundamental reforms, highlighted by educational reforms. The sustained support of the court for these reforms, it must be said, was extraordinarily important in the context of China's centralized and autocratic political systems. Reforms had been undertaken before 1900, some with a modern educational component such as the Tongwen Guan, the Jiangnan Arsenal, and the Fuzhou Shipyard. These had been sporadic, however, a series of experiments rather than a coordinated movement. The results, though noteworthy, were modest at best.

Militating against sustained reform in the nineteenth century was China's conviction that it was the sole center of the civilized universe. The idea that China was one nation among many in an alien world order had no appeal whatsoever. Although forced to sign unequal treaties after 1842, China's leaders clung to the hope that the Western powers would tire and go away, leaving China supreme in its old world. All hopes of a return to the old order were shattered, however, by China's military defeat by Japan in 1894–95. That defeat was followed by further defeats, the failure of the Hundred Days' Reform of 1898 and the anti-foreign Boxer Uprising of 1898–1900, with its punitive settlement. China, now knocked off its high pedestal and reduced to a subordinate position, suddenly regarded the status of equal as not only acceptable but even desirable. To achieve equality, however, required radical reforms such as those that had transformed Meiji Japan into a Western-style power capable of inflicting defeat on a nation like China.

These developments formed the immediate background of the Qing dynasty's remarkable Xinzheng reforms of 1901–10, perhaps the most consequential of which were educational reforms. Preliminary educational reforms of 1902 and 1904 culminated in the astonishing abolition of China's 1,200-year-old civil service examination system in September 1905. Sponsored by conservative reformers such as Liu Kunyi and Zhang Zhidong, these changes produced revolutionary outcomes. They fundamentally restructured and reoriented China's entire culture of learning. A complex new system of graded formal schooling, teaching unfamiliar modern subjects, replaced China's time-honored *keju* (examination) system, which was centered around the Confucian classics. The new school system was constructed entirely around a foreign model, Meiji Japan's modern educational system. Never before in Chinese history had the state altered a core element of life so abruptly or so directly from a foreign model. Other foreign models followed. Their collective influence on China was so enduring and transformative that the topic of education and society in twentieth-century China is incomprehensible without a consideration of Sino-foreign interactions.

No essay in the present section catalogs these foreign influences on state education in China. The broad phases and sources of influence are well-known: phase 1 (early 1900s), Meiji Japan; phase 2 (early 1920s), American models associated with John Dewey; and phase 3 (the 1950s), Soviet models. None of these borrowings took hold in China without considerable adaptation, a point stressed by Gang Ding in the last essay of this section and well illustrated in the essay by Yutaka Otsuka. Ironically, in this section it is not state educational initiatives that best illustrate the process of adaptation. It is, rather, nonstate Christian mission schools. The full story of Christian mission schools in China remains to be told. This volume begins the process of a more analytical understanding of foreign mission schools and China, in their mutual adaptations and accommodations at local, provincial, and national levels.

As Russian scholar Nina Borevskaya points out in the opening essay of this section, "Searching for Individuality," her study focuses less on the influence and incorporation of foreign ideas by state and nonstate agencies and more on the approach of liberal educators in Russia and China to individual-oriented educational philosophies, rooted in a Western, and especially American, pedagogy. Her analysis, anchored in a review of the idea of "human being" in the Confucian tradition of China and in the Orthodox Christian tradition of Russia, offers an informed discussion of the search by Chinese liberal educators in the 1910s and 1920s for a new individual in China and by Russian liberal educators of the same time period of education for self-realization and individuality. The new Soviet state of the 1920s endorsed the notion of education as a way to mold a "new person for a new socialist society." Russian liberal educators endeavored to achieve collectivist goals through individual self-realization. In Russia, as in China but for different reasons, the search for individuality through education in the 1920s ended prematurely.

In the 1980s and 1990s, interestingly, both China and Russia revived an interest in individual-oriented pedagogy. Educators drawing from both foreign experience and their own past, including the 1920s, engaged in lively debates, explored by Borevskaya, that reveal at once the complexities of views within China and within Russia, the vastly different cultural backgrounds of the two nations, and the constraints upon both as liberal educators commit themselves to the search for individuality. The topic of the search for individuality might easily have been undertaken for either China or Russia independently. Examining both countries in two similar time periods is a richly rewarding approach. Modern humanistic ideas have influenced educational philosophies in Russia and China in unexpected ways. Particularly interesting is that "Russia's longer humanistic tradition and stronger democratic trends" have influenced Chinese pedagogical liberalization. Going one step further, Borevskaya concludes that in the West, the wellspring of humanism, "individualism as an educational principle has already reached its apogee and pedagogues there are increasingly looking toward the categories of collectivism found in Eastern pedagogical traditions." The time has come, she suggests, for "a dynamic combination of alternate traditions as a means to reinvigorate Chinese, Russian, and Western education."

Douglas Reynolds's essay opens a subset of three essays focusing on foreign mission schools. In the nineteenth century mission schools were associated in most minds with Western gunboat diplomacy and what might be called Christian imperialism. Because of their Christian component, mission schools were objects of Chinese suspicion, unacceptable as models, and subject to attack. Only the unequal treaties protected them. Chinese official unease with mission schools culminated in a 1906 communiqué from the new Ministry of Education declaring mission schools unauthorized and unregistered and their graduates ineligible for public employment and other privileges. (These restrictions were lifted after the Revolution of 1911.) During the 1920s, or phase 2 of state educational reforms, mission schools were required to register with the state and to conform to new government regulations. In phase 3, after 1949, mission schools were essentially nationalized, ending a century of existence in China.

The history of mission schools in China was uneven, arousing occasional waves of criticism and attack. It was these very pressures and attacks, Reynolds argues, that forced mission schools to accommodate and adapt themselves to Chinese demands. As Chinese Christians were entrusted more and more with leadership responsibilities, they acquired a direct stake in a "Chinese Christianity" independent of foreign missionaries and foreign funding. This laid the foundations for the explosive growth of Christianity in China since 1979, long after foreign missionaries had gone. Official reports now put the number of Chinese Christians at about fourteen million in 1997, or "fourteen times as many as in 1949." Former mission schools are perhaps the most important single reason for these unexpected numbers.

Ryan Dunch's discussion of the Anglo-Chinese College (ACC) of Fuzhou, 1881–1956, resonates with many of Reynolds's themes but also raises doubts about certain conventional views about Christianity in nineteenth-century China. ACC, for example, does not fit the mold of a simple foreign "imperialistic" imposition on China. Its founding was the immediate result of Chinese rather than foreign money and vision. Its full English name, Anglo-Chinese College, conveys a foreignness not so apparent in its Chinese name, Heling Yinghua Shuyuan or, after 1928, Heling Yinghua Zhongxue. Its Chinese name highlights the school's specific debt to Chinese benefactor Zhang Heling, a wealthy local merchant who donated ten thousand dollars (U.S.) in 1881 on condition that English instruction be offered. The Methodist Episcopal mission board in New York and a majority of its missionaries in Fuzhou opposed instruction in English. Their view was overridden, however. Local Chinese Methodist preachers, who had been empowered to help make Methodist church policy in the field and who in 1877 outnumbered the foreign missionaries by thirty to five, sided with Zhang Heling and instituted the policy of English instruction against the wishes of the foreign mission board. If this is nineteenth-century imperialism, it is of a very ingenious sort. At the outset of his article Dunch points out that "mission-run schools tend to be neglected in scholarly treatments of the history of modern education in China." The prominent overall place of mission schools in Fujian province, documented by Dunch, highlights the seriousness of this neglect. The Fujian case demands that the scholarly community write mission schools into its research agenda. In this volume Dunch's essay and those of Reynolds, Cui Dan, and Heidi Ross begin to rectify this neglect.

The Anglo-Chinese College offers a particularly fine case study because it both confirms and questions conventional wisdom about mission schools in

China. ACC, like most other prominent mission schools, came under anti-Christian and Chinese nationalist attack in the mid-1920s. Steep enrollment declines followed, and in 1927 it closed it doors. It reopened in 1928, registered under Chinese law, with a Chinese president and a majority Chinese Board of Trustees. Another commonality is that, like leading mission schools everywhere, some of its best students were radicals, who after 1939 formed a Communist Party cell within the school. ACC—like Shanghai's McTyeire School for Girls—inculcated an ethos of service to society, nation, and the world. Also like McTyeire, in the 1950s both schools ceased to exist, having been absorbed into China's new educational system. In the 1980s and 1990s, in another commonality, both have been partially revived with funds from generous alumni overseas. A further similarity is that during the Cultural Revolution ACC's president from 1928 to 1948, Chen Zhimei, came under attack not just as a Christian but as a rightist and imperialist spy. The attacks broke Chen's health and contributed to his death in 1972. Officially exonerated in 1979, today Chen Zhimei enjoys an "extraordinary reverence" among alumni. In contrast to most mission school experience in China (or at least to conventional views of that experience), ACC was founded with Chinese participation and a determining voice in setting school policies. As early as 1899, student tuition fees met most of the school's running costs, enabling it to be essentially self-financing. And during the War of Resistance against Japan, from 1937 to 1945, ACC retreated three hundred kilometers into the interior, more in the manner of wartime universities than high schools.

Dan Cui focuses her attention on British Protestant educational activities in China and what she terms the nationalization of Chinese education in the 1920s. Exploring first the social gospel background of British educational endeavors in China, Cui elucidates this major force behind Christian mission education. Her separate discussions of elementary, secondary, and higher education and of medical and popular education (featuring the impressive British museum in Jinan) and her distinction between schools in large cities, smaller cities, and town-villages provide a framework and approach for future studies of mission education in China. Her observation that lower-level schools affiliated themselves with higher mission schools and functioned as feeders reflects the experience of the three Bai sisters cited by Reynolds. British missions, generally less well funded than American missions, actively pursued interdenominational cooperative or union arrangements. This draws attention to the phenomenon of Western mission groups transcending denominational lines, anticipating in a sense China's post-denominational Christian church after 1949, under the rubric of the Three Self Patriotic Movement.

Cui's thesis that the 1920s marked the turning point in "transferring educational administration to Chinese control" is well taken. It is necessary to remind ourselves, however, as Cui herself suggests, that this process of sinification long predated the 1920s. The commitment to Chinese leadership of the Chinese church, exemplified by the Anglo-Chinese College as far back as the 1880s, was a principle affirmed by many foreign missionaries at the turn of the century. The 1920s should be seen not as a sudden and grudging departure, therefore, but as a culmination of forces long in the making.

Yutaka Otsuka's article on Japanese involvement in higher education in Manchuria sets out to look at institutions inherited by Japan after creation of the puppet state of Manchukuo in 1932. Its primary case is a richly detailed narrative and analysis of the Harbin Polytechnical University (HPU). Founded by Russian initiative in 1920, this school utilized Russian as its language of instruction, was guided by "Soviet-style rules and curriculum," and had a majority of Russian students (Chinese constituted a mere 19 percent of its graduates). Its early organization anticipated changes adopted by many Chinese universities after 1949, when China formally adopted the Soviet model of education.

In the interim, from 1937 to 1945, HPU came under direct Japanese control. During this period it followed the Japanese model of education and utilized Japanese as its language of instruction. To Japan's credit, nearly 50 percent of HPU graduates during those years were Chinese, a contrast with the Soviet era. From 1945 to 1950 HPU returned to joint Sino-Soviet management and a Soviet model of education. Because of its rich experience with Soviet-style education, after 1950 and under sole Chinese control, this university became a model for Chinese state-run industrial universities with a Soviet-style administration. Otsuka's interest in Soviet influences on Chinese education complements Nina Borevskaya, without duplicating the latter's specific interest in "searching for individuality." Although Manchukuo came increasingly under Japanese direction and the Harbin Polytechnical University became more "Japanized," HPU maintained a relatively constant number of Chinese students in its ranks. The Japanese-controlled environment of Manchukuo allowed for the orderly recruitment and integration of Chinese students. This contrasts, ironically, to Tō-A Dōbun Shoin in Shanghai (discussed by Reynolds), which was founded on the ideal of a joint education for Chinese and Japanese. The Shanghai school gave up the idea of a joint education after less than a year. When it tried to reinstitute joint education in the late 1910s and 1920s, it ran into problem after problem. Over the years Tō-A Dōbun Shoin became steadily more Japanese, ending up as a school essentially of the Japanese, by the Japanese, and for the Japanese. Unlike HPU, this unique Shanghai institution exercised no meaningful influence on Chinese education or society.

The final essay, by Chinese scholar Gang Ding, returns to the two time periods investigated by Nina Borevskaya, the 1920s (and 1930s, in the case of Ding) and the 1980s and 1990s. Both authors regard these decades as seminal in the history of education in twentieth-century China. Ding is particularly interested in the 1920s and 1930s and the 1980s and 1990s as "turning points" for Chinese educators in consciously absorbing foreign educational influences. Instead of blindly copying foreign models (as Ding alleges to be the case of late-Qing borrowings from Japan—a misleading allegation, in my view), educators in these decades actively adapted foreign borrowings to Chinese needs and imperatives.

The internationalization of Chinese education endured best, Ding argues, when it interacted creatively with nationalization—that is, when foreign borrowings were selectively chosen and creatively adapted to Chinese realities. In the 1920s and 1930s Cai Yuanpei and Tao Xingzhi, giants of educational theory and practice in twentieth-century China, are most frequently cited to exemplify the nationalization of international educational ideas. In the 1980s and 1990s the process of internationalization has been revived based on a further selective adaptation of foreign theory and practice. Policy documents, government regulations, and official statements reveal the expanding horizons of China's approach to education. They testify likewise to the complexity and vitality of current policies and practice as China ushers in the new millenium.

In China, going back at least to the Tang dynasty (618–907), education has been the primary instrument by which the Chinese state has molded and indoctrinated its members. China of the twentieth century has been heir to the Chinese faith in the transformative powers of education. Remolding and reindoctrinating citizens through education have occurred remorselessly since early 1900, around unstable constellations of power brokers. Elsewhere in this volume Zheng Yuan speaks of continuities with China's Confucian past, as competing authorities invoke Confucian values to inspire or impose social harmony and control. The evidence marshaled is substantial and significant. But the more dramatic story of twentieth-century China lies in its discontinuities with the past.

Foreign interactions are responsible for China's most radical discontinuities of the twentieth century. For the first time in China's long and unique history, China has had to reinvent itself according to outside rules (European, American, Japanese, Soviet). Modern education to make China strong has been a constant goal of Chinese authorities. Models and formulas were sought from abroad. At the same time, institutions imposed on China by outsiders were made China's own. Whether through the process of borrowing or of absorbing outside impositions, Chinese society and government have been transformed by foreign influence as never before. Without reference to the transformations from foreign interactions, China of the last century is incomprehensible. The six essays that follow testify to this.

Searching for Individuality: Educational Pursuits in China and Russia

Nina Y. Borevskaya

This essay is a comparative study of educational reforms in China and Russia in the twentieth century. Unlike previous studies of this subject, the emphasis is not so much on the influence and incorporation of foreign ideas by state and nonstate agents but on the actual ideas and activities of liberal educators in Russia and China during two periods in which both countries experienced revolutionary change: the period that began with the Russian Revolution of 1917 and continued through the 1920s; and the period from 1989 and through the 1990s. Specifically, this essay compares how Chinese and Russian liberal educators approached the issue of a child-oriented educational philosophy that was rooted in a Western, especially American, individual-oriented pedagogy. It examines common trends as well as the divergence of the Chinese approach to personality and individualization in the educational process. The latter is understood to be a result of both ontological and socio-historical differences. Throughout this essay, I proceed from the premise that the rationale for the pursuit of individuality in both countries must be located in their respective internal conditions and can therefore be properly understood only in the context of their differing cultural and historical traditions. At the same time, I also believe that regardless of the great disparities in their dominant cultures—Confucianism in the case of China and Russian Orthodox Christianity in the case of Russia—the two traditions also had much in common with each other with respect to their approaches to human subjectivity.

Human Beings and Personality in Chinese and Russian Cultural Traditions

A brief discussion of some key concepts in the Chinese and Russian philosophical traditions may be of assistance in analyzing contemporary debates and the specific character in which these predicaments become manifest in pedagogical practice. As a point of departure, I share the conviction of some Chinese scholars that there are certain maxims within the Confucian tradition that hindered the realization of individual-oriented education in China.[1] Here I wish to identify four such maxims.

The first maxim was that of the "Unity of Heaven and Humans" (*Tian ren he yi*). I concur with those PRC philosophers who ascribe the lack of individuality (*gexing*) in modern China to this formula, which generated a theoretical assumption that a human being as Heaven's creature could not be singled out from a host of other things in the Universe and therefore possessed neither an autonomous nature nor a superior value.[2] A second Confucian maxim that served to inhibit the development of a concept of individual autonomy held that "human beings are by nature alike, only learning makes them different" (*xing xiang jin ye, xi xiang yuan ye*), along with the related principle that "among those who are educated there are no distinctions" (*you jiao wu lei*). The philosopher Mozi (470–391? B.C.E.) similarly compared human nature to unbleached linen, which could be dyed different colors by education.[3] A third maxim was that all human virtues are derived from the *xin* (heart and mind) and that all evils and corruption derive from *qing* (sensuality) and *yu* (flesh and blood desires). In this formulation the role of *xin* is to control, subdue, and restrict *yu*. The Neo-Confucian philsopher Zhu Xi (C.E. 1130–1200) affirmed this understanding when he reiterated the ancient Mencian dictum of "destroying the flesh to reach humanity (*sha shen cheng ren*) as well as Xunzi's (298–238? B.C.E.) call to "struggle against feelings and desires" (*fan yuqing*) and to "abide the heavenly principles, subdue human desires" (*cun tian li, mie ren yu*).[4] Finally, the fourth maxim to be mentioned here was the Confucian priority given to social relationships and love for others (*ren*) while subduing one's own "self" (*keji fuli*). According to the early Confucian philosopher and statesman, Dong Zhongshu (179–104 B.C.E), "Humanity as a law presupposes love of others, but not of oneself" (*ren zhi fa zai ai ren bu zai ai wo*).[5] Such an unambiguously negative approach to human nature as egoistic was inherited by the Neo-Confucians and continued to prevail throughout the late imperial period. Compelled to feel ashamed of one's egoistic aspirations, a human being thus had no chance to express his or her individuality.[6]

Taken together, these four maxims illustrate that in those areas of traditional Chinese education in which Confucian orthodoxy dominated, a human being was not categorized as an individual, much less as a subject or personality. In contrast to the Chinese legacy, Russian philosophers as early as the eighteenth century began to challenge Christian religious dogmas with an anthropocentric approach that fostered the affirmation of a human being as an individual and a subject with intrinsic value. In doing so, they came close to affirming the human being as an independent personality. As early as the eighteenth century, the Russian philosophic-religious tradition was becoming enriched with ideas absorbed from the European Renaissance, with the result that by the nineteenth century it had grown opposed to the earlier Orthodox Christian approach to a human being as a "vessel of evil." A human being was now defined as an individual close to God, hence obtaining a special value. Vissarion Belinsky (1810–48) was the first Russian pedagogue to claim that the human being's task was to be a human being first and only thereafter a citizen. According to him, individuals should love one another because they are human beings, and schools must first nurture individuals. Belinsky propagated "a fanatic love of individual freedom and independence that could be implemented only in a society based on truth and valor."[7] Similarly, turn of the century Russian philosophers like V. Solovjov, N. Berdiajev, and Leo Tolstoy invariably treated the concept of an individual as having an indissoluble connection with individual autonomy and relative freedom from society. It was on the basis of these respective philosophical foundations that Chinese and Russian pedagogues confronted the unprecedented social, political, and psychological challenges of the early twentieth century.

The Revolutionary Syndrome of the 1920s: The Chinese "New Citizen" and the Soviet "New Person"

The unsuccessful attempt to restore the Chinese monarchy in 1916 was followed by a decade of concerted efforts to achieve educational independence and modernization led by liberal educators such as Tao Xingzhi, Cai Yuanpei, Jiang Menglin, Chen Heqing, Huang Yanpei, Yan Yangchu (James Yen), and others, many of whom had received education in Europe and the United States. Proclaiming "national salvation through education," they formed part of a broad-based New Culture Movement whose goal was nothing less than the creation of a new civilizational paradigm for China. For these educational reformers the struggle for national freedom and independence was inseparable from the struggle for individual freedom, because they envisaged a new

China as a free civil society. They therefore came to the conclusion that the cultural task of molding a "modern" Chinese "person" was the core problem of modernization.

The New Culture impetus for educational reform was grounded in the efforts of the previous generation of intellectual reformers led by Kang Youwei, Liang Qichao, and others, who challenged aspects of the Confucian tradition by claiming that individual autonomy was a basic human characteristic. In Liang's words, the individual's development derived from his or her "spiritual emancipation," which in turn presupposed the right to a critical outlook as well as freedom of action (with respect to marriage, e.g.).[8] According to some PRC scholars, the main difference between the earlier generation of liberal intellectuals and the post-1911 generation of reformers and revolutionaries lay in the way they delineated their goals: while the former saw themselves struggling for "peoples' rights" (*minquan*), the latter enriched this goal with the concept of "human rights" (*renquan*).[9] In the educational domain this change was reflected in an emphasis upon individual-oriented education.

Disagreements between left-wing and, after 1921, Communist Party intellectuals, on the one hand, and noncommunist liberal educators, on the other, were often explicitly manifested in their respective approaches to the question of the individual. These differences, however, were not as clear-cut in the 1920s as they later became. Early revolutionaries such as Yun Daiying also raised their voices against the old educational system, which was accused of "maiming" individual personality, and even Mao himself proclaimed, in one of his earliest works, that "the final goal of a human being is to realize one's self . . . there is nothing more important than to develop utterly his physical and spiritual potency."[10] Yet, the younger generation of intellectuals who received their education after the 1911 Revolution were more likely to be inspired by the achievements of European (especially German and French) educational thought and the humanistic individualism of Kant and Rousseau than by Adam Smith. Kant's morality, which called for a positive concern for the well-being of all individuals with whom one interacts, resonated more closely with the reform agenda of the post-1911 generation of radicals than did the arguments of British political economists, that individuals both are and ought to be concerned only for their own advantage. Similarly, Rousseau's argument that human societies are not the natural setting for human life, whose natural condition is one of individual independence and freedom, accorded well with the aspirations of Chinese intellectuals who saw their task as waging a struggle against state tyranny. Leo Tolstoy's concept of "free education" was also popular among Chinese educational innovators; Cai

Yuanpei, for example, urged that Tolstoy's model of schooling be introduced to China on an experimental basis.[11]

Redefining the meaning of *personality* became a core problem for intellectuals who assumed that the "new education" was incompatible with the traditional educational paradigm and its key problem: the Confucian approach to a separate human being. Tao Xingzhi approached this problem in terms of a tradition/modernity dichotomy, arguing that the crucial difference between traditional agrarian society and the modern industrial one lay in their approach to the value of a human being. In a similar vein Jiang Menglin stressed that China's backwardness in relation to the Western world stemmed from underdevelopment of the individual, and he challenged the Confucian notion that an individual's conditional value was manifested exclusively through a system of social roles in which individuals expressed their "belonging" and "submission" to a community, whether national or family. Instead, he claimed that the new individual's value was simply as "you, me, he," an ultimate human value expressing a right to autonomy. Jiang came close to the notion of "personality" in a Western sense when he called for the nurturing of an individual with "an independent spirit, who has the courage to declare his own position."[12]

By promoting concepts such as *zili, zidong, zijue* (self-support, spontaneous initiative, self-consciousness), liberal educators like Jiang and Tao emphasized not simply students' learning style but also their approach to life in general: an individual's ability to organize his or her life independently and by relying on his or her own innate potency. The notion of innate potential was in turn closely related to the question of individual nature. The liberal educators' image of an individual was delineated as an independent and active person in a social system in which the state was losing its traditional priority. Thus, Liang Qichao spoke of *xinmin* (new citizen) as an "individual with a reformist mind, initiative and able to rule"; Jiang Menglin described the modern Chinese person as someone who was both a personality and a citizen, not just a family member; and Cai Yuanpei referred to the individual as a personality who could become a respected and integral part of a state, as in ancient Greece. Chen Heqing accurately summed up these aspirations as the quest to nurture "a human being, a Chinese, a modern Chinese."[13]

Proponents of a new education challenged the Confucian approach to a human being's biological nature: "An individual's value exists in yours, mine and his inherent nature" (Jiang Menglin); and "Respect nature, develop the individual" (shang ziran, zhan gexing) (Cai Yuanpei).[14] According to this view, liberal educators in the 1920s delineated the difference between "old" and "new" education in terms of the ability to promote a spontaneous development of the individual's nature. In contrast to the traditional pedagogy, whose main goal was to transfer cognitive knowledge, the innovative pedagogy advocated by liberal pedagogues insisted that the main task was to cultivate students' ability to excavate knowledge by themselves. Thus, Cai Yuanpei asserted that a teacher ought "to learn the internal laws of a child's nature, and choose proper methods to support it"; a teacher, like an experienced gardener, "pours water on dry plants, supports the weakest, warms the frozen, feeds the wasted."[15] Cai, following Wang Guowei, presumed that aesthetic education was a means of solving the Confucian puzzle of how to suppress egoistic aspirations. Likewise, Tao Xingzhi's educational philosophy emphasized the nurturing of "knowledge, feelings, thoughts" (*zhi, qing, yi*), which expressed his desire to combine rationality with sensuality. He enriched the principle of "life education" by maintaining that "an aesthetic life is an aesthetic education."[16] Tao also stressed that "teaching methods must correspond to an individual's learning efforts."[17] Liberal Chinese educators thus emphasized the potential for spontaneous self-development and regarded the individual's moral autonomy as an inner impetus guiding the process of self-development. Assuming that the individual was a subject entailed enbracing core features of democratic theory: creativity and activity, initiated by an individual as the means to his or her self-realization and self-development.

Through their efforts to redefine personality the liberal pedagogues also made substantial contributions to the underdeveloped field of child psychology in China. Through their pedagogical techniques and philosophy they directed attention to specific aspects of child psychology, such as the acquisition of knowledge through games. Applying Dewey's child-centered philosophy and practice, they demanded that schools become not just student centered but, more important, child centered. Chen Heqing, in particular, stressed the need to respect the child's personality and to protect his or her naïveté and innocence. Chen was among the pioneers of child psychology in China, who sought to establish that "a child is not just 'a small man,' his psychology is different from that of adults, and childhood is not just a preparatory period for adult life, but possesses its own value."[18]

The liberal pedagogy of the 1920s had its limits, however. Many of the educators mentioned here, for example, continued to conceive of the crucial goal of education in terms of cultivating *tecai* (special talent) and *rencai* (human talent), traditional terms whose meaning resonated with the emerging modern concept (pioneered, in fact, by the Soviet state in the 1920s) of "human capital," in which educational goals are subordinated to the needs of the state. Moreover, the individualism of Chinese liberal pedagogues in the

1920s was of a humanistic character and never opposed collectivism. Thus, a 1919 statement stated that the goals of education were to "cultivate an all-round personality, develop a republican spirit . . . private morals for one's own existence and public morals to serve the community and the state."[19]

Unlike the revolutionary wing of the intelligentsia, who also claimed the need to develop personality but who, in fact, never went further than mere declarations, China's liberal pedagogues took concrete steps to implement an individual-oriented pedagogy. They initiated and, with the help of their influential American colleagues and financial and political backers, implemented a complex educational reform, promulgated in 1922, which proclaimed the importance of the individual and the child as a "center of education." For a short period as chancellor of Beijing University, Cai Yuanpei was able to implement his main thesis—that individuality presupposes an independence of views and aspirations that are realized through democratic disputes—by inviting the representatives of opposing parties and ideologies to give lectures. Tao Xingzhi pursued the same policy in his school at Xiaozhuang, where he invited teachers of different political orientations and declared his campus "a free territory." Through their activities they sought to combine the indigenous *shuyuan* (academy) tradition of free discussion and student initiative with the innovations of American Progressivism, such as the Dalton plan, which emphasized individual responsibility. They also elaborated new curricula and teaching materials, introduced new heuristic methods, and sought to foster students' self-education. Tao's accent on student creativity, self-realization, self-activity, and self-management was realized in the Xiaozhuang Normal College, where education was combined with physical labor and the use of student-instructors was introduced.

During the same period of the 1920s, Russia was in essence China's classmate. Both had the same teacher. Interestingly, Russia's educational search for personality ended with results very different from China's. In both China and Russia the educational search for personality in the 1920s was to be found not in the mainstream of official policy but in the alternative theories proposed by liberal educators. While no specific interactions can be traced between Russian and Chinese educators in this domain during the 1920s, parallels existed because the rise of individual-oriented pedagogy was closely related to democratic influences at work in both societies. While Chinese revolutionaries applied the Soviet model of mass education, with its emphasis on rebuilding society, liberal educators in both countries developed a theory of alternative schools based upon the model of American Progressivism.[20] The active essence of human nature was a fundamental principle of American Progressivism, rooted in Protestant morality. This principle conflicted to some degree with the Russian Orthodox approach to a human being and even more so with the Chinese Taoist principle of *wuwei* (nonactivity), which oriented pedagogy toward "communicating with the Truth" by meditation and the accumulation of wisdom.

Superficially, both Russian and Chinese educators had the same aim: to liberate the individual's mind and enable his or her independent approach to life through the search for personality. Thus, like his Chinese colleagues, the Soviet theorist Blonsky criticized the traditional schools for cultivating "the spirit of passive submission to authority and an uncritical way of thinking."[21] Chinese and Russian students of Dewey's humanistic individualism had much in common. For example, a comparison of two schools, Tao Xingzhi's Xiaozhuang or Yucai School and Shatsky's First Experimental Field School of the People's Commissariat of Education, reveals an amazing coincidence of experiments in areas such as labor education, aesthetic education, and students' involvement in self-government. The American observer W. Kilpatrick, who visited an experimental rural school organized in the USSR by S. Shatsky and later traveled to Xiaozhuang, was impressed by the similarities of the two schools and told Tao Xingzhi about the identical ideas of his Russian colleague.[22]

At the same time, however, the different civilizational backgrounds and cultural traditions of the two countries gave rise to equally important differences in the individual-oriented approaches of Russian and Chinese educators. The humanistic trend that was evident in the first decade of Soviet education had at least two central characteristics that set it apart from the similar trend under way in Chinese educational circles in the 1920s. One was a degree of official state support for a liberal pedagogy that was absent in China. The other was a greater integration of liberal educational philosophy with other disciplines in terms of research and application. Let us begin with the first difference. The first generation of Soviet leaders sought to portray themselves, in educational terms, as the legitimate heirs of Russian indigenous and world humanistic trends. The first "new schools" embodying an individual-oriented pedagogy in Russia appeared at the end of the nineteenth century as a product of the combined influence of Russian philosophers, writers, and educators. In 1911, six years before the October Revolution, a prominent Russian educator declared that the main goal in reforming education was "not the individualization of teaching, but the educating of an individuality."[23] Seven years later, in 1918, the official Soviet Declaration on the Unified Labor School confirmed that "the personality remains the highest value in the socialist culture." N. K. Krupskaya, Lenin's wife and a high-ranking official at the People's Commissariat of Education, actively supported the innovations that were proposed by liberal educators. The declaration was implemented by instituting an innovative "complex" curriculum that included experimental research learning (laboratory experiments and labor), field excursions and projects, the Dalton plan, studio system learning based on a free schedule (which was intended to replace classroom-based learning), and the abolition of examinations—all of which were intended to stimulate individual activity and creative initiative.

The Russian innovative approach to developing a human being also differed from that of Chinese liberal educators in the 1920s in that the former presupposed an integration of all kinds of human knowledge, including literature, anthropology, psychology, and the intellectual traditions of the Russian non-Orthodox Church, which regarded a human being as God's crowning creation. Within this holistic framework, special emphasis was laid on the biological characteristics of an individual. As early as the first half of the nineteenth century, Russian educators had promoted the idea that education should be directed not only toward differences in individuals' mental abilities but also to differences in his or her physiological-psychological characteristics as well. Thus, during the first Soviet decade schools were expected to undertake biological and psychological tests of students as part of their efforts to develop a child-oriented pedagogy. Russian educators in the 1920s went further in their theoretical pursuits than their Chinese colleagues, embarking upon close studies in areas such as genetic psychology. This included efforts by Blonsky and others to determine the age-based characteristics of students, the psychological mechanisms that determined an individual's innate orientations, and the mechanisms that shaped individuals' interactions with the world of external incentives (the latter, which included formal education, were evaluated for their capacity to modify or stimulate genetically determined characteristics). In focusing upon genetic psychology, Blonsky and others adopted the position that the goal of education could not be externally determined but, instead, had to stem from a child's original nature. The development of personality was understood as a process of interaction between a person's innate characteristics and the external world, made up of the world of nature, social values, and culture. The role of education was therefore to awaken inherent abilities and creativity.

There were deep disparities, however, between the liberal pedagogues' understanding of individual activity and the Marxist approach of the Soviet state. While liberal educators regarded individual learning activity as a means of self-realization and interaction with the surrounding world, Marxist educators stressed the power of education to mold a "new person for a new socialist society." Russian liberal pedagogues also envisaged a human being as a citizen (i.e., they agreed that individual existence was embedded in national, historical, and social contexts), but for them the individual as citizen was also part of their belief in socialism as a free civil society. This resulted in an inevitable and increasing clash between the advocates of "free choice" and "self-development," on the one hand, and the official goal of "molding a new person for a new socialist society," on the other. The paradox of the Soviet school in the 1920s was thus to be found in its awkward efforts to combine individualism with collectivism. Liberal experiments such as the Dalton plan, which were intrinsically oriented to student's individual efforts, were implemented in studio group classes, in order "not to break the principle of collectivism." Learning activities that were originally intended to cultivate individual responsibility were reduced to mean an individual's responsibility to "struggle" for the fulfillment of collective goals, such as the targets of the five-year "industrial-financial plan."[24] In general, both Russian and Chinese searches for individualism were of a humanistic character and never opposed collectivism. But the clash between the liberals' call for individual self-development, on the one hand, and official demands for molding a personality, on the other, represented the essential tension between the traditional monological and future dialogical cultures in both countries.

The Individualization of Education in China and Russia in the 1980s and 1990s: Similar Patterns?

Historical events between the 1930s and the 1970s seriously constrained the further development of child-centered education in both China and the USSR. The anti-Japanese war, revolution, and the subsequent period of socialist construction in China shifted the focus to mass education for sociopolitical change and economic development. In Russia in 1931 the Soviet Communist Party, envisaging rapid industrialization, issued a decree that unambiguously put an end to all alternative experiments in education and established a new educational paradigm well suited to the needs of a totalitarian state. At different periods during the following half-century, Chinese state and non-state agencies followed the "Soviet gymnasium" model and adopted those aspects of Soviet education that were concerned with mass-oriented education into the framework of a unified school system. According to the recent evaluations of some Chinese scholars, China after 1949 failed to "make a timely transition from cognitive pedagogy to a pedagogy aimed at satisfying the demands of a human being and society."[25]

In the 1980s, when Chinese and Russian educators sought reform, they drew both from foreign experience and from the indigenous humanistic trends of the 1920s. For many Chinese and Russian intellectuals the crisis of belief, morality, and values in the post-totalitarian era was not simply a crisis of political ideology but was also a deeper crisis of self-identity.[26] Yet, while some of the school reforms that were adopted in the 1980s, including individualization of teaching methods and a diversification of types of schools, appeared to be similar in both countries, the extent and significance of the reforms actually depended on the degree of democratization of the whole society. As we shall see, there were significant differences between the two countries in this respect.

Reformist calls for a more individually oriented pedagogy provoked ardent debates among Chinese educators in the 1980s and 1990s. Opponents of such reforms labeled them "tricks of the Western bourgeoisie," while proponents of reform claimed that "there are those who confuse the development of an individual with the growth of individualism; this is a big mistake."[27] Gu Mingyuan argued, correctly in the opinion of this author, that the existing system was unable to educate the kinds of personnel needed for a market economy and scientific progress.[28] New kinds of cadres were required, Gu said, who did not simply obey their leaders' commands but who were autonomous, creative, daring, and capable of undertaking unusual decisions and initiative with a sense of individual responsibility. Some scholars responded that such characteristics were lacking in the Chinese national character, while reformers maintained that the fault lay not with the Chinese people but with the existing educational system.[29] One scholar even charged that the existing PRC educational system was simply incapable of producing Nobel Prize winners.[30]

The search for personality in the reform era was restricted in its early phase by the official goals of educational reform as expressed in the 1985 "Decision on the Reform of the Educational System" and the 1986 Compulsory Education Law. These documents affirmed that the main goal of education was "to improve the nation's quality" (*tigao minzu suzhi*) by training new types of talent (*rencai*) for modernization. Within this policy context the search for personality entailed tapping natural talents (*tiancai*) by determining individual abilities. Educators successfully revived the Confucian maxim that one should "teach according to (students') abilities" (*yincai shijiao*), while theorists stressed the importance of early development of students' skills, mental potency, and nonmental abilities. To this end some experimental schools were established in the 1980s that emphasized student initiative, introduced elective courses and individual tutoring, and organized extracurricular activities according to students' individual interests and abilities. In most schools, however, the new emphasis on the individual translated into the practice of concentrating teacher attention on gifted pupils while ignoring the individual needs of the majority of students. Critics also charged that, even among the gifted students who were lavished with individual attention, "the development of abilities often substitutes for the development of individuality."[31]

During the 1980s Russia, China's former schoolmate in the class of individual-oriented pedagogy in the 1920s, aroused deep interest among Chinese reformist educators and scholars, who looked to contemporary Russian educational experience and experimentation as often as they looked to Piaget, Dewey, Bloom, Bruner, or Maslow. The special attraction of the Russian search for personality to China's democratic-minded educators lay in the humanistic nature of the former and the common collectivist heritage of the two countries. With Russia's officially proclaimed transition from orthodox Marxist ideology to "universal human values" in the late 1980s, Russian philosophers and educators began to elaborate a new educational paradigm within the framework of humanism. Enriched by the modern achievements of anthropology and educational psychology, this new paradigm was based on an explicit assumption that the state exists for the individual. It asserted that a genuine humanization of education presupposed the construction of circumstances and incentives directed toward the nurturing of personality and a new system of values. This breakthrough provided a strong impetus to some Chinese scholars, who admitted that "the Soviet Union is far ahead of us in recognizing an individual's development, in that this principle is specified in the (Russian) Constitution, and that its practical implementation is much more scientific."[32]

Before the 1980s official Chinese pedagogy was heavily influenced by the ideas of the famous Russian pedagogue I. A. Kairov. According to Kairov, an individual's inherent characteristics, social surroundings, and education constituted three independent determinants of a human being's development. Kairov's conception represented a step toward the acknowledgment of biological characteristics. The next step took place under the influence of Russian pedagogy in the 1960s, in which Chinese scholars accepted the equal importance of both social and biological factors in an individual's development. By the end of the 1980s Chinese scholars challenged the official, purely sociological understanding of individual development with arguments concerning the interrelationships of social and biological factors. Even the most daring of Chinese innovators, however, while proclaiming the individual as the starting point of education, nonetheless also insisted that their view of education did not presume the separation of education and society and that it presupposed the existence of individuals as social beings.[33] What they did do, however, was

to challenge the official understanding of *social* by insisting that human beings' social nature extended beyond the framework of class affiliation.[34] And
they argued that only when individuality ceased to be regarded as fostering
"anarchism and a lack of responsibility, discipline and order" could education
begin to provide for the future development of the whole society.[35]

The late 1980s thus saw the beginnings of genuine "great leap forward" in
the development of the notion of personality in China. The political climate
changed after June 4, 1989, however, and for a period PRC officials repudiated
all efforts aimed at introducing humanism as a theory that stressed the existence of the self beyond social boundaries. Indeed, the very term *self* was
rejected as a "bourgeois" conception. It was not until late 1992, after Deng
Xiaopoing's criticism of the leftist wing of the Party and his demand to
accelerate all aspects of modernization, that Chinese liberals were able to take
the next step: to probe the notion of a personality as a subject possessing his
or her own self-consciousness. By this time a new Russian Law on Education
had already proclaimed "an individual's free development" as one of the core
principles of state policy.[36] Chinese law meanwhile continued to define the
goal of education as "improving the nation's quality," but the Russian model
served to foster further humanistic pursuits by Chinese intellectuals.

From 1992 onward Chinese scholars resumed their theoretical investiga-
tions in search of educational models for the development of personality and
individuality. For instance, the previous acknowledgment that biological nature played an important role in individual development stimulated new
research into emotional learning, first begun in China in the 1920s, as a
component of cognitive learning. Previously, a rational approach had dominated, whereby emotional education was regarded as equivalent to either
aesthetic or moral education. Reformers in the 1990s called for a new approach of "educating the emotions," which acknowledged the core importance of emotional motivations in the learning process: a child as a subject
could efficiently absorb curriculum only in cases when he or she assimilated a
need for it through a process involving both mental and emotional choice.
Emotional learning was said to be based on children's innate feelings of
affection, joy, and self-esteem, which it was the job of the school (and teachers) to protect and nurture. Genuine individualization (*rengehua*) was thus
understood as inseparable from emotional reflection and internalization of
the teaching material.[37]

In a further example of the resumption of interest in personality, some
Chinese scholars proposed a spiritual dimension to the quest for individ-
uality—thereby reviving another trend that had originated in the 1920s.
Some scholars raised the banner of apriorism, according to which the goal of

education was to assist a human being in recalling his or her spiritual consciousness. Zhang Ling echoed a Russian Christian concept when he claimed
that pedagogy had to treat a human being as "a physical, spiritual and social
creature." Zhang criticized Chinese schools for elevating material over emotional (spiritual) discourse.[38] This reminds us of Tolstoy's assumption that
a human being's development was intrinsically a matter of spiritual self-
realization, the essence of which was to overcome biological and social determinants of behavior. Tolstoy's spirituality was located in the domain of
religion—a human being's divine origin—as was that of the Chinese Christian philosopher Lu Xiaofeng, who in the early 1990s claimed the status of an
individual to be prior and greater than that of a state, nation, or ethnic and
cultural tradition, and that individuals possessed a value that transcended
national or cultural boundaries. Thus, by the middle of the 1990s the humanistic tendencies that had emerged in China in the previous decade had advanced to a new stage: whereas China's liberal pedagogues in the 1980s had
spoken in rather general terms of the "human being" as the logical starting
point of education, their successors in the 1990s defined their subject more
precisely as a "real person in real life" (*xianshi shenghuo ren*). This shift
represented a further challenge to the official pedagogy, which, insofar as it
was modeled on a concept of the individual, imagined ideal human beings.[39]

Subjectivity and self-realization emerged in the 1990s as primary concerns among Russian and Chinese education scholars. In the early 1990s a
group of leading Russian educational theorists proposed that Russian education should henceforth proceed from the premise that a human being was at
once a biological organism, a social personality, and a self-conscious individual. Education ought therefore to involve training, socialization, and self-
realization.[40] Chinese scholars also challenged the view that students were
primarily objects of socialization. The first step toward affirming subjectivity
was the same in both Russia and China: to claim that a student was concurrently both object and subject in the educational process. This premise also
implied that teachers, as individuals, were also subjects and that therefore
teacher-student relationships could be explained in terms of subject-to-
subject relationships based on mutual respect and equality—a daring challenge to the traditional leading role of a teacher. In this way Chinese notions
of subjectivity were freed from a narrow practical interpretation, in which
subjectivity referred only to subjects engaged in market-based competition or
to a juridical person, and obtained a more profound pedagogical meaning.
Chinese educational theorists insisted that a student was an independent
personality, and, like their Russian colleagues, they proclaimed his or her self-
realization as the main goal of education. Educators in both countries also

accused the existing educational system of using examinations, marks, and punishments to restrain student's subjectivity. They claimed that only when the teaching process guaranteed the development and enhancement of the subjective characteristics of each participant would the educational system be capable of nurturing individuality.[41]

To summarize, the writings of Chinese and Russian educational theorists in the 1990s on the topic of individual subjectivity were characterized by two shared features. First, scholars in both countries inherited a traditional holistic approach that conceived of an individual as an undivided unity of biological, social, and self attributes. Second, scholars in both countries defined personality as an inherently self-developing and self-regulating system, one that was not rigidly determined by either biological or sociological factors. The former presupposed that each individual should be approached as a spontaneous subject with a variety of aspects, while the latter implied that the conversion of latent potential depended not only on an individual's inherent characteristics and external circumstances but on the formation of his or her self-consciousness and capacity for personal choice and self-determination. In the words of one Chinese writer, "A human being is not simply a product of a combination of genetic characteristics and surroundings, a human being is a product of his own choice."[42] This understanding of the nature and development of personality was held up by reformist educators in both countries as the basis upon which to design the goals, content, and methods of an individual-oriented pedagogy.

Of course, the relative emphases of individual-oriented pedagogy were somewhat different in the two countries, reflecting the different historical and cultural backgrounds. Thus, for example, while Russia's individual-oriented pedagogy emphasized such functions as self-reflection and the construction of a self-image, Chinese theorists tended to focus rather more on self-improvement and self-discipline—aspects of personality that were closer to the traditional concept of self-cultivation (*xiu ji*).[43] Nonetheless, I believe that the acknowledgment of self-development and self-determination represented a breakthrough in Chinese pedagogy: a turning point from authoritarian-based education to education for freedom. Even though Chinese pedagogues—unlike their Russian counterparts in the 1990s—steadfastly refrained from using the expression "education for freedom," they nonetheless appear to have had this concept in mind when they quoted Marx: "the free development of each individual is a necessary condition for the free development of society."[44]

It may be argued that Russian educators proceeded further toward an understanding of the individual than their Chinese colleagues in some respects.

For example, right through the mid-1990s Chinese educational theorists found it impossible to justify the use of the term *individualism*, with its heavy negative political connotations in the contemporary Chinese context. By contrast, Russian educational theorists in the 1990s were not only free to use *individualism*, but they also succeeded in infusing the term with a sophisticated theoretical significance. They did so by insisting that it be defined as an internal intellectual and moral independence that was linked with self-discipline, self-estimation, and self-improvement. In particular, these Russian theorists emphasized the importance of the cultural environment and civilizational values in assisting individuals to impose self-restrictions on their freedom of action and to manage, by means of self-regulation, the eternal inner conflict between biological and individual urges and social imperatives. As one Russian writer explained: "A personality as a subject achieves its individual meaning only through a combination of cultural elements . . . The more perfectly an individual is able to master these cultural elements, the more freedom (not willfulness) he possesses."[45] In other words, the ability of individuals to assume responsibility for their actions and to act autonomously within the limits of existing social and cultural constraints involved the ability to impose inner constraints on one's freedom.

Thus far we have been discussing the search for personality among Chinese educational theorists in the 1980s and 1990s. But to what extent did Chinese educators actually succeed in implementing these reform ideas? Since the late 1980s a number of experiments aimed at developing an individual-oriented pedagogy were initiated at primary and junior middle schools in Shandong, Zhejiang, and Henan.[46] The starting point for all such experiments involved the effort to improve teaching. The experimental schools organized special training courses for teachers, who were required to pass exams demonstrating their aesthetic abilities in dancing, singing, drawing, and reciting poems. Fostering new relationships between teachers and students was another focus of the experiments. Teachers were supposed to demonstrate trust and respect for students and to take into consideration their emotional reactions. For example, teachers in the experimental schools were required to compile comprehensive files for each student that included not only a record of marks but also a listing of school achievements, special abilities, aspirations, and pertinent psychological observations and physical data. In some experiments designed to improve their self-evaluation, students were asked to provide subjective assessments of their abilities and aptitudes on a standard questionnaire, and the responses were then compared with teachers' assessments.[47]

Fostering a positive learning environment was another goal of the experimental schools. In the Shandong schools teachers were encouraged to smile throughout the lesson in order to create a joyful learning atmosphere.[48] School activities were designed to stimulate students' desire to uncover data and solutions and to participate in class discussions and competitions. In all such experiments and competitions "personal success" was considered key. Teachers were instructed in how to create "situations of success." This included avoiding excessive criticism (in one Shandong school, e.g., Saturday was designated as "the day without any critics"); rewarding good performance; and organizing students into "mutual support" groups. Some experiments endeavored to raise students' self-esteem by giving every student an opportunity to exercise leadership.

In the final analysis, however, all such experiments undertaken since the late 1980s in the name of individual-oriented pedagogy were aimed primarily at developing academic abilities rather than individual characteristics and outlook. Thus, the process of "individualization" often entailed neglect of the majority of students while concentrating teachers' attention on the gifted few. Similar tendencies are also observable in Russian schools since the 1980s, where the pace of experimentation was much greater (by the mid-1990s 15 percent of Russian schools were involved in experiments to foster "education for freedom"). In Russia, however, experiments were also undertaken to implement individual-oriented teaching methods for slow learners. Very few schools in China were involved in such experiments. Finally, the possibility of a curriculum that promotes the validity and advantages of alternative viewpoints remained for the most part out of reach. Such a curriculum, with its implication of pluralism, remained elusive not only in China but also even in Russia at the end of the 1990s.

Conclusion

The search for personality in China at the end of the present century represents a restoration and further development of pursuits that were first begun in the 1920s. The pedagogical search for personality in the 1980s and 1990s built upon notions first developed by educators such as Tao Xingzhi, Cai Yuanpei, Chen Heqing, and others and then further enriched them with recent insights drawn from psychology, anthropology, and philosophy. What this meant was that the original 1920s liberal concern for nurturing personal subjectivity, creativity, and self-consciousness remained in the 1980s and 1990s, but these qualities were now seen to arise from within self-developing and self-regulating human beings rather than being molded by external influences, as liberal educators of the 1920s had believed. Whereas the innovative pedagogues of the 1920s had stressed the significance of the individual within a social context, those of the 1990s approached a notion of individuality based on the concept of an autonomous self.

The most liberal Chinese pedagogues realized that modernization presupposed core changes in personality and that only a democratization of education could create the conditions necessary for nurturing modern characteristics such as independence and the spirit of equality, freedom, and citizenship. In their search for personality Chinese pedagogues drew from the humanistic breakthroughs of indigenous philosophers and assimilated global humanistic trends, including those emanating from their Russian neighbor. Of course, given their different historical backgrounds and cultural heritages, as well as their differing social conditions during the 1980s and 1990s transition period, the term *individualization* obtained a different meaning in the educational paradigms of China and Russia. In China individualization was expressed primarily in the form of innovations in teaching methods, geared mainly toward nurturing the academic abilities of gifted students (often grouped together in special "key" schools), while in Russia additional steps were taken toward creating and implementing a new educational paradigm of "education for freedom." In addition, Chinese pedagogical reforms were more restricted in their spread, being confined mainly to experimental schools in a few provinces, while in Russia by the late 1990s some 15 percent of all schools were engaged in efforts to implement education for freedom.

The search for personality arose concurrently and independently in both countries, and in both cases it led toward a form of humanistic individualism. In the last decade, however, owing to Russia's longer humanistic tradition and stronger democratic trends, Russian influence on Chinese pedagogical liberalization has become increasingly influential. At the same time, it must be pointed out that, in the longer term, successful promotion of humanistic trends in education may be closely linked to a country's internal stability and economic growth. Seen from this perspective, although China began reform at a much lower level of economic development than Russia, by the 1990s China was economically vibrant as well as politically stable, while Russia demonstrated decline in both realms. Thus, although the impetus and desire for pedagogical reform may be similar in both countries, the long-term results may well depend on conditions outside and beyond the control of the education sector. At the same time, it is also important not to exaggerate the trend toward individualization in the two countries. Neither society was ready or prepared to accept and implement the ideas of humanistic individualism and a dialogical culture in the late 1990s. What we are discussing here is, rather, a series of theoretical breakthroughs and some experiments that have established a foundation for the future.

Finally, I also assume that big countries, like big numerals, have some common trends in their development. In Russia and China one such common trend has been the value each society has historically placed on collectivism, coupled with a corresponding opposition to individualism. For many developed Western countries, individualism as an educational principle has already reached its apogee, and pedagogues there are increasingly looking toward the categories of collectivism found in Eastern pedagogical traditions. China and Russia may be located at the opposite end of the pendulum: while attempting to create a new educational philosophy based on the individual, educators in both countries remain acutely aware of what they regard as the negative consequences of extreme individualism in the West. In this sense they have not rejected collectivism in total but are, rather, searching for new forms of collectivity, each member of which can also be an individual. This notion conforms with the tradition of modern Chinese democracy: Cai Yuanpei predicted, for example, that the future of humankind lay not in competitive struggle between individuals but in their mutual support. In his view the ideal personality had two modes: one possessed of an individual character and the other possessed of a mass character, each one struggling with and supplementing each other.[49]

Scholars in many countries have emphasized the traditional Chinese holistic approach to a human being. Such a holistic approach was also found in Russian pedagogy and philosophy (it dominated the thought of Blonsky and P. Kapterev) and, indeed, is characteristic of most humanist pedagogies (including that of Dewey). A holistic approach to the human being offers wide potential for a humanistic pedagogy because it presupposes the harmony and spirituality of an individual and because it considers human nature in a broad context encompassing not only society but nature and the cosmos as well. Such a perspective may be of core importance in postmodern societies in which human beings are valued not exclusively on the basis of their abilities but on their very humanity. In this respect some contemporary Chinese theorists have advanced the view that spirituality can minimize the negative effects of a commodity society, by enabling individuals to transcend their economic interests and material instincts and "obtain the specific features of a free personality and of an ideal person for a future communist society."[50] Similarly, many scholars in both the West and the East have emphasized the potential for mutual enrichment of alternative concepts, such as supplementing individuality with a notion of collectivism in which individuals may realize themselves through collective consciousness. I concur with those educators who urge a dynamic combination of alternate traditions as a means to reinvigorate Chinese, Russian, and Western education.[51]

NOTES

1. I am quite aware of the fact that these maxims received many different interpretations in the history of Chinese philosophical thought. I assume, however, that outside the scholarly debates they became a part of imperial Confucianism's orthodoxy and thus existed as dogmas until the end of the empire.

2. Liu Gang, "Jiaoyu zhexuezhong you quan rende lilun yanjiu jinzhan he cunzaide wenti" (Some problems and prospects in the human being theory in the philosophy of education), in *Analysis and Perspectives in Chinese Pedagogy after the Third Plenum of the CCP* (Beijing: 1988), 197. In the Russian philosophical tradition this is one of the most confusing terms, with about seventy definitions in contemporary Russia. Until recently, the term was often used as a synonym for *personality*. Nowadays, however, it is often used to mean the unity of an individual and his or her personality, a whole independent closed microcosm in which all elements interact. See B. G. Matunin, "Lichnost ili individualnost?" (Personality or individuality?), *Pedagogica* 3 (1993): 14; and V. I. Genetinsky, "Individualnost kak predmet pedagogicheskoi antropologii" (Individuality as a subject of pedagogical anthropology), *Sovetskaya Pedagogika* (Moscow) 9 (1991): 47.

3. Guo Qijia, *Zhongguo jiaoyu sixiang shi* (The history of Chinese pedagogical ideas) (Beijing: Jiaoyu kexue chubanshe, 1987), 15, 52.

4. The challenge to the Confucian approach on this issue came from the Daoist tradition, whose philosophers, beginning with Ji Kang and Liu Xue and continuing among some Ming-Qing thinkers, never accepted that transcendental *tianli* (heavenly principles) were incompatible with human nature and its biological passions. See Guo, *Zhongguo jiaoyu sixiang shi,* 178.

5. Dong Zhongshu, cited in Guo Qijia, *Zhongguo jiaoyu sixiang shi,* 157.

6. On this issue, too, one can also locate challenges to orthodoxy emanating from within the Chinese philosophic tradition. On this question the challenge emanated from Mozi, who took the first step toward individual self-esteem with statements like "One who loves people is included as an object of this love as well" and "Love yourself and others equally." Of course, this remains a far cry from the Christian concept of "love thy neighbor as one loves oneself." Moreover, Mozi justified love of oneself only when it did not contradict the interests of the state. Nonetheless, in many Russian scholars' estimation, Mozi was the first Chinese philosopher to investigate the problem of the correlation between individual and collective interests. See M. L. Titarenko, *Drevnekitaisky Filosof Mo Di, Yego Shkola i Ucheniye* (Ancient philosopher Mo Di, his school and ideas) (Moscow: 1985).

7. Cited in P. F. Kapterev, "Istorija Russkoj Pedagogiki" (A history of Russian pedagogy), *Pedagogy* 5 (1994): 54–57.

8. Liang Qichao, cited in Liu Qi, "Gexing, qunxing, shehui" (Individuality, masses, society), *Huadong Shifan Daxue xuebao: Jiaoyu kexueban* (Journal of East China Normal University, pedagogical issue) 2 (1989): 3.

9. Zhu Zhimin, "Jin xiandai zhongguode jiaoyu yu 'Wusi' " (Modern education in China and the May Fourth Movement), *Jiaoyu yanjiu* 6 (1989): 7.

10. Cited in Wang Shubai, "Mao Zedong zaoqi lunli sixiang chushuo" (Preliminary investigation of Mao Zedong's early ethical ideas), *Qiusu*, no. 6 (1983).

11. Cai Yuanpei, *Cai Yuanpei xuanji* (Selected works of Cai Yuanpei), vol. 3 (Beijing: Zhonghua shuju, 1984), 174.

12. Cited in Wang, "Mao Zedong zaoqi lunli sixiang chushuo."

13. Guo Qijia, *Zhongguo jiaoyu sixiang shi*, 382–84, 467; Liu Qi, "Gexing, qunxing, shehui," 1.

14. Liu Qi, "Gexing, qunxing, shehui," 2; Cai Yuanpei, *Cai Yuanpei xuanji* 3:174.

15. Cai Yuanpei, *Cai Yuanpei xuanji* (Selected works of Cai Yuanpei), 3:174.

16. *Yi Tao wei shi, xian shen jiaoyu* (Learn from Tao, dedicate your life to education) (Nanjing: Nanjingshi jiaoyu xuehui, 1990), 71.

17. *Yi Tao wei shi, xian shen jiaoyu*, 86.

18. See Guo Qijia, *Zhongguo jiaoyu sixing shi*, 459.

19. Zhu Zhimin, "Jin xiandai zhongguode jiaoyu yu 'Wusi,' " 8.

20. Hubert O. Brown, "American Progressivism in Chinese Education: The Case of Tao Xingzhi," in Ruth Hayhoe and Marianne Bastid, eds., *China's Education and the Industrialized World* (Armonk, N.Y.: M. E. Sharpe, 1987).

21. V. G. Prianikova, "Antropologo-gumanisticheskoje napravlenije v otechest-vennoi pedagogike" (The anthropological-humanistic trend in our country's pedagogy), *Pedagogy* 2 (1995).

22. *Yi Tao wei shi, xian shen jiaoyu*, 72; and G. J. Maximova, *Vzaimosvijaz tvorcheskikh idei i opita S. T. Shatskogo s kontseptsijami i praktikoi zarubezhnoi pedagogiki* (The interrelationship of S. T. Shatski's creative ideas and experience with the experience of foreign education) (Moscow: Academy of Pedagogical Sciences, 1991), 18.

23. J. Z. Gilbuch, "Idei differentsiirovannogo obucheniya v nashei pedagogike" (Individual-oriented ideas in our pedagogy), *Pedagogy* 5 (1994): 83.

24. R. B. Vendrovskaya, *Shkola 20-kh godov: pojiski i rezultati* (School in the 1920s: explorations and results) (Moscow: International Pedagogical Academy, 1993), 11–13, 30.

25. Hu Xiaofeng, "Guanyu gengxin jiaoyu sixiang jinxing chuangye jiaoyude tanlun" (Exploring the issue of renewing educational thought and implementing creative pedagogy), *Renmin ribao* (People's Daily) 16 (January 1989): 5.

26. Hu Zhongpin, "Ren shi jiaoyude chufadian" (Human beings, the starting point of education), *Jiaoyu yanjiu* 8 (1989): 34.

27. Gu Mingyuan, "Jiaoyu kexue ying cong 'Wusi' jingshen zhong xiqu shenmo yingyang" (What kind of nourishment should educational science absorb from the spirit of the May Fourth Movement?), *Jiaoyu yanjiu* 6 (1989): 5.

28. Ibid.

29. Meng Wangjin, "Zhongguo chuantong wenhua beijingxia de guomin xinli yu jiaoyu" (People's psychology and education under Chinese traditional culture), *Jiaoyu yanjiu* 2 (1992): 73–76; and Li Qingmin, "Shiying yu chaoyue: deyu dui xiandaihua

shehuide yingda" (Adaptation and transcendence: the response of moral education to modern society), *Jiaoyu yanjiu* 8 (1989): 11.

30. Sun Xining et al., "Rende zhutixing neihan yu rende zhutixing jiaoyu" (On the meaning of human beings' subject nature and subject education), *Jiaoyu yanjiu* 10 (1995): 10.

31. Dai Ruqian, "Gexing fazhan yu jiaoyu gaige shiyan" (Personality development and educational reform experiments), *Jiaoyu yanjiu* 7 (1989): 35.

32. Dai Ruqian and Wan Shiqi, " 'Fahui techang' bing bu dengyu 'fazhan gexing' " ("Tapping talents" is not equal to "personality development"), *Jiaoyu yanjiu yu shiyan* (Educational research and experiments) 3 (1990): 24. See also Kuang Pinghe, " 'Xin siwei' tuidong xiade Sulian jiaoyu gaige" (The Soviet Union's educational reform is promoted by the "new thinking"), *Jiaoyu yanjiu* 6 (1989): 24–29.

33. Hu Zhongpin, "Ren shi jiaoyude chufadian," 36.

34. Huang Ji, *Jiaoyu zhexue* (Philosophy of education) (Beijing: 1985).

35. Dai Ruqian and Wan Shiqi, " 'Fahui techang' bing du dengyu 'fazhan gexing,' " 25.

36. *Zakon Rossiiskoy Federatsii ob obpazovanii* (Russian federation law on education) (Moscow: Novaya shkola Press, 1992), 4.

37. Zhu Xiaoman, "Qinggan jiaoyude yishi jiqi teshu jizhi" (The sense and mechanism of emotional education), *Jiaoyu yanjiu* 7 (1993): 44–45.

38. Zhang Ling, "Jiaoyu mudi ziwo shixian shi qiantan" (An elementary investigation of self-realization theory as an educational goal), *Jiaoyu lilun yu shixian* 9, no. 2 (1989): 6.

39. Fu Songtao, "Xianshi shenghuo ren shi jiaoyuxuede loji qidian" (Human beings in real life is the logical starting point of pedagogy), *Jiaoyu yanjiu* 6 (1996): 26.

40. A. A. Bodalev et al., "Kontseptsija vospitanija uchascchejsia molodiozhi" (The concept of bringing up youth at schools), *Pedagogy* 3–4 (1992): 11–19.

41. Zhang Tongshan, "Luelun ren shi zhuti yu ketide tongyi" (A discussion on the unity of a human being as a subject and an object), *Jiaoyu yanjiu* 2 (1990): 47; and V. V. Gorshkova, *Problema Subyecta v Pedagogike* (The problem of a subject in pedagogy) (Leningrad: Rossijski gosudarstvenni pedagogicheskii Universitet, 1991), 12.

42. Ye Lan, "Shidai jingshen yu xin jiaoyu lixiangde goujian" (The moral symbol of a new era and the construction of a new educational ideal), *Jiaoyu yanjiu* 10 (1994): 5.

43. The Confucian meaning of *self-cultivation* was not identical, however, to the modern concepts of self-improvement and self-discipline. While Confucian self-cultivation (*xiu ji*) referred to mental (*xin*) reflection to train one's own nature (*zhi xing*) in order to learn from and to serve Heaven (*zhi tian*), the modern notions of self-improvement and self-discipline referred to the realization of personality for the benefit of the individual and society.

44. Sun Xining et al., "Rende zhutixing neihan yu rende zhutixing jiaoyu," 37.

45. B. M. Bim-Bud, "Antropologicheskiye osnovanija teorii i practiki obrazovanija" (The anthropological basis for educational theory and practice), *Pedagogy* 5 (1994): 3.

46. Expert Group, "Cujin chuzhongsheng gexing zuiyou fazhande shiyan tansuo" (An experiment in making the students in junior middle schools develop the best personalities), *Jiaoyu yanjiu* 1 (1994): 64.

47. United Group, "Xiaoxuesheng zhutixing fazhan shiyan yu zhibiao tixide dianli cepin yanjiu" (A joint study of the experiment in developing primary students' subjectivity and the establishment of an indicator system), *Jiaoyu yanjiu* 12 (1994): 59.

48. Tian Bing, "Guanyu cujin ertong gexing quanmian hexie fazhande tansuo" (Explorations in promoting all-round harmonious development in children's personality), *Jiaoyu yanjiu* 3 (1994): 65.

49. Cited in Chen Jingpan, *Zhongguo jin xiandai jiaoyujia zhuan* (Biographies of modern and contemporary Chinese educators) (Beijing: Beijing Shifan Daxue chubanshe, 1987), 133.

50. Sun Xining et al., "Rende zhutixing neihan yu rende zhutixing jiaoyu," 35.

51. Chinaeva, "Problemi perestroiki shkoli," 22; and H. W. Stevenson and J. Stingler, *The Learning Cap: Why Our Schools Are Failing and What We Can Learn from Japanese and Chinese Education* (New York: Summit, 1992).

Japan's Involvement with Higher Education in Manchuria: Some Historical Lessons from an Imposed Educational Cooperation

Yutaka Otsuka

Although there are differences in degree, all countries in the process of educational development are influenced by and exhibit relationships with other countries. This can be seen in the adoption of foreign educational theories, systems, practices, and customs and in the phenomenon of students studying abroad. While there are examples in which this relationship is voluntary, there are also examples in which it has been imposed. The aim of this essay is to examine Japan's involvement in higher education in China's northeast region, formerly known as Manchuria (Manzhouli), from the late nineteenth century to 1945.

Japan's first involvement in former Manchuria came when Japan imposed military rule over territory occupied during the Russo-Japanese War (1904–5). At that time permission was also granted to establish the privately run Jinzhou Academy in Manchuria. When Japan subsequently acquired the Guandong District and areas adjoining the South Manchuria Railway, it also took over the educational administration of those areas. From the outset Japan asserted control over the region's primary schools. Eventually, it also assumed management control over such institutions of higher education as the Lüshun (Port Arthur) Technical Institute (Lüshun gongke xuetang) and the Southern Manchurian Medical Institute (Nan Manzhouli yixuetang) (from 1922 these institutions were raised to university status and became the Lüshun Technical University (Lüshun gongke daxue) and the Manchurian

Medical University, respectively (Manzhou yike daxue). The Lüshun Technical University (established in 1909) and the Manchurian Medical University (established in 1911) were based on the policy of so-called culturally camouflaged armament (a strategy for advancing Japanese influence in the three Northeast Provinces through investment in cultural enterprises) put forward by Goto Shimpei, the first president of the South Manchuria Railway Company, and in accordance with Japan's Imperial Ordinance relating to Special Schools.[1] Although some Chinese students were permitted to enter both universities, they were essentially Japanese universities that happened to be on foreign soil. As such, they differed significantly from the institutions of higher education that were established within China by Chinese.

Eventually, with the setting up of Manchukuo as a Japanese puppet state in 1932, Japan formally transferred the administrative power that it had held up to that point over to Manchukuo. Even after this transfer of authority, Lüshun Technical University and the Manchurian Medical University continued to be run as Japanese universities. This essay, however, does not seek to investigate the character of the Japanese universities that were set up in China. Rather, it examines the influence that Japan exerted on Chinese universities in Manchuria from the late nineteenth century and, especially, on those institutions that continued to exist as universities in the Japanese puppet state of Manchukuo from 1932–45.

Japanese Influence on Higher Education Institutions Prior to the Manchurian Incident

The *State of Manchuria Education Yearbook* (edited by the Ministry of Education), published in March 1934, describes the institutions of higher education that existed in China's northeast region before the Manchurian Incident of 1931, which was followed by Japan's formal annexation of the region. "During the period of the former regime in the north-east the following universities existed. In Fengtian (Mukden) Province, the Northeastern University (Dongbei daxue), the Northeastern Jiaotong University, (Dongbei jiaotong daxue) and the Private Fengyong University (Sili Fengyong daxue) and, in the Jilin Province, the Jilin University (Jilin daxue). These universities were established so that the Chinese authorities of the time could train their supporters. Chinese administrators also occupied posts as directors of these universities and financed them. Although there is some evidence that random schools were established, there is not the slightest sign that they were intended to cultivate gifted people. When considering the facts, it is clear that the Chinese authorities took the good name of education and used it as a tool to grasp political power. After the Manchurian Incident, when their political power collapsed, all of these universities disappeared. The only ones that still exist to this day are the Medical College in Harbin and the Teacher Training School run by Xingdong Special District."[2] The *Second Education Yearbook of the Manchurian Empire,* published one year later, in December 1935, states that, aside from the four universities mentioned earlier—Northeastern, Jiaotong, Fengyong, and Jilin—"there were two universities (one industrial and one legal) run under Soviet authority in Harbin."[3]

On the other hand, according to Minagawa Toyoji, who held the posts of director of the General Affairs Bureau of the Ministry of Education and director of the Education Bureau of the Ministry of Public Welfare, there were some thirty institutions of higher education in Manchuria prior to the Manchurian Incident.[4] The discrepancy can be put down to differences in the definition of what constitutes a university or institution of higher education. If one were to take a more jaundiced view, it may have been that the editors of the official yearbook felt it necessary to underestimate the number of genuine institutions of higher education before 1931 in order to play down the extent of the damage to higher education caused by the Manchurian Incident. Setting aside the exact number of institutions, even Minagawa Toyoji charged that the thirty institutions that he claimed existed before Japanese rule were mere "hollow shells of universities and colleges which were so far removed from the form of government, the condition of the people, and primary and secondary education, that they were trying in vain to keep up appearances. As a result education lost its equilibrium and this laissez-faire attitude led to the appearance of swarms of pseudo-politician students, who, forgetting the role of students, acted as pawns of the military authorities and ran wild with anti-Japanese sentiment."[5]

It is difficult to accept the yearbook's assertion that "there was not the slightest intention of cultivating gifted people," nor does Minagawa Toyoji's description of "shells of universities" reflect the facts. In reality significant efforts were being made toward improving higher education in the northeast region prior to the Manchurian Incident. It is instructive to look at an example of one such institution, the Northeastern University. The University Foundation Preparatory Committee was formed in July 1922 in Fengtian Province, with Wang Yongjiang serving as its chair. At the outset it was supposed to be jointly managed by the three northeastern provinces, but in the end Jilin decided to found its own university and withdrew from the effort. Fengtian and Heilongjiang Provinces financed the institution on a 9:1 ratio. Northeastern contained four faculties: Literature, Law, Science, and Engineering. The

Faculty of Literature included English and Russian literature departments, while the Law Faculty contained the departments of politics and law. The Faculties of Science and Engineering contained the departments of mathematics, physics, and mechanical, electrical, and civil engineering. In 1923 Wang Zhaofan was made head of the literature and law faculties, and Zhao Houda became head of science and engineering. Yet the following year Zuo Yaoxian succeeded Zhao, who had contracted an illness while engaged in the purchase of experimental equipment in Germany. Subsequently, Wang Yongjian became president, and on October 24, 1924, he formally opened the university. More than three hundred preparatory course students were granted admission to the university in its first year following entrance examinations, which had been held the previous July. Students entered the regular course after one year of preparatory study.

Eventually, the Manchurian warlord Zhang Xueliang became president, and Northeastern University entered a new phase of development. Zhang was responsible for the construction of new school buildings, even donating some of his personal funds. Under the northern warlords' administration, even such famous institutions as Beijing University and Qinghua University were faced with worsening underfunding and late or nonpayment of staff wages. The annual budget of Beijing University was 900,000 yuan and that of Qinghua 1,200,000 yuan at the end of the 1920s. While nonpayment of wages certainly did not occur at Northeastern University, its annual expenditures rose to 1,500,000 yuan, more than the budgets of both Beijing and Qinghua University.[6] Indeed, Northeastern University began to attract scholars from all over the country.

On September 18, 1931, however, with the Manchurian Incident, the situation at Northeastern University changed drastically. On September 19 all military establishments and government institutions fell into the hands of the Japanese Imperial Army. But because Northeastern University was a cultural institution, even the Japanese army did not dare to occupy it. Instead, the Japanese army publicly dispatched the Japanese principal of the South Manchuria Middle School to calm fears and urge students to continue attending classes. He even went as far as to offer financial assistance on behalf of the Japanese army. These measures were meant to prevent Northeastern University from relocating. This offer was refused, however, and the teachers and students decided to evacuate to Beiping (Beijing). On September 22 they all set off by car for Beiping, but, due to the hurried nature of their departure, they were unable to transport the university's books, maps, machines, and equipment, and these were all lost.[7]

Jiaotong University and the private Fengyong University, which also fled the northeast after the Manchurian Incident, merged with Northeastern in 1932. Jilin University, which had been elevated to a university from its former status as the Jilin Junior Law College (Jilin falu zhuanke xuexiao) in 1929, stopped functioning.[8] After the Manchurian Incident many existing universities ceased operating, while others, not wanting to stay in the northeast under Japanese occupation, decided to move to areas such as Beiping, which had not been ravaged by the fires of war. Other higher technical schools also stopped operating. Thus, we can concur with the observation that, "with the founding of Manchukuo, all institutions of higher education from the former regime period were closed down immediately."[9] It is necessary, however, to confront the unpleasant truth that with the Japanese occupation almost all existing educational institutions either fled the northeast or were destroyed.

Subsequently, Japanese authorities in Manchuria recorded that "after due consideration of the need for their establishment, the current situation and so on, and together with the announcement of the Regulations for Private Schools, approval was granted for the establishment of the Mukden Medical College, the Harbin Medical College and the St. Vladimir Special School."[10] In 1933 Harbin Medical College was a private institution, but, because its funding had ceased, it was now supported financially by the Education Bureau of the Special District of the Northeastern Provinces and thus became effectively a state institution. In 1934 there were eighty-four registered students. The private Mukden Medical School had originally been established by the United Free Church of Scotland and had ninety-eight students.[11] It now became the Mukden Medical College. It would have been very difficult for the Japanese authorities to abolish this college because of its connection to Britain, which was the major foreign power in China at the time and with whom Japan enjoyed friendly relations. Other schools that continued to exist because of their close relationships with foreign countries were St. Vladimir College and the Harbin Polytechnic University.

On the other hand, independent institutions of higher education in Manchuria were established in rapid succession. Among these newly established schools, which were under the direct control of the Manchukuo Ministry of Education, were Fengtian Agricultural College, Harbin Agricultural College, Xinjing Livestock Veterinary College, Xinjing Law College, Fengtian Law College, Fengtian Technical College, and Xinjing Technical College (all three-year universities); plus Fengtian Medical College, Harbin Medical College, Jiamusi Medical College, and Harbin College (all four-year universities). In addition, the Xingan, Longjing, and Qiqihar Pioneer Medical Colleges (two years) were established with the aim of providing doctors for newly settled areas. Private educational institutions included the Northern Manchuria College (commerce three years, industry four years), Fengtian Pharmaceutical Training Center (three years), Fengtian College of Commerce (two years), and others. Institutions that were under the direct control of the State Council's premier included Jianguo University and Datong Academy, the latter a civil servant training institution. There were also two types of teacher-training institutions, one for primary education and one for secondary education. The latter had a three-year training period and admitted graduates from a four-year national higher school (both men and women were admitted), while the former also had a three-year training period and admitted persons with at least three years of education at a national higher education school. In addition, there was also the Xinjing Central Teacher Training Facility and, in Fengtian, the Provisional Agricultural Teacher Training Center.[12]

In summary, it is possible to identify three developments relating to the rise and fall of institutions of higher education in the northeast after the Manchurian Incident and the establishment of Manchukuo. First, as described earlier, a number of universities (such as Northeastern University) disappeared, some of which managed to survive elsewhere. Second, there were also universities that continued to exist in the northeast by adapting to the new situation and making the necessary changes to ensure their future survival. A third development was the birth of completely new Machukuo-based institutions of higher education. All of these developments contain important aspects that shed light on the background of Japanese influence on education in this region. Universities that ceased to exist or migrated, however, were no longer exposed to Japanese influence and interference, while the study of the newly established institutions is of limited value because of the lack of background against which a comparison may be made. It is therefore by tracing the path of the second of these developments—the survival and adaptation of Chinese higher educational institutions under Japanese colonial rule—that we can best discover the specific nature of Japanese involvement with higher education in Manchukuo. If we can analyze this process in detail, then the differences between universities before and after Japanese involvement should become clear, and the differences should bring to light the exact nature of Japanese influence. The specific experience of Harbin Polytechnical University (Haerbin gongye daxue) is selected for a case study. As will be described in greater detail later, this university was founded with the backing of the Soviet Union, and its transition from a Soviet to a Japanese institution makes it an extremely interesting case.

Harbin Polytechnical University under the Administration of the Chinese Eastern Railway Company

The Harbin Polytechnical University, originally known as the Harbin Sino-Russian Technical School, was established in 1920 to provide personnel for the Chinese Eastern Railway Company (also known as the Northeastern China Railway Company and the Northern Manchuria Railway Company), which was created under a contract between the Russian and Qing governments. On August 5, 1920, the School Foundation Committee was established, made up of representatives from the Northeastern China Railway Company, the Harbin City Council, and the Chamber of Commerce, among others. Song Xiaolian, president of the Northeastern China Railway Company was appointed as honorary chair, while T. R. Holwat, director of the Northeastern China Railway Company, was appointed as chair, and A. A. Cherkov was named school principal. In addition, a committee was set up to plan the curriculum under S. Ophenberg. Foundations were laid for the running of this university in accordance with Soviet-style rules and curriculum.[13]

The university formally opened on October 17, 1920, and classes began the following day. The language of instruction was Russian. A preparatory course was put in place from the very outset. Its main aim appears to have been Russian language education for the predominantly Chinese students.[14] The preparatory course took three years and was divided into beginner, intermediate, and advanced levels. Each level took approximately one year. Graduates of the advanced class were able to enter the first year of the regular course. Initially, there were seventeen students enrolled in the preparatory course, and their fees were 150 rubles per year, reduced to 100 rubles for children of workers employed by the Chinese Eastern Railway Company. The preparatory course existed until it was finally abolished in 1955, although it was suspended from 1937 to 1945 during the Manchukuo Period.[15]

The regular course was made up of two departments, the Department of Railway Construction and the Department of Mechanical and Electrical Engineering. As there were some Russian students in the Department of Railway Construction[16] who had already completed a year at Russian universities, first- and second-year students were admitted together, and there was only one class for each academic year. A total of thirty-six subjects were offered by the department. At the Department of Mechanical and Electrical Engineering there was only one class for all students, and thirty-nine subjects were taught. The course was based on a credit system and took four years to complete. There were no standard teaching materials, and students would listen and take notes during the classes. Both written and oral examinations were carried out, and a five-point result-assessment system was used. In the first year those who failed three subjects had to repeat the year. Those who failed only two subjects had to retake the examinations, but if they failed one or both examinations they too would be required to repeat the year. In order to graduate, students had to take written and oral examinations on their graduation projects.

Each student paid three hundred rubles per year in fees, but for children of workers employed by the Chinese Eastern Railway Company this was reduced to 200 rubles. Food expenses ranged from 30–35 rubles per month. A total of twenty students from each new intake would be government scholarship students who received support amounting to sixty rubles per month. In addition, Holwat scholarships worth three hundred rubles per year were awarded to five students every year.[17]

In April 1922 the Harbin Sino-Russian Technical School was renamed Harbin Sino-Russian Technical University. The existing departments became the Faculty of Railway Construction and the Faculty of Mechanical and Electrical Engineering, the courses were extended from four to five years, and high school graduates were admitted for the first time. During the 1923–24 academic year female students were also admitted for the first time, and by the end of 1923 there were some 347 students attending. In September 1924 General Zhu Qinglan, commander of the Chinese Eastern Railway Company's Railway Protection Army, took over as head of the University Administration Association, and the following month the first batch of students graduated. All 22 graduates of the Faculty of Railway Construction gained the title of engineer. The following year 25 students graduated from the Faculty of Mechanical and Electrical Engineering, along with 8 students from the Faculty of Railway Construction. The main reason why there were so few graduates compared to the number of admissions is that the requirements to move up to the next academic year at Harbin Sino-Russian Technical University were so rigorous that most students were not able to graduate or gain their engineering qualifications.[18] In addition, some students quit the course due to financial constraints. In the spring of 1925 a decision was made to permit the best of the graduate students to remain at the university to carry out research and to teach.

On December 4, 1925, Cherkov, the first university president, resigned due to illness, and in his stead Vostorgov took over the post. This ensuing period saw great changes to the university's organizational structure. Most important, the basic theoretical subjects common to the two existing faculties were rationalized into single classes called "teaching and research sections" (*jiaoyan shi*). A total of seventeen teaching and research sections and two teaching and research groups (*jiaoyan zu*) were put in place at the university.[19] After the communist victory in 1949 this practice of organizing academic activity into sections and groups, modeled on the advanced educational and research organizations of Soviet universities, was introduced to many universities across China. It is noteworthy that all of these changes had already been effected at Harbin Polytechnical University in the 1920s. In 1928 the Faculty of Railroad Construction was reorganized as the Faculty of Construction. This faculty eventually became the Faculty of Civil Engineering and Construction, and during the 1950s it was further reorganized into the Harbin Institute of Civil Engineering and Architecture.

On February 4, 1928, the university ceased to be under the Chinese Eastern Railway Company and was placed under the control of the Republic of China's Special District of the Northeastern Provinces. Its name was changed to the Technical University of the Special District of the Northeastern provinces, and, along with the change of name, it now became a state-run university. Administration and funding was provided by the Special District, and all financial support from the Chinese Eastern Railway Company ceased. Yet, notwithstanding the formal change of administration, following the requisition of the Chinese Eastern Railway by the Soviet government, an extraordinary conference was called by the Special District administration and the railway's board of directors. This heralded the start of a seven-year period of joint Sino-Soviet administraiton of the university, which was now renamed Harbin Technical University. Throughout the period from February 1928 to March 1935, the administration of Harbin Technical University was ostensibly based on the principle of equality between China and the Soviet Union. The university's board of directors was made up of five representatives from each country. In reality, however, in the same way as General Zhang Xueliang had previously held the post of chair while the Russian vice director of the Chinese Eastern Railway, Cherkin, had held the post of vice chair, so the Chinese now held the main post while the Soviet side had the subordinate post. The president of the university was Liu Zhe and the vice president, Vostorgov.

There were 815 registered students in the 1928–29 academic year. In the spring of 1931 graduate students were recruited for the first time, as a result of which three Chinese students gained admission. After two years of study they earned the right to study abroad, albeit at their own expense. In the 1930–31 academic year departments were established within each faculty. The Faculty of Mechanical and Electrical Engineering now contained departments of Electrical Engineering, Mechanical Engineering, and Industrial Arts and Manufacturing, while the Faculty of Construction included the Departments of Road Transport, City Construction, and Architectural Engineering. A third department, that of Commercial Transportation, was added in 1931 but was subsequently abolished in 1935.[20]

The Founding of Manchukuo and the New School System

The Manchurian Incident occurred just as the development of Harbin Technical University was unfolding. After Manchukuo came into being in 1932, its government employed twenty-six engineers from the Chinese Eastern Railway Company (although only eighteen held real jobs) as educators and administrators at Harbin Technical University. At the same time, twelve Soviet lecturers and staff members were dismissed. The course of study was also reduced from five to four and a half years, and university funding was cut back. To illustrate the reduction in funding the Manchukuo government provided fifty-three thousand rubles in 1933, but this was no more than a quarter of the budget necessary to run the university. In 1934 the budget was further reduced to twenty-five thousand rubles. As a result of these unstable circumstances, a great many students left the university.[21]

Japan employed both soft and tough approaches to achieve its objective of acquiring all railways in the northeast of China. On March 23, 1935, an accord was signed stipulating Japan's takeover of the Chinese Eastern Railway Company, which up to that point had been under joint Sino-Soviet management.[22] Under the terms of this accord, the Japanese and Manchukuo governments agreed to pay the Soviet Union 170 million yuan in compensation (some 30 million yuan of this figure consisted of severance pay for Soviet staff and workers), while Chinese interests in the company were simply requisitioned by Manchukuo. In this way the right to administer Harbin Technical University passed from the Chinese Eastern Railway Company to the Manchukuo Ministry of Education (and later to the Ministry of Public Welfare). From late March to October 1935 the university was shut down, and additional Soviet teachers were dismissed.[23] In addition, the Manchukuo Ministry of Education launched a purge of the university's "communist faction" on July 1, which resulted in the expulsion of a number of students.[24] Nevertheless, when the university reopened in October, Russian remained the medium of instruction as before, and Russians continued to hold leading academic and administrative positions in the university. A. K. Popov was dean of the important Faculty of Mechanical and Electrical Engineering, and Gregorvitch was dean of the Faculty of Construction.

Important changes were about to occur, however. Beginning October 8, 1935, education throughout the university was carried out in accordance with a new policy. There were around 350 students and 29 teachers in the university at this time. From this point until the announcement of the New School System in 1937, the mode of organization, administration, and teaching at Harbin underwent what can be termed a transitional period of gradual Japanization. During this period the post of university president was held first by Liu Menggeng, who had held the job since 1933, and then by Wang Yuqing from 1935.[25]

On January 1, 1936, Harbin Technical University was renamed the National Harbin Technical Higher School, and the course of study was reduced to four years, but the existing departments and faculties remained unchanged. Funding was now provided by the Manchukuo Ministry of Education. In April of the same year students from the North Manchuria College, which had been founded by the YMCA, and over a hundred students who had left university in the spring of 1935, passed the entrance examinations and were admitted to National Harbin Technical Higher School. It was from this point that the institution underwent rapid evolution, and its structure changed drastically. In May 1936 the two existing faculties were abolished, and six departments were put in their place: Electrical Engineering, Mechanical Engineering, Chemistry, Mining, Construction, and Architectural Engineering. In October the school's Soviet-style management practices were scrapped. Thus, the curtain closed on the period of Soviet-style education at Harbin Technical University. Nonetheless, since its establishment in 1920, the Harbin Technical University (including all previous incarnations) had produced a total of 1,093 graduates following a Soviet model of education and using the Russian language as the medium of instruction. If we divide this total between the two faculties, 644 students graduated from the Faculty of Mechanical and Electrical Engineering (58 percent), and 458 students graduated from the Faculty of Construction (42 percent). Fully 81 percent of the graduates were Russian (including Poles), and 19 percent were Chinese.[26]

Despite the many changes effected at Harbin Technical Higher School shortly after the formation of the state of Manchukuo, it would be a further six years before the Manchukuo government promulgated a New School System in 1937. The New School System affected each university, and all were fundamentally altered. With the reorganization of universities under the new system, Harbin Technical Higher School and two state-run schools, the Higher Agricultural School and the Xinjing Medical School, were designated as Manchukuo's Industrial, Agricultural, and Medical state universities, respectively. The basis for these changes was the "Universities Edict" (*daxue ling*), an imperial decree announced on May 2, 1937, and the "Regulations for State and Private Universities" (*Gong si li daxue guicheng*) issued by the

Ministry of Public Welfare on December 28 in the same year. In examining these documents, it is possible to discern many provisions that bear the influence of Japan.[27] In the first place, Article 7 of the "Universities Edict" states that "university courses shall be three years long. If necessary this can be extended by up to one year." This reflected current Japanese practice but departed from the standard practice in China, in which Article 21 of the Nationalist government's 1929 "University Organizational Law" stipulated that "the period of instruction at universities shall be five years for medical colleges, and four years for all others." Since Japanese universities had adopted a three-year system (four for medicine) under the 1918 "Imperial Ordinance Relating to Universities," one could be justified in thinking that Manchukuo had copied Japan rather than China in this matter.

A second example of Japanese influence on the New School System concerned the terminology used to denote the head of a university. Article 12 of the "Universities Edict" stated that "university presidents and teachers may discipline students where necessary for educational purposes." The term *Xuezhang* to denote the head of a university is used as though it were perfectly normal. Yet it is possible to see Japanese influence even in this simple matter of terminology. Heads of universities in China were called *Xiaozhang*, while the term *Xuezhang* was never used.

A third example concerned the popular festivals that were established as national school holidays. Under Article 11 of the "Regulations for State and Private Universities" we can see that all the Japanese holidays are included in accordance with antithetical to the official slogan "Japan and Manchuria, one virtue, one heart." The Birthday of the Emperor, Empire Day, the Anniversary of the Birth of Emperor Meiji, as well as the Memorial Day of Emperor Puyi's Visit to Japan are all listed in the article as official school holidays. Similarly, in Article 11 there are also regulations stating that commemoration rites should be conducted as part of normal school business. The regulations stipulated that on New Year's Day, National Foundation Day, and the Memorial Day of Emperor Puyi's Visit to Japan "the president, teachers and students shall sing the national anthem of Manchukuo and the national anthem of Japan," while "the president of the university shall read aloud the Imperial Edict Commemorating Emperor Puyi's Visit to Japan" and "shall bow down before the national flags of both Manchukuo and Japan." The rites for Empire Day, the Birthday of the Emperor, and the Anniversary of the Birth of Emperor Meiji were to be conducted as follows: "The president, teachers and students will sing the Manchukuo and Japanese national anthems" and "worship the Imperial Palace from afar." The president "shall read aloud the Imperial Edict Commemorating Emperor Puyi's Visit to Japan" and "bow down before the national flags of Manchukuo and Japan." There can be no sign of Japanese influence more emphatic than this.

Some of the regulations did show signs of Manchukuo autonomy, however slight. Article 4 of the "Regulations for State and Private Universities" stipulated that the academic year should begin on January 1 and end on December 31. The academic year in China at that time ran from August 1 to July 31 of the following year, while in Japan it ran from the April 1 to March 31 of the following year. The Manchukuo practice could thus be interpreted as showing some slight and exceptional evidence of Manchukuo autonomy in the midst of obvious Japanese influence over most educational practices of the time.

Harbin Polytechnical University under the New School System

Under the New School System Harbin Technical Higher School became a state-run industrial university, and preparations had advanced a step toward making it a genuine Manchukuo university. On May 26, 1938, the "Organizational Regulations for Harbin Polytechnical University" were announced, followed by the Harbin Polytechnical University Regulations, which were published in June of the same year.[28]

The "organizational regulations" clearly stated that Harbin Polytechnical University was to be placed under the control of the Ministry of Public Welfare. It also stipulated that there should be one president appointed by the emperor, under whom were to be fifteen teachers, one dean, and one commissioner appointed by the prime minister. In addition, there was to be a total of ten assistant teachers appointed by the prime minister or another minister (no more than five were to be appointed by the prime minister), plus three government clerks, one librarian, and fourteen assistants appointed by a minister.

Of these latter posts the dean was second in command and "administered student discipline and accommodation in accordance with the orders of the president." The post was occupied by Colonel Ozawa Toyokichi, who had resigned from service with the army first reserve in order to take up the position. It was distinct, however, from that of a military officer attached to a school for the purpose of military drill and education. The latter was filled by Colonel Takanarita from the Japanese Imperial Army, who instructed the Japanese students, and by Captain Nagai Sen from the Manchukuo Army, who instructed the Manchurian students. Both were seconded to the university and employed on a full-time basis.[29] The commissioner, who acted as a kind of secretary-general, was in charge of the university's clerks and other minor officials below him.

It is interesting to take note of the titles assigned to assistant professors and assistants. When China first introduced the modern university system at the end of the Qing, the terms used for teachers—*zheng jiaoxi, fu jiaoxi,* and *fen jiaoxi*—had their origins in ancient tradition and seemed to hark back to an earlier period. Teaching assistants were termed *zhu jiao.* Later, it seems likely that China was influenced by the Japanese "Imperial Ordinance Relating to the Imperial Universities" for the Japanese system of professor–assistant professor (*jiashou–zhu jiaoshou*) system was adopted. Later still, from the latter half of the 1920s, the professor–associate professor (*jiaoshou–fu jiaoshou*) was adopted.[30] The term *zhushou* was never used in China, however, and even to this day the term *zhujiao* is still used. Japanese influence was thus clearly visible when it came to the choice of titles for university president and assistants.

The Harbin Polytechnical University Regulations specified the establishment of six departments: Civil Engineering, Construction, Electrical Engineering, Mechanical Engineering, Applied Chemistry, and Mining and Metallurgy and fixed the length of the course at four years. These six departments took the place of the two faculties (Construction and Electrical and Mechanical Engineering) of the Chinese Eastern Railway Company administration period and were not radically different from the six departments established immediately after the formation of the state of Manchukuo. The only difference was that the Department of Architectural Engineering, which subsequently briefly became the Department of Railway Construction, changed again to become the Department of Civil Engineering.[31] Additionally, Metallurgy was added to the Department of Mining, and the Chemistry Department became the Department of Applied Chemistry.

Course lengths immediately following the promulgation of the New School System were as follows. Fengtian Agricultural University, the Faculty of Commerce at the North Manchurian College, the Harbin College of Dentistry, and the Fengtian Pharmacology Training Center all had three-year courses. The Xinjing Medical University, the Harbin Medical University, and the Fengtian Medical School, along with all other medical institutions, had four-year courses, as did the Harbin Polytechnical University and the Faculty of Industry at the North Manchurian College (formed out of the merger of St. Vladimir College and Harbin Overseas Russian College).[32] There were numerous medically related institutions of higher education in Manchukuo, for which four-year courses were not uncommon.[33] If we look at a sample of twenty-one institutions of higher education five years later, in 1943, we can see that a total of seven institutions offered four-year courses. Among them were four medical colleges and three nonmedical institutions, including Harbin Polytechnic University, National Harbin College, and the Faculty of Industry at the private North Manchurian College. Ten institutions operated under a three-year system, including Fengtian Agricultural College, Xinjing Polytechnical University, Fengtian Polytechnical University, and others. In addition, there were four institutions offering a two-year course, including the Bei'an Pioneer Medical School.[34]

Thus, Harbin Polytechnic University was one of the few industrially related institutions to have a four-year course under the New School System. This may be viewed as a remnant from the earlier period of Soviet administration, when most courses ran for four to five years. Yet, because Xinjing and Fengtian Industrial Universities, both of which had been established by the Manchukuo government, offered three-year courses, the Council of University Presidents eventually decided to standardize the period of instruction for universities, and Harbin was forced to adopt the three-year system.

The upshot was that no students were admitted to the university in the spring of 1943, as the changeover was being implemented. The first students to enter the university under the new three-year system did so in the spring of 1944.[35] This change notwithstanding, Article 3 of the Harbin Polytechnic University Regulations as well as the Manchukuo government's Regulations for State and Private Universities both stipulated that "the academic year shall begin on 1st January and end on 31st December." As noted earlier, the choice of academic year appeared to suggest an element of elusive Manchukuo autonomy in the educational sphere, however slight. In fact, upon closer examination it emerges that the spring entry date was adapted to the needs of Japanese middle school students, who graduated at the end of March. Indeed, it became increasingly the norm for students to enter Manchukuo universities in April and to graduate in March.

Under the New School System, Harbin Polytechnic University also moved away from the credit system, which had been in use up to this point, and adopted a rigid academic year system. This meant that students had to complete the required number of academic years regardless of how many credits they may have earned. Later, however, as the war progressed, many students graduated early. The foreign language studied at the university also changed from Russian to Japanese, the preparatory course was abolished, and only graduates of four-year middle schools were admitted. In addition, only Japanese, Chinese, and Korean students could enter, while Russian students were actively denied admission. Most of the Russian teaching staff left the university at this point. In their stead came Japanese teachers, who were employed in increasing numbers as more and more Japanese students entered the university.

The person who was in charge of overseeing this transformation to a Japanese-style polytechnical university was Suzuki Masao, who served as president of Harbin Polytechnical University for more than eight years, from the time he took up the post in May 1937 until Japan's defeat on August 15, 1945. After graduating from the Architectural Department of Tokyo Higher Technical School, Suzuki entered the South Manchuria Railway Company. By the time he took up his position at Harbin Polytechnical University, he was a veteran of many varied posts in the field of technology, having worked in numerous departments of the South Manchuria Railway Company[36] before leaving the company after his final post as head of the railway's construction. While employed at the railway company, Suzuki had also managed to accumulate a decade of teaching experience as part-time lecturer at the South Manchuria Technical School and the South Manchuria Technical College.[37] It appears that he was appointed to the post of president of the university in light of his varied technical and academic experience.

According to the recollections of Dean Ozawa, there were many problems in need of immediate solution as the university was transformed from a Russian to a Japanese institution. Ozawa listed the most urgent tasks facing the new president in 1937 as follows:

1. To enable students under the present Russian-style system to graduate quickly (in about two years) by introducing a special fast-track course. To persuade Russian teachers who are department heads or degree holders to consent to taking new posts at other universities and to make the remaining Russians transfer away from the university in due course.
2. To ensure the fullest use of existing facilities in each department and to give priority to the new applied chemistry experimental equipment and fit it out for the first academic year. To equip other departments suffering from equipment shortages on a year-by-year basis in a well-planned manner.
3. To pay for the cost of buying technical books in Japanese and other foreign languages, most of which were needed in the first academic year. To create a convenient university library with a store of tens of thousands of specialized technical books (including books in Russian and other foreign languages) by completely revamping the existing library.
4. To realize the necessary building work for which there were strong

budgetary demands within the first academic year, by building upon the existing foundations of ruined school buildings in the northeast part of the campus. To tackle the problem of a shortage of classrooms and laboratories for the new term of the next academic year.

5. To concentrate all efforts toward acquiring existing land and buildings around the university in order to provide new school buildings and student dormitories in accordance with site expansion plans, thus bringing the university to completion and preparing for its future development.

6. To inspire confidence in the new authority of Harbin Polytechnical University by ensuring that suitable people are employed as department heads and teachers and through smooth internal management of the university. To recruit suitable departmental heads, not from any one particular Japanese university but from many and without bias.

7. To implement a new policy on annual admission quotas for Japanese students, having admitted a hundred exclusively Manchurian students in the first academic year.[38]

It appears that most of these problems were solved and plans realized within the first two to three years of Suzuki's tenure as president. It was the human dynamics of this process, however, that are most fascinating. First, the dismissal of the teaching staff at the Russian Language Department and indeed of all the Russian personnel was carried out on May 6, 1937, the day that Suzuki took up his post as president. The Russian Language Department itself was abolished at the end of 1938. Soviet influence had been stamped out. There were no more than four Russian names on the staff register during the remaining Manchukuo period: Biliarev, Grisalovitch, Biebrodosky, and Suvchich.[39] All were White Russians emigrés who were no longer Soviet nationals.

The Japanese teaching staff subsequently buried any remaining traces left by the former Russian teachers. The new heads of departments were drawn from the following Japanese universities, in accordance with the policy of not favoring specific institutions. The head of the Department of Civil Engineering was Ōsaki Toraji, who was a graduate of Kyoto University and had left a post as a teacher at the Nagoya Higher Technical School. The head of the Construction Department was Imai Hideo, a graduate of the Tokyo Kuramae Higher Technical School, while the head of the Department of Electrical Engineering was Kanaya Kazuhide, a graduate of Waseda University who came to Harbin from the Electrical Engineering Testing Center. The head of the Department of Mechanical Engineering was Goto Ryuzaburo, a graduate of Lüshun College who came to Harbin from the South Manchuria Railway Company. The head of the Department of Applied Chemistry was Matsuo Shunichi, a graduate of Kyushu University. The head of the Department of Mining was Umezaki Kakuichi, a graduate of Waseda University, and the head of the Department of Metallurgy was Sato Tsuneyoshi, who was an associate professor at Kyushu University.

But, while the policy against preferential hiring appears to have been followed at the level of department heads, within each department were many teachers and assistant teachers who had graduated from the same university or college as the department head. Thus, for example, all of the teachers in mathematics and physics were graduates of the Physics Department of Tohoku Imperial University.[40] As a result, while the university staff as a whole was clearly made up of graduates of many different universities, academic cliques formed in each of the departments in what could perhaps be called a typical Japanese fashion.

As mentioned above, Russian students were denied admission, and a policy of favouring the admission of Japanese students was implemented. In the first academic year (1937) one hundred exclusively Manchurian students were admitted, and there was only one Japanese among those who graduated in that first intake.[41] But in the following year there were twenty-eight Japanese students (table 1). Table 1 also shows that Manchukuo's higher-education institutions at the time were all small-scale, and among them only Harbin Polytechnical University and the Fengtian Pharmaceutical Training Center admitted Japanese students. Subsequently, however, every institution increased its intake of Japanese students. In the case of Harbin Polytechnical University, by 1943 the number of Japanese and Chinese students was almost equal. Still, by 1943 only Xinjing Medical College had fewer Chinese students than five years previously. While the other institutions had also increased their numbers of Japanese students, this did not result in a corresponding decline in the number of Chinese students admitted; on the contrary, their numbers also increased. In summary, these statistics reveal that in every Manchukuo institution of higher education, with the exception of Xinjing Medical College, Japanese students did not steal opportunities from Chinese students or drive them away, as some scholars have assumed. A more appropriate understanding of the situation is that there was increasing enrollment in all institutions of higher education and that most of this increase was monopolized by Japanese students.

From the implementation of the New School System in 1937 until the end of the war in 1945 there were a total of eight annual student intakes at Harbin

TABLE 1. Changes in the Composition of Teachers and Students by Ethnicity

Institutions	Year	Teachers				Students			
		Japanese	Chinese	Others	Total	Japanese	Chinese	Others	Total
Fengtian Agricultural College	1938	15	29	1	45	0	281	8	289
	1943	41	22	0	64	94	339	11	444
Harbin Polytechnical University	1938	34	22	19	75	28	266	47	341
	1943	79	31	0	110	243	296	3	542
Xinjing Medical College	1938	15	5	0	20	0	271	11	282
	1943	56	24	0	80	149	152	6	307
Harbin Medical College	1938	23	10	0	33	0	224	16	240
	1943	58	12	2	72	204	315	23	542
Northern Manchurian College	1938	8	1	39	48	0	4	242	246
	1943	9	2	24	35	6	11	246	281
Fengtian Pharmaceutical Center	1938	27	1	0	28	27	216	0	233
	1943	19	8	0	27	27	123	0	150

Source: The Manchukuo Survey on Educational Matters, 1938 ed., 102–4; and the Manchukuo Survey on Educational Matters, 1943 ed., 62–63. "Others" includes Russians, Koreans, Mongolians, and others. There were many Russian students at the Harbin Polytechnical University and at the North Manchurian College, which was run by the YMCA.

Polytechnical University. Table 2 shows the number of students who graduated or who otherwise "finished" their studies at the end of the war, by department, for each of these intakes. In addition, figure 1 shows changes in the ethnic composition of the university's graduating students (in addition to Chinese and Japanese there were also small numbers of Koreans and Mongolians among graduating students) for each intake. As previously described, the number of Chinese students increases somewhat, while the number of Japanese students rose dramatically after 1937. Even by 1943, however, there were still more Chinese than Japanese students attending Harbin. But, while there were consistently more Chinese than Japanese students enrolled in the university, many more Japanese students graduated than Chinese students. What factors are responsible for the differences between the number of Chinese and Japanese graduates?

It has been generally asserted that the academic training at Harbin Polytechnical University was extremely rigorous. This is illustrated by the large number of students who were unable to pass the examinations and were

TABLE 2.   Changes in the Numbers[a] of Graduates at Harbin Polytechnical University by Department

| Department | Nationality | INTAKE | | | | | | | | Total |
		I	II	III	IV	V	VI	VII	VIII	
Civil	Japanese	0	2	5	7	18	22	29	40	123
Engineering	Chinese and others	12	16	14	21	14	14	5	6	102
Architectual	Japanese	0	3	3	3	16	14	23	28	90
Engineering	Chinese and others	11	14	18	21	11	22	6	3	106
Electric	Japanese	0	3	5	11	8	14	22	22	85
Engineering	Chinese and others	9	13	11	8	10	10	7	4	72
Mechanical	Japanese	1	3	4	7	9	19	34	38	115
Engineering	Chinese and others	6	16	9	15	12	7	11	1	77
Applied	Japanese	0	6	7	4	5	12	21	17	70
Chemistry	Chinese and others	13	9	16	16	5	7	2	1	69
Mining	Japanese	0	3	5	5	7	12	21	17	70
	Chinese and others	4	11	15	15	12	4	5	3	69
Metallurgy	Japanese	0	0	3	3	6	10	9	19	50
	Chinese and others	6	6	8	3	4	8	4	4	43
Total	Japanese	1	20	32	40	69	103	152	193	610
	Chinese and others	61	85	91	99	68	72	40	21	537

Source: COBOP *Membership List* (Harbin: Harbin Institute of Technology Alumni Association, 1959 and 1985).

[a]In each cell, the top row of the numbers represents the number of graduates of Japanese nationality, whereas the bottom row represents the number of graduates of Chinese and other nationalities.

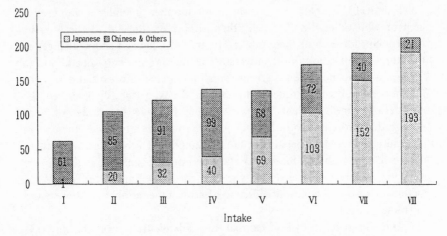

Fig. 1. Variations in the Number of Students Graduating from Harbin Polytechnical University (From COBOP, *Membership List* [Harbin: Harbin Institute of Technology Alumni Association, 1959 and 1985].)

weeded out. All students were required to take the same written examinations regardless of ethnicity or background. A score of one hundred points represented full marks, while those who scored less than 40 percent in one subject and those who, even if they exceeded 40 percent, failed to score 60 percent in three subjects failed. Failing the examination twice meant expulsion. For example, of the twenty-five students who entered the Department of Electrical Engineering in the third intake in February 1939, eight were forced to repeat the first year, a further eight failed to make it through to the third year, and only fourteen students made it to the fourth year. One of these students subsequently had to leave the university due to illness, so that in the final analysis no more than thirteen students, or just over half of those admitted, managed to graduate.[42] The university's Alumni Association later recorded a total of sixteen graduates, but, setting aside this discrepancy, the fact that only about half of each intake managed to graduate amply illustrates how tough the course was.[43]

Perhaps the most important factor affecting the differing graduation rates of Japanese and Chinese students was that Japanese was designated, however unreasonably, as the official language of Manchukuo, and Chinese and other non-Japanese students therefore had to take lessons in what for them was a foreign language. It should certainly come as no surprise that most of the students who quit the course were non-Japanese. There were also differences in the dormitories' dietary treatment of Japanese and non-

Japanese students. "Circumstances gradually improved, but in the beginning the staple food for Japanese students was white rice, and for Manchurian students it was millet or gaoliang."[44]

From among the non-Japanese graduates who had survived these severe trials came "first-class engineers" (the highest engineering title awarded) as well as university lecturers and those who used their expertise to gain administrative posts. The 1985 edition of the Alumni Association membership list includes Chinese graduates such as Qiu Linshu (Department of Civil Engineering, fifth intake), a first-class engineer of the Jilin Railway Company; Zhao Jingxin, vice president of Harbin Architectural Engineering College (Department of Construction, fifth intake); He Zengming, vice president of the Beijing Construction Materials Engineering College (Department of Electrical Engineering, sixth intake); Chen Yiling, vice president of the Anshan Steel College (Department of Metallurgy, sixth intake); and Pei Chao, director of the National Planning Committee's Bureau of Overseas Economics. The list also includes graduates working in the Democratic People's Republic of Korea, including Lee Jong Auk, national vice chairman (Department of Applied Chemistry, fourth intake); Lim Kei Chul, minister of light industry (Department of Applied Chemistry, sixth intake), and others too numerous to mention. Including these examples, Harbin Polytechnical University altogether produced over six hundred Japanese, Chinese, Korean, and Mongolian graduates over the entire period from March 1935 to August 1945.

The Waning of Japanese Power and the Revival of the Soviet Model

With the end of the war on August 15, 1945, the fate of Japanese teachers and students at Harbin Polytechnical University changed dramatically. At the time of Japan's defeat, the situation at the university had already begun to deteriorate. The seventh and eighth intakes had already begun the new three-year course, but the number of Chinese students admitted was extremely low due to the worsening war situation, and Japanese students were finding it impossible to complete their studies due to military conscription.[45] The harsh reality of defeat brought further fundamental changes to the university.

The late Professor Saito Kazuo of the Department of Applied Chemistry reflected at the time that "the surprising thing about facing the end of the war at Harbin was that all the Manchurians stopped speaking Japanese, there were outbreaks of violence in the city, and then after four or five days the Soviet soldiers set upon the Japanese nationals with guns and swords. The pillaging had begun. Even at my home, every day two or three Soviet soldiers would kick down the front door and make off with watches, jewels and the like. The shirts and western clothes did not fit so they just left them. It gradually became worse and I began to fear for my life, so I moved some futons down to the coal cellar and hid there." Subsequently, this same professor took refuge in students' houses. "Fortunately, when it grew dark in the evening, Mr. Li Run Liang, a Manchurian student who had been an assistant, and others like him would bring me pork and bread. I was deeply moved and came to understand that human love really does transcend racial considerations."[46]

Eventually, Saito ventured into Harbin city and was arrested by the Chinese Communist Party Army. He was taken into custody for alleged "thought crimes" along with Yoshibashi, commander of the military police, the vice president of the Manchurian Central Bank, the president of the Xinjing Publishing Company, and Suzuki, the president of Harbin Polytechnical University. Yoshibashi, the bank vice president, and the publisher were executed, but the two men from Harbin Polytechnical University were released. President Suzuki was subsequently detained as an architectural engineer for the Harbin city government until his return to Japan in September 1953. Professor Saito was likewise detained to carry out chemistry-related work in Harbin, Dongan, and Fengtian, until his return, also in 1953. A considerable number of Harbin Polytechnical University's Japanese teaching staff shared similar fates. Nor did the university's students emerge unscathed. A Japanese student who was in the student dormitory on August 20, 1945, relates the following tale. "Chinese soldiers clutching rifles surrounded us. The officer in charge was waving his pistol and shouting 'Get out front! Get outside! Put your hands in the air! Both of them!' From that point on our journey to Hailin and Mudanjiang as prisoners had begun. Even though we were students we were placed among captives taken from the Japanese Imperial Army."[47]

Meanwhile, immediately after the ending of the war, the China Changchun Railway Company (the former Chinese Eastern Railway and South Manchuria Railway) once again came under joint Sino-Soviet management, based on the Sino-Soviet Agreement signed in 1945. Accordingly, Harbin Polytechnical University was also placed under the control of the China Changchun Railway Company, which was to provide funding for the university. Harbin Polytechnical University, however, was in a state of turmoil. The classrooms, laboratories, and lecture halls were filled to overflowing with waste consisting of Japanese Imperial Army equipment and surplus matériel, and all educational activities had been suspended. At this juncture the China Changchun Railway Company mobilized the students and teachers of Northern Manchuria College to carry out repairs and a thorough overhaul of the university. On November 24, 1945, the Administrative Bureau of the China Changchun Railway Company issued the following instructions concerning the university:

> All teaching staff who left Harbin Polytechnical University during the period of administration by the Chinese Eastern Railway Company will be recruited to return to the university, and all Russian students from the Northern Manchuria College's Faculty of Industry will be admitted to the university. The university will re-open on 1st December 1945 and classes will begin formally on 6th December.
>
> All departments established during the period of administration by the Chinese Eastern Railway Company—architectural engineering, mechanical and electrical engineering and transportation economics—will be revived, as will the preparatory course. A. B. Ozov from the Administration Bureau's Transportation Construction Section of the China Changchun Railway Company is appointed to the post of university president.[48]

This represented the first step toward reestablishing the original Soviet-style industrial polytechnical university that had disappeared after the Manchurian Incident. The course of study reverted to five years, and, perhaps most symbolic of the end of the Japanese model and the rebirth of the Soviet one, Russian was restored as the language of instruction in all classes. The titles of the teaching staff were quickly returned to the former Soviet nomenclature of "professor—associate professor—assistant." At this stage the course design and curriculum were still drafted by the teaching staff themselves, but the basic content was broadly similar to that of Soviet industrial institutions of higher education. In addition, evening classes were established for some of the first-year students, and two preparatory classes were set up for those students who were unable to keep up with the normal daytime classes. The preparatory classes were separated into ones aimed at Russian students whose results in the basic subjects were not sufficient to allow them to advance to the regular course and others aimed primarily at Chinese students to prepare them for admission to the regular course through supplementary Russian-language classes.[49]

In 1944 a fourth department, that of Oriental Economics, was added. This department was established with the aim of nurturing a coterie of Russian specialists deeply versed in the Chinese language and the Chinese economy. In 1947 the Department of Transportation Economics became the Department of

Engineering Economics, and a fifth department, that of Cargo Economics, was created.[50] Finally, in 1949 Feng Zhongyun, chair of the People's Government of Songjian province, took up the post of university president. A further three departments were also established at this time: Mining and Metallurgy, Chemistry, and Aeronautical Engineering.[51]

Conclusion

Following the establishment of the People's Republic of China on October 1, 1949, changes toward a Soviet-style model quickened at Harbin Polytechnic University. In 1950, as part of the agreement to return Chinese assets, the university came under the sole jurisdiction of the Chinese government, as it remains to this day. At the same time, however, China's entire higher educational system was being reorganized and overhauled in the early 1950s, taking the Soviet Union as its model. Just as the People's University became the model for institutions devoted to the humanities and social sciences, Harbin Polytechnic University became the model for state-run industrial universities under a Soviet-style administration.

Japanese involvement in the history of Harbin Polytechnic University lasted for fourteen years following the Manchurian Incident in 1931, and the university was under direct Japanese control for a period of eight years from the introduction of the Manchukuo New School System in 1937 until the end of the war. This study has revealed that the most representative changes in the Japanization of the university concerned the language of instruction and the rise in the proportion of Japanese professors and students during the latter period. Second, signs of Japanization were also discernible in aspects such as course length, titles of teaching staff, and university customs and ceremonies. The *Harbin Polytechnic University Review*, published in 1952, recorded that "in the period of violation by Japanese imperialism from 1935 to 1945, many unwarranted and indiscriminate alterations were made concerning course length, the educational system, and the establishment of faculties and departments. This led to the deterioration of original standards and of the quality of education."[52] It is certainly true that the course was shortened, and it is natural that standards should decline under wartime conditions. The lack of historical materials and related sources that were available for this essay means, however, that there remains much work to do in revealing the extent of deeper Japanese influences at the university. For instance, there is a need for comparative analysis of the curriculum and educational content for each stage in the history of departments like that of Mechanical and Electrical

Engineering. These departments were in place from the founding of the university and experienced, in turn, the Soviet model, the Japanese model, and then a revived Soviet model. Such an analysis would reveal much more clearly the true nature and extent of Japanese influence on education in Manchuria. It is more difficult to determine cultural differences in the theories and scientific principles of fields such as mechanical engineering between countries than it is in the humanities. Yet, if any differences can be detected, then they should clearly illuminate patterns of influence stemming from relationships with Russia and Japan. This may be a fruitful area for further research.

Finally, any evaluation of this period as a whole must acknowledge that, whatever justifications may be offered, the adoption of the Japanese model was certainly not an independent choice for Manchuria. There is no disputing the fact that it was the result of coercion, and any evaluation must therefore be negative and extremely damning. Nonetheless, it should also be acknowledged that, while Harbin Polytechnic University was following the Russian model, until it was abandoned following the Manchurian Incident, only 19 percent of those who graduated were Chinese. During the following Japanese period, 46.7 percent of graduates were Chinese (including small numbers of Korean and Mongolian students), almost as many as the number of Japanese graduates. Furthermore, the departments of Metallurgy and Chemistry were abolished at the end of the war, during the rapid reintroduction of the Soviet model, in an effort to eradicate all Japanese influence. Yet they were subsequently revived using foundations that had been laid earlier during the Manchukuo period. Japanese contributions to the existence of these two departments should surely be recognized.

NOTES

1. Suzuki Kenichi, "Tosansyo niokeru Nihon no Kyoiku Jigyo" (Japan's Educational Undertaking in Three Northeastern Provinces), in *Nit-Chū Kyōiku Bunka Kōryū to Masatsu* (Sino-Japanese Educational and Cultural Exchanges and Conflicts), ed. Hiroshi Abe (Tokyo: Daiichi Shobō, 1983), 199–216.

2. Wu Qiang, ed. *Dongbei lunxian shisi nian jiaoyu shiliao, di yi ji* (Materials on Educational History during Fourteen Years Occupation in Northeast Region, no. 1) (Changchun: Jilin jiaoyu chubanshe, 1989), 106.

3. Ibid., 316.

4. Toyoji Minagawa, *Mansyukoku no Kyōiku* (Education in Manchukuo), ed. Manzhou Diguo Jiaoyu Hui (Educational Association of the Manchurian Empire, 1939), 190.

5. Ibid., 190.

6. Wang Zhenqian, Qiu Qing, and Jiang Kefu, eds., *Dongbei Daxue shigao* (Manuscript of History of Northeastern University) (Changchun: Dongbei Shifan Daxue chubanshe, 1988), 10.

7. Ibid., 33.

8. Ibid., 53.

9. Minagawa, *Mansyukoku no Kyoiku,* 190.

10. Ibid., 190–91.

11. *Dongbei Daxue shigao,* 106–7.

12. Ibid., 52. *Da Manzhou Diguo nianjian* (Great Manchurian Empire Yearbook of 1944) (initial issue) states that the term of study at Fengtian Technical College and Xinjing Technical College was four years, but these colleges in fact adopted a three-year system.

13. Harbin Institute of Technology Alumni Association, ed., *COBOP Membership List,* 1959 ed., 76; *Haerbin Gongye Daxue jianshi* (Brief History of the Harbin Institute of Technology) (Haerbin: Haerbin gongxueyuan chubanshe, 1985), 1.

14. Harbin Institute of Technology Alumni Association, ed., *COBOP Membership List,* 1964 ed., 62.

15. *Haerbin Gongye Daxue jianshi,* 2.

16. Harbin Institute of Technology Alumni Association, *COBOP Membership List,* 62.

17. *Haerbin Gongye Daxue jianshi,* 2.

18. Ibid., 3–4.

19. Ibid., 4.

20. Ibid., 5–6.

21. Ibid., 6.

22. Jiang Niandong et al., eds., *Wei Manzhouguo shi* (History of Pseudo Manchukuo) (Changchun: Jilin renmin chubanshe, 1980), 249. While Japan had purchased proprietary rights to the North East China Railway from the Soviet Union for a modest sum, the Soviet Union occupied the railway again upon Japan's surrender. China was dissatisfied with this Soviet action. Akira Ishii, *Chū-Sō Kankeishi no Kenkyu,* 1945–1950 (A Study on the History of Sino-Soviet Relations, 1945–1950) (Tokyo: Tokyo University Press, 1990), 258.

23. Harbin Institute of Technology Alumni Association, *COBOP Membership List,* 62.

24. *Haerbin Gongye Daxue jianshi,* 7.

25. Harbin Institute of Technology Alumni Association, *COBOP Membership List,* 63.

26. Ibid. The brief history of the Harbin Institute of Technology, however, describes how "new students were admitted to the Russian Language Department in October 1936 but it was then decided to abolish the department in December" (*Haerbin Gongye Daxue jianshi,* 7). Therefore, it is uncertain exactly when Russian-style education was discontinued.

27. Wu Qiang, *Dongbei lunxian shisi nian jiaoyu shiliao, di yi ji,* 585–94.

28. Ibid., 605–10.

29. Kazuo Saito, *Watashi no Jinsei Kaiko* (My Life Reminiscences) (Mr. Kazuo Saito's Posthumous Manuscripts Publishing Association, 1989), 16.

30. See Otsuka Yutaka, "Chūgoku no Diagaku Kyojushoku" (Professorship in China), in *Daigaku Kyojushoku no Shiteki Hensen to Syoruikei ni kansuru Kenkyu* (Study on the Historical Development of Professorship and Its Typology) (Tokyo: National Institute for Educational Research of Japan, 1989), 77–101.

31. *Haerbin Gongye Daxue xiaoyou lu* (Record of Alumni of Harbin Institute of Technology), volume for 1937–45 Haerbin: Haerbin gongye daxue 1985 ed.), 1.

32. Ministry of Education (Manchukuo), ed., *Manzhou Diguo xueshi yaolan* (Manchurian Empire Survey on Educational Matters), 1938 ed. (Manchukuo Ministry of Education, 1939), 101–2.

33. Minagawa, *Mansyukoku no Kyoiku*, 73.

34. Ministry of Education (Manchukuo), ed., *Manzhou Diguo xueshi yaolan* (Manchurian Empire Survey on Educational Matters), 1943 ed. Manchukuo Ministry of Education (n.d.), 62–63.

35. Saito, *Watashi no Jinsei Kaiko*, 20.

36. *Showa Jinmei Jiten* (Who's Who of the Showa Era), vol. 4: Section on Overseas Territories (Tokyo: Nihon Tosho Center, 1987), 155.

37. Masao Suzuki, "Kaiso" (Reminiscences), in *COBOP Membership List*, 9–10.

38. Ibid., 9–10.

39. *Haerbin Gongye Daxue xiaoyou lu*, 1985 ed., 1–3.

40. Saito, *Watashi no Jinsei Kaiko*, 26.

41. According to Hiroshi Inagaki of Kobe Women's Univeristy, who is himself a graduate of Harbin Polytechnic University and worked there as an assistant professor, the only Japanese student was Isamu Shiramizu of the Mechanical Engineering Department.

42. *Haerbin Gongye Daxue jianshi*, 8.

43. *Haerbin Gongye Daxue xiaoyou lu*, 1985 ed., 31–32.

44. Saito, *Watashi no Jinsei Kaiko*, 26.

45. Ibid., 77.

46. Ibid., 28.

47. Araki Toru, "Kakubo ni matsuwaru Hanashi" (A Story Concerning College Cap), in Harbin Institute of Technology Japanese Alumni Association, ed., *Nangan*, 1991 ed., 15.

48. *Haerbin Gongye Daxue jianshi*, 10–11.

49. Ibid., 10–11.

50. Ibid., 10.

51. *Dongbei Jiaoyu* (Education in the Northeast), 2:13 (1949): 13.

52. *Haerbin Gongye Daxue gaikuang* (An Introduction to Harbin Institute of Technology) (Haerbin: Haerbin gongye daxue 1952), 1.

Christian Mission Schools and Japan's Tō-A Dōbun Shoin: Comparisons and Legacies

Douglas R. Reynolds

Introduction: Christianity and China

In 1939 Mao Zedong expressed a view about foreign cultural policies and Christian endeavors in China that became more or less official after 1949:

> Furthermore, the imperialist powers have never slackened their efforts to poison the minds of the Chinese people. This is their policy of cultural aggression (*qinlue zhengce*). And it is carried out through missionary work, through establishing hospitals and schools, publishing newspapers and inducing Chinese students to study abroad. Their aim is to train intellectuals who will serve their interests and to dupe the people.[1]

Few Western scholars up through the 1970s would have argued strenuously against this position, at least as applied to the nineteenth century, when China was the victim of crude Western aggression. For most of the nineteenth century, even in the face of serious challenges inside and out, China's long-established ideals and institutions remained basically intact. Christianity undermined and subverted them. Simply stated, as in a recent study of Christianity in nineteenth-century China, "Missionaries came to China with the intention of displacing Chinese beliefs, values, and rituals with Christianity."[2]

In Chinese treaty ports, under the unequal treaties that ended the Opium War, Christianity was legalized in 1844. Outside of treaty ports, a ban of 1724 that labeled Christianity a "heterodox doctrine"[3] remained in force. The ban was freely ignored, and Christianity was carried well into the interior by, among others, "God's Chinese Son,"[4] in his devastating Taiping Revolution of 1850–64. Coincidentally, between 1856 and 1860 the Arrow Wars provided foreign powers a pretext to coerce the Chinese court into officially lifting the ban for all of China in 1860.[5] Thereafter, missionaries traveled throughout the country, protected by unequal treaties and backed by gunboats. The fears and resentments aroused by Christian activities over the next forty years, 1860–1900, triggered more than four hundred incidents known as *jiao'an* (literally, "religious cases") in almost every province of China. These anti-Christian *jiao'an*, well documented in official records, culminated in the ferocious Boxer upheavals of 1899–1900.[6]

Early into the twentieth century *jiao'an* declined sharply in numbers and intensity. This decline occurred for both Chinese and foreign reasons. The Chinese court, for its part, changed strategies and opened China up to the outside world in a series of remarkable reforms after 1901.[7] Foreigners, for their part, humbled by the Boxer trauma and inclined to welcome China's post-Boxer reforms, became more sympathetic and responsive to Chinese concerns and needs. Missionaries in growing numbers shifted emphasis to "good works" from mere conversion, inspired partly by the social gospel discussed by Dan Cui in the present volume.

The consequences of these developments for China were enormous. In 1905, for example, China abolished its time-honored civil service examination system, and in 1911 China's 2,100-year old imperial system itself collapsed. These core changes cut off China's elites from their intellectual and institutional moorings. For centuries China's cultural past had been a source of towering pride and strength. Now that rich past struck many as a travesty and source of self-delusion, the cause of unbearable humiliation and suffering. So extreme was the reaction that after 1915, during the May Fourth era, the cultural and political avant-garde of China essentially rejected China's past. An ideological and intellectual vacuum developed. Elites now turned to outside ideas that promised to make China modern and strong. In the new mix of ideas, Christianity, despite sporadic anti-Christian outbursts such as in the 1920s, secured a certain legitimacy, aided by the fact that national leaders such as Sun Yat-sen (Sun Zhongshan, 1866–1925)[8] and, after 1930, Chiang Kai-shek (Jiang Jieshi, 1887–1975) were avowed Christians.

It was not Christianity, however, but rival Marxism that triumphed by midcentury. "A Western heresy that could be used against the West," as Conrad Schirokauer so aptly termed it,[9] Marxism promised to undo Chinese national humiliation and the effects of foreign imperialism. After the victory of Marxism in 1949, foreigners on the losing side (including Christian missionaries and

educators) found themselve expelled, and their various institutions were nationalized and absorbed into the new state system. From 1949 to 1957 Christianity and other religions reached an accommodation with the new authorities.
This was followed by conflict that culminated in the Cultural Revolution.[10]
Tony Lambert, after examining these various periods, concluded in 1991: "For
the thirteen-year period 1966–79 institutional Christianity was completely
eradicated in China."[11]

Twice before, Christianity had appeared and then disappeared from
China. It first arrived during China's cosmopolitan Tang dynasty (618–907),
after which it vanished for reasons that are not clear. Its second coming took
place during the Pax Mongolia period of China's Yuan dynasty (1279–1368),
after which it vanished again. A third appearance occurred during the late
Ming (1368–1644) and Qing (1644–1912) dynasties. After its 1724 ban Christianity might well have vanished again. "Had missionaries after 1835 gradually
ceased coming to China instead of increasing in numbers," Kenneth Scott
Latourette wrote in 1929, "the Church would probably have passed out of
existence within a few generations, leaving behind it no permanent mark."[12]

In this telling, the disappearance of Christianity after 1949 ought to have
been expected. What was not expected was a remarkable resurgence of
Christianity—the "Christianity fever"[13] of the 1980s and 1990s. Most startling
of all, the number of Christians today vastly exceeds anything in China's past.
An official State Council report of October 1997 puts that number at four
million Catholics and about ten million Protestants, or "14 times as many as in
1949."[14] Foreign observers offer estimates as high as ten million Catholics and
fifty to sixty-five million Protestants.[15]

Whatever the exact numbers, even the lower official figures are surprising and unexpected. They are a wake-up call to historians. The topic of
Christianity in modern China demands reexamination. The present volume
looks at education and society in twentieth-century China. Christian mission
schools, or *jiaohui xuexiao*, were a major influence, a fact widely recognized.
Yet the real connection between education, society, and mission schools has
scarcely been examined. This essay takes a broad look at Christian mission
schools. It looks at the numbers of schools and their teaching staffs, their
policies and practices, and considers their possible legacies. The sources of
information are published primary and secondary materials, which, when
viewed with fresh eyes, open up new lines of inquiry.

My interest in the topic of education and Christianity in China is twofold. One is personal, deriving from my parents, who were educational missionaries in China from 1947 to 1951.[16] The other is academic, around my
research field of modern Sino-Japanese cultural interactions. For twenty years

I have researched and published about Tō-A Dōbun Shoin (East Asia Common Culture Academy, later University), a remarkable Japanese school in Shanghai, 1900–1945, that offered its students a unique and original area studies–type curriculum.[17] Although it was a foreign educational institution in China, Tō-A Dōbun Shoin's goals, policies, and practices were fundamentally different from those of Christian mission schools. Looking at Christian mission schools and at Tō-A Dōbun Shoin together highlights special features of both. Mission schools, whatever their limitations, were committed to and achieved a surprising degree of indigenization, meaning education for, of, and by Chinese. Tō-A Dōbun Shoin, a school with enviable strengths, was committed to and achieved a superior education not for Chinese but for Japanese. The school's founding ideal was for a joint education of Chinese and Japanese together, but this was dropped before any real implementation. The subsequent contrast between these institutions' commitments and achievements accentuate features not apparent when looking at each separately.

Christianity and the Question of Indigenization

The Boxer trauma of 1899–1900 had a powerful impact on Chinese and foreigner alike. The painful settlement imposed on China prompted the court to carry out far-reaching reforms, launched by the Empress Dowager's Reform Edict of 29 January 1901.[18] As for foreigners, the impassioned antiforeignism of the movement shocked many into moving away from confrontation toward cooperation, with counterparts in China now more active, forthcoming, and determined.

New Christian initiatives reflected trends of the late nineteenth century, including the question of how to make the Chinese church more truly "Chinese."[19] Known as indigenization (*bense yundong;* also *bense jiaohui,* the indigenous church) or sinicization (*Zhongguohua*),[20] this concern surfaced at the 1907 China Centenary Missionary Conference (Chuanjiao Bainian Jinian Huiyi) commemorating the one hundredth anniversary of the arrival in China of Robert Morrison (1782–1834), the first Protestant missionary to China. The missionaries in attendance passed a resolution aimed at their home churches, which declared: "(b) That [home churches supporting mission work in China] should abstain from claiming any permanent right of spiritual or administrative control over [Chinese] churches."[21] This principle of the autonomy of the Chinese church was reaffirmed and elaborated at the landmark World Missionary Conference in Edinburgh in 1910.[22] Even before China's 1911 Revolution, then, Christian leaders both foreign and Chinese had openly committed themselves to the principle of a Chinese church based on self-administration (*zili* or *zizhi*), self-supporting (*ziyang*), and self-propagation (*zichuan*)—terms encountered in both English and Chinese at the time.

The extent to which the Chinese church before 1949 was indigenized is hotly debated.[23] Whatever its extent, the concern about indigenization per se points to a fundamental characteristic of Christianity. Christianity is a universalistic faith. It assumes that all adherents will ultimately be independent and autonomous, bound by no earthly authority. This is not unique to Christianity. It is inherent in all universalistic, proselytizing faiths—in "Indian" Buddhism[24] and in "Arabic" Islam, for example. It is inherent in universalistic *secular* creeds or systems such as in "Chinese" Confucianism, adopted outside of China by Korea's Yi dynasty (1392–1910), by Japan's Tokugawa authorities (1603–1868), and by Vietnam's Later Le dynasty (1418–1789). This applies to "Western" Marxism, adopted in Russia, China, Cuba, and elsewhere. Belief systems that are universalistic do indeed expect to spread and to alter minds through indoctrination and conversion. If spread by force, these may well provoke the charge of cultural invasion or imperialism. Over the long run, however, a universalistic faith is implicitly and necessarily *anti*-imperialistic, rejecting control by an outside authority.[25]

Foreign proselytizers take for granted (and look forward to the day) that converts will become self-propagating and self-supporting, so that foreign personnel and funds can be withdrawn. Even at the earliest stages native assistants and leaders are necessary to achieve foreign mission objectives. "From the beginning," as Latourette wrote in 1929, "missionaries had expressed the hope that the Chinese would ultimately take over entire responsibility for the Church. . . . Many, indeed, were more eager to pass over authority than were some of the Chinese to accept it."[26]

Indigenization equates with success. Christian "success" in East Asia is manifest today in the existence of an independent "Korean Christianity"[27] (which counts more Presbyterians than any other country in the world), "Taiwan Christianity,"[28] "Japanese Christianity,"[29] "Vietnamese Christianity," and "Chinese Christianity." These Christian communities take pride in sending their own missionaries overseas, including back to the Christian West.[30]

The essential meaning of Christian universalism is captured poignantly in the following declaration by a Naga Christian in Assam, northeastern India:

> Europeans do not have the monopoly on Christianity. . . . Christianity came to Eurupe from Asia and some Indians were Christians 500 years before the Europeans. When Europeans became Christians they made it a European indigenous religion.

Now I, like many Nagas, am a Christian, but I am not a European. I have a relationship with my God. Now my God can speak to me through my dreams, just as happened to my Angami ancestors. I don't have to be like the Anglicans or the Catholics and go through all those rituals. I don't need them. What I am talking about is Naga Christianity—an indigenous Naga Christianity.[31]

Western missionaries in China might not have used these exact words, but the process of indigenization was at work as an implicit long-term goal. It was occurring not only in the churches but at mission schools, to which we now turn.

Mission Schools in the Twentieth Century: Increasing Indigenization

The years 1901 to 1914 were a period of unprecedented growth of Christianity in China.[32] "At last that fabric which had so far been impermeable was crumbling," writes Latourette. "The missionary, moreover, profited, at least for a time, by his association with the forces which were chiefly responsible for the change."[33] A surge in numbers followed—numbers of missionaries; numbers of Chinese converts, church workers, and ordained ministers; numbers of mission schools and teachers; and numbers of church-related institutions.[34] The jump in numbers is suggested by the work of the Swiss Basel mission among Hakka in Guangdong province:

> In 1876 there were 4 Basel mission stations, 16 outstations, 11 schools, and 953 communicants spread over the Hakka regions of Guangdong. By 1913, the mission had grown to include 18 mission stations, 108 outstations, and 80 schools (including a theological seminary, 2 normal schools, a middle school, 4 secondary schools, 13 boarding schools, and a total of 3,097 students). There were 2 hospitals, several dispensaries, 72 European staff, 271 Chinese staff, and 6,699 communicants.[35]

Such surges, evident also in areas served by better-funded missionaries from the United States and Great Britain,[36] solidified the foundation for growth.

Of primary interest to this article is the evidence of indigenization, and its extent. In churches, mission schools, hospitals, in every kind of Christian institution, Chinese were taking leadership positions, impelled by a combination of foreign limitations and overextension, growth in the number and sophistication of Chinese Christians, Chinese nationalistic agitation, Chinese government policies, and survival strategies dictated by circumstances like the War of Resistance of 1937–45.[37]

In terms of mission schools the best summary evidence available dates back nearly seventy years, to Latourette's *History of Christian Missions in China.* Latourette draws on a rich array of published reports, culminating in the ambitious (and audaciously titled) report of 1922, *The Christian Occupation of China.*[38] Latourette's most cited source for the years after 1910 is *The China Mission Year Book.* Published under this name from 1910 to 1925 (nos. 1–13 [1910–25]), it was renamed *The China Christian Year Book* in 1926 (nos. 14–21 [1926–39]). The name change in 1926 is deeply meaningful, because it signaled a shift away from the old centerpiece of "mission," meaning *foreign* mission, to the new centerpiece of "Christian," meaning *Chinese* Christian.

To elaborate on the meaning of the shift, the yearbooks for 1910 to 1916 and again for 1918 include the tables "Statistics of the Work of Protestant Missions in China."[39] These tables were mission centered—organized alphabetically by "Name of Society or Mission." They were dropped as of 1923. Their discontinuance reflected a dual process at work, one, the diminution of mission-centered thinking and leadership within the Chinese church and, the other, the rise of Chinese-centered thinking and leadership. Nothing documents this process better than the following. Nationwide meetings of Christian leaders, sometimes called Jidujiao Quanguo Dahui or National Christian Conference, had been held in Shanghai in 1877, 1890, 1907, 1913, and 1922. At meetings one, two, and three the participants were almost exclusively foreign. At the fourth meeting, in 1913, attendees were predominantly foreign. In 1922 more than half of the representatives were Chinese. The 1922 conference formed a new body, the National Christian Council (Zhonghua Jidujiao Xiejinhui). Consisting of one hundred members, a majority of whom were Chinese, this body replaced the foreign missionary–dominated leadership organization of earlier years.[40]

Mission schools, the evidence suggests, were ahead of the national leadership in their "Chineseness." For the six years 1913 through 1917 and 1920, annual statistics report the "total teaching force" of mission schools. Broken down into the subcategories of foreign men, foreign women, Chinese men, and Chinese women, these include a fifth subcategory of "Non-Christian Chinese Teachers." Table 1 adds a sixth category, which calculates Chinese as a percentage of the total teaching force. Beyond these figures *The China Christian Year Book* for 1929 reports that, as of 1926 for the East China Region (where foreign missionary numbers were high), 81 percent of the teachers at Christian middle schools were Chinese (274).[41] Of the teachers who were Chinese, a growing number, significantly, were graduates of Chinese Christian colleges and universities. A

1926 statistical table reveals that of 2,822 Christian college graduates surveyed 840, or 25.3 percent, were employed as mission school teachers.[42]

As for Christian *middle* schools and their numbers, those peaked in 1924 at 339 schools, as reported by the 1929 yearbook. Many Christian middle schools closed in 1925 as a result of the anti-Christian agitation of 1925–26.[43] By 1927–28 fewer than 100 mission middle schools were holding classes; by 1928–29 the number was back up to 164 schools (308). *The China Christian Year Book* for 1932–33 reports 196 middle schools operating in 1930 and 240 in 1932 (262–63). The same issue states, significantly, that the majority of members of boards of directors of these schools were now Chinese (264). This development, the result of government policies, gave Chinese a more direct stake in mission schools and dramatically accelerated the process of sinicization.

A broader statistical overview of mission schools is provided by Zhang Li and Liu Jiantang, for all levels and up to 1934.[44] As of 1914, Zhang and Liu report over 12,000 mission schools of all levels and types, enrolling more than 250,000 students. The anti-Christian agitation of 1925, followed by the stock market crash of 1929 (which sharply reduced foreign giving), caused the collapse of weaker schools. By 1934 only 6,593 mission schools remained. These schools were overwhelmingly at the primary or elementary level, but their numbers included 260 middle schools[45] (up from 164 in 1928–29), 7 seminaries, 3 medical schools, and 13 colleges and universities. The universities included professional schools or departments such as for medicine, law, agriculture, engineering, commerce, and education.

Systematic statistical reports for mission schools were discontinued in the 1920s, in part a casualty of developments described later. In 1922 *Christian Education in China*, a comprehensive report prepared by the China Educational

TABLE 1.   Total Teaching Force

Year	Foreign Men	Foreign Women	Chinese Men	Chinese Women	Chinese as Percent of Total Teaching Force	Non-Christian Chinese Teachers
1913	382	562	4,497	1,939	87.2	NA
1914	400	561	5,216	1,988	88.2	468
1915	476	633	5,941	2,528	88.4	726
1916	463	747	6,610	2,743	88.5	619
1917	405	592	7,635	2,998	91.4	755
1920	356	601	9,274	3,502	93.0	760

Source: From Dong Baoliang, *Zhongguo jiaoyushi gang: Jindai zhibu* (A general history of Chinese education: Modern period) (Beijing: Renmin jiaoyu chubanshe, 1993), 345–46.

Commission of sixteen prominent Chinese and foreign educators, was published in English and Chinese. Detailing educational statistics for the year 1920, its impact was immediate and arresting, in ways neither anticipated nor desired. Latourette remarks:

> The report attracted the attention of government educators to this system of schools—often better equipped and more efficient than anything else in a community—independent of the Chinese state and largely under foreign control. The intense nationalism of the day witnessed this development with a fear which was not unmixed with envy and before many years came the attempt to bring mission institutions under strict governmental supervision and to reduce to a minimum their foreign and religious character.[46]

Frenzied nationalism in fact had prompted Chinese governments, beginning in 1924, to take steps to bring Christian mission schools under state control.[47] Typical of the regulations are those issued by Beijing in 1925, as reported by Cyrus Peake in 1932:

> On November 16, 1925 the Ministry of Education of the Peking government promulgated regulations which insisted that all private schools have a Chinese President or Vice-President, that more than half the Board of Directors be Chinese, that religious propaganda should not be conducted, that the curricula conform to those of the Ministry of Education and that attendance upon religious courses be not compulsory.[48]

Somewhat later, in February 1928, the Ministry of Education at Nanjing issued similar regulations. Widely implemented, the effect of these various regulations was to accelerate the process of Chinese Christian institutions emerging "independent of foreign missions, autonomous in operations, and indigenous in ideas and leadership."[49]

In 1997 a woman named Bai Yongda reminisced about herself and her two eldest sisters, who had attended mission schools at successive levels. From an elementary mission school for girls in their local *zhen*, or town, in Hebei province, the two sisters had proceeded to a girls' mission school for middle grades in Baoding *fu*, or prefecture, and finished at a girls' senior high mission school in Beijing. The elder of the two sisters went on to graduate from National Beiping Normal University (Guoli Beiping shifan daxue) and devoted her life to education in various parts of China; the second graduated from Hebei Provincial Medical College (Hebei shengli yixueyuan) and during the War of Resistance served with a Red Cross medical team in southern Shaanxi province. Her dream, to make her way to communist areas of northern Shaanxi, was cut short by her early death due to illness. Bai Yongda herself, ten years junior to the sister who died, graduated from the renowned Christian Ginling College, or Jinling daxue, in Nanjing.

Inspired by a 1920 photograph of these sisters and their classmates at the local girls' elementary school, Bai published her comments in a popular series called *Old Photographs*. Her supplemental note is both revealing and suggestive:

> Supplementary note: The study of "mission schools" (*jiaohui xuexiao*) has taken new strides among historians in recent years. Mission schools were established by Protestant [missionaries] as necessary supplements to evangelism, because of the differences they encountered between Chinese and western cultures. But, speaking objectively, they also served to augment [Chinese] education just when the late-Qing government had abolished the old examination system and was instituting a brand new educational system. This was no small aid to China, in advancing its modernization. [Mission schools] increased opportunities for young boys and girls (especially girls) to attend school. For example, at the time had there been no Fanzhen Girls' Elementary School (Fanzhen nüzi xiaoxue) in our town of Xin'an (in fact there was no other girls' school, or coed elementary school, but only a boys' elementary school), it would have been impossible for my two eldest sisters to pave the way for the nine of us brothers and sisters not just for elementary schooling but for university education. Statistics reveal that at the time, 38.2 percent of all American missionary expenditures in China went to education. Many of China's most famous schools and universities ewre *jiaohui xuexiao,* such as Yanjing (Yenching University), Xiehe (Peking Union Medical College), Huiwen (Hwei Wen Girls' High School, Nanjing), Sheng Yuehan (St. John's University, Shanghai), Jinling (Ginling College, Nanjing), Dongwu (Soochow University), Zhijiang (Hangchow Christian College), Xiangya (Yale-in-China, Changsha), Huaxi (West China Union University, Chengdu), and Lingnan (Canton Christian College or, after 1926, Lingnan University). Leighton Stuart made his name in education. One of the above, Jinling Daxue, was my alma mater.

A further reason I treasure this photo is this: in the 1930s, my mother Liu Shuzhen served as principal of this school, although only in name (*mingyi*), because of her financial support or "backing" of the school. *Neither of my parents were Christian* [emph. added], but because three daughters attended this school (including third daughter Yongci), they were more than happy to extend their support and assistance.[50]

The Chinese government centralized China's educational bureaucracy in the late 1920s, and yet, as Suzanne Pepper reminds us, local elites remained a primary source of supplemental funding even for *public* schools.[51] Mission schools depended for survival on donations by local elites, including non-Christians, who valued good education regardless of sponsorship.[52] Yet appointing a non-Christian donor, such as Bai's mother, principal of the mission school is something I had not expected. That and other surprising dimensions of mission schools—many mentioned by Ryan Dunch in this volume—beg for examination. Bai Yongda's comments, it should be noted finally, were written for popular Chinese consumption rather than for a Christian or Western audience. This makes them particularly compelling.[53]

Tō-A Dōbun Shoin: Decreasing Indigenization

Tō-A Dōbun Shoin (East Asia Common Culture Academy) was planned and founded in 1899–1900, perfectly timed to benefit from the explosive anti-Western and anti-Christian sentiment of the Boxer era. That sentiment, however, was not its primary inspiration. In the aftermath of Japan's military victory over China in the Sino-Japanese War of 1894–95, Japanese had developed a certain contempt toward China[54] and seemed disinterested in their China ties. This prompted the concern of Konoe Atsumaro (1863–1904), a visionary imperial prince who had studied in Europe from 1885 to 1890.[55] While in Europe, Konoe had acquired a somewhat apocalyptic view of future East-West relations: "We are fated to have a struggle between the white and yellow races," he declared in a sensationalist article in January 1898, "and in that struggle Chinese and Japanese will both be regarded as the sworn enemies of the whites."[56] Given such an eventuality, Konoe devoted a major part of his later years, until his premature death in 1904, to cultivating ties and exchanges with China. Tō-A Dōbun Shoin, sponsored by Konoe's Tō-A Dōbunkai (East Asia Common Culture Association), founded in 1898 in Tokyo, emerged as that association's most ambitious, enduring, and significant endeavor in China.[57]

In the planning stages of Tō-A Dōbun Shoin, Prince Konoe traveled to China in October 1899 and discussed establishing a school with both Governor-Generals Zhang Zhidong (1837–1909) and Liu Kunyi (1830–1902). Liu invited Konoe to set up his school in Liu's jurisdictional capital of

Nanjing. Just seven months later, in May 1900, Nanjing Tongwen Shuyuan (Nankin Dōbun Shoin, or Nanjing Common Culture Academy) opened its doors to Chinese and Japanese students at the upper high school level.

The previous December, Konoe had unveiled his founding hopes for the school in a recruiting circular sent out to prefectural governors and assembly heads around Japan:

> The instruction of Chinese students, centered around the Japanese language, will instill scientific thinking in them, and arouse a sense of nationhood (*kokka teki kannen*). They will live in dormitories, just like our Japanese students. It is hoped that by bringing Japanese and Chinese students together, close friendships and prolonged mutual help and mutual support will serve greatly to expedite our future dealings.[58]

The man Konoe handpicked as coordinator (and longtime headmaster, 1900–1923) seemed a perfect choice. Nezu Hajime (1860–1927), a recognized China Hand, or *Shina tsu,* was known in military, business, government, and organizational circles. His interest in China had developed as a military academy classmate in the mid-1880s of Arao Sei (1859–1896), a fellow budding China Hand. During the Sino-Japanese War of 1894–95 Nezu had served in the army with distinction and had been decorated. More germane to his appointment by Konoe, he had served from 1890 to 1893 as assistant to Arao Sei at the latter's impressive pioneering school in Shanghai, Nisshin Bōeki Kenkyūjo (Japan-China Trade Research Institute),[59] the spiritual predecessor of Tō-A Dōbun Shoin. Nezu spoke good Chinese and was devoted to Neo-Confucianism of the Wang Yangming or O Yomei School.

It was at Konoe's bidding that Nezuo found himself back in China in early 1900, where he met with Liu Kunyi, Zhang Zhidong, and Chinese educators. During that time Nezu authored two brief but important essays in classical Chinese: "Xingxue yaozhi" (Aims of Learning) and "Lijiao gangling" (Principles of Education).[60] These incorporated key phrases and reformist notions then in vogue in China and served as the founding principles for Tō-A Dōbun Shoin.

Liu Kunyi was delighted. Already in December 1899, after the outbreak of Boxer violence in the north, Liu had expressed appreciation that the educational efforts of Tō-A Dōbunkai were "unrelated to any religion"[61]—a jab at Christian mission schools. A half-year later, in a letter to Konoe, Liu lauded "Lijiao gangling," remarking that its balanced concern for both Chinese classics and Western subjects manifested "both *ti* and *yong*" (*you ti you yong*)[62]— Chinese principle and Western practical learning. This was high praise, indeed.

These founding ideals were well suited to China of the moment. Unfortunately, they were never realized. The Nanjing school had twenty-three Japanese and thirty Chinese students. The first-year program of the Chinese students consisted solely of language instruction in Japanese and English languages and Chinese literature. The program for Japanese students was hardly any better, with only two qualified Japanese teachers, no real headmaster (Nezu, headmaster beginning in April after the designated headmaster fell ill, was absent from Nanjing nearly the entire time), and proper instruction only in Chinese and English. By early summer the campus was in turmoil, and Boxers loomed on the horizon. Governor-General Liu urged the Japanese to evacuate to the safety of Shanghai. The Japanese departed in late August, leaving behind the school's Chinese students. The Japanese never returned.[63] The new school in Shanghai, rechristened Tō-A Dōbun Shoin, opened to much fanfare in late May 1901. This and other Japanese cultural initiatives of the moment caught the eye of the astute Rev. A. P. Parker of Shanghai, who lost no time in sounding the alarm. *The Chinese Recorder* of July carries Parker's warning, formidably titled "A New Japanese Invasion of China":

> An invasion of ideas instead of one of arms. A propaganda of education instead of one of coercion. A subtle attempt to make a conquest of China by means of mental rather than physical forces.

> Such is, in brief, the condition of things now rapidly coming to the front in China under the Japanese program, as indicated by their methods of procedure during the past few years.[64]

Had Rev. Parker realized that the dream to train Chinese and Japanese students together had been jettisoned, the alarm he sounded might have been muted.

The fundamental reason for Tō-A Dōbun Shoin's retreat from joint education was economic. Japan, struggling to industrialize, was poor. Arao, Konoe, and now Nezu had stretched themselves to the limit to devise ways to finance their unconventional schools in China. Unlike Western countries, Japan had no home missionary societies or wealthy philanthropists to fund exotic educational programs abroad. Hard choices had to be made. In deciding to drop Chinese students and concentrate on building up a program for Japanese students alone, there was no apparent struggle or debate. A compromise solution was reached. Japanese—and only Japanese—were to be trained in China, at Tō-A Dōbun Shoin in Shanghai; Chinese were to be trained in Tokyo, at a school founded in 1901, named Tōkyō Dōbun Shoin (Tokyo

Common Culture Academy), which existed from 1901 to 1922.[65] These several developments rendered moot the question of indigenization, so pertinent to the story of Christian mission schools.

Since indigenization is not an issue for Tō-A Dōbun Shoin, the remainder of this section concentrates on the process by which Tō-A Dōbun Shoin *as a foreign educational institution in China* became more and more "foreign" while insulating itself from the revolutionary currents and struggles of China. Although offering a magnificent area studies–type training, the school became more and more a school *of the Japanese, by the Japanese, and for the Japanese.* Instead of sinicization and indigenization, there is a persistent "Japanization." The comparison with mission school brings into sharp relief this essential characteristic of Tō-A Dōbun Shoin while accentuating the neglected (but significant) indigenization process of Christian mission schools.

It is well to remind ourselves of Tō-A Dōbun Shoin's humble institutional status. Until 1921 its main course of study was a three-year program offered to graduates of Japanese middle schools, emphasizing commercial studies, or *shōmuka.* Not until 1921 was it elevated to a four-year specialized higher school, or *senmon gakkō,* which, because of its overseas location, remained under the jurisdiction of Japan's Foreign Ministry rather than Ministry of Education. It was subsequently raised to the status of a comprehensive university, or *daigaku,* but this occurred only in 1939, in anticipation of Japan's wartime and postwar needs.

The modest formal institutional standing of Tō-A Dōbun Shoin must be kept in mind for at least two reasons: one, it makes all the more remarkable its many impressive achievements;[66] and, two, it serves as a necessary reminder that neither Tō-A Dōbun Shoin nor its graduates were in a position to influence Japanese policy toward China meaningfully. As Takeuchi Yoshimi pointed out many years ago, despite the special qualifications of Dōbun Shoin graduates, "the path to the top of both government and business was closed" because of Japan's elitist system of hiring and promoting.[67]

In terms of Sino-Japanese cooperation and understanding, the initial years of Tō-A Dōbun Shoin, up to the Russo-Japanese War of 1904–5, could be considered the school's "finest hour." In July 1901 Governors-General Liu Kunyi and Zhang Zhidong submitted their landmark joint memorial calling for fundamental educational reforms. An imperial edict of 2 October 1901 pronounced this and two other Liu-Zhang joint memorials on reform China's official guidelines for reform.[68]

The opportunity this afforded was seized upon by Nezu Hajime. After meeting separately with Liu and Zhang to discuss Yangzi region educational needs, Nezu reported to Tō-A Dōbunkai in Tokyo on 20 December 1902:

"Middle schools are to be set up in prefectures (*fu*), and elementary schools are to be set up in districts (*zhou*) and counties (*xian*). The jurisdiction under Zhang Zhidong alone has fifty prefectures and one hundred forty districts and counties. One person per prefecture means fifty people needed for middle schools; and one person per elementary school means one hundred forty persons needed." Nezu also reported to Liu and Zhang, on personnel needs: "Beginning the year after next, every April our Dbun Shoin will be producing around one hundred graduates. Why not hire them?" Both showed interest.[69] A handful of Dōbun Shoin graduates were indeed hired to teach in Yangzi region Chinese government schools after 1904. Their numbers turned out to be insignificant, however, compared to graduates drawn to the more lucrative opportunities that unexpectedly opened up to the north (and which Nezu cultivated assiduously). After Japan's victory over Russia in the Russo-Japanese War of 1904–5, Japan acquired vast Russian interests in Manchuria. This was a watershed in modern Sino-Japanese relations. Before the war the Japanese government lacked a unified continental policy; with the spoils of war, a coordinated policy quickly began to take shape. The logic of imperialism now made Japan more aggressive toward China. Tō-A Dōbun Shoin became caught up in this process. As early as April 1908, more than one-third of Dōbun Shoin graduates were employed in Manchuria and North China, serving chiefly Japanese firms. The consequence of this trend, in terms of earlier understandings and ideals, was a radical reorientation of the school and its graduates both away from their Yangzi base area and away from employment for Chinese benefit.[70] Ide Saburo (1862–1931), a sensitive observer with experience in China dating back to the 1880s, filed a report in 1910 commissioned by the Japanese Foreign Ministry, in which he warned: "One urgent need is to win the hearts and minds of the Chinese people." Ide strongly endorsed a proposal to create a university in Nanjing (called Nanjing daxue) to educate the children of local elites.[71] Japan, however, lacked the resources and the will for such a major undertaking. Thus, while Tō-A Dōbun Shoin was moving away from its founding vision of education for Chinese in China, Christian mission schools were multiplying at every level and educating ever larger numbers of Chinese students. The contrast is striking.

In the middle 1910s the Japanese government noted with alarm that it seemed to be losing the cultural battle for China to the West.[72] Spurred by the examples of the United States and Great Britain utilizing Boxer indemnity funds for educational and cultural programs for Chinese, the Japanese Foreign Ministry instructed Tō-A Dōbun Shoin in 1918 to establish a Chinese Student Division (Chūka Gakuseibu), using Boxer indemnity funds paid to Japan. Meant to accommodate a class of fifty Chinese students each year beginning in

1919, the recruitment effort for 1919 was halted because of May Fourth–related anti-Japanese sentiment. For 1920 Tō-A Dōbun Shoin did manage to recruit six students for the program. The problems of the program remained legion, however: problems of recruiting good Chinese students, political agitation by those students, and their subversion of Japanese classmates by spreading "dangerous thoughts" (*kiken shisō*). A program designed to graduate fifty Chinese students per class had, after ten full classes, graduated a total of only forty-eight students—and the division was shut down in 1934.[73]

Anti-Japanese agitation among Chinese students at Tō-A Dōbun Shoin would best be compared to antiforeign student agitation on the campuses of Christian colleges and universities. That critique, however, is beyond the scope of this study. At the very least we have to recognize that neither Tō-A Dōbun Shoin nor Christian colleges fully controlled their own destinies during the volatile 1920s. Neither can be faulted entirely for their unhappy experiences with Chinese students. On the other hand, Tō-A Dōbun Shoin must be faulted for several measures that made it more "Japanese," which accordingly made it more "alien" and inhospitable to Chinese. In April 1921, at the very time Tō-A Dōbun Shoin was struggling to attract more Chinese students, the school, which until then had observed the Chinese academic year of August to June, switched over to the Japanese school year of April to March. Also beginning in April 1921, Tō-A Dōbun Shoin embarked on a six-month campaign to build an endowment fund from those Japanese companies that employed its graduates and benefited from its training programs and publications. The campaign was a success. That success, however, tied the school more closely to the Japanese donors and their business agendas.[74] From a strictly Japanese point of view, these efforts were perhaps desirable and necessary, since they coincided with Tō-A Dōbun Shoin's elevation to a four-year *senmon gakkō*, effective April 1921. But for Sino-Japanese relations their implications were negative.

Two separate initiatives, one in 1923 and the other in 1935, solidified the school's cultural ties to Japan and away from China. The timing of this trend was quite astonishing, given the rampant Chinese nationalism of the period. It suggests a certain institutional disconnect between Tō-A Dōbun Shoin and its Chinese setting. In 1923 a tower was erected on campus called the Peace in Asia Memorial Tower (Sei-A Hyōshō no tō). A very "Japanese" action, this monument featured a dedicatory inscription of 1920 by headmaster Nezu, celebrating the deeds of unnamed Japanese patriots, or *shishi,* who had risked their lives to found the school and bring peace to Asia.[75] In hindsight the memorial seems a modest step when compared to the completion and dedication in November 1935 of a large Shinto shrine, or *jinja,* on the campus. Proposed by headmaster Ōuchi Chōzō (1874–1944) in April 1934—the very same year that Tō-A Dōbun

Shoin closed its failed Chinese Student Division—Sei-A Jinja enshrined the spirits of Konoe Atsumaro, Arao Sei, and Nezu Hajime with memorial tablets to 649 other martyrs to the cause of the school and its predecessor, in typical Shinto fashion.[76]

Japanese Shinto, the indigenous religion of Japan, is unlike Buddhism, Christianity, or Islam. It is *not* universalistic but is particularistic, tied to the Japanese people and ultimately to their homeland and its mythic origins. If dissociated from these elements, Shinto is rendered meaningless.[77] The connection is evident in the expression "Where Japanese go, there go *jinja.*"[78] In Manchuria between 1905 and 1945 more than three hundred *jinja* were erected. These shrines were fundamentally "of the Japanese and for the Japanese,"[79] in the words of Shinto scholar Sagai Tatsuru. With the demise of the Japanese puppet state of Manchukuo, and the return of Japanese to their homeland, these shrines ceased to function.

Tō-A Dōbun Shoin, by 1923 and accelerating over the years, became caught up in Japanese particularism and Shinto ritualism. This detached the school further, at least institutionally, from China and its people. (This institutional detachment, it must be emphasized, only partially affected Dōbun Shoin students, who prided themselves on their good reputations in Shanghai, whose streets they walked freely, in school uniform and without incident.) On their long research field trips students would encounter and report on anti-Japanese sentiment. They were prevented by the school and after 1930 by the Japanese consular police, however, from siding with Chinese nationalism or taking a critical view of Japan's own accelerating militarism and expansion.[80]

In November 1937 Tō-A Dōbun Shoin's twenty-year-old campus was destroyed by fire, including its valuable Chinese library and unique museum collection. The next month the school requisitioned the fine campus of the nearby Jiaotong University (Jiaotong daxue), which provided handsome quarters prior to the school's elevation to university status in December 1939—an upgrade to assist in its "great mission" (*dai shimei*) of training administrative personnel for Japan's expanded role in the "guidance of East Asia" (*Tō-A no keirin*).[81] With this development Chinese individuals (except Chinese from Taiwan, who matriculated as Japanese citizens) cease to play a part in the plans, programs, or leadereship of this *now totally foreign university* in China.

Mission Schools and Tō-A Dōbun Shoin: Comparative Legacies

It was as a "totally foreign university" that Tō-A Dōbun Shoin Daigaku was expelled from China after the war, in 1946. It left behind no core of Chinese students and few alumni, because Chinese students and staff were almost nonexistent. Nor did it leave behind a distinctive campus or facilities, because its wartime campus simply reverted to Jiaotong University. The "legacy" of Tō-A Dōbun Shoin ended up not in China but in Japan, among Japanese students, alumni, and staff, where it lives on today.

The Japanese alumni association of Tō-A Dōbun Shoin, known as Koyūkai, or Friends of Shanghai Association, and based in Tokyo's downtown government center of Kasumigaseki, has endeavored since the school's expulsion to keep alive its memory and to support and promote Sino-Japanese friendship. Efforts include publications, research, training, and various special programs to inform the Japanese public about China. They are carried out variously through Kazankai (successor to Tō-A Dōbunkai), Koyūkai, and Aichi Daigaku, or Aichi University, in Toyohashi City—established in 1946 to receive students from Tō-A Dōbun Shoin Daigaku and other colonial universities in Taiwan, Korea, and Manchukuo, whose education had been interrupted by the war's abrupt end.

Aichi University celebrated its fiftieth anniversary in 1996 and is increasingly active in China-related endeavors. It houses the valuable Kazan Bunko collection of China research materials of the prewar Tō-A Dōbunkai; it houses and preserves student records and research reports from Tō-A Dōbun Shoin; it undertakes joint research projects with Chinese universities and institutions, and in April 1997, under authorization of the Ministry of Education, it admitted the first group of 180 students into its Faculty of Modern Chinese Studies (Gendai Chūgoku Gakubu), the sole faculty in Japan devoted to a four-year program of modern Chinese studies. Gendai Chūgoku Gakubu, with a projected enrollment of 770 students (120 of them foreign students, including some from Korea), with its mandatory Chinese-language semester at Nankai University in Tianjin during a student's freshman year, with instruction in Chinese by Chinese professors teaching courses on modern Chinese history, Chinese culture, Chinese society, and Chinese law, and with a Master's program, may well emerge as the real successor to Tō-A Dōbun Shoin Daigaku.[82] Like Tō-A Dōbun Shoin, it seeks to recruit Japanese students from every part of Japan.

Though these activities benefit Sino-Japanese relations and understanding, they serve primarily Japanese needs and interests. As Aichi University's China program grows, it might well come closer to Tō-A Dōbun Shoin's founding ideal of a joint education on China for Japanese and non-Japanese together.

As for Christian mission schools, their legacy resides *inside* of China. That legacy is visibly alive in those few cases in which alumni have come together to revive their alma mater, as in the cases of the Anglo-Chinese

College of Fuzhou and the McTyeire School for Girls in Shanghai, reported on, respectively, by Ryan Dunch and Heidi Ross in this volume. When renewed links have been accompanied by promises of hard currency from outside of China, the Chinese government has been amenable to gatherings, rememberings, commemoratings, and even reopenings.

In most cases, however, the legacy of mission schools is not so visible. It is subterranean. It surfaces here and there, part of the powerful undercurrent fueling Christianity's growth in numbers in the 1980s and 1990s. In 1979 my father and I returned to Wuhu for our first visit since 1951. My father, Dr. Hubert Reynolds, wanted to find former colleagues and friends from Cuiwen Zhongxue (Cuiwen Middle School, or Wuhu Christian Academy), where he had taught from 1947 to 1951. (The campus of Cuiwen Middle School serves today as a core part of the campus of Anhui Normal University, or Anhui Shifan Daxue, which regards Cuiwen as forerunner of its Middle School Attached to Anhui Normal University, or Anhui Shifan Daxue Fushu Zhongxue).[83] We located Wan Shuyong, school principal from 1934 to 1952,[84] as well as the former school pastor, in a residential compound, where they and Muslim and Buddhist leaders had been relocated during the Cultural Revolution. These men and their families had suffered severely for their faith. Their faith had been tested and—judging by their confident manners and glowing faces—had emerged stronger for it.

My father and the men greeted one another tearfully, as old friends and fellow Christians. These Chinese Christians had survived on their own. They did not ask for anything. They said only, "Pray for us," and my father replied, "Let us pray for each other." They spoke of other Christian leaders in Anhui and nearby provinces. I was impressed by their quiet faith and determination and by their optimism. But I did not know the meaning of what I was seeing.

Now, twenty years later—in light of this study and of a May 1999 return visit to China with former Wuhu missionary Dr. Joseph M. Smith—it is clear that what I witnessed was evidence of a *Chinese* Christianity from before 1949, a faith that had been sinified both culturally and personally. Like the Naga who declared, "What I am talking about is Naga Christianity—an indigenous Naga Christianity," Chinese had arrived at an indigenous Chinese Christianity. No mere abstract article of faith, Christianity had become internalized as Chinese assumed the positions of leadership and control of their own Christian lives and institutions. Since 1949 the process of indigenization has solidified around China's Three-Self Patriotic Movement (Sanzi aiguo yundong), centered around the three principles of self-administration, self-support, and self-propagation. Before 1949 Chinese Christian ties to foreigners inspired the saying "One more Christian, one less Chinese." Just fifty years later, in 1999 when I queried non-Christian Chinese about Chinese who were Christians, not one person intimated that there was anything unpatriotic or "un-Chinese" about being both Chinese and Christian. The shift in attitude is remarkable, almost beyond imagination. Mission schools, as centers of education *for the Chinese, of the Chinese, and by the Chinese* (including non-Christians), were an important vehicle for arriving at this point.

In the 1920s, 1930s, and 1940s, as mission schools were becoming *more Chinese* in their struggle to adjust to new Chinese laws and nationalist sentiment, Tō-A Dōbun Shoin was becoming less Chinese and *more foreign*, accommodating itself to Japanese laws in order to award more prestigious Japanese degrees to its students. Increasingly, the education offered was *for the Japanese, of the Japanese, and by the Japanese.*

Foreign educational institutions in China have played roles enormously complex and varied, having vastly different outcomes. Seeds from the past, whether Chinese, Japanese, or Western, are cross-fertilizing today to create hybrids still in the making. To understand their impact on education and society in twentieth- and twenty-first-century China requires observers to keep their eyes open and minds alert to unexpected and sometimes astonishing developments, some only just unfolding.

NOTES

1. Mao Zedong, "The Chinese Revolution and the Chinese Communist Party" (December 1939), in *Selected Works of Mao Tse-tung*, vol. 2 (Peking: Foreign Languages Press, 1965, 1967), 312.

2. Jessie G. Lutz and Rolland Ray Lutz, *Hakka Chinese Confront Protestant Christianity, 1850–1900; With the Autobiographies of Eight Hakka Christians, and Commentary* (Armonk, N.Y.: M. E. Sharpe, 1998), 3.

3. The imperial order banning Christianity appeared under the subtitle "Destroy Heterodox Doctrines in Order to Render Honor to Orthodox Learning." For a discussion, see Paul A. Cohen, *China and Christianity: The Missionary Movement and the Growth of Chinese Antiforeignism, 1860–1870* (Cambridge: Harvard University Press, 1963), 11–15. See also Cohen's essay "Christian Missions and Their Impact to 1900," in John K. Fairbank, ed., *The Cambridge History of China*, vol. 10: *Late Ch'ing, 1800–1911*, pt. 1 (Cambridge: Cambridge University Press, 1978), 545, also, 552–53.

4. The term *God's Chinese Son* is from Jonathan D. Spence, *God's Chinese Son: The Heavenly Kingdom of Hong Xiuquan* (New York: W. W. Norton, 1996). Spence looks carefully at the conversion and Christian theology of Hong Xiuquan, founder and leader of the Taiping movement.

5. Kenneth Scott Latourette, *A History of Christian Missions in China* (New York:

Macmillan, 1929), 271–81, discusses the terms of the conventions that opened China's interior to Christianity.

6. Archival records of late-Qing *jiao'an* are reproduced with punctuation in the impressive multivolume series, *Jiaowu jiao'an dang* (1860–1911) (The Zongli Yamen Archives on Christian affairs and on cases and disputes involving missionaries and converts [1860–1911]) (ser. 1–7) (Taihei: Institute of Modern History, Academia Sinica, 1974–81). For an invaluable study, see Zhang Li and Liu Jiantang, *Zhongguo jiao'an shi* (A history of Anti-Christian incidents in China) (Chengdu: Sichuan sheng shehui kexueyuan chubanshe, 1987), 388–648, which conveniently discusses and analyzes leading *jiao'an* for the years 1861–1911; a careful listing of these *jiao'an*, with brief descriptions and documentation, appears on pages 776–886.

7. Douglas R. Reynolds, *China, 1898–1912: The Xinzheng Revolution and Japan* (Cambridge: Council on East Asian Studies, Harvard University, 1993), examines China's post-1901 reforms. A revised version of this study, translated into Chinese by Li Zhongxian (Chung-yin Lee) and with added citations to original documents in published collections, is Ren Da (Douglas R. Reynolds), *Xinzheng geming yu Riben: Zhongguo, 1898–1912* (Nanjing: Jiangsu renmin chubanshe, 1998). For reform efforts dating back to 1895, see Douglas R. Reynolds, ed. and trans., *China, 1895–1912: State-Sponsored Reforms and China's Late-Qing Revolution—Selected Essays from Zhongguo Jindai Shi*, a double issue of *Chinese Studies in History* (Spring–Summer 1995).

8. See Zhou Xingliang, "Sun Zhongshan yu Xifang Jidujiao" (Sun Zhongshan and Western Christianity), *Wen-Shi-Zhe* (Literature, history, philosophy [Jinan]), no. 6 (1995): 74–82; reprinted in *Zhongguo Jindai Shi* (Modern Chinese history), no. 2 (1996): 114–22.

9. Conrad Schirokauer, *A Brief History of Chinese and Japanese Civilizations*, 2d ed. (San Diego: Harcourt Brace Jovanovich, 1989), 490.

10. Richard C. Bush Jr., *Religion in Communist China* (Nashville: Abingdon Press, 1970), examines religion broadly in revolutionary China. Bob Whyte, *Unfinished Encounter: China and Christianity* (Harrisburg, Pa.; Morehouse Publishing, 1988, 1990), looks more specifically at Christianity, providing an informed history and analysis by period.

11. Tony Lambert, *The Resurrection of the Chinese Church* (London: Hodder and Stoughton, 1991), also 12, 161.

12. Latourette, *History of Christian Missions*, 196. For the Tang and Mongol periods, see 51–77. See also the appropriate sections of the carefully researched study of Samuel Hugh Moffett, *A History of Christianity in Asia*, vol. 1: *Beginnings to 1500* (San Francisco: HarperCollins, 1992).

13. " 'Christianity Fever': The Growth of the Church" is the title of chapter 9 of Lambert, *Resurrection*, 142–57. Lambert's is a well-documented study from a fundamentalist Christian perspective.

14. "Freedom of Religious Belief in China" (State Council Information Office, October 1997), *Beijing Review* 40, no. 44 (November 3–9, 1997): 20, also 13. This report is also available under the title of "White Paper—Freedom of Religious Belief in China" (Information Office of the State Council of the People's Republic of China, October 1997), on the Internet at www. china-embassy.org under "Issues and Events."

China's 1982 census reported three million Christians, or "three times the number in 1949." Ten years later, in 1992, the official figures were 3.5 million Catholics and 5.5 million Protestants. See *China Facts and Figures Annual,* vol. 13 (Gulf Breeze, Fla.: Academic International Press, 1989), 370; and vol. 17 (1993), 460, respectively. The 1993 issue remarks: "One of the paradoxes of China is that Christianity may be growing at a more rapid rate under today's repressive regime than it did when missionaries were free" (460).

15. For foreign figures, see the reports of such groups as Amnesty International, the Holy Spirit Study Center in Hong Kong, and Human Rights Watch. A thoughtful report, "How to Count the Number of Christians in China: Questions and Answers" (September 1997), by Amity News Service, Hong Kong, is available on the Internet at www.hk.super.net/~amityhk/96_4_sp2.htm.

16. My parents, I. Hubert Reynolds (Ren Lede), Ph.D. (1914–93), and Harriet Robertson Reynolds (Ren Ruide), Ph.D. (1910–88), were missionary educators, with doctorates in cultural anthropology. They served with the Christian Church (Disciples of Christ) first in China from 1947 to 1951 and then in the Philippines, from 1952 until their deaths. In China they were associated with Cuiwen Zhongxue (Cuiwen Middle School, or Wuhu Christian Academy), in Wuhu, Anhui province, about which more is said at the end of this article.

17. See Douglas R. Reynolds, "Chinese Area Studies in Prewar China: Japan's Tō-A Dōbun Shoin in Shanghai, 1900–1945," *Journal of Asian Studies* 45, no. 5 (November 1986): 945–70.

18. Translated in Reynolds, *China, 1898–1912,* 201–4.

19. Whyte, *Unfinished Encounter,* 98–101 and 117–28, examines nineteenth-century missionary antecedents of indigenization. Lutz and Lutz recount the story of the Basel Mission in Guangdong, where congregations were "founded by Chinese evangelists rather than missionaries" (*Hakka Chinese,* 3). Also see Latourette, *History of Christian Missions,* 423–29 and 665–80.

20. Yamamoto Sumiko, *Chūgoku Kirisutokyo shi kenky: Purotesutanto no "dochakuka" o chushin to shite* (Studies on the history of Christianity in China: with special reference to the "indigenization" of Protestant churches in the first half of the twentieth century) (Tokyo: Tokyo Daigaku Shuppankai, 1972), 51–68 and 291–327. Also see Zhang Li and Liu Jiantang, *Zhongguo jiao an shi,* 661–70.

21. *China Centenary Missionary Conference Records,* 439, quoted in Latourette, *History of Christian Missions,* 674.

22. Latourette, *History of Christian Missions,* 669–80, discusses the Edinburgh Conference and its guidelines for future mission work in China.

23. Daniel H. Bays, "The Growth of Independent Christianity in China, 1900–1937," in Daniel H. Bays, ed., *Christianity in China: From the Eighteenth Century to the Present* (Stanford: Stanford University Press, 1996), 307–16, is an excellent introduction to the complex issues of indigenous Christianity in China. Whyte, *Unfinished Encounter,* 122–23, 124–28, 161–62, 179–82, 202–5, 340, 400–401, 415–16, provides additional comments on the promises as well as the limitations of the indigenization process of the Chinese church.

24. Arthur F. Wright, *Buddhism in Chinese History* (Stanford: Stanford University

Press, 1959), recounts the tortuous path by which an independent Buddhism emerged in China.

25. In the case of Christianity one partial exception to this rule involves the Roman Catholic Church, centered in the Vatican and around the pope. Certain matters decided by the pope are considered doctrinally binding on all church members. In no other branch of Christianity or Buddhism or Islam—or Confucianism or Marxism (despite the best efforts of some)—do "infallible" doctrines or dogma emanate from a single center. The Chinese quarrel with the Vatican is spelled out in "White Paper— Freedom of Religious Belief in China," 6 and 7.

26. Latourette, *History of Christian Missions,* 802, also 672. For specifics of the period 1901–14, see 672–80; and for the period 1918–26, see 801–11.

27. Donald N. Clark, *Christianity in Modern Korea* (Lanham, Md.: University Press of America, 1986), offers a brief summary treatment. A more recent study is Chang Geun Hwang, "Political and Social Factors in the Establishment of Buddhism and Christianity in Korea: Social Change and Acculturation by the Acceptance of Foreign Religions in Korea" (Master's thesis, University of Georgia, 1992).

28. See Murray A. Rubinstein, *The Protestant Community on Modern Taiwan: Mission, Seminary, and Church* (Armonk, N.Y.: M. E. Sharpe, 1991).

29. Carlo Caldarola, *Christianity: The Japanese Way* (Leiden: E. J. Brill, 1979), discusses the acculturation of Christianity to Japan, around the Mukyokai, or Non-Church, movement.

30. In a reversal involving Buddhism, the Japanese, who had received Buddhism from Korea and China, sent Japanese Buddhist missionaries to China in the late nineteenth and early twentieth centuries. This theme is explored in Douglas R. Reynolds, "Japanese Buddhist Mission Work in China and the Challenge of Christianity, 1868–1915" (paper presented at the 1989 symposium, "History of Christianity in China Project," University of Kansas, Lawrence, June 18–23, 1989).

31. *The Naga Nation and Its Struggle against Genocide: A Report Compiled by IWGIA* (International Work Group for Indigenous Affairs) (Copenhagen: IWGIA Document no. 56, 1986), 106–7. This passage is partially quoted in Richard M. Eaton, "Comparative History as World History: Religious Conversion in Modern India," *Journal of World History* 8, no. 2 (Fall 1997): 271.

32. Protestant missions emphasized education open to all and at every level. Roman Catholic missions tended to emphasize education of Catholics alone and chiefly at lower levels. This article limits itself to Protestant educational efforts.

33. Latourette, *History of Christian Missions,* 532.

34. Ibid., esp. 527–685.

35. Nicole Constable, "Christianity and Hakka Identity," in Bays, ed., *Christianity in China,* 161–62. Constable adds that by 1948 the Basel mission had close to twenty thousand communicants (162).

36. Latourette, *History of Christian Missions,* 534–35, 569, makes a direct connection between industrial wealth and mission giving in the United States and Great Britain.

37. Timothy Brook, "Toward Independence: Christianity in China under the Japanese Occupation, 1937–1945," in Bays, ed., *Christianity in China,* 317–37, addresses this interesting question.

38. *The Christian Occupation of China: A General Survey of the Numerical Strength and Geographical Distribution of the Christian Forces in China,* made by the Special Committee on Survey and Occupation, China Continuation Committee (Shanghai: China Continuation Committee, 1922).

39. Masako Nohara, my graduate research assistant, spent many hours examining and gathering statistics from this and other published sources. It is a pleasure to acknowledge her assistance.

40. Latourette, *History of Christian Missions,* 796–97, also 801–9.

41. This same issue reports that at boys' middle schools a majority of the students were from non-Christian families (276).

42. The table, from Xu Wentai, "Shouhui daxue jiaoyu quan! Tiaoyueshang de baozhang" (Recover China's educational rights! With treaty guarantees), *Minfeng 7,* no. 3 (March 1926), is reproduced in Dong Baoliang, *Zhongguo jiaoyushi gang: Jindai zhi bu* (A general history of Chinese education: modern period) (Beijing: Renmin jiaoyu chubanshe, 1993), 345–46. For an authoritative overview of Christian higher education in China, see Jessie Gregory Lutz, *China and the Christian Colleges, 1850–1950* (Ithaca: Cornell University Press, 1971).

43. Ka-che Yip, *Religion, Nationalism, and Chinese Students: The Anti-Christian Movement of 1922–1927* (Bellingham: Western Washington University Press, 1980), examines anti-Christian agitation in relationship to questions of education and Chinese nationalism. See also Jessie G. Lutz, *Chinese Politics and Christian Missions: The Anti-Christian Movements of 1920–28* (Notre Dame, Ind.: Cross Cultural Publications, 1988). At the height of the crisis, *The China Christian Year Book* for 1926 declared resolutely: "Christian education is passing through a time of opposition and danger. It is in times like this that Christianity has always flourished" (233).

44. Zhang Li and Liu Jiantang, *Zhongguo jiao'an shi,* 685–90.

45. *China Christian Year Book* for 1934–35 (267) gives the same number of 260 Christian middle schools in 1934.

46. Latourette, *History of Christian Missions,* 787–88. With regard to *Christian Education in China: The Report of the China Educational Commission of 1921–1922* and to the commission itself, see ibid., 786–87. The other primary source of Christian information, the *Chinese Recorder* (monthly; 1868–1935), is also short on statistics for the 1920s.

47. Latourette, *History of Christian Missions,* 814–15, conveniently summarizes the issues and measures.

48. Cyrus H. Peake, *Nationalism and Education in Modern China* (1932; rpt., New York: Howard Fertig, 1970), 151.

49. Bays, *Christianity in China,* 309, cites these criteria to define a fully independent Chinese church.

50. Bai Yongda, "Bashinian qian Baiyang Dianbian de xiangzhen nüzi xiaoxue" (The Baiyang dian bian town girls' elementary school eighty years ago), in *Lao zhaopian* (Old photographs) (Jinan: Shandong huabao chubanshe, 1997), 3:70.

51. Suzanne Pepper, *Radicalism and Education Reform in Twentieth-Century China: The Search for an Ideal Development Model* (Cambridge: Cambridge University Press, 1996), 65–73. That mission schools may fit into this pattern is suggested by Ryan Dunch in the present volume.

52. Foreign acknowledgment of Chinese support is evident in the category of "Chinese Contributions" in the statistical tables for "union educational work," in *China Mission Year Book,* issues 1915 to 1919. The information is spotty, however.

53. The small volumes, *Old Photographs,* are a series published for profit and sold at small bookstores for a popular Chinese readership. Print runs reflect the rapid growth of that readership: vol. 1 (1997), no figures; vol. 2, no figures; vol. 3, 60,000 copies; vol. 4 (1998), 240,000 copies. My friend Dr. Edward Krebs ran across *Old Photographs* while browsing subway bookstalls in Beijing and at small bookstores in Nanjing. He presented me with a set, for which I am most grateful.

54. Donald Keene, "The Sino-Japanese War of 1894–95 and Its Cultural Effects in Japan," in Donald H. Shively, ed., *Tradition and Modernization in Japanese Culture* (Princeton: Princeton University Press, 1971), 121–75, brilliantly probes this problem.

55. Marius B. Jansen, "Konoe Atsumaro," in Akira Iriye, ed., *The Chinese and the Japanese: Essays in Political and Cultural Interactions* (Princeton: Princeton University Press, 1980), 107–23, is a masterful essay on Prince Konoe.

56. Konoe Atsumaro, "Dōjinshu dōmei, tsuketari Shina mondai kenkyū no hitsuyō" (Racial alliances, with reference to the necessity for studying the China problem), *Taiyo* 4, no. 1 (1 January 1898), as translated in Jansen, "Konoe Atsumaro," 113–14.

57. Douglas R. Reynolds, "Training Young China Hands: Tō-A Dōbun Shoin and Its Precursors, 1886–1945," in Peter Duus, Ramon H. Myers, and Mark R. Peattie, eds., *The Japanese Informal Empire in China, 1895–1937* (Princeton: Princeton University Press, 1989), 224–27, offers details on the founding of Tō-A Dōbun Shoin and its parent organization, Tō-A Dōbunkai (East Asia Common Culture Association), with appropriate citations to Japanese primary and secondary source materials.

58. Quoted in *Tō-A Dōbun Shoin Daigaku shi: Sōritsu hachijū shūnen kinen shi* (A history of Tō-A Dōbun Shoin University: commemorating its eightieth anniversary), comp. Koyūkai (Tokyo: Koyūkai, 1982), 79; translated in Reynolds, "Training Young China Hands," 229.

59. Reynolds, "Chinese Area Studies," details the founding and unique curriculum of the Japan-China Trade Research Institute.

60. *Tō-A Dōbunkai shi* (A history of Tō-A Dōbunkai), comp. Tō-A Bunka Kenkyūjo (Tokyo: Kazankai, 1988), 325–27, reproduces the Chinese originals of these essays; *Tō-A Dōbun Shoin Daigaku shi,* 715–18, reprints the essays in Japanese translation.

61. Reported in *Tō-a Dōbunkai shi,* 204.

62. Quoted in ibid., 210.

63. For more detail, see Reynolds, "Training Young China Hands," 230–32.

64. Rev. A. P. Parker, "A New Japanese Invasion of China," *Chinese Recorder* 32, no. 7 (July 1901): 356.

65. Reynolds, "Training Young China Hands," 233 n. 85, provides information and citations for this Tokyo school, designed to prepare Chinese students for entrance into regular Japanese institutions of higher learning.

66. For these, see ibid.; and Reynolds, "Chinese Area Studies."

67. Takeuchi Yoshimi, "Tō-A Dōbunkai to Tō-A Dōbun Shoin" (Tō-A Dōbunkai and Tō-A Dōbun Shoin), in Takeuchi Yoshimi, *Nippon to Ajia: Takeuchi Yoshimi*

hyoronshu daisankan (Japan and Asia: vol. 3: Collected essays of Takeuchi Yoshimi) (Tokyo: Chikuma Shobō, 1966), 389.

68. Reynolds, *China, 1898–1912*, 132–33, discusses the joint memorials.

69. Report of Nezu Hajime to the fall membership meeting of Tō-A Dōbunkai, 20 December 1902, in *Tō-A Dōbunkai shi*, 354.

70. Reynolds, "Training Young China Hands," 245–46, discusses this issue, with tables and citations.

71. See ibid., 236–40, 247.

72. Abe Hiroshi, ed., *Nit-Chū kyōiku bunka kōryū to masatsu: Senzen Nihon no zai-Ka kyōiku jigyō* (Japanese-Chinese educational and cultural exchange and conflict: Japanese educational activities in prewar China) (Tokyo: Daiichi Shobō, 1983), addresses many questions related to this serious concern of Japan. See also the informed and sensitive article of Sophia Lee, "The Foreign Ministry's Cultural Agenda for China: The Boxer Indemnity," in Duus, Myers, and Peattie, *Japanese Informal Empire*, 272–306.

73. Reynolds, "Training Young China Hands," 258–61, provides details of the Chinese Student Division, with citations.

74. Ibid., 256, offers a brief discussion, with citations.

75. *Tō-A Dōbun Shoin Daigaku shi*, 122, reproduces the full inscription.

76. Ibid., 143–45, contains a photograph of this impressive shrine structure and an account of its dedication and history.

77. D. C. Holtom, *Modern Japan and Shinto Nationalism: A Study of Present-Day Trends in Japanese Religions* (Chicago: University of Chicago Press, 1943), discusses at length the fundamental differences between Japanese Shinto and universalistic religions like Buddhism and Christianity. See esp. chap. 6, "The Overseas Expansion of State Shinto."

78. Sagai Tatsuru, *Manshu no jinja koboshi* (The rise and fall of Japanese Shinto shrines in Manchuria) (Tokyo: Fuyo Shobō Shuppan, 1998), includes the expression "Nipponjin no yuku tokoro jinja ari" (Where Japanese go, there go *jinja*) as a subtitle of this book on the cover page only. See also 13, 14, 259, and 294.

79. Ibid., 13, 293. The Japanese expression is "Nipponjin ni yoru Nipponjin no tame."

80. Reynolds, "Training Young China Hands," 260–61, discusses Japanese student leftist activism and the disciplining of students by school and consular police authorities.

81. *Tō-A Dōbun Shoin Daigaku shi*, 155.

82. *Aichi Dagaku Gendai Chūgoku Gakubu* (Faculty of Modern Chinese Studies, Aichi University) (1996), is a richly illustrated, twenty-two page oversized catalog introducing the program.

83. See *Anhui shifan daxue fushu zhongxue xiaozhi, 1903–1986* (History of the attached middle school, Anhui Normal University, 1903–1986), comp. Huang Weiqing and Hu Bangnai (Wuhu: *Anshida Fuzhong xiaozhi* Weiyuanhui, 1987), 1–2, 78.

84. Cuiwen Zhongxue in 1926 responded to governmental directives by establishing a Chinese board of directors, which appointed a Chinese principal. It was they who

oversaw Cuiwen's evacuation to Chongqing after Japanese troops occupied Wuhu in 1937. Cuiwen had been founded in 1903 by a Canadian missionary and a local Chinese Christian. After 1912 it became a "union institution" supported by the Christian Church (Disciples of Christ), or Jiduhui, and the American Advent Mission Society, or Laifuhui. In 1924 it expanded from a four-year program to a six-year program of middle- and upper-middle schools, and in 1932 this boarding school for boys became coed. Ibid., 1, 4, 6, 78.

Mission Schools and Modernity: The Anglo-Chinese College, Fuzhou

Ryan Dunch

On the evening of October 31, 1993, the ground floor of the three-star Minjiang Hotel in Fuzhou was filled to overflowing with around seven hundred alumni of the Fuzhou Anglo-Chinese College (Heling yinghua shuyuan) (ACC), a Methodist mission school disbanded nearly forty years before, in 1956. These men and women, few of them younger than sixty and some in their nineties, had come from all over China and as far afield as the United States, Austria, Indonesia, and Taiwan to attend a banquet in honor of the 112th anniversary of the school's founding in 1881. The sumptuous meal was hosted and paid for by Chen Lin (1915–97), a Chinese-American businessman and 1936 graduate of the college, and it was followed by speeches from the principal and other dignitaries and the singing of the old school songs in English and Chinese.

For the participants this gathering was more than just a celebration of the past. In 1988, at the instigation and with the support of many of these same alumni, a new Anglo-Chinese College had opened as a private secondary school in Fuzhou. By the time of the banquet the new ACC had students in all six secondary grades, and that morning a brand-new building for the school, splendidly located close to the pre-1949 campus on the south bank of the Min River, had been officially opened. The new building had one wing named after Dr. Chen Zhimei, the principal of the school from 1928 to 1948, and the other named after Chen Lin, whose initial donation of U.S. $200,000 in 1988 had made the new building possible. At the end of the banquet Chen Lin announced, to sustained applause, a further gift of RMB 3,700,000 (roughly U.S. $440,000) toward a college-level program in connection with the new ACC.[1]

While Chen Lin's generosity was instrumental in the reopening of the school in 1988, his sense of loyalty toward his alma mater was widely shared among alumni of more modest means. A stone plaque on the new ACC building records gifts for construction of the building or operation of the school from twenty-four different individuals or groups, including alumni and former missionary teachers. These donations (in the United States, Hong Kong, and Taiwan currencies) ranged in magnitude from Chen Lin's $200,000 down to U.S. $1,000.[2] The importance of the ongoing financial support of ACC alumni is reflected also in the quarterly alumni newsletter, published since the spring of 1989, which lists in each issue donations received during that quarter, sometimes running to over two hundred names.[3]

Just as telling as the hundreds of alumni who gave money to reestablish and sustain their old school was the large number of alumni in their sixties, seventies, and even eighties who gave their time to serve as teachers and administrators in the new ACC. The majority of the faculty in the 1993–94 academic year, when this writer lived in Fuzhou, consisted of alumni who were devoting their retirement years to recreating and carrying forward the ACC spirit to a new generation.

What was it about this spirit that was important enough to these alumni for them to give their time, energy, and financial resources to passing it on? What did the old ACC mean to its students and alumni? These alumni had lived out very different lives since graduating from the school in the conflict-ridden years of the 1930s and 1940s. Some had become successful and wealthy as entrepreneurs and professionals in capitalist settings abroad; most, however, had remained in China, some rising to high rank within the Chinese Communist Party and government. Some of the alumni were Christian, but many others were not. Yet all of them agreed that the legacy of their schooling in the Anglo-Chinese College was worth passing on to the next generation, and they summed up that legacy in the words of the school's motto, drawn from the words of Christ to his disciples in the Sermon on the Mount: "You are the light of the world" (*er nai shi zhi guang* [Matt. 5:14]).

This succinct phrase can bear many meanings, and for most of the alumni today its significance is unrelated to its original point of reference in Christianity. As the latter part of this essay explores, for them it denotes the life of service, which they see as the basic ethos of the old ACC: each individual should seek to accomplish something for others, to bring light to the world through a life that benefits others. That is, the meaning of one's individual life must be assessed in relation to the wider human community.

As we shall see through the history of the school, this wider community meant, in the first instance, the nation, and the students and alumni of ACC came to see patriotism expressed through service as the highest embodiment of the ACC spirit. Implicit in this ideal is an organic conception of the nation, a conception of the nation in which each individual is a participant, a citizen with a responsibility toward the whole. This conception of the nation is fundamentally and radically modern, not only in relation to China but in terms of world history; it is the corollary of the new reality of mass politics that has accompanied the transformation of the world into a patchwork of sovereign nation-states over the last two centuries.[4] In China, as elsewhere, the emergence of this conception of the nation went hand in hand with the replacement of the taboos, ritual, and hierarchy of the ancien régime with a new model of politics as a domain of public discussion and mass action.

This essay argues that the modern conception of the nation and the role of the individual in it was embedded in the educational mission of the Anglo-Chinese College from its beginnings in the missionary milieu of the late nineteenth century right through to its demise as a separate institution after 1949. Throughout those seven decades the Anglo-Chinese College aimed to prepare students to play a role in the transformation of China and thus to locate the meaning of their lives in relation to the nation, and this basic orientation was absorbed by many more of its students than converted to Christianity. In other words, to understand the significance of this school in historical terms we must look beyond the specifics of curriculum and career to an underlying reconfiguration of the self in relation to the nation.

While this organic conception of the nation was quite novel in China when the Anglo-Chinese College was founded in 1881, it became widely shared by Chinese nationalists of all stripes during the Republican period, and it is shared by ACC alumni of diverse backgrounds today. As this essay shows, missionaries, Chinese Christians, liberal modernizers, and Communists could all come together around the ideal of patriotic service that the school motto signified. In China in the 1990s, however, the orientation toward public service and patriotism that was so basic to pre-1949 Chinese nationalism can no longer be taken for granted, and worry is frequently expressed about the values of youth in the increasingly fragmented, consumerist, and (arguably) postmodern world of urban China today. Against this background it becomes evident that the reestablishment of the school by its alumni represents an attempt by the older generation to pass on to today's youth the orientation of the individual toward a life of service that they imbibed from the old ACC and which they remain united in affirming.

The Place of Mission Education in Pre-1949 China

Educational change was clearly a fundamental dimension of the social and political changes in China in the first half of the twentieth century, and schools run by Christian missions, particularly Anglo-American Protestant missions, were a significant feature of the educational landscape over that period. Yet for several reasons mission-run schools tend to be neglected in scholarly treatments of the history of modern education in China. First, these works have in the main focused on government education to the neglect of private education in general, including mission schools.[5] Second, while several important books have dealt with the articulation in policy of a modern educational system in the 1900s, the actual implementation of new educational policies through the upheavals of the Republican period has received less systematic attention.[6] Third, despite the substantial literature on colleges and college students in the Republican period, elementary and secondary education have been little studied.[7]

Given these gaps in the literature, some preliminary remarks on the place of mission schools in China before 1949 are in order. I believe that it is necessary to place mission education in the context of the total educational picture over the first half of the twentieth century, concentrating less on policy and theory and more on practice. From this perspective the central question becomes, what place did mission schools have in the provision of educational opportunities in urban and rural China over this period? If we look at the actual provision of education over the long term, it is evident that the plans for a rational, standardized, nationwide system of government schools devised during key periods of innovation (the years after 1905 or the 1920s) were never fully realized, due to the political instability and fluctuating finances of all levels of government in Republican China, and that mission schools, and private schools in general, remained important educational providers, particularly at the elementary and secondary levels, throughout the Republican period.[8]

This contention can be illustrated by several examples from Fujian province. In 1923 church sources reported that one-third of all elementary education in the province was being provided in Protestant schools.[9] In 1930, according to provincial government statistics, fully 60 percent of the middle schools in the province and nearly 40 percent of the primary schools were private schools.[10] In many of the more remote counties (and some less remote) the only secondary education available was in private schools, which in many instances were mission schools.[11] As late as 1940, Protestant schools accounted for 45 of the 11 schools of lower middle school grade or higher in

Fujian province, outnumbering both government schools (41) and non-mission private schools (the remaining 24).[12]

Detailed information for Changle County, on the coast southeast of Fuzhou, helps to show the importance of mission schools in the Republican period. The American Board mission (ABCFM) began operating a girls' school there in the 1890s, adding a boys' primary school in 1911. Building on this foundation, in 1922 the mission extended each of these schools to lower middle school level. These schools, which combined into one coeducational school in 1931, continued to operate until being turned over to the revolutionary county government in 1949. There was no government-run middle school in the county until 1942, and two efforts in the 1920s and 1930s to found other private lower middle schools both failed after only a few years. Thus, for two decades, from 1922 until 1942, the mission school remained virtually the only secondary educational institution in the county.[13]

The role of the mission school system as a ladder of mobility between rural areas and Fuzhou (and from there to the world beyond) can be shown from data in a local gazetteer from Gutian, a mountainous and isolated county to the northwest of Fuzhou. Two Protestant missions, the Methodist Episcopal Board of Foreign Missions (American) and the Church Missionary Society (Church of England), worked in Gutian from the 1860s on, and by the 1890s both had formed an extensive series of elementary schools, capped by boarding schools for girls and boys in the county seat.[14] The gazetteer, published in 1942, lists all the men and women from Gutian who went on to higher education beyond the county, including graduates from high schools, postsecondary professional programs, and universities in China and abroad.[15] Overall, out of a total of 471 men who completed some level of education beyond that offered in Gutian, a minimum of 162, fully one-third of the total, went through the Protestant educational system. Of the 169 high school graduates listed, 133 (79 percent) received their diplomas from the Protestant high schools in Fuzhou.[16] The figures for women are even more striking, for they show that the Protestant schools were practically the only channel for Gutian women to acquire a higher education, right through until the early 1940s, when the gazetteer was compiled. Of the 162 women listed, at least 157 (97 percent) graduated from Protestant schools, including all 7 of those who earned university degrees abroad and all 30 of the graduates of Chinese universities.[17]

In practice, then, mission education was a significant part of the educational picture on the ground in Fujian. Who were the students of mission schools, and what impact did their schooling have on them? The stereotype of mission school students is that they were chiefly the children of Christian converts, were from the lower classes, and were cut off by their foreign education from full participation in the life of the nation.[18] During the anti-Christian and recovery of educational sovereignty movements of the 1920s, mission schools were commonly portrayed as slave factories, aimed at dulling the patriotic consciousness of students and turning Chinese youth into the obedient puppets of the imperialists.[19] If this were a full picture of mission schools and their students, then those schools and students would indeed be irrelevant to one of the most important aspects of the history of education in modern China, the role of education in the development of nationalism and political consciousness. It is far from being a full picture, however, as this essay will show for the case of the Anglo-Chinese College.

Historical Sketch of the Anglo-Chinese College

In the early period of Protestant missions in China, education was generally seen as of secondary importance to evangelism, and the teaching of English or of secular subjects in mission schools was frowned upon. The Anglo-Chinese College in Fuzhou, which not only taught English but used English as the language of instruction, was the first mission school in China to break this pattern, and one of the fascinating aspects of the story of the college is that the initiative and aspirations of Chinese Christians were instrumental in forcing this change, *against* the wishes of the Methodist Episcopal mission board in New York and the majority of the Methodist missionaries in Fuzhou. This development was made possible by the particular structure of the Methodist system of church government, in which the annual conference of ordained preachers was the governing body of the church in each area, with the power to hear and approve reports and to decide appointments, promotions, salaries, and pastoral questions.[20] In 1877 the Fuzhou Methodist Church was detached from the direct authority of the mission society and constituted as an annual conference in its own right, consisting of thirty ordained Chinese preachers and five missionaries.[21] Under this system the Chinese preachers held a substantial majority over the missionaries, and they soon began to press the mission for a greater emphasis on education, particularly education for women and girls, and a higher grade of education, including English instruction, for boys. They were supported by two of the missionaries, Nathan Sites and Franklin Ohlinger, but the other missionaries were opposed, particularly to English instruction, since they believed it imperative that education remain subordinate to evangelism. In January 1881 a wealthy merchant and recent convert, Zhang Heling (Diong Ahok, d. 1890), offered Ohlinger ten thousand dollars to purchase a site for a college on the condition that English would be taught in it. With the backing of the Chinese pastors, Ohlinger accepted the gift, bought a site, created a Board of Trustees, and that year opened an Anglo-Chinese College (named Heling yinghua shuyuan in honor of its bene-factor), with himself as its president.[22]

The Chinese preachers desired higher educational standards because they saw education and evangelism not as two distinct tasks but as comple-mentary aspects of the Christian effort to convert, reform, and regenerate China. This broad conception of the task of the church was reflected in the program of the College, which aimed to provide the youth of China with facilities for obtaining a thorough general education according to the stan-dards that prevailed in European and American colleges.[23] To critics who charged that the teaching of English would draw students away from the pastorate and toward secular employment, Ohlinger replied grandly:

> We do not propose to teach English (as some of our opponents persist in saying) but to give a thorough general education which besides many other things embraces a knowledge of the English language. We do not train men to be cooks and butlers for the foreign merchants, but men who shall be leaders of thought, who shall carry the banner of Christian-ity and western Science into every part of these Eighteen Provinces.[24]

For Ohlinger the task of mission education was not to make converts in any narrow sense: it was to nurture Chinese Christians who would be intellectu-ally equipped to take the lead in reforming and transforming China, along the lines of what Ohlinger saw as modern, Christian, scientific civilization. His models were the burgeoning denominational colleges in the United States, and he dreamed of eventually adding faculties of law, theology, and medicine to the school.[25]

For the first thirty-five years of its existence the Anglo-Chinese College offered an eight-year program, divided into four years each of preparatory and college work, arranged on the general lines of an American college course, though not as extensive, being arranged with reference to the needs of this country and time, as the 1893–94 catalog put it.[26] In addition to English, the Bible in Chinese and English, and a classical Chinese education, the course included geography and history, international law, mathematics (including algebra and trigonometry but not calculus), botany, chemistry, physics, geol-ogy, and astronomy.[27] The evidence available indicates that graduates of this eight-year course attained high levels of mastery both of English and of the Chinese classical curriculum. Following the founding of the Fukien Christian

University in 1916, the Anglo-Chinese College relinquished its claim to being a college-level institution and adopted a six-year secondary program. It did, however, retain the English name Anglo-Chinese College and in its Chinese name only substituted the term *zhongxue* (middle school) for the more imposing literary title *shuyuan* (academy) when forced to do so to register with the government in 1928.[28]

From small beginnings the Anglo-Chinese College grew into the largest mission school in China and the largest school of any sort in Fujian Province by the early 1900s. From an initial handful the student body grew to ninety by 1888 and ballooned to over three hundred in the reform climate of the later 1890s and 1900s.[29] Enrollments continued to grow during the early Republican period, peaking at over five hundred in the early 1920s, before plummeting in the political turbulence that swept Fujian and all China from 1925 to 1927. Facing political unrest and demands for registration from the new Kuomintang government, the school closed for reorganization in the fall term of 1927.[30] It reopened the following spring, under a Chinese president and a new Board of Trustees, in which Chinese members were for the first time in the majority. By 1930 it was once again one of the largest and wealthiest schools in Fujian, with a faculty of 50, a student body of 458, and a budget exceeded only by the largest government middle school.[31] Enrollment remained high during the war years, when the school was forced to move inland to the small town of Yangkou on the upper reaches of the Min River. In the fall of 1937 the school had the highest enrollment in its history, 650, and two years later the number still stood around 550.[32] After the war the enrollment, augmented by the admission of girls to the school after 1940, boomed again, reaching 1,200 in 1949 before falling after Liberation.[33]

Thus, while the Anglo-Chinese College never quite became the collegiate-level institution that Ohlinger had envisioned in 1881, it was an important and well attended school throughout the seventy-odd years of its existence. Despite the periods of political upheaval, it was also well respected within Fuzhou society for most of that time; important officials of the province attended its graduation ceremonies from 1898 on, and in the Republican period the promotional publications of the school carried endorsements and calligraphic tributes from provincial government leaders and important national figures.[34]

Although there were some scholarships available for poor students and for the sons of Protestant preachers, the tuition fees of the Anglo-Chinese College were relatively high throughout its existence.[35] In 1899 the president boasted that the college was practically unique among mission schools in China in paying for its own current expenses (barring the salaries of the missionary teachers).[36] As the high fees imply, the school attracted the sons of the commercial and political elite as well as those of Protestant families.[37] The high fees may also be one reason why the rate of graduation was quite low. In 1895 it was reported that the college had enrolled a total of 347 boys since 1881, and the student body then numbered 133.[38] Only 9, however, had graduated from the full eight-year course by that time. By 1940 the number of alumni who had studied for one year or more in the school stood at around 10,000, while graduates numbered only around 1,000.[39] An important factor in the low graduation rate was the fact that over the first few decades of its existence, a few years study in the Anglo-Chinese College sufficed to secure many young men a well-paid position in the customs service, the post office, or in foreign businesses trading at Fuzhou.[40] One such figure was Lin Sen, the head of state in China under the Kuomintang from 1931 to 1943, who was a member of the initial class in 1881 but left after a couple of years of English study to take up an appointment in the customs service.[41]

For the most part only general or anecdotal evidence on the thousands of nongraduate alumni is available, but we can be more precise about the identities and occupations of ACC graduates to 1916, since a 1917 catalog in Chinese for the college lists the names of all 157 graduates to that date and the occupations at that time of 130 of them (14 had died, and for 13 no occupation is given). Fourteen were pursuing further studies (4 in China, 10 in the United States), so their occupations are also unclear. Of the remaining 116 graduates, a total of 46, or nearly 40 percent, worked in education, a little over half of them in Protestant schools, the remainder in government or unspecified schools. Forty (34.5 percent) were in some form of government service (aside from education), 30 of whom were in the modern Sino-foreign bureaucracies, the maritime customs (11), the post office (9), and the salt administration (10).[42] Nineteen were in business or commerce, a minority as compradores in the big foreign *hongs* (Standard Oil, Jardine Matheson) or in the banking and mining sectors; most in business apparently worked for themselves. Two graduates were working as the interpreters for the U.S. consuls in Fuzhou and Xiamen. Medicine accounted for 6 of the graduates (including the 2 military physicians numbered earlier), and another 5 were in church or YMCA work.

Locations are specified for 121 of these 157 graduates. While many of them (46, or 38 percent) had remained in Fuzhou, a larger number were dispersed around China, 10 in other parts of Fujian and 41 beyond the province (including 2 in Hong Kong and 1 in Taiwan). Many of those working in other parts of China were in the customs, post, or salt services. Another 24 were further afield: 13 in Southeast Asia, mostly in Manila or the Straits Settlements, and 11 in the United States (ten of them as students).[43]

This source gives only a synchronic snapshot, not a full picture of the career trajectories of these graduates. Some of those listed as educators in the Christian schools were also ordained clergymen. From other sources it is clear that a good number of them were returnees from universities in the United States or Britain. The proportion in business is strikingly small and the proportion in government service very high. Overall, the best term to characterize this data is *professionalism;* the great majority of the graduates of the Anglo-Chinese College entered the growing professional elite, consisting of educators, Western-style medical doctors, civil servants, business managers, and church workers. This elite was also an international one. One graduate, Xue Fenshi (Alfonso Sycip, 1903), was a leading member of the Chinese community in Manila; another, Yin Xuecun (Dr. S. C. Yin, 1898), studied in the United States, Canada, and Britain and became a prominent physician and community leader in Singapore.[44] In 1920 the president of the college received a warm welcome and generous pledges for new college buildings when he visited former students in Beijing, Tianjin, Amoy (Xiamen), and the Philippines.[45]

The general conclusion that ACC graduates went mainly into white-collar professional work appears to hold true for the Republican period also, although the evidence is less full. Many of the elderly alumni active in supporting the school in the 1990s had retired from careers as school and college faculty, engineers, and administrators. Figures for 1937–39 graduates show that 79 out of the total of 136 (58 percent) went on to further study, 3 of them in military academies and the remainder in regular colleges and universities. Of the 39 who went straight to work after their graduation, only 9 went into business (all of them in the class of 1937, which graduated before the outbreak of the war). Educational work (6), government employment (21, with 10 of them in the customs, post, salt, or banking systems), or military service (3) accounted for the remainder.[46] The same publication, dated 1940, gives statistics on the fields of study selected at university by 103 recent ACC graduates: the professional majors of engineering and medicine were the most popular choices, with 14 students each, followed by the various pure sciences and social sciences with a total of 18 each. Only 10 chose humanities majors.[47]

Impact of the School on Its Students

In the remainder of this essay we will return to the question posed at the beginning: why do the present-day alumni demonstrate such an intense and costly loyalty to the school? What was the impact of the Anglo-Chinese College on its students, and why did it have such an impact? As stated earlier, I believe that the Anglo-Chinese College left a deep imprint on its students not in spite of its status as a mission school but because of it, for the whole thrust of the education offered in the college from 1881 to the 1950s was explicitly to prepare students to play a role in the transformation of China. The specifics of the transformative task were seen differently across the generations and by different individuals: participation in the Republican revolution in 1911, social service and gradual change in the 1930s, armed resistance to Japan in the 1940s, and Communist-led social revolution for some. Through all these changes, however, the college taught its students to see the meaning of their individual lives in relation to the wider communities of the nation and the world. "You are the light of the world," the school motto proclaimed, and students interpreted this to mean that their individual lives must count toward bringing light to the world, through service to others. A sense of responsibility, a realization that every man is in a very real sense his brother's keeper, is how one alumnus summed up the schools ethos in 1920.[48]

The impact of this ethos on students and alumni is evident in their political involvements through the first half of the twentieth century, which are traced in the remainder of this essay, beginning with the anti-American boycott of 1905. This boycott spread through the port cities of China in the summer of that year, in protest against the exclusion law, which prohibited Chinese coolies from entering the United States and led to long periods of detention and demeaning examinations for all Chinese, coolies or not, who sought to enter the United States. In Fuzhou, as in other cities, students were at the center of the boycott movement, and students of ACC and other mission schools took part with government school students in protest rallies and in the founding of a Fujian Public Association for the Protection of Laborers during the summer.[49]

For ACC students the issue had a personal face, for three graduates of the college sent to the United States for further study had been held in detention at their point of entry for several months, despite having valid student visas.[50] Before news of the boycott had even reached Fuzhou, the U.S. consul in the port, himself a devout Methodist and chairman of the ACC board, had given two lengthy addresses in the college chapel at the request of the faculty, teachers, monitors, and students of the Anglo-Chinese College and accepted from them a petition signed by 350 Chinese teachers and students of the college outlining their objections to the exclusion laws.[51] This document shows a clear understanding both of American history and of the policies governing the treatment of Chinese in the United States. Announcing themselves, on the one hand, grateful for the education and the Christian influence they had received from Americans, yet, on the other, duty bound as loyal Chinese subjects to protest, the petitioners juxtaposed the United States' treatment of Chinese people with its self-image as a Christian nation and its self-proclaimed values of liberty and equal rights, equal rights that Americans had shed blood to extend to blacks and Cubans yet now denied to Chinese. In considering the races of the world, no matter how ignorant and how base the Chinese may seem to be, still they are not inferior to the negroes, the petition states. "[We Chinese] do not quite understand why your people in China [i.e., the missionaries] preach the doctrine of Love, while in America you treat Chinese worse than any other nation, nay, even the negroes! If you really love God you must prove your love to Him by first loving the brethren whom you can see on this earth . . . that is, the Chinese; only thus would the missionaries' words carry weight in China."[52]

As it was in other Chinese cities, the anti-American boycott was a turning point in the development of nationalist consciousness and political activism in Fuzhou.[53] In the years after 1905 there was an extraordinary proliferation of political activity in the city, expressed in the founding of scores of voluntary associations for social reform and in the establishment of new magazines and newspapers that gave voice to the developing sense of nationalism. By the end of the decade many of these associations and publications had become nodes of revolutionary sentiment, and in 1911 some of them provided the organizational base for the revolution in Fujian.[54] The teachers, alumni, and students of the Anglo-Chinese College played important roles in the politics of these years, and several of them held prominent positions in the Republican government of the province after the revolution of 1911.

The most important of these new associations in Fuzhou was the Qiaonan gongyishe (South-of-the-Bridge Public Welfare Society, hereafter the Qiaonan Society), formed early in 1907. Appealing to all scholars and merchants of spirit (*you zhi shishang*) south of the bridge (over the Min River, i.e., in the Cangqian suburb of the city), it sponsored public lectures, reading rooms, and a branch of the Anti-Opium League, a public association formed the previous year to aid in the official opium suppression effort.[55] Later it published a newspaper and started a physical training association and a fire brigade (both of which became revolutionary militia units in 1911), and in the fall of 1911 it became the base for the revolution in Fujian.[56] When Sun Yat-sen (Sun Zhongshan) visited Fujian in 1912, he contributed the calligraphy for a plaque acknowledging the society's importance in the revolution.[57]

Extant reports of the Qiaonan Society and the related fire brigade (Minnan jiuhuo hui, or South-of-the-Min Fire Brigade) show that several alumni and students of the Anglo-Chinese College were involved in these societies.[58] Particularly prominent in them was Chen Nengguang (Bingtai), son of a Methodist preacher and an 1896 graduate of ACC.[59] After his graduation Chen Nengguang had entered the newly established postal service in Fuzhou as its first bilingual clerk.[60] He resigned from the postal service in September 1907 and took up an appointment as the interpreter for the U.S. Consulate in Fuzhou, where his political activism became something of an embarrassment for the consul.[61] At some point before 1911 Chen became a member of the Revolutionary Alliance (Tongmenghui), and after the revolution he was made head of the Foreign Affairs Department of the new provincial government, a position for which his fluency in English and his connection with the U.S. Consulate in Fuzhou must have equipped him well. In subsequent years he held high posts in the customs, the Fujian government office to suppress opium cultivation, the province's salt administration, and the post office.[62]

Another alumnus of the Anglo-Chinese College who became politically prominent in the final years of the Qing dynasty was Chen Zhilin (Zhiting, b. 1878), a vice president of the Fujian Provincial Assembly, the representative assembly created in 1909 in the course of the ill-fated Qing constitutional reforms. Chen, who at age thirty in 1909 was one of the youngest members of the assembly, was a native of south Fujian, but his family seems to have had extensive commercial interests in Fuzhou and probably resided there.[63] Chen had both classical and Western educational credentials, for in 1903 he both graduated from the Anglo-Chinese College and earned the *juren* degree in the final administration of the ancient examination in the province.[64] After graduation Chen spent some time in charge of new government schools in Fujian and also traveled through British Malaya and the Dutch East Indies in 1904 and 1905. Extant records indicate that Chen Zhilin was one of the most fiery and confrontational of the young Turks in the Fujian Provincial Assembly. He appears to have functioned as the assembly's expert on provincial finance, often questioning the governor-general's deputies on financial matters.[65] That he was seen by peers as having expertise in financial administration is confirmed by the fact that he was made head of the provincial Board of Finance directly after the 1911 revolution and retained the post for several years.

Both Chen Nengguang and Chen Zhilin were nationalists who supported political reform in China, by means of revolution if necessary. Both also, clearly, made no secret of their Christian adherence, looked back with gratitude on their education in the Anglo-Chinese College, and saw no conflict between their Christianity, their ACC education, and their nationalism. In 1906, at a banquet celebrating the twenty-fifth anniversary of the school, Chen Nengguang proposed that the alumni raise money for a clock tower to mark the occasion and himself pledged the large sum of fifty silver dollars on the spot for that purpose.[66] Chen Zhilin was forthright about the value of Christianity and schools like ACC for China. In 1909 the YMCA and the Methodist Church held a reception for the newly convened Provincial Assembly, and in his speech to the gathering Chen described the mission of the Protestant Church as reforming society, raising the morality of the people, and developing their knowledge. He attributed his election to public office to his education in the Anglo-Chinese College and stated that, "as our nation comes to recognize the value of the church schools, the day will come when you gentlemen [of the church] will also be elected," as he had been.[67]

In addition to these politically prominent alumni, the students of the Anglo-Chinese College were deeply involved in the events that led up to the overthrow of the Qing dynasty, including the revolutionary battle itself. Student radicalism was by this time an important political force all over China, fueled by the rapid growth of the student population following the educational reforms of the decade.[68] In 1910 a group of ACC students, using the college as the contact address, founded a society called Jingxing she, or Awakening Society, and began publishing a patriotic magazine, *Jingxing bao*.[69] This magazine, which carried articles on current events, foreign threats to Fujian, and patriotism and citizenship, was distributed through the Qiaonan Society, bookstores, companies, and medical establishments in Fuzhou; through various institutions (including one church) in the different counties and regions of Fujian; in Shanghai, Hankou, and Hong Kong; and in Paris and the United States, through Fuzhou men (one of them an alumnus of the Anglo-Chinese College) studying there.[70]

In the spring of 1911 these students started a new periodical, the tone of which was dramatically more anti-Qing, racialist, and pro-republican than *Jingxing bao*. This monthly periodical, *Minxin* (Hearts of the People), became so popular that the first four issues had to be reprinted within a few months of publication to meet the demand for back issues.[71] The magazine carried material on the anti-Manchu Taiping Rebellion and on the U.S. Constitution. Its May 1911 issue openly commemorated the seventy-two martyrs executed after the failed Huanghuagang uprising in Guangzhou the month before and quoted the revolutionary leader Sun Yat-sen's three principles of ethnic nationalism, sovereignty, and democracy.[72]

Radical views and Christian belief seem to have been wholly compatible for these young journalists, for one of them was, in addition to his journalism, both the president of the student YMCA and a secret member of the Tongmenghui. In March 1911 this man became the first student in the college, and reportedly in the whole city, to signal his rejection of Qing authority by cutting off his queue.[73] Other ACC students soon followed his example.[74]

By the spring of 1911 the Tongmenghui had recruited a considerable number of the students of the Anglo-Chinese College, and many ACC students were being trained for revolution under the auspices of the Physical Training Association (Tiyu hui) set up by the Qiaonan Society. This association, which met after school hours close by the ACC campus, was training its members in military drill, with real firearms under the guise of physical education.[75] During the battle for Fuzhou on November 9 and 10, 1911, members of this Physical Training Association formed the nucleus of a student militia that played an active role in the fighting, and one ACC student was killed by Manchu troops during the battle.[76] Missionary accounts of the revolution focus on the relatively minimal bloodshed and the sacrificial spirit of this young Christian student and others like him.[77] Some other foreign observers were less impressed, however, with the conduct of the revolution and the role of ACC students in it. The British consul in Fuzhou saw some Manchus being executed by a Chinese party composed almost entirely of young students belonging to the American Presbyterian [should be Methodist] Mission. "This mission," he continued, "has been training large numbers of young revolutionaries and was rumored to have been importing American rifles and bayonets surreptitiously, labeled as jam and other American groceries." "At any rate," he stated, "it was an American fluted bayonet that a Chinese youth of 20 in a new foreign uniform dug into the stomach of a captive Manchu soldier a few minutes after he had informed me, in excellent American, that he was one of Mr. Gowdy's Christians!"[78]

Were the president of the college, John Gowdy, and the other American missionary teachers as deeply implicated in the revolutionary activity of their students as the British consul supposed? Remembering that the school had a student body of over three hundred and only about a half-dozen missionary teachers, it seems most likely that they were not fully aware of that activity. In this case the inherent difficulty of keeping informed on an institution of that size was heightened by the fact that the Methodist mission had been short-staffed throughout the first decade of the century. Gowdy, the senior Methodist (male) missionary in the city, had only been in Fuzhou since 1902; the other missionary teachers had come still more recently and may not have had the language mastery or contacts to know what was beneath the surface in the college.

Nevertheless, while they may not have encouraged revolutionary involvement directly, the foreign teachers of the college certainly favored political reforms in China and were markedly supportive of the revolution when it took place, so much so that they, and the Methodist missionaries more generally, were criticized by the other missions in Fuzhou for failing to maintain neutrality where China's domestic politics was concerned.[79] Overall, it is likely that the intellectual climate in the Anglo-Chinese College predisposed students to favor political change in China and perhaps also to prefer republican political institutions on the American model to other political forms.[80]

The compatibility between Christianity and patriotism evident in 1911 continued through the first dozen years of the republic, but it changed in the 1920s as a new generation of Chinese natonalists, influenced by Soviet terminology, began to regard Christian missions as a form of cultural imperialism.[81] Beginning in 1922, an Anti-Christian Movement, which declared both that religion and science were incompatible and that Christianity was a means by which imperialists oppressed weaker nations, spread through student circles across China. This was followed in 1924–25 by the Recovery of Educational Sovereignty Movement, which advocated bringing all mission schools under government control.[82] In Fuzhou the agitation came to a head in the spring of 1927, when a coalition of radical teachers and students in the main mission schools attempted to take over their institutions and turn them over to the new Kuomintang provincial government, forcing many of the schools, including the Anglo-Chinese College, to close for a semester and some for a full year.[83]

Ultimately, however, the Kuomintang government was content to have Christian missions keep funding and operating schools in China, provided that they register with the government, that Chinese people run them, and that religious observances and instruction be made purely voluntary.[84] These changes were welcomed by some missionaries and many Chinese Christian educators, including the man who becames the first Chinese president of the Anglo-Chinese College, James L. Ding (Chen Zhimei, 1896–1972).[85] The son of a Methodist preacher from Gutian County, Chen Zhimei had graduated from the college in 1915 then gone to the United States to study at a Methodist school in Iowa, Cornell College.[86] Graduating in 1918, Chen returned to Fuzhou and worked as a YMCA secretary. In 1921 he joined the faculty of the Education Department in the newly founded Amoy (Xiamen) University, where he taught until accepting the presidency of ACC at the beginning of 1928.[87]

As noted at the start of this essay, Chen Zhimei led the school for twenty years, right through the hardships of the war against Japan, and he left a deep impression on the Anglo-Chinese College and on the lives of its students. One wing of the school building opened in 1993 is named after him, and the many published reminiscences of ACC alumni often pay homage to his memory.[88] These reminiscences highlight his role during the war, when he led the migration of the school inland to the small market town of Yangkou, three hundred kilometers from Fuzhou. This move, involving as it did over five hundred students, thirty-two teachers, staff, and their households, presented numerous logistical difficulties. More important, however, were the difficulties of morale, particularly during those periods when Fuzhou was actually under Japanese occupation, cutting many of the students off from regular contact with and financial support from their families. In these periods Chen and his staff had to work hard to keep up the morale of the students and engage in creative financial management in order to provide for the livelihood as well as the education of the students.[89]

In his writings from the war years, it is clear that Chen Zhimei saw the task of the school as building up China's capacity for reconstruction through armed resistance, as the title of one school publication of the time phrased it.[90] That is, the task of education was not just the short-term one of training students to be patriots and fighters, but neither was it to equip students merely to be part of the reconstruction effort after someone else won the war. Resistance to foreign aggression and readiness to serve society in a positive sense were seen as going hand in hand, and shaping the character of the students according to this twofold agenda was central to Chen Zhimei's vision of the role of the Anglo-Chinese College during the war years. To this end the school encouraged student involvement in extracurricular activities and social service efforts, particularly ones addressing the problems of rural China, with which the move to Yangkou brought many students into close contact for the first time. ACC students in Yangkou held discussions on international affairs and the national situation; spread patriotic propaganda through speeches and plays, cartoons and wall posters, and Fujianese opera performances; and spent months in rural settings throughout inland Fujian as part of a government-run mass education movement.[91]

Chen Zhimei's emphasis on developing student character and leadership qualities through extracurricular activities and practical social service did not originate with the war years but runs throughout his tenure as president of the school. Indeed, in its stress on the individual's place in the wider community of the nation it echoes Franklin Ohlinger's nineteenth-century vision of the school cultivating men who shall be leaders of thought, who shall carry the banner of Christianity and Western science into every part of [China], or the YMCA stress on moral education (*deyu*), which was so characteristic of the Chinese Protestant milieu of Chen Zhimei's youth.[92]

In another sense, however, the linking of patriotism with character development, and both with their concrete expression in service to society, was a deliberate response of Christian schools to the challenge to their very existence posed by Chinese nationalism and student radicalism in the 1920s. Finding themselves under attack for subverting students' patriotism, Christian schools tried to show themselves to be, on the contrary, sympathetic to that patriotism while simultaneously challenging their students to express their patriotism through constructive practical service rather than (implicitly, destructive) radicalism and protest.[93]

Thus, upon assuming the presidency of the school in the spring of 1928, after it had been forced to close for a semester by political unrest and student protests, Chen swiftly began emphasizing constructive patriotic service such as the furthering of mass education as a key element in the school's program. During his first semester as president, Chen set up some monetary prizes in recognition of such service; these had a real influence in directing the expression of student patriotism toward more constructive efforts, wrote one missionary at the end of that semester.[94] Chen Zhimei put it this way in 1928:

> The spirit of our young students is admirable. What they need is the guidance of competent leaders. The College will endeavor to keep alive this glowing patriotism and direct the enthusiasm toward proper channels.[95]

Chen Zhimei's emphasis on character was also a response to the political context of the late 1920s in another respect. The insistence of the Kuomintang government that religious observances must be made voluntary in Christian schools before they could be registered forced those schools to rethink their fundamental purpose. If students could not be required to attend chapel services and the like and if their freedom of religion had to be respected, clearly the reason for the existence of the schools could not be seen as converting every student to Christianity. In that case, however, why have Christian schools at all? What distinguished them from government schools or other private schools?[96] For Chen Zhimei, as for many others (Chinese and missionary) in the Christian education system in the late 1920s and 1930s, the answer lay in the Protestant stress on character formation and social service. In the words of a school brochure from the early 1930s, "the Anglo-Chinese College is distinctive [vis-à-vis private and government schools] in the field of moral and religious teaching, and in cultivating in every student strength of character and spirit of devotion to public service."[97]

The Anglo-Chinese College's wartime emphasis on character and service, then, had general roots in the history of mission education going back to the nineteenth century and specific ones in the attempt of the school and others like it to respond to the challenges of 1920s nationalism. How did students react to this emphasis? As already noted, the ACC motto was and is "You are the light of the world," and Chen Zhimei was given to summing up the school's charge to its students in those words. While Chen Zhimei was certainly aware of the Christian derivation of the motto, for most of the students it had no necessary relationship to Christianity, as far as can be discerned from published memoirs.[98] Christian or not, however, the students of ACC embraced its call to devote their lives to the service of society, and the alumni of the school in the 1990s still summed up the spirit of ACC in the words of the motto. Moreover, this spirit of dedication to the service of society was clearly what they were seeking to pass on to Chinese youth in the 1990s by establishing and supporting the new ACC. Significantly, the motto, in Chen Zhimei's calligraphy, is prominently displayed on the new school campus, carved in stone above the assembly ground.[99]

Emphasis on service and self-sacrifice was hardly unique to Protestant Christianity in China in the 1930s and 1940s, and students could translate the general injunction to be the light of the world into several different frameworks for action. For a significant proportion of them, involvement in the Communist Party underground seemed the most valid form of constructive patriotic service available. The Party established a cell among the students of the college in the summer of 1939, and over the next decade many ACC students were recruited into the Communist Party through it. At least twenty-four ACC alumni were executed as Communists in the 1940s, and many ACC alumni rose to high office in the Party and government after 1949.[100]

It is not clear how much Chen Zhimei and his staff knew about the Communist infiltration of the student body, but we do know that Chen remained in broad sympathy with the patriotism of his students even when it took them toward Communism. On more than one occasion he drew on ACC's prestige and its independence as a mission school to prevent the Kuomintang government from arresting or harming Left-leaning members of the faculty or the student body. During the Yangkou years the police wanted to arrest Chen Hengting, a non-Christian faculty member who included material on dialectical materialism and socialism in his courses on ethics. In the name of academic freedom and the need for education to remain nonpartisan, Chen Zhimei protested this attempted interference in the school and prevented the arrest, and Chen Hengting is cited by a number of alumni as an influence in raising their awareness of Marxism.[101] On another occasion the secret police planned to arrest two ACC students who were underground Party members, but Chen Zhimei prevented it. When one of the two was subsequently arrested and executed after organizing a protest by rickshaw pullers, Chen Zhimei took the considerable political risk of openly holding a memorial service for him at the school.[102]

At the beginning of 1947 Chen Zhimei and his wife went to the United States at the invitation of the Methodist mission board, to visit churches and raise financial support for the school. They remained in the United States until the sumer of 1948, when Chen resigned as president of ACC after twenty years in that office. By that time it was clear that the Kuomintang government would probably not be able to retain control of the country, and friends in the United States urged the couple to remain there and get their family out. The mission board offered to employ Chen if they chose to remain in the States. They insisted on returning to Fuzhou, however, so Chen could take up a new position as educational secretary for the Methodist Church in south China.

Tragically, during the Cultural Revolution Chen Zhimei's return in 1948 formed the basis for an accusation that he was an imperialist spy, in addition to being a Christian and a rightist. Chen Zhimei was the most heavily targeted of all the Protestant victims of the Cultural Revolution in Fuzhou, and his health was broken by the ordeal. He died in 1972, at the age of seventy-five, and the injustice of his treatment is certainly one reason for the extraordinary reverence for his memory expressed by ACC alumni in the 1990s. In 1979 his name was officially cleared by the provincial Party Committee, and in 1982 the ACC alumni association held a service marking the tenth anniversary of his death in the hall of the Fujian People's Political Consultative Conference.[103]

Conclusion

Three conclusions about mission schools emerge from the history of the Anglo-Chinese College recounted in this essay. Most obviously, mission schools cannot lightly be dismissed as irrelevant or marginal to the history of education in modern China. The Anglo-Chinese College was an important school, and its history relates closely to the broader picture of the relationship between education and social and political change. It was also an institution that, notwithstanding its foreign origin, curriculum, and personnel, was embedded in Chinese society and substantially shaped by Chinese people throughout its existence.

Second, mission schools were harbingers of modernity on many levels. ACC students studied modern subjects and moved primarily into modern professional careers; most important, however, they absorbed a modern concept of China as a nation made up of citizens, each of whom had a role to play in the life of the nation. This orientation of the self toward the nation was embedded in the educational mission of the Anglo-Chinese College from its beginnings in 1881, and its impact on ACC students and alumni across the generations is evidenced by their political activism over the decades covered here.

The third point brings us back to where this essay began, the reestablishment of the school by its alumni in 1988. Like other institutions, schools do not remain the property of their founders, even when they are mission boards, but are perpetuated by those who take it upon themselves to interpret and propagate the legacy or spirit of the institution, as the alumni of ACC have done since 1988. This essay began by asking what it was about the spirit of ACC that was important enough to cause these hundreds of elderly men and women to give of their time and resources in order to pass it on. As it has shown, the ideal of patriotic service, which could be embraced by people of diverse backgrounds and political persuasions, was at the heart of the ethos of ACC. In refounding the school in contemporary China, the alumni of the Anglo-Chinese College are simultaneously embodying the ideal of public service and seeking to pass it on to today's youth, through constant invocations of the old ACC: its motto, its school song, its leaders (especially Chen Zhimei), and its spirit.

The invocation of the old school in the service of the new was evident on July 13, 1996, when the third class to pass through all six years of secondary school in the new ACC graduated. At the commencement ceremony, held in the Zhimei Memorial Hall of the new building, ACC President Zheng Xian gave a speech that would have sounded very familiar to Chen Zhimei's generation. Zheng urged the graduates to remember that the molding of personality and character had been a more important part of their schooling than the acquisition of knowledge and skill, crucial though they were. While the graduates might still have some years of learning ahead of them, "eventually you will begin to give," Zheng told them, "and when you have something to give to others, when you serve others, you live up to the ACC spirit. In the future you might eventually forget what your teachers have done for you at this school," he concluded, "but I do sincerely hope that you will never forget [the] ACC motto: 'you are the light of the world.' "[104]

NOTES

1. "ACC Moves Ahead—A Sketch of the 112th Anniversary of ACC" (article in English published by ACC). I attended this banquet. For Chen Lin's biography, see *Yinghua tongxun* (ACC news) 33 (3/97).

2. Plaque on ACC building, dated October 1993.

3. See, for example, *Yinghua tongxun* 12 (December 1991): 10–11.

4. Benedict Anderson, *Imagined Communities: Reflections on the Origins and Spread of Nationalism,* rev. ed. (London: Verso, 1991); E. J. Hobsbawm, *Nations and Nationalism since 1780: Programme, Myth, Reality,* 2d ed. (Cambridge, New York, and Melbourne: Cambridge University Press, 1992); esp. chap. 3; and "Mass-Producing Traditions:

Europe, 1870–1914," in Eric Hobsbawm and Terence Ranger, eds., *The Invention of Tradition* (Cambridge: Cambridge University Press, 1983).

5. For example, Chen Qitian, *Zuijin sanshinian Zhongguo jiaoyu shi* (History of Chinese education in the last thirty years) (1930; rpt., Taipei: Wenxing shudian, 1962); David D. Buck, "Educational Modernization in Tsinan, 1899–1937," in Mark Elvin and G. William Skinner, eds., *The Chinese City between Two Worlds* (Stanford: Stanford University Press, 1974), 171–212.

6. For example, Sally Borthwick, *Education and Social Change in China: The Beginnings of the Modern Era* (Stanford: Hoover Institution Press, 1983); William Ayers, *Chang Chih-tung and Educational Reform in China* (Cambridge: Harvard University Press, 1971); Marianne Bastid, *Educational Reform in Early Twentieth-Century China*, trans. Paul Bailey (Ann Arbor: Center for Chinese Studies, University of Michigan, 1988). An important exception to the pre-1911 policy focus is Buck, "Educational Modernization."

7. For example, Wen-hsin Yeh, *The Alienated Academy: Culture and Politics in Republican China, 1919–1937* (Cambridge, Mass.: Harvard University Press, 1990); Jeffrey N. Wasserstrom, *Student Protests in Twentieth-Century China: The View from Shanghai* (Stanford: Stanford University Press, 1991). On the Christian colleges, see Jessie G. Lutz, *China and the Christian Colleges, 1850–1950* (Ithaca: Cornell University Press, 1971).

8. On the impact of this instability on government schools, see Buck, "Educational Modernization," 210–11.

9. Eddy Lucius Ford, *The History of the Educational Work of the Methodist Episcopal Church in China: A Study of Its Development and Present Trends* (Foochow: Christian Herald Mission Press, 1938), 203; cf. Milton T. Stauffer, ed., *The Christian Occupation of China* (Shanghai: China Continuation Committee, 1922), app. A, viii.

10. *Fujian sheng jiaoyu tongji* (Educational statistics for Fujian Province) (Fuzhou: preface Fujian jiaoyuting, 1931), n.p. A similar proportion of private to government secondary schools pertained in 1946; see *Fujian ziliao huibian* (Compiled Materials on Fujian) 1 (1957): 195–207.

11. See breakdown of schools by counties in *Fujian sheng jiaoyu tongji*.

12. Qiu Daogen, ed., *Kangjian zhong de Fujian sili xuexiao* (Fujian private schools during reconstruction through resistance) (Fuzhou: N.p., 1940), statistical app., p. 1. For simplicity I have tried to use the term *mission school* throughout this essay; strictly, these schools should be termed *church schools* after the late 1920s, when the KMT registration requirements forced missions to commit management of the schools to the Chinese church bodies.

13. *Changle xian jiaoyu zhi* (Gazetteer of education in Changle County), ed. Fujian sheng Changle xian jiaoyu zhi bianzuan weiyuanhui bangongshi (Office of the Editorial Committee of the Gazetteer of Education in Changle County, Fujian Province) (N.p.p., 1991), 29, 39–40; cf. *Zhonghua Jidu jiaohui Minzhong xiehui nianjian* (Yearbook of the Mid-Fukien Synod of the Church of Christ in China) (1948): 90–91.

14. *Gutian Jidujiao zhi* (Gazetteer of [Protestant] Christianity in Gutian), ed. Gutian xian Jidujiao sanzi aiguo yundong weiyuanhui (Gutian County Committee of the Protestant Three-Self Patriotic Movement) (N.p.: preface 1989), 33–36. In 1923 the

Methodists alone were operating a total of 85 schools in the county: 42 girls' schools, with 43 teachers and 574 students, and 42 boys' schools, with 53 teachers and 1,021 students. Ford, *Methodist Episcopal Education in China*, 23–24, citing a report to the Methodist China Central Conference in 1923.

15. The list occurs in the *xuanju* section, which in imperial times listed degree holders. The highest schools in Gutian were *chuzhong* (middle) schools. The list does not give dates of graduation.

16. The breakdown is: 5 of 35 who had studied overseas (only 24 of those graduates); 24 of 49 graduates of Chinese universities; none of 28 military/police graduates, 80 normal/technical graduates, 69 law and government (*fazheng*) graduates, and 41 vocational school (*shiye*) graduates; 133 of 169 high school graduates. This figure is a minimum only, since others of these men could have gone through Gutian church schools without it.

17. The remaining 125 women listed are 5 graduates of vocational or normal courses, who may or may not have had a church connection, and 120 high school graduates, all from church schools in Fuzhou. *Gutian xianzhi* (Gutian county gazetteer), comp. Huang Chengyuan et al. (N.p.p., 1942), *juan* 15: (*xuanju zhi*), 79b–96.

18. See, for example, the description by Republican educator Kuo Ping-wen, *The Chinese System of Public Education* (1915; rpt., New York: AMS Press, 1972), 64, quoted in Borthwick, *Education and Social Change*, 56.

19. For this rhetoric, see *Juejiao* (Sever relations) 1 (24 August 1925); and *Fuzhou xuesheng* (Fuzhou students) I (10 February 1928): 9. On the recovery of the rights movement, see Jessie G. Lutz, *Chinese Politics and Christian Missions: The Anti-Christian Movements of 1920–1928* (Notre Dame, Ind.: Cross-Cultural Publications, 1988).

20. The dates, place, and officers of each session of the conference are listed in *Fuzhou Meiyimei nianhui shi* (History of the Foochow Conference of the Methodist Episcopal Church), ed. Lin Xianfang et al. (Fuzhou: [Methodist Church], 1936), 227–31; and in the English minutes for each year, for example, *Minutes of the Foochow Annual Conference of the Methodist Church* (1938), 434–36.

21. Walter N. Lacy, *A Hundred Years of Chinese Methodism* (Nashville: Abingdon-Cokesbury Press, 1948), 79–81.

22. For the politics around the founding of the school, see Dana Robert, "The Methodist Struggle over Higher Education in Fuzhou, China, 1877–1883," *Methodist History* 34, no. 3 (1996): 173–89.

23. *Constitution of the Anglo-Chinese College* (Foochow: 1887), in Methodist Archives, Acc. 79-16, 1459-4-2:09.

24. Ohlinger to Fowler, 9 August 1881, quoted in Robert, "Methodist Struggle over Higher Education."

25. Ibid.

26. *Catalogue of the Anglo-Chinese College, Foochow, for the Nineteenth Year of the Emperor Kuang-hsu, 1893–1894*, 20, in Methodist Archives, Acc. 79-16, 1459-4-2:09.

27. Ibid., 22–24; cf. Ford, *Methodist Episcopal Education in China*, 149–50; *Constitution of ACC* (1887).

28. Ford, *Methodist Episcopal Education in China*, 256–58; *Minutes of the Foochow Conference* (1928), 63.

29. Ford, *Methodist Episcopal Education in China,* 151–52; C. M. Lacey Sites, ed., *Educational Institutions of the Methodist Episcopal Church in China* (Shanghai: Methodist Publishing House, 1907), 4, in Methodist Archives, Acc. 79-16 1459-3-3:01; Julean H. Arnold, "Educational Activity in Foochow, China," 205, in *Report of the [U.S.] Commissioner of Education for the Year Ended June 30, 1907,* 1: 191–220.

30. For enrollment statistics for the 1920s, when mission recordkeeping was particularly full, see the Educational Statistics sections of each year's *Annual Report of the Missionary Society of the Methodist Episcopal Church.*

31. On the reorganization of the school, see *New A.C.C. Spirit* (May 1928): 1–3, in Ohlinger Papers, YDS RG 23-11-209. The 1930 statistics are from *Fujian sheng jiaoyu tongji.* According to this source, the only larger middle schools in 1930 were two government schools with 633 and 532 students, 60 and 62 staff, respectively. Only the larger of these exceeded ACC in expenditure, and in per capita terms ACC's expenditure was higher.

32. *Anglo-Chinese College after Twenty-two Months of War: China's Reconstruction through Armed Resistance* (Foochow: Christian Herald Industrial Mission Press, 1939), 6, pamphlet in Ohlinger Papers, YDS RG 23-11-209.

33. David Lin to Constance Ohlinger, 31 May 1950, in Ohlinger Papers, YDS RG 23-9-179. On the admission of girls, see *Yinghua zai Yangkou, 1938–1945* (ACC at Yangkou, 1938–1945), special issue of *Shunchang wenshi ziliao* (Materials on Shunchang history) 11 (1993): 213–15.

34. George B. Smyth to Rev. A. J. Palmer, 28 February 1898, in Methodist Archives, Miss. 1/1 1259-6-2: 43; *Forty Years After: The Anglo-Chinese College, Foochow, China, 1881–1921,* 7; *New ACC Spirit* (May 1928: 1, both in the Ohlinger Papers, YDS RG 23-11-209; *Sili Fuzhou Heling yinghua zhongxue liushi zhou xiaoqing jinian kan* (Commemorative volume for the sixtieth anniversary of the Anglo-Chinese College, Fuzhou) (N.p.p., 1940), 3–12.

35. Fees for 1906 are given in Lacey Sites, *Educational Institutions of the Methodist Episcopal Church,* 4–5. During the war ACC remained one of the most costly of private middle schools in Fujian although much cheaper than comparable schools in neighboring Guangdong; see Qiu, *Kangjian zhong de xuexiao,* statistical app., p. 9–10.

36. George B. Smyth to Rev. A. J. Palmer, D. D., 27 March 1899, in Methodist Archives, Miss. 1/1, 1259-6-2: 43. Space forbids a detailed exploration of the financing of the school here; information for the late 1920s and early 1930s can be found in Fuzhou Municipal Archives 19-10-178, *Yinghua zhongxue sili xuexiao xiaodonghui sheli chengbao shixiangbiao* (Report of establishment of board of trustees of private school for ACC itemized chart), 018, 033. For finances during the war years, see Qiu, *Kangjian zhong de xuexiao,* statistical app., p. 2–4, 9–10.

37. Sites, *Educational Institutions of the Methodist Church,* 4; *Yinghua liushi zhou xiaoqing jinian kan,* 34.

38. John D. Fryer, ed., *Educational Directory for China* 1 (1895): 40.

39. Qiu, *Kangjian zhong de xuexiao,* statistical app., 3.

40. Fryer, *Educational Directory for China* 1 (1895): 40.

41. On Lin, see Howard L. Boorman and Richard C. Howard, eds., *Biographical Dictionary of Republican China* (New York: Columbia University Press, 1971), 379–82.

42. On these three services, see Albert Feuerwerker, *The Foreign Establishment in China in the Early Twentieth Century* (Ann Arbor: Center for Chinese Studies, University of Michigan, 1976), chap. 4. The remaining ten government employees were road and rail administrators (3), diplomats (1), legislators (2), provincial government bureaucrats (1, in the Finance Department), and military men (3, 2 of them physicians with the army/navy).

43. *Heling Yinghua shuyuan zhangcheng* (Catalog of the Foochow Anglo-Chinese College) (N.p.p., 1917), 16–19.

44. On Xue/Sycip, see the biography of his brother Xue Minlao (Hsueh Min-lao or Albino Sycip, another nongraduate alumnus of ACC), in Boorman, *Biographical Dictionary of Republican China;* I am indebted to Edgar Wickberg for alerting me to the ties of the Sycip brothers to ACC. On Yin, see Song Ong Siang, *One Hundred Years History of the Chinese in Singapore* (Singapore: Oxford University Press, 1984), 422–23.

45. *Minutes of the Foochow Conference* (1920), 103–4.

46. Occupations for the remaining eighteen graduates are unspecified.

47. Remaining categories were agricultural science (4), military affairs (3), tax management (1), and unknown (21); *Yinghua zhongxue liushi zhou xiaoqing jinian kan*, 38–39.

48. Rev. Uong Gang Huo (Wang Ganhe), in *Forty Years After*, 12, Ohlinger Papers, YDS RG 23-11-209.

49. *Xinwen bao* (News) Guangxu 32/5/15 [July 6, 1906], reprinted in *Meiguo huagong jinyue jishi erbian* (Continued record of the American treaty excluding Chinese laborers) (N.p.p.: Pingdeng she [Equality society], 1905), p. 2, 15b, in Fujian Provincial Archives, *ziliao* collection, 2-8-18. Cf. *Minbao* (Fujian daily), Guangxu 32/5/15 [July 6, 1906], enclosed in USDS, *Despatches from U.S. Consuls in Foochow*, 6/21/05, Gracey to Department, no. 167.

50. USDS, *Despatches from U.S. Consuls in Foochow*, 6/7/05 [June 21, 1905], Gracey to Department, no. 164, 2.

51. Ibid.

52. The text of the petition, dated 2 June 1905, is enclosed in USDS, *Despatches from United States Ministers in China, 1843–1906*, 7/26/05 [July 26, 1905], Rockhill to Department, no. 38.

53. Mary Clabaugh Wright, "Introduction: The Rising Tide of Change," 10, in Mary Clabaugh Wright, ed., *China in Revolution: The First Phase, 1900–1913* (New Haven and London: Yale University Press, 1968), 1–63.

54. For more on this period, see chaps. 2 and 3 of my Ph.D. dissertation, "Piety, Patriotism, Progress: Chinese Protestants in Fuzhou Society and the Making of a Modern China, 1857–1927," Yale University, 1996.

55. Zheng Lansun [Zuyin] et al., ed., *Fujian xinhai guangfu shiliao* (Historical materials on the Xinhai Revolution in Fujian) (Liancheng, Fujian: Jianguo chubanshe, 1940), 5. On the Anti-Opium League (*Qudu she*), see Joyce Ann Madancy, "Ambitious Interlude: The Anti-Opium Campaign in China's Fujian Province, 1906–1917" (Ph.D. diss., University of Michigan, 1996).

56. Zheng, *Fujian xinhai guangfu shiliao*, 5; *Zhonghua minguo kaiguo wushi nian wenxian* (Collected documents on the fiftieth anniversary of the founding of the

Republic of China) (Taipei: Editorial Commission of the Collected Documents on the Fiftieth Anniversary of the Founding of the Republic of China, 1964), 1, 12, 85.

57. *Zhonghua minguo kaiguo wushi nian wenxian,* part 1: vol. 12, 70, 85.

58. For more on Protestant involvement in these societies, see Dunch, "Piety, Patriotism, Progress," 115–29.

59. Zheng, *Fujian xinhai guangfu shiliao,* 3; *Yinghua shuyuan zhangcheng,* 16; *Fuzhou Meiyimei nianhui shi,* 90–91.

60. Fukien Post Office, Native Staff Record: Clerks and Inland Agents from 1897 to 1908, first entry; in Fujian Provincial Archives, 56-1-1. Bilingual clerk was the highest grade of appointment open to Chinese.

61. *Fuzhou Meiyimei nianhui shi,* 90. On Chen's political activities while in the employ of the consulate, see U.S. National Archives, USDS 3823/109, Gracey to Department no. 318, 14 August 1909, and encl.; USDS 3823/114, Gracey to Department no. 321, 27 August 1909, and encl. I thank Joyce Madancy for showing me these documents.

62. Zheng, *Fujian xinhai guangfu shiliao,* 116–20, 143; *Fuzhou Meiyimei nianhui shi,* 90.

63. Tahara Teijiro, comp., *Shinmatsu minsho Chugoku kanshin jimmeiroku* (Biographies of Chinese officials and gentry of the late Qing and early Republic) (Dalian: Chugoku kenkyukai, 1918), 383; Xu Youchun et al., eds., *Minguo renwu da cidian* (Dictionary of Republican biography) (Shijiazhuang: Hebei renmin chubanshe, 1991), 1009; Gaimusho johobu (Information Division, Ministry of Foreign Affairs, Japan), *Kaitei gendai Shina jimmeikan* (Revised biographical dictionary of contemporary China) (Tokyo: N.p., 1928), 199.

64. *Yinghua shuyuan zhangcheng,* 16b; Chen Yan, comp., *Fujian tongzhi* (Fujian gazetteer) (Fuzhou: N.p., 1938), *xuanju zhi, juan* 14, 33b.

65. *Dierci Fujian ziyiju yishi suji lu* (Minutes of the second session of the Fujian Provincial Assembly), 4 (Xuantong 2/9/8–10 October 1910), 4ff.; *Dierci Fujian ziyiju yishi suji lu* 8 (Xuantong 2/9/17–19 October 1910), 4–5; *Dierci Fujian ziyiju yishi suji lu* 12 (Xuantong 2/9/29–31 October 1910), 9.

66. *Qingnian* 9, no. 4 (May 1906): 4–5. A total of $1,050 was pledged that night.

67. *Fuzhou Meiyimei nianhui lu* (Minutes of the Foochow Annual Conference of the Methodist Episcopal Church) 33 (1909): *juan shang,* 7.

68. See, for example, Joseph W. Esherick, *Reform and Revolution in China: The 1911 Revolution in Hunan and Hubei* (Berkeley and Los Angeles: University of California Press, 1976), 40–58; Sally Borthwick, "Students and Revolutionary Culture in Late Qing Schools," *Papers on Far Eastern History* 19 (March 1979: 91–109).

69. On the society and its aims, see Zheng, *Fujian xinhai guangfu shiliao,* 29.

70. Based on an examination of issues no. 4 and 5 in the Fujian Provincial Library. Distribution points are listed on the back cover of *Jingxing bao* 5 (Xuantong 2/9/15–17 October 1910).

71. For a lengthy discussion of this publication, see Ding Shouhe, ed., *Xinhai geming shiqi qikan jieshao* (Introduction to 1911 Revolution era periodicals) (Beijing: Renmin chubanshe, 1983), 3: 667–81.

72. Based on an examination of the first three issues, dated Xinhai 2, 3, and 4 months, in Fujian Provincial Library.

73. Qi Xuan; see Pan Zuchang, "Xinhai geming Tengshan renwu yiwen" (Anecdotes on Tengshan personalities in the 1911 Revolution), *Cangshan wenshi* 6 (October 1991): 46.

74. Ding Xiancheng, "Xinhai geming qianhou Fuzhou jiaohui xuexiao de aiguo yundong yu geming zhanzheng de huiyi" (Reminiscences of the patriotic movement and revolutionary war in Fuzhou mission schools before and after the 1911 Revolution), *Fuzhou wenshi ziliao xuanji* 1 (1981): 66; cf. photograph in *Fujian wenshi ziliao* 27 (1991): front plates.

75. Zheng, *Fujian xinhai guangfu shiliao*, 27–28.

76. Wang Tiefan, "Fujian Tongmenghui zai Cangshan mimi zhizao zhadan" (The secret manufacture of bombs in Cangshan by the Fujian Revolutionary Alliance), *Cangshan wenshi* 6 (1991): 17–18; Zheng, *Fujian xinhai guangfu shiliao*, 48, 53; Huang Naishang, *Fucheng qishi zixu* (Autobiography at age seventy) (1919), in Liu Zizheng, *Huang Naishang yu Xin Fuzhou* (Huang Naishang and the New Fuzhou), (Singapore: Nanyang xuehui, 1979), 200.

77. S. Moore Sites, *Nathan Sites: An Epic of the East* (New York: Fleming H. Revell and Co., 1912), 205–6; YMCA Archives, box 23/52, Brockman to Lyon, 4 December 1911.

78. Great Britain, Public Records Office, Foreign Office Archives, FO 228/1800/35, 20 November 1911.

79. Thomas E. Korson, "Congregational Missionaries in Foochow during the 1911 Revolution," *Chinese Culture* 8, no. 2 (1967): 86–87; YMCA Archives, box 2, A. Q. Adamson Quarterly Report, July–September 1911; CMS Archives G1 CH4/o 1911/253, Dr. B. van Someren Taylor to Dr. Baring-Gould, 17 November 1911; USDS, *Records . . . Internal Affairs of China*, 893.00/1005, Thompson to secretary of state, 20 December 1911.

80. On the United States as a model for Chinese Protestant revolutionaries, see Dunch, "Piety, Patriotism, Progress," 213–31.

81. See Chow Tse-tsung, *The May Fourth Movement: Intellectual Revolution in Modern China*, (1960; rpt., Stanford: Stanford University Press, 1967), 354–55 n. g.

82. Kenneth Scott Latourette, *A History of Christian Missions in China* (1929; rpt., Taipei: Cheng-wen, 1973), 694–99, 812–15. The fullest treatment of the anti-Christian movements of the 1920s is Lutz, *Chinese Politics and Christian Missions*.

83. On the movement in general in Fuzhou, see *Fujian wenshi ziliao* 13 (1986): 154–85; for ACC in particular, see *Annual Report of the Board of Foreign Missions of the Methodist Episcopal Church* 109 (1927): 101–2; *Minutes of the Foochow Conference* (1927): 71–74.

84. *Zhonghua minguo fagui huibian* (Shanghai: Zhonghua shuju, 1933), bian 9, 175–78; Fujian jiaoyuting, ed., *Sili xuexiao lian xuzhi* (Guide to the registration of public schools) (N.p.p., 1927).

85. For Chen's views, see *New A.C.C. Spirit* (May 1928): 2–3, Ohlinger Papers, YDS RG 23-11-209.

86. Graduating along with Chen in 1915 was William Hung (Hong Ye), later a noted historian and dean of Yenching University. Susan Chan Egan's biography of Hung gives an evocative account of both the Anglo-Chinese College in the early Republic

and the life of ACC graduates studying in the United States in the 1910s; Egan, *A Latterday Confucian: Reminiscences of William Hung (1893–1980)* (Cambridge: Council on East Asian Studies, Harvard University, 1987), chaps. 5–8. Chen Zhimei is mentioned on 45, 62.

87. *Chen Zhimei xiaozhang jinan ji* (Memorial album of President James Chen) ([Fuzhou]: Yinghua zhongxue xiaoyouhui, 1990), 6.

88. *Chen Zhimei xiaozhang jinian ji*; and *Wo yu Yinghua* (ACC; and I) ([Fuzhou]: Yinghua zhongxue xiaoyouhui, 1992); *Yinghua zai Yangkou.*

89. Chen Yunji and Zheng Xian, "Yinghua zhongxue neiqian Yangkou de jingguo" (Experiences of the Anglo-Chinese College while inland at Yangkou), 161–65, in *Yinghua zai Yangkou*; Edith Simester letter to Dear Friends, 8 September 1939, in Ohlinger Papers, YDS RG 23-9-178.

90. *Anglo-Chinese College after Twenty-two Months of War: China's Reconstruction through Armed Resistance.*

91. Chen Zhimei, "Qianyi shang Yang hou de Yinghua," in Qiu, *Kangjian zhong de Fujian sili xuexiao*, 33–34; *Anglo-Chinese College after Twenty-two Months of War*, 3–7; *Yinghua zai Yangkou*, 141–60.

92. On the YMCA in Fuzhou, see Dunch, *Piety, Patriotism, Progress*, 133–44, and chap. 5.

93. For the responses of Christian schools to 1920s nationalism, see Chester S. Maio and Frank W. Price, *Religion and Character in Christian Middle Schools: A Study of Religious Education in Christian Private Middle Schools of China* (Shanghai: China Christian Educational Association, 1929).

94. *New A.C.C. Spirit* (May 1928): 3; F. C. Havighurst letter to Gustavus Ohlinger, 8 June 1928, in Ohlinger Papers, YDS RG 23-9-178.

95. *New A.C.C. Spirit* (May 1928): 3.

96. See Miao and Price, *Religion and Character in Christian Middle Schools*, esp. chap. 2.

97. *A Bulwark of Christian Influence: Facts about Anglo-Chinese College*, in Ohlinger Papers, YDS RG 23-11-209.

98. See Yang Weiping, "Yinghua jingshen—*er nai shi zhi guang*" (The ACC spirit—"You are the light of the world"), in *Wo yu Yinghua*, 106–7; writing of five alumni who became distinguished scientists, Yang glosses the meaning of the motto as "the determination to spend one's every effort on behalf of the nation and of humanity."

99. Cf. a photograph of the motto in Chen's hand in *Chen Zhimei xiaozhang jinianji*, front section.

100. *Yinghua zai Yangkou*, 230–67; *Jingtao* (Tide: Commemorative Publication of Fiftieth Anniversary of Graduation of Tide Class, 7 July 1993, 24.

101. See "*Yinghua zai Yangkou*," 62–80.

102. *Chen Zhimei xiaozhang jinianji*, 4–5.

103. *Chen Zhimei xiaozhang jinianji*, 6; author interview with Mrs. Katharine Pih and Mrs. Emily Lau (daughters of Chen Zhimei), Queens, N.Y., 17 February 1995.

104. *Yinghua tongxun* 31 (September 1996): 2; cf. Zheng's 1997 commencement speech in ibid., 36 (September 1997): p. 4.

British Protestant Educational Activities and the Nationalization of Chinese Education in the 1920s

Dan Cui

This essay examines the British Protestant educational activities in China during the 1920s.[1] The 1920s was an important period in the history of British mission education in China. On the one hand, the decade witnessed the fruition of the missionary commitment to education, born of social gospel theology. During the nineteenth century British Protestant missionaries in China had confined their efforts mainly to evangelical activities and met with comparatively little success. By the turn of the century, however, British missions were becoming increasingly imbued with a social gospel spirit. This branch of theology originated in eighteenth-century Britain as a Protestant response to social problems engendered by the Industrial Revolution. The social gospel stressed the idea of Jesus as a social reformer and the Christian responsibility to confront social ills.[2] In its missionary context it led to growing involvement in a range of social welfare activities, including education. In 1910 the Edinburgh World Missionary Conference enshrined commitment to social responsibility as the basis of Protestant mission work, and by the following decade the social gospel had entered its golden age both at home and abroad.

The pioneer of the social gospel in China was Timothy Richard.[3] Richard, a British missionary who spent forty-five years in China, recognized a potential to convert millions of Chinese to Christianity through education, medicine, and literature. By the 1920s his strategic vision had taken firm hold. British missionaries increasingly appeared in China not as evangelists but as mediators of Western civilization. Christianity was to be presented as "the central ingredient of an integrated package of westernization."[4]

On the other hand, the 1920s also witnessed the rise of mass nationalism in China, which often was strongly opposed to missionary activity. In the realm of education, in particular, the 1920s was the decade of the nationalization of foreign educational institutions. By nationalization I mean both the legal obligation, imposed by China's national governments beginning in 1925, of foreign educational institutions to register with government and meet official regulations as well as a broader movement for the devolution of administrative control over educational institutions to local Chinese (for other perspectives on the movement for recovery of educational sovereignty, see the essays by Gang Ding and Ryan Dunch in this volume). This essay examines both the achievements and the challenges facing British mission education during the 1920s. Based on British mission archives, it first describes the structure and character of mission school education, including medical education. It then examines how British mission educational institutions responded to the demands for nationalization. Finally, the essay ends with a brief examination of one area of British mission educational activity that was highly influential but largely untouched by nationalization, the realm of popular education.

School Education

In 1921 the Conference of Representatives of Missionary Societies of Great Britain and Ireland decided that their educational role in China should lay mainly in transplanting the British model of primary and secondary education into China while strengthening their involvement in higher education through intermissionary cooperation.[5] As a result, by the late 1920s British educational institutions had become an integral part of the Chinese education system. This section looks first at the emphasis British missions placed on elementary education. It is followed by an examination of British mission-sponsored secondary schooling and higher education.

Elementary Education

Throughout the 1920s elementary schools constituted the largest number of British mission schools in China. Compared to earlier periods, British missionaries in the 1920s devoted increased attention to rural primary education, expanding many four-year schools into full six-year ones and developing the schools located in mission residential stations into educational models for the surrounding countryside. School management was also revised during the 1920s, and the number of trained Chinese teachers greatly increased.

British missions sponsored two types of elementary schools. Four-year schools were dotted throughout the countryside. Most of them were located beyond the mission residential stations and were run either by missionaries or local Chinese churches. Some missions established rural educational funds to help develop these schools, and some village schools also became centers of mission-sponsored agricultural experimentation or demonstration, providing specific forms of vocational training. Many of the schools, however, remained weak and poorly developed.[6]

Greater progress was made in developing full six-year elementary schools.[7] These schools, many of which were established during the 1920s, were usually located in mission residential stations, normally in a city or town, and provided student boarding. Regarded by the missionary societies as models of British mission-sponsored elementary education, they enjoyed superior funding and facilities compared to the four-year schools in the countryside. Kindergartens were sometimes attached to these schools, which usually also served as feeders to the local mission secondary school. Most children, however, never advanced beyond the junior primary level. And, although the six-year schools were generally of higher quality, they were fewer in number and constituted only a small proportion of the total mission school enrollment. In 1920 there were a total of 57,259 pupils enrolled in primary schools established by the major British missions, more than 85 percent of whom were attending four-year village schools.

Most British missions regarded primary education as an integral part of mission education. (Only one, however, the China Inland Mission (CIM), concentrated its efforts almost entirely on primary education.)[8] The schools emphasized basic knowledge and artistic and physical training courses such as music, drawing, dancing, games, drill, and gymnastics. A mandatory public health course was added to all schools in the 1920s. In addition, the schools also included courses from the public school curricula. And, since the majority of pupils did not advance to middle school but entered life directly from elementary education, many British missions also began to offer vocational and handicraft training courses.

One of the major achievements of British mission primary education during this period lay in training Chinese teachers. In the senior classes teachers specifically attempted to direct students' interest toward the study of teaching methods and class management. Additionally, graduates of junior primary school were often recruited as teachers in the schools' kindergartens and junior classes. In 1920 there were already 2,930 Chinese teachers, two-thirds of whom were men. By 1930 mission-trained Chinese teachers constituted 94.7 percent of the total.[9]

In 1920 there were a total of 6,391 mission primary schools. By 1936 the number had fallen to around 3,000. The number of schools expanded until the mid-1920s, when the anti-Christian movements and the campaign for restoring educational sovereignty led to a decline. The number of mission elementary schools declined steadily from the late 1920s as the Nationalist government took over the major responsibility for elementary education.[10] Still, there were 99 million children in China old enough to go to school, yet less than 4 percent of them were able to do so. Thus, British missions, which tended to devote more attention to elementary education than did many other missions, performed a valuable role in shouldering part of the responsibility for elementary education that an insufficient government school system was unable to provide.

Secondary Education

Before 1920 secondary schooling constituted the weak point in British mission education. But in the 1920s middle schools run by British missions became the backbone of Christian education and even of the Christian community in China. Investment in secondary education became the main focus of British mission educational work, with the Church Missionary Society (CMS), English Presbyterian Mission (EPM), and London Missionary Society (LMS) leading the way. In 1920 there were eighty British mission middle schools, equal to 28 percent of all Christian secondary schools in China. Like their primary school counterparts, they were spread across roughly two-thirds of Chinese territory.

British mission secondary education can be divided into four main types: large city, small city, town-village, and union schools. Generally speaking, the large city–based schools included both junior and senior levels and provided full six-year courses. Some even had precollege departments or departments with a college standard. English was the teaching medium in these schools, which invariably retained a larger number of foreign staff than other types of secondary schools. Their teachers were usually better qualified and their equipment and facilities superior to that of other secondary schools. Almost all were boarding schools. Not only did they serve as the main feeders of Christian universities, but they also prepared candidates for official departments and commercial circles. Their graduates were invariably city oriented, and, because the teaching language was English, they were assured of plentiful enrollments. High tuition fees ensured that the majority of students came from wealthy merchant and official families.

Middle schools in the smaller cities were always located in the mission residential stations. Like the big city schools, most were boarding schools. Unlike the former, however, the majority possessed only junior departments, and English was a subject of study but not the medium of instruction. Chinese teachers accounted for the majority of the staff, who worked under the supervision of foreign missionaries. The widespread use of vernacular-trained, non-collegiate teachers was a major feature of these schools, which, unlike the big city schools, oriented their efforts toward meeting the skilled labor requirements of smaller towns and rural districts. During the latter half of the 1920s these schools increasingly specialized in rural subjects.

The third category, town-village schools, were a special type of rural secondary boarding school whose main purpose was to train teachers for village primary schools. Some of them provided only two-year middle school courses, while others functioned as middle school departments within existing higher primary schools. Finally, union middle schools jointly founded by British and American missions were another means whereby the missions attempted to enlarge their sphere of secondary education. In some regions cooperation with American missions became the major means for British missions to participate in secondary education.

In the early 1920s only a minority of British middle schools, mostly those located in large cities, were able to offer the full six-year secondary course. In fact, the majority of secondary schools contained both elementary and secondary departments, with far fewer students in the latter. Generally speaking, however, standards were maintained and progress was conspicuous throughout the 1920s. Teaching quality in particular improved greatly over the decade. The majority of principals had high academic backgrounds, and the schools also managed to secure a significant number of British and Chinese university graduates as science teachers. These highly qualified British and Chinese staff were not only efficient teachers but helped to raise the schools' scholastic standards.

Beginning in 1922 British mission secondary schools introduced a triple-track curriculum. On completing the second year, students were allowed to choose one of three courses: general, vocational, or university. The general course followed that of British state-run schools and emphasized humanities and sciences. The vocational option included business, engineering, teacher training, pre-medicine, agriculture, and industrial training, while the university option prepared senior secondary graduates for entrance to Christian colleges and universities. A number of the most outstanding schools even provided their own first- and second-year university-level courses.[11]

The influence of British mission-run secondary education cannot be underestimated. Only around 5 percent of children who graduated from government schools went on to middle school. Secondary education remained a weak link in the state-run system throughout the Republican period. This effectively left secondary education as the special preserve of missions. British mission schools universally reported increasing enrollments during the 1920s. British mission secondary schools were particularly strong in the treaty ports, where they were respected and admired among China's westernizing middle classes. Through Anglo-Chinese secondary schools, British educators brought their own ideals of British culture and methods of education; in the words of one observer, the syllabus they offered was "completely based on British norms."[12] The schools were conducted strictly along the lines of British state-run middle schools. The staff character, class arrangements, the tutorial system, and the encouragement given to athletics all reflected this influence.

Not surprisingly, these institutions became one of the most productive fields for creating a body of anglicized Chinese professionals and business people.[13] British mission-run secondary schools embodied the prestige and influence of the British educational model in China. Their high quality was respected by government and well-known locally. Moreover, many British secondary schools affiliated themselves with specific mission colleges and universities and became their important feeders. By supplying an increasing number of graduates for postsecondary education, the schools also stimulated the development of mission colleges and universities.

Higher Education

Conventional wisdom is that British missions in China paid relatively little attention to higher education. This statement, while it is generally true, requires some modification. While American missions assumed a dominant role, British missions were the second largest participant in higher education among the Protestant community. The LMS, Baptist Missionary Society (BMS), CMS, Wesleyan Methodist Missionary Society (WMMS), Friends Foreign Mission Association (FFMA), and Society for the Propagation of the Gospel (SPG) showed the greatest interest in higher education. Yet British missions rarely operated higher educational enterprises by themselves. Instead, they contributed personnel, materials, and, occasionally, funding to seven cooperatively run institutions. The following brief overview illustrates some of the precise forms of British mission involvement in Chinese higher education.

Several British missions were involved in higher educational work since the early part of the twentieth century. The British FFMA and CMS had only a very small financial share in the West China Union University (WCUU), which was established in 1910. Yet British missionary educators shouldered important teaching and administrative responsibilities in the university, and in the early 1920s 21 percent of its freshmen were graduates of British mission-run secondary schools in Sichuan. In addition, the FFMA built a permanent university middle school, and both missions had their own colleges.[14]

The University of Hong Kong, established in 1912, is a second example of British mission involvement in higher education. Although not a mission institution, the LMS and CMS shared in its work from the beginning, and many missionary educators remained there for their entire careers. The Church of Christ in China also assisted in running the university for a period during the late 1920s. It was the only higher educational institution run on a purely British university model in all of China.[15]

A third example of British mission involvement in Chinese higher education was the Guangzhou Christian College (CCC, or Lingnan). Established in 1915, it was maintained by an interdenominational board of trustees to serve all the churches of South China. One of its most distinctive features was that it was strongly rooted in Chinese society, drawing a larger measure of support from Chinese sources than any other Christian college. By 1931 Lingnan had 284 undergraduates and 38 graduate students as well as more than 1,200 summer school students and was the leading higher educational model in South China.[16] Also in South China, the Fujian Christian University (FCU) was established in 1916, supported by four church bodies, including the British CMS. While most of its funding came from American sources, British mission middle schools across South China became its most important feeders. The university had 109 students in 1924 and 74 undergraduates and 20 graduates in 1929.[17]

The Central China University (Huazhong) was founded in Wuchang in 1929 by four Christian institutions based in Central China. The British LMS and WMMS contributed most of the university's land. As the youngest mission university, its establishment did much to promote higher education in Central China. Even in 1933 it was still one of only three university-level institutions in Hubei.[18] The Beijing Christian University (Yanjing) was founded in 1909. Although the majority of its trustees were American citizens, five British missionaries of the LMS and SPG were also represented. J. B. Tayler exercised a wide influence through his studies and lectures in social science, and the university's research achievements, especially in the humanities, were known nationwide.

Yanjing exemplified the notion of universities as both training centers and academic bases.

Shandong Christian University (SCU, or Qilu), the first union higher educational institution, was established in 1904 by the BMS and the Board of Foreign Missions of the Presbyterian Church in the United States. A British missionary educator served as president for six years from 1921 to 1927, and a total of seven British missions participated in running it. The BMS, in particular, played a critical role in initiating, building, and developing the university. Until 1935 half the cost of the College of Arts and Sciences was borne by the BMS. Qilu was unique in several respects. It was the only union university granted a charter by act of the Parliament of Canada. It also set an example by using the Chinese national language (*guoyu*) to teach Western subjects and was the only union university that provided specialized training for rural areas. In 1931 there were 235 undergraduate and 35 postgraduates.[19]

Medical Education

In addition to their efforts in developing school education, British missionaries, along with other Western missionaries, were pioneers of modern medical training. In 1913 the CMMA resolved that foreign physicians had no permanent place in China and, if the church was to have lasting influence, provision of medical education for the Chinese themselves had to be emphasized.[20] A systematic education and training strategy was put in place, and by the 1920s the training of Chinese successors was regarded as the principal project of mission medical work.

The majority of regular mission-sponsored medical colleges were established around 1910. In order to promote efficiency and economy, the larger missions of Great Britain, United States, and Canada, along with those of some other countries, merged their resources to create five medical colleges with attached hospitals. These were located in Beijing (two colleges), Jinan, Fuzhou, and Chengdu. In addition, British missions ran their own colleges in Mukden and Hangzhou and were also involved in the work of the Medical College at Hong Kong University.

Several institutions are particularly worthy of mention. The Medical School at Qilu University in Jinan, Shandong, established in 1914, constituted the second most important medical school in China after the Beijing Union Medical College (PUMC). Between 1915 and 1929 the school produced 220 graduates; in 1928, 105 graduates were employed in fifty-seven hospitals scattered over fifteen provinces.[21] The Medical School at Qilu emerged as a national model for the teaching of Western medicine in Chinese (Mandarin).

It founded the Qilu Translation Bureau for the purpose of translating standard Western medical works into Chinese. This work, which was carried out in close cooperation with the CMMA, constituted the mission's chief translation enterprise in China. British missionaries constituted the majority of the bureau's best-known translators and editors. Under British leadership the bureau made important contributions in revising out-of-date books and initiating standard Chinese medical terms. From 1918 to 1932 the bureau, together with the CMMA (later the CMA), edited and translated or revised a total of fifty-three medical professional works. Most of the up-to-date medical literature in Chinese before the mid-1930s was their work.[22]

Also worth mentioning is the Moukden (Mukden) Medical College (MMC), opened in 1912 and the only mission medical college in Northeast China. The MMC was also the earliest medical mission school to register with the government (in 1917). It admitted women students in 1924 and thus became a major training center for both male and female doctors in Northeast China. After the Hangzhou Medical College was taken over by the government in 1927, the MMC became the only medical school in China run on British lines. Although it was in name a union college founded jointly by the United Free Church of Scotland (UFS), Presbyterian Church in Ireland (PCI), and the Danish Lutheran Mission, British staff constituted over 70 percent of the faculty. In addition, the curriculum was based on a Scottish model, and the college aimed to duplicate the standard of Scottish universities, offering a five-year course that was later extended to six and then seven years. By 1929 the college had produced 176 graduates, many of whom went on to become well-known specialists, directors, and superintendents of hospitals throughout the country. Although not the largest, it was certainly the most respected and prestigious medical school in China. Like the medical school at Qilu, the MMC used Chinese as the language of instruction.[23]

Finally, the Hangzhou Medical Training College was set up in 1910 by the CMS. In addition to training physicians, it also included a Pharmacy Training College, Maternity Training College, Men's Nurses' School, and Women's Nurses' School. In April 1927 it was taken over by the new Nationalist government. Although short-lived, the institution played a valuable role in training Chinese medical personnel for Zhejiang province and for CMS hospitals in other provinces. In particular, the quality of the college's foreign-trained midwives were widely recognized, making it an important British-style medical educational center of the 1920s.[24]

British missions also made important contributions to the development of nursing in China. The first modern nurse in South China was trained by the LMS. One of the most important institutions in the development of modern nursing in China was the Nurses' Association of China (NAC). Jointly founded in 1912 by four British and four American missionary nurses, the NAC curricula was eventually adopted by all of the nursing training schools in China, and in 1922 the organization was accepted as a full member of the International Council of Nurses in Geneva. Between 1918 and 1932 the NAC published a total of fifty-seven books on medicine and nursing, which became standard teaching materials in nurse training courses.[25]

Mission hospitals were the main centers for training nurses and produced a larger number of nursing staff than the mission medical colleges. In both, however, the main teaching emphasis was on care for the sick and the prevention of illness. Most nursing schools offered three- or four-year programs run along British or American lines and used Chinese as the medium of instruction. By the late 1920s some larger schools had begun to offer specialized courses in areas such as public health nursing, industrial nursing, child welfare, and maternity services; some also provided special midwifery courses. Medical missions also began to train professional Chinese midwives after 1920. Nearly all mission-based women's hospitals participated in midwifery training schemes, and many started regular midwifery training schools.[26]

In 1915 there were a total of 36 mission nursing schools with 272 students in all of China. By the early 1920s thorough nursing training programs existed in only around 40 percent of mission hospitals. British missions (including those of Canada and New Zealand) operated 29 nursing schools with 295 students. In 1929 the total number of mission nursing schools had grown to 125, with 1,600 students. By 1935 all British mission hospitals had shouldered responsibility for training nurses with the exception of seven small cottage hospitals. The NAC, which had only 231 members in 1920, counted 2,456 members in 1935. It is also worth noting that the number of female nurses surpassed the number of male nurses in the late 1920s, signaling the breakdown of the old taboo hindering women nurses from entering men's wards and the beginning of the era of nursing as a mainly female profession in China.[27]

A further British mission contribution to the development of medical education lay in training hospital technicians. This effort was prompted by the serious lack of trained medical staff and the potential for an increased division of medical labor within the modern hospital. In 1920 George Hadden proposed the creation of an Institute of Hospital Technology under the auspices of the CMMA. The institute began work in 1923 at the ACM hospital in Anqing, Anhui, with Hadden in the lead, but a shortage of funds forced the institute's relocation to the British Hankou Union Hospital in 1928. Here its courses soon included laboratory, pharmacy, and anesthetics training as well as an increasing emphasis on hospital administration. By 1938 the institute had trained 483 students from ninety-seven mission hospitals across China. By 1935 around forty British mission hospitals had also taken on the task of training hospital technicians.[28]

Finally, the contribution of British missions to the development of modern medical education in China extended beyond the development of individual institutions and training programs. The medical curriculum in these mission institutions reflected the high academic standards of their home countries and the educational and professional background of their founders. They all stressed basic scientific and hospital-oriented clinical training in both laboratory and wards. Foreign-trained Chinese doctors thus acquired the latest essential medical theory as well as valuable practical training from worthy role models. In the process of their education they were exposed to higher scientific ideals and the best traditions of the Western medical profession. Second, the institutions of higher medical education attracted women students considerably earlier than did other scientific enterprises in China. By the mid-1920s all mission-based medical colleges had opened their doors to men and women on equal terms. Third, by the 1920s nearly all major British missions had adopted a policy of encouraging medical education by providing bursaries and scholarships and offering their Chinese doctors opportunities for further training.

Perhaps the single greatest contribution of British mission medical education lay in training Chinese medical talent, including native teachers. By the late 1920s the number of Chinese staff outnumbered foreign staff in British mission-based medical educational institutions. The proportion of Chinese and foreign doctors in mission hospitals in 1920 was 55 percent and 45 percent, respectively; by 1930 it was 67 percent and 33 percent. In 1915 there were a total of 119 Chinese doctors and 509 Chinese nurses working in mission hospitals and dispensaries; in 1930–31 mission medical institutions employed 410 Chinese doctors and 700 Chinese nurses, and by 1935 they employed 634 Chinese doctors and 1,656 Chinese nurses. By the mid-1920s Chinese medical staff shouldered the main burden in many inland mission institutions. All of this meant that missions devoted much greater efforts to training a native medical corps in the 1920s than they had in the previous decade. British missions played a central role in this endeavor.[29]

The Nationalization of Christian Education

The 1920s were an important decade in the history of British mission education in China not only because they marked a period of unprecedented growth and development of the mission educational enterprise. The 1920s also marked an important turning point for British missions in transferring educational administration to Chinese control. This transfer of control, which took place in the late 1920s, has often been portrayed, especially in PRC sources, as a compulsory action forced upon a reluctant missionary establishment by the new Nationalist government and a rising tide of Chinese nationalism, the latter most forcefully expressed in the anti-Christian, antiforeign, and rights recovery movements of the mid- and late 1920s. The reality, however, was considerably more complex than this reading of history allows.

In the first place many British mission schools had started to adopt the new 6-6-4 government educational system of 1922 (namely, six years of primary school followed by a further six years of middle school and four years of higher education, with the exception of medical colleges) before the outbreak of the antiforeign movement (1925) and the campaign to recover educational rights (1926). The Conference of Missionary Societies of Great Britain and Ireland had introduced a similar educational principle and had called upon its British missions in China to adopt the system. In the course of implementing the 6-6-4 school system, mission institutions had therefore consciously or unconsciously prepared the conditions for their eventual nationalization. This early voluntary movement by missions toward the new educational system helped to facilitate the successful integration of British mission schools into the national educational system after 1928.

In addition, many mission institutions had adopted the government curricula well before their nationalization in the late 1920s. This was because the more that mission schools approximated government schools in their programs and standards, the more assured was their long-term status and position in Chinese society. Although mission institutions were not an integral part of the state educational system, neither did their presence threaten the government system; rather, their existence was supplementary to the government system. The mission educational enterprise represented an attempt to meet real needs and give assistance to the huge educational task confronting China.

In 1924–25 the Chinese government at the time required all private mission-based educational institutions to register with government, develop Chinese leadership, transfer administrative rights to Chinese responsibility, and offer religious education on a voluntary basis only. Even before these regulations were promulgated, however, missionary educators had on numerous occasions spoken out about the need to transfer educational control to Chinese Christians, and many missions had admitted the desirability of bringing Chinese leaders into positions of responsibility for shaping and carrying out educational policy.[30] As early as 1922, it was proposed that "teaching and administrative positions must be filled by Chinese as rapidly as Christian men and women with requisite ability can be secured"; that "Chinese membership on boards of management of schools should be very largely increased and should eventually displace foreign missionaries entirely"; and that "foreigners should be employed only for services for which there is as yet an inadequate number of competent Chinese, and the foreigners who are thus employed should be thoroughly qualified for their specific task."[31] Calls were issued for the number of Chinese teachers and administrative members in mission schools to be raised to 50 percent of staff.[32]

Individual institutions implemented their own plans and targets for recruiting and training Chinese for positions of responsibility. In 1920 the authorities of the Moukden Christian College instituted a new policy that the college's senior Chinese teachers should be admitted to the faculty; in 1923 the British Joint Board of the Qilu Medical School suggested securing a larger proportion of Chinese professors. The same year Chinese principals were appointed to the EPM's largest middle schools as well as to Westminster College and the Yunnan Boys' School. By 1925 the WMMS had evolved a scheme for transferring control of its educational work to the Chinese church in South China. Thus, the inclination of British missions toward educational nationalization had been made clear in the early 1920s, although the speed of handing over control to the Chinese naturally varied from place to place.[33]

All of this suggests that, while mission and state schools constituted two formally independent systems of education before the late 1920s, relations between the two had actually grown considerably closer since 1920. From this date onward mission schools had begun to initiate a series of efforts designed to integrate mission schools more closely with the state school system, embracing the 6-6-4 system, adopting the government curriculum, and declaring an intention to relinquish administrative control of the schools to local Chinese. The issue of educational devolution had thus been raised—by the missions themselves—and concrete preparations for transferring educational control to Chinese already were under way well before the 1926 campaign to restore educational rights. The evidence clearly contradicts the claim made by some observers of this period that missionary educators were bent on maintaining control over their schools' educational system forever. Why then the charge, so often heard in historical accounts of this period, that missions were forced by government action and popular pressure to relinquish control over education?

Disagreements over the proposed pace of educational devolution and the right of missionaries to choose their own successors made conflict between missions and the forces of Chinese nationalism inevitable in the late 1920s.

Many missionaries expressed the view that their Chinese colleagues were not sufficiently prepared or mature to take on the full responsibility of administering large educational institutions. Instead of full and immediate devolution of power, they advocated a gradual evolutionary transfer of responsibility from missionaries to local Chinese as the best means of addressing the problem while preserving educational quality and standards. Above all, missionaries insisted on the right to choose their own trained Chinese Christians as successors.

As proof of their sincerity, British missions could point to the fact that their elementary schools had already been transferred to Chinese control by the early 1920s; that around half of all British mission secondary schools had been placed under direct Chinese control by 1925; and that plans were in place for the eventual devolution of all secondary schools to Chinese control. The mission preference for an evolutionary process of educational devolution conflicted, however, with increasing Nationalist-inspired demands for immediate and radical change in the status of mission educational institutions. As a result, devolution of control over the remaining 50 percent of British mission secondary schools, as well as over British higher educational institutions, took place after the 1926 Nationalist Party–orchestrated campaign for restoring educational rights, as part of a government-mandated action.

The rising tide of Chinese nationalism from the mid-1920s made it increasingly plain that Chinese politics would no longer tolerate the existence of a parallel school system operated by foreigners. Once this became clear, a more radical pace of change than was envisaged by liberal missionary educators became inevitable. The deciding factor, however, may well have been the May Thirtieth Movement of 1925. The upsurge of radical nationalist feelings that followed this incident, in which British police in Shanghai fired upon unarmed Chinese student demonstrators, killing many, rendered it impossible for nationalist Chinese to wait patiently for the missions' evolutionary plan to unfold, and conflict between the two sides quickly spilled out into the open. British missions, as representatives of the leading foreign power in China and the nation whose troops were responsible for the May Thirtieth incident, became easy targets of nationalist enmity.

As reported by contemporary missionary observers, the nationalist outpouring against mission schools after 1925 expressed numerous concerns. First, Chinese nationalists denounced mission educational work as a subtle form of Western propaganda, designed to advance the cause of Western civilization and to bring about the destruction of Chinese culture, the most precious heritage that China possessed.[34] The religious purpose of mission schools was to develop Christian personalities. But in the opinion of critics mission schools did not pay enough attention to Chinese subjects, and even cultivated a stu-

dent habit of detesting Chinese subjects. Antiforeign and antireligious senti-
ments were thus intermingled in nationalist opposition toward mission
schools.[35] Second, Christianity and religious education were believed by many
to be remote from China's actual needs. Many mission students looked forward to employment in cities, where the chances for a good income and social
advancement were better, and had "no appetite" for rural work.[36] Third, by the
late 1920s many Chinese were becoming more and more convinced that China
could hope for nothing in the way of sympathy and support from Christian
missions in its struggle for independence from Western countries. Both of the
country's leading political parties, the Guomindang (GMD, Nationalist), and
the Chinese Communist Party (CCP), advocated anti–imperialist struggle.
And, since Britain was the leading foreign power in China at the time, British
mission schools naturally became a focus of criticism.

The changes to mission education began in 1925 when the Ministry of
Education insisted that foreign-run schools register with the government. The
Nationalist government, which came to power in 1928, imposed even stricter
regulations. Significantly, Chinese staff and students in mission schools appear to have been overwhelmingly in favor of government registration, according to internal mission reports. These reports also stated that it was common
for Chinese staff to regard the mission school as a foreign place, owned and
run by foreigners, with Chinese having little say in its operation.[37] The initial
reaction of some British missions, however, was to resist registration. Many
missionaries expressed deep concern over the strict limits that new government regulations imposed on religious teaching in schools. Most missionaries
considered it perfectly legitimate for Chinese governments to seek to exercise
general control over what was being taught in the country's schools.[38] But
many also claimed a right to provide Christian teaching to the children of
Chinese Christians.[39] When the new Nationalist authorities refused to make
any concession on the issue, mission schools were forced to decide whether to
register with the government or close.

Many Christian schools remained closed for more than a year during
1927–28. In 1927 only 100 or so British mission middle schools remained open,
but by 1928–29 the number had risen to 172.[40] By the end of the decade most
British missions had agreed to register their schools with the national government. The majority of missions also took concrete measures to address the
criticisms of their Chinese staff. An increasing number created Chinese-
staffed boards of directors and elected Chinese principals and deans. In 1923
the ratio of Chinese to foreigners in mission universities was one to one; in
1932 it was two to one; and by 1936 it was four to one. In the spring of 1929,
85.2 percent of Christian middle schools had Chinese principals; by the early

1930s the figure had risen to 90 percent. By 1933 all British mission educational institutions had registered with the government and complied with the new regulations.[41]

The 1920s was thus a critical transitional phase in the history of British mission education in China. The decade witnessed a definitive devolution of educational control into Chinese hands, but at the same time official registration gave mission educational institutions a permanent legal status in China: Christian education was taken into the orbit of the national educational system. The value of Christian schools was thereby formally recognized, and their continued existence was legally encouraged by government and throughout Chinese society rather than discouraged. Registration also aided the cause of achieving a more uniform standard of education in China. Nationalization and standardization was beneficial not only to the continued development and progress of mission schools but to the exchange of talent between mission schools and government ones. As an important integral part of Chinese education, Christian institutions were in a position to wield more power in promoting the transformation of Chinese society.

After nationalization foreigners became a minority on the boards of trustees of mission schools, and foreigners were no longer allowed to serve as principals or headmasters. Yet almost all of the posts subsequently held by Chinese principals were secured by mission-trained graduates. Individual missionaries were now welcomed as experts, advisors, cooperators, and even ordinary employees in institutions in which foreigners had formerly been absolute leaders.[42] With the formal structures of foreign control removed or dismantled, mission schools proceeded to cultivate within their institutional confines the patriotic and national atmosphere of the times under the energetic leadership of Chinese Christians. They were able to cooperate with government in more productive ways and on a much larger scale than was previously the case.[43] Finally, while government exercised administrative control of mission schools, the schools were still dependent to a large extent on mission funds to maintain themselves.[44]

Popular Education

One area of British mission educational activity that was not greatly affected by nationalization but which remained a crucial feature of British religious and cultural influence in China during the 1920s was the diverse field of popular education. No account of British mission educational activity in China in the 1920s would be complete without reference to the vigorous and flourishing enterprise of popular education. The considerable resources British missionaries devoted to various forms of popular education reflected their commitment to the social gospel that demanded popular education be regarded as an integral part of mission social reform. Popular education included a diverse array of activities ranging from anti–illiteracy campaigns[45] and public hygiene to translation and publishing,[46] public lectures, amateur societies, and the establishment of some of China's earliest modern museums. A brief examination of the latter three activities may serve to illuminate the significance of this aspect of British mission education.

The giving of "Public Lectures" became a compulsory responsibility of British missions in the 1920s. Specialist speakers were recruited to deliver lectures on topics such as "Evolution," "Mountaineering and the Great Earthquake in Japan," "Cambridge," "Ancient British Monuments: Avebury and Stonehenge," "The Country That Shakespeare Knew and Loved," "The Panama Canal," "Mexico," "The New Internationalism," "An Evening with Dickens," "Marine Engines," "Arithmetic," "Geography," "Hygiene," and "History of Sinn Fein."[47] Likewise, the British YMCA and YWCA also regarded introducing new knowledge as the major aim of popular educational activities, the participants of which, according to the reminiscences of former missionaries, were mainly non-Christian young people.[48]

Often mission social clubs located in cities and towns were formed along YMCA and YWCA lines. The BMS social center at Zhoucun and the International Institute of the FFMA in Chongqing were typical in that they included reading rooms and recreational facilities open to all. Indeed, British missionaries were often enthusiastic initiators and advocates of various social sports and recreational activities. As a result, British-style football, tennis, badminton, table tennis, and snooker became widely popular in areas of South China where missionaries were active. Besides sports and recreational activities, British missionaries were also active in organizing various societies and institutions, such as the Societies of Science and Arts, Beijing Society of Natural History, Photographic Society and Energetic Society, and the Fujian Scientific Society. Their activities and public lectures attracted many young people and aroused their strong interest in science and Western learning.[49]

British efforts were also instrumental in the development of modern museums in China. The first Western-style museum in China was founded in the late nineteenth century by a British institution, the (North) China Branch of the Royal Asiatic Society. Yet as late as 1920 there was no national public museum in China, and even by 1929 there were only thirty-one public museums and three private museums in the entire country.[50] By the 1920s the church regarded museums as an important part of popular education and intellectual culture, capable of attracting—and educating—both elite and illiterate audiences. Indeed, British mission-sponsored museums in the 1920s enjoyed an extraordinary popularity among the Chinese public.

In 1887 J. S. Whitewright founded what was destined to become one of the most influential British museums in China at Qingzhou. In 1905 a large grant from the trustees of Robert Arthington, a British millionaire from Leeds, enabled Whitewright to transfer his idea to Jinan, in Shandong province, where the museum enjoyed expanded quarters with greatly improved facilities for staging exhibits. In 1917 the museum merged with Qilu University and henceforward functioned as its extension department but was maintained entirely by the British Baptist Missionary Society. The museum's avowed aim was the enlightenment of Chinese people of all classes concerning Western civilization. The exhibits, on subjects ranging from agriculture to forestry, public health, and modern science and technology, included reproductions of a Scottish orphanage, hospitals, and asylums for the blind, all run by Christian charity enterprises. A perfect model of a Bristol main street was displayed as the epitome of a Western city, while a picture of the British Houses of Parliament served as background for a textual account of Western forms of government. Western achievements in science and engineering such as aforestation, river control, and irrigation; methods of preventing blight and eliminating crop pests; improved wells; sanitation; as well as modern inventions such as steamers, engines, and machinery of various types were all represented by photographs and working models. In the words of the museum's organizers, "Everything is magnificent and stirring as well as fascinating."[51]

If the museum's attendance figures are any indication, local Chinese visitors would appear to have agreed with this assessment. The museum soon averaged more than one thousand visitors a day, and its popularity continued to grow. Between January and September 19, 1922, the museum recorded a whopping 434,000-plus visitors to the museum and lecture hall. So popular had the facility become that from 1925 it remained open every night of the week. The record for a single day was made on January 30, 1933, when a total of 12,635 visitors attended.[52] Described as "the most effective piece of university extension work which can be found in Asia, if not in the world" and as "the greatest single cultural enterprise in China," the museum also attracted representatives from various educational organizations who came to study and learn from its experience. Many were struck by the sheer number of items exhibited. J. R. Mott wrote, "I see more points of contact in this institution than any others I have visited in the world." Taken together, the exhibits often served to contrast the modernity of the West with the backwardness of China, as can be seen from this remark by a prominent Chinese observer: "Stuffed birds and animals of various countries were displayed, and also machinery and engines for different occupations—the primitive ones as still used in China compared with the time- and labor-saving inventions of the west."[53]

One might well ask what impression Chinese visitors gleaned from this and similar mission-organized cultural displays on subjects as diverse as modern Western labor-saving inventions, Scottish orphanages, and Shakespeare's England. The British missionaries in these cultural institutions dedicated themselves to popular education and to the well-being of the local Chinese communities. The institutions they ran were China's best popular educational centers for developing intellects, popularizing common scientific knowledge, and advancing enlightened ideas on social reform. They also sought to elevate popular morals and taste and to serve as civilizers. They therefore played an important role in the process of ideological persuasion.

Conclusion

The educational purpose of British missions in China changed significantly during the course of the 1920s. Evangelism receded and was replaced by a social gospel commitment to developing education as a means of reforming and improving society. This entailed a commitment to all forms and levels of education, from elementary education to advanced medical colleges, literacy classes to the translation and publication of advanced scientific texts. Then, in the latter part of the decade, British mission schools responded to the urgent demands for nationalization, registering with government and handing over administrative control of mission schools to local Chinese, most of whom were mission school graduates. "Serve the nation" became one of the mission schools' slogans.

It is true, generally speaking, that mission educational institutions did not pay enough attention to Chinese subjects, and this was a legitimate focus of Chinese criticism of mission schools in the 1920s. Yet British mission institutions, along with those of other Christian missions, did play a vital part in forming the minds of several recent generations of Chinese. Such institutions attracted many young people who yearned for new knowledge and new thoughts. They were the best source of Western learning in China. Historical experiences had taught the Chinese that whichever nation was able to quickly, wisely, and most directly make use of the ready-made and advanced results of human creation and invention would be able to join the list of advanced nations of the world. The Chinese embraced modern education on this basis, as the major means for increasing a nation's quality and pushing forward social progress. British mission education flourished in part because it fulfilled this strongly felt need. It also had long-lasting effects. Thousands of mission-trained graduates contributed to China's twentieth-century social upheaval and changed the very structure of society. Its results in this respect alone have been of inestimable value.

NOTES

1. The following abbreviations are for names of missionary societies. When these abbreviations are used in the notes, they also indicate the source of archival materials.

ACM, American Church Mission.

BMS, Baptist Missionary Society, located in Angus Library of Regent's Park College, University of Oxford (Minutes/Reports/Correspondence and Papers).

CBMS, Conference of British Missionary Societies, located in the Library of School of Oriental and African Studies (SOAS), University of London (Minutes/Reports: China Continuation Committee, 1913–1921; and the National Christian Council, 1922–1932).

CIM, China Inland Mission, located in (1) its headquarters at Sevenoaks, Kent, England; (2) the SOAS Library, University of London (Report/Minutes/Annual Accounts).

CMMA, China Medical Missionary Association.

CMS, Church Missionary Society, located in Heslop Room, the Central Library of Birmingham University (Letters, Procis Books and Original Papers, Papers of Medical Department in 1920 and 1931: Minutes/Correspondence/Memoranda/Reports).

EPM, English Presbyterian Mission, located in the SOAS Library (combining interviews with former missionaries) (Papers/Reports/Correspondence).

FFMA, Friends Foreign Mission Association (after 1927, FSC, Friends Service Council), located in Friends' House Library, Euston Road, London (Minutes/Correspondence/Reports).

LMS, London Missionary Society, located in the SOAS Library (combining interviews with four former missionaries) (Reports/Incoming Letters/Correspondence).

PCI, Presbyterian Church in Ireland, (1) parts of its archives are located in Edinburgh (see the UFS); (2) Headquarters Library of the PCI in Belfast, Northern Ireland; (3) Library of Queen's University in Belfast; (4) Public Record Office of Northern Ireland in Belfast (combining interviews with eight former missionaries) (Minutes/Reports/Correspondence).

PN, Board Of Foreign Missions of the Presbyterian Church in the United States.

SPG, Society for the Propagation of the Gospel.

UFS, United Free Church of Scotland, located in (1) National Library of Scotland; (2) Library of New College, University of Edinburgh; (3) Department of Manuscripts, Edinburgh University Library; (4) Headquarters Library, Church of Scot-

land in Edinburgh (combining interviews with ten former missionaries in Scotland) (Reports/Minutes/Correspondence/Papers).
WMMS, Wesleyan Methodist Missionary Society, located in the SOAS Library (General Correspondence/Synod Minutes/Correspondence).

2. On the origins of the social gospel, see Alan D. Gilbert, *Religion and Society in Industrial England: Church, Chapel and Social Change, 1740–1914* (London and New York: Longman, 1976).

3. Timothy Richard, *Forty-Five Years in China* (London: Longman, 1916). See also Jiang Wenhan, "Li Timotai he Guang Xuehui" (Timothy Richard and the Christian Literary Society for China) *Wenshi ziliao xuanji* 43 (March 1964).

4. C. Peter Williams, "British Religion and the Wider World: Mission and Empire, 1800–1940," in Sheridan Gilley and W. J. Sheils, eds., *A History of Religion in Britain: Practice and Belief from Pre-Roman Times to the Present* (Oxford and Cambridge, Mass.: Blackwell, 1994), 384, 403.

5. London Missionary Society, North China, "Incoming Letters," box 24, George B. Barbour, Beijing, 10 February 1924, 4.

6. On rural educational funds, see the Financial Committee reports, annual distribution of grants for LMS, North China. On the vocational training provided by village-level mission primary schools, see Baptist Missionary Society (hereafter BMS), English Baptist Mission Minutes of Foreign Conference held in Taiyuanfu, 24–25 March 1930.

7. Baptist Missionary Society, "Minutes of the Fourth Inter-Provincial Conference," 1924.

8. CIM also retained many features of mission elementary education from the late nineteenth century, such as an almost equal number of Sunday school pupils and day school/boarding school pupils and a much greater emphasis on religious education.

9. Milton Theobald Stauffer, ed., *Zhonghua guizhu*, trans. Cai Yongchun (Beijing: 1985), 1195, 1197.

10. WMMS, Veneration of ancestors and Christianizing the Home Movement—Hankou, 1931, Wuchang Chairman, box 966; *Chinese Recorder* 61:469; *China Year Book* (London) (1931):317.

11. UFS, Minutes of Foreign Mission committee, 1922.

12. Ruth Hayhoe and Marianne Bastid, eds., *China's Education and the Industrialized World Studies in Cultural Transfer* (Armonk, N.Y. and London: M. E. Sharpe, 1987), 47. See also WMMS, Wuchang District Report 1931; and LMS, Central China Report 1923.

13. *Missionary Herald of PCI* (1920–22):152; and (1930):99; LMS, Report of C. W. Knott, 1930, Griffith John School, Hankou, 30 December 1930; FFMA. CH/6 Letters from China 1928–31, Alfred Davidson to H. T. Silcock from Chungking, 2 May 1931.

14. FFMA, China Committee, 11/VIII/20, see University Budget for 1921; CMS, G1/CH3/L3 1926, Minutes of Committee of 15 December 1926.

15. CMS. G1/CH1/P4, 6 November 1923, no. 67; LMS, South China, Correspondence file in/out, box 27, article in *Hong Kong Post*, 25 January 1930, "Opening of a New College."

16. LMS, South China, Correspondence file in/out, box 27, see the letter from O. D. Wannamaber, 26 March 1931. Each academic year Lingnan ran two summer schools.

17. CMS, G1/CH4/O 1929, Nos. 6, 19, and 4. In 1924, 56 percent of FCU freshmen came from British mission middle schools; in 1927 the figure was 40 percent.

18. LMS, Correspondence files in/out, box 25, see Minutes of Annual Meeting Supervisory Committee China Union Universities Central Office, 3 October 1928, New York; WMMS, see Central China College, Wuchang, China, President's Report for the Year 1932–33.

19. BMS, SCU Student Body Statistics for the fall semester 1926.

20. Resolution of the CMMA, January 1913 in *Chinese Recorder,* 44:595.

21. BMS, *Challenge of China,* 26; Annual Report of BMS 1930, 22. See also BMS, CH/64 SCU, F. Oldrieve, SCU Foreign Staff in Residence, May 1928.

22. LMS, North China, Incoming letters, box 23-1922, see Bernard Upward's letter to F. H. Hawkins, 13 March 1922; BMS, Annual Report of BMS 1924, 97; Conference of British Missionary Societies (CBMS). Area File, Asia, China, Medical FBN 19, box 407, E/T China 61 (2), micro. 13.

23. See Douglas Christie, *Thirty Years in Moukden, 1883–1913* (Constable) (London: 1914). Also UFS, Minutes of Foreign Mission Committee, UFS, May 1928 to September 1929, 300; MMC Central Committee Minutes, 8 July 1925; UFS, Anglo-Chinese College (ACC), 7548/D/35–39, file 21, 1930, to the Indemnity Committee (British Indemnity Fund); and UFS, MMC Report, 1934, 13.

24. CMS, M/Y CH2 1920, file 1, Zhejiang 12, memorandum of notes of interview between Dr. J. H. Cook and Bishop Molony, 26 May 1920; G1 CH2/O 1918–1922, file 2, G1 CH2/O 1921, no. 45; CMS, G1 CH2/O 1922, 36; G1 CH2/O 1923–25, file 1, 1923, 10.

25. Report for 1926 and 1927, by E. Hope Bell, LMS, Central China, Reports, box 10–1927; WMMS, China, box 1091, Wuchang District, Missionaries on Furlough, notes from Sister Gladys Stephenson's letter to Mr. Andrews, 22 January 1928; WMMS, China Hubei General, box 965, Report of Committee on Nursing Policy, 1928.

26. EPM, Overseas Lingdong, Shantou, General Correspondence, Minutes, Reports, Correspondence, 1924, box 33, file 5, Shantou W.M.A. Council, 22 January 1924, 49th meeting; UFS, Report on Foreign Missions: Submitted to the General Assembly of the United Free Church of Scotland 1924, 73; and 1926, 76.

27. *Zhonghua guizhu,* 1201, 713; CBMS, London, Asia Committee, E/T China, FBN 19, box 409, no. 12, see the statistics of mission medical work, 1–39; WMMS, China Hubei, box 965, Wuchang chairman, see Sister Gladys Stephenson's *Nurses' Association of China.*

28. WMMS, China Correspondence Hubei, box 962, Hubei chairman 1923, from medical secretary on 13 June 1923; CBMS, London. Asia Committee, FBN 19, box 407, Micro. 18, "Institute of Hospital Technology."

29. Zhao Hongchun, *Jindai zhongxiyi lunzheng shi* (Modern Chinese history of controversy between Western and Chinese medicine) (Shijiazhuan: 1982), 35; Wang Zhixin, *Zhongguo jidujiao shigang* (Historical outline of Christianity in China) (Shanghai: 1930), 332. See also W. G. Lennox's paper, CMJ, vol. 46; K. C. Wong, *Lancet and Cross,* preface.

30. "Jidujiao xuexiao zai Zhongguo jiaoyu xitong zhong sozhan diwei" (The place of Christian schools in the Chinese educational system), *Xin jiaoyu* 4, no. 3 (March 1922).

31. E. W. Wallace's address "The Work of the China Educational Committee," from the National Christian Conference held in Shanghai, 2–11 May 1922. See also "Jidujiao jiaoyu zhi congzhi yu jingshen" (The Purpose and Spirit of Christian Education), *Xin jiaoyu* 5, nos. 1–2 (August 1922).

32. LMS, memorandum of Evangelistic and Educational Policy in the East China District, 1923.

33. LMS, C. G. Sparham to F. H. Hawkins on 11 June 1923, Shanghai; *Missionary Herald of the PCI,* (1920–22), 28; EPM. Amoy Council Minutes, July 1922. See also the latter's educational report of the South China District for 1925.

34. Paul Monroe, "Chinese Attitude toward Western Culture," *North China Standard,* 22 January 1929.

35. Wu Leichuan, "Jiaohui xuexiao de yiwang ji jianglai" (The past and future of mission schools), *Jiaoyu jikan* 3, no. 1 (March 1927); Yang Zheng, "Jidujiao jiaoyu zhi jianglai" (The future of Christian education), *Qingnian jinbu* 93 (1926). For the missionary perception of antireligious/antiforeign sentiment directed at mission schools, see also CBMS, London, Asia Committee, China: Education, FBN 20, box 410, E/T China 64 (1) no. 1, "The Registration of Mission Schools and Colleges with the Chinese Government," by F. H. Hawkins of the LMS (London, 1926).

36. LMS, North China, Correspondence file in/out, box 28-1930, see P. L. McAll to F. H. Hawkins, 22 March 1930; LMS, South China, Correspondence file in/out, box 25, Micro. no. 430.

37. CBMS, London, Asia Committee, China: Education and Government, box 410, E/T China: 64(1–3), no. 2, see the article by F. H. Hawkins.

38. LMS, South China, Reports, box 6-1930, see Decennial Report, from T. C. Brown.

39. LMS, South China, Reports, box 6-1927, see "Reports for Year 1927" of the LMS D.C., 9; BMS, CH/64, Wilson to Rowley, 20 September 1927; EPM, Overseas Lingdong, Shantou, individual correspondence, H. C. Wallace, box 44, file 4, 30 June 1927.

40. On the decision whether to maintain or close individual schools, see EPM, Foreign Mission Committee, Report on the Anglo-Chinese College, Amoy, August 1927.

41. FFMA, China 1927, CH/5/4, Letters from Missionaries, "A Brief Report of Our Christian Educational Institutions," 1 June 1927; LMS, Correspondence file in/out, box 28-1930, P. L. McAll to F. H. Hawkins, the secretary of LMS, 20 March 1930; EPM, Overseas General Correspondence, South Fujian, 1931, box 12, file 2, Minutes of Amoy Mission Council, 3–13 February 1931.

42. "The Claims of the New China," *The Friend: A Religious and Literary Journal* (London), n.s. 68, no. 67 (1927):391.

43. Yuan Bojiao, "Jidujiao xuexiao yu jiaoshi" (Christian schools and teachers), *Jiaoyu jikan* 3, no. 2 (June 1937).

44. Educational grants from mission home boards topped the budgets of British missions in China throughout the 1920s, with home board grants accounting for about 60 percent of mission educational income.

45. In 1923 the missionary writer Garland reported that an estimated 90 percent of non-Christian Chinese were illiterate but that perhaps as many as 40 percent of Chinese churchgoers could read in the vernacular, thanks to missionary efforts to teach illiterates basic knowledge of the Bible and simple Chinese characters using local vernaculars. CIM, S. Garland, "The Problem of China's Illiteracy" *China's Millions* 31 (October 1923):156.

46. The Christian Literature Society for China, founded in 1887 and staffed mainly by British specialists trained in journalism, published 322 books between 1918–32, of which 208 were secular books. Roughly one quarter of the society's published output concerned social reform. The Religious Tract Society, founded in 1884, also became an enthusiastic advocate of social reform in the 1920s, publishing some 76 tracts and 22 books on issues ranging from anti-footbinding, anti-opium, anti-superstition, public health, and sexual equality over the course of the decade. The Guang Xue Publishing House in Shanghai published 57 secular books and pamphlets from 1918 to 1932. Mission publishing efforts were aimed at both elite and popular audiences; as explained in an earlier section of this essay, significant efforts were also undertaken in the translation and publishing of medical and scientific texts.

47. See the Report by C. H. B. Longman, Tianjin for 1926, A Year of Recovery, LMS, North China, Reports, box 9-1926; also LMS, South China, Incoming letters box 22- 1920, "Union Church Literary Club," by W. Season, *South China Morning Post* (Guangzhou).

48. Interviews with M. Garvie on 14 October 1992 in Scotland, Rev. Colin Corley on 31 January 1993, and Dr. A. J. Weir on 1 Feb. 1993 in Belfast. All three were British YWCA and YMCA missionaries in China.

49. "Societies and Institutions," in *China Journal of Science and Arts* (1920–30); also Physical Training College of Chengdu, ed., *Zhongguo jindai tiyu shi ziliao* (Historical materials on the history of physical education in China) (Chengdu: Sichuan jiaoyu chubanshe, 1988), 259.

50. Jiaoyubu. *Diyici Zhongguo jiaoyu nianjian* (First China Education Yearbook) (Shanghai: Kaiming shudian, 1934), 880.

51. BMS, Annual Report for the Year of 1921. See also "The Late John Sutherland Whitewright," in *China Journal of Science and Arts* 4, no. 3 (March 1926):126.

52. H. R. Williamson, *British Baptists in China* (London: 1957), 202–3; BMS, Minutes of Inter-Provincial Conference, 1925, 55; BMS, Minutes of China Sub-Committee Conferences, no. 9, 114.

53. The quotation from J. R. Mott is in the BMS pamphlet, *The Story of Jinanfu*. The other quotation is from Wu Lien-teh, *The Plague Fighter: The Autobiography of a Modern Chinese Physician Wu Lien-teh* (Cambridge: University of Cambridge Press, 1959), 515.

Nationalization and Internationalization: Two Turning Points in China's Education in the Twentieth Century

Gang Ding

This essay looks at educational development in the twentieth century through the complex and interwined movements of nationalization and internationalization. These twin movements emerge as the main forces propelling reforms and changes in Chinese education. During the twentieth century Chinese educators encountered varied foreign knowledge patterns and influences and became more and more proactive in utilizing them to pioneer their own national path toward educational development.

This essay takes the relationship between nationalization and internationalization as its focus and seeks to probe this relationship in depth. Adopting the methodology of comparative history, it examines a number of themes in two crucial periods during the century, first, the 1920s and 1930s and, second, the 1980s and 1990s. On the basis of this discussion certain patterns appear that help us to understand educational development over the century.

The First Turning Point: The 1920s and 1930s

In the 1920s China turned from a situation in which one external model exercised a dominant influence over its modern educational development, that of Japan, to one in which a range of external models were used eclectically to develop a road to educational reform that constituted a kind of search for a new Chinese identity. This took place in the context of intense conflict between Chinese and foreign cultural and educational ideas. The special challenge, and difficulty, that faced educators of the period was how to manage the relationship between Chinese and foreign educational experience in such a way as to benefit China's own educational development.

In this period education was one of the most important elements in overall social reform. Educational reform involved debates over past traditions as well as comparisons between Chinese and Western educational theories, systems, and practices, as a basis for taking stock of educational practice in the period. The intention was to adopt the most beneficial aspects of Western educational experience and explore a pathway toward national educational development. In this section three themes that illustrate this process of exploration will be pursued.

The Establishment of Modern Universities

From the late Qing to the Revolution of 1911, as confrontation between Chinese and Western cultural and educational ideas intensified, political reform was initiated, and the traditional examination system was abolished. A large number of schools and colleges patterned after Western and Japanese models sprung up, characterized by such innovations as the integration of arts and sciences, the development of specialist higher programs, the organization and timetabling of teaching by discrete classes, and annual graduation, all features that might be seen as a kind of foundation for a modern higher education system in China.

These innovations, however, were somewhat superficial, due to the fact that the foreign models were not always fully understood or adapted to the Chinese context. The Japanese model had the deepest influence on China's educational system over this period, because it was found appropriate in terms of national spirit and linguistic compatability. The 1902 document entitled "Qinding daxuetang zhangcheng" (Imperially Approved School Regulations) stated that China had taken the school systems of many countries into consideration, but in fact there was not a great deal of evidence to support this claim. The Chinese system was actually a very close copy of the Japanese system, and, even though it was revised seven times, there was little sense of a spirit of independence in the document.

Before a new school system was promulgated by the new republic, which emerged after the Revolution of 1911, a provincial educational conference was convened. Once again, the Japanese educational system was taken as the main reference point.[1] Apparently, people saw the Japanese system as a successful model that had transformed suitable aspects of Western education and culture for its own purposes and felt it would promote reform. By the late 1910s, however, many problems became evident, including an overmechanistic approach to education, a tendency to emphasize social good and inhibit the development of individuality, and the neglect of scientific research into education. These problems stimulated people to turn away from the utilitarian considerations that had shaped modern education up till then and adopt an approach that reflected a deep inner search for a modern Chinese identity.

Although the New Culture Movement of May 4, 1919, was still trammeled by traditions, in their efforts to promote social progress, the main activists took quite radical positions in both their rhetoric and their activities.[2] Still they did not totally negate tradition nor advocate a wholesale Westernization. Rather they considered traditional and contemporary ideas from both China and the West, evaluating their successes and failures and seeking a path to national development based on both theory and practice. One might see this as a transition from critiquing tradition to critically absorbing tradition, from a rather holistic copying of external patterns to a more eclectic selection of what was suited to China. In this process one can see the way in which these educational reformers reflected on the interconnection between nationalization and internationalization as they tried to modernize education. A striking example is the emphasis they put on the model of the classical academy, or *shuyuan,* as they worked to establish a modern higher education system.

Cai Yuanpei was a strong supporter of higher education reform in the early twentieth century, and he was convinced that the establishment of modern structures of higher education, patterned after Western models, did not bespeak any real change in the deep character of the institutions. He commented that "the movement to uphold Western learning was merely a matter of surface copying, and gave little attention to research."[3] The main reason why so-called modern higher institutions, which the Chinese established through their own efforts, had such meager achievements was this lack of attention to scholarly research. Cai Yuanpei emphasized the point that high-level scholarship should be the main purpose of universities. He felt that not only had Western institutions of higher learning emphasized scholarly research, but this emphasis was also characteristic of the educational traditions of China's *shuyuan.* The *shuyuan*'s tradition of free research and self-sponsored development played a positive role in stimulating China's modern universities toward fundamental reform.[4]

In Cai Yuanpei's plan for university reform he insisted on scholarly research as a main purpose and direction of development, and his efforts in founding and popularizing university research institutes were instrumental in advancing modern higher education in China. Hu Shi also believed that it was essential to promote the free development of scholarly research and self-study if modern higher education were to be effective. He commented that "knowledge simply crammed into the head is not of much use, but the only truly reliable knowledge is that gained through self study. The ability to study independently is the only essential requirement for scholarship."[5] He also pointed out that "self study and research constituted the true spirit of the *shuyuan,*" and he promoted self-initiated research.[6]

Qinghua University's research institute for Chinese national studies was established with Hu Shi's encouragement, and he saw it as emulating "the traditional *shuyuan* and the British university system, with research methods based on self study under the guidance of a professor."[7] His emphasis on research had a tremendous influence on Chinese universities of the time. Both Cai and Hu advocated a blend of the traditions of the *shuyuan* with those of Western universities, and this was a formative influence on China's modern university system, resulting in a large number of research institutes and centers developing within the universities and a system of graduate education taking shape.

At that time the young Mao Zedong also played a significant role in the reform of Chinese higher education. He also emphasized scholarly research and academic freedom, but he was particularly concerned about making scholarship widely available to ordinary people. He established the Hunan Self-Study University (Hunan zixiu daxue), consciously drawing upon features of both the traditional *shuyuan* and Western schools. It aimed to adopt "methods of self-initiated activity, to foster research into all areas of scholarship, in order to discover truth, to create talent and to ensure that culture was spread to ordinary people and scholarship was diffused widely in society."[8] This institution had considerable influence on higher education at the time. Mao's approach was somewhat different from that of Hu Shi and Cai Yuanpei. While they advocated that academics be in control of higher-learning institutions, his main concern was to break through the mystique that tended to surround academic work and to make it possible for everyone to have access to academic knowledge. He thus opposed the institutionalization of higher learning and advocated a populist approach and nonformal learning. From the time that Mao established the Hunan Self-Study University up to the Yan'an period, many nonformal institutions of higher learning were set up, and these models had considerable influence on the development of higher education after 1949. This was closely linked to Mao's early appreciation of the *shuyuan* tradition of scholarship.

We might say that the reforms that were carried out in Chinese universities in the period just after May Fourth were a product of the interaction between Chinese and Western culture. The direct reason for this was the dissatisfaction felt by Chinese scholars at the kinds of copying of Western models that had been undertaken in the late Qing period. If we probe to a deeper level of significance, we can see that reformers of the time made a concerted effort to meld dimensions of the *shuyuan* with aspects of Western higher education as they sought to nationalize Chinese universities. In the different emphases they placed on the *shuyuan* tradition, two quite different directions emerged, one that brought about a kind of regularization of the higher education system and the other that encouraged a range of nonformal higher-learning institutions.[9]

The Establishment of a Modern School System

The reform of the school system was another important theme in China's educational development over the century. This process was not only a matter of the establishment of standards within education itself but also had intimate connections with the overall evolution of the social culture.

From the late Qing, when Western ideas about school systems were first introduced, Chinese traditional patterns of schooling were challenged. They had had little concept of differentiation on the basis of age, grade, or curricular organization. After the Sino-Japanese War of 1894–95, the Chinese felt an even greater urgency over the matter of reforming their school system. This was because Japan had demonstrated in that war how quickly it had been possible to become strong and raise the quality of its people through a new education system based on Western models. From the establishment of the 1902 educational system to the reform of the system in the early Republican period, and right up to the 1922 Regulation for Reform of the Education System, a lot of attention was paid to elementary and secondary education.

It is well-known that the Imperial Regulations of 1902 were mainly a copy of the Japanese system of education. Even though they constituted China's first modern education system, there were still traditional features in evidence, such as the requirement that all pupils in primary and secondary schools should read and recite the classics. Although it was divided into grades and levels in a way that had the external appearance of a modern system, its spirit was still permeated by the notion of "Chinese learning for basic principle, Western learning for practical application."[10]

After the collapse of the Qing dynasty in the Revolution of 1911, Cai Yuanpei, who was briefly minister of education in 1912, established a new school system. It was three years shorter in duration than the one that had been established in 1902. What had originally been higher education colleges were now called university preparatory colleges, and university-level study was basically unchanged. The main changes were at the elementary and secondary levels, with elementary education reduced from nine to seven years and secondary education from five to four years. Also, women were finally given a recognized place within the education system. The most important element of this reform was the abolition of the traditional practice of reading and reciting the classics and the special privileges given to graduates, which made possible a unified system for both women and men.[11] While it is clear that this reformed system of the early republic remained closer to the Japanese system than those of Europe and America, one can nevertheless see some of the special characteristics introduced by those who were running education at the time, in their determined fight against traditional practices and their efforts to develop a national spirit in education.[12]

With the May Fourth Movement of 1919 Chinese people began to realize that only they themselves could change China's fate. This was a time when movements against imperialism and feudalism reached their high point. On the one hand, a sense of conflict between traditional and modern, Eastern and Western, culture pressed people into seeking some kind of impetus for the development of education and a new foundation for the rejuvenation of the nation. On the other hand, efforts to eliminate the remnants of feudalism and to realize democratic educational goals, initiated mainly by such American returned scholars as Hu Shi, Jiang Menglin, and Tao Xingzhi, resulted in the widespread influence of John Dewey's educational ideas.

In May 1919 Dewey visited China, and during the two years and two months of his stay he gave lectures all over the country. He emphasized individualism in children's development as the basic element in a democratic education and the relationship between schools and social progress. His lectures had a significant influence in Chinese education of the time. Most scholars see the most important result of Dewey's influence as the new system of education adopted in 1922, which affirmed individual development and emphasized adapting to society's needs as important standards. It directly adopted the American patterns of six years of primary, three years of lower secondary and three years of upper secondary education. Nevertheless, it is important to understand that this was not merely a matter once again of copying a foreign system of education, even though it is true that Dewey's ideas did support the democratic movement in education.

In 1915 the educational associations of various provinces had gathered together for the first time to hold a national education conference. At that time the Hunan provincial association put forward a motion for reforming the school system that proposed the complete abolition of the existing system in favor of a national education system.[13] In 1920 the sixth national education conference issued a "proposal for reforming the school system" that was based on motions proposed by Anhui, Fengtian, Yunnan, and Fujian. It invited all provincial education associations to study the proposal and decided that a motion to adopt a new school system should be the first item for consideration at the seventh national education conference the following year and that other motions should only be discussed afterward.

In October 1921 the seventh national education conference was held in Guangzhou, and this motion was the first item on the agenda. In fact, there were eleven different reform motions from various provinces, but the draft put forward by Guangdong province was the most detailed and thorough. Before preparing this draft, Guangdong educators had made a systematic study of various foreign school systems, including those of England, the United States, France, Germany, and Japan, analyzing their strong and weak points. They had also summarized international trends in educational developments in each province, including historical antecedents, the influence of differing customs, and the ways in which foreign systems had had an influence. In terms of social context they had studied social organizations, financial organizations, and political organizations. The scientific aspect of their research had included psychology, physiology, and philosophy. The motion finally put forward was based on a comparative study of other countries' experience and a summary of research on the practical situation in China. It combined both scientific research and the suggestions gathered from participants at the conference.[14]

The original draft from Guangdong was taken as the basis for the motion, and it was revised in light of the other provincial drafts. The final standards of the "School System Motion" were as follows: (1) develop the spirit of education for common people, on the basis of republicanism; (2) adapt to the needs of social evolution; (3) develop individual personality in young people and give them freedom of choice; (4) pay attention to national economic strength; (5) leave plenty of space for flexibility in different regions; and (6) ensure that education can be popularized. The school system was to have three levels: elementary, intermediate, and higher. There was little dispute over how higher education should develop, but there were heated debates over elementary and intermediate education. Finally, it was decided that there should be six years of elementary education, divided into two stages of four and two years; the six years of secondary education were to be divided into two periods of three years each. Divisions of four to two years or two to four years were also tolerated.[15]

It is undeniable that this system was influenced by Dewey's educational ideas and the American education system, but it was also the result of active choices made by Chinese educators and based on their analysis of the realities of their own system. First of all, as Tao Xingzhi stated when commenting on this motion, four kinds of attitude were important in changing the school system: "a readiness to discuss in a modest and open way and investigate various experiments so as to establish a system that takes all needs into account"; "care in studying the experience of foreign education systems and in discerning what is valuable to learn from them, without following them blindly or giving up one's own views"; "a welcoming of the new school system, while still looking back to see if anything important has been lost"; "a recognition of the fact that a new school system is only the first step in a long journey, and many other problems will still need to be resolved."[16] If we take Tao's four points into account in reflecting on the process of establishing a new school system, we can definitely see that they informed the changes very closely. For example, while secondary school was to be six years, there was flexibility about whether this would be three and three, two and four, or four and two, with each region being allowed to make its own decision on the matter. The "Proposal for the Reform of the School system issued by the President" also allowed this flexibility.[17] Later, as it was implemented in each province, there were adaptations to local conditions. Hu Shi made the point that these variations in the secondary school system supported diversity and adaptation to local conditions and broke the old models of absolute conformity.[18] What is most notable is the fact that this was a movement that came from the bottom up and went through intensive discussion by representatives of many provinces. It was thus flexible and adaptable, and some features of it, such as the general structure of six years primary, three years lower secondary, and three years upper secondary, managed to remain in place even after the Soviet-inspired reforms of the 1950s. By contrast, the systems adopted in the late Qing were less suited to Chinese conditions, and their influence was less long lasting.

In addition, we should take note of one issue that has generally been ignored. That is the fact that many people preferred to keep a seven-year primary education rather than accept the reform to six years. For example, Yu Jiaju criticized the six-year primary school in an article published in the *Shishi xinbao* (New Times), putting forward the argument that the Chinese language was too difficult for students to reach the desired objectives in six years.[19] This opinion was widely representative of other educators, who were particularly concerned about a possible drop in standards as a result of shortening the length of primary schooling. Hu Shi made the point, however, that it was possible to reduce the length of schooling without compromising standards. "With the use of the vernacular in teaching, many difficulties can be removed and teaching efficiency can be greatly enhanced."[20] The crux of the matter was reforming pedagogy, in Hu's view. One of the major reforms of the May Fourth period was the movement to the wide use of the vernacular instead of classical Chinese, and this had profound effects on school education at the time. That is why Hu Shi saw this as the foundation for the reform of the elementary education system.

Education for the Common People and the Vernacular Movement

The first objective set for the 1922 education system was to "develop the spirit of education for the common people on the basis of republicanism." In fact, education for the common people was the most fundamental of the education movements in the period from May Fourth to the 1930s and 1940s. It was boosted by the democratic spirit that pervaded the May Fourth Movement and became a wide-reaching and influential tide of ideas. The republic took this as its foundation and the popularization of education was a commonly shared slogan. Most of the educational trends of the time, activities such as popular lecture groups, the work study movement abroad, vocational education, and the stimulus to go from the cities into the villages, were all closely associated with this movement.

There can be no doubt that Western democratic education had some influence in all of this. Yet Chinese educational thinkers and practitioners, facing the realities of their own social development, made their own unique contributions to democratization as they promoted the movement of education for the common people. Tao Xingzhi's ideas about "life education" might be seen as one example.

As one of the promoters of education for the common people, Tao ensured that his theory of life education ran through the whole process of the movement he was engaged in. The theory had three essential elements: life itself is education; society is itself a school; and teaching, learning, and doing are all integrated in one. There can be no doubt that this theory was deeply influenced by Dewey's educational ideas, yet Tao felt that Dewey's ideas implied bringing a part of life and a part of society into the school, like placing a few twigs in a bird cage, and that this would be a kind of artificial life and artificial society. By contrast he advocated the idea that education must be a part of life itself before it can gain the power of a true life education.[21] "Education must run through life itself before it can express the energy to become true life education."[22] While Dewey saw the classroom as a kind of miniature of society, Tao felt that the integration of teaching, learning, and knowing was not simply a method of education but an expression of life itself.[23] He saw the whole of human life as a world of educational activities, in which teaching, learning, and doing were integrated and formal and informal education were intertwined. Tao's idea of life education, in a word, was to impose education on life itself, to allow life to determine education, and to have a true education through living. "The theory of life education is an educational theory through which a semi-colonial and semi-feudal China struggles for freedom and equality," to use Tao's own words.[24] Tao's school, Xiaozhuang, and his system of using "little teachers," and other practices exemplified the efforts of educators of his period to absorb ideas and methods from the international arena and apply them to reforming national education.

The threads of nationalization and internationalization that were woven through the movement of education for the common people were also clearly reflected in the vernacular movement and the concomitant reforms in the teaching of the Chinese language and literature. Lu Xun made the point that "the so-called language and literature of China is not something that belongs to ordinary people." In fact the vast majority of people were illiterate due to the fact that cultural education had not been made widely accessible. "This wretched country in which even the written word is not accessible to people is daily deteriorating. The vernacular newspapers of the late Qing and the literary revolution of the May 4th movement of 1919 were aimed at changing this situation."[25] The reason it was so difficult to make cultural education accessible to common people lay in the difficulty of classical Chinese. For that reason advocacy of the vernacular became a strong trend.

In the Westernization movement and the constitutional reform movement of the late Qing, a great deal of knowledge was imported from the West and widely disseminated, leading to the birth of a new culture and new language, largely associated with the bourgeoisie. The reform of the written language was seen as essential to the task of rejuvenating the nation. The reality of this became evident in the work done to translate both literary and scientific texts, with an emphasis on making the written word conform to the spoken word. Both Western books and ancient Chinese texts were translated into the vernacular, and many new textbooks were prepared in the vernacular. By the end of the Qing there were about fifty kinds of textbooks already in the vernacular, about ten newspapers in different regions, and over one thousand five hundred novels.[26] In spite of this, the teaching of Chinese in primary and secondary schools remained very traditional, with an emphasis on "maintaining the national essence" as well as reading the classics and showing respect to Confucius. Nevertheless, those publications that translated or introduced ideas from abroad had a tremendous impact on education, and gradually the new ideas found their way into the language textbooks.

The May Fourth Movement, which was a kind of continuation of the vernacular movement of the late Qing, promoted a unification of language practices across the country—that is, the movement for a national spoken language (*guoyu*), which could also be described as a common language and is now known as *putonghua*. The vernacular promoted by the May Fourth Movement was in fact the national language. The movement to popularize the national language had a tremendous influence on school education, along with the complementary ideas of literature in the national language and a literary national language. In 1916 certain leading personalities in Beijing established a national language institute, and in 1918 this institute formally promulgated a phonetic syllabary. By 1922 all primary school textbooks were published in the vernacular and the amount of teaching materials available at primary and secondary levels in classical Chinese began to decrease. Thus, the national language movement went ahead with unprecedented momentum.

Teaching in the national language led in turn to reforms in teaching methodology. Western methodologies were introduced and experimented with, including George Herbart's notion of a five-phase approach to teaching, William Kirkpatrick's idea of designing pedagogy around children as the center, and the Dalton system invented by Helen Parkhurst. The national language institute also absorbed many ideas about educational testing and experimentation from the United States and Europe.[27] Nevertheless, it was the system of little teachers, developed by Tao Xingzhi, that shaped the movement for mass literacy most directly. The three most important language texts for the new school system, which were drafted in 1923 by a committee of the National Education Association responsible for course standards for the new school system, promoted methods of self-study, discussion, comparison, and note taking drawn from Tao's work.

The national language education movement, which followed upon earlier vernacular movements, opened up a new debate over popular language and literature in the 1930s. As Chen Zizhan noted at the time, "the contemporary vernacular literature is really something that belongs only to one class, the intellectuals, and it is not what is truly needed by the ordinary masses of people." As a result, the term *popular language* replaced *vernacular,* and language teaching was aimed primarily at "the 80% of the total population made up by peasants, crafts people, industrial workers, vendors and small business people." "Just as the vernacular had to be promoted in the past, to remedy the defects of the old classical language, now the popular language must be promoted, to remedy the defects of the vernacular."[28] Tao Xingzhi explained the concept of the popular language in the following way: "It is the language and literature representing the progressive consciousness of ordinary people . . . it is the language which ordinary people speak, hear, read and write with pleasure."[29] The emphasis here was on reforming a kind of vernacular that had been detached from the life and consciousness of ordinary people and on creating a situation in which speech and writing were linked and in which language was close to people's consciousness and integrated with life itself. We can see that this popular language movement was a kind of continuation of the vernacular and national language movements, and its main purpose was to further popularize the national language and bring it closer to ordinary people.

This effort to popularize language use was naturally beneficial to the popularization of education. It is true that the May Fourth Movement was strongly influenced by Western democratic theories of education, yet, if we consider the fact that language and literature are the vehicles of education, we can see that this was also a movement toward the nationalization of education. The outcomes of the movement had a deep influence on school education in China and on social reform. Tao himself felt that this movement caused Chinese educational reform to be advanced by twenty years, compared to other areas.[30]

The Second Turning Point: The 1980s and 1990s

China's education entered a new period of development in the 1980s and 1990s. After several stormy decades of socialist development, finally the radical approach to educational reform through mass movements was set aside in favor of a more cumulative approach to change, based on the gradual acquisition of experience and a new venture in opening up to the world. As an advocator of modernization, Deng Xiaoping put forward new directions for education, indicating that the cultural conflicts of the past were over and China was ready to absorb all that was of value in the world's experience and adapt it in realistic ways to China's own development. There was a conscious effort to both nationalize and internationalize Chinese education, in order to establish a socialist education system that had Chinese characteristics and to project a new image of China on the world educational stage.

The Reasons for Educational Reform

One of the main issues that faced educational circles in the 1980s was how to treat the educational influences of the Soviet Union. In the 1950s, as a result of the policy of Western countries of isolating China, China chose to adopt the Soviet model for its educational development. Soviet experts and teachers could be found in virtually every province of China and Soviet texts were translated or Soviet materials edited to provide textbooks in nearly every field of knowledge. In the field of education I. Kairov's theories had a particularly strong influence.

Kairov's pedagogy was published in Chinese in 1950, and educational circles studied it systematically and at length, taking it as the basis for educational theory and for standards of criticism. Later, when relations between China and the Soviet Union deteriorated, Kairov's theories were repudiated, and during the Cultural Revolution they were subject to thorough criticism. This criticism had a strong political bias, however, and related academic issues were blurred. Only in the 1980s was there a renewed consideration of Kairov's work, and then the focus of the academic debate was on whether education should be developed along formal academic lines or whether the emphasis should be put on the relation between education and social practice. Objectively, Kairov's pedagogy played a positive role in China's educational development, yet its tendency to overemphasize academicism had resulted in a rigid form of education, divorced from practical life. It was therefore logical that the assessment of Kairov's educational thought and influence in the early 1980s led to a concern about how to give greater importance to the relation between education and social practice.[31]

China's experience of learning from the Soviet Union in education in the 1950s was not a matter of simple imitation, of course. Some international scholars maintain that the Soviet model in China, with its focus on classroom teaching and textbooks, was a typical academic pattern, while Mao's emphasis on links between education and society was a typical revolutionary pattern. China's educational development between the 1950s and the late 1970s was then interpreted as a series of swings between these two patterns.[32] Others see China's educational development as a polymer-type of phenomenon and insist that China began from its own national reality in building a model that intended to combine formal and informal education, a regular school system with work-study schools and part-time schools.[33] It was not a matter of simply copying the Soviet Union without any critical reflection.

The reevaluation of Kairov's pedagogy in the 1980s was conducted at a time when China's education faced new developments. It was less a matter of evaluating one particular theoretical contribution than of reflecting on the whole process of China's experience in introducing and absorbing international influences. Thus, educational circles in China broadened their vision beyond a consideration of Kairov's pedagogy to include Zankov and other Russian theorists while also looking at the educational development experience of other countries. Many books were written or translated on foreign educational systems and theories, with a major focus on such developed regions as Europe, North America, and Japan.[34] These discussions were the herald of reforms in national education, and the main focus of debate over the nature of education in the late 1970s was on how to detach Chinese education from the influence of the Soviet Union. Understanding the relation between education and the forces of production was a main issue, also the related question of whether education was part of the superstructure.[35] The role of education in building socialism in the Chinese context was gradually clarified, through an analysis of China's own historical experience and through comparative studies of the experience of other countries in education and economic development.

In 1983 Deng Xiaoping put forward his famous call that "education should face modernization, the world, and the future." Throughout the rest of 1983 and 1984 there were lively discussions in China concerning the new technological revolution, and a new enthusiasm for reform in educational circles was stimulated. Education was given more importance than ever before, as the primary channel for communicating and mastering modern science and technology. As the policy of making economic development the center point in modernization became firm, education became a priority. The promulgation of the document entitled "Outline of the Reform and Development of China's Education" in February 1993 and the holding of several national education conferences confirmed the strategy of developing the economy through scientific advances and through improving the quality of labor. Thus, throughout the 1980s and 1990s both the theoretical and practical ideas and experiences of other countries were absorbed, as Chinese education went through many changes and reforms.

The reform of higher education was particularly remarkable. Take the structure of the higher education system as an example. In 1980 the Regulations regarding Academic Degrees in the People's Republic of China were formulated and adopted by the State Council. Formal higher education was divided into three levels—short cycle, regular undergraduate, and graduate study—and a reasonable set of structures for higher-level study took form.[36] As for curricular emphasis, the fields of finance and economics, law and political science, as well as a range of applied humanities, were rapidly expanded to meet the needs of economic development. Between 1980 and 1991 the number of graduates in engineering increased by a factor of 3, and in humanities by a factor of 4.5. In finance and economics the increase was by a factor of 51, and in law and political science by a factor of 112.[37]

In curricular development there was a clear breakthrough in terms of getting away from the tendency to extremely narrow specialization under Soviet influence, and many interdisciplinary programs developed. While there had been only two academic levels under the Soviet model, with departments being directly under the central administration of higher institutions, colleges were formed between the department and institution level in the 1980s. The college structure helped to foster cooperation among related subject areas and in some cases nurtured collaboration across the humanities, social sciences, and natural sciences. Many universities of science and technology became more comprehensive in nature, with new departments in the humanities and management science added to the engineering sciences. Moreover, students were required to pay fees, and the old system of centrally mandated job assignments for all graduates was replaced by a system that allowed employers and institutions to enter into negotiations over the placement of graduates. This change was vital in enabling higher education to respond to the needs of social and economic development.

In the transition from a planned economy to a market economy, China's universities gradually clarified their three main tasks: forming human talent, pursuing high-quality scientific research achievements, and offering various kinds of service to society. The tide of economic reform gave impetus to the reform of higher education, and horizontal relations among higher institutions and between them and other social and economic organizations became a kind of flash point of attention. These included collaboration among different types of higher institutions, collaboration across various disciplines and programs, and the development of jointly managed institutions. There were also many collaborations between higher institutions and enterprises, involving scientific and technical cooperation, the joint running of research centers and enterprises, and the establishment of centers for developing research in engineering. The international activities of Chinese higher institutions went beyond sending students to study abroad, to include cooperation in scientific research and even collaboration in managing higher institutions. Particularly notable were the joint programs for graduate education.[38] After the rapid proliferation in the number of higher institutions in the 1980s, the issue of the relative scale and size of universities gained attention in the 1990s. The tendency toward amalgamation among higher institutions in the 1990s might be seen as a logical development arising from the collaborative ties among institutions formed in the 1980s. This tendency became stronger and stronger throughout the 1990s.

These changes in higher education had parallels in other levels of the education systems. Vocational and technical education was given special importance, and its large-scale development led to reforms in the structure of secondary education and became an effective pillar of support for socioeconomic development. Studies of the German dual-track structure of vocational education and close linkages with enterprises and social practice led to a tendency for vocational education to be closely linked to related trades and in many cases to be managed by the trades themselves. Even basic education began to move away from its longtime attachment to an examination-bound model, in which "academic knowledge was of first importance" and "success in climbing the academic ladder took precedence." The new emphasis was on raising the overall quality of the people, and the reforms in education might be seen as a carefully thought out, rational approach that cut through the tides of economic development. They demonstrated how China's education was reforming itself from within through a process of reflection on its evolution and future development.

While priority was given to higher education in the 1980s, there was a shift in emphasis toward the overall education system in the 1990s. The "Outline of the Reform and Development of China's Education," published in 1993, demonstrated a macroscopic conception of the adjustment of the overall education structure. The implementation proposal for this document delineated the task in the following way: "taking nine-year compulsory education as the foundation, run academic upper secondary schooling well, expand vocational and continuing education on a large-scale, and develop higher education appropriately, giving special effort to improving the quality and standards of regular undergraduate education." The implementation proposal demarcated four regions by level of economic development in the country and set standards for the full implementation of nine-year education accordingly, with appropriate guidelines for each region.[39] This change illustrated the shift in emphasis that had taken place from higher education to basic education.

The educational developments of the 1980s were greatly affected by Western economic theories, as it was a period when a number of important works on the economics of education were translated into Chinese.[40] Most important of all was the theory of human capital and the work of the American scholar T. W. Schultz, with its conviction that investment in education would fuel economic growth. This provided a theoretical foundation in China for policies of educational expansion, especially the expansion of higher education. In the 1960s the expansion of higher education in the West and in some developing countries had also been based on this theory, yet the oil crisis of the 1970s had led to reflection on and criticism of aspects of human capital theory.[41]

China should have learned from this lesson, yet the introduction of human capital theory coincided with an enormous enthusiasm for higher education development, and so the lesson went unheeded. The expansion of higher education was far too rapid for the level of economic development, resulting in an oversupply of highly educated professionals relative to the numbers of people with a general cultural education and good technical skills. This was to be expected for an agriculture-based economy as it moved toward fuller industrialization. Yet under the auspices of human capital theory China repeated, in the 1980s, the error other countries had made at an earlier period. In the 1990s China's education has shifted focus, as a result of reflection on its own development experience. Coincidentally, a research report issued by the World Bank in 1995, based on the analysis of educational policies around the world over the previous ten years, made the point that investment in basic education would be likely to have the highest social reward for middle- and lower-income countries and so should be given priority.[42] This was precisely what China had discovered, and it showed how educational developments in China were beginning to repeat patterns already seen earlier in other parts of the world.

The Evolution of the Education System

In 1979 the presidents of four Shanghai universities made an appeal in the *People's Daily* for higher education institutions to have greater autonomy, both in terms of their internal management and their relations with local and national government bodies.[43] There was an enormous response around the country to this appeal. In fact, the problems identified were rooted in the centralized system of administration that had been established in the early 1950s. This system had been challenged in 1958, with some institutions being put under local control. Yet, after the end of the Cultural Revolution, the system of centralized administration had been reinstated, and it had historic links with the national planned economy. As the centrally planned economic system gradually gave way to a market system, the problems of the closed and rigid system of educational administration were increasingly recognized, and there was a widely felt desire for educational system reform. In the 1980s the reform of the economic system gave a direct impetus to the reform of the educational system, which entered the national agenda. During this period educators were very active in researching foreign education systems, and this work was an important backdrop to the first major reform document: the Decision on the Reform of the Education System made by the central Committee of the Chinese Communist Party, promulgated on May 27, 1985.

This document stressed the relation between educational development and social development and set out the main directions for the reform of the educational system. In basic education policies, regulations, and the implementation of educational development were transferred to provincial and local governments. In higher education there were to be three levels of administration—national, provincial (including autonomous regions and municipalities), and urban, in the case of major cities. Higher institutions were assured considerable autonomy, including greater control over their own finances, some flexibility in enrolling students outside of the national plan, as well as control over decisions about teaching content and scientific research. Also, encouragement was given to various kinds of independent social organizations to run schools or colleges. At the secondary level emphasis was placed on technical and vocational education, and several streams of secondary education were fostered.

As a result of this decision, the State Education Commission was established, in place of the Ministry of Education, with responsibility for broad educational policy, and most provinces and municipalities followed suit, establishing provincial and municipal education commissions, charged with carrying out reform in the basic education system. The main approach was one of having schools run on three levels and managed on two levels. That meant that the county managed all senior secondary schools, while junior secondary schools and primary schools were managed by the township, and primary schools were actually run by the villages. Similarly, cities administered schools at the level of the city and the city district. This approach of running schools on three levels was a successful outcome of the educational reform of the 1980s.

In terms of the length of basic education a new direction had been set forth in the 1980s and was stipulated in the "Law of Compulsory Education of the People's Republic of China" issued on April 12, 1986. Here it was stated that "the state supports a nine-year compulsory education system, while provinces, autonomous regions, and municipalities will decide on the pace of implementation in accordance with regional economic and cultural development conditions." After a few years of experience the state made further regulations concerning the implementation of compulsory education: "The state announces the basic education system . . . provinces, autonomous regions and municipalities have autonomy to decide the education system of their locality."[44] As a result of this change, different localities put in place different patterns for basic education, including a six-three system, a five-four system, and a nine-year integrated system. Although the six-three-three system remains common, many provinces and municipalities have adopted a five-four-three system, after Beijing Normal University demonstrated the superiority of this system through experimentation and research.

In comparison with basic education, structural reform in higher education has proceeded much more slowly, in spite of an earlier start. Barriers between higher and lower levels and between institutions under different administrative authorities have been harder to break down.

In the 1990s people's thoughts were once again liberated as a result of Deng Xiaoping's speeches during his southern inspection tour in February 1992, when he put forth a whole series of theories and guidelines for developing socialism with Chinese characteristics. Further to that, the Fourteenth Congress of the Chinese Communist Party convened in October 1992, confirmed the establishment of a socialist market economy, and provided a theoretical basis for the outline of educational reforms, which had been discussed over many years. On February 13, 1993, the Central Committee of the Communist Party and the State Council issued the "Outline of the Reform and Development of China's Education," whose starting point was the evolution of a socialist market economy and which put forward many significant proposals addressing practical problems.[45] In 1994 the State Council issued its own implementation suggestions for the "Outline of the Reform and Development of China's Education," with the principle that compulsory education should be implemented in accordance with the cultural and economic conditions of each region, as discussed earlier.[46] It also put considerable emphasis on developing alternative streams for technical and vocational education, following on primary, lower, and upper secondary schooling, so there would be a suitable balance between vocational and academic educational opportunities and the possibility of flow between the two sectors. Another innovation was opening up opportunities for various social organizations and individuals to run schools while maintaining the government's core responsibility for education. In rural education efforts were made to integrate academic, vocational, and higher education in ways that made possible the integration of science, education, and agricultural development. Generally, both rural and urban education were further improved in the wake of the publication of the "Outline on the Reform and Development of China's Education."

Nevertheless, "higher education poses the most difficult problem in the reform of the overall system of educational administration," a comment made by Party Secretary General Jiang Zemin.[47] Little progress was made in terms of reforming the macroscopic system of higher education administration during the 1980s. The basic reason for this lay in the fact that the system had been organized during the 1950s along the lines of China's six large geographical regions and major industrial sectors that were managed by national-level ministries. There was a lot of duplication of programs among provincial-level institutions and national institutions run by major sectoral ministries, and there were real barriers to cooperation among these institutions. The "Outline for Reform" proposed a system whereby higher institutions should be managed on two levels, national and provincial, but with the main responsibility being at the provincial level. The old system with institutions being completely self-reliant and self-contained, responsible only to the authority that managed them, was to be done away with, and the movement of major management responsibilities to the provincial level was to allow for more effective coordination of the work of different institutions.

One of the main outcomes of this policy was a tendency for institutions with overlapping roles to become affiliated or even amalgamated. Since 1994 many provinces and municipalities have reorganized higher education to achieve greater efficiency. Shanghai provides a good example. Under the planned economy there had been fifty higher institutions, with nineteen belonging to major sectoral ministries and commissions at the national level and fourteen belonging to municipal departments and commissions. These different allegiances had made it extremely difficult for them to achieve any coordination of effort in serving Shanghai's rapidly paced restructuring and urban renewal. In 1994, however, under the impetus of the policies announced in the "Outline of Reform," the Shanghai government put forward the policy of "joint establishment, collaborative establishment, amalgamation and adjustment,"[48] whereby a total reorganization was undertaken. Major national universities such as Fudan, Jiaotong, and Shanghai Foreign Studies University were now jointly managed by the municipal government and the State Education Commission, and numerous local institutions were amalgamated, such as the newly established Shanghai University, involving the merger of four local institutions. In other cases local institutions were amalgamated within national ones. For example, Tongji University absorbed the Shanghai Urban Construction College (belonging to Shanghai Municipality) and the Shanghai Industrial College of Construction Material (belonging to the General Bureau of the State Industry of Construction Material).[49] A parallel case is East China Normal University, a national keypoint university under the State Education Commission, which has recently absorbed a number of local teacher-training institutions, setting a pattern for the integration of general academic education and continuing professional education.

In international practice the relations between central and local government in managing education have been diverse. France and the former Soviet Union have typified centralized patterns of management, while the United States and Canada have been characterized by decentralized patterns. Centralization has some benefits in terms of the implementation of state policies and the ability of national governments to initiate reform, but it has tended to disable local initiative and hinder the adaptation of education to local socio-economic development. Decentralized systems have just the opposite effect. In the 1980s and 1990s China's educational reform was based on a thorough study of the historical experience and trends of other countries and basically adopted the approach of increasing the administrative jurisdiction of provinces and localities and establishing a more appropriate balance of decision-making power at central and provincial levels. This readjustment of the authority structure of central and local governments was seen as suited to the development of the socialist market economy. It should not be seen as an all-out decentralization but, rather, a matter of seeking a pattern suited to China's own national situation, which drew upon a careful study of international experience.

Conclusion

This essay has considered two different periods, which were turning points in the development of China's education, and explored the relations between international influences and a conscious building of national identity. The two periods selected for consideration are only cases or examples, but they can help us reflect on this complex process.

The process of China's education opening up to the outside world in these two periods took place against a historical background of rapid social change, but there were also interesting differences. During the late Qing the approach had been to adopt one unitary model as a means of liberation, while during the 1920s and 1930s the pressures of nationalism caused China to move away from imitating one foreign model and take the experience of other countries selectively as a point of reference. This insistence on eclecticism in what was introduced had the important effect of allowing diverse ideas to be incorporated into the development of the national education system. In the opening up of China's education after 1978, there was a process whereby international experience was taken as a reference point in an overall adjustment of the national system.[50] This is a relatively objective assessment of the situation. Nevertheless, what should be particularly emphasized is that, whether the approach be one of eclecticism or of an overall absorption of external influences, the critical issue is the initial standpoint for considering the needs and possibilities of change.

The situation of the 1920s and 1930s was completely different from that of the late Qing, although educational circles in China in both periods felt that China was behind and the West was strong and that China had to learn from the West. The difference was an insistence on an eclectic approach in the second period. As Hu Shi expressed it, the purpose in introducing Dewey's education theories was to criticize traditional education and also the way in which foreign models had been copied holistically, rather than critically and eclectically, "to awaken the nation's consciousness so that all Chinese would turn their efforts to a fundamental educational reform."[51] The process of selecting diverse elements and integrating them within China's own emerging practice was a kind of expression of the search for national identity and national strength in a situation of cultural conflict between China and the West. It was neither a matter of all-out negation of traditional Chinese culture nor of all-out Westernization. This was because valuable elements of traditional culture and personal practical experience of reform became an ongoing resource within the process itself, a resource that underlay the rhetoric of establishing a new value system based on eclectic foreign influences. This shows clearly that, if there is no self-consciousness, no clear standpoint in the process of national reform, there will be neither the possibility nor the necessity of reform. None of the outward movements, such as the establishment of modern universities, the modern schooling system, and the vernacular movement, could have had this kind of deep influence on Chinese education. Of course, the process of selecting foreign reference points and the emergence of China's own educational model is a worthy subject for research, but of greatest interest is the evolving consciousness of national identity and standpoint. The degree of maturity reached in terms of consciousness really determined the effectiveness of reform efforts. International influences were essential to reform, but they could only be effective once there was a foundation for reform in the people's own national consciousness. Otherwise, there would be a loss of national identity and a sense of confusion over the direction the nation should take.

At the same time, national identity was not simply a matter of the revival of traditions. National traditions could only become a vital source of inspiration in a situation in which international influences were being combined with practical experience in the reform process. Thus, we might say there is a kind of necessity for national identity building and international influence to complement each other, on the basis of a foundation of independent thinking.

If we take this perspective to consider the reforms of the 1980s and 1990s, it is immediately evident that the starting point was very different from that of the 1920s, although there was a similar process of a deepening self-consciousness as the reforms unfolded. By the late twentieth century China had already clearly established a socialist education system having Chinese characteristics. While this system embodied respect for tradition, it was also committed to openness and reform. During the 1990s the development of theories of educational reform and experiments of educational practice at the national level made more and more evident China's increasing maturity and depth of experience in balancing international influence with national identity formation.

If we take a longitudinal view of the two turning points during the century, we can see that these turning points were not merely a matter of an external impact, followed by a response from within. The facts show that the simplistic logic of the dominant culture exerting its power does not enable us to explain or evaluate China's educational experience over the century. Certainly, we cannot underestimate the importance of external cultural influences in China's educational development, but we must also recognize that it was not simply a matter of China progressing from a lower to a higher cultural level. Rather, it was a matter of the creation of a new cultural complex, which drew upon the best of foreign cultures and reached a higher level through a kind of dialectic between universal and particular, an integration of diversity and unity.

China's educational experience also demonstrates the fact that genuine reform development can only take place in a situation in which there is a conscious critical assessment of traditional culture and a discriminatory absorption of external cultural influences. Any reform that does not succeed in stimulating a people's motivation to develop themselves and that is not upheld by some kind of internal impetus to revolution will have difficulty in creating a profound sense of national consciousness and in being able to represent itself effectively in an international milieu.

NOTES

1. This at least was the view of Tao Xingzhi, as expressed in an article, "Zhongguo jianshe xinxuezhi de lishi" (The history of China's new school system), in *Xin Jiaoyu* 4, no. 2 (January 1922): 240.

2. In 1917 Chen Duxiu clearly put forward a slogan that "China's education must learn from the West." See Chen Duxiu, "Xiandai xiyang jiaoyu" (Western education in modern times), *Chen Duxiu wenzhang xuan* (Chen Duxiu's selected papers) (Beijing: Sanlian shudian, 1984), 1:218.

3. Cai Yuanpei, "Beida chengli 25 zhounian jinianhui kaihuici" (The speech at the twenty-fifth anniversary of Beijing University), in Gao Pingshu, ed., *Cai Yuanpei jiaoyu lunzhu xuan* (Cai Yuanpei's selected works on education) (Beijing: Renmin jiaoyu chubanshe, 1991), 449.

4. Cai Yuanpei, "Zhonguo jiaoyu de lishi yu xianzhuang" (The history and status quo of education in China), in Gao, *Cai Yuanpei,* 498.

5. Jiang Menglin and Hu Shi, "Women dui xuesheng de xiwang" (Our expectations in students), in Hu Shi, *Hu Shi xuanji* (Selected works of Hu Shi) (Taibei: Wenxing shudian, 1966), 8:1–10. This article was first published in *Xin Jiaoyu* 2, no. 5 (September 1920).

6. "Qinghua guoxue yanjiuyuan zhangcheng" (The charter of the Qinghua institute of Chinese studies), *Qinghua Zhoukan* 360 (1925).

7. Hu Shi, "Shuyuanzhi shi lue" (A brief history of the classical academy system), *Dongfang zazhi* 21, no. 3 (1924).

8. "Hunan zixiu daxue zuzhi dagang" (The outline of the organization of the Hunan self-study university), *Wusi shiqi de shetuan* (The social organizations during the period of the May Fourth Movement) (Beijing: Sanlian shujian, 1979), 1:75.

9. Ding Gang, "The *Shuyuan* and the Development of Chinese Universities in the Early Twentieth Century," trans. Ningsha Zhong, in Ruth Hayhoe and Julia Pan, eds., *East-West Dialogue in Knowledge and Higher Education* (New York: M. E. Sharpe, 1996), 218–44.

10. Qu Xingui and Tang Liangyan, eds., *Zhongguo jindai jiaoyushi ziliao huibian, xuezhi yanbian* (A collection of historical materials of Chinese education in modern times—evolution of the school system) (Shanghai: Jiaoyu chubanshe, 1991), 291–328.

11. *Dierci zhongguo jiaoyu nianjian* (The second yearbook of China's education), 1948, 256.

12. According to Jiang Weiqiao, he studied many documents of foreign school systems translated by Chinese overseas students, when he began to draft a new school system. He found that most of the foreign school systems had not fit into the Chinese situation. Thus, the new school system of China had to follow the Japanese school system. Considering the phenomenon in the early years of the Republic of China, especially the characteristics and experiences in primary schools, Jiang thought that it would be very appropriate for China to adapt the Japanese school system and add domestic courses. See Jiang Weiqiao, "Minguo jiaoyubu chu she shi zhuangkuang" (The beginning of the Ministry of Education in the Republic of China), in Shu Xincheng, ed., *Jindai zhongguo jiaoyu shiliao* (The historical materials of education in modern China) (Shanghai: Zhonghua shuju, 1928), 4:195–98.

13. "Hunan sheng jiaoyuhui tiyi: gaige xuexiao xitong an" (The motion for the reform of the school system), in *Quanguo jiaoyuhui lianhehui baogao* (The report of the national educational association), (Beijing: Quanguo jiaoyuhui, June 1915).

14. Jin Zengcheng, "Guangdong tichu xuezhi xitong caoan zhi jingguo jiqi chengli" (The proposal and establishment of the school system by Guangdong province), *Jiaoyu*, 4, no. 2 (January 1922): 175–86.

15. "Xuezhi xitong caoan" (The draft of the school system), *Xin Jiaoyu* 4, no. 2 (January 1922): 307–10.

16. Tao Xingzhi, "Women dui xinxuezhi caoan ying chi zhi taidu" (The right attitude toward the drafting of the new school system), *Xin Jiaoyu* 4, no. 2 (January 1922): 127–30.

17. *Xin Jiaoyu* 5, no. 5 (1922): 1032.

18. Liao Shicheng, "Guanyu xinxuezhi de yige jinji wenti" (An urgent issue of the new school system), *Xin Jiaoyu* 5, no. 4 (1922): 187.

19. Qu and Tang, *Zhongguo jindai jiaoyushi ziliao huibian,* 878.

20. Hu Shi, "Guanyu xinxuezhi de ganxiang" (A reflection of the new school system), *Xin Jiaoyu* 4, no. 2 (January 1922): 191.

21. Tao Xingzhi, "Puji xiandai jiaoyu zhi lu" (The approach to the popularization of modern education), *Tao Xingzhi jiaoyu wenxuan* (Beijing: Jiaoyu kexue chubanshe, 1981), 164.

22. Tao, "Shenghuo ji jiaoyu," in *Tao Xingzhi jiaoyu wenxuan,* 1981, 109.

23. Tao, "Xiang Hu jiaoxue taolun hui ji," in *Tao Xingzhi jiaoyu wenxuan,* 1981, 88.

24. Tao, "Tan shenghuo jiaoyu," in *Tao Xingzhi jiaoyu wenxuan,* 1981, 267.

25. Lu Xun, "Qie jieting zawen, zhongguo yuwen de xinsheng" (Essays, the new life of Chinese language and literature), in *Lu Xun zawen xuan* (Selected Essays of Lu Xun) (Shanghai: Shanghai Renmin chubanshe, 1973).

26. Tan Bian, *Wan qing de baihuawen yundong* (The vernacular language movement in the late Qing dynasty) (Wuhan: Hubei renmin chubanshe, 1966).

27. Zhang Longhua et al., eds., *Zhongguo yuwen jiaoyu shigang* (An outline of the history of language and literature education in China) (Changsha: Hunan shifan daxue chubanshe, 1991), 185–92.

28. Chen Zizhan, "Wenyan-baihua-dazhongyu" (Classical style prose–vernacular language–the popular language), in Xuan Haoping, ed., *Dazhong yuwen lunzhan* (The debate over the popular language and literature) (Shanghai: Qizhi shuju, 1935).

29. Tao Xingzhi, "Dazhongyu yundong zhilu" (The way of the popular language movement), in *Tao Xingzhi jiaoyu wenxuan,* 1981, 53–54.

30. Tao, *Tao Xingzhi jiaoyu wenxuan,* 1981, 170.

31. Guo Sheng et al., eds., *Xin zhongguo jiaoyu sishi nian* (Forty years of education in China) (Fuzhou: Fujian jiaoyu chubanshe, 1989), 624–35.

32. Theodore Hsi-en Chen, *Chinese Education since 1949: Academic and Revolutionary Models* (New York: Pergamon Press, 1981).

33. Ronald F. Price, "Convergence or Copying: China and the Soviet Union," in Ruth Hayhoe and Marianne Bastid, eds., *China's Education and Industrialized World* (Armonk, N.Y.: M. E. Sharpe, 1987), 159–60.

34. Guo Sheng et al., *Xin zhongguo jiaoyu sishi nian,* 529–30.

35. Li Kejing, "Guanyu jiaoyu benzhi taolun de qingkuang" (On the nature of education) *Zhongguo shehui kexue* (Social sciences in China) 4 (1980).

36. Two drafts of the regulations of academic degrees were made in the period 1954–57 and in the period 1961–64, but they were not put into practice. The contemporary one was the third one, carried out after 1 January 1981.

37. Liu Fonian et al., eds., *Zhongguo jiaoyu de weilai* (The future of Chinese education) (Hefei: Anhui jiaoyu chubanshe, 1995), 4.

38. Yang Deguang and Jin Xinghuo, eds., *Zhongguo gaodeng jiaoyu gaige de shijian yu fazhan qushi* (The practice and development trends of the higher education reform in China) (Shanghai: Tongji daxue chubanshe, 1990), 176–83, 352–53.

39. Guojia jiaoyu weiyuanhui, ed., *Xin de lichengbei: quanguo jiaoyu gongzuo huiyi wenjian huibian* (A new milestone: a collection of documents of the national educational conference) (Beijing: Jiaoyu kexue chubanshe, 1994), 56.

40. Jin Xibin, *Cong cihou dao chaoqian: 20 shiji renli ziben xueshuo, jiaoyu jingjixue*

(From lagging to leading: the human resources capital theories in the twentieth century, educational economics) (Jinan: Shandong jiaoyu chubanshe, 1995), 333–34.

41. Ibid., 64–65.

42. Education and Social Policy Department, World Bank, *Priorities and Strategies for Education* (New York: World Bank, 1995).

43. *Renmin Ribao*, "Shanghai sisuo daxue fuzeren huyu: gei gaodeng xuexiao yidian zizhuquan" (The presidents of the four universities in Shanghai appeal to the government: giving some autonomy to universities), 6 December 1979.

44. "Zhonghua renmin gongheguo yiwu jiaoyufa shishi xize" (The implementation methods of the compulsory education law of the People's Republic of China), in Bangongting, Guojia jiaoyu weiyuanhui, ed., *Zhongguo jiaoyu gaige he fazhan wenxian xuanbian* (The selected documents of the reform and development of China's education) (Beijing: Renmin jiaoyu chubansh, 1993).

45. Guojia jiaoyu weiyuanhui, *Zhongguo jiaoyu gaige he fazhan wenxian xuanbian*, 63–87.

46. Ibid., 99–120.

47. Ibid., 21.

48. Ibid., 187.

49. The present Tongji University has been formed by the former Tongji University of the State Education Commission, Shanghai Urban Construction College of Shanghai Municipality, and the Shanghai Industrial College of Constructing Materials of the General Bureau of the State Industry of Constructing Materials.

50. Marianne Bastid, "Servitude or Liberation? The Introduction of Foreign Educational Practices and Systems to China from 1840 to the Present," in Ruth Hayhoe and Marianne Bastid, eds., *Industrialized World: Studies in Cultural Transfer* (Armonk, N.Y.: M. E. Sharpe, 1987), 3–20.

51. Jiang Menglin and Hu Shi, "Women duiyu xuesheng de xiwang" in Hu Shi, ed., *Hu Shi xuanji* (Selected works of Hu Shi) (Taipei: Wenxing shudian, 1966), 8:1.

Part 2

State and Society in Chinese Education

Stig Thøgersen

The expansion of modern schooling in twentieth-century China has, to a very large extent, been spurred by visions of education as a key element in the construction of a strong nation-state. For the late Qing reformers education was already an important instrument in the struggle for national survival, and after the 1911 revolution the schooling of the Chinese population, first mainly understood as the elite but later also including the urban poor and the rural masses, was placed close to the top of the national political agenda. The expansion of education accelerated further after 1949, when the Communist government saw education as a prerequisite for economic reconstruction as well as for class-based revolution. In this sense the 1986 law on nine years' compulsory education marked the logical, but probably only preliminary, conclusion of a century-long, state-sponsored drive to educate the Chinese people.

As we are approaching the end of the century, these protracted efforts must be characterized as a quantitative success, with the official enrollment rate for the school-age population running as high as 98.5 percent by 1995.[1] This figure may be somewhat inflated, and basic education is still facing towering problems connected to the low economic priority it is given, to persisting poverty in some regions, to the lack of qualified teachers, and to special conditions in many areas inhabited by non-Han ethnic groups. Yet the general trend up through the century, in spite of all setbacks caused by war, internal turmoil, and mistaken policies, has been that the educational level of the Chinese population has been rising, with more students now attending school for more years than ever before.

This spread of modern education in China has been closely intertwined with the process of state formation. In the nineteenth century, before the Xinzheng reforms, the imperial state played a very limited role in the planning and provision of education, particularly at the elementary level. The remarkable uniformity of curriculum, textbooks, and even teaching methods across differences in time and space in late imperial China was the result of the ideological hegemony of Confucianism and of state control over the civil service examination system, and thereby over social mobility. It was not a matter of active state interventions in the field of education, since state-sponsored schools at the basic level were a drop in the sea compared to schools run by families, lineages, local communities, and private teachers. As the modern Chinese state under Republican and Communist rule gradually penetrated traditional social structures and communities, however, its role inside the expanding education system was strengthened. At the same time the schools contributed significantly to the formation of a citizenry whose norms and values supported the legitimacy of the state.

The nature of the state and the process of state formation, rather than the level of industrialization or urbanization, played the most decisive role in the development of national education systems and the spread of mass education in Europe and the United States, as Andy Green has convincingly demonstrated. According to Green's analysis, "the formation of national [education] systems occurred first and fastest in countries where the process of state formation was most intensive,"[2] especially as a reaction to external military threats, major internal transformations such as civil wars and revolutions, and perceived economic underdevelopment compared to competitor countries. It is therefore not surprising to find a strong link between education and state formation also in twentieth-century China, where all these conditions have been present for longer or shorter periods of time. What is interesting is how the nature of this link changed over time in the specific Chinese context and how different social groups and actors took part in the grand national project of educational expansion.

On the one hand, educational reforms designed by the central authorities deeply influenced basic features of Chinese society. New ideas and concepts introduced through schools and education campaigns challenged well-established social norms in fields as diverse as social hierarchy, gender relations, patterns of authority, health and perceptions of the body, eating habits, child rearing, and career patterns. On the other hand, if we reduce Chinese local communities, families, and individuals to the role of passive objects of a transformation process engineered by shifting central governments, we certainly miss the dynamics of educational change. The Chinese population has often met educational reforms with skepticism or even resistance, sometimes violently, as when angry villagers burned down late Qing "modern schools." More often they tacitly selected and exploited those elements in the reformed school system, which they found useful, twisting the intended content of other components and ignoring the rest. This often left reformers seriously frustrated because policies that looked promising on paper turned out to have unforeseen results. The essays in this section explore, in different ways, these patterns of interaction between state and society during the century-long drive for the expansion of education in China.

The section opens with Zheng Yuan's essay on the changing status of Confucianism in the curriculum during the first half of this century. This topic concerns the explicit moral-political aims of the education system, a terrain where the direct influence of the central state apparatus is evident. Since the first transformation of Confucian academies and charitable schools into modern schools around the turn of the century, every step of educational reform has involved attempts on the part of the state to penetrate society and transform those norms and values that were seen as blocking the way of progress, variously defined. Changing ideologies have been disseminated through the textbooks and "hidden curricula" of Imperial, Republican, and Communist schools, and shifting types of knowledge and terminology have been established as legitimate and advantageous to China's development, while others have been brushed aside or suppressed. The basic assumption, however, that education is a forceful remedy in the efforts to "raise the quality of the population," a term used in present PRC official parlance, has been a constant feature in the ideology of successive regimes. Yuan's essay demonstrates how Confucian orthodoxy during the first half of this century was used by varying political rulers to lend legitimacy to their rule and to counterbalance the diffusion of liberal ideas inside the education system. Yuan also shows us, however, how Cai Yuanpei and other reform-minded intellectuals resisted this type of indoctrination and did their best to ignore it in their daily educational practice.

The following two essays by Glen Peterson and Stig Thøgersen focus on rural China and offer further examples of the interaction between central policies and local responses and of the complexity of the interests involved in the social field of education. Until the establishment of rural production teams in the 1950s, village schools were in many ways outposts of state power in rural society, and even today they represent an important channel of influence for the central authorities. Glen Peterson discusses the rural literacy campaigns of the 1950s and their roots in pre-1949 experiences of reformers inside and outside of the Chinese Communist Party (CCP). Besides giving a detailed and multifaceted account of the strategies and considerations behind CCP policies in this field, his essay also deals with a series of fundamental issues concerning the relationship between education and power. The literacy campaigns of the 1950s were inseparable from the collectivization of agriculture, and the vocabulary taught to the peasants was determined by the demands raised in the socioeconomic process. This leads Peterson to question the empowering effects of the literacy achieved by the participants and to turn our attention to the fact that the literacy campaigns were part of a larger development that bound the peasants physically to their village or production team and mentally to the discursive world of the Party. The essay also shows that, while literacy campaigns certainly are tools and manifestations of social and political control, the qualifications acquired by the learners can also be individually and collectively used in ways that were definitely not intended by the authorities.

Stig Thøgersen looks at the same complex of state, community, and individual interests in rural education from the point of view of one village in Shandong province. The essay's starting point is the feeling among social reformers and revolutionaries throughout the twentieth century that Chinese rural education has been in a state of almost constant crisis because of its inability to provide the villagers with the skills they need to promote social and economic development in the countryside. A closer analysis of the careers of teachers, doctors, artisans, and managers in the village shows that in spite of all attempts at making education "useful" to the rural population schooling has only played a marginal role in the transmission of economically relevant skills. Learning through participation and apprenticeship, on the other hand, which has been widely despised, or at best ignored, by educational reformers throughout the century, has been absolutely essential inside practically all trades. Yet one reason why most families have insisted that their children attend "irrelevant" academic-type schools has been that a superior performance here has been an important selection criterion for attractive positions inside the villages, besides offering the remote possibility of gaining access to a university.

Ningsha Zhong and Ruth Hayhoe discuss the relationship between state and society in yet another field, the governing of Chinese universities. After a discussion of the concept of autonomy in the Chinese context and a historical introduction that, interestingly, brings us back to Cai Yuanpei as a key figure in the discussion of academic freedom in China, Zhong and Hayhoe present a detailed case study of how three universities in Sichuan province have taken advantage of the possibilities of limited self-government offered to them in the post-1978 reform era. The authors find that Chinese universities enjoy a considerable degree of autonomy in some respects. The newly won status of higher education institutions as legal persons makes it possible for them to design their own institutional profiles, make important financial decisions, and conduct a number of reform experiments. The three universities studied here made ample use of this space for maneuver in the highly competitive field of higher education. In this sense Chinese universities have a larger degree of independence from direct state influence than, for example, higher education institutions in Japan. While academic freedom is still limited and the possibility for students and teachers to organize politically is practically nonexistent, this essay shows that Chinese universities have much to say about how they manage their own daily affairs, certainly an important aspect of autonomy.

The final essay by David K. K. Chan and Ka-Ho Mok focuses on the resurgence of private education in the reform era, a trend that is the result of recent policies of decentralization and diversification and which holds great potential significance for state-society relations. The private schools, which can be found at all levels from primary school to university, operate under the title of *minban,* or people-run institutions, a term that was earlier only used to describe second-rate schools run by local communities without much support from the government. The social reality of the new *minban* schools, however, is fundamentally different. Private primary schools are often elite institutions demanding high fees and therefore catering to the needs of the most wealthy social strata, and they can be seen as an effect of, as well as a contribution to, the growing social and interregional inequality in post-Mao China. For this reason their success appears to cause certain worries among political leaders. At the other end of the scale, private universities enjoy less prestige than state-run institutions and are struggling hard to gain the power over certification from the State Education Commission. Chan and Mok further show how this development in the field of education reflects more fundamental changes in the role of the state. They use the term *quasi-marketization* to describe the process taking place in social policy in which market conditions gain influence in areas that used to be governed exclusively by the state.

Through all five essays in this section runs the notion that most of the frictions and tensions in the interface between Chinese state and society that have surfaced during this century are somehow reflected in the history of education. Intimately linked to processes of social reproduction, political and ideological transformation, and economic development the field of education has been and still is a contested site where all players on the political and social scene struggle to implement their visions of China's future.

NOTES

1. State Statistical Bureau, ed., *China Statistical Yearbook 1996* (Beijing: China Statistical Publishing House, 1996), 637.

2. Andy Green, *Education and State Formation: The Rise of Education Systems in England, France and the USA* (Houndsmill and London: Macmillan Press, 1990), 309–10. See also John Boli, *New Citizens for a New Society: The Institutional Origins of Mass Schooling in Sweden* (Oxford: Pergamon Press, 1989).

The Status of Confucianism in Modern Chinese Education, 1901–49: A Curricular Study

Zheng Yuan

During the first half of this century the Qing court, the Republican government in Beijing, and the Nationalist government in Nanjing all made significant strides toward developing modern education.[1] The authorities' attitudes
toward freedom of thought in schools also changed dramatically, however,
during this period. Until the abolition of the civil service examinations and
the promulgation of a modern school system in the early years of this century,
Confucianism, as the official state orthodoxy, had dominated Chinese education for more than two thousand years. The purpose of this essay is to
examine the changing status of Confucianism in modern Chinese education
between 1901 and 1949. More specifically, I intend to scrutinize the curricula
adopted by modern schools under the three successive regimes. I argue that
fluctuations in the status of Confucianism in the curricula can serve as an
indicator of the state's desire to assert political control over education. This
analysis of curricular changes may also contribute to an understanding of a
paradoxical phenomenon, which I call "conservative reform," or "authoritarian modernization."

Before beginning, it may be helpful to offer the following observation.
Since the main aim of this essay is to illuminate official attitudes toward
freedom of thought in education, the main focus is placed on educational
decrees and official curricula. China was a centralized country. All of the
central governments discussed here required that public and private schools
throughout the country follow their regulations. Generally speaking, we may
say that schools were most likely to obey these central directives during the

late Qing period and that they enjoyed the greatest degree of freedom from central regulations during the early years of the Republic (1912–26). Under the Nationalist government that took power in 1927, uniform regulations were well implemented in elementary and secondary education. Some universities and colleges, however, especially those whose chancellors and professors were trained abroad, complied with central regulations in public but ignored them whenever it was possible or desirable to do so. The main feature of higher education during this latter period, as Yeh Wen-hsin has pointed out, was not so much a consensus on cultural beliefs and educational ideals as a concession to the high-handedness of the Nationalist authorities.[2]

The Last Pillar of the Last Monarchy

China's modern school system did not come easily. Beginning with the Opium War of 1840, China was repeatedly defeated by the armed forces of industrialized countries. Although the government launched a "self-strengthening" movement that included the setting up of some Western-style schools, the national crisis only deepened. In the 1890s Liang Qichao and other reform-minded scholars and officials came to a realization that the government had merely created a few foreign language, military, and technical schools, whereas what China needed most were people who understood Western and Chinese politics.[3] In 1898 the young Guangxu emperor was persuaded of this view and launched a reform movement.

Among the reform edicts dealing with the economy, culture, and the military was the June 10 order that the academies (*shuyuan*) in the provincial capitals be converted into modern colleges (*gaodeng xue*); that those in the prefectural capitals become secondary schools (*zhongdeng xue*); and that those in the counties be converted into elementary schools (*xiaoxue*).[4] This was the first time in history that a Chinese government had decided to establish a countrywide modern school system consisting of institutions of higher education, secondary education, and elementary education. The reform movement came to a sudden and unexpected end, however, when the Empress Dowager Cixi, with the help of conservative Manchu officials, deposed the young emperor and resumed her regency. On November 13, 1898, she ordered that the traditional Confucian academies not be converted into modern schools. The program of educational modernization was thus aborted.[5]

After suppressing the reform movement, the Empress Dowager and the conservatives at court placed their hopes on the poor and superstitious peasant militants, the so-called Boxers, whose slogan was "Support the Qing, destroy the foreign." With official encouragement, the Boxers attacked foreign missionaries and legations. When foreign troops invaded to fight the Boxers, the court declared war on the foreign countries. The Chinese army and the Boxers were defeated, however, and the court fled to Xi'an. Again, China was forced to accept a humiliating settlement. Now it was Cixi who decided to launch a reform movement. Soon after the court returned to the capital, an imperial edict was issued in January 1901, ordering high officials to scrutinize Chinese and Western systems and to present reform proposals within two months.

The aim of the reform, however, was to save the authoritarian dynasty from collapse, and therefore it was not allowed to challenge the old ideology, Confucianism, which had been the theoretical basis for China's paternalistic government since Emperor Han Wudi (140–87 B.C.E) chose it as the state orthodoxy. Thus the reform edict stated: "There are principles of morality that are immutable throughout the ages, but no methods of governance that are unchangeable. What are immutable are the three Bonds and the Five Constant Virtues, which are like the sun and the stars shining steadfastly upon the earth. What can be changed is regulation A or regulation B, which is adjustable as strings on a musical instrument." The Three Bonds and the Five Constant Virtues are basic principles in Confucianism. The former are the bond of loyalty on the part of subject to ruler, of filial obedience on the part of son to father, and of submission on the part of wife to husband. The latter are humanity, righteousness, propriety, wisdom, and faithfulness, which Confucians held were human beings' innate virtues. Here propriety meant following the traditional norms, especially respecting and obeying the elders and the superiors. Thus, the imperial edict laid down the guideline of a conservative reform: assimilate foreign practices and technology in order to strengthen the existing authoritarian government. This was in fact the same attitude expressed in the famous slogan of the self-strengthening movement, "Chinese learning for basic principles, western learning for practical uses."[6]

After various proposals were presented to the court, reforms in education, the military, judiciary, and government structure began. In September 1901 the court ordered that all academies be converted into modern schools: those at the provincial capitals into colleges (*da xuetang*), those at the prefectural capitals into secondary schools (*zhong xuetang*), and those in the counties into elementary schools (*xiao xuetang*).[7] This was the same decision that had been promulgated in the 1898 reform edict; even the wording was very similar. This decree marked the formal establishment of a countrywide modern school system in China.

The court stipulated that all modern schools should teach mainly the Confucian *Four Books, Five Classics,* and Confucian ethics while making history, Chinese and foreign politics, science, and technology subsidiary courses. The aim was to equip children with a solid Confucian moral foundation and practical abilities.[8]

In August 1902 the court promulgated detailed regulations for the new schools. One article stated: "Whether the countries of Europe, the United States, or Japan, each country is founded upon its own distinct principles. China is also founded upon its own traditional political beliefs and customs. Anyone at school found guilty on reliable evidence of openly advocating heterodox theories, of violating state laws, and of transgressing against the Confucian moral code, will be either dismissed or punished."[9] On the grounds of tradition and customs, the Qing government persisted in maintaining the status of Confucianism as the unchallengeable orthodoxy and the core of education and resisted foreign liberal and democratic theories. Here people might well ask, "What if the tradition and customs were bad?" The reality was that Confucianism supported imperial autocracy, while Western theories would undermine the court's authority.

The government thus kept a wary eye on Western thought while establishing the Western-style modern school system. Coincidentally, soon after the 1902 school regulations were issued, Chinese students in Japan, influenced by foreign liberal theories, launched a large-scale protest movement. They even sent home propaganda and open letters. As a result, both the school regulations and their author, Minister of Education Zhang Baixi, an ethnic Han Chinese, were fiercely criticized by conservatives, especially Manchu officials.[10] In June 1903 the court ordered a Manchu official Rongqing and the most famous conservative reformer Zhang Zhidong together with Zhang Baixi to revise the school regulations. According to the memorial presenting the revised version to the throne, Zhang Zhidong, the famed formulator of the slogan "Chinese learning for basic principles, western learning for practical uses," played the key role.[11]

The revised regulations were promulgated by the court in January 1904 and were to remain in force until the end of the dynasty. One article stated that, "Recently students are frivolous and arrogant: some openly advocate preposterous ideas and some presumptuously interfere with state affairs." The article went on to cite a saying from Confucius' *Analects:* "A noble man does not consider things outside his position," and then declared "What a student's position requires is to strictly observe school discipline and to be proficient in his studies." Therefore, the article stipulated, all students were forbidden to comment on state affairs; otherwise, they would be punished.[12]

According to the 1904 regulations, institutions of elementary education mainly included lower elementary schools (*chudeng xiao xuetang*), higher elementary schools (*gaodeng xiao xuetang*), lower vocational schools (*chudeng shiye xuetang*), general vocational supplementary schools (*shiye buxi putong xuetang*), and apprentice schools (*yitu xuetang*). Lower elementary schools were for children aged six to eleven. The curriculum consisted of moral self-cultivation (*xiushen*), Confucian classics, Chinese, arithmetic, history, geography, nature, and physical education. Moral self-cultivation was taught two hours a week, with the main content being Confucian ethics. The Confucian classics were taught two hours a day. Together these two courses amounted to 47 percent of the total teaching hours.[13]

Higher elementary schools were for eleven- to fifteen-year-olds. The curriculum included moral self-cultivation, Confucian classics, Chinese, arithmetic, Chinese history, geography, nature, drawing, and physical education. Moral self-cultivation was taught two hours a week and Confucian classics two hours a day. Together they amounted to 39 percent of the total teaching hours. In addition, all lower and higher elementary school pupils were required to spend half an hour each day at school to review by themselves the Confucian classics already taught.[14] The original 1902 regulations, however, had assigned only one hour a day to the teaching of Confucian classics in lower and higher elementary schools.[15] The 1904 regulations also stipulated that foreign languages were not to be taught in lower and higher elementary schools, so that pupils could develop a good command of Chinese language in order to study the Confucian classics well.[16]

In addition to strengthen Confucian moral and political education in regular academic schools, the 1904 regulations also extended to vocational education. Moral self-cultivation was included in the curricula of all lower vocational schools, general vocational supplementary schools, and apprentice schools.[17] These vocational training institutions were aimed at children of poor families, who would study while working or take jobs as laborers after a short period of schooling. Too much teaching of the Confucian classics, which are difficult to understand, would scare these children and their parents away and therefore hinder the government's policy of developing vocational education. Thus, the 1904 regulations did not stipulate how much time should be devoted to moral self-cultivation in vocational schools. In 1907 the government issued more detailed regulations for the apprentice schools, which assigned one hour a week to this course.[18] One hour a week did not seem like much. What was important, however, was that the course maintained the status of Confucianism as the absolutely correct code of behavior that everyone should follow.

According to the 1904 school regulations, institutions of secondary education mainly consisted of secondary schools (*zhong xuetang*), lower normal schools (*chuji shifan xuetang*), and middle vocational schools (*zhongdeng shiye xuetang*). Secondary school education lasted five years, and its curriculum included moral self-cultivation, Confucian classics, Chinese, foreign language, history, geography, mathematics, physics, and chemistry, a total of twelve courses. Moral self-cultivation was taught one hour per week. As in elementary schools, the course in Confucian classics occupied the most important part of the curriculum: nine hours per week. Together these two courses amounted to 28 percent of the total teaching hours. In addition, students were required to spend half an hour each day at school to review by themselves the Confucian classics already taught.[19] The original 1902 regulations, however, had assigned only three hours a week to the teaching of Confucian classics.[20]

Lower normal schools, with a five-year program, were for training students to be elementary school teachers. The curriculum included moral self-cultivation, Confucian classics, Chinese, pedagogy, history, geography, mathematics, physics, chemistry, and penmanship. The number of teaching hours devoted to moral self-cultivation and Confucian classics were the same as in secondary schools, amounting to 28 percent of the total classroom instruction time. Students were also required to spend half an hour each day at school to review by themselves the Confucian classics already taught. One of the articles in the 1904 regulations stated: "Confucius and Mencius were the founding fathers of Chinese education. Teacher-training must strictly follow the instructions of the Confucian classics and elucidate their important meaning, and must not, in the slightest degree, contradict their spirit, and create strange ideas."[21] As in the lower vocational schools, moral self-cultivation was also a mandatory part of the curriculum in the middle vocational schools.[22]

University education under the 1904 school system was made up of three stages: higher preparatory schools (*daxue yubeike / gaodeng xuetang*), the university (*fenke daxue*), and the graduate school (*tongru yuan*). The university, located in the capital, consisted of the colleges of Confucianism (*jingxue ke daxue*), politics and law, arts, medicine, science, agriculture, engineering and business, comprising a total of eight colleges, each with programs of three or four years. In the 1902 school system, the university included seven colleges, with Confucian classics and Neo-Confucianism (*lixue*) as merely two of the departments in the college of arts. Now, however, they became the most important college of the university, consisting of eleven departments teaching Confucian classics and Neo-Confucianism, respectively.[23]

Higher preparatory schools included the one attached to the university (*daxue yubeike*) and those in the provinces (*gaodeng xuetang*, formerly the colleges). They offered three different year-long programs to prepare students to enter the university. One was for those who planned to enter the colleges of Confucianism, politics and law, arts, and business. The curriculum consisted of such courses as ethics (*lunli*), Confucian classics, Chinese, foreign languages, and economics. The second program was intended for those who planned to enter the colleges of science, engineering, and agriculture. The curriculum included ethics, Confucian classics, Chinese, foreign languages, and mathematics. The third program was for those who planned to enter the college of medicine. The curriculum included ethics, Confucian classics, Chinese, foreign languages, and zoology.[24]

The 1902 school regulations had stipulated that the content of the course in ethics consist of not only traditional Chinese ethics but also foreign ethics. It included "the ethical thought of worthies since the Three Dynasties and Hans and Tang times, . . . as well as distinguished foreign personages' sayings and life stories." The 1904 regulations stated, however, that foreign ethics were "different from China's" and stipulated that the course in ethics should teach only Neo-Confucian theories, which the court described as "inheriting the thought of Confucius and Mencius honestly and rigorously." According to the 1902 regulations, students who planned to enter the colleges of politics, arts, and business were to take the courses in ethics and Confucian classics, while those who planned to enter the colleges of sciences, engineering, agriculture, and medicine were to take the course in ethics only. The 1904 regulations, however, required all students in the higher preparatory schools to study both courses. Nobody was exempt from the course in Confucian classics.[25]

In addition to the university and the higher preparatory schools, higher normal schools (*youji shifan xuetang*) and higher vocational schools (*gaodeng shiye xuetang*) were also institutions of higher education in the 1904 school system. Higher normal schools, with a four-year program, trained teachers and administrators for secondary schools and lower normal schools. Total classroom instruction time was about thirty-six hours per week. The courses in ethics and Confucian classics were taught three hours per week in the first year, eight hours per week in the second year, seven hours per week in the third year, and six hours per week in the fourth year. In the higher vocational schools the students were also required to take the course in ethics.[26]

As in past centuries, Confucius was described in the 1904 school regulations as "The Most Holy Former Master" (*zhisheng xianshi*) and "The Sage" (*shengren*). On Confucius' birthday, as well as on the first and the last day of each semester and the first day of each month, teachers and students in all modern schools were required to gather in the auditorium and to *kowtow* (*koutou*) before Confucius' memorial tablet.[27] Confucius was still to be treated as a God, and Confucianism was still the inviolable holy writ.

The Qing court, while recognizing that the traditional Chinese schools and the civil service examinations were out-of-date, was determined not to allow the modernization of education to weaken the traditional orthodoxy. On the contrary, the court hoped to strengthen Confucian education with the modern schools, which offered well-organized and continuous instruction proceeding from the elementary school level to the university level. This was made manifest in the preamble of the 1904 regulations, which stated that after elementary and secondary school education, all students will "have studied ten Confucian classics and understood their basic meaning, more than the graduates of the traditional schools and academies studied and understood in the past. . . . So it is not merely that the sacred classics will never be neglected, but that from now on the studies of Confucian classics will flourish as never before."[28] The preamble went on to make the argument that "the curricula now laid down for various modern schools do not neglect the traditional studies of Confucian classics, of Neo-Confucianism, of Chinese history and of classical literature"; on the contrary, "there are now fixed schedules for teaching and studying, which are much more systematic than the civil service examination candidates studied in the past. These candidates did not have regular teachers, and they often had nobody to teach them. Their teachers usually did not have fixed schedules, and the instruction was inevitably shallow and disordered. . . . Therefore, modern school students will have a better command of the traditional learning which was the main content of the civil service examinations, while the modern schools also teach the new learning which the civil service examination candidates never understood."[29]

Up until this point the traditional civil service examinations had remained in force. From February 1904 to September 1905, however, Japan and Russia fought a war in Northeast China over privileges in China and Korea, while all China could do was watch. Once again, the humiliated country felt how weak it was. The war spurred the Qing court to carry out further reforms. In 1905 the civil service examinations were completely abolished, and the traditional school system that prepared students for the civil service examinations was dismantled.[30] Practical efforts were made to expand the modern school system, while the court also strove hard to maintain the status of Confucianism. In March 1906 the court issued an edict on "The Aims of Education," which included teaching students "to be loyal to the monarch," "to worship Confucius," "to care about public good," "to have a martial spirit," and "to value practical studies" (*zhongjun, zun Kong, shanggong, shangwu, shangshi*). All schools throughout the country were ordered to inscribe these few "aims" on a board and to put them on prominent display as guiding principles.[31]

The 1904 school regulations had made no provision for the education of girls. In March 1907 the Qing court decided to set up government elementary schools for girls (*nüzi xiao xuetang*) and to create lower normal schools for women (*nüzi shifan xuetang*) to train teachers for these elementary schools. As explained by Paul Bailey in this volume, the decision was motivated by anxiety over women's changing status and position in society. Thus, the government proclaimed that "great emphasis has always been placed on feminine ethics throughout all the ages of Chinese history. Prime importance should be attached to this in women's education today, in the hope that female students do not violate the Confucian norm for graceful behaviors and are not contaminated by undisciplined bad habits." The curriculum of elementary schools for girls included moral self-cultivation, Chinese, arithmetic, needlework, and drawing. The curriculum of lower normal schools for women included moral self-cultivation, Chinese, arithmetic, pedagogy, and needlework. Moral self-cultivation, which mainly inculcated Confucian ethics, was the most important course in all of these schools for women and girls.[32]

During the final years of the dynasty the court adjusted some of the school regulations for practical reasons while continuing to insist on the primacy of Confucianism in the curricula and aims of education. Thus, the Ministry of Education reported in 1909 that some secondary school students were more interested in science, while others were interested mainly in arts, and that it was difficult for one to study all subjects well. In May 1909 the government responded to this problem by adopting the German model of splitting secondary school education into two programs. While both continued to teach the original twelve courses, program 1 assigned more time to the teaching of Confucian classics, Chinese, history, and geography, and program 2 assigned more time to the teaching of mathematics, nature, physics, and chemistry. The classroom instruction time for moral self-cultivation remained the same in both programs, while that for Confucian classics increased to ten hours per week in program 1 and decreased to three hours per week in program 2.[33]

A second problem centered on the length of schooling. According to the 1904 regulations, elementary school education lasted as long as nine years. In 1909 the Ministry of Education reported that, although lower elementary schools were popular in cities and towns, very few had been set up in rural areas due to lack of funds and qualified teachers. The court approved the ministry's proposal to allow some lower elementary schools, especially those in rural areas to reduce the program by one or two years. The following year the court rejected this lack of uniformity and ordered that all lower elementary schools should offer a four-year program rather than the original five-year program as stipulated in the 1904 regulations. The number of courses and teaching hours were also reduced. In the first two years the amount of classroom instruction was reduced from thirty hours to twenty-four hours per week, and the course in Confucian classics was omitted. In the third and fourth years classroom instruction was still thirty hours a week, and Confucian classics were taught five hours a week. The amount of time spent on the course in moral self-cultivation remained at two hours per week throughout the four years of lower elementary schooling.[34]

Finally, the court also had to contend with challenges to its notions of curricular orthodoxy. The 1906 "Aims of Education" had made it clear that "worshipping Confucius" also meant "resisting heterodox doctrines," namely Western liberal and democratic theories. Therefore, any viewpoint contradicting Confucianism was not allowed to circulate in schools. In 1909 the Ministry of Education banned a textbook of Chinese that was intended for use in elementary schools for girls because it contained the word *equality,* a concept that contradicted the cardinal Confucian bond of submission on the part of a wife to her husband.[35] The same year the ministry also banned an ethics textbook. This book, translated from Japanese, was inclined toward utilitarianism and included a preface by the famous liberal educator Cai Yuanpei, which criticized the Confucian *Four Books and Five Classics.* The authorities denounced the book as mixing up Western and Chinese ethics and the preface as preposterous.[36]

In its last decade the Qing court was extremely weak. Nonetheless, most officials, including some provincial governors-general who were notoriously powerful both militarily and economically, remained loyal to the dynasty. This continued loyalty in the face of a rapidly deteriorating situation suggests why the court was willing to adjust some of the school regulations for practical reasons but continued to insist on Confucianism as the sole orthodoxy in education. Confucian loyalty was the last pillar of the shaky monarchy.

The Emergence of a Much-Repeated Slogan

The late Qing reforms were both limited and too late. Although the government disliked Western liberal and democratic theories and tried its best to suppress them, some of these theories still managed to circulate in society, gradually eroding the last pillar of Qing rule. In such circumstances resentment on the part of the majority Han ethnic group toward the Manchu court grew steadily after the turn of the century. Finally, the monarchy was overthrown, and a republic was established in January 1912. Intellectuals and officials who had been influenced by Western thought were excited by this development. The first Republican education minister was the liberal educator Cai Yuanpei. He immediately criticized the former Qing dynasty's "Aims of Education" and declared that the compulsion "to worship Confucius goes against freedom of worship." In January 1912 his ministry therefore eliminated the course in Confucian classics in elementary schools, secondary schools, and normal schools (*shifan xuexiao,* formerly the lower normal schools).[37] From July to August the ministry convened a national conference on education, which resulted in the decision to repeal the regulations requiring schools to hold regular rituals for worshiping Confucius.[38]

After much discussion the Ministry of Education promulgated a series of new regulations between September 1912 to August 1913, which established the first school system of the republic. Under the new system institutions of elementary education included lower elementary schools (*chudeng xiaoxue xiao*), higher elementary schools (*gaodeng xiao xuexiao*), lower vocational schools (*yizhong shiye xuexiao*), and vocational supplementary schools (*shiye buxi xuexiao*). The course in Confucian classics disappeared from the curricula of these schools, while the course in moral self-cultivation remained, although its content was now dramatically modernized. The morals course was to "teach the practical elements among the virtues of filial piety and fraternal duty (*xiaoti*), loving relatives (*qinai*) . . . and gradually extend to one's responsibility to society and the country, in order to arouse an enterprising spirit and cultivate love of one's community and the country. . . . Rudimentary knowledge of the legal system of the republic should also be taught."[39] Here "filial piety and fraternal duty" as well as "loving relatives" were vestiges of Confucian ethics, while the requirement to arouse an enterprising spirit and to teach legal knowledge contradicted Confucianism.

Secondary education included secondary schools (*zhong xuexiao*), normal schools (*shifan xuexiao*), and middle vocational schools (*jiazhong shiye xuexiao*). The course in Confucian classics was also eliminated from the curriculum at this level. Moral self-cultivation remained in the teaching schedules of these schools, but its content was changed.[40] Yet, many contemporary sources, including the often-cited *Diyici Zhongguo jiaoyu nianjian* (First China Education Yearbook), as well as many recent scholarly articles claim that the course in Confucian classics was still being taught in the normal schools. If this observation is accurate, how do we explain it? Most of the commonly cited regulations on normal schools, although originally formulated in 1912, were revised in 1916.[41] In the standard curriculum issued in March 1913 for normal schools, there was no course in Confucian classics.[42] The course was reintroduced, however, when the regulations were revised in 1916.

Under the 1912–13 school system higher education included universities (*daxue*), higher normal schools (*gaodeng shifan xuexiao*), and specialized schools (*zhuanmen xuexiao*). It was stipulated that a university should consist of two or more of the seven designated colleges—namely, arts, science, law, business, medicine, agriculture, and engineering. The college of Confucianism was abolished. The philosophy department of the college of arts included two divisions: Chinese philosophy and Western philosophy. Confucianism was taught, together with other schools of thought, in the Chinese philosophy course but only to Chinese philosophy majors, who were also required to study Western philosophy, Indian philosophy, and other philosophies.[43]

After completing the undergraduate course, students had the option of applying for graduate study. Before taking the graduate courses, however, students were encouraged to attend preparatory classes (*yuke*) attached to the universities. The preparatory schools offered three year-long programs similar to those stipulated by the 1904 school regulations. Program 1 was intended to prepare students to enter the colleges of arts, law, and business, while program 2 prepared students for the colleges of science, engineering, agriculture, and the pharmaceutics department of the college of medicine. Program 3 prepared students to enter the therapeutics department of the college of medicine. Ethics was one of the subjects in program 1, but it no longer included Confucian morality.[44] Ethics was also taught in the higher normal schools and in the preparatory program of the schools of law and politics, the latter of which belonged to the category of specialized schools. In the higher normal schools the ethics course consisted of moral philosophy, the history of Western ethics, and the history of Chinese ethics.[45]

Because Confucianism had lost its previous status as state orthodoxy and because there was now no unchallengeable government ideology, Western liberal and democratic theories spread quickly in the schools and through some sections of society. There was, however, a long history of autocracy in China, and the Qing regime itself had suppressed Western thought until its collapse. Therefore, although intellectuals, especially young students, were far more open-minded than their forebears, many of those in power in the new republic remained steeped in Confucianism. President Yuan Shikai had played an important role in the late Qing reforms. Now, having effectively sidelined Sun Yat-sen (Sun Zhongshan), the first president of the republic, he wanted to continue down a path of conservative reform. He first abolished the parliament and then tried unsuccessfully to make himself emperor. What is more interesting for the purposes of this essay is that, in order to achieve his goal, Yuan strove to restore Confucianism to its former orthodox position while at the same time endeavoring to combat liberal and democratic theories emanating from the West.

Like the Qing court before him, the Republican president stressed the differences between China's alleged national essence and foreign cultures, describing the former as "the foundation of the country." "Recently," he said, "scholars detest and reject old learning, and have lost the spirit of independence. . . . It is urgent to make every effort to promote the old learning and develop traditional culture, in order to preserve the spirit of independence and protect the foundation of the country from damage."⁴⁶ It is thought-provoking to note that the slogan "develop traditional culture" (*fazhan guyou wenhua*), which we hear time after time, was first put forward by Yuan Shikai under these circumstances. In January 1915 the president issued his own "Principles of Education," which were similar to those of the Qing dynasty a decade previously. One of the principles he enunciated was "to follow the instructions of Confucius and Mencius" (*fa Kong Meng*). Yuan elaborated on what this meant: "[Confucius] takes 'not offending against superiors and not creating disorders' as the root of humanity. [He] also says, 'A noble man does not consider things outside his position.' "⁴⁷ Obviously, by reviving Confucianism, Yuan Shikai hoped that schools would continue to nurture students to be obedient subjects.

Following Yuan Shikai's instructions, the Ministry of Education had issued an earlier directive in June 1914 stipulating that Confucianism was to be the guiding ideology of textbooks on moral self-cultivation and in the textbooks for teaching Chinese in elementary and secondary schools. Existing textbooks that did not include the teachings of Confucius or contradicted them were to be revised.⁴⁸ Then, when Yuan Shikai promulgated his "Principles of Education" the following year, he personally ordered that the course in Confucian classics be restored into the curricula of elementary and secondary schools and that a University of Confucianism (*jingxue yuan*) be set up in the capital. The Ministry of Education complied by revising the regulations on normal schools in January 1916 and ordered the reintroduction of the course in Confucian classics into the curriculum.⁴⁹

At this point the Qing monarchy had only recently been overthrown, and liberals and democrats still had high hopes for the future. Indeed, their morale was further buoyed by the fact that the central government's political control was not yet tightly established. Open-minded scholars therefore published numerous articles sharply criticizing the reactionary activities of Yuan Shikai and his followers and trumpeting new theories from the West. This was the famous "New Culture Movement" that began around 1915 and later merged with the May Fourth Movement of 1919. The effect of the movement was to make more and more scholars and officials aware of the political uses to which Confucianism had been put in the past and the present. Yuan Shikai died in June 1916. In September his "Principles of Education" were formally annulled. Shortly afterward, all existing government directives aimed at reviving Confucianism in education were also repealed.[50] Educators and students were about to enjoy a rare moment of freedom of thought in Chinese history.

In order to spread their message of cultural renewal, the leaders of the New Culture Movement unfurled the banner of "literary revolution" and advocated the replacement of the classical written language by the northern-based vernacular. Use of the vernacular as a written language subsequently spread rapidly. In April 1920 the Ministry of Education ordered that all textbooks for citizen schools (*guomin xuexiao*, formerly the lower elementary schools) written in the classical language were to be replaced by textbooks in vernacular by the end of 1922.[51] Soon after that, the textbooks for schools at all levels were rewritten in the Beijing-based vernacular formerly known as Mandarin (*guanhua*, literally "official speech") and now renamed as the "national language" (*guoyu*). This was an important event. From then on the spoken and written languages were unified. What students studied was this modern language, and classical written Chinese became a dead language that was out of use and difficult to understand. Naturally, as a result, the Confucian classics, which were written in the classical language, also came to be considered antiques belonging to the past.

Chinese intellectuals' field of vision became progressively broader and broader during the period of the New Culture Movement and the May Fourth Movement. Since the late Qing, Chinese educators had mainly taken Japan as their model. Now Chinese intellectuals would learn directly from the more liberal Western countries, especially the United States. American educators were invited to China. Among them the most influential was the leading educational thinker John Dewey, who spent more than two years in China lecturing in more than ten provinces from 1919–21. The fifth annual conference of the National Education Association was held in October 1919, at which Dewey made an influential speech. Under his influence the conference passed a resolution declaring that "educators should not be required to achieve any kind of 'aims' or to adhere to any theory because this fetters students. No matter what the 'aims' or theory may be, they will create a single mold in education [in which all students are cast.] . . . Therefore, from now on, the so-called 'aims of education' should not be discussed or revised, but rather they should be resolutely abandoned!"[52] It was unprecedented for these representatives of educators throughout the country to announce openly that it was wrong for a government to impose its ideology and political principles on education.

The conference also decided to work out a new school system. After three years of public discussions and debates, the National Education Association's seventh annual conference adopted an American-style school system, which was approved and promulgated by the government in November 1922, replacing the 1912–13 system. Educators also formulated a set of standard curricula in concert with the new school system, which was issued by the Ministry of Education in May 1923 for trial implementation. "Moral self-cultivation" was a concept borrowed from Confucianism, which implied the attitude of "not considering things outside one's position." Now this course in both elementary and secondary schools was revised as "civics" (*gongmin*), a modern concept from the West.[53] Other remaining vestiges of Confucianism also faded, but this would soon prove to be only temporary.

A Traditional Saying Is Revived

The first decade and a half of the Republic, also known as the Beijing government era, saw great progress in culture and the economy overall. Yet the development of democracy was rough, and the political situation remained unstable. Gradually, this led to the destruction of a laissez-faire attitude toward education and the revival of Confucianism. In the southernmost province of Guangdong, the Nationalist Party set up a rival government to counter that of the northern warlords. Helped by the Communist International, the Nationalists reorganized their party and established a centralized Soviet-style party apparatus. In January 1924 they began to "partify" education (*danghua jiaoyu*)—to make education into a political tool of the Party. Obviously, the effect of this policy was to stifle the emerging freedom of thought in schools. Not content with politicizing the content of education, in July 1926 the Nationalist authorities ordered all school staff and students, from government university professors and clerks to private elementary school pupils, to join the Party.[54]

The same month the Nationalist Party launched a Northern Expedition with Chiang Kai-shek (Jiang Jieshi) as the commander in chief and was soon able to conquer several Chinese provinces. In April 1927 Chiang purged the Communists from the Nationalist Party and made Nanjing his capital. The Nationalist Party became the national government. At this time Chiang's power was still contained by opponents within the Party, and the Republican government in Beijing still controlled several provinces. The famed liberal educator Cai Yuanpei was appointed a member of the Educational Administrative Committee in April, and, when the committee was replaced by the Grand Academic Council (*daxue yuan*) in June, Cai was named chair of the council, making him the top official in charge of education. Cai Yuanpei advocated education free of political control and disagreed openly with the policy of partification of education.

Yet the situation was changing. Chiang Kai-shek managed to out-maneuver his opponents within the Party and became the supreme leader of the Nationalist government in early 1928. Heavily influenced by a mixture of Confucian paternalism, Japanese military authoritarianism, and the Soviet concept of party dictatorship, Chiang immediately began to assert control over education. The Nationalist troops conquered Beijing in June 1928 and overthrew the Republican government there. At the August plenary session of the Party's Central Executive Committee, Cai Yuanpei was fiercely criticized for pursuing the independence of education from politics. Realizing that his ideals stood no chance of being implemented, he resigned from the chair of the Grand Academic Council in protest.[55]

The Nationalist authorities formally overturned Cai's educational policy at the Party's Third National Congress held in March 1929. The resolutions of this congress severely criticized Chinese educators for introducing Western theories and charged that education in its present guise "lacked a dominant ideology, only parroting prevalent theories and aping others at every step." As a result, it was "necessary to replace the previous laissez-faire attitude with state educational policies" and to make the Party's official ideology—the Three Principles of the People—the guiding basis for education.[56]

As John King Fairbank has pointed out, the Three Peoples' Principles were only the Nationalist Party's nominal ideology, because they were really a set of goals, more than an ideology.[57] These principles were far from enough to expel the sophisticated Western theories that had crept into Chinese educational thought and practice over the previous two decades. Therefore, Chiang Kai-shek adopted the prominent Nationalist theorist Dai Jitao's advice and resorted to Confucianism, claiming that Confucianism represented the theoretical basis of the Three People's Principles. According to him, these principles had "inherited the ethical thought of Yao, Shun, Yu, Tang, King Wen, King Wu, Duke of Zhou, Confucius, and other ancient sages and raise this thought to a new plane of development. The Three Principles of the People are born of the [Confucian] morality of humanity and righteousness."[58] In this way Confucianism was mixed with the Nationalist Party doctrines and once again became official orthodoxy.

Having overthrown the warlord government based in Beijing, the Nationalists abolished the parliamentary system, announcing that the Party's National Congress would substitute for a parliament.⁵⁹ So it was the party, and not the parliament, that came to decide educational policies in the Nationalist state. Following the Party's Third National Congress, school curricula were revised. Because China was a centralized country and the modern school system had been introduced by the central government from abroad, the government assumed responsibility for laying down the revised curricula for all schools. The promulgation of the 1922 school system, however, had marked the maturation of China's modern school system. Subsequent reforms, including this one, merely adjusted the 1922 system by designating obligatory courses for higher education. More significant was the issuing of a revised detailed curricula for schools at elementary and secondary levels. In August 1929 the Ministry of Education issued a series of course programs and regulations that stipulated that "party doctrines" (*dangyi*) was to become an obligatory course in all elementary schools, secondary schools, and higher educational institutions.⁶⁰ As part of the course content, Confucianism was formally reintroduced into the curriculum.

Meanwhile, during the Beijing government era (1912–27), students had been very active in striving for freedom and democracy. Now the Nationalist authorities also imposed tight restrictions on student activities. In December 1930 Chiang Kai-shek issued a decree that students be forbidden to strike and hold rallies without authorization; otherwise, the government would "punish them as reactionaries." The decree specifically stated that "a student should devote himself/herself exclusively to studies, cultivate the mind, and follow the ancient instruction that '[a noble man does] not consider things outside [his] position.' "⁶¹ It was no coincidence that the Qing court, Yuan Shikai, and Chiang Kai-shek all cited this same saying from Confucius' *Analects*. Their purpose in advocating Confucianism was simply to command the people's obedience: to be loyal to the ruler, to work hard to increase the country's wealth, but not to consider political affairs.

Following the establishment of the Nationalist government in Nanjing in 1927, the 1922 school system was still in force. Under the liberal educator Cai Yuanpei's leadership, there had been a brief trend toward the merger of vocational schools with normal schools and secondary schools. Yet the authoritarian modernizers who assumed power in 1927 did not want people who had acquired vocational and professional knowledge to consider anything beyond their own jobs. After Cai Yuanpei's resignation, the government gave priority to the development of vocational education and teacher training, and in 1932 it decided to separate vocational and normal schools from secondary schools.⁶²

The Ministry of Education accordingly issued a set of new curricula between October 1932 and March 1933. The course in party doctrines was renamed "citizen training" (*gongmin xunlian*) in elementary schools and "civics" (*gongmin*) in secondary, normal, and vocational schools.[63] The course content, however, did not change much. The Ministry of Education stipulated that the goal of the course in citizen training was to "develop traditional Chinese ethics" and to "instill the [traditional] concepts of propriety, righteousness, honesty and shame (*li, yi, lian, chi*)." It was furthermore to teach pupils "to show filial obedience to parents" as well as "to obey the instructions of parents, elders and officials" and "to obey collective decisions."[64] Traditional Chinese ethics emphasized collective discipline. Since China was not a democratic society, in practice this latter goal meant obedience to those in power.

Under the one-party dictatorship the problems of official corruption and inefficiency grew to serious proportions. In the history of imperial China, time after time, authoritarian reformers such as Wang Anshi (1021–86) of the Song dynasty and Zhang Juzheng (1525–82) of the Ming dynasty strove to resolve problems of this kind by strengthening the absolute power of the central government and by tightening control over the thinking of officials and scholars, from among whom officialdom was recruited. Chiang Kai-shek inherited this tradition. He took Western theories of freedom and democracy as obstacles to commanding obedience. In February 1934 Chiang staged a New Life Movement to inculcate Confucian and fascist ideas, in the hope that officials throughout the country would obey the ruler as soldiers obey the commander. The status of Confucianism was further elevated, and the worship of Confucius was formally resumed. In July 1934 the Party's Central Executive Committee stipulated that on Confucius' birthday classes were to be suspended and commemorative assemblies held in all schools. Participants at these assemblies were to bow three times to Confucius' portrait, sing the commemorative anthem for Confucius together with the anthem of the Nationalist Party, and listen to speeches on Confucius' life and thought and on the relationship between Confucianism and the Three Principles of the People.[65] In this way Confucianism was restored to a status of official orthodoxy.

Japan launched a full-scale war of aggression against China in July 1937. During the war Chiang Kai-shek strove to increase his power, further tightening his grip on education and strengthening the inculcation of Confucian values. In April 1938 the provisional National Congress of the Nationalist Party passed a resolution declaring that "the management [of schools] must be very rigid, . . . and all the institutions of secondary and higher education should be managed with military discipline."[66] When giving "instruction" (*xunci*) to the third national conference on education in March 1939, Chiang

Kai-shek ordered that the moral principles of "loyalty, filial obedience, humanity, love, faithfulness, righteousness and peacefulness" be considered the proper standards of conduct for youths and all students and that the traditional virtues of "propriety, righteousness, honesty and a sense of shame" become the motto for the schools throughout the country.[67]

In 1938 the Ministry of Education revised the textbooks for elementary and secondary schools yet again. Chiang Kai-shek ordered that the moral teachings of the Confucian classics *The Spring and Autumn Annals (Chunqiu)* and *The Book of Rites (Liji)* should form the kernel of the textbooks on "citizen training" and "civics."[68] The ministry also issued a revised curriculum for elementary schools in 1942, in which the course in citizen training was renamed "collective training" (*tuanti xunlian*). As pointed out earlier, traditional Chinese ethics emphasized collective discipline and were hostile to individual freedom. The content of this course was in fact barely changed from its earlier version, and the aim of the course was still "to develop traditional Chinese ethics" and "instill the concepts of propriety, righteousness, honesty and shame." Even the Ministry of Education itself admitted that, "although citizen training has been renamed collective training, its goal is almost the same."[69]

Higher education underwent a similar process of curricular revision. From July to November 1938 the Ministry of Education issued a series of lists of obligatory courses for universities and colleges, in which the course in party doctrines was renamed "Three Principles of the People" (*sanmin zhuyi*), while its content remained unchanged. Following Chiang Kai-shek's handwritten instruction, the ministry also promulgated a directive in May 1942 that an obligatory course in ethics (*lunli xue*) be added to the curricula of all higher educational institutions, whose purpose was to instill traditional Chinese morality, mainly Confucian ethical theories.[70]

In March 1943 Chiang Kai-shek published *China's Destiny (Zhongguo zhi mingyun)*, in which Chiang highly praised Confucianism and heavily criticized Western liberal and democratic theories.[71] In April of the same year the government ordered all teachers and students in collegiate and secondary schools to study and discuss this book carefully. Wen Yiduo, a famous professor of the Southwest United University (*Xinan lianhe daxue*), responded with indignation: "Is this really our astute leader's thought? The May Fourth Movement (which fiercely criticized Confucianism and enthusiastically advocated liberal and democratic theories) gave me tremendous inspiration. *China's Destiny* openly declares war against the May Fourth Movement. I just can't bear it!"[72]

Interestingly, in the occupied territories, the Japanese invaders were also vigorously advocating Confucianism under the slogan "Restore traditional Eastern culture and ethics" (on Japanese educational influence in Manchuria, see the essay by Yutaka Otsuka in this volume). In Manchuria the Japanese at first ordered that the course in party doctrines in schools at all levels be temporarily substituted with the teaching of the Confucian *Four Books and Five Classics*. They then formally replaced this practice with a course in moral self-cultivation, which aimed to instill the Confucian virtues of "loyalty, filial piety," "fraternal duty," and so on and which interpreted obedience as the most important moral principle. At the same time, a course in Confucian classics was added to the curricula of secondary and college-level schools. In coastal China, meanwhile, the Japanese ordered students and pupils to study *The Analects, Mencius, The Book of Filial Piety (Xiaojing)*, and *The Three Character Classic (Sanzijing)*.[73]

Japan surrendered in August 1945. During the last years of Nationalist rule on the mainland, Confucianism retained the status it had held during the War of Resistance. In January 1948 the Ministry of Education issued a revised curriculum for elementary schools and again renamed the course in collective training "citizen training." The fourteen virtues instilled in this course included "filial obedience, loyalty [to the ruler] and respectfulness [to elders and superiors], honesty and a sense of shame" as well as "humanity and love, propriety."[74]

Concluding Observations

In this essay I have used the term *conservative reforms* to describe a major theme of curricular reform in China from the late Qing period until the end of the republican era in 1949. In the context of modern China *conservative* denotes the authorities' intention of maintaining or restoring the traditional autocratic form of government. *Reforms* denotes their efforts to introduce modern science, technology, educational systems, and economic practices from foreign countries. This paradoxical joining of political conservatism with reform policies represented a continuation, in the global age, of the traditional authoritarian reform pattern of imperial China, as seen in the efforts of premodern reformers such as Wang Anshi and Zhang Juzheng. As we have seen, to a certain extent political and cultural conservatism and bold reforms were not mutually exclusive. Indeed, I would argue that some features of modernization, including reforms in education, the economy, and the military, are perfectly compatible with autocracy and can even be helpful to the survival of dictatorship.

Any new idea must represent a transcendence of traditional or existing ideas. Creativity is the ability to break through traditions. Yet right up to modern times, almost without exception, there was always an unchallengeable orthodoxy in Chinese classrooms—a solid wall that teachers and students dared not surmount. This impaired the creativity of both students and their teachers. Democracy and liberalism are Western ideas that contradict Chinese traditions. Leaders in the East, who would rule their countries autocratically, often seek to use the notion of an indigenous cultural tradition as a weapon to combat democratic and liberal theories. In the first half of the twentieth century, whenever the Chinese authorities attempted to suppress these ideas, they strove to advocate Confucianism and traditional Chinese culture, of which the Confucian spirit was the core. This is not to say that Confucian thinkers were of evil intention but that some of the basic elements in their theories, such as those that advocate paternalism and require people to concentrate on their moral self-cultivation, have always been exploited by dictators throughout Chinese history.

During the late Qing reforms the court strove hard to suppress Western democratic and liberal theories by continuing to advocate Confucianism. This had profound consequences. When the republic was established, democracy lacked a firm foundation: President Yuan Shikai tried to destroy it, and the politicans and most people were ignorant of it.[75] When Chiang Kai-shek, a Confucian authoritarian educated in traditional and modern schools during the late Qing reforms, learned party dictatorship from the Soviet Union and achieved sufficient military strength to control the country, the congenitally feeble democracy was completely wrecked.

NOTES

I am grateful to Douglas R. Reynolds and Kathy Shen for their helpful comments on earlier versions of this essay. I would also like to thank Qiu Ke and Wang Jianzhong for generously lending me the use of a quiet cottage in which this essay was prepared.

1. The Japanese invasion in 1937 caused a brief interruption, but the development resumed in about one year. See Zheng Yuan, *Zhonghua wenhua tongzhi: xuexiao zhi* (Comprehensive annals on Chinese culture: the school gazetteer) (Shanghai: Shanghai renmin chubanshe, 1997), 226, 271, 304–5.

2. Wen-hsin Yeh, *The Alienated Academy: Culture and Politics in Republican China, 1919–1937* (Cambridge, Mass.: Council on East Asian Studies, Harvard University, 1990), 2–3.

3. Liang Qichao, "Xuexiao yulun," *Yinbingshi heji* (Complete works from the Ice-Drinker's Studio) (Beijing: Zhonghua shuju, 1989), bk. 1, 60–64; Zhu Shoupeng,

comp., *Guangxuchao donghualu* (East gate chronicle of the Guangxu Emperor's reign) (Beijing: Zhonghua shuju, 1958), bk. 4, 61–64.

4. Chen Baochen et al., comps., *Dezong jinghuangdi shilu* (Beijing: Zhonghua shuju, 1987), 420, 504–5.

5. Ibid., 430, 654–55.

6. Chen Baochen et al., *Dezong jinghuangdi shilu*, 476, 273–74. Translated with reference to Douglas R. Reynolds, *China, 1898–1912: The Xinzheng Revolution and Japan* (Cambridge, Mass.: Council on East Asian Studies, Harvard University, 1993), 201.

7. Chen Baochen et al., *Dezong jinghuangdi shilu*, 486, 419–20.

8. Ibid., 486, 419–20.

9. Shu Xincheng, comp., *Zhongguo jindai jiaoyushi ziliao* (Materials on modern Chinese educational history) (Beijing: Renmin jiaoyu chubanshe, 1962), 2:549–50.

10. Zhao Erxun et al., *Qingshi gao* (Draft history of the Qing dynasty) (Beijing: Zhonghua shuju, 1976), 12, 107, 3132. For the student movement in Japan, see Li Xisuo, *Jindai Zhongguo de liuxuesheng* (Modern China's overseas students) (Beijing: Renmin chubanshe, 1987), 154–61.

11. Shu Xincheng, *Zhongguo jindai jiaoyushi ziliao*, 1:197.

12. Ibid., 209.

13. Shu Xincheng, *Zhongguo jindai jiaoyushi ziliao*, 2:420–24.

14. Ibid., 435–39.

15. Shu Xincheng, *Zhongguo jindai jiaoyushi ziliao*, 2:400, 406–9. In the 1902 system primary schools were for children aged about five to nine, lower elementary schools were for nine- to twelve-year-olds, and higher elementary schools were for twelve- to fifteen-year-olds.

16. Shu Xincheng, *Zhongguo jindai jiaoyushi ziliao*, 1:204, 206.

17. Ibid., 2:754–56, 775, 783.

18. Paul Bailey, *Reform the People: Changing Attitudes towards Popular Education in Early 20th Century China* (Edinburgh: Edinburgh University Press, 1990), 112.

19. Shu Xincheng, *Zhongguo jindai jiaoyushi ziliao*, 2:508, 512–14.

20. Ibid., 499.

21. Ibid., 675, 677, 683–86.

22. Ibid., 757–64.

23. Ibid., 551, 578–80.

24. Ibid., 568.

25. Ibid., 539–41, 568–75.

26. Ibid., 692–99, 766–73.

27. Zhao Erxun et al., *Qingshi gao*, 12, 107, 3141.

28. Shu Xincheng, *Zhongguo jindai jiaoyushi ziliao*, 1:203–4.

29. Ibid., 215.

30. See Zheng Yuan, *Zhonghua wenhua tongzhi: xuexiao zhi*, 206.

31. Zhu Shoupeng, *Guangxuchao donghualu*, bk. 5, 5492–96.

32. Shu Xincheng, *Zhongguo jindai jiaoyushi ziliao*, 3:810–15.

33. Ibid., 2:517–25.

34. Liu Jinzao, *Qingchao xu wenxian tongkao* (Shanghai: Shangwu yinshuguan, 1935),

2, 106, 8655; Wu Yanyin et al., *Zuijin sanshiwunian zhi Zhongguo jiaoyu* (Chinese education in the last thirty-five years) (Shanghai: Shangwu yishuguan, 1931), 4, 15.

35. Jiaoyu bu, *Diyici Zhongguo jiaoyu nianjian* (First China Education Yearbook) (Shanghai: Kaiming shudian, 1934, hereafter DYNJ), 5:121.

36. DYNJ, 5:121; Gao Pingshu, comp., *Cai Yuanpei quanji* (Complete works of Cai Yuanpei) (Beijing: Zhonghua shuju, 1984), 1:168–69.

37. Zhongguo dier lishi dangan guan, comp., *Zhonghua Minguo shi dangan ziliao huibian* (Collection of archival materials on Republican Chinese history) (Nanjing: Jiangsu renmin chubanshe, 1981), 2:474–62.

38. Zhou Tiandu, *Cai Yuanpei zhuan* (A biography of Cai Yuanpei) (Beijing: Renmin chubanshe, 1984), 56–57.

39. Shu Xincheng, *Zhongguo jindai jiaoyushi ziliao*, 2:456.

40. Ibid., 535–37, 731–36, 789–94.

41. Jiaoyu bu, comp., *Jiaoyu fagui huibian* (Collection of educational regulations) (Beijing: Jiaoyu bu, 1919), 201. This document is reprinted in Shu Xincheng, *Zhongguo jindai jiaoyushi ziliao*, 710–26.

42. Jiaoyu bu, comp., *Jiaoyu fagui huibian*, 223–90. Reprinted in Shu Xincheng, *Zhongguo jindai jiaoyushi ziliao*, 2:731–36.

43. Shu Xincheng, *Zhongguo jindai jiaoyushi ziliao*, 2:652–53.

44. Ibid., 253.

45. Jiaoyu bu, comp., *Jiaoyu fagui huibian*, 234–46, 381.

46. Shu Xincheng, *Zhongguo jindai jiaoyushi ziliao*, 1:267–68.

47. Ibid., 253.

48. Ibid., 3:1069–71.

49. Ibid., 1:263, 267; 2:710–12.

50. DYNJ, 1:4; 3:308; Wu Yanyin et al., *Zuijin sanshiwunian zhi Zhongguo jiaoyu*, 19.

51. DYNJ, 3:592.

52. Ibid., 1:9.

53. Ibid., 3:190, 422.

54. Ibid., 5:128, 142.

55. Zhou Tiandu, *Cai Yuanpei zhuan*, 277–78; Gao Pingshu, *Cai Yuanpei nianpu* (A chronicle of Cai Yuanpei's life) (Beijing: Zhonghua shuju, 1980), 93.

56. DYNJ, 1:8, 17.

57. John King Fairbank, *China: A New History* (Cambridge, Mass.: Harvard University Press, 1992), 285.

58. Xiong Mingan, *Zhonghua Minguo jiaoyu shi* (A history of education in Republican China) (Chongqing: Chongqing chubanshe, 1990), 122.

59. *Zhongyang ribao*, 4 October 1928.

60. DYNJ, 2:62; 3:142, 191, 422.

61. *Jiaoyu zazhi* 23, no. 1 (1930):175–76.

62. DYNJ, 3:374–75.

63. Ibid., 2:51; 3:192, 423. The ministry did not issue separate curricula for vocational schools at this time but followed the example of the secondary and normal schools. See Guangdong jiaoyu yuekan she, comp., *Zhongyang ji Guangdongshen xianxing*

jiaoyu fagui (Current national and Guangdong provincial regulations on education) (Guangzhou: Guangdong jiaoyu yuekanshe, 1949), 141–66; Jiaoyu bu jiaoyu nianjian bianzuan weiyuanhui, *Dierci Zhongguo jiaoyu nianjian* (Second China education yearbook, hereafter DENJ) (Shanghai: Shangwu yinshu guan, 1948), 1030.

64. DENJ, 217.

65. Jiaoyu bu canshishi, comp., *Jiaoyu faling* (Educational regulations) (Shanghai: Zhonghua shuju, 1947), 108–9.

66. DENJ, 11.

67. Ibid., 81–83.

68. Ibid., 355.

69. Ibid., 210.

70. Ibid., 496–503.

71. Jiang Zhongzheng, *Zhongguo zhi mingyun* (China's destiny) (Chongqing: Zhengzhong shuju, 1942).

72. Zhang Xianwen et al., *Zhonghua Minguo shigang* (An outline history of the Republic of China) (Zhengzhou: Henan renmin chubanshe, 1985), 595; Xiao Di, ed., *Jiachui xiansong zai chuncheng* (Teaching and studying in Kunming) (Kunming: Yunnan renmin chubanshe, 1986), 146–46.

73. Yanan Shishi wenti yanjiuhui, ed., *Riben diguo zhuyi zai Zhongguo lunxianqu* (Japanese imperialism in occupied territories of China) (Shanghai: Shanghai renmin chubanshe, 1958), 226; Shishi wenti yanjiuhui, ed., *Kangzhan zhong de Zhongguo wenhua jiaoyu* (Chinese culture and education in the war of resistance) (Beijing: Zhongguo xiandaishi ziliao bianji weiyuanhui, 1957), 9, 37.

74. DENJ, 208, 215.

75. For an interesting analysis of politicians' ignorance of democracy at this time, see Jin Guantao and Liu Qingfeng, *Kaifang zhong de bianqian* (Changes since the adoption of Open-Door policies) (Hong Kong: Chinese University Press, 1993), 170–74.

Peasant Education and the Reconstruction of Village Society

Glen Peterson

The pursuit of mass literacy for nation building and economic development has been a central theme in the history of reform and revolution in China throughout the twentieth century. Inspired originally by Darwinian fears of national extinction and the accompanying belief that the key to Western strength lay in the "quality"—educational and otherwise—of its citizens, the mass literacy movement that developed after 1900 in China expressed the complicated desire of successive generations of Chinese rulers—from late Qing reformers and warlord modernizers to Guomindang and Communist nation and state builders—to reform and uplift the lower classes. The twentieth century has seen what Charles Hayford terms the emergence of a "broad, continuous three-pronged literacy movement" in China, involving efforts (1) to reform the written and spoken language; (2) to expand and reform the formal school system; and (3) to promote informal or nonschool forms of "social" education.[1] It is this latter aspect of nonformal education, viewed in its post-1949 context that the present essay seeks to address.

More specifically, this essay attempts to examine the social and political construction of literacy campaigns in the Chinese countryside during the critical first decade of the People's Republic. It begins by tracing the Chinese Communist Party's changing conception of the political and economic signifi-cance of literacy and then seeks to show how state educational ideologies were related to major rural societal and political transformations of the 1950s. The theory and practice of peasant literacy education is thus used to shed light on state-society relations as well as on the Communist Party's views of how peasants ought to participate in social and political life. Finally, I also try to understand how villagers themselves received and regarded the education and schools they were offered. The main arguments may be summarized as follows. First, I want to suggest that, contrary to what is often assumed, the early PRC state was not possessed of a consuming interest in mass literacy. Rather, I argue that early 1950s approaches to "peasant education" were heavily conditioned by the Party's wartime experience in popular education, which emphasized political mobilization more than literacy acquisition. Second, I argue that universal literacy did not emerge as a truly urgent priority in the countryside until the mid-1950s, in conjunction with state efforts to collectivize rural society. The great national literacy campaigns of the middle and latter 1950s should therefore be understood within the larger context of an emerging political economy of collectivization and, more particularly, with the state's steadily increasing efforts to limit and control, by means of a host of administrative and fiscal measures, the physical as well as social mobility of rural residents. Third, I also try to show how villagers themselves, far from being passive recipients of state educational aims, were able actively to separate those aspects of the official pedagogy that they regarded as either useful or necessary in economic or political terms from other aspects that they deemed fit to oppose or ignore. Villagers frequently resisted, rebuffed, feigned compliance with, or simply disregarded official literacy prescriptions and instead used literacy for nonstatist and occasionally even antistate purposes. Thus, while this essay underlines the role of the state in constructing social and political realities, it also seeks to expose the gap that frequently existed between state aims and popular thought and action. By viewing state-society relations through the lens of literacy campaigns and popular education, this essay aims to raise anew the vexed question of how scholars can comprehend the phenomenon of state power and its impact upon ordinary citizens and daily life in the People's Republic of China.[2]

Popular Education and the Pursuit of National Wealth and Power: The Early-Twentieth Century Origins of Peasant Education

The concept of peasant education (*nongmin jiaoyu*) adopted by China's post-1949 leaders had a long lineage in modern Chinese educational thought, which predated not only the communist revolution but the Chinese communist movement itself. The roots of the idea stretch back to the earlier concept of social education (*shehui jiaoyu*), borrowed from the Japanese (*shakai kyōiku*) at the turn of the century and introduced into China for the first time in 1902.³ Inspired by elite fears that Japan's industrialization was leading—as it had in the West—to increasing class differentiation and social conflict, social education sought to overcome social fissions by inculcating the importance of social unity, patriotism, and the collective interest. The formal school system was not only of little use in this effort but was regarded by many social and educational critics as a leading destroyer of social unity, the reason being that the formal school system, in its relentless pursuit and training of the very best talent for the nation's modernization, bred a kind of ruthless, competitive individualism as a matter of necessity and ideal. Thus, for politicians and social critics who fretted over the socially divisive costs of modernization— and who for historical and philosophical reasons tended to regard social cohesion as the key to national strength—the preferred means for inculcating the importance of the collective interest involved nonformal educational activities, conducted *outside* the formal school system.

The term *social education* was soon used to describe an enormous variety of officially sponsored activities and institutions whose function was to inform, educate, and persuade citizens. As an example, the social education department set up under the first Republican Ministry of Education in 1912 was responsible for matters ranging from religion and rites to science and art, museums, libraries, and all matters concerning popular ceremonies and customs (*tongsu liyi*) as well as literature, music, theater, recreational facilities, and even zoos and parks.⁴

The avowed aims of social education were embedded in a modernizing discourse that contrasted the ideals of modern citizenship with the backwardness of China's unruly and localistic peasant cultures. As in Japan, social education was from the beginning directed primarily at the lower classes and was closely connected with increasing elite and state efforts to supervise and "reform" popular culture in the name of nation and state building. The intellectual-led and self-proclaimed "New Culture" movement of the 1910s, with its mission of educating and enlightening the "people" (thereby revealing an ironically Confucian predisposition among members of an avowedly iconoclastic movement), served to galvanize what Charles Hayford describes as the emerging "patriotic and modernizing populism."⁵ By the 1920s the intellectual movement to enlighten the lower orders had invented a plethora of new terms describing its mission, including *poor people's education* (*pinmin jiaoyu*), *common people's education* (*pingmin jiaoyu*), and *mass education* (*minzhong jiaoyu*).

By the 1930s social education in its rural reconstructionist form led by James Yen, Tao Xingzhi, and other dedicated reformers also came to represent a powerful critique and alternative to the much criticized formal school system, with its alleged bookish elitism, urban bias, and divorce from the genuine educational needs of China's rural millions. As advocated and practiced by Yen and Tao, social education came to stand for education that was not only patriotic in content but economically useful; schooling that was dedicated to aiding and improving the livelihood of the rural poor, in ways that the formal school system was—as an early 1930s League of Nations educational mission to China report concluded—thoroughly incapable of achieving.[6]

The Chinese Communist Party and Peasant Education before 1949

The Chinese Communist Party also embraced the concept of social education. Social education was formally incorporated into the CCP educational program during the Jiangxi Soviet period. In 1934 the secretary of the Communist Youth League, Kai Feng, described social education in the Jiangxi Soviet as "very broadly defined . . . including not only supplementary adult education and the literacy movement but also clubs, Lenin rooms, dramas, play activities, singing, lectures, libraries, etc."[7] Like the Republican Ministry of Education, the Department of Education in the Jiangxi Soviet included a separate section for social education, with branches that extended to the provincial, county, and district levels. Indeed, one scholar has gone so far as to suggest that, despite official claims to the contrary, the Jiangxi Soviet government accorded greater importance to social education than regular schooling. While the Soviet government lacked the fiscal and bureaucratic resources to implement its stated goal of free universal regular schooling, social education proved to be a cheap and effective means of reaching mass audiences.[8]

Significantly, the term *social education* was dropped from Party vocabulary in the late 1930s in favor of the more overtly class-conscious *worker-peasant education* (*gongnong jiaoyu*). Signaling the birth of Marxist educational thought in China, the rectification was clearly intended to distinguish the CCP theory and practice of education from that of "bourgeois" educators and politicians, whom the Communists now accused of harboring a bourgeois conception of society without social divisions or classes. As noted, the original motive underlying social education (which noncommunist educational reformers continued to uphold) had been to assuage class conflict and promote social harmony. This motive first came under attack by the CCP in 1929, when, as Paul Bailey has pointed out, the Chinese Marxist educator Yang Xianzhang published a polemic denouncing all education that was divorced from radical politics. Yang argued that, without genuine political or social change, education functioned primarily to perpetuate the existing class structure and to reproduce a submissive working class.[9] By contrast, *worker-peasant education* implied educational activity that was both consciously class based and linked to wider social and political struggles.

The revised understanding of popular education formed the basis of subsequent efforts to develop peasant education in the Party's wartime base areas. By 1949 the CCP had developed a wide and imaginative repertoire of popular educational techniques—from literacy classes to public lectures, opera, and traditional storytelling—for mobilizing peasants for "war and production." In the years immediately following the 1949 revolution, however, an important debate ensued over the legacy of the Party's wartime educational experience and, more important, whether that experience should continue to serve as a model for the future.

The Contested Priorities of Early Postrevolutionary Peasant Education

How important a priority was mass literacy in the new state? The question is not easy to answer, in part because in China, as in other large, poor, and nationalistic "Third World" nations, literacy campaigns were endowed with a politico-symbolic and even spiritual significance that went well beyond their pragmatic and often rather limited pedagogical ambitions. The image of communist revolutionaries teaching illiterate peasants how to read in rustic classrooms, by candlelight in the evenings and in open fields during the day, was an integral part of the revolution's mystique. The revolutionaries themselves generously encouraged this mystique, for they were aware that the literacy crusade was one of the communist movement's most powerful legitimating symbols. Understanding the priority accorded to mass literacy is also complicated by the highly ritualized nature of most official discourse on the subject: official pronouncements constantly referred to the historical necessity of universal literacy for "building socialism" (*shehuizhuyi jianshe*), while Lenin's famous dicta that "it is impossible to build a socialist society on a foundation of mass illiteracy" and that "illiterates stood outside politics" were widely and routinely quoted in official China in the 1950s, as was Mao's similar injunction that "New China cannot be established on a foundation of eighty percent illiteracy." Western scholars have by and large taken this devotion on faith.[10] In fact, however, the CCP approach to mass literacy in the early 1950s was considerably more complex—and more divided.

Two contending impulses stimulated peasant education in the new state. One originated in a functionalist conception of literacy's role in fostering bureaucratic and economic rationalization. As Party work shifted from military and political struggle to the complex administrative and management tasks of state building and planned economic development, literacy was increasingly regarded as a functional requisite for local leaders and villagers alike. The second stimulus, however, emanated from the Party's accumulated wartime experience in the North China base areas: it stressed the popular mobilizational uses of education more than literacy's presumed capacity to facilitate bureaucratic rule. In the early 1950s these two impulses collided. It is tempting to attribute the ensuing conflict over educational policy to a split between Communist Party "ideologues," on the one hand, and Ministry of Education "experts," on the other.[11] This interpretation, however, overlooks the full range and complexity of the ideological and political influences that weighed upon the formation of PRC mass education policy.

One of the most significant indicators of this complexity was the appearance in 1949 of renowned classical scholar Ma Xulun as minister of education in the new PRC state. Ma was the preeminent representative of an older generation of classically educated scholars and linguists who became leaders of the post-1949 literacy movement. Born in 1884, Ma was a renowned philologist whose earliest written works predated the 1911 revolution but whose greatest scholarly contribution—a textual criticism of the *Shuowen jiezi*, a first century C.E. analytical dictionary of characters—appeared in 1957. Ma taught Chinese philosophy at Beijing University for nearly two decades between 1916 and 1936, during which time he continued to publish on subjects as varied as the philological study of Zhou dynasty stone drum inscriptions, philosophies of Laozi and Zhuangzi, and modern language reform. As an early supporter of Sun Yat-sen's Revolutionary Alliance, his scholarly interests were combined with an equally long and distinguished career of political activism, serving variously as director of propaganda in the Guomindang's Beijing headquarters, vice minister of education in the Nanjing government, and cofounder of the China Association for the Promotion of Democracy. During the May Fourth Movement he led teachers and university professors on a strike in support of protesting students, yet in the 1920s he emerged as one of the most articulate critics of the *baihua* movement to replace the classical language with a vernacular script.[12]

Where do we locate a person like Ma Xulun in the universe of PRC officialdom? Assuming that his presence was more than simply a tactical device to legitimate Mao's claim that New China was also a "New Democracy" in which noncommunists could and did participate, it is nonetheless clear that Ma does not fit easily into the "expert" category. Indeed, to describe Ma Xulun as an expert in the sense in which that term is normally employed in discussions of Chinese politics—as a modern technocrat—would be seriously to misunderstand Ma's intellectual world and that of many of his contemporaries. Ma represented not modern technocracy but the elite traditions of classical scholarship, at least some of whose post-1911 practitioners and leaders opted to support the communist revolution. Ma's significance for understanding the politics of the PRC literacy movement lies in the unique perspectives and ideas he brought to bear upon the literacy issue. Specifically, Ma brought to the literacy movement an elite classically educated scholar's erudite knowledge and appreciation for the extraordinary historical depth and complexity of the Chinese written language. Surveying China's illiteracy problem from the vantage point of more than a half-century of philological scholarship, Ma was predisposed to reject utopian promises of quick solutions, stressing instead the intricacies of the written culture. He combined a long-term commitment to simplifying the Chinese script in order to make it more accessible (he headed the official committee for the reform of the Chinese written language in the 1950s) with constant reminders to officials and educators of the inherent richness and complexity of the written culture.

Ma made these views clear at the First National Worker-Peasant Education Conference in September 1950 (attended by both Mao and Zhu De). He described the twin goals of worker-peasant education as raising the "cultural level and political level" (*wenhua shuiping he zhengzhi shuiping*) of workers and peasants, in order to "develop and consolidate the people's democratic dictatorship." He also claimed that these twin efforts had a profound economic significance as well, since without them it would be impossible to inculcate the "new laboring attitude and creative spirit" needed to develop the national economy. In order to achieve these goals, he argued, basic literacy instruction must now take precedence over the pre-1949 mobilizational uses of mass education. In fact, Ma was openly critical of the Party's wartime record in raising popular literacy levels, informing delegates that New China had inherited a large corps of peasant cadres with impeccable revolutionary credentials—but with "no education." An official Ministry of Education statement, bearing Ma's imprint, was equally blunt: it claimed that, while mass education in the wartime base areas had been enormously successful in raising peasants' political consciousness and mobilizing them to fight the Japanese invaders, the accomplishments in terms of spreading literacy were simply "not very great." Similarly, Qian Junrui, a senior educational official, asserted that of the three kinds of peasant education promoted in the wartime base areas—political education, technical education, and basic literacy instruction—only the first two were given priority, while literacy education had been deliberately neglected. According to this view, the Party's long years in the wilderness had produced a "guerilla mentality" (*youji xiqi*), which regarded education purely as a mobilizational tool for inciting mass struggle.[13]

Recent scholarship confirms this view of the Party's pre-1949 educational record. Political mobilization among the rural populace was a multimedia enterprise in which visual and oral media predominated over written communications. Benedict Anderson has recently reminded us of the critical role played in twentieth-century revolutions by the advent of radio, which enabled revolutionaries to "bypass" printed media and reach illiterate audiences directly.[14] Long before the dissemination of modern mass communication technologies, however, the Chinese communists were engaged in a creative effort to develop nonliterate means for mobilizing popular support. Indeed, such means became the very hallmark of the "Yanan way" in popular education. Some of these technologies—such as the use of pictorial magazines, cartoons, revolutionary songs, peasant dances, and public announcements—were borrowed from the Soviet Red Army.[15] Others were drawn from the popular culture itself and from a venerable repertoire of traditional elite means for communicating with illiterate village audiences, including the use of woodblock prints, folk songs, storytelling arts (*quyi*), and popular opera. Theater was a particularly crucial vehicle because, as Barbara Ward explained, "it was the popular theater, not books, which disseminated . . . the major part of what ordinary people in the matshed audience knew about the vast complex of Chinese culture and values—both orthodox and heterodox."[16]

It is worth remembering, moreover, that Mao himself was one of the most steadfast advocates of such nonliterate techniques for reaching and mobilizing peasant audiences. Whenever Mao attacked the shortcomings of formal schooling—and this attack represented one of the unswerving continuities in Mao's educational thought, from the New Culture Movement to the Cultural Revolution—it was usually from the perspective of the greater mobilizational efficacy of nonbook learning. "The greatest achievements of the peasant associations," Mao wrote in 1927,

> are always to do with popularizing political propaganda: some simple slogans, picture books, and lectures . . . the results are extremely wide-ranging and rapid . . . Can opening ten thousand law and political science schools succeed in popularizing politics among the peasants, men and women, young and old, in such a short time as the peasant associations have been able to do (using these methods)? . . . I think not.[17]

By the 1940s these ideas had become firmly entrenched in the Party's approach to peasant education. Thus, David Holm, a leading Western student of CCP cultural policies before 1949, writes that "visual and oral media were far more important for mass work than media for which literacy was required."[18] And, according to Helen Chauncey's research, peasant education in the wartime base areas was "stripped of much of its basic pedagogical functions and devoted instead to general political mobilization." Mass education was viewed as "a means of explaining to [peasants] the importance of base area political tasks at any given time" and took as its motto "political understanding first, literacy second."[19]

As noted earlier, beginning in 1950 the Ministry of Education under Ma Xulun's direction attempted to give greater priority to basic literacy instruction. In the end, however, the ministry's first policy statement on "Opening up Peasant Sparetime Education" was an ambiguously worded document that embodied the tension between literacy education and political mobilization. "Now that the country is united," the directive began, peasant spare-time education "ordinarily should take literacy and learning culture as the priority" (*nongmin yeyu jiaoyu yiban de yi shizi xue wenhua weizhu*).[20] Yet it then went on to list the specific conditions under which this new emphasis was to be forsaken and literacy instruction either reduced or even, in certain circumstances, proscribed. Thus, the literacy movement was to commence only in the "old liberated areas" of the country (mainly north China), where land reform had already been carried out and the new state was firmly in control. Even in these areas, however, the emphasis on literacy instruction was to be reduced "on the occasion of major political tasks" (*yuyou zhongda zhengzhi renwu*) and be replaced by "current political affairs education" (*shishi zhengzhi jiaoyu*). As for the "newly liberated areas" and "semi-old base areas" (*banlao qu*), land reform had not yet been carried out and the "struggle against feudalism was just in the process of unfolding." In these areas peasant education was to follow the wartime model of "taking political and current affairs education as the priorty" and of "utilizing every possible method." Only when "peasants demand it and conditions permit" was this to include the basic literacy instruction. In general, the newly liberated areas and semi-old base areas—in other words, the vast part of China—were to embark on a full-scale literacy movement only after the land reform had been successfully carried out.

Ma Xulun had earlier warned education cadres against the impossibility of simply decreeing the abolition of illiteracy, urging instead that illiteracy in China would only be eliminated "gradually" over an extended period. Perhaps reflecting this view, the initial goals of the literacy movement were rather modest. They were also openly elitist in their choice of target group: priority was to be given to village cadres, activists, and youth, while only the first two groups were required to master one thousand characters and to possess a preliminary ability to "read, write and calculate" within three to five years.[21]

China's entry into the Korean War in November 1950 and the ensuing radicalization of domestic politics had an immediate impact on peasant education policy. The Ministry of Education responded by directing village-level winter schools to resume their wartime function of mobilizing peasants for political struggle and called upon local officials to root out any educators who still insisted that "learning culture" was more important than political mobilization.[22] The literacy movement resumed briefly in 1952–53, but it soon came under criticism again, this time for defying the official policy of gradualism. In late 1953 leading officials of the literacy movement were accused of pursuing an "adventurist" line that neglected the difficulty and the necessity of conducting the literacy movement with properly trained teachers, adequate supplies of textbooks, proper school facilities, and the like. This, too, represented an attempt by critics of the wartime guerilla model of peasant education to replace it with a more "regular" (*zhenggui*) system of standardized schools and literacy programs. The net result of all of these developments, however, was that the literacy movement on the whole made little discernible progress throughout the first half of the 1950s.[23]

Collectivization: Literacy Expansion and Social Contraction

The economic, social, and political pressures for literacy rose dramatically following Mao's mid-1955 appeal for rapid collectivization.[24] Within months of Mao's July 1955 speech, which accused local cadres of attempting to restrain popular enthusiasm for collectivization and called for its immediate implementation, the literacy campaign was revived on a national scale with unprecedented fervor. On March 29, 1956, the Central Committee and State Council jointly issued an "anti-illiteracy decree" calling for the elimination of illiteracy in the countryside within five to seven years. Provinces, counties, and townships were instructed to draw up specific plans and timetables for implementing the decree.[25] In the weeks and months that preceded and followed this announcement, Chinese peasants and urban dwellers alike became swept up in the largest and most dramatic literacy campaign in the country's history. The campaign entered a brief lull in 1957, only to be revived with even greater fervor during the Great Leap Forward of 1958–60. Altogether as many as eighty million persons may have received some form of literacy education within the space of four years, from 1956 and 1960, more than at any other period before or since in the history of the People's Republic.

At this point we would do well to reflect on the meaning of the literacy campaign. In recent years scholars in many different disciplines have begun critically to reexamine many of the assumptions that have guided conventional approaches to the study of literacy. Supposedly "scientific" and "objective" definitions like "functional" literacy have been shown to "necessarily be derived from prior assumptions about the nature and functions of literacy in society which, in turn, connect to contestable views on citizens' rights and the good life."[26] When viewed from this perspective, the question of *who* defines literacy becomes critical. As Alexander Woodside writes, literacy conceptions are "normative prescriptions . . . [that] may serve as ruling elites' images of what is possible and desirable with respect to the way they and the social classes below them will participate in economic and social life."[27] If we accept this view, then it becomes clear that a particular concept of literacy represents "a political and even moral abstraction beyond the reach of empirical data."[28] Prescribed definitions of literacy are ideological statements.

Understanding how China's leaders conceived of the meaning of *literacy* among the rural population therefore requires understanding the purposes— social, economic, and political—they expected literacy to serve in the new political economy. The literacy objectives prescribed in 1956 were closely connected to the political and economic objectives of collectivization. The anti-illiteracy decree defined literacy among peasants as mastery of fifteen hundred characters plus the ability to comprehend popular (*tongsu*) books and newspapers, write simple notes and keep basic accounts, and perform simple calculations using the abacus. The 1956 literacy definition of fifteen hundred characters was more ambitious than the thousand-character goal adopted by the Political Affairs Council in 1950 and reaffirmed in 1953 but less so than the three thousand–character definition adopted by the Jiangxi Soviet in the 1930s. Perhaps more significant, it was also substantially less than the minimum four thousand–character standard required of senior primary school graduates in the 1950s. Most important, unlike literacy education for regular schoolgoers, the purpose of which was to initiate students into the world of academic learning and prepare them to climb the school ladder, peasant literacy instruction was terminal in nature. It was to be based upon the principles of "integrating the practical" (*lianxi shiji*) and of "learning in order to apply" (*xue yi zhi yong*) and was to proceed "from [that which is] close to [that which is] far [*you jin ji yuan*]"—meaning that local production-related knowledge was to be given greatest priority.[29]

Starting in the mid-1950s, peasant literacy training emphasized the inculcation of local economic competencies and the importance of being a rural production team worker, along with a rudimentary instruction on the state structure and official ideology. These goals were spelled out in late 1955 by Lin Handa, secretary-general of the National Anti-Illiteracy Association. As a former schoolteacher who had spent three years in Colorado before 1949 studying for a doctorate in education, Lin became the first head of the worker-peasant education division within the Ministry of Education in 1950. He subsequently played a leading role in virtually all of the major state bodies for literacy and mass education, becoming vice chair of the Anti-Illiteracy Work Committee in 1952, vice minister of education from 1954 to 1957, and a prominent member of the Committee for Reform of the Chinese Written Language.[30] Lin's 1955 sharply worded, incisive analysis of the literacy campaign's purpose stands as one of the crucial, and hitherto largely overlooked, official statements in the history of the PRC literacy movement.[31]

Starting from the premise that "what should be taught" was a sociopolitical question as well as a pedagogical issue, Lin launched a blistering attack on the traditional method of literacy instruction involving the memorization of a prescribed number of individual (*danzi*) unrelated characters. This type of literacy training led, in Lin's view, to the creation of artificial numeric standards of literacy, which failed to take into account that reading and writing were above all social activities. He then went on to assail the traditional educational philosophy on which it was based, which held that "the purpose of eliminating literacy is simply to be able to recognize characters, and the purpose of being able to recognize characters is to enable one to *study*" (emph. added). In Lin's view nothing was more detrimental to the state's purpose of spreading literacy in the countryside than the persistence of the traditional notion that the purpose of becoming literate was to enter the world of academic learning. It explained why the "best" students in village literacy classes—the ones who attended regularly, did not come late, and scored highest—were not the cadres, activists, and members of the village labor force whom the state had intended as the chief targets of the literacy campaign but were, rather (Lin noted with obvious chagrin), "young girls and old village women." The reason why young girls and old women had so regrettably become the best students was because others were too busy to attend classes that only taught students how to recognize characters and were unconcerned with the practical purposes of reading and writing. Similarly, Lin argued that the reason why workers were making more rapid literacy progress than peasants was because workers followed the experience of the Soviet Union in striving for ways to use literacy to improve technology and production, while in the countryside the reason why "activists are not as good as the masses" and "men are not as good as women" was because literacy training was still divorced from daily needs.[32]

The solution, in Lin's view, was to integrate village literacy instruction more closely with the bureaucratic-economic requirements of collectivization. Lin followed Mao in proposing a three-tiered model of basic literacy training for peasants.[33] Subsequently enshrined in the 1956 anti–illiteracy decree, it remained the official foundation for rural literacy instruction throughout the collective era. Literacy instruction was to begin with mastery of several hundred characters related to the daily practices of collective living. This included such activities as the reading and recording of work points, labor assignments, accounts, and receipts as well as learning to read and write the characters for local persons and places, names of local institutions such as the production team, brigade, and supply and marketing cooperative, and names of local crops, farm implements, and the like. The second-level primer would consist of an additional several hundred characters of vocabulary centered on county institutions, including the names of county-level administrative and political organs and place and personal names. Finally, the third-level primer was to consist of three to four hundred characters of vocabulary related to the province and center, including the state structure, official ideology, and major state personalities.[34]

All of this suggests the need for a degree of caution when considering the "empowering" effects of literacy in the Chinese countryside after the mid-1950s. Vivienne Shue and others have described how the institutional reorganizations of Chinese agriculture in the 1950s added up to an "encystment" of rural communities, a paradoxical turning inward in economic and social terms even as the village's links with the state became unprecedentedly more direct.[35] The official ideology of peasant literacy embodied in the three-tier literacy model contributed to this process of encystment through its attempt to foster localized economic competence and solidary bonds among local communities, together with a limited incorporation into the world beyond the production team on terms and in ways determined by the state. Literacy expansion was accompanied by a process of social contraction, in which the boundaries of villagers' economic and social existence shrank to a historic minimum.[36] If this were indeed the case, then, far from empowering Chinese peasants, the 1950s literacy drive may merely have made possible the opposite: the historically unprecedented entrapment of rural production team members within bureaucratic webs of communication and control.

But how well did it work? Any attempt to evaluate the effectiveness of this entrapment must begin with the observation that Chinese leaders themselves have repeatedly been disappointed by the failure of literacy campaigns to achieve their stated objectives. Inadequate fiscal resources; lack of trained teachers; shortages of textbooks, paper, and writing utensils; not to mention bureaucratic wrangles, local cadre "commandism," and bureaucratic inertia—the literacy campaign was compromised by a host of difficulties, large and small.[37]

In addition to bureaucratic obstacles and institutional bottlenecks, there is also the question of popular responses to the literacy campaign. It is significant that the anti-illiteracy decree created a new, officially stigmatized social category of "culturally blind" (*wenmang*) persons. Whereas illiteracy was traditionally an anonymous feature of village society, those who could not read or write now suddenly found themselves members of an officially labeled outcast group to be pitied, cajoled, and compelled into learning. The literacy campaign spawned enormous social and political pressures for villagers to "cast off their blindness" (*tuomang*).[38] The stigmatization of illiterates furthermore lent an inquisitorial tone to the literacy campaign that was reminiscent of earlier Soviet literacy campaigns. Krupskaya's own dramatic description of the tensions that accompanied a typical literacy campaign meeting in the Soviet Union could just as easily apply to China: "In the front rows sit the liquidators (of illiteracy), the organizers of the campaign and the *aktiv*. . . . At the back and on the side, crowded shoulder to shoulder, stand the masses who are to be taught—tense, motionless, listening. . . . They are waiting, tensely waiting: What does it mean? Is it serious, or is it just talk?"[39] As Sheila Fitzpatrick points out, Soviet illiteracy "liquidators" seemed "constantly on the brink of treating the village as occupied territory and its illiterate population as the enemy."[40] China's literacy campaign organizers copied directly the militarist strategy and vocabulary of the Soviet campaign. Just as the Soviet Komsomol (Youth League) spoke of raising a "cultural army" to "attack" illiterates, Youth League members in China were the "advance troops" (*xianjun*) of the literacy campaign, conducting propaganda work and procuring study benches, desks, and lamp oil, while literacy instructors were described as "anti-illiteracy assault troops" (*saomang dui*), based in anti-illiteracy "command posts" (*zhihui bu*) spread across the country.

Popular resistance to the literacy campaign was widespread and common. Many peasants apparently regarded memorizing characters as a difficult and time-consuming task with few immediate rewards. In the heat of the collectivization campaign, when local cadres were constantly pressuring team member for production increases, the thought of spending evenings or lunch breaks in the fields learning characters was often greeted with dismay, if not open resistance. Peasants were frequently said to be of the opinion that "taking part in the cooperative movement is like riding a train but participating in a literacy class is like riding an ox cart"; while others were skeptical of the campaign's aims: "a hen fed in the morning can't lay eggs by afternoon."[41]

The official view was that collectivization would stimulate popular demand for literacy. But in Guangdong many parents actually withdrew their children from school so they could join the newly formed production teams, a phenomenon that led to mass drop-outs in some parts of the province.[42]

Villagers were not the only ones to resist; local officials were sometimes equally adept at deflecting campaign demands. Local cadre resistance appears to have often been motivated by concern that literacy work interfered with production. Farming yielded immediate tangible results, whereas the fruits of literacy work were less obvious, took longer to achieve, and were difficult, if not impossible, to quantify. This, combined with the fact that local officials were far more likely to be castigated by their superiors for failing to meet production quotas than for failing to meet literacy targets, meant that literacy efforts often took a backseat to agricultural production in the scheme of local priorities. Contemporary accounts of the literacy campaign complain of several "deviationist" tendencies, including a belief that literacy work was "neither here nor there" (*ke you, ke wu*); a tendency to regard literacy work as simply a quota-filling exercise; and, at the extreme, local efforts to ban literacy classes entirely, on grounds that they represented an unjustified diversion of scarce economic and labor resources.[43] Besides such open expressions of defiance, opposition frequently also took the form of feigned compliance, passive evasion, and other "everyday forms of peasant resistance."[44]

It would be wrong, of course, to assume from this description that villagers were simply *not interested* in becoming literate; on the contrary, a variety of compelling motives existed for actively participating in the literacy movement, ranging from the desire to learn and gain access to the vast storehouse of written culture to more instrumental reasons. For villagers the leap from private family farming to bureaucratic collectivism entailed participating on a daily basis in a new literate world revolving around work points (*gongfen*), task lists, team ledgers, receipts, accounts, promissory notes, personal records, permission slips, and other written practices associated with the collective economy. From the state's point of view, these written practices represented concrete expressions of "building socialism" in the countryside. From the point of view of villagers–turned–production team members, however, mastering this "work point literacy" may have meant nothing more than the acquisition of a necessary set of "survival skills" for coping in the new collectivized rural order.[45] Such survival skills, moreover, were not limited to work point–related matters alone. They also entailed mastery of a new political vocabulary as well. Michael Schoenhals has recently demonstrated the extent to which formalized language has formed an integral aspect of political power in China since 1949. The PRC state strove through an administered system of formalized language to construct a formal discourse for describing social reality, one that would be far more effective in regulating public expression than outright censorship.[46] The literacy campaign served as the state's vehicle for inculcating this formalized language of revolution among non-schoolgoers.

Mastering the state language was an act of political survival but could also be an expression of political ambition. In China, as elsewhere, the state language was never truly hegemonic in a Gramscian sense. Its deployment by citizens is perhaps best understood as a linguistically based political skill— mastered, manipulated, and wielded for advantage in certain social and political circumstances. We get a sense of the ambiguous power of this state language from Gu Hua's novel *A Small Town Called Hibiscus,* in which Gu describes an unpopular village cadre fond of uttering phrases like *Marxism-Leninism* and *class struggle,* which "pour(ed) from her lips . . . for hours at a stretch . . . as if she had been to a college to learn revolutionary terminology." Gu's subtle message captures the curious combination of alert respect and contained mockery that characterized popular attitudes toward the state language.[47]

Finally, we ought to be cautious about attributing too much power to the state in its effort to limit and control the popular uses of literacy. Literacy, it must be conceded, is not a socially and politically neutral "technology of the intellect" but a form of social practice whose meaning and significance derives from the particular institutions and social structures in which it is embedded. As one scholar has recently noted, literacy training that is limited to "a very restricted range of printed materials, especially instructions, labels, signs, application forms . . . [and other] types of communication whose function is to . . . institutionalize existing social arrangements" might well have the net effect of "domesticat[ing] and subordinat[ing] the previously illiterate person further rather than . . . increas[ing] his or her autonomy and social standing."[48] And yet there is much evidence to suggest that Chinese peasants, having acquired basic reading and writing abilities, frequently used their newfound skills for nonstate or even antistate purposes. John Burns has shown how in the 1960s peasants occasionally used "big character posters" and other forms of written expression to expose the wrongdoings of local cadres, while recent research by Kevin O'Brien and Lianjiang Li demonstrates that the use of such written complaints (*gaozhuang*) was on the rise in the 1990s.[49] A quick glance at "street literature" sold at roadside book stalls in contemporary Chinese cities also reveals the continuing lack of fit between the official discourse and popular written culture, the latter of which now embraces everything from "pornography" (variously defined) and modern science fiction to traditional hand-copied, mimeographed, and, more recently, formally published *fengshui* manuals.[50] Finally, the tradition of the written word providing access to the supernatural appears to be alive and well in rural China today, if recent reports of emperor worship, glyphomancy, and circulation of magical texts are any indication.[51]

The use of the written word to expose official fallacies, to defy orthodoxy, and even to challenge the state's very moral and political legitimacy: all of this suggests that literacy is more socially and politically neutral than state leaders may have believed or hoped. The mass literacy project of the Maoist era cannot be understood apart from the state's larger political project of creating a new class of peasants–turned–production team members who were bound legally and permanently to their collectives and whose primary state-imposed economic obligation was to produce agricultural surpluses for China's rapidly industrializing cities. State-sponsored "work point literacy" contributed— along with ration cards, official residency status, and other forms of bureaucratic control—to the socialist state's "pinning down" of the Chinese peasantry to the land during the Mao era. We ought to be careful, however, to distinguish these larger—and largely state-intended—institutional consequences from the more personal ones.

NOTES

1. Charles W. Hayford, "Literacy Movements in Modern China," in Robert F. Arnove and Harvey J. Graff, eds, *National Literacy Campaigns: Historical and Comparative Perspectives* (New York: Plenum Press, 1987), 155.

2. For a thoughtful consideration of the various issues involved in this debate, see Vivienne Shue, "Powers of State, Paradoxes of Dominion: China 1949–1979," in Kenneth Lieberthal et al., *Perspectives on China: Four Anniversaries* (Armonk, N.Y.: M. E. Sharpe, 1991), 205–25.

3. The following paragraphs are heavily indebted to Paul Bailey, *Reform the People: Changing Attitudes towards Popular Education in Early Twentieth Century China* (Vancouver: University of British Columbia Press, 1990), 3, 69–71, 142–44, 191, 193, 263–64.

4. Bailey, *Reform the People,* 143–44.

5. Hayford, "Literacy Movements in Modern China," 153–61, esp. 156; Bailey, *Reform the People.*

6. For a trenchant critique of the formal school system during the republican era, see *The League of Nations Mission of Educational Experts: The Reorganization of Education in China* (Paris: League of Nations Institute of Intellectual Cooperation, 1932). On the rural reconstruction movement, see Charles W. Hayford, *To the People: James Yen and Village China* (New York: Columbia University Press, 1990).

7. Cited in Wang Hsueh-wen, "A Study of Chinese Communist Education during the Kiangsi Period," pt. 3, *Issues and Studies* 4, no. 9 (June 1973): 68. (Translation slightly modified).

8. Wang Hsueh-wen, "A Study of Chinese Communist Education during the Kiangsi Period," pt. 1, *Issues and Studies* 4, no. 7 (April 1973): 67.

9. Bailey, *Reform the People,* 266. See also Alexander Woodside, "Problems of Education in the Chinese and Vietnamese Revolutions," *Pacific Affairs* 49, no. 4 (Winter 1976–77): 650.

10. Glen Peterson, "State Literacy Ideologies and the Transformation of Rural China," *Australian Journal of Chinese Affairs* 32 (July 1994): 99.

11. See, for example, *Vilma Seeberg, Literacy in China: The Effects of the National Development Context and Policy on Literacy Levels, 1949–1979* (Bochum: Brockmeyer, 1990), 55–62. Seeberg refers to a constant alternation in PRC literacy policy between what she calls "Maoist Radicalism" (defined as a "mass politicization approach" to education led by the Communist Party) and a more pragmatic "manpower needs"–based approach, or "Moderate Policy," emanating from the Ministry of Education.

12. Ma served as minister of higher education after the ministry was divided in 1952 and was also vice chair of the Culture and Education Committee of the Government Affairs Council, forerunner of the State Council. For a detailed biography of Ma's life and contributions, see Jinyang xuekan xuekan bianji bu, comp., *Zhongguo xiandai shehui kexuejia zhuanlue* (Biographical sketches of contemporary Chinese social scientists), 10 vols. (Taiyuan: Shanxi renmin chubanshe, 1983), 2:10–31. See also Donald W. Klein and Ann B. Clark, eds., *Biographical dictionary of Chinese Communism, 1921–1965,* 2 vols. (Cambridge, Mass.: Harvard University Press, 1971), 1:465–68.

13. Ma Xulun, "Guanyu diyici quanguo gongnong jiaoyu huiyi de baogao" (Report concerning the first all-China worker-peasant education conference), in Zhonghua renmin gongheguo jiaoyubu gongnong jiaoyusi, ed., *Gongnong jiaoyu wenxian huibian* (nongmin jiaoyu) (Compendium of documents on worker-peasant education [peasant education]) (Beijing: N.p. 1979), 13. See also "Ma Xulun buzhang zai diyici quanguo gongnong jiaoyu huiyi shang de kaimu ci" (Minister Ma Xulun's opening speech to the first all-China worker-peasant education conference), in *Gongnong jiaoyu wenxian huibian* (nongmin jiaoyu), 6. See also Zhongguo jiaoyu nianjian bianji bu, ed., *Zhongguo jiaoyu nianjian, 1949–1984* (Chinese educational yearbook, 1949–1984) (Beijing: Zhongguo dabaike quanshu chubanshe, 1984), 575; and Qian Junrui, "Wei tigao gongnong de wenhua shuiping manzu gongnong ganbu de wenhua yaoqiu er fendou" (Strive to raise the cultural level of workers and peasants and satisfy the cultural needs of worker-peasant cadres), *Renmin jiaoyu* 3, no. 1 (May 1951): 12–16.

14. Benedict Anderson, *Imagined Communities: Reflections on the Origin and Spread of Nationalism,* rev. ed. (New York and London: Verso, 1991), 54 n. 28.

15. David Holm, *Art and Ideology in Revolutionary China* (Oxford: Clarendon University Press, 1991), 221–69.

16. Barbara Ward, "Regional Operas and Their Audiences: Evidence from Hong Kong," in David Johnson, Andrew J. Nathan, and Evelyn S. Rawski, eds., *Popular Culture in Late Imperial China* (Berkeley: University of California Press, 1985), 187. Since Song times local magistrates had propagated agricultural techniques using cartoons posted on *yamen* walls. Public poster campaigns were the favored means of local gentry seeking to defame Christian missionaries in the late nineteenth century. See Evelyn Sakakida Rawski, *Education and Popular Literacy in Ch'ing China* (Ann Arbor: University of Michigan Press, 1979), 15; and Paul Cohen, *China and Christianity: The*

Missionary Movement and the Growth of Chinese Antiforeignism, 1860–1870 (Cambridge, Mass.: Harvard University Press, 1963). On Party efforts to co-opt traditional storytelling arts, see Chang-Tai Hung, "Re-educating a Blind Storyteller: Han Qixiang and the Chinese Communist Storytelling Campaign," *Modern China* 19, no. 4 (October 1993): 395–426.

17. From Mao's 1927 "Report on the Investigation into the Peasant Movement in Hunan," reprinted in "Xuexi he guanche Mao zhuxi de jiaoyu sixiang: wei jinian zhongguo gongchang dang de sanshi zhounian er zuo" (Study and implement Chairman Mao's educational thought: commemorating the thirtieth anniversary of the Chinese Communist Party), *Guangdong jiaoyu yu wenhua* 3, no. 4 (August 1951): 1–7.

18. Holm, *Art and Ideology*, 21. See also Chang-tai Hung, *War and Popular Culture: Resistance in Modern China, 1937–45* (Berkeley: University of California Press, 1994), 221–69; and Peter J. Seybolt, "The Yenan Revolution in Mass Education," *China Quarterly* 48 (1971): 641–69.

19. Helen R. Chauncey, *Schoolhouse Politicians: Locality and State during the Chinese Republic* (Honolulu: University of Hawaii Press, 1992), 191.

20. Ma Xulun, "Guanyu diyici quanguo gongnong jiaoyu huiyi"; "Ma Xulun buzhang zai diyici quanguo gongnong jiaoyu huiyi." See also "Jiaoyubu guanyu kaizhan nongmin yeyu jiaoyu de zhishi" (Ministry of Education directive on opening up peasant sparetime education), 14 December 1950, reprinted in *Zhongguo jiaoyu nianjian*, 895.

21. "Jiaoyu bu guanyu kaizhan nongmin yeyu jiaoyu de zhishi."

22. See "Jiaoyubu guanyu jiaqiang jinnian dongxue zhengzhi shishi jiaoyu de zhishi" (Ministry of Education directive on strengthening political and contemporary affairs education in this year's winter schools), in *Gongnong jiaoyu wenxian huibian* (nongmin jiaoyu), 23–24; and, in the same source, "Jiaoyubu guanyu jiaqiang nongmin yeyu jiaoyu zhong kangmei yuanchao shishi jiaoyu de zhishi" (Ministry of Education directive on strengthening education on the facts of the Resist America Support Korea campaign in worker-peasant sparetime education), 19–20.

23. These events are discussed more fully in chapter 2 of my book *The Power of Words: Literacy and Revolution in South China, 1949–1995* (Vancouver: University of British Columbia, 1997).

24. Mao's appeal for immediate collectivization was delivered in a speech to a meeting of provincial and regional bosses in Beijing in July 1955. The speech appears to have stunned members of the central committee, who had just recently reaffirmed the need for a gradualist approach. The level of astonishment—and opposition—to Mao's unilateral reversal of this policy is suggested by the fact that the Party's leading cadre journal for policy studies, *Xuexi* (Study), subsequently published two full issues without even mentioning Mao's speech. The full text, with accompanying editorials in support, was finally published three months later in the October issue, once the supremacy of Mao's view had been fully established. See *Xuexi* 11 (October 1955), the entire issue of which is devoted to the subject.

25. "Zhonggong zhongyang, guowuyuan guanyu saochu wenmang de jeuding" (Chinese Communist Party Central Committee, State Council decision concerning the elimination of illiteracy), 29 March 1956, reprinted in *Zhongguo jiaoyu nianjian*, 895–97.

26. Kenneth Levine, *The Social Context of Literacy* (London: Routledge and Kegan Paul, 1986), 41. Levine's book belongs to a burgeoning revisionist literature on the

social and political context of literacy, which is multidisciplinary and spans a wide range of time periods and national histories. See also Brian V. Street, *Literacy in Theory and Practice* (Cambridge and New York: Cambridge University Press, 1984); and Harvey J. Graff, ed., *Literacy and Social Development in the West: A Reader* (Cambridge and New York: Cambridge University Press, 1981).

27. Alexander Woodside, "Real and Imagined Continuities in the Chinese Struggle for Literacy" (paper presented to the UCLA Education in China Workshop, February 1989), 11.

28. Hayford, "Literacy Movements," 168.

29. The campaign was to be directed at villagers aged fourteen to fifty years and was to be completed among 70 percent of this age group within five to seven years. See "Zhonggong zhongyang, guowuyuan guanyu saochu wenmang," 896.

30. Jinyang xuekan bianji bu, eds., *Zhongguo xiandai shehui kexuejia zhuanlue,* 4:159–68.

31. The speech was published in two parts: "Wei shehui zhuyi jianshe kaizhan saomang gongzuo" (Open up anti-illiteracy work for socialist construction), *Wenhui-bao,* pt. 1, 2 November 1955; pt. 2, 3 November 1955, reprinted in *Union Research Institute* L0364 42222.

32. Lin, "Wei shehui zhuyi jianshe kaizhan saomang gongzuo," p. 1.

33. Lin Handa, "Wei shehui zhuyi kaizhan saomang gongzuo," pt. 2. The idea appears to have originated with Mao, after he observed the experiences of a Shang-dong collective in establishing "workpoint recording classes" (*jigong xuexi ban*) for team members. See Zhonggong zhongyang bangong ting, ed., *Zhongguo nongcun de shehui zhuyi gaochao: xuanben* (Socialist high tide in China's villages: selections) (Beijing: Renmin chubanshe, 1956), 362–64.

34. An estimated thirteen to eighteen months of continuous spare-time study was required to complete the three primers (equivalent to fifteen hundred characters in total). See Lin Handa, "Wei shehui zhuyi kaizhan saomang gongzuo," pt. 2. See also Hu Yaobang, "Guanyu nongcun saochu wenmang gongzuo" (Concerning anti-illiteracy work in the villages), *Renmin ribao,* 16 November 1955, in *Union Research Institute* L0364 42222.

35. Vivienne Shue, *The Reach of the State: Sketches of the Chinese Body Politic* (Stanford: Stanford University Press, 1988), 132–33.

36. In terms of both geographic and social mobility the "liberated" Chinese peasant was much less free than his or her forebears in the freewheeling societies of the late imperial and republican eras. The late imperial state was able to regulate social mobility to a degree through the manipulation of examination quotas and by the very social appeal of the examination system itself. But, in a society with a thriving free market in land and extraordinary population pressures, it was largely powerless to control the increasing geographic mobility of its subjects: witness the spectacular internal and external peasant migrations of the late imperial period, to the exasperation of Qing emperors.

37. Peterson, *Power of Words,* chap. 6.

38. On the social construction of deviance and the use of labels, see Howard S. Becker, *The Outsiders: Studies in the Sociology of Deviance* (New York: Free Press, 1973).

39. As quoted in Sheila Fitzpatrick, *Education and Social Mobility in the Soviet Union, 1921–1934* (Cambridge: Cambridge University Press, 1979), 162.

40. Fitzpatrick, *Education and Social Mobility in the Soviet Union*, 162.

41. "Zenyang jiasu saochu nongcun wenmang gongzuo" (How to speed up anti-illiteracy work in the villages), *Guangming ribao*, 28 November 1955, in *Union Research Institute* Lo364, 42222; *Zhongguo nongcun de shehui zhuyi gaochao: xuanben*, 365.

42. Lin Liming, "Guanyu dangqian jiaoyu gongzuo zhong de jige wenti" (Some problems concerning peasant educational work), *Guangdong jiaoyu*, 10 April 1956, 6.

43. "Jiji xuexi he dali guanche guanyu saochu wenmang de jueding" (Enthusiastically study and thoroughly implement the decision concerning eliminating illiteracy), *Renmin jiaoyu* 4 (1956): 6; "Zuodao shengchan, saomang liang buwu" (Accomplish production and eliminate illiteracy, miss neither). *Guangming ribao*, 4 December 1955, in *Union Research Institute* Lo364 4222.

44. On "everyday forms of resistance," see James C. Scott, *Weapons of the Weak: Everyday Forms of Peasant Resistance* (New Haven: Yale University Press, 1985).

45. The notion of literacy as a set of "survival skills" for coping in a changed sociopolitical order is drawn from Ben Eklof's important study of the growth of Russian peasant education, *Russian Peasant Schools: Officialdom, Village Culture, and Popular Pedagogy, 1861–1941* (Berkeley: University of California Press, 1986).

46. Michael Schoenhals, *Doing Things with Words in Chinese Politics: Five Studies* (Berkeley: Institute of East Asian Studies, University of California, Berkeley, 1992).

47. Gu Hua, *A Small Town Called Hibiscus*, trans. Gladys Yang (Beijing: Panda Books, 1983), 109. On the social uses of state language in the PRC, see also Perry Link, *Evening Chats in Beijing: Probing China's Predicament* (New York: W. W. Norton, 1992), 173–91. On the use of revolutionary language in the French Revolution, see Lynn Hunt, *Politics, Culture and Class in the French Revolution* (Berkeley: University of California Press, 1984), 19–26.

48. Levine, *Social Context of Literacy*, 41.

49. John P. Burns, "Political Participation of Peasants in China," in Victor C. Falkenheim, ed., *Citizens and Groups in Contemporary China* (Ann Arbor: Center for Chinese Studies, 1987); and *Political Participation in Rural China* (Berkeley: University of California Press, 1988), esp. 148–51. For the recent situation, see Kevin J. O'Brien and Lianjiang Li, "The Politics of Lodging Complaints in Rural China," *China Quarterly* 143 (September 1995): 756–83.

50. For a telling survey of some of this literature, see Perry Link, "Fiction and the Reading Public in Guangzhou and Other Chinese Cities, 1979–1980," in Jeffrey C. Kinkley, ed., *After Mao: Chinese Literature and Society* (Cambridge, Mass.: Council on East Asian Studies, Harvard University, 1985), 221–74. On the recent surging popularity of the *fengshui* tradition, see Ole Brun, "The Fengshui Resurgence in China: Conflicting Cosmologies between State and Peasantry," *China Journal* Issue 36 (July 1996): 47–65.

51. See, for example, Ann S. Anagnost, "The Beginning and End of an Emperor," *Modern China* 11, no. 2 (April 1985): 147–76; and "Politics and Magic," *Modern China* 13 no. 1 (January 1987): 40–61.

Learning in Lijiazhuang: Education, Skills, and Careers in Twentieth-Century Rural China

Stig Thøgersen

Almost since the introduction of new schools around the turn of the century and with great force since the late 1920s, critics have found Chinese rural education to be in a state of crisis rooted in a basic incongruity between the needs of the villages, on the one hand, and what the schools have had to offer, on the other. The school system has repeatedly been accused of having an urban bias and of being geared mainly to select a minority for further education, while the losers who had to remain in or return to their villages learned little that could help them improve their rural communities. This opinion has been couched in many different ways by educational reformers such as Tao Xingzhi, Yan Yangchu (James Yen), Liang Shuming, and Mao Zedong.[1] In official Chinese post-Mao phraseology it has typically been expressed as in the following statement by Zhang Jian, a senior figure in the PRC education establishment:

> At the moment village education is, in varying degrees, separated from the realities of agricultural production, from peasant life, and from village reconstruction, and there is a serious tendency to one-sidedly emphasize promotion rates. This has led to a situation where the quality of the labourers is very low, which seriously obstructs the development of the productive forces.[2]

The contradiction between education for rural development and education for social selection that Zhang refers to is a universal problem in late-developing countries.³ Neither the high degree of awareness about the issue in China nor the numerous attempts to solve it throughout the twentieth century seem to have fundamentally changed the situation: according to Chinese educators from the State Education Commission down to village schoolteachers, the school system's contribution to rural development is still not satisfactory.

In the eyes of the critics from the 1920s to the present day the school system itself has to bear most of the blame for this miserable state of affairs, but the users of the system, the rural students and their parents, have also repeatedly been accused of obstructing a more healthy development, because they have insisted on gaining access to the higher levels of education, and thereby to residence in a city, without considering their own "objective needs" for more practical qualifications. Whenever one of the many attempts to make education relevant to the rural areas has failed, from the "village schools" (*cunxue*) of the Rural Reconstruction Movement in the 1930s to the agricultural middle schools of the late 1950s to the participation in productive work of the 1970s to the vocational and agricultural middle schools of the 1980s and 1990s, a particular rural mentality has been seen as one of the main culprits.

Behind this critique of rural schooling, significantly consistent across political and historical borderlines, lie two assumptions. One is that it is the task of the school system not only to provide rural students with general qualifications but also to prepare them specifically for their future work roles. This assumption has had wide-ranging consequences for the Chinese discourse on practical learning in spite of the fact that the role of rural schools in spreading vocational skills has probably been marginal even during the most radical periods.

The other assumption is that the academic aspirations of rural children and youths are irrational, "backward," "feudal," "traditional," or whatever label successive generations of progressive Chinese reformers have put on ideas and attitudes with which they did not sympathize. In their view academic-type schooling could only be said to have paid off in the few cases in which it actually enhanced the student's social and geographic mobility, when, in other words, education enabled the student to escape village life. Academic achievements beyond literacy and numeracy were thus considered irrelevant, or at least incomplete, to people who would live the rest of their lives as "peasants."

The aim of this essay is to reexamine these consistent "problems" in twentieth-century Chinese rural education from the perspective of a single village and its inhabitants rather than from that of the reformers and policy makers. The essay will address two main sets of questions: First, how has the historical relation developed up through the twentieth-century between general and vocational schooling, on the one hand, and the qualifications that people in China's villages need to perform their roles in rural economic life, on the other? If it is true that the rural school system has been incapable of transmitting relevant knowledge and skills, how have people in China's villages actually acquired their qualifications? Second, which social experiences and strategies lie behind the persistent preference of rural families for general, academic-type schools? What has been the role of such formal schooling in forming the careers and working lives of the vast majority of Chinese villagers who did not advance to postsecondary education and urban jobs?

The discussion of these two related issues is part of a larger study of the educational history of Zouping county in Shandong, where I have conducted about ninety life history interviews on learning experiences and their consequences for people's lives and careers.[4] The starting point will be Lijiazhuang, a village of around one thousand inhabitants in Qingyang township. The focus will be on the qualifications and skills that are actually present in Lijiazhuang, on the ways in which they have been acquired and transmitted up through the twentieth-century and on the role of education and training in the social strategies of individuals and families.

Zouping county is economically above average for Shandong, but it is not a boom area, and Qingyang is one of its least-developed townships. Lijiazhuang is situated on rather meager soil at the foot of a mountain, and its inhabitants have a long tradition of working as itinerant blacksmiths. Although rural industrialization has just reached the village in the last few years, agriculture has never been the sole source of income in Lijiazhuang, and several occupations are historically represented in the village.

After talking to a number of informants, it became clear that some villagers stood out because of their specialized professional skills. The eight schoolteachers constitute the most obvious group, and the three doctors are also clearly visible in the social landscape.[5] Both professions are now tied to the formal education system, but the historical development of these ties turned out to be distinctly different. In addition, there is a large group of people who mastered more or less complicated crafts: the electrician, a few carpenters and masons, people making and selling food products like *doufu* and *mantou*, and, most important, several blacksmiths. Finally, there are people with commercial and managerial skills, primarily the Party secretary and the village head, who both played key roles in Lijiazhuang's only village enterprise.

There are, of course, people in Lijiazhuang with other important types of knowledge and skills, related to agriculture and household work, for example, but in this essay I shall limit the discussion to what appear to be the four groups that were socially most prominent: teachers, doctors, artisans, and managers. Most of the examples will be drawn from Lijiazhuang, but experiences from other parts of Zouping will also be included to illustrate a number of points that did not surface in the Lijiazhuang interviews. The names of the village and its inhabitants have been changed to protect their privacy.

The School Teachers

Professionalization is, of course, a key term in the relationship between schooling and work, and the teachers are of particular historical interest here because they were the first occupational group for which training became institutionalized in schools and for which the authorities established specific qualification requirements. Professionalization of the teaching corps began in the first decade of this century, but, as the following discussion will show, it has been a complicated and still unfinished process.

The traditional Chinese village teacher, the *sishu xiansheng,* who dominated village education in Zouping until the late 1920s and played an important role right up to 1949, was originally a product, normally a residual product, of the imperial civil service examination system. The traditional school (*sishu*) taught basic reading skills and the Confucian canon to boys, and the teacher learned his profession by imitating his own teachers rather than through pedagogical studies. Before setting up his school, he had to make an arrangement with a family, a lineage, or a village who wanted him to teach their offspring, but he needed no official recognition, and his activities were not registered by any higher-level authority. The teachers of these schools held a mixed reputation.[6] Arthur Smith, a late-nineteenth-century American missionary observer who lived in Shandong for many years found the village schoolteacher to be a pathetic figure of low social prestige with no knowledge of anything except the Chinese classics (and often not even much of that), limited intellectual abilities, and no practical skills.[7] The reform-minded Chinese intellectuals of the 1920s and 1930s likewise tended to see the schoolmaster as a parochial, conservative, and dull representative of a doomed culture. In later CCP sources, especially in propaganda directed toward the new generation of teachers, the traditional schoolmaster is depicted in equally grim colors, normally as an intellectual day laborer, the humiliated victim of ruthless landlord exploitation.

To all these critics, however, the traditional teachers also represented an obstacle to their own reform projects. A less-partisan observer like Liao T'ai-ch'u, who conducted a survey of education in Wenshang county in Shandong in the 1930s, also found some traditional teachers who knew "practically nothing about the world either old or new," but on the whole he found that they held relatively high prestige and were "definitely superior" to their modern school colleagues.[8] Life histories from Zouping tend to confirm the picture drawn by Liao. Rather than being itinerant scholars desperately looking for an income, most traditional schoolteachers seem to have been local personalities of rather high reputation who often had other skills besides mere literacy.[9] For example, the most prominent *sishu* teacher in Lijiazhuang during the Republican period had studied under his father-in-law for many years and was known as an expert on the *Book of Odes* and the *Book of Changes*. He was often invited by neighboring villages to set up school for their children, was recruited to teach in a prominent modern school in the 1930s, and even after 1949 he sometimes entertained his fellow villagers with stories and quotations from the classical literature. Another Lijiazhuang *sishu* teacher practiced as a traditional doctor when he was not teaching, a combination that appears to have been quite common. Several teachers were reknowned for their command of Chinese high culture and were invited to contribute their calligraphy on such occasions as weddings. Although the abolition of the examination system in 1905 had cut off the traditional civil service career track for people with a background in the classics, their special expertise and talents continued to be both respected and in demand in the rural backwaters well into the twentieth-century.

Traditional teachers were paid a modest salary by their students' families, normally in grain. In addition to this they were entitled to free meals, an arrangement in which the parents took turns inviting them home. Though Zouping teachers who depended on teaching as their sole source of income were not rich even by the local standards of the time, their students remembered them as being better off than the average peasant family. The teaching profession, in other words, was a reasonably attractive alternative to agricultural work for those who had received some education but who lacked the socioeconomic background, the connections, or the luck to advance further up the social ladder.

Following the introduction of modern schools around the turn of the century, the provincial leadership in Shandong recognized teachers' training as a key link in educational reform. Already from 1902 specific teachers' training was offered in Jinan, the provincial capital, the effects of which reached Zouping through a scheme that allowed each county to send two students to the provincial capital for advanced modern studies to supplement their traditional qualifications with the teaching skills required by the new schools. In 1904 a short-term teachers' training course with ten students was organized in the county seat of Zouping in order to upgrade some of the local *sishu* teachers. In 1907 the county magistrate established a lower teachers' training school, and each of the thirty school districts into which Zouping was divided was ordered to send one teacher to the course and pay his costs. After graduation in 1908 those who had attended the course were granted the right to set up a modern school in their home district.[10] Through such courses, which among other things taught pedagogical theory, the idea was introduced in Zouping that teaching was a job demanding specialized professional training and that teachers should go through an official endorsement procedure before they could open a school.

The courses in 1904 and 1907 portended a protracted effort on the part of the state for gaining control over teachers' training. Nonetheless, for many years traditional schoolmasters, more or less untouched by the new ideas, continued to dominate rural schools in Zouping, and in spite of repeated efforts to reeducate them most stuck to their old ways and switched their schools back to *sishu* mode whenever central control slackened.

From the 1920s, however, a new type of teacher appeared on the scene who had received most or all of his training in modern schools. The careers of these people mainly followed two channels. One went through the teachers' training schools, which had become attractive to rural youths for several reasons. First, tuition was free, in contrast to general middle schools, and the students were even granted a modest stipend. This was, of course, in order to attract people to a profession that was in high demand but in which income and career prospects were modest. Second, during almost the entire Republican period teacher training was the only type of school education with a vocational aim offered inside the borders of Zouping county.[11] For other types of training students would have to cover the costs involved in moving to Jinan or even further away. These factors combined to make teachers' training the most obvious choice for students from less-wealthy families who wanted to continue their education beyond the level of higher primary school, whether or not they were interested in becoming village teachers.[12]

The second route to teaching jobs led through general secondary or even tertiary education. The unstable sociopolitical conditions during the period made it difficult even for university graduates to find suitable jobs, and this, often combined with a radical political ambition of changing the face of China's villages through education, made several Zouping students return at least temporarily to work in the education sector of their home county.

By 1930 still only one-third of the Zouping schoolteachers had been through teachers' training,[13] but the professionalization of the teaching corps was greatly enhanced when Liang Shuming established the headquarters of his Rural Reconstruction Movement (RRM) in the county in 1931.[14] A teachers' training school set up by the RRM attracted a large group of local youths who came to play a major part in the later educational development of Zouping. The career of one of these teachers, Yang Nianjiu, may serve to illustrate.

Yang was born in 1912 and attended both modern and traditional schools for several years before he enrolled in the Zouping teachers' training school in 1933. Here he was deeply influenced by the progressive educational ideas of Zhang Zonglin who was the school's director for a year and who had earlier worked with Tao Xingzhi in Xiaozhuang.[15] Yang graduated after four years and continued his career as a teacher in a number of modern local schools, of which an anti-Japanese school near Lijiazhuang was the most prominent. In periods when the local school system broke down because of war and unrest, however, he reverted to teaching in local *sishu* using the whole traditional set of reading primers and teaching methods. After 1950 he became headmaster of a school in Zouping town that supervised five village schools and played a major role in building up a network of rural schools in the area.[16]

Yang Nianjiu was the prototype of the professionally trained teacher who after 1949 was sent by the county education bureau from one village to another depending on the needs of local school authorities. In the early years of the People's Republic teachers of this kind dominated village schools. In 1950 more than 90 percent of the Zouping teachers were employed by the county (*gongban*), while less than 10 percent were hired and paid by their own village (*minban*).[17] During the anti-rightist campaign of 1957, 115 Zouping teachers and education cadres were branded as rightists, and professional expertise in general was treated with disregard,[18] but by 1962 the teaching corps was still predominantly professional, with 75 percent of the Zouping *gongban* primary schoolteachers being graduates of different levels of teachers' training schools.[19]

The expansion of both primary and secondary school enrollment during the Cultural Revolution decade was so massive, however, that it became impossible for the educational system to train enough teachers. The number of teachers in primary and secondary schools doubled between 1962 and 1971, from two thousand three hundred to four thousand seven hundred,[20] and teaching again became deprofessionalized as senior and junior middle school graduates were handpicked to fill positions as village teachers. By 1977 almost half of all Zouping primary schoolteachers had only a primary or general secondary school background.[21] Whereas the professional teachers were assigned jobs through the Education Bureau of the county administration, the new teachers were appointed by the village leaders from among the local youth. This meant that the teaching profession once again became an alternative to agricultural work for young villagers with an above-average general educational background. The careers of two Lijiazhuang teachers may serve as illustrations.

Lin Zhonghua was born in 1944. When he graduated from the township higher primary school in 1957 he was the only child from his village who gained admission to junior middle school. After graduating in 1960, he returned to his production brigade as an accountant, and in 1968 the brigade appointed him *minban* teacher in the village school. When I interviewed him in the mid-1990s, he had been teaching there ever since. During the collective period he received full work points (ten points a day) and a small supplementary salary. When the brigade distributed its land in 1983 he got his share and furthermore received from the village a growing cash income, which by 1993 had reached 140 *yuan* a month.[22]

Han Weimin had almost been forced into a teaching career by his poor health and lack of physical strength. He finished junior middle school in 1973, but because of his health problems the brigade did not recommend him for further studies. Instead, he repeated the entire junior middle school course in another school where the academic standard was higher, and, finally, in 1976 Lijiazhuang hired him as a *minban* teacher. From 1987 to 1991 he was professionally upgraded through a correspondence course that gave him the same credentials as a teachers' training school graduate. He felt that this course had taught him much about Chinese language and mathematics but hardly anything about teaching, psychology, and such.[23] Interviews with several other young men and women confirmed that from the 1950s onward many of those who had done well academically had taught for some years in the village school.

In the 1980s and 1990s it again became the intention of the State Education Commission to professionalize the teaching corps, but this is a slow process, and it works mainly through an upgrading of the present teachers, as in the case of Han Weimin. Out of the eight teachers who taught in Lijiazhuang in 1996 only one, the school headmaster, had attended a teachers' training school. In 1992 the county administration officially claimed that 92 percent of Zouping primary schoolteachers were graduates of teachers' training schools,[24] but this probably referred mainly to teachers with a general middle school background supplemented by later on-the-job training. The professionalization of the teaching corps was thus far from completed by the 1990s, and the role as village teacher was still primarily filled by people who had done well in the school system but who had not been able to escape rural life through educational advancement and who lacked the economic and social resources for entering more profitable occupations. In this respect their social position was not far from that of the traditional schoolmaster.

The market economic reforms of the 1980s and 1990s had obviously reduced the attraction of the teaching profession, and the county administration openly admitted that many male teachers were leaving their positions to take up more lucrative jobs, particularly in the commercial sector.[25] Teaching now appealed more to young women, to whom it represented an alternative to tedious household work. For several young female informants their ambition in life was to become a teacher. While I have no statistics on the gender distribution of different generations of Zouping teachers, in the several schools I visited older teachers were normally men, the middle-aged were mixed but most of them male, while the majority of young teachers were female.[26]

In relation to the questions asked at the beginning of this essay, it should first be noted that teaching was the first occupation in which school-based professional training was offered in rural China and that it has been essential to the state, before as well as after 1949, to gain control over the teachers through training and certification, not least for ideological and political reasons. In spite of these intensive and long-term efforts, however, most twentieth-century village schoolteachers have been products of the general school system rather than of professional training, and in most cases they have learned the art of teaching by imitation rather than by school-based instruction. The job as a teacher has been relatively attractive to village youths, at least compared to agricultural labor, and the way to achieve it has been by demonstrating academic talent inside the general school system.

The Doctors

The training of village doctors and other medical personnel has gone through a process that differs from that of teachers' training in several respects. The two professions had quite different origins in traditional society. While the traditional village teachers had attended schools or even academies, the most common way to become a traditional medical practitioner was through apprenticeship training. Sometimes medical skills were combined with classical studies and transmitted from father to son inside literati families, but in most cases the training did not differ in essence from trades that are normally thought of as "manual." One of the most famous Zouping practitioners, for example, was Wang Fengming, born in 1878 and a specialist in healing broken bones. He learned his skills from an elderly doctor in another village who, after Wang's protracted pleadings, finally accepted him as his apprentice. For five years he studied his master's healing techniques, including different types of *qigong* and martial arts, without ever seeing a textbook. When Wang finished his training he was as illiterate as when he had started, and later in his career, when he wanted to study a manual of Chinese medicine, he had to ask other people to read it aloud for him while he memorized it sentence by sentence.[27]

From the turn of the century, when the first modern medical schools were established in Shandong, Western medicine was introduced to Zouping first by the British Baptist Mission and later, in the 1930s, by the Rural Reconstruction Movement. At the national level there were several efforts to register and certify medical doctors and organize them in a nationwide health care system. Already in 1915 the National Medical Association had urged the government to register all doctors, and regulations to this effect were promulgated in 1928–29.[28]

There were also strong forces in Republican China who wanted to regulate the activities of traditional practitioners, but they were not very successful, and in the rural areas in particular the Republican state never had as much control over the medical profession as over the teachers.[29] Unlike modern schools, pre-1949 clinics with Western-style doctors were almost exclusively found in the urban centers, and the traditional healers who dominated the profession in rural areas were largely ignored by the officials. Likewise, although the school curriculum was reformed several times during the first decades of the twentieth century, a number of essential skills held by traditional teachers, literacy first of all, were still highly relevant in the new school system. By contrast, traditional medical practitioners operated inside a knowledge system fundamentally different from that of their Western-style colleagues, and they could not easily be retrained. At the same time the field of education was so politically important that the authorities felt an urgent need to control the teaching corps right down to the village level, while traditional doctors represented no similar political threat to the Nationalist ideology. Furthermore, traditional doctors relied to a wide extent on orally transmitted methods, which they guarded like trade secrets and would only pass on to a few carefully selected students, who were often family members. As a result of all these factors, and also because there was no alternative to traditional medicine in the rural areas, the village practitioners in Zouping were allowed to exist outside the state system of registration and certification to a much larger extent than were the traditional teachers, and their training was formalized and institutionalized much later than the professional training of teachers. As late as 1953, there were 183 doctors and pharmacists in Zouping county who worked in the Chinese medical tradition and had been trained as apprentices in the traditional manner, compared to only 52 who practiced Western-style medicine.[30] At this time there was still no medical school inside the county.

From the introduction of collective health care in 1958, and particularly with the barefoot doctors of the 1970s, the medical profession, like teaching, became a main escape route from agricultural labor for talented rural youths. The total number of medical personnel in the county grew from 235 persons in 1953 to more than 2,000 in 1976,[31] and the privatization of the 1980s did not reduce the number. A health school was established inside the county hospital in 1965, which enrolled 64 students in a three-year course, but following the graduation of the first class the school offered only short-term courses to nurses and barefoot doctors. When graduates from other medical schools were assigned jobs in Zouping, they would be posted to the county town rather than in the villages,[32] while the village practitioners were selected locally for short-term training.

Three life histories may serve to show the role of family background, school education and professional training in the formation of this rapidly expanding occupational group. Chen Rongwen, born in 1934, was the youngest son in a family of illiterate farmers, and when he showed academic talent his father decided to invest in his education. His schooling was interrupted by war and economic problems, but in 1954, at the age of twenty, he was finally enrolled in the prestigious No. 1 Middle School in Zouping as the first Lijiazhuang student since the Revolution in 1949. Before that time only two persons from the village, both from landlord families, had received secondary education. Because of his father's death, however, he had to leave school after only one and a half years and was subsequently assigned different jobs in the township administration and in the Communist Youth League. Due to health problems, he returned to Lijiazhuang in 1960 and began studying Western-style medicine on his own. After a few years of self-study he began to practice as a doctor, and for more than ten years he was the only Western-style medical worker in Lijiazhuang. Between 1980 and 1988 he was also village head (*cunzhang*).[33]

From the 1960s more and more women started to work in the health sector. There was no female doctor in Lijiazhuang when I visited the village, but the career of Wang Yingxiu from a nearby village provides an example of a woman who rose to relative prominence in her village through the medical field. She was born in 1951, and after finishing lower primary school she was among the 50 percent or so of her class who were accepted to higher primary school (years five and six). She failed the entrance examination to the No. 1

Middle School in 1964 and never went to the agricultural middle school, which had been willing to accept her. Instead, the brigade selected her for training as a barefoot doctor, the first woman in the village's history to acquire medical training. The training was based on learning through participation, and she followed a trained doctor for about two months. Immediately after the course, she started as a medical worker, and in the same year she joined the Communist Youth League. In 1970 she became a full-time medical worker (*weishengyuan*) in her home village. Since 1975 she had regularly taken courses and passed examinations in health care and medicine and was now officially classified as a doctor trained at the specialized middle school (*yishi*). In terms of political influence she was head of the village Women's Federation, and her brother was the village Party secretary.[34]

The third career to be discussed here is that of Zhang Licai, who by 1996 was the youngest and most active doctor in Lijiazhuang. Born in 1968, he had attended the local village school and passed the exam to the township keypoint middle school as the only one from his class. In 1985, after studying an extra year in junior middle school to improve his chances, he was accepted to the senior section of the Zouping No. 1 Middle School, again as the only Lijiazhuang student that year. Here he also studied for four years, one year more than the norm, but was still unable to pass the national university entrance examination. Instead, he took a one-semester course at an unofficial medical school in Tai'an. After one month of practice in Tai'an and one month in the local Qingyang township hospital, he was called back to Lijiazhuang to take over the village clinic. His father was a traditional Chinese doctor with a high educational level for his generation, and Li's real interest was also in the field of traditional medicine. He had realized, however, that people did not trust young traditional doctors and so only practised Western medicine. He was professionally supervised by the township hospital, which arranged regular courses for village doctors to bring them up to specialized middle school level. Zhang Licai was married to one of the village schoolteachers, who was from a family that, like his own, had long traditions in education.

These personal histories illustrate how medical service at the village level has been, and to a large extent still is, provided by people who have acquired their knowledge from self-study, practice, and work participation rather than from schools. Like the schoolteachers, many village doctors have been professionally upgraded since the late 1980s and will sooner or later receive official credentials and figure as *zhongzhuan* graduates in the statistics, but their routes into the profession have generally been unorthodox, and their main skills have not been acquired through formal schooling. On the other hand, we find again, as with the teachers, that excellent school performance seems to have been a major element in creating the doctors' careers. The two male Lijiazhuang doctors had both been outstanding students by village standards and had had strong academic aspirations. They had advanced further in the school system than any of their classmates but had failed to make the final step away from the village. Also, Wang Yingxiu had done well in school and had been close to gaining a place in No. 1 Middle School.

At the same time, the social ascendency of Chen Rongwen and Wang Yingxiu to the position of doctors may also have been linked to the political rise of their families and lineages. Right up to 1987 the village leaders appointed young people to be trained for one year as medical workers in township- and county-level clinics and hospitals, and this procedure was, of course, open to influence from the more powerful families. Chen and Wang both held or had held positions of political authority, and so did members of their closest family. The Chen lineage, to which we shall return later, was the largest lineage in Lijiazhuang by 1949. Economically, its members were at the medium level, and, though no one from this lineage was classified as landlords, they had several literate members. After 1949 they came to dominate village politics completely, and village heads and brigade or village Party secretaries were normally recruited among the Chens.

The young doctor trained in the 1980s, on the other hand, seems to have had no similar political connections and no political ambitions either. He had another important asset, however: a family tradition for education and for the medical profession. It seems that both families with political and cultural capital have seen promising career prospects for their offspring in the medical profession.

After 1987 professionalization of the medical field gathered momentum in Zouping. In that year the state demanded that village doctors should reach the level of specialized middle school graduates, and, as only 30 percent of the existing corps of doctors could live up to this criterion at the time, the county health bureau decided to open a specialized middle school offering three-year courses in both Western and Chinese medicine as well as to upgrade courses for former barefoot doctors. The first graduates found jobs in hospitals or in the army, but by 1996 most of these attractive posts had already been filled, and the school leader expected more students to return to work in the clinics of their home villages in the future.[35]

It was interesting to note that many of the medical students, like the young primary schoolteachers, were female. According to the school's headmaster, many family heads found that the medical profession offered clean, respectable, and relatively well-paid jobs that were suitable for girls, and the girls scored high enough in the entrance exams to the specialized middle school to gain access. If this trend continues, the professionalization of the medical sector at the village level will be paralleled by a distinct feminization of this sphere of work.

The Craftsmen

The land around Lijiazhuang is not fertile, and agricultural production alone has never been enough to keep the villagers alive. As far back as people could remember, many male villagers had supplemented the family income by working as itinerant blacksmiths on the Jiaodong peninsula, in Hebei, and even in Manchuria. Interestingly, the richest families in the village—those who were classified as landlords after 1949—were, in fact, master blacksmiths rather than large landowners.[36]

Accounts of apprenticeship in pre-1949 urban China tend to emphasize two aspects above all: the systematic and elaborate nature of the training with contracts, rituals, and a gradual learning process proceeding from the most menial tasks to the more complicated; and the appalling living conditions and ruthless exploitation of the apprentices.[37] Rural apprenticeships seem to have been more moderate in both respects, probably because they very often took place inside the family, where the master was at the same time the father or uncle of the apprentice. One elderly blacksmith told me that master-apprentice relations in the village, according to what he had heard, had been quite formal before the fall of the Qing dynasty. In those days, he said, a blacksmith always went through a four-year apprenticeship. During the first three years he only got board and lodging, but during the fourth year he received a small salary and a complete set of tools and was then regarded as a skilled worker (*shifu*).[38] At least from the 1920s onward, however, when the interviewees had their personal experiences, such rules and procedures were not strictly applied.

In spite of the rather informal relationship between different categories of workers, there was still a clear hierarchy among them, at least until the 1960s. Only some men in Lijiazhuang had the status of *shifu*, and they would take their fellow villagers along to work far from home for several months at a time. Some men in the group only did simple manual work with little skill involved and never advanced to the *shifu* level, while others were taught to perform gradually more complicated tasks. One man had started as an apprentice with his uncle when he was sixteen and had received a small but gradually rising salary, paid in grain because of the inflation. During the first two years he had only been tending the hearth while watching his uncle work, but after this period he had hammered out iron under supervision until his training terminated, when he was twenty-one.[39]

An apprentice learned more than just manual skills, as blacksmiths were also required to know how to use the abacus. One man recalled how he had made and repaired farm implements in a poor region of Hebei where the villagers were so impoverished that they could only afford to pay him at the end of the year. He therefore had to learn the basic principles of bookkeeping from his grandfather in order to keep track of how much they owed him.[40]

In Republican times the apprenticeship system coexisted well with both traditional and modern schools, and it was quite normal for a Lijiazhuang boy to study a few years with an old-style teacher then enroll in a modern school if it were available and, finally, enter training as a blacksmith when he was physically strong enough.

Ironwork had determined the fate of Lijiazhuang in more than one way. During the 1940s the men avoided being drafted to the contending armies of the civil war by traveling as journeymen, and this meant that the number of both "revolutionary cadres" and people with "historical problems" in the village was comparatively low. After the revolution a collective iron workshop was established that provided the village with a good income to compensate for the poor soil. After the decollectivization of the 1980s, however, this workshop was dissolved when its workers went out traveling again to try their own individual luck on the labor market. This time, however, they were not making and repairing agricultural implements as they had done before. Instead, they would cut up scrap iron into smaller pieces or fill other types of unskilled and temporary positions in factories where the skilled jobs were taken by regular workers. The mechanization of iron production itself was probably the main reason behind this diminution of the Lijiazhuang blacksmiths from skilled to unskilled laborers. But it also seems that an erosion of the traditional technical skills had taken place during the intervening decades because they had not been continuously developed and updated. The result was that Lijiazhuang's economic status had declined since the mid-1980s compared to other villages in the district.[41]

In 1995 a new village-owned enterprise opened in Lijiazhuang in the buildings formerly housing the collective workshop. The enterprise was a subcontractor to a factory in the township and produced spare parts for motorcycles. There were four skilled workers, all from Lijiazhuang, and all former workers in the township enterprise, where they had also been trained as apprentices for a half-year. These four workers now each had an apprentice, but the work procedures in the new factory were technically simple, so the training was quite informal and only lasted a few months. The factory also employed nine unskilled workers. As I will show later, the factory was actually run by the politically dominant Chen lineage, for whom the enterprise represented an attempt to achieve prosperity through a technical field in which they had some traditions and experience.

By 1996 the richest people in the village were apparently not, however, from the politically dominant lineage. According to one informant, the economically most successful villagers came from the families of old master blacksmiths, who had been classified as landlords or rich peasants after the Revolution. These families had been able to transmit their technical skills to their offspring, who were now making good money in skilled jobs outside the village.[42]

This brief outline of the history of blacksmithing in Lijiazhuang shows how the economic destiny of a rural village depends not only on the development of its agriculture but also on the type and level of the technical skills of its labor force. In a similar way artisans who worked in their own and neighboring villages as masons or carpenters also possessed their own special skills. Like the schoolteachers and medical practitioners, they also engaged in agriculture, but they supplemented their income substantially through their crafts.

What has been the role of the school system in the training of such artisans in rural China? My interviews in Lijiazhuang clearly demonstrate that none of the attempts at bridge building between the worlds of schooling and the crafts had been very successful. In fact, schooling had had no discernible impact on the transmission of skills among blacksmiths and carpenters during any period under study.

Vocational education developed slowly in the Chinese countryside. Between 1906 and 1908 secondary-level schools in languages, law and politics, medicine, commerce, industry, handicrafts, agriculture, and fishery were established in Jinan and other larger Shandong cities, and in 1910 a small agricultural school opened in Zouping, but, though it survived until 1933, it remained insignificant.[43] The Rural Reconstruction Movement of the 1930s paid much attention to the dissemination of practical skills and knowledge among the villagers, but their primary target group was young adults rather than schoolchildren, and vocational training was never part of the curriculum in their primary schools.

The post-1949 school system has tried to increase compatibility between school and work in two main ways: through labor education and practical work as part of the general curriculum for all students and in agricultural and vocational schools at the secondary level. Although there is no space for a detailed discussion of these types of training here, a few remarks on the impression they made on my informants may shed some light on the effects they have had in a village like Lijiazhuang.⁴⁴

All Lijiazhuang students who had attended school since the 1950s had experiences with labor education (*laodong ke*) and participation in practical work at school, although such experiences had been most intensive in the late 1950s and during the Cultural Revolution decade (1966–76). Practically all of them had welcomed it as a break in the daily routine of lectures and tests and as a chance to leave the stifling atmosphere of the classroom. As a way of transmitting vocational qualifications, however, labor education had little effect. The skill content in pulling up weeds or feeding pigs was limited, and most of the children had already learned to perform such tasks at home. Another problem was that practically all of the work done by students was related to agriculture, not to specific crafts. Labor education was probably important for economic reasons (schools were partly financed through their own production), for ideological reasons (as part of the celebration of work as a central value in communism), and even for didactic reasons (important points in, e.g., biology or physics could be illustrated in practice), but it did not prepare students for the world of work.

Turning to vocational schools at the secondary level, by far the most common type has been the agricultural middle schools. Such schools only flourished in Zouping during three relatively short periods (1958–1961, 1964–1965, and 1980–1982), and the villagers always regarded them as second-class institutions for children who could not gain access to general middle school. I talked to a number of graduates from these schools, and they generally felt that the courses in agriculture had been useful because they had increased their theoretical understanding and introduced them to modern farming methods. It was interesting to note, however, that few of them still had agriculture as their main source of income. Because they had received a secondary education, which few villagers did in the 1950s and early 1960s, they had been led onto other career tracks and were now often engaged in small-scale industry, commercial activities, or administration.⁴⁵

It should be added that some other villages in Zouping had different stories to tell about the transmission of vocational skills. In Nanbeisi, a cluster of small villages in the mountains, a combined primary and secondary school had integrated vocational training and work in school factories into the general school curriculum from the early 1970s and soon became a provincial-level model unit in this field. It trained local construction workers, textile workers, tractor mechanics, and other skilled workers and established local industries in which the graduates were allocated jobs.⁴⁶ This school was quite unique in the county, however, and, although its success demonstrates the potential of the vocational school strategy, its practical impact has been confined to its immediate surroundings.

Another, and so far equally unique, model was being followed in the most wealthy village in Zouping, Dongguancun, which is now part of the county seat. This village opened several enterprises in the wake of the market economic reforms in the 1980s and soon lacked qualified laborers. The village leadership first decided to pay the way for Dongguancun students through specialized secondary or even tertiary education, and later the village opened its own vocational school, which trained junior middle school graduates from the entire county for posts as skilled workers, technicians, and administrative personnel in the booming village enterprises.[47] This type of vocational training was apparently more successful than previous experiments with county-run vocational middle schools, probably because the link to the employer was so strong. Yet the model demands a well-developed industrial base, and no one therefore expected other villages to follow the example of Dongguancun in the foreseeable future.

In conclusion, the training of artisans in Lijiazhuang was never successfully integrated into the school system. Apprenticeship was the traditional way to learn a trade and continued to be so up through the twentieth century. In China's urban areas skilled workers' training schools (*jigong xuexiao*), often based in large enterprises, created a new framework for apprenticeship by combining it with school-based instruction. In this context apprenticeship could be reinterpreted as members of the revolutionary working class training their own successors. In the countryside, however, vocational education remained weakly developed and geared only to agriculture. Villagers were primarily seen as "peasants," and their handicraft skills became symbols of the past rather than the future. The apprenticeship system was left to deteriorate slowly, and the skill level of the artisans probably dropped as a result of this process.

Managers and Businessmen

Managerial skills are hard to identify and particularly hard to trace historically. I will define them here quite broadly as the technical and interpersonal skills needed in business and management, such as knowing the written and unwritten rules of business transactions, knowing how to get loans, make budgets and keep accounts, how to create and maintain good relations with other actors on the economic and political scene, and how to organize production and manage the workforce.

The pre-1949 training of shopkeepers and businessmen in Zouping resembled that of other professions (i.e. apprenticeship, usually inside the family). Commercial families sometimes arranged for their children to be taught calculation skills in the traditional *sishu*,[48] but the real training would take place in shops, often in Zhoucun, a nearby commercial center with hundreds of businesses in all trades. In 1919 the Zhoucun Commercial School was established, representing a new trend of school-based training of skilled persons for the commercial sector. The school was financed partly by the Zhoucun Chamber of Commerce and partly by the Nanyang Brothers Tobacco Company, and the curriculum contained a combination of general subjects and training in commercial skills. The school survived until the Japanese occupation. It trained more than one thousand people, and the large majority of graduates actually found jobs in the commercial sector. This was the first case in the Zouping area of a vocational school rooted in a growing local demand for skilled labor caused by economic development.[49]

The communist takeover required a transmission of business and community leadership skills in the villages from those classified as rich peasants and landlords to the politically more reliable classes. In Lijiazhuang there was no revolutionary tradition and no one who had gone through communist cadre training before 1949, so the new leaders had to be found among the poor and middle peasants. The life histories of the present village Party secretary and the village head may serve to illustrate the careers of two generations of post-1949 leaders

The Party secretary Chen Rongbin was born in 1940, and because of the civil war and the poverty of his family he received less than three years of regular schooling as a boy. In 1956 he attended the village evening school, reached elementary school level after two years, and the following two winters he was in a group of five young villagers who, in a concrete example of skill transmission from the old to the new "masters of the country," were taught arithmetic and the use of the abacus by an old rich peasant. This training qualified Chen for a job as an accountant, first in his production team and later in his brigade. His membership in the Party led him to the post of village head and later vice secretary of the village Party branch. In 1976 he was made Party secretary of a factory run by the commune (later the township), a big step up the social ladder that involved moving to Qingyang, the seat of the commune administration. He stayed there for almost a decade before he was sent back, much against his will, and made Party secretary of his home village in 1985.

During his stay in Qingyang, Chen Rongbin received political training at the county Party school, and he also attended a one-month course in quality control. He gained administrative experience and established connections to many important people in Zouping's industrial sector, and he was the prime mover when the village factory started up in Lijiazhuang in 1995, producing spare parts for the factory in Qingyang, where Chen used to work. Both his sons had done well in school but had failed to gain admission to higher education. He had then arranged for them to be trained as apprentices in the factory in Qingyang, where he was Party secretary, after which they returned to the Lijiazhuang factory as foremen. His youngest child, a daughter, was the first girl in Lijiazhuang to graduate from a specialized secondary school. She had studied business and had become the youngest female department head in a large department store in Zouping town. The secretary himself was a member of the village factory's leadership group and was responsible for the daily production.[50]

The village head, Chen Gang, was born in 1963 as the second son of Chen Rongwen, the autodidact doctor mentioned earlier. He finished senior middle school in 1979, but the academic level in this local school was very low, and after a few months as a village schoolteacher he decided to re-enroll in 1980 in an agricultural technical school (*nongye jishu xuexiao*) in another commune. He graduated two and a half years later but never engaged in agriculture. Like so many other young men in Lijiazhuang, he traveled to the northeast, instead, and got a temporary job in a factory in Shenyang after his uncle had taught him the basic skills of a blacksmith. He returned to Lijiazhuang in 1989, when he replaced his father as village head. The agricultural technical school he had attended was rated as the best vocational school in the county at the time, so his educational background counted among the highest in the village. When I first met him in 1993 he had recently started Lijiazhuang's only private enterprise but did not make any profits from it. By 1996 he had become director of the newly established village-owned factory. He had a wide net of contacts to other village heads and small entrepreneurs in the area. His wife had been the first female senior middle school graduate in Lijiazhuang. She had originally wanted to become a teacher, but her father demanded that she worked in the fields instead. She was now a housewife and worked on the family land.[51]

These two examples may serve to illustrate how political capital after the introduction of the market-oriented reforms in the 1980s could be transformed into socioeconomic success through managerial skills that had been accumulated in the collective era. Many other people in the village had tried to establish small shops, sell clothes in urban markets, or run other businesses, but on a more individual basis and without much success. The reason the village head and the Party secretary were able to start an enterprise that provided jobs and incomes in the range of 600–800 yuan a month to more than a dozen people cannot be reduced to the fact that they had *guanxi* (connections) inside the system. They had also acquired, through their careers as cadres at the lowest levels, the managerial skills needed to get loans to buy equipment, identify business partners, set up contracts, and keep accounts. This was not so much the result of direct training inside the Party apparatus, as the courses and meetings they had attended at the Party school had been mostly of an ideological nature. It was, rather, a question of having concrete experience with industrial production and management.

That Lijiazhuang is not an isolated case in this respect is illustrated by a recent survey on the background of enterprise managers in Huantai county, close to Zouping. Here Ray Yep found that, "while political capital matters, non-political attributes such as management skills and knowledge are equally important in explaining the rise of enterprise managers in rural China during the reform era." At the village level, however, the cadres had few competitors in regard to managerial skills and experience, and most managers of village enterprises were therefore Party secretaries or deputy secretaries, as opposed to the township level, where the cadres met fiercer competition from people who had acquired managerial and technical skills outside the Party apparatus.[52]

Another point worth noting is how the Party secretary consistently kept his children's educational careers in view. He had let all three of them study as far as they could in the general school system, and when they failed to advance further he had placed them in the best kind of vocational training available to people at the educational level they had reached. This meant that his daughter had been able to move up the sociogeographic ladder to the county seat, while his sons possessed the technical qualifications necessary to occupy two of the four skilled positions in the factory. In a similar way the village head and his wife invested much hope and energy in the education of their children who were still in primary school. The transmission of qualifications inside lineages and from generation to generation was obviously an important element in the ongoing process of social stratification in the rural areas. The Chen lineage in Lijiazhuang used a broad-spectrum strategy in which they maintained the hope of sending some younger members to higher-level schools while at the same time recognizing the importance of both technical and managerial skills for those who remained in the village. Education and training were crucial elements in the personal and collective ambitions of people in Lijiazhuang.

Conclusion and Perspectives

The preceding broad outline of the history of four occupations in Lijiazhuang and their relations to the educational system through the twentieth century leads back to the questions asked at the beginning of this essay: How have people in Lijiazhuang acquired the skills from which they make a living? To the best of my knowledge there was only one out of the approximately one thousand inhabitants of the village whose career had advanced from general schooling to school-based vocational or professional training to an occupation in the field for which he or she had been trained. This one person was the school headmaster who had gone from junior middle school via a teachers' training school to a teaching position. Everyone else had received their training through participation in work supplemented by self-study and/or short-term courses along the way. It is doubtless correct that the preparation for an increasing number of urban jobs and professions has moved away from apprenticeship and learning through participation and into educational institutions, and this is even true for some jobs in the county town of Zouping. The effects of this trend in a village like Lijiazhuang, however, are still negligible. For all practical purposes vocational training in Lijiazhuang still takes place outside the school system.

In light of this fact it is surprising how the apprenticeship model has been ignored in both Chinese and Western research on Chinese rural education. Several tendencies seem to gang up to keep this way of learning, which is and always has been absolutely essential to rural economy, out of our perspective. Already the reformers of the 1920s and 1930s, represented in Zouping by the Rural Reconstruction Movement, felt that learning should be liberated from the feudal and traditional ideas permeating rural society and placed in schools where it could be accompanied by progressive ideology. In the 1930s, therefore, village schools in Zouping, staffed by young people trained by the RRM, started to teach the villagers how they should dress, wash, cook their meals, and bring up their children. The transmission of knowledge and skills that took place inside the family and in the rural community could simply not be trusted and was therefore largely ignored by the reformers.

While we do have a number of detailed accounts, particularly from urban areas, of apprenticeship in the first half of the century from persons who actually went out and observed what was happening, the topic almost completely disappeared from both Chinese and the Western research agendas after 1949. There are several reasons for this: inside the bureaucratic structure, apprenticeship training and even skilled workers' training schools were placed outside the auspices of the educational administration; politically, apprenticeship was seen as a type of exploitation (people in Lijiazhuang even stopped using the term *apprentice* because of its class content); and, ideologically, PRC propaganda promoted the idea that the learning of practical skills now was, or at least should be, located inside the school system, by "combining theory and practice" in vocational and agricultural schools, for example, or in physical labor classes.

The effect of this official representation on our understanding of post-1949 Chinese education has been quite significant; in the voluminous literature in the field, from scholarly works to World Bank reports, we hardly find anything on apprenticeship in rural areas. The case may serve to illustrate how Chinese ideological constructs and bureaucratic structures control our view of Chinese social reality. Social activities for which an office and a professional hierarchy are responsible are so much more visible in China than are those fields that fall outside or between the bureaucratic sectors.

More important, it may be assumed that the authorities' (Republican as well as Communist) mistrust and neglect of the traditional learning model for artisans and professionals led to declining skill levels in the rural workforce, thereby increasing rural-urban inequalities. The schematic view of a society sharply divided into an "urban" and a "rural" population, as exemplified in the household registration system, seems to have blinded the authorities to the fact that villagers were not just, and in many cases not even primarily, "peasants" who tilled the land. They were also artisans whose vocational skills had to be maintained, developed, and continually updated. This task was far beyond the capacity of the school system because villagers' expectations of this system went in a totally different direction.

This brings us to the question of why villagers have preferred academic-track schools. My interviews left little doubt that most people in Zouping perceived the Chinese educational system as being "useful" and "relevant" exactly *because* it performed the role of a giant sorting machine that made it possible for the most talented to escape the monotony of village life. When villagers recounted their educational careers for me, regardless of which historical period they had attended school, they would almost invariably describe their school experience as an elimination race in which economic or political obstacles, lack of intellectual ability, or simply bad luck had forced them to drop out at a certain stage. The theme that was second in prominence among interviewees saw schooling as a process in which they had acquired a set of general qualifications. The school had taught them significant general skills such as reading and writing and had also made them better persons and/or exposed them to new thoughts and ideas. Only in the third place, if at all, did they talk about school as a place where they had acquired knowledge and skills that made it possible for them to fill their present work role.

Some village children do get access to university, and the handful of Lijiazhuang people who had achieved this was enough to keep a flickering hope alive in many families whose offspring showed academic talent. More important, however, several individual careers showed that formal competence in academic school subjects, as measured in examination results, was used inside the village to identify those young people who were suited for careers outside agriculture. When a brigade or village needed a teacher, an electrician, a barefoot doctor, an accountant, or a technician, they would select for training someone who had done well in school. From the 1950s to the mid-1970s political and social criteria were used to screen out a minority of students with "bad class background," but even at that time the remaining pool of young people was large enough to leave room for choice, and good school performance was a prerequisite to being selected for an attractive job. Even during the Cultural Revolution decade most interviewees felt that the students who had been selected for higher education or for skilled positions inside the village had been among the brightest heads of their generation.

Rural social mobility through education is not just a question of gaining admission to tertiary-level schools. Some posts inside the village are clearly more attractive than others, and general schooling is one way to get them. The idea that talented persons (*rencai*) are best identified through academic tests, even when the job in question has little or no academic content, has found expression throughout the twentieth century both in the way people have planned their careers and in the way they have actually been selected. In other words, when families in Lijiazhuang consistently preferred general schools over agricultural schools, it was not because they necessarily held any illusions about their children's chances of ending up as engineers or college professors but because the cultural values that they and their fellow villagers attached to general, academic-type schooling meant that this type of schooling most significantly increased the opportunities for upward social mobility, not only for those who got away from the village but also for those who stayed there.

NOTES

1. For Tao, see Barry Keenan, *The Dewey Experiment in China: Educational Reform and Political Power in the Early Republic* (Cambridge, Mass.: Harvard University Press, 1977); for Liang, see Guy S. Alitto, *The Last Confucian: Liang Shu-ming and the Chinese Dilemma of Modernity*, 2d ed. (Berkeley: University of California Press, 1986); for Yan, see Charles W. Hayford, *To The People: James Yen and Village China* (New York: Columbia University Press, 1990). Suzanne Pepper, *Radicalism and Education Reform in Twentieth-Century China: The Search for an Ideal Development Model* (Cambridge: Cambridge University Press, 1996), contains an illuminating discussion of the radical tradition in Chinese educational thought.

2. Zhang Jian, "Nongcun jiaoyu gaige xuyao yanjiu de jige wenti" (Some problems in rural education reform that need to be researched), in Zhang Jian, ed., *Zhongguo jiaoyu de fangzhen yu zhengce yanjiu* (Research on political line and policies in Chinese education) (Beijing: Zhongguo jiaoyu chubanshe, 1992), 169–78.

3. D. Berstecher, ed., *Education and Rural Development: Issues for Planning and Research* (Paris: Unesco, International Institute for Educational Planning, 1985).

4. The interviews were carried out during three visits in 1992, 1993, and 1996. I was allowed to select the villages I wanted to work in as well as my interviewees without interference from officials. I am grateful for the help of the Foreign Affairs Office of Zouping County, of Ni Anru, Shandong University, and, most of all, of my interviewees.

5. I will use the word *doctor* in a broad sense about all medical practitioners regardless of their educational background.

6. For a discussion of different images of the schoolmaster in later Qing literary works, see Allan Barr, "Four Schoolmasters. Educational Issues in Li Hai-kuan's Lamp at the Crossroads," in Benjamin A. Elman and Alexander Woodside, eds., *Education and Society in Late Imperial China, 1600–1900* (Berkeley: University of California Press, 1994), 50–75.

7. Arthur H. Smith, *Village Life in China: A Study in Sociology* (New York: Fleming H. Revell Co., 1898), 102.

8. Liao T'ai-ch'u, "Rural Education in Transition: A Study of the Old-Fashioned Chinese Schools (Szu Shu) in Shantung and Szechuan," *Yenching Journal of Social Studies* 4, no. 2 (February 1949): 19–67.

9. Literacy alone was, in fact, of much practical value in late Qing and Republican China, and literate people could assist fellow villagers in many fields. See Evelyn S. Rawski, *Education and Popular Literacy in Ch'ing China* (Ann Arbor: University of Michigan Press, 1979); and James Hayes, "Specialists and Written Materials in the Village World," in David Johnson, Andrew J. Nathan, and Evelyn S. Rawski, eds., *Popular Culture in Late Imperial China* (Berkeley: University of California Press, 1985), 75–111.

10. An Zuozhang, ed., *Shandong tongshi, jindai juan* (A general history of Shandong, the modern times) 2 vols. (Jinan: Shandong renmin chubanshe, 1995), 2:528–29; "Zouping xian jiaoyuzhi" bianzuan lingdao xiaozu: *Zouping xian jiaoyuzhi* (Zouping county education gazetteer) (Jinan: Shandong sheng chuban zongshe Huimin fenshe, 1990), 285; *Zouping xian zhi* (Zouping county gazetteer) (1915; rpt., Taiwan: 1972), 360.

11. The only exception was a sericultural school run by the county administration from 1910 to 1933, but this school seems to have held little prestige. *Zouping xian jiaoyuzhi*, 305–6.

12. The nearest middle school was found in neighboring Changshan county. Zouping did not get its own middle school until 1942.

13. *Zouping xian jiaoyuzhi*, 372.

14. Alitto, *Last Confucian*, 238–78.

15. Zhang Zonglin was one of China's most prominent specialists on preschool education and was influenced by the most progressive European and American theories of his time. See Zhang Lu, ed., *Zhang Zonglin youer jiaoyu lunji* (Zhang Zonglin's selected works on the education of children) (Changsha: Hunan jiaoyu chubanshe,

1985); Zhang Lu, ed., *Zhang Zonglin xiangcun jiaoyu lunji* (Zhang Zonglin's selected works on rural education) (Changsha: Hunan jiaoyu chubanshe, 1987).

16. Interview no. 19, 1992.

17. *Zouping xian jiaoyuzhi*, 374.

18. Ibid., 377.

19. Ibid., 372.

20. Ibid., 144–47, 176–79.

21. Ibid., 373.

22. Interview no. 15, 1993.

23. Interview no. 6, 1996.

24. Interview no. 5, 1992.

25. Ibid.

26. For an interesting discussion of the effect of market reforms on gender relations in rural Shandong, see Ellen Judd, *Gender and Power in Rural North China* (Stanford: Stanford University Press, 1994).

27. Qu Yanqing, "Ren shu ji shi liu yu hou ren" (His contemporaries benefited from his kindness, his reputation still lives in posterity), *Zouping wenshi ziliao xuanji* (Selected materials on Zouping history and culture) 3 (1986): 215–21.

28. Ka-che Yip, *Health and National Reconstruction in Nationalist China. The Development of Modern Health Services, 1928–1937* (Ann Arbor: Association for Asian Studies, Monograph and Occasional Paper Series, no. 50, 1995), 15, 58–59.

29. For an interesting view on rural health care and health education through the twentieth century, including the conflict between traditional and modern medicine, see C. C. Chen (in collaboration with Fredericia M. Bunge), *Medicine in Rural China: A Personal Account* (Berkeley: University of California Press, 1989).

30. Shandong sheng Zouping xian difang shizhi bianzuan weiyuanhui, eds., *Zouping xianzhi* (Zouping county gazetteer) (Beijing: Zhonghua shuju, 1992), 806.

31. *Zouping xianzhi*, 1992, 806–7.

32. *Zouping xian jiaoyuzhi*, 315–16.

33. Interview no. 11, 1993.

34. Interview no. 3, 1993.

35. An opposite trend of deprofessionalization may be at work at the same time, however, because the privatization of rural medicine combined with the market economic reforms leaves more room for unofficial healers and herbalists who have received no formal medical education and who work outside any state control.

36. Interview no. 29, 1996. In his ethnography of a prerevolution Shandong village Martin C. Yang also found that the artisans made more money than the farmers, but people still preferred to engage in agriculture because of the value they attached to owning land. See Martin C. Yang: *A Chinese Village. Taitou, Shandong Province* (London: Kegan Paul, 1947), 25–27. In Lijiazhuang the blacksmiths appear to have held considerable prestige.

37. John S. Burgess, *The Guilds of Peking* (New York: Columbia University Press, 1928); Liao T'ai-ch'u, "The Apprentices in Chengtu during and after the War," *Yenching Journal of Social Studies* 4, no. 1 (August 1948): 1103–20.

38. Interview no. 19, 1993.

39. Interview no. 21, 1993.

40. Interview no. 19, 1993.

41. Interview no. 29, 1993.

42. Interview no. 29, 1996. I was unable to interview these families, because the men did not work in the village, but the quality of the houses they were building indicated that my informant's opinion was correct.

43. *Shandong tongshi, jindai juan,* 529; *Zouping xian jiaoyuzhi,* 305–6. The agricultural school changed its specialization to sericulture in 1912.

44. For a broader discussion of vocational and labor education in China, see, for example, Matthias Risler, *Berufsbildung in China. Rot und Experte* (Hamburg: Mitteilungen des Institut für Asienkunde Nr. 179, 1987); Jan-Ingvar Löfstedt, *Practice and Work in Chinese Education: Why, How and How Much,* (Stockholm: University of Stockholm, Center for Pacific Asia Studies, Working Paper no. 5, 1987); Stig Thøgersen, *Secondary Education in China after Mao: Reform and Social Conflict* (Aarhus: Aarhus University Press, 1990), 94–117.

45. There are too few agricultural school graduates among my informants to justify any firm conclusion, but it is well-known that farmers with more schooling often do more off-farm work than others (see, e.g., Dennis Tao Yang, "Education and Off-Farm Work," *Economic Development and Cultural Change* 45, no. 3 [April 1997]: 613–32), and it seems likely that agricultural schooling, contrary to the intentions of the planners, has a similar effect.

46. Interview no. 31, 1996.

47. Interview no. 2, 1996.

48. Interview no. 13, 1992.

49. Ziboshi Zhoucun qu jiaoyuzhi bangongshi, *Zhoucun qu jiaoyuzhi 1840–1985* [Zhoucun district educational gazetteer 1840–1985] (N.p.p., 1987), 184–86.

50. Interviews nos. 10, 1993, and 17, 1996.

51. Interviews nos. 12 and 13, 1993.

52. From an unpublished chapter of a doctoral thesis by Ray Yep, Oxford University, 1997.

University Autonomy in Twentieth-Century China

Ningsha Zhong and Ruth Hayhoe

In this essay we wish to explore the concept of university autonomy that is emerging at present in China and clarify some of the features that distinguish it from the Western concept. We begin with some reflections on key terms in the Chinese discourse in part 1 and then, in part 2, develop a broad historical overview of the ways in which autonomy was understood in classical China and in the three main periods of modern China's development. In part 3 we analyze the reform period, since 1978, and seek to understand how the autonomy of contemporary Chinese universities is taking shape within the particular conditions provided by the Dengist reforms. Finally, in part 4 we look at three universities under different jurisdictions in China's Southwest region and explore the ways in which they have asserted some autonomy in responding to the opportunities provided by the present environment.

University Autonomy and Chinese Ways of Knowing

Many terms in the Chinese language can be used to translate *autonomy,* but two strike us as particularly important: *zizhiquan* (autonomy as independence) and *zizhuquan* (autonomy as self-mastery). Autonomy as independence is widely used in political contexts, such as China's autonomous regions, but in the context of the higher education literature the term is usually associated with Western universities. It implies the need for universities to avoid external interference and suggests autonomy as an end in itself. It has the connotation of political sovereignty in the Chinese language and so is highly sensitive.[1] The second term, autonomy as self-mastery, implies that universities and colleges should be encouraged to act upon their own and respond to social needs within the framework of government policies. The idea of autonomy as self-mastery involves the liberation of the minds of university members on a deep level and from a practical perspective: daring to think and daring to do things. This term avoids political controversy, with reference to the leadership of the Chinese Communist Party (CCP) on campus. The contemporary scholarly literature on higher education in China tends to use autonomy as self-mastery to analyze changes taking place in universities over the reform period.[2]

Two important concepts that are often used in conjunction with autonomy as self-mastery are "responsibility" (*zeren*) and "legal persons" (*faren*). The concept of responsibility is drawn from the responsibility system (*zeren zhi*) adopted in agriculture and industry and reflects the fact that Chinese universities have a strong orientation toward serving society. All government policies that involve the delegation of new powers to universities come along with new responsibilities, particularly financial ones. Universities are expected to meet more and more of their own financial needs through offering a range of services to government, industry, and society more generally. The term *legal persons* expresses the new status universities have, for example independent of the government administrative structures in which they were formerly lodged. The Education Law of 1995 rules that higher education institutions should be self-governed and specifies the new powers delegated to them. Their activities are now to be regulated by law, rather than by administrative fiat from above.[3] In practice the new status of universities as legal persons is expected to protect their interests and enhance their freedom of action.

The literature linked to the concept of autonomy as self-mastery (*zizhuquan*) can be traced back to the early part of the reform period. At a provincial government meeting on university governance in 1979, Zhao Ziyang, then Party secretary of Sichuan province,[4] announced that the provincial government would give universities some autonomy so that they could create alternative funding sources, on condition that they would not ask for more money from the government.[5] Autonomy as self-mastery thus emerged first as a practical initiative encouraging universities to subsidize government provision for their needs. An early study carried out by Cheng Hongsheng,[6] a university vice president, pointed out that university autonomy in China took the reform of enterprise as its reference point, with a focus on practical activities for institutional development. Autonomous procedures for making internal regulations and implementing a kind of responsibility system were developed in many institutions. Some of the ingredients of autonomy included the freedom to select students and staff, to design curricula within certain limitations, and to allocate income from the state and private sources.

We believe the concept of autonomy as self-mastery is rooted in Chinese intellectual traditions and is expressive of deep features of Chinese culture. At the same time, such dimensions as the notion of universities as legal persons, and as corporate bodies, are linked to the Western tradition. There university autonomy is understood as both institutional and ideological independence from government interference and is rooted in a long historical tradition in which the universities constituted a kind of third force, between state and church.[7] Hayhoe's book on China's universities[8] traces the introduction of the Western idea of university autonomy and academic freedom in the development of China's modern universities between the late nineteenth and the early twentieth centuries, through the leadership of scholars such as Ma Xiangbo, Cai Yuanpei, and Hu Shi. In a sense the present period is providing a new phase of experimentation in institutional development, with dimensions of the Western models that were influential in the Nationalist period being revived.

The literature linked to the Chinese intellectual tradition provides a somewhat different picture of the role of intellectuals and their institutions within Chinese society. Pepper sees the failure of radical change in recent decades as resulting from the control of professional educators, rooted in a tradition in which intellectuals shared power with rulers. She suggests that the history of Chinese higher education be rewritten as a history of how professional educators gained not only autonomy but the capacity to direct social change through the established educational system.[9] Within this framework the practical autonomy enjoyed by Chinese intellectuals could be examined in particular institutions and periods over China's long history. Examples include studies of the Song dynasty, such as that of de Bary and Chaffee,[10] of the Ming dynasty, such as that of Meskill,[11] and of the Qing dynasty, such as that of Elman and Woodside.[12] This practical autonomy is in turn related to epistemological traditions very different from those of the West. Li Zehou defines a dominant thread of Chinese epistemology as pragmatic rationality, whereby one obtains knowledge through concrete action rather than by abstract thinking. "A gentleman is slow in speech, but quick in action" and "Listening to one's speech but trusting one's action" are two quotes from Confucius that illustrate this emphasis.[13] In Chinese culture knowing has always been focused on action. It is both participatory and creative—"tracing" in the sense of etching a pattern and of following it. To know is to realize and to make real. The path to the truth is not given but is made in the treading of it. Actions are always a significant factor in the shaping of one's world. It is the group, however, more than the individual, that is the subject of knowing and action.[14] This point is particularly relevant to understanding Chinese universities' experience in the reform period.

We are thus sketching out an initial concept of university autonomy in the Chinese context, which emphasizes the initiation of action and the mastery of the skills for action. Autonomy as self-mastery (*zizhuquan*), the contemporary manifestation of the Chinese concept of autonomy, has historical roots in both the modern period and the premodern period. We see it as a feature of Chinese culture, which we will seek to explore and interpret in relation to this historical context.

Autonomy as Self-Mastery in China's Historical Experience

In this highly condensed reflection on China's historical experience of autonomy with relation to higher education, we deal first with the long dynastic period, when certain persistent patterns can be identified, then with three historical stages after 1842 that saw very rapid changes: the late Qing (1842–1911), the Republican period (1911–49), and the socialist period (1949–78). Traditionally, China had two levels of education, basic and higher education. While basic education focused on literacy and common knowledge, higher education led students to specialized knowledge of the classics and skills for governing the state. The theoretical foundation of education for much of this long history was Confucianism, and the value of education was viewed in relation to its impact on human government and its contribution to the establishment of a harmonious social order.

In the light of Confucianism higher education was closely linked to state administration. One product of this link between higher education and state administration in traditional China was the national higher education system, which was composed of official and private institutions. Official institutions emerged in the western Han dynasty (206 B.C. to 25 B.C.), with the establishment of the Central College (*taixue*) in 124 B.C.E.[15] During the Sui dynasty (581–618) the Central University (*guozijian*) was established as both the highest level of academic institution and the highest administrative organ for education. As a teaching institution, the Central University had several colleges, including the college for sons of the state (*guozixue*), the central college (*taixue*), the college for the four studies of Confucianism, history, metaphysics, and literature (*simenxue*), language (*shuxue*), and mathematics (*suanxue*). As an administrative body, it was responsible for inspection and academic standards in official schools at the provincial, prefectural, and county levels.[16]

By the Ming dynasty (1378–1644) a complete national higher education system had taken form, composed of the National University in the capital and about 1,700 institutions in provincial, prefectural, and county areas, with more than four thousand teacher-officials.[17]

Parallel to the official institutions were private institutions of higher learning such as the *shuyuan* (academies). The first academy was associated with the official library in the late Tang dynasty (618–907), and by the Song (960–1279) academies had emerged as teaching and research institutions. There were 173 at one count, with the 4 most famous being the Bailudong (the cave of the white deer), Yingtianfu (response to the sky), Yuelu (the foot of the high mountain), and Shigu (the stone drum).[18] Many academies were located away from cities and towns, in places of natural beauty and cultural appeal.[19] They were largely founded and funded by individual gentry, scholars, or governmental officials, but some got official support through grants of land.[20] Focusing on the study of Neo-Confucianism and practical knowledge, academies provided an alternative learning experience to that of governmental schools. They made an important contribution to Chinese higher education in terms of developing methods of self-study, classroom discussion, and academic debates (*jianghui*).[21] The informal character of these institutions placed them at the opposite pole from the official state institutions and provided a space for independent critical inquiry and even oppositional politics. Their approach to knowledge and the role of the intellectual, however, was fundamentally similar to that of the state institutions.

The other product of the link between higher education and state administration was the imperial examination system, which began in the Sui dynasty (581–618) with the establishment of the "department of advanced scholars" (*jinshike*),[22] developed into its mature form in the Tang dynasty (618–907), and lasted until 1905. In the Ming and Qing dynasties (1368–1911) the imperial examination system took the form of formal examinations at provincial (*xiangshi*), metropolitan (*huishi*), and palace (*dianshi*) levels. Three different titles associated with these examinations were granted to those who had passed. The titles of "recommended person" (*juren*) at the provincial level, "selected scholar" (*gongshi*) at the metropolitan level, and "advanced scholar" (*jinshi*) at the palace level[23] can be regarded as parallel to the degrees of the bachelor, the master, and the doctor in Western universities. The impact of these titles on students and their families was very different in China, however, than in the West. The titles not only qualified Chinese scholars for official positions but also gave privileges to their families.

Both higher learning institutions and the civil service examination system had a profound influence on national politics. The most important aspect was the creation of a contingent of intellectuals at various levels: scholar-officials in the government, teachers and students in both official and private institutions, and gentry in broad areas of society. For the most part these intellectuals identified themselves not with a particular institution but, rather, with the whole system of education and the state. Their connection to the state is the key to understanding the continuity of Chinese higher education through the dynastic period. It also sheds a great deal of light on the way in which intellectuals have behaved and the concept of autonomy that has emerged over the modern period.

Although the structures of traditional higher education were undermined and finally collapsed, between 1842 and 1905, the influence of the Confucian intellectual tradition has continued, shaping higher education development toward the integration of university learning and national development. This is especially reflected in the idea of Chinese learning as the essence and Western learning for its usefulness,[24] which became a central theme in Chinese higher education development in the period between 1842 and 1911 and determined the structure of the Imperial University, later called Beijing University. It was founded in 1898 as one of the first modern universities. In these new institutions structure and curricular content of European universities were transplanted, but Confucianism was still maintained as the guiding ideology. Zhang Hengjia, the general superintendent of the National University of Beijing from 1903 to 1905, explained the reason in the following words:

> Now foreign influences are very strong. To resist them, we must educate our people to work out a better government and country. We must cultivate self-esteem and independence. We must evaluate our history and promote love and respect for the emperor and parents. We learn from Europe and America for their wisdom, but we can gain virtue only from Confucianism. Our teaching principle is to learn positive things from others, discard our shortcomings, correct our mistakes, and keep what is good in our tradition.[25]

A positive attempt was being made to form an approach to higher education development that had Chinese characteristics.[26] This approach particularly emphasized the government's leading role in fostering modernization through higher education. By the first decade of this century there were 128 officially recognized higher education institutions of various levels, three of which were regarded as universities.[27]

After the Revolution of 1911 successive Republican and warlord governments made great efforts to develop a modern educational system, setting new aims and moving away from Zhang Zhidong's formula, on the surface at least. The goal of education had changed from preparing personnel for official-dom to preparing personnel with practical skills for the wider needs of soci-ety. The University Act of 1912 promulgated the aim of the university as "teaching high levels of learning and cultivating talent with general knowledge for the needs of the state."[28] In 1922 the government changed the educational system to follow the American pattern, reducing the length of study and adopting more practical aims of training specialists for all fields needed by society.[29]

A national system of higher education gradually took shape, composed of universities, independent colleges, and higher specialized schools. In the public sector there were two kinds of institutions: national institutions that were controlled and funded by the central government and local public institutions that were controlled and funded by the provincial and municipal governments. Universities were mostly controlled by the central government and represented the highest level of scholarship and prestige. Local economic development and civil conditions very much influenced local public institu-tions, making for great differences among different regions.

In the private sector there were religious institutions and independent institutions. The religious institutions were founded and continued to be funded by Christian churches, mainly in the United States, Canada, and Europe. They had been among the earliest higher education institutions and became integrated into the national education system after 1927, while still being funded by churches.[30] The independent institutions were founded and funded by individuals, associations, or social groups and had some parallel to traditional academies. Both types of private institutions flourished in this period, and a few won national reputations such as Yanjing University (1919) for its focus on liberal education and law and Nankai University (1919) for its focus on economics and social sciences.[31]

By 1947 there were 207 higher education institutions, including 74 na-tional, 54 provincial, and 79 private ones. There was a total of 20,133 faculty members, 155,036 students, and 424 graduate students.[32] The development of these institutions had transformed the Chinese intellectual community. Uni-versity teachers had become a professional group that took leadership in advancing various specialist knowledge areas, while they and their students were also extremely active in various types of protest movement.[33] Higher education was less closely linked to the bureaucratic system institutionally than ever before, even though the national government still assumed a major responsibility for it, with 61.4 percent of all higher institutions being public and 38.6 percent being private.

In 1949 the People's Republic of China was established under the leadership of the Chinese Communist Party. At the First National Conference on Education in 1950, Qian Junrui, the deputy minister, announced the aim of Chinese education as serving socialism and fostering economic development. The decision of the Chinese government to reshape the higher education system on the example of Soviet education was discussed.[34] To realize this aim, the Chinese government took over all private institutions, including over twenty universities and colleges funded by the churches. In 1952 the government began to reorganize the higher education system, in order to ensure a fair geographic distribution of opportunity and a direct service to socialist construction through the training of specialists in specific areas. The new system had eleven types of institutions, based on subject matter: comprehensive, engineering, teacher training, agriculture, forestry, medicine, finance, law and political science, music, fine arts, and sports. There were graduate, undergraduate, and short-cycle undergraduate studies, but no degrees were conferred, nor was the development of institutional identity encouraged. A system of specialties was introduced, through which a standard nationwide curriculum was linked to the practical needs of society for specialists and fitted in with a national system for planning.[35] Effectively, the map of higher education was redrawn, with the academic departments of all of the former universities and colleges reorganized into a new set of higher institutions, designed according to patterns introduced from the Soviet Union.[36]

In this overview of the history of Chinese higher education, one theme remains relatively constant, that is, autonomy as a kind of administrative power and the ability of intellectuals to use that power in initiating action in order to serve society. Traditionally, this can be seen in intellectuals' collective authority and the integration of higher education within the state administration. The notion of university autonomy was implicit in traditional times, and its essence is most vividly conveyed by the following comment of a nineteenth-century British admirer: "The whole of China may be said to resemble one vast university, which is governed by the scholars who have been educated within its walls."[37] No group identified itself with a particular institution within the higher education system, but all established intellectuals shared power with the emperor. They organized the government and formed schools, constituting government officials and school members. Within the bureaucratic system of the state they enjoyed the right to control and regulate knowledge on behalf of the emperor.

In modern times the Western value of university autonomy informed the development of Chinese universities.[38] It was redefined, however, in a context very different from that of the West. We have noted three layers to the meaning of *autonomy* in Chinese universities in this period. The first layer is closely related to issues of national sovereignty in a period of imperialism. The second takes up the relationship between higher education and the government within the context of a developing modern state. The third deals with the practical expression of autonomy at the operational level in Chinese institutions, a significant aspect in light of the pragmatic rationalism that characterizes Chinese epistemology.

In terms of the first layer the concept of autonomy became linked to the freedom and independence of China's modern universities in the face of foreign imperialism. When China did not have political independence, it was impossible for Chinese higher education to have true autonomy. In the late Qing some foreign governments frequently interfered with hiring issues at the National University of Beijing.[39] In the 1930s the Japanese purposely targeted universities in their bombing attacks, as they knew that university intellectuals provided a focal point of resistance.[40] Christian missionary control over some twenty universities and colleges was also an issue of educational sovereignty. In an earlier section of this volume, Dan Cui described in some detail the diverse concerns of the Chinese and of missionaries over the issue of nationalization. It was only after 1949 that all forms of foreign control and pressure, including that of the church, were finally lifted.[41] For many Chinese people an increase of autonomy for China in the larger international context and in relation to imperialism was one of the most important achievements of the 1949 revolution.

The second layer of the meaning of *autonomy* in the Chinese context relates to the relationship between higher education institutions and the government. The main issue is whether higher education institutions should or could be independent from national politics. The Western concept of university autonomy as independence from direct governmental control influenced Chinese intellectuals in their struggle to form credible modern universities over the first half of the twentieth century. Higher education institutions had a defined legal status, and university teachers began to form into a professional group devoted mainly to teaching and research.[42] For various reasons, however, higher education institutions were not able to become independent from national politics.

Of particular note in this regard was the work of Cai Yuanpei (1868–1940), who tried to integrate the traditional value of higher education as a social agent to improve government and society with the Western spirit of autonomy. In his position as minister of education in 1912, he advocated the independence of education from the control of both national politics and religion and suggested that education should have its own independent administration, funding, ideas, and content. In 1927 he tried to establish a national academic council, which would give academics statutory power to govern the whole education system, independent of the Nationalist Party and of state bureaucratic structures. This experiment ended after one year, however, having gained neither the approval of the Nationalist Party and government nor the support of leaders within the education system.[43]

For the Chinese Communist Party the idea of the independence of higher education from the state or national politics was not acceptable. After 1949 the Chinese government adopted the Soviet model, integrating its higher education into the social, economic, and political development of the country. All higher education institutions became public and were put under government control. A small number were administered directly by the Ministry of Education, a somewhat larger number by central ministries and agencies, and others by provincial governments. Their relationship with the Communist Party and with various sectors of government put universities and colleges in a position in which they had to operate as a part of the socialist bureaucracy. Teachers were integrated into the state personnel system as cadres, a status that weakened their identity as a professional group. Students graduating from formal higher education institutions were guaranteed positions as state cadres.

A third layer of *autonomy* can be explored in terms of the operational settings of the university. Here the focus is on the freedom of the university as a collective group to create its own agenda and initiate action based on that agenda within the local, national, and international context. Once again, it was Cai Yuanpei who made the most important historical contribution at this level. When he became chancellor of Beijing University in 1917, he set the aim of the university as the pursuit of higher learning, encouraged academic and ideological freedom, and fostered science and democracy on campus. Cai's management model, which had been inspired by his years of study at the universities of Berlin and Leipzig, was to have considerable influence on Chinese universities in the Nationalist period. Cai's chosen phrase for university autonomy was *professorial governance* (*jiaoshou zhixiao*), and at the heart of this process was the university council. A university council was established at Beijing University as the highest decision-making body. Constituted by the president, deans of the colleges, and chairs of the departments as well as representatives of all of the professors, it made all regulations governing the internal life of the university, determined the establishment of subjects, examined the faculty's professorial titles and students' academic records, and controlled the budget. During Cai's period of office the university council passed "the Organization Act of the Association of Professors in Universities and

Colleges" (1917) and "the Internal Organization Act" (1919), which established the power of professors on campus and regulated the ways in which that power was to be used.[44] The mechanisms of democracy established at Beijing University under Cai gave the university continuity over time and made it an influential model throughout the Nationalist period.

After 1949 higher education became fully integrated into the new socialist system, and autonomy at this level no longer seemed important. Individual universities and colleges had very little room to operate, except in the arena of nonformal education, where there was considerable freedom, since graduates were not given access to the state cadre system. Admission into higher education was determined by a national, unified set of entry examinations. When students graduated, universities were responsible to dispatch them to positions within the state bureaucracy, which the government had arranged. The curriculum was strictly regulated, with detailed curricular plans and course outlines centrally established for each of the hundreds of specializations. These had an almost lawlike authority.[45] The hiring of teachers for higher education was regulated through the state labor and cadre system, in accordance with macro planning processes. There was thus no possibility of universities taking independent initiatives or exercising genuine intellectual autonomy. Compliance with and conformity to the requirements of the socialist state was largely assured through the patterns of the system itself. Those intellectuals who had the courage to express independent and critical opinions in the Hundred Flowers Movement of 1956 paid a very high price.[46]

University Autonomy and the Reforms since 1978

At the Third Plenary Session of the Eleventh Congress of the CCP in December 1978, the Chinese leadership announced a plan of economic reform. It started from the countryside in the late 1970s and was expanded to urban areas in the early 1980s. In the 1990s the reform went into all domains of the economy to establish a market economy with socialist characteristics.[47] This is sometimes described as a planned commodity economy with such qualities as multiple ownership of the means of production with the state and collective bodies controlling most of the national economy, diverse development of private enterprises, a distribution system based on contribution, and capitalist mechanisms such as the stock system, joint and foreign ventures, the tax system, the role of banks, and small business.

Within the national context of economic reform, universities and colleges no longer fit into the national development of a market economy. They have therefore been called upon to adapt to ongoing social change. Government policies provide a framework for this process. In 1985 the Central Committee of the CCP issued an important decision on educational reform, calling upon universities and colleges to prepare more and more talented and qualified personnel for economic development. The reformed higher education system was to have an appropriate structure, diverse programs, and multiple levels and types of institutions. In addition to educating high-level professionals, the new mandate called on universities to conduct scientific research independently, commercialize research results, and solve theoretical and practical problems, which emerged during modernization. The decision outlined the main areas relating to academic programs, personnel, and finance, in which the government would delegate greater power and responsibility to individual institutions.[48]

In 1986 the State Council issued a detailed policy statement, granting universities and colleges the following new rights: to enroll a certain number of self-paid or industry-sponsored students and develop cooperative relationships with government and business organizations; to allocate the funds provided by the government and the funds generated by themselves; to select construction companies to carry out capital planning, design, and construction; to appoint and dismiss the vice president, administrative officers, teachers, and staff and to approve professorial titles of associate professor in most universities and that of professor in a few universities; to develop programs and to select teaching materials and methods; to do research; to participate in community services; to accept donations from external units; to amalgamate with other legal bodies; to spend self-generated funds according to their own priorities; and to participate in foreign exchanges and to send people to study abroad or to invite foreign scholars for academic purposes.[49]

In 1993 the Central Committee of the CCP and the State Council issued an "Outline for the Reform and Development of China's Education." It confirmed the principle of autonomy (*zizhuquan*) and urged universities and colleges to establish mechanisms of self-regulation and responsibility. The outline announced plans to strengthen the legal status of universities and colleges.[50] This culminated in the first comprehensive educational law, promulgated in 1995. *Autonomy* (*zizhuquan*) is made explicit in the law. The law defines universities as legal persons subject to supervision by the government. The president is the legal representative of the university, responsible for both academic matters and administration. Universities and colleges have the following rights: to govern themselves under their charter and organize teaching activities and student admission; to control registration and internal discipline; to issue diplomas and certificates; to hire faculty members and other staff and reward or punish them; to manage and spend funds allocated to the institution; to reject any individual or organization's illegal interference into teaching and learning activities in the institution; and to enjoy all other rights granted by law. They also have the following responsibilities: to abide by the law; to carry out government policies and ensure educational quality; to protect the rights of students, teachers, and staff; to provide students and their guardians with information on their performance in appropriate ways; to set up standards for fees according to the state's regulation and publish an itemization of the fee structure; to be subjected to supervision according to the law.[51]

All these policies provide guidelines for universities and colleges as they move into a new era. They have left considerable space for universities and colleges to take action and to fulfill visions they define for themselves. As a result, a novel set of activities has emerged under the rubric of university autonomy, and there has been a ferment of discussion around the concept itself. Autonomy as a way of thinking and a code of action has become explicit in this period.

The first layer of the meaning of autonomy, discussed earlier, is related to the sovereignty of Chinese universities. There is still an awareness of educational sovereignty in this period, and little change is expected to the stance adopted in 1949. Although the Chinese government has invited foreign educators to come to teach and to run joint educational institutions, it has protected educational sovereignty through maintaining universities as public institutions and affirming the CCP's leadership on campus.

The second layer of the meaning of *autonomy* can be seen in the adjustments being made in the relationship between higher education and the state. While the CCP's leadership in higher education continues, the government has given new powers to universities, allowing them to govern themselves within the framework of the policies elaborated here. Universities have been given the status and rights of legal persons, and the only limitations on their independence of action are their responsibilities under the law. State policy development since 1991 has given universities new opportunities to contribute to national development through such high-profile projects as the 2/1/1 program, the purpose of which is to develop one hundred key universities and some key programs to a level of excellence consonant with the best in the world during the twenty-first century.[52] These universities are expected to play a prominent role in national modernization.

The third layer of the meaning of *autonomy* is examined through the operational settings of universities. Practical autonomy can be seen in three aspects of university life: academic matters, personnel, and finance. The idea of professorial governance developed by Cai Yuanpei in the Nationalist period has been revived, with the reestablishment of the status of academic staff after the Cultural Revolution and the restoration of the presidential responsibility system. Autonomy can be seen in the space universities now have to make their own internal policies, within the framework of government policies, and to take action based on policies they have developed themselves. The most important areas of initiative have been in student admission and job placement, the adjustment of program definitions and directions, the appointment of administrators, the creation of alternative sources of funds, the allocation of government funds, and international academic exchange. In all of these areas the government no longer gives instructions but leaves it up to universities and colleges to consider how they should act and respond to the needs and conditions they find around them. This is quite unprecedented in the history of higher education since 1949.

Case Studies in University Autonomy

In this last section of the essay we will explore the actual experience of three Chinese universities during the reform period, all in the southwestern province of Sichuan. Sichuan Union University (SUU), located in Chengdu, is a national comprehensive university, administered directly by the State Education Commission. Chongqing Industry and Management Institute (CIMI) is located in the city of Chongqing and is administered by the Ministry of Armament Industry. Chongqing Teachers' College (CTC), also located in Chongqing, is a provincial-level institution, under the administration of the Sichuan provincial government. In the autumn of 1996 Ningsha Zhong spent several months in these two cities, carrying out intensive interviews with three groups: academic and Party leaders, faculty members, and students. Her focus was on clarifying how the concept of autonomy was understood by these members of the university community in the practical context of recent reforms and how it had found expression in action. The three cases sketched out here will thus illustrate different facets of autonomy as experienced by members of these three different institutions.

Sichuan Union University

Sichuan Union University (Sichuan lianhe daxue) is the new name given to the merger of two institutions, Sichuan University and Chengdu Science and Technology University, which had formerly been one institution before 1949. SUU has gained a lot of attention most recently as a new model of Chinese higher education, a multiversity with liberal arts, pure sciences, engineering, economics, management, law, and other applied sciences and arts. University autonomy was an essential precondition to the development of this model through the imagination and efforts of members of both universities.[53]

In 1995 SUU had an academic staff of four thousand three hundred and a student body of twenty-five thousand, including one thousand five hundred graduate students, making it the largest university in China. It boasted two academicians on its faculty, sixty-nine doctoral student supervisors, and a number of nationally distinguished younger scholars. Every year it attracted more than one hundred foreign students and about five hundred researchers and teachers from other parts of China there for various kinds of academic upgrading.[54]

SUU's origins can be traced back to the founding dates of the Sino-Western School (Zhongxi xuetang, 1896–1902), the province's first modern tertiary institution, and two traditional academies (Jingjiang Shuyuan, 1704–1902, and Zunjing Shuyuan, 1875–1902). In 1902 the provincial governor, Kui Jun, amalgamated these three institutions to form the Sichuan provincial institution of higher education (Sichuan shengcheng gaodeng xuetang). Modeling itself after Beijing University, it became a comprehensive university with four colleges: arts and sciences, teacher training, sports, and preparatory study for university. The first president was Hu Jun, a holder of the highest traditional academic title, advanced scholar (*jinshi*), and a member of the Hanlin Academy.[55]

From 1911 to 1927 the institution's status as a provincial comprehensive university was lost, and from 1916 to 1926 it was closed down, by order of the central government.[56] In 1926 the institution was restored under the name of National Chengdu University, and in 1931 the Nationalist government approved the establishment of National Sichuan University (NSU). It was based on the amalgamation of National Chengdu University, National Chengdu Normal University, and Public Sichuan University, an institution focusing on applied sciences. The university made the transition from a local institution to a national one in terms of teaching objectives, faculty origins, student sources, structures, and material conditions in subsequent years, with the help of direct funding from the central government. In 1949 NSU had 5,057 students, 371 faculty members, and 614 staff. Its six colleges embraced engineering, agriculture, law, sciences, liberal arts, and teacher training, and under them were twenty-five academic departments and two semi–independent research institutes.[57]

Under the Communist regime it continued to be recognized as a national comprehensive university, but its institutional identity underwent drastic change, as it was made to conform to the newly adopted Soviet model. The nationwide restructuring of higher education that took place in 1952 left Sichuan University with only two subject areas: arts and sciences. Its law college was merged with the Southwestern Law and Politics Institute located in Chongqing; its engineering college was formed into an independent institute, Chengdu Engineering Institute (later Chengdu Science and Technology University); its agriculture college merged with the Sichuan Agriculture Institute located in Ya'an; and its teacher training college moved into Sichuan Teachers' College located in the north of downtown Chengdu. As a national comprehensive university within the new model of higher education that had been adopted, it still enjoyed the highest academic status in the province and, indeed, in the whole southwestern region. It was one of fourteen universities nationwide having this position. In 1960 it was delineated as one of the national keypoint universities affiliated with the Ministry of Education.

After being moved out of Sichuan University in 1952, the Chengdu Engineering Institute was combined with departments and colleges of other universities in certain areas of engineering and became a highly specialized institution, focusing on mechanical engineering, hydroelectricity, and applied chemistry. In 1978 its name was changed to Chengdu Science and Technology University, and it became a national keypoint university. In the beginning of 1993 Beijing put forward its ambitious project to develop one hundred world-class universities for the twenty-first century (dubbed the 2/1/1 program), which was highly attractive to universities under the jurisdiction of central government agencies, due to the funding and the prestige it promised. One of the conditions for entering the project was based on institutional type. What Beijing wanted to encourage was the redevelopment of comprehensive universities in the Western rather than the Soviet sense, institutions that combined the arts, basic sciences, and such applied fields as engineering, agriculture, and medicine. Since neither Sichuan University nor Chengdu Science and Technology University could meet the requirements of the project on their own, the leaders of the two universities began to consider a merger. They had been one institution before 1949, and both were now affiliated with the State Education Commission, factors that greatly facilitated the move toward amalgamation. In May 1993 the SEC approved their merger, and in July 1994 the two universities officially joined as one under a new name, Sichuan Union University. This merger was described as "a breakthrough in the stereotype for decades that tech-oriented institutions should be divorced from arts and pure sciences."[58]

Being among thirty-five keypoint universities affiliated to the SEC, Sichuan Union University is the first and, so far, the only case of such an amalgamation. The merger has served to strengthen considerably the university's position in the national higher education system.[59] Although SUU mainly turns out specialists for important state projects and national enterprises, as well as teachers for higher education institutions, as a teaching and research university it has considerable breadth in its training objectives. This is reflected first of all in research. As a national keypoint university, SUU is far ahead of the other two institutions we will be considering. It has been involved in dozens of key state projects and other contracted research and has obtained millions of yuan in research funds each year. Its curriculum has also been significantly broadened by recent changes. There are now 109 undergraduate specialties, 90 master's programs, 31 doctoral programs, 5 national keypoint subjects, and 3 postdoctoral study areas. In governance one of its striking innovations has been its ability to develop cooperative relationships with the provincial and municipal governments, which have provided tremendous financial support for its bid to enter the 2/1/1 project.[60] In terms of internal governance, the power of the president and of academic faculty over all academic affairs has been affirmed, and freedom to adjust internal administrative and staffing structures has been obtained.

The authority and power of the president has emerged as a notable aspect of the change, due to the fact that the present president is a high-profile scientist and doctoral supervisor who is widely respected in his administrative as well as academic role. Under presidential administration several academic committees have been set up to supervise and guide academic development. The degree committee is responsible for decisions about conferring degrees on students at all levels; the subject development council is in charge of the development of new programs and specialties; the academic title committee approves the academic titles of faculty members and administrators; and the text development council supervises the writing and publication of textbooks. Professors and associate professors are members of these committees, all of which are chaired by the president. With the help of these committees, the university manages academic planning, program development, the appointment of teachers, finance, foreign exchange, and the overall direction of university development, within the policies of the CCP and the State Council.

On its own initiative SUU has established an intermediate structure of administration, the college, between the university and department. The university is divided into fourteen colleges and departments, which have been grouped in such a way as to encourage the cross-fertilization of related fields. The development of these colleges has been a significant expression of autonomy, with all decisions made within the university. Although the university is still managed mainly at the university and department levels at present, especially in terms of funding procedures,[61] it will be interesting to see how the colleges develop in the future and the way in which they find their place in the overall administrative structure of the university.

Another administrative innovation has been the creation of positions for presidential assistants, who help the president in everyday work, in many cases being given titles of director and deputy director in the president's office and in the Party committee office. These individuals provide the practical infrastructure for executing the academic decisions that are being made.

In October 1996 SUU celebrated its one hundredth anniversary, taking the founding of the Sino-Western school in 1896 as its origin, rather than its establishment as a provincial university in 1902 or a national university in 1931. It stands out as a model of university reform through amalgamation, a model not only of combining liberal arts, pure sciences, and technology but also a model of the reuniting of institutions that had been separated under the Soviet model in 1952. What is strikingly different from the reforms of that era is that university members in both institutions themselves chose to merge in the present period. This is an example of autonomy as self-mastery, the freedom to determine one's own institutional future in a climate in which diversity is tolerated and different choices are being made around the country.

Chongqing Industry Management Institute

In contrast to SUU, Chongqing Industry Management Institute (Chongqing gongye guanli xueyuan) is a relatively small institution and one of the youngest degree-granting institutes of higher education in China, yet it might be viewed as a case study of one of China's fastest-growing institutions. Here autonomy as self-mastery can be seen in the vigorous action taken to seek institutional development through cooperation with various different groups in the wider society.

CIMI is affiliated with the Ministry of Armament Industry (or China Northern Industry Corporation Group) and specializes in industrial management and engineering.[62] Located in the center of the Yangjiaping district of the city of Chongqing, its campus is less than one-seventh of the size of SUU. In 1995 CIMI had an academic staff of 327 and a student body of 3,168 in full-time programs and another 1,000 in adult learning. These numbers probably mean little to others, but they are a matter of tremendous pride to CIMI's members, in light of the fact that the institute was only reestablished as a higher education institution in 1986 after a relatively brief but turbulent history.

In their recently published institutional history the origin of CIMI was identified as the eleventh technical school of the Ministry of Armament Industry affiliated with the ministry's twenty-first factory. This school was established in 1940 by the Southwestern Armament Industry Corporation of the Nationalist government. Li Chenggan was the first principal, and he was also director of the twenty-first factory of the Ministry of Armament Industry. He was a scientist in electronic engineering, who had graduated from Tokyo Imperial University in the first decade of this century. Under his leadership the school focused on mechanical technology and trained students through work-study programs. By 1949, 1,068 students had graduated from the school.

After the People's Republic of China was founded, the school became a secondary-level professional training school and continued to serve the armament industry. In 1965 it was raised to the level of a university, offering four-year undergraduate programs and given the name of Chongqing Industry Institute. It focused on work-study programs, as an alternative model to the regular higher education institutions, with students spending half of their time studying on campus and half of their time working in factories belonging to the armament industry.[63] With the outbreak of the Cultural Revolution one year later, however, it was made into a factory to make meters and electronic parts. Only in 1983 did the Ministry of Armament Industry reestablish the institute to meet the increasing demands for skilled personnel in the sector. It was now named Chongqing Industry Management Institute, with programs in engineering, business, and management, and its first group of 150 students were enrolled in 1986. In 1990 the State Council gave it degree-granting status.

One of the interviewees commented that CIMI had a history that has not left them with any burdens.[64] Rather, its historical experience has been a kind of resource, inspiring contemporary members to take new initiatives, particularly in the area of cooperative education and linkages with industry. As a new institution of higher education, its teaching and research resources have been limited, but its members have tried to create something new by making the most of the particular opportunities available to it. The most important of them arise from its affiliation with the armament industry, which has resulted in a special emphasis on discipline as well as a commitment to fostering the practical ability of students.

The curriculum focuses on engineering and industrial management, which are being interpreted in a broader sense than ever before. Specialities in electrical engineering, mechanics, and computer science areas have been added to its engineering program, and industrial management has been expanded to include a wide range of business practices. The guiding principles for curriculum development have been internally defined in the following way: facing society and expanding knowledge areas in all directions; facing the future and sticking to reform and renovation; facing grassroots areas and serving the armament industry; and facing CIMI's reality and developing its own special characteristics.[65] Under the guidance of these principles CIMI has moved away from the former sectoral and geographic limitations imposed upon it and has sought cooperation with many different agencies, including enterprises of different types and foreign corporations as well as the government. It has eleven academic departments, twenty-nine degree and nondegree programs, and two master's programs.

A strong leadership has been regarded as an important factor in CIMI's rapid development. Full cooperation between the presidential administration and the Party Committee characterizes the governance, with a centralization of power in the institute's leading group. It includes the president, five vice presidents, the Party committee secretary, and the chair of the Party discipline committee. Highly efficient and disciplined, the leading group has displayed a remarkable ability to formulate policies and initiate action based upon these policies. This efficiency and effectiveness is attributed by some to the traditions of the armament industry. In academic administration the president is highly regarded and respected by all as a leader, a practitioner, and an entrepreneur.[66]

The most notable aspect of university autonomy in CIMI is the complete freedom to initiate action that provides supplementary financial resources. As a sectoral institute, CIMI is funded by the Ministry of Armament Industry under the unitary funding formula of the state. In addition, CIMI has benefited greatly from its links to the armament industry and its history of being a factory for over twenty years. After it was restored as a higher educational institution in 1986, it still kept a part of the factory in order to allow for student internships. By 1994 the factory had expanded to employ a workforce of five hundred employees, with the addition of an auto parts facility. The institute has also established a construction firm. This has enabled it not only to serve external clients but also to save money by undertaking all of its own construction work for institutional development. In their own words, institute members do not allow their own "fertilizing water" (money) to irrigate other people's fields.[67] By 1995 the institute's business income had reached ten million yuan, making up about one-third of its total budget.[68]

Beside the income from manufacturing activity, CIMI has actively sought support from society. In 1993 it developed about thirty partners within the sectoral industry, which made donations adding up to 750,000 yuan in that year.[69] In 1994 the Automobile Technology Education Foundation of the Southwest Armament Industry was established, and CIMI became a member. In that year the foundation invested 4,200,000 yuan in CIMI to build an automobile school, and in 1995 it gave another 4,800,000 yuan for the school's further needs. In 1995 CIMI launched several more cooperative ventures. Three vocational schools were founded through cooperative relations with various partners. One was a tourist school established in cooperation with the Wanyou Travel Company, the second a land management school in cooperation with the government of Chongqing, and the third a driver training school in cooperation with the Hongkong Xingzhao Development Corporation. In 1996 CIMI began to develop international cooperative programs with Centennial College in Ontario through its adult education college.

One purpose of these cooperative efforts was financial, and in this CIMI was very successful. In 1995 the institute's funding sources fell into three categories, with about ten million each coming from the government, cooperating partners, and business activities. While the funds from partners are unlikely to be consistent year by year, funds from government are steady, and those from business activities are expected to increase.

A second purpose for cooperative activities was academic. One of the problems that troubled the leadership was that the institute was too young to have a high academic standing. Without an adequate academic standing, it would be hard to maintain its success. Thus, it was important to develop cooperative academic programs as a means of enhancing its academic status in the sectoral educational system, which has about twenty higher education institutions. When the 2/1/1 program was launched early in 1993, it was clear to the CIMI leadership that the institute had absolutely no chance of becoming one of the top one hundred higher institutions. Therefore, they developed their own approach to lessening the gap that existed between them and the major national universities. It was one of collaboration in developing graduate-level academic programs. In 1993 CIMI developed a master's program in industry with the North China Industry Institute and Sichuan Union University. In 1994 it signed the contract to prepare graduate students in business management with Sichuan Union University. These initiatives were taken through its own efforts, with little reference to the central ministry it is affiliated with.

Through cooperative training programs with industry and collaborative academic programs with more prestigious institutions, CIMI has developed a successful model of a sectoral university under a central government ministry profiting from vigorous local linkages. Although it has a relatively short history, it is regarded as innovative and progressive. Its cooperative activities have fueled a rapid academic expansion. In addition, it is able to provide greatly enhanced services for the local area and for the sector. While other universities are struggling to survive and find adequate resources to maintain the quality of their academic programs, CIMI is flourishing, both academically and financially. In 1995 it was singled out for praise by the provincial government as a model of institutional development in the province.

Chongqing Teachers' College

The third institution in our case study, Chongqing Teachers' College (Chongqing shifan xueyuan) is a medium-sized degree-granting institution affiliated with the provincial government and focusing on the academic and professional training of secondary school teachers. It is in Shapingba district, the cultural center of Chongqing, where there are seven universities and colleges and several prestigious keypoint secondary schools at the primary and secondary levels. Its campus is about the same size as that of CIMI but is located right in the commercial center of the district, next to a railway station and a long-distance bus station, which link the city to all areas of the region and the country. The convenience of this location has been one of the most important conditions enabling it to attract faculty members and self-paying students. In 1995 the college had 436 faculty members and 4,500 full-time students as well as 2,400 students in various types of adult learning. It had fourteen bachelor's programs, six master's programs, nineteen diploma programs, and about thirty programs in adult learning.

CTC was founded in December 1953 by the government of Chongqing City as a junior college to prepare teachers for lower secondary schools. It had six specializations: Chinese, mathematics, physics, chemistry, geography, and biology. Deng Ken, director of the municipal educational bureau and a revolutionary veteran, acted as the first president (1954–56). In 1954 the provincial government took over the control of the college, and enrollment increased steadily. In 1959 it was raised to the university level, with four-year study programs, and took the name of Chongqing Teachers' College.[70] It enjoyed a modest expansion of programs and enrollment in 1959–60. That, however, was the last year of institutional expansion.

In the retrenchment period of the early 1960s the central government adjusted the plan for teacher education, and CTC was reduced once again to a junior college, with three-year study programs. Its specialties were cut from nine to four, including Chinese, mathematics, biology, and geography, and many facilities, programs, faculty, and students were transferred to Sichuan Teachers' College in Chengdu, about five hundred kilometers away from Chongqing. In the years between 1961 and the outbreak of the Cultural Revolution in 1966, the college continued to reduce its enrollment, and by 1965 there were only about six hundred students on campus.

In 1966 the college stopped operation, as did most other universities and colleges at that time. In 1972 it reopened and began to develop slowly but steadily. Its yearly student intake was about three hundred on average from 1972 to 1976. By 1976, the last year of the Cultural Revolution decade, there were five departments and seven programs: Chinese, mathematics, physics and chemistry, history and geography, and foreign languages, with about nine hundred full-time students in three-year programs. In addition it took vigorous steps to develop informal education programs over this period, mainly distance education programs in Chinese and mathematics. The number of registered students in these programs reached thirty eight thousand by 1976, with twenty eight thousand in Chinese and ten thousand in mathematics. They were divided into 370 classes and over 5,000 study groups.[71]

In January 1978 the State Council once again raised CTC to the university level, with four-year study programs, and in 1981 it was granted power to confer bachelor degrees. In 1987 the college enrolled its first group of master's degree students, marking a move toward greater academic prestige in its programs. Entering the 1990s, the college faced considerable challenges in the market, which required it to reform its internal management system and adapt to the economic transition.

Compared with SUU and CIMI, it faces greater limitations in the market economy. These arise mainly from its professional orientation and subject areas. As a teachers' college that continues to be subject to government planning requirements, it is unable to benefit from some of the reform policies that have given greater autonomy to other institutions.[72] Furthermore, with programs that are mainly based on arts and science, the college has fewer resources than those with a wide range of specialities in technological areas and opportunities to undertake consulting services for government or industry. As a provincial institution, located in a poor province with a population of over one hundred million, its development is limited by local economic conditions.

The central issue that concerns its leadership is an endemic shortage of funds. Like CIMI, Chongqing Teachers' College has no chance of entering the 2/1/1 program and obtaining extra government subsidies through that route. Unlike CIMI, it has no manufacturing or commercial base, which would enable it to generate revenues, nor does it have any parallel to CIMI's wide connections within the mechanical and armaments industries. Its leaders has therefore had to look for their own pattern of development, based on their own traditional area of strength—teaching.

In 1992 the college set up an ad hoc committee to design a reform plan.[73] Curriculum enhancement and program innovation was seen as the most important focus of development. The decision was made to maintain and extend its basic commitment to teacher education while at the same time opening some programs in other areas. Four new teacher education programs were opened as well as new programs in tourism management and film and video. In addition, extensive curricular revision resulted in a reduction in the number of theoretical courses in favor of new courses in the applied arts and technologies. The leadership recognized that it was impossible to gain a reputation for excellence in all areas at once, so a focused effort was made to develop nine courses that could be recognized as keypoint courses within the college and three that gained provincial recognition as keypoint courses: English, mathematics, and ancient Chinese. Excellence in foreign languages and computer science was fostered through enforcing student participation in national-level tests, while demanding internal regulations were established to ensure high standards of teaching and learning.[74]

Through curriculum change and the improvement of teaching the college has enhanced its academic reputation and succeeded in attracting an increasing number of students on a self-funding basis. It also has flourishing adult learning programs, which have benefited from the advantageous geographical position of the campus and access to good transportation facilities. In 1995 it was able to generate ten million yuan on its own, in addition to a government allocation of fifteen million. Most of this came through student fees in its formal programs outside of teacher education and its many adult learning activities.

Like SUU and CIMI, CTC's governance structure has been one of a presidential responsibility system under the supervision of the Communist Party. What has been notable about the Party's role in recent years has been the practical nature of its contribution to institutional development. This has included recovering land originally belonging to the college, which had been occupied by various companies during the Cultural Revolution, and accumulating money to build an eight-floor training center to house adult learning programs. While all important issues relating to personnel, finance, and overall planning have to be discussed in the Party committee, academic program development is largely left to academic leaders. The main responsibility of the Party committee is for Party membership development, policy studies, the administration of cadres, and students' moral education.

Toward a Chinese Concept of University Autonomy

We began this essay with some reflections on the term that is currently used to express the idea of autonomy in Chinese higher education: *zizhuquan,* or autonomy as self-mastery. We noted the difference in emphasis expressed in this term from the notion of autonomy as independence (*zizhiquan*), which is often used in the Chinese literature with reference to the experience of Western universities. We then tried to explore the context for this term in China's intellectual tradition, in which institutions of higher learning tended to be closely integrated within the imperial bureaucracy and traditions of knowledge had a strong orientation toward action.

In considering the modern history of higher education in China, we noted the emergence of relatively independent universities of diverse types in the Nationalist period. Their status was established and protected through national legislation, and both professors and students were able to develop a new sense of professionalism and relatively autonomous groupings around academic activity as well as sociopolitical protest.[75] This was fairly novel in relation to the past.

With the reorganization of colleges and departments that took place in 1952, all higher institutions were reshaped to fit Soviet-defined patterns of higher education and became absorbed within the socialist bureaucracy. It afforded them neither an independent legal status nor the opportunity for self-initiated academic or social action. The three institutions described in our case study illustrate the ways in which higher institutions were subjected to the vicissitudes of political change over the period from the early 1950s up to 1978. Expansion, retrenchment, and even closure came about as a result of such major national movements as the Great Leap Forward and the Cultural Revolution, with university members having little possibility of developing the individual identities of their institutions or responding in creative ways to their external environment.

Since 1978, however, a whole new situation has unfolded, giving individual universities unprecedented opportunities to take new initiatives on their own and culminating in the educational law of 1995, which has given each institution the status of a legal person. Under this status universities bear both the responsibilities and limitations that the law imposes upon them but are otherwise largely free to provide for their own financial health and to plan their own future development. Such provisions and plans depend very heavily on the differential conditions enjoyed by different types of institutions.

Each of the three institutions in our case study displayed a different approach to development. SUU became a model of combining arts, sciences, and engineering and a celebrated case of the merger of two major institutions. CIMI made its name as a model of cooperative education, in both its academic programs and its fund-raising activities. CTC capitalized on its strengths as a teacher education institution to develop excellence in professional and adult education programs, which could attract a wide range of new students.

The new status of Chinese universities as legal persons is an important factor in these new developments and reflects the integration of important elements of the Western tradition of university autonomy, which has influenced China since early in the century. It is interesting to note, by way of contrast, that Japan's imperial universities still remain an integrated part of the Japanese bureaucracy and do not enjoy the status of legal persons. While academics in Japan enjoy academic freedom far beyond that of Chinese academics, in the sense of freedom to express divergent and oppositional political views, they do not enjoy the kind of freedom of collective action or financial responsibility that Chinese universities have recently gained.[76] For their part Chinese academics are not free to participate in organized critical and oppositional activity to the state, as evident in the extensive literature around the Tiananmen tragedy. The fate of the autonomous organizations of students and professors, which took shape in those fateful months, is well-known, and it is interesting to note that it was the concept of autonomy as independence (*zizhiquan*) rather than autonomy as self-mastery (*zizhuquan*), which was used to describe these organizations.

If we conclude with some reflection on the three layers of autonomy that have been noted in China's historical experience, we might say that Chinese universities have displayed a remarkable freedom of action on the third layer, the operational settings of universities, as they have responded with vigor and ingenuity to social needs and opportunities. Their effectiveness in collective action has required the cooperation of all groups on campus, and the role of campus Party organizations has been largely one of support and facilitation.

On the second layer, that of the relationship of universities and government, both government policy and recent legislation have provided for a greater degree of freedom from government intervention than has been experienced since 1949. As the new system of market socialism matures, we anticipate that the status of universities as legal persons is likely to become a more and more significant element in fostering conditions for independent action. It is not clear, however, whether or to what degree this will lead to independence from local Party involvement or indeed to oppositional politics in relation to the ruling Party.

Finally, with reference to the third layer, national sovereignty, as China gains increasing confidence and respect in the international community, there is likely to be less and less concern about international influences that might be seen as unacceptable external intervention. Rather, we may see a situation in which some aspects of the success of Chinese universities in developing new roles and identities produces a model that could be emulated elsewhere.

Chinese epistemology has always emphasized knowledge in action, and our study has tried to focus on what university members are doing, quietly yet effectively, as their way of expressing their newfound autonomy. It may be some time before they gain the kind of negative freedom, which might be seen as a core value of Western liberalism and is expressed in the concept of autonomy as independence (*zizhiquan*), or protection from external intervention. They are, however, already showing a positive freedom expressed in the concept of autonomy as self-mastery (*zizhuquan*) in their daily activities, and this may be the most valuable lesson they have to show the world.

NOTES

1. Autonomy as independence was introduced through the democratic movement in the 1980s as a call for intellectual freedom from the Communist government. One of the promoters was Fang Lizhi, then a professor and the vice president of the Chinese University of Science and Technology in Hefei. He advocated the university's complete independence from the Communist Party, using the expression *daxue zizhi* (university autonomy as independence). According to him, the university should be an independent ideological center. He also thought that intellectuals should be independent of the working class and establish their own identity. Of course, the Communist government did not like the idea and responded quickly, taking a stern stance against this approach. See Li Lun, "Lun Fang Lizhi de daxue duli" (On Fang Lizhi's claim of university independence). *Gaodeng jiaoyu* (Higher education) 5 (1987): 15–20. "Minzhu banxue juebuneng baituo dang de lingdao" (Democratic management of universities does not mean to be independent of the leadership of the Party), *Renmin ribao* (People's daily), Overseas edition, 17 January 1987. The further development of Fang's ideas in the lead up to the Tiananmen events is well-known.

2. We examined three educational journals—*Gaodeng Jiaoyu* (Higher education), *Shanghai Gaodeng Jiaoyu* (Higher education in Shanghai), *Jiaoyu Yanjiu* (Educational research)—from the early 1980s to the present and found the most common term used for university autonomy was *zizhuquan*.

3. "Zhonghua renmin gongheguo jiaoyufa" (Education law of the People's Republic of China), *Renmin ribao*, Overseas edition, 23 March 1995.

4. From the 1975 to 1980 Zhao Ziyang was the Party secretary of Sichuan province. In 1980 he became the premier of the State Council and the director of the State Reform Committee of the Economic System. In 1987 he was the acting general-secretary of the Central Committee of the CCP, and in 1988 he was vice chairman of the military committee. After the June 4 Incident he was dismissed from all positions in the Party and government for his disloyalty to the Party and showing sympathy for the student movement. Zhao was one of the main figures promoting economic reform

in the 1980s and was responsible for making many policies directly related to practical changes. See *Zhongguo renwu nianjian: 1989* (Who's who in China 1989) (Beijing: Huayi chubanshe, 1989), 276–77.

5. *Sichuan gaodeng jiaoyu he zhongdeng jiaoyu nianjian* (The yearbook of Sichuan higher education and secondary education) (Chengdu: Sichuan jiaoyu chubanshe, 1988), 26.

6. Chen Hongsheng, "Guanyu gaodeng xuexiao zizhuquan de tantao" (On autonomy of higher education institutions), *Renmin jiaoyu* (People's education) (December 1980): 6.

7. Hastings Rashdall, *The Universities of Europe in the Middle Ages* (Oxford: Clarendon Press, 1895), vol. 1, chap. 1.

8. Ruth Hayhoe, *China's Universities, 1895–1995: A Century of Cultural Conflict* (New York: Garland Publishing, 1996).

9. Suzanne Pepper, *Radicalism and Education Reform in Twentieth-Century China: The Search for an Ideal Development Model* (Cambridge: Cambridge University Press, 1996).

10. W. Theodore de Bary and John W. Chaffee, eds., *Neo-Confucian Education: The Formative Stage* (Berkeley: University of California Press, 1989).

11. John Meskill, *Academies in Ming China: A Historical Essay* (Tucson: Association for Asian Studies by the University of Arizona, 1982).

12. Benjamin Elman and Alexander Woodside, eds., *Education and Society in Late Imperial China: 1600–1900* (Berkeley: University of California Press, 1994).

13. Li Zehou, *Zhongguo xiandai sixianghshi lun* (On the history of modern Chinese thought) (Hefei: Anhui wenyi chubanshe, 1994), 34–35.

14. Roger Ames, trans. and comm., *Sun Tzu: The Master of Warfare* (New York: Ballantine Books, 1993), 49–67.

15. Xiong Mingan, *Zhongguo gaodeng jiaoyushi* (A history of Chinese higher education) (Chongqing: Chongqing chubanshe, 1983), 71, 89.

16. Chen Qingzhi, *Zhongguo jiaoyushi* (A history of Chinese education) (Taibei: Taiwan shangwu yinshuguan, 1963), 216.

17. Chen, *Zhongguo jiaoyushi*, 373–80.

18. Sheng Langxi, *Zhongguo shuyuan zhidu* (The system of Chinese traditional academies) (Shanghai: Zhonghua shuju, 1934), 18.

19. Sheng, *Zhongguo shuyuan zhidu*, 41.

20. Xiong, *Zhongguo Gaodeng jiaoyushi*, 187.

21. Mao Lirui, "Xu" (Preface), in Xiong, *Zhongguo gaodeng jiaoyushi*, 3–4.

22. Xiong, *Zhongguo gaodeng jiaoyushi*, 152.

23. Before attending these formal examinations, one had to pass preliminary tests to be qualified. Xiong, *Zhongguo gaodeng jiaoyushi*, 254–55.

24. This slogan was put forward by Zhang Zhidong, a leading scholar-official of the late Qing. See "Quanxue pian" (An exhortation to learning), in Gu Mingyuan et al., ed., *Zhongguo jiaoyu daxi* (The encyclopedic series of Chinese education) (Wuhan: Hubei jiaoyu chubanshe, 1994), 2: 1718–19.

25. Zhang Hengjia, "Guangxu sanshinian daxuetang zongjiandu Zhang Hengjia zou kaiban yubeike bing zhao shifansheng dagai qingxing zhe" (The report about preparing

for the opening of the preparatory study department and the enrollment of students in teacher training), in Zhu Youxian, et al., ed., *Zhongguo jindai xuezhi shiliao* (Historical materials of the modern Chinese educational system) (Shanghai: Huadong shifan daxue chubanshe, 1985), vol. 2, bk. 1, 840–41.

26. Mao, "Xu" (Preface), in Xiong, *Zhongguo gaodeng jiaoyushi*, 5.

27. Xiong, *Zhongguo gaodeng jiaoyushi*, 316.

28. "Daxue ling" (The university act), in Shu Xincheng, ed., *Xiandai zhongguo jiaoyushi ziliao* (Materials of the modern Chinese educational history) (Beijing: Renmin jiaoyu chubanshe, 1962), 647–49.

29. "Xuexiao xitong gaige an" (The reform plan for the school system), in Gu, *Zhongguo jiaoyu daxi*, 4:2200–2. First printed in *Xin jiaoyu* (New education) 5, no. 5 (1922).

30. William Purvance Fenn, *Christian Higher Education in Changing China, 1890–1950* (Grand Rapids, Mich.: W. B. Eerdmans, 1976), 242. See also the essays by Dan Cui and Douglas Reynolds in this volume.

31. Yanjing University was established in 1920 through the merger of three religious universities: Tongzhou Xiehe daxue (1905), Beijing Huiwen daxue (1870), and Huabei Xiehe nüzi daxue (1905). It remained private until 1952. See Chen Lishong and Cheng Xi, "Jianxiao jingguo" (The founding of the university) in Dong Ding et al., eds., *Xuefu jiwen: sili yanjing daxue* (The records of universities: private Yanjing university) (Taibei: Nanjing chuban youxian gongsi, 1982), 1–3. Nankai University started in 1919 and registered with the government as a private institution in 1925. In 1945 it became a public institution. See Wang Wenjun et al., eds., *Nankai daxue xiaoshi ziliaoxuan* (Selected materials of the history of Nankai university) (Tianjin: Nankai daxue chubanshe, 1989). See also Chiang Yung-chen, "Social Engineering and the Social Sciences in China, 1898–1949" (Ph.D. diss., Harvard University, 1986).

32. Xiong, *Zhongguo gaodeng jiaoyushi*, 384. First published in *Di er ci zhongguo jiaoyu nianjian* (The second yearbook of education in China) (Shanghai: Shangwu yinshuguang, 1948).

33. John Israel, *Student Nationalism in China, 1927–1937* (Stanford, Calif.: Stanford University Press, 1966).

34. Guojia jiaowei chengren jiaoyusi, *Zhongguo gaodeng hanshou jiaoyu, dashiji, wenxian, ziliao* (Chinese higher-distance education) (Beijing: Renmin daxue chubanshe, 1994), 3.

35. A department has several specialties. Each specialty forms into a teaching and research division (*jiaoyanshi*), with a group of teachers. Academic activities are usually conducted through these divisions. The teaching and research division is the grassroots academic unit in the university. The central government has control over how many specialties there should be in the higher educational system. In 1953, 215 kinds of specialties were approved by the government. See Liu Yifan, *Zhongguo dangdai gaodeng jiaoyu shilue* (A brief history of Chinese contemporary higher education) (Wuhan: Huazhong ligong daxue, 1991), 24–25.

36. Hayhoe, *China's Universities 1895–1995: A Century of Cultural Conflict*, 73–90.

37. C. T. Downey, 1838, quoted in Teng Ssu-yu, "Chinese Influences on the Western Examination System," in *Harvard Journal of Asiatic Studies* 7, no. 4 (1942): 290.

38. Hayhoe, *China's Universities, 1895–1995.*

39. On August 10, 1898, the Italian Embassy presented a memorandum to the premier's office requiring that the National University of Beijing establish the department of Italian language and hire Italian teachers. On September 16 the Italian ambassador sent another memorandum requiring this to be done. At the same time, the German ambassador also asked the university to hire a certain number of German teachers. On August 28, 1898, the president of the National University of Beijing replied to all these inquiries that the running of the university was an internal affair of China and that the German and Italian ministers should not interfere with it. See Zhu, *Zhongguo jindai xuezhi shiliao*, vol. 1, bk. 1, 678–83.

40. Hubert Freyn, *Chinese Education in the War* (Shanghai: Kelly and Walsh, 1940).

41. The political differences between the United States and Communist China, exacerbated by the Korean War in the early 1950s, resulted in the Chinese government's determination to take over the control of all denominational institutions in China. The process began in the early 1950s and ended in 1953. All religious and private institutions were integrated into the public system. Liu, *Zhongguo dangdai gaodeng jiaoyu shilue*, 3–5.

42. Ruth Hayhoe and Ningsha Zhong, "University and Civil Society," in Timothy Brook and B. Michael Frolic, eds., *Civil Society in China* (Armonk, N.Y.: M. E. Sharpe, 1997).

43. Allen B. Linden, "Politics and Education in Nationalist China: The Case of the University Council, 1927–1928," *Journal of Asian Studies* 28, no. 4 (August) 1968: 763–76.

44. "The Internal Organization Act," passed in December 1919, established the internal governance structure as follows: the university council as the highest judicial body, authorized to make laws; the administrative committee as the executive body with the president as head and representatives of professors as members; the office of academic affairs to supervise academic studies; and the office of general affairs to manage personnel and general affairs. See Liu Dehua et al., eds., *Zhongguo jiaoyu guanlishi* (A history of Chinese educational administration) (Jinan: Shandong jiaoyu chubanshe, 1990), 393–94.

45. Ruth Hayhoe, *China's Universities and the Open Door* (Armonk, N.Y.: M. E. Sharpe, 1989), 18–21, 30–37.

46. Roderick MacFarquhar, *The Hundred Flowers Campaign and the Chinese Intellectuals* (New York: Octagon Books, 1974).

47. This summary of the economic development in the reform period was given by Li Tieying in his article on the reform of economic system. See *Renmin ribao*, May 12, 1994.

48. Guojia jiaowei zhengce faguisi, ed., "Zhonggong zhongyang guanyu jiaoyu tizhi gaige de jueding" (The decision on reform of the educational system by the central committee of the Chinese communist party), *Shiyi jie sanzhong quanhui yilai zhongyao jiaoyu wenxian* (Important education documents since the third plenary of the eleventh congress of the Communist Party) (Beijing: Jiaoyu kexue chubanshe, 1992), 182–89.

49. Goujia jiaowei zhengce faguisi, ed., "Gaodeng jiaoyu guanli zhize zanxing guiding" (The temporary provisions of higher education administration) (Beijing: Guojia jiaowei, 1992), 227.

50. Zhonggong zhongyang, guowuyuan, "Zhongguo jiaoyu gaige he fazhan gangyao" (Outline for the reform and development of Chinese education), in Buojia jiaowei bangongting, Guojia jiaowei, *Zhongguo jiaoyu gaige he fazhan wenxian xuanbian* (Selected documents on Chinese education reform and development) (Beijing: Renmin jiaoyu chubanshe, 1993), 13.

51. *Renmin ribao,* overseas edition, March 23, 1995.

52. Hayhoe, *China's Universities,* 259–60.

53. When Ningsha Zhong was visiting Sichuan Union University in October 1995, the university was organizing people to write a history of Sichuan Union University. At the time there were two publications about SUU's history. One is *Sichuan daxue shigao* (The history of Sichuan University), which ends in 1949 when the People's Republic of China was established. The other is *Chengdu keji daxue xiaoshi* (A history of the University of Chengdu Science and Technology). It is expected that the new history will have a new perspective, viewing the two universities as part of one tradition.

54. *Sichuan daxue jianjie* (Sichuan Union University brochure) (Chengdu: Sichuan Union University, 1995).

55. Sichuan daxue xiaoshi bianxiezu, *Sichuan daxue shigao* (A history of Sichuan University) (Chengdu: Sichuan daxue chubanshe, 1985).

56. The Qing government differentiated national and provincial universities, requiring a national university to have eight subject areas, a provincial one three. In the University Act (1912) a national university had to have not less than two subject areas. In 1924 the central government issued the National University Provisions, which stated that a national university could have one to several subject areas. See Xiong, *Zhongguo gaodeng jiaoyushi,* 314, 361, 734.

57. Sichuan daxue xiaoshi bianxiezu, *Sichuan daxue shigao.*

58. *Sichuan daxue jianjie,* 1995.

59. At the end of 1995 SUU successfully passed the first evaluation of the SEC and became one of the first universities to join in the 2/1/1 project (field notes, January 16, 1996).

60. The government of Sichuan province decided to give SUU the following support for the 2/1/1 project: (1) 150 million yuan for development in the coming years; (2) all of the preferable policies and support that the provincial government gives to its own affiliated institutions of higher education; (3) tax deductions for teaching and living facilities; (4) incentive for large and medium-size enterprises to support the university. See Sichuan daxue xiao bangongshi, *Sichuan daxue nianjian* (Sichuan University yearbook) (Chengdu: Sichuan daxue chubanshe, 1994), 334.

61. One of the problems in the state administrative system is that it does not have an appropriate administrative rank for the college. At present the administrative rank of the university is equal to that of the prefecture and the administrative rank of the department to that of the county. Since there is no administrative division between the prefecture and county, there is no relevant rank for the college. The good thing is that the university is allowed to adjust the administrative structure according to its own situation and resources. In SUU one of the efforts was the publication of regulations for administrative management at three levels (interview with a Party worker at SUU, October 10, 1995).

62. *Chongqing gongye guanli xueyuan: xiaoshi 1940–95* (Chongqing industry management institute: history 1940–95) (Chongqing: Chongqing gongye guanli xueyuan, 1995), 152–54.

63. The model of half-work and half-study in Chinese universities was based on nonformal education for adults. In 1964 the central government decided to expand this practice into the formal higher education system. CIMI became one of the institutions called upon to participate.

64. Interview with a faculty member at CIMI, January 12, 1996.

65. *Chongqing gongye guanli xueyuan: xiaoshi 1940–1995,* 1995, 97.

66. Interview with an administrator at CIMI, December 20, 1995.

67. *Chongqing gongye guanli xueyuan: xiaoshi 1940–1995,* 1995, 121.

68. Interview with an administrator at CIMI, December 20, 1995.

69. One Canadian dollar was worth about six yuan at the time.

70. *Chongqing shifan xueyuan xiaoshi* (A history of Chongqing Teachers' College) (Chongqing: Chongqing shifan xueyuan, 1995).

71. *Chongqing shifan xueyuan xiaoshi,* 61.

72. For instance, graduates are still subject to centralized job placement policies, and there are no tuition fees for those students in teacher training programs. For those students who are not in teacher training, tuition fees are kept much lower than in SUU and CIMI.

73. *Chongqing shifan xueyuan xiaoshi,* 143.

74. Interview with an administrator at CTC, November 14, 1995.

75. Jeffrey Wasserstrom, *Student Protests in Twentieth Century China: The View from Shanghai* (Stanford: Stanford University Press, 1991).

76. For example, Japanese national universities are not able to contract with such government agencies as JICA or the OECF to undertake development projects on behalf of the Japanese government. This is due to the fact that they have no independent legal status but are an extension of the government's educational bureaucracy in their institutional identity. Academic freedom is fiercely protected by the faculty councils, which are the key governance and decision-making bodies of each university faculty, but these councils have no financial or legal autonomy. Ruth Hayhoe, "Barriers to the Internationalization of Japanese Universities," in William Cummings and John Hawkins, eds., *Japanese Educational Exchange* (New York: SUNY Press; and Tokyo: Tamagawa University Press, 1998).

The Resurgence of Private Education in Post-Mao China: Problems and Prospects

David K. K. Chan and Ka-Ho Mok

A phenomenon of considerable significance is presently taking place in Chinese education: after more than three decades of state socialism, China is experiencing a resurgence in private education. Following the founding of the People's Republic of China in 1949, education in China was placed under state control as part of a system of "bureaucratic centralism" in which ruling groups and administrative elites exercised central planning for social and economic development.[1] It was only at the end of the 1970s, with the inauguration of the post-Mao economic reforms, that the Chinese Communist Party (CCP) began to diversify the provision of educational services, in the process allowing the establishment of schools by the private sector. After a halting start, private education in China has undergone rapid development and transformation within the last decade, particularly in major urban centers. This essay examines how China's flourishing market economy and the policy of decentralization adopted by the post-Mao leadership have contributed to the rise of private schooling in recent years and considers some of the problems and prospects for the future of private education in China.

Decentralization and Privatization

During the Mao era the central state exercised substantial control over the provision, financing, and management of schools. Since 1978, however, it has continuously reduced its level of financial subsidy to education by re-emphasizing the importance of individual responsibilities and by encouraging local communities, social organizations, and private individuals to create additional educational opportunities at the local level. This process has involved a necessary devolution of financial responsibility and decision-making power from the central state to the localities.[2] The 1985 Decision on Reform of the Educational System called for greater local responsibility, diversification of educational opportunities (including a significant expansion in vocational education), decentralization of power to school authorities in the governance of school affairs, and the creation of multiple channels of educational funding.[3] Central authorities reiterated their support for decentralization and diversification of educational services over the next several years, culminating in a series of important policy and legislative decisions in 1993. In the official Program for Reform and Development of China's Education, promulgated in 1993, the CCP Central Committee affirmed that "the national policy is to actively encourage and fully support social institutions and citizens to establish schools according to laws and to provide correct guidelines and strengthen administration." Article 16 of the program called for "people in all walks of life" to run schools and even invited "international cooperation" in the effort to increase educational opportunities.[4]

The same year the State Education Commission declared that "the government has to change its function from direct control to managing schools through legislation, funding, planning, guiding policies and other necessary means."[5] Meanwhile, as the central government confirmed its intention to shift from direct control over the educational sector to providing the legal framework for educational development, further edicts were issued stressing the obligation of all educational institutions to conduct their affairs in accordance with the respective state ordinances and regulations.[6] Basic education (defined here as primary and middle school) is now implemented according to the principle of "sponsorship at three levels, management at two levels" (*sanji banxue, liangji guanli*). In practice this means that senior secondary schools are sponsored by counties and managed by county authorities; junior secondary schools are sponsored by townships and managed by township authorities; and primary schools are sponsored by villages but managed by township authorities because of the absence of formal state structures at the village level. Under this system educational financing since the early 1990s has come to rely heavily upon local initiatives, as the state's contribution to total educational spending has declined to around 12 percent.[7]

The result has been a steady privatization of many aspects of the provision of basic education, as local authorities respond to the central government's reduced funding by attempting to carve out "multiple channels" (*duoqudao*) of local financing. In addition to local government subsidies, they include educational surcharges added to local taxes; miscellaneous fees (*zafei*) levied on parents of schoolchildren for everything from the use of school desks to winter heating charges; increased tuition fees; and funds raised from overseas Chinese and from compatriots in Hong Kong, Macau, and Taiwan.[8] The rise of self-supporting or fee-paying students has proved a popular means of raising school finances in prosperous regions where parents can afford the higher costs. In Dashi township in Guangdong province, for example, school principals acquired the discretion to admit nonscheme students who are self-supporting (*zifei sheng*). In another instance students in Guangdong's Panyu county not only pay tuition fees but are also required to make regular financial contributions to the development and management of schools. Similar studies show that the intake of self-supporting students is on the rise in other regions as well.[9] Table 1 shows the relative contribution of "multiple funding channels" and state budgetary appropriations to improvements in school operating conditions for the period 1981–91. In all provinces except the poorest inland provinces, multiple funding channels made up well over 50 percent of total contributions, rising to more than 80 percent in some provinces.[10]

In addition to public schools that are sponsored by local governments but seek an increasing proportion of their financing from "multiple sources," mostly private, there are also an increasing number of privately owned schools. Officially, all schools that are run by the nonstate sector are registered as *minban,* or "people-run," schools. They include a wide variety of schools run by different "social forces" (*shehui liliang*), including collectives, business enterprises, and private entrepreneurs. In China the terms *private* and *minban* are frequently used interchangeably, while proprietors of the former will often prefer, for political reasons, to employ the latter label to describe their schools. For these reasons it is extremely difficult to gauge the exact number of purely private schools that have emerged in China in recent years. Suzanne Pepper has painstakingly collated figures published in official Chinese sources, reprinted in table 2, that reveal the changing proportion of *minban* schools and enrollments to the regular national system.[11]

At least two main types of basic-level private schools have emerged in China in recent years. One is the "elite" private schools that have been established in major urban centers. These schools charge tuition fees that are extremely high by Chinese standards and cater mainly to the children of newly rich families in the economically well-developed coastal cities and provincial capitals. The first elite private school was established on June 16, 1992, in Chengdu in the interior province of Sichuan and was named Guangya Elementary School. Subsequently, many more such schools were established in the various regions of China, including the Jinghua Private Elementary School and Private Zhengze Middle School, both in Beijing; Xinshiji Elementary and Middle Schools in Shanghai; Xiaozhuang Experimental School in Nanjing; Zhonghua Yinghao Elementary and Middle Schools in Conghua, Guangdong province; and the Private Chaoneng International School in Huizhou, also in Guangdong.[12]

TABLE 1.   Comparison of Contributions by Government Appropriation and Multiple Channels of Funding (MCF) to the Improvement of Operating Conditions in Schools, 1981–91 (1 = RMB 100 million)

Place	Total Contribution	State Appropriation	Multiple Channels of Funding	MCF Percentage Total
Beijing	24.57	10.91	13.66	55.59
Tianjin	18.87	6.99	11.88	62.96
Hebei	39.76	8.72	31.04	78.07
Shanxi	26.53	8.42	18.11	68.26
Inner Mongolia	15.37	7.65	7.72	50.23
Liaoning	39.8	17.9	21.9	55.03
Jilin	24.43	8.03	16.4	67.13
Heilongjiang	23.22	6.3	16.92	72.87
Shanghai	39.35	18.95	20.4	51.84
Jiangsu	39.06	6.35	32.71	83.74
Zhejiang	45.25	14.37	30.88	68.24
Anhui	49.8	18.6	31.2	62.65
Fujian	35.95	11.6	24.35	37.73
Jiangxi	21.48	6.44	15.04	70.01
Shangdong	55	7.28	47.72	86.76
Hennan	102.96	31.07	71.89	69.82
Hubei	42.02	7.98	34.04	81.00
Hunan	94.76	13.99	80.77	85.24
Guangxi	35.48	9.19	26.29	74.09
Guangdong	106.91	38.07	68.84	64.39
Hainan[a]	6.09	3.87	2.22	36.45
Sichuan	58	24	34	58.62
Guizhou	16.77	13.67	3.1	18.49
Yunnan	40.2	28.3	11.9	29.60
Tibet	2.2	2	0.2	90.90
Shannxi	25.07	3.98	21.09	84.12
Gansu	12.65	6.99	5.66	44.74
Qinghai	8.87	7.036	1.84	20.74
Ningxia	4.69	1.83	2.86	60.98
Xinjiang	10.8	6.97	3.83	35.46
Total	1065.91	357.45	708.46	66.47

Source: *China Education News*, September 8, 1992, 1.
[a]Figures for Hainan reflect the situation for the 1988–91 period.

In addition to the elite private schools, there are also an increasing number of privately owned schools set up since 1992 catering to ordinary citizens. Such schools "have moderate facilities and charge fees that are quite low, yet their quality is by no means poor as they are under constant pressure to improve their conditions in order to retain and attract students."[13] In fact, one of the reasons such schools have appeared in increasing numbers at the primary level in rural areas in recent years is that they often charge less in fees and tuition than local public schools, where tuition and miscellaneous fees

TABLE 2.   Private (*minban*) Schools and the National System, Number of Schools (and of Students in Parentheses) (Students: millions)

	Private Schools			National System	
	1991(a)	1992(b)	1993(c)	1994(d)	1993(e)
Kindergartens		13.8 (0.53)		16,990 (0.72)	165,197
Elementary/Secondary	1,199	1,600 (0.2)			
Elementary	655	863 (0.05)	4,000 (0.65)	4,030 (0.65)	696,681 (124.2)
Secondary	544	6,773 (0.13)		851 (0.13)	96,744 (53.8)
Junior Secondary Only			550		
Tertiary				800	1,065 (2.5)
SEC Approved		10		15	
Others		40			
Province		500			
Nonformal[a]		10,000		30,000	

Source: Private schools: (a) *Zhongguo jiaoyu bao,* November 24, 1992, 2; (b) *Renmin ribao,* August 4, 1993 (article by Zhu Kaixuan), 3; elementary and secondary breakdown only, in Xinhua News Agency (Chinese), (Beijing), March 18, 1993 (report by Li Tieying), trans. in FBIS-CHI-93–052 (March 19, 1993), 19; (c) *Zhongguo jiaoyu bao,* January 18, 1995 (speech by Zhu Kaixuan); (d) Xinhua News Agency (English), (Beijing), June 17, 1994, in FBIS-CHI-94-118 (June 20, 1994), 36; edited versions of the same report also in *Guangming ribao,* June 20, 1994, and *Zhongguo jiaoyu bao,* July 1, 1994. (e) *Zhongguo tongji nianjian,* 1994 (Statistical Yearbook of China, 1994), edited by Guojia tongji ju (Beijing: Zhongguo tongji chubanshe, 1994), 557–61. Private schools are not listed as a separate category in this compilation, nor is there any indication about whether they are included within the figures shown. Presumably they are not, at least at the tertiary level. Secondary-level figures do not include skilled workers schools (*jigong xuexiao*). State Statistical Bureau preliminary aggregates for 1994 include total student enrollments only. They are at the elementary, secondary (exclusive of skilled workers schools), and tertiary levels: 130 million, 56.4 million, and 2.8 million, respectively (*Renmin ribao,* March 1, 1995).

[a]Nonformal training schools, programs.

have escalated as a result of the recent policy of educational decentralization and progressive withdrawal of central state funding.

Both types of private school have increased rapidly in number since 1992, following Deng Xiaoping's Spring Festival tour of the country's southern provinces, in which he used the occasion to reaffirm the central government policy of rapid reform and opening. In Guangdong, the prosperous southeastern coastal province that presently leads the country in the growth of private education, there were already 125 private schools at the end of 1992. The next year, following Deng's tour, a further 45 private schools were established in the capital of Guangzhou alone (including tertiary institutions), while from 1993 to mid-1995 an estimated 690 new *minban* and private schools appeared across the whole of the province.[14]

Privatization Trends in Tertiary Education

In 1950, before the nationalization of higher education, 39 percent of China's 227 universities were private, a significant number of which were missionary related.[15] In 1952 all private higher education institutions were transformed into public ones along the lines of the Soviet model adopted by China's leaders. Strict state control and funding, along with a mandatory system of state allocation of jobs for graduates, was an integral feature of tertiary education in China for the next twenty-five years, until the late 1970s.

Since 1978, however, decentralization of funding has created new needs and opportunities for privatization in the tertiary education sector. As with basic education, reduction of central state funding has increased the pressure on tertiary educational institutions to seek out "multiple channels" of funding and income to make up for the loss in state funds. A rapid increase in the number and proportion of self-supporting students has been one means of achieving this goal. Aided by the state's decision to allow students to choose their own career paths after graduation, recruitment of self-supporting students in higher educational institutions in Zhejiang, one of China's most rapidly developing provinces in the reform period, jumped from a mere 404 students in 1986 to 2,549 in 1989. In nearby Shanghai the number of self-supporting students in tertiary institutions rose from 829 in 1987 to 13,438 in 1994. Similar increases were reported in other provinces, with the highest increases in the most prosperous regions.[16] In addition, the major financial sources for research activities among Chinese universities are no longer derived from the central government. In 1993, according to one report, research grants were largely from nonstate budget funds raised by individual institutions of higher learning: 22,932.54 thousand yuan as compared to 4,111.73 thousand yuan from the central state.[17]

The most significant development, however, and one that poses the greatest potential challenge to state control of education has been the appearance in recent years of privately owned tertiary institutions. These institutions have flourished as a result of the increased demand for skilled scientific and management personnel generated by the post-Mao economic reforms and by the demand for credentials among private job seekers in the growing market economy. Thus, the period 1978–82 saw the creation of over 100 *minban* tertiary institutions across the country, while a further 170 *minban* tertiary institutions appeared during the period 1982–86.[18] Chinese sources sometimes use the term *daxue* (university) rather loosely to denote such institutions. In fact, the vast majority are not full-fledged universities as such, since they have not been certified by the central government to award degrees and diplomas. Most are technical or vocational colleges whose curricula are mainly market driven and oriented. We will return to the issue of accreditation.

The response of the State Education Commission, the official body responsible for overseeing education policy, to this resurgence of private tertiary institutions has been to attempt to regulate their existence and activities through a series of edicts. Beginning in 1987, the commission promulgated a set of "Provisional Regulations on Social Forces Running Schools." The regulations attempted—with only limited success—to impose a set of standard rules for the governance and conferring of diplomas in *minban* tertiary schools. For the next four years, until 1991, the State Education Commission attempted to carry out a kind of "rectification" campaign intended to weed out institutions that failed to conform to the commission's regulations and compel them to either improve or face closure. In the face of these pressures representatives of *minban* tertiary institutions mounted their own counterefforts to resist central demands and to win greater autonomy from the State Education Commission. A first national conference on *minban* tertiary education was held in Wuhan, Hubei, in January 1989, with more than seventy *minban* tertiary institutions represented. Many conference attendees seized upon the opportunity to criticize excessive restrictions and lack of support from the State Education Commission; the conference itself ended with a plea for the country's educational authorities to "liberate their thinking," accept new ideas, and strengthen their consciousness about the need for reform.[19] A meeting of presidents and directors of *minban* tertiary institutions was held in Beijing from February 20–26, 1992, which resulted in proposals to the central government for the further development of private tertiary education. A few months later, in the spring of 1992, Deng Xiaoping's call to quicken the pace of reform strengthened the position of proponents of private education.

In August 1993 the State Education Commission enacted a set of "Provisional Regulations for Establishment of People-Run Schools for Higher Education."[20] The regulations contained a total of seven chapters covering the legal status of *minban* tertiary education, criteria for the establishment of such institutions and for their evaluation by the State Education Commission, formal procedures for applying for official certification, and laws for the administration and governance of institutions. The legal basis of *minban* tertiary education was thus firmly secured.

Discussion

In a recent article the scholar of Chinese education Jing Lin pointed out that the contemporary resurgence of private education in China "raises intricate and important questions concerning the issue of social equality, educational quality and efficiency, reform in public schools, and the relationship between education and economic development."[21] Indeed, the recent surge in private education is not without problems. In the first place the elite education offered by some of these private schools contradicts the official spirit and principles of a government that remains avowedly socialist. The development of private education, by adding to the progressively widening gap between official rhetoric and social reality in China, might further erode whatever thin crust of legitimacy the CCP still retains among its citizens. On the other hand, the contradiction may also mean that the future of private education is not entirely secure. In 1995 the vice premier of the State Council, Li Lanqing, openly criticized the development of private educational institutions, arguing that the existence of such "aristocratic" schools was contradictory to socialist ideals. While recognizing that the category of *minban* schools made significant contributions to the development of education, Li believed that privately run schools for profit had fostered a host of social and economic problems.[22] Among the problems was that tuition fees at some private schools were so expensive as to be quite beyond the reach of most ordinary people. The tuition fee for a single semester at an elite private middle school can be as high as U.S. $1,200, compared to an average fee per semester in ordinary public schools of only U.S. $25. One private school in Sichuan province charged students 180,000 yuan upon admission, in addition to more than 4,200 yuan in tuition fees. Students who enroll in Jinghua School, an elite private primary school in Beijing, have to pay a 30,000 yuan charge for the construction of school buildings, plus a further 14,000 yuan annually for tuition fees.[23]

Arguably, such "patrician" schools may contribute appreciably to the problem of the increasing disparity between rich and poor in China. Public opinion on the issue, however, is not straightforward. A recent opinion poll conducted by the Guangzhou Modern Education Research Institute concerning parents' attitudes toward private education reported that over 54 percent of respondents approved of private schools but did not wish to encourage such a development, while only around 30 percent of respondents actually opposed private schools because they contributed a widening of the gap between rich and poor. The response may be related to the fact that, while most private schools charge higher fees than public schools, only about 40 percent of private schools are in an elite class of their own catering exclusively to China's new rich, according to one estimate.[24]

Other problems in basic-level private education can also be identified. First, the school authorities often face high expectations from parents that cannot be met. After sending their children to reputedly elite private schools, parents sometimes complained to the press that there was a huge gap between the projected image of the school and its reality. Second, shortages and frequent changes in the teaching staff of private schools have hampered not only the schools' administration but students' learning. For instance, the managing team of the Yinghao School in Conghua, Guangdong, has had to attempt to attract teachers across the country because qualified and experienced teachers in the nearby provincial capital of Guangzhou are reluctant to teach in the rural county, despite the relatively handsome salaries the school offers. Difficulty in recruiting and retaining teachers in private schools may be related in part to the heavy workload and to the nature of the students in such schools. Many teachers working in the new "patrician" schools find they have to deal with a host of unexpected academic, behavioral, and personal problems on the part of their students. Unlike the state-run schools, which streamline the top students, many of the students who enroll in private schools come with lower academic standards. For example, teachers in the Nanyang private primary school complained that around 30 percent of their students had both disciplinary and academic problems. Teachers of the Yinghao School we visited described their students as being the "four poors": psychologically poor, academically poor, behaviorally poor, and disciplinarily poor.[25]

A third problem currently confronting basic-level private educational institutions is whether they can continue to ensure a steady intake of students. For many schools it will require years of operation to build up a solid reputation before steady enrollments are assured. In the meantime many schools must spend an inordinate amount of time and resources simply on the recruitment and retention of students. Finally, many basic-level private schools face financial difficulty, especially in situations where the enterprises that own the schools fail to ensure stable gains and profits from their other activities sufficient to finance school operations and expenditures.

The problems currently confronting private tertiary education are in some cases similar but occur on a much different level. The major problem facing private tertiary institutions concerns admissions. Students with the highest grades prefer admission to state-run keypoint universities or to other public universities, leaving private institutions to recruit those students whose academic standing was not high enough to gain admission to public institutions. And, since the majority of private tertiary institutions remain uncertified by the central government, graduates of private schools also face inferior job prospects. Graduation from certified institutions, which are usually public ones, carries greater prestige and affords better job prospects in general.

A second problem for many private tertiary institutions concerns financial constraints. In order to meet their recurrent operational expenditures, private institutions sometimes enter into agreements with other enterprises, such as providing commissioned courses for the enterprise's staff. This kind of fee-for-service approach, however, can easily lead to compromised standards that fail to meet those laid down by the central authorities

In response to such problems, the central government has recently devoted substantial attention to the passage of laws and regulations intended to govern the operations of private educational institutions at all levels. The most significant of these recent measures was the passage of a new Education Law in 1995.[26] The law's avowed purpose is to facilitate the elimination of illiteracy and implementation of nine years of compulsory basic education. Comprised of some ten chapters and eighty-one clauses, the law sets out a series of directives governing the country's basic-level educational institutions including school management, financing, minimum facilities, as well as the rights and duties of educators and students. Stressing decentralization of management and financing, the law also lays out criteria for the establishment of overseas-funded schools, including international schools, and other private schools. The law grants educational institutions more autonomy in areas such as financing, management, student enrollments, and staff recruitment in return for conformity with central standards and regulations.

Despite an obvious discomfort and anxiety over the apparent growing popularity of private education, it appears that the central state is caught in a dilemma. On the one hand, it welcomes private educational undertakings, including even those by foreign educational organizations and foundations, as a useful and necessary means for spreading basic education; on the other hand, it deplores the setting up of educational institutions on a purely profit-making basis and urges that monies thus gained from such schools should be reinvested for further educational development, rather than constitute a return on investment.[27] The authors of this essay are of the view that the state has already largely lost control over basic-level private schools, despite recent efforts to regulate their existence. The simple reason is that such schools appear to have a strong basis of support among local people, which makes it difficult for the central state to curb their momentum.[28]

The same cannot be said, however, for private tertiary education. Here the state wields considerably greater power to shape and control the activities and existence of private institutions. The State Education Commission's 1993 "Provisional Regulations for the Establishment of People-Run Schools for Higher Education" were officially intended, in the words of one group of researchers, to "actively encourage, correctly direct the building and operation of people-run higher education schools, to protect the legal rights and privileges of people-run higher education, and to improve the governance and administration of people-run higher education schools."[29] But, while there is official support for the development of private tertiary education, evidence suggests that the State Education Commission may actually be engaged in an acute political struggle with the proponents and representatives of private tertiary institutions. The commission's single most powerful weapon in this struggle is its power to extend or withhold certification. Without official certification schools find it difficult to attract students, and graduates face reduced job prospects. In 1994 there were altogether more than eight hundred *minban* tertiary institutions across China, a mere eighteen of which had been certified by the State Education Commission.[30]

The response by proponents of private tertiary education has been to seek greater autonomy from the State Education Commission. Specifically, their strategy has centered on the establishment of a separate commission for *minban* education independent of the State Education Commission and possessed of its own certification powers. The National *Minban* Tertiary Education Commission was formally established in May 1995 in Beijing under the auspices of the China National Association for Adult Education. More than 150 representatives from over 106 *minban* tertiary institutions across the country met to create a common platform for the further development of private tertiary education. Forty delegates were elected to form a standing committee. The commission also launched an official bimonthly publication, entitled *Minban jiaoyu tiandi* (The World of People-Run Education). At a recent regional seminar on private higher education in the Asia-Pacific Region, attended by the authors, representatives of the commission disclosed their intention of asserting their professional autonomy from the State Education Commission by attempting to win over the authority of accreditation and certification of *minban* tertiary institutions from the State Education Commission.[31] It remains to be seen whether the *Minban* Tertiary Education Commission will achieve this aim.

Conclusion

In a recent article Linda Wong has drawn attention to the privatization of many aspects of social welfare in post-Mao China.[32] The shifting of service provision responsibilities from the state to the nonstate sector and the market suggests that a paradigmatic change in social policy has taken place.[33] Irrespective of whatever official terminology is used to describe this current social policy trend—whether *marketization, commodification,* or *socialization*—the unassailable central fact is that the role of the state in the social policy arena is declining.

China thus appears to have joined a global trend toward what some analysts have termed "quasi-marketization" of social policy.[34] In societies where social policy has undergone a process of quasi-marketization, social welfare provision operates in a relatively competitive market setting within the public sector. Social welfare is conceived as a set of mutual obligations and responsibilities between "purchasers" and "providers." Resources are allocated by the market rather than the state, though the latter may retain a significant regulatory role. Proponents of this approach argue that it leads to greater clarity of the responsibilities of "purchasers" and "providers," more effective resource management, and greater efficiency in the delivery of social services.

The recent boom in private educational institutions and the partial privatization of many funding features of public institutions, including the increased importance of self-financing students and other "multiple funding channels," suggests that a "quasi-market" is beginning to evolve in China's educational sector. It is important, however, not to exaggerate the extent of this development. At present the split between the purchaser and the provider of education has not crystallized in China as it has in some Western countries.[35] It would also be too much to say that a fully fledged "internal market" currently exists within the public education sector. Currently, the private sector plays only a limited, rather peripheral role in the educational sector. It would perhaps be more accurate to say that developments in recent years, especially since 1992, point toward an increasing shared responsibility between state and nonstate sectors in providing education. The state, meanwhile, continues to wield enormous influence and power, especially at the tertiary level, through its ability to either extend or withhold certification of private schools.

Even though the central state did not deliberately set out to promote private education, the persistent emphasis on decentralization and diversification of educational services has created ample space for private education to grow. The change has produced numerous positive results, both direct and indirect. Not least has been the revitalization of local initiative after decades of rigid central control. Through the reinvigoration of local initiatives, individual efforts, and overseas support, the central government has encouraged a more direct relationship between those who provide educational services (the providers) and those who pay for and consume them (the purchasers). Set within the present context of rapid economic growth and change, this more direct relationship arguably has contributed to a closer integration between the economic field and the educational sector, as purchasers demand education that is geared to current economic opportunities. Decentralization and privatization have also contributed to growing autonomy and flexibility in school governance, a growing assertion of professional autonomy on the part of local educators, and the refocusing of curricula toward a more practical and vocational orientation. Finally, an unintended but no less significant consequence of the current privatization trend has been the development of the concepts of consumers' rights on the purchasers' side and of professional accountability on the providers' side—concepts that are taken for granted in capitalist society but which were virtually unknown in China's socialist society until recently.

Finally, it goes without saying that, while the resurgence of private education has been made possible by a relaxation of central control, its stature as a significant sociocultural phenomenon of the post-Mao era is firmly linked to the changes in China's social structure wrought by the economic reforms introduced since 1978. In a word, Chinese society has become more plural. In place of the former monolithic social structure, there is emerging a greater degree of social differentiation and a variety of avenues and options where previously none existed. Seen from this perspective, private education caters to, and is a manifestation of, this process of pluralization.

Seen from a public policy perspective, the major negative consequence of educational decentralization and privatization is increased disparity, among social groups and across regions. Public perception and official criticism of elite-based private schools as "aristocratic" is one indication that private

education is a potentially explosive social issue. The long-term regional implications of educational decentralization also deserve serious consideration.
Emphasizing "multiple channels" of educational funding, particularly from
nongovernmental sectors, has opened the way for a widening of regional
disparities in education, with the poorer western and inland provinces lagging
far behind the richer southern and eastern coastal provinces. During the Mao
era the inland and less-developed provinces were advantaged by preferential
allocation of state financial and human resources investment, but this advantage has been gradually fading as the mandates of centralized planning give
way to the dynamics of a market economy.[36] Decentralization of educational
financing has put regional disparity into sharper focus as funding for individual schools is increasingly determined by the economic strength of localities.
In 1995 Shanghai's per capita gross domestic product was U.S. $1,900, about
ten times that of Guizhou's figure of U.S. $194. One recent analysis suggests
that China is evolving three broad regions of educational development—
advanced, medium, and developing—based on expenditures per student,
enrollments in primary and junior secondary schools, and retention rates in
primary schools.[37] Even within the highly developed coastal provinces of
Guangdong, Jiangsu, and Zhejiang, serious regional disparities exist in terms
of educational opportunities, resources and school facilities, teacher qualifications, and student achievements. Whether these disparities will be reduced or
exacerbated in the future remains an open question.

NOTES

1. On the concept of bureaucratic centralism in education, see J. Laoglo, "Forms of
Decentralization and Their Implication for Education," *Comparative Education* 31, no.
1 (1995): 5–29.

2. On educational decentralization since 1978, see Kai-Ming Cheng, "Issues in Decentralizing Education: What the Reform in China Tells," *International Journal of
Educational Research* 21, no. 8 (1994): 799–808. For the process and implications of
educational decentralization in Guangdong, a province where there has been a rapid
development of private education in recent years, see the following: K. W. Cheung and
P. T. Iu, "Power Negotiation between the Center and Locale: Development of Higher
Education Policy in Guangdong in the 1980s," in J. Cheng and Stewart MacPherson,
eds., *Development in Southern China: A Report on the Pearl River Delta Including the
Special Economic Zone* (Hong Kong: Longman, 1995); Ka-Ho Mok, "Professional Autonomy and Private Education in Guangdong Province," *Leeds East Asia Papers* 41 (1997):
1–40; and Y. Liang, "Zhujiang sanjiaozhou gaodeng jiaoyu de hongguan fenxi ji fazhan
duice" (Macroanalysis and development strategies of higher education in the Pearl
River delta), in Jiajiang Huang et al. eds., *Gaige dacao zhong de zhujiang sanjiaozhou*

jiaoyu (Education in the Pearl River delta amid tides of reform) (Guangzhou: Gaodeng jiaoyu chubanshe, 1993).

3. Chinese Communist Party Central Committee, *Decision of the Central Committee of the Communist Party of China on Reform of the Educational System* (Beijing: Chinese Communist Party Central Committee, 1985). For analyses of the implications of the reform, see Kai-Ming Cheng, "Issues in Decentralizing Education," 799–808; and also Suzanne Pepper, "Regaining the Initiative for Education Reform and Development," in C. K. Lo, et al., eds., *China Review 1995* (Hong Kong: Chinese University Press, 1995).

4. Chinese Communist Party Central Committee, *Program for Reform and Development of China's Education* (Beijing: Chinese Communist Party Central Committee, 1993).

5. State Education Commission Policies and Law Department, *Law and Regulation on Basic Education of the People's Republic of China* (Beijing: Beijing Normal University, 1993), 6.

6. See Kai-Ming Cheng, "Education: Decentralization and the Market," in Linda Wong and Stewart MacPherson, eds., *Social Change and Social Policy in Contemporary China* (Averbury: Aldershot, 1995).

7. Hu Ruiwen, "Jiushi niandao Zhongguo jiaoyu de jinzhang yu 2010 nian zhanwang" (China's education in the 1990s and the prospects in the year of 2010) (paper presented to the Fifth International Conference on Chinese Education "Towards the 21st Century," August 13–19, 1997, Chinese University of Hong Kong).

8. For examples of this trend, see Ka-Ho Mok, "Marketization and Decentralization: Development of Education and Paradigm Shift in Social Policy," *Hong Kong Public Administration* 5, no. 1 (March 1996): 35–56.

9. See Cheng, "Education: Decentralization and the Market."

10. Reprinted here from Leslie Nai-kwai Lo, "The Changing Educational System: Dilemma of Disparity," in Joseph Y. S. Cheng and Maurice Brousseau, eds., *China Review 1993* (Hong Kong: Chinese University Press, 1993), 22, 17.

11. Reprinted here from Suzanne Pepper, "Regaining the Initiative for Education Reform and Development," in C. K. Lo, Suzanne Pepper, and K. Y. Tsui, eds., *China Review 1995* (Hong Kong: Chinese University Press, 1995), 18, 21.

12. See Ka-Ho Mok, "Retreat of the State: Marketization of Education in the Pearl River Delta," *Comparative Education Review* 41, no. 3 (August 1997): 260–76; and Ka-Ho Mok and David K. K. Chan, "The Emergence of Private Education in the Pearl River Delta: Its Social Implications," in Stewart MacPherson and Joseph Y. S. Cheng, eds., *The Economic and Social Developments in South China* (London: Edward Elgar, 1996). See also Jing Lin, "Private Schools in China," *Chinese Education and Society* 29, no. 2 (March–April 1996): 5–9; and "The Development and Prospect of Private Schools in China: A Preliminary Study" (paper presented at the Annual Meeting of the American Educational Research Association, New Orleans, April 4–8, 1994).

13. Jing Lin, "Private Schools in China," 3.

14. Guangdong Yearbook Editorial Committee, *Guangdong Yearbook 1994* (Guangzhou: Guangdong nianjian chubanshe, 1994). See also Y. Liang, "Zhujiang sanjiaozhou gaodeng jiaoyu."

15. *China National Institute of Educational Research: A Study of NGO-Sponsored and Private Higher Education in China* (Beijing: UNESCO, 1995), 4–5.

16. See Yuan Zhengguo, "Chinese Higher Educational Changes: From 'State Model' to 'Social Model' " (paper presented at the International Symposium on Education and Socio-Political Transitions on Asia, May 29–31, 1995, at the University of Hong Kong); Pepper, "Regaining the Initiative"; Yin Qiping and G. White, "The Marketization of Chinese Higher Education: A Critical Assessment," discussion paper (Brighton: Institute of Development Studies, University of Sussex, 1993).

17. Ying-chu Ng and Sung-ko Li, "Measuring the Research Performance of Chinese Higher Education Institutions: An Application of Data Envelopment Analysis" (PRC Papers on China, School of Business, Business Research Center, Hong Kong Baptist University, July 1997).

18. China National Institute of Educational Research, *A Study of NGO-Sponsored and Private Higher Education,* 10.

19. Wei Yitong and Zhang Guocai, "A Historical Perspective on Non-governmental Higher Education in China" (paper presented at the "Regional Seminar on Private Higher Education in Asia and the Pacific," Xiamen, Fujian, October 30–November 3, 1995), 7–8.

20. State Education Commission, "The Provisional Regulation for the Establishment of People-Run Schools for Higher Education," in China National Institute of Educational Research, *A Study of NGO-Sponsored and Private Higher Education.*

21. Jing Lin, "Private Schools in China," 4.

22. *Ming Bao,* January 12, 1995.

23. *Asian Relations,* no. 2 (Winter–Spring 1994); Yang Xiong, "Zhongguo minban jiaoyu wuzi, taqing jiqi rencheng yuanyin de fenxi" (An analysis of the characteristics and reasons for the formation of private educational models in China), in Wu Zhuimin, ed., *Zhongguo jichu jiaoyu fazhan yanjiu* (Research on the development of Chinese basic education) (Shanghai: Shanghai jiaoyu chubanshe, 1997), 234–38.

24. Xi Ling, "Sili xuexiao duowei toushi" (A multidimensional perspective on private schools), *Shehui,* no. 3 (Shanghai: 1994), 34. On the public opinion survey, see *Open Times* (May 1995).

25. Interview with administrators and teachers at the Yinghao School conducted during a field visit in December 1994; *Open Times* (May 1995): 57–58.

26. *Renmin Ribao,* March 12, 1995; *Wen Hui Bao* (Hong Kong), March 13, 1995.

27. See the report in *Da Gong Bao* (Hong Kong), March 17, 1995.

28. As an illustration of this popularity, consider the private Guanghua Primary School in the Pearl River Delta region of Guangdong province. The school, which originally planned to open with only 100 students, was eventually forced to admit up to 150 students as a result of pressure from local parents.

29. Wei Yitong and Zhang Guocai, "Historical Perspective," 10.

30. China National Institute of Educational Research, *A Study of NGO-Sponsored and Private Higher Education,* 11. By 1997 the total number of *minban* higher institutions across the country had risen to one thousand two hundred, of which only twenty-two were officially recognized by the State Education Commission (pers. comm. with Professor Yutaka Otsuka of Hiroshima University).

31. "A Burdensome Historical Mission: Summary Report on the First Meeting of the National *Minban* Tertiary Education Commission," issue no. 3/95 (cumulative no. 15) (June 20, 1995), 5–6. The Regional Seminar on Private Tertiary Education in Asia and the Pacific was held October 29–November 2, 1995, at Xiamen University in Fujian province, China.

32. Linda Wong, "Privatization of Social Welfare in Post-Mao China," *Asian Survey* 34, no. 4 (1994): 307–25.

33. C. Chan and N. Chow, *More Welfare after Economic Reform? Welfare Development in the People's Republic of China* (Hong Kong: Center of Urban Planning and Environmental Management, University of Hong Kong, 1992). See also X. S. Jiang, "Lun woguo shehui zhengce de chuantong moshi ji zhuanbian" (A discussion of our country's traditional social policy model and its transformation), *Shehuixue yanjiu* (Beijing), (1992). For a comparative perspective, see J. Le Grand and R. Robinson, eds., *Privatization and the Welfare State* (London: George Allen and Unwin, 1985).

34. See J. Le Grand and W. Bartlett, eds., *Quasi-Marketization and Social Policy* (London: Macmillan, 1993).

35. See S. Harrison and G. Whistow, "The Purchaser-Provider Split in Health Care: Towards Explicit Rationing" (paper presented to the Twenty-second Annual Conference of the Regional Science Association, Oxford, September 1991).

36. Stanley Rosen, "The Impact of Economic Reform on Chinese Education: Markets and the Growth of Differentiation" (paper presented to the Conference on Social Consequences of Chinese Economic Reform at the John K. Fairbank Center, Harvard University, May 22–24, 1997). See also Gong Fang, "Zhongguo jingji fazhan de qüyühua ji qi dui gaodeng jiaoyu de yingxiang" (The regionalization of China's economic development and its effects on higher education), *Jiaoyu yanjiu* (Educational research) 9 (1988).

37. State Education Commission and Shanghai Institute for Human Resources Development, *Zhongguo Jiaoyu Jingfei Fazhan Baogao, 1996* (Annual development report on China's educational finance) (Beijing: Jiaoyu kexue chubanshe, 1997). See also Jacques Lamontagne, "Educational Disparities in Mainland China: Characteristics and Trends," in Lin Bih-jaw and Fan Li-min, eds., *Education in Mainland China* (Taipei: Institute of International Relations, National Chengchi University, 1990), 130–51.

Part 3
Gender Representation and Identification

Heidi Ross

Gender provides a compelling context for understanding the relationship between education and society, and the role of schooling in consolidating or destabilizing state-society relations. The essays in this section explore the social and individual consequences for diverse groups of girls and women of formal schooling promoted by missionaries, nationalists, professional educators, feminists, entrepreneurs, and philanthropists. Each essay depicts the state and schools as gendered spaces in which knowledge, social responsibility, and personal allegiance are perceived by women in ambiguous and frequently contradictory ways. Because China's first schools for girls were intimately connected to the state-building project, evaluation of their outcomes has required that we grapple with "the problem of nationalism." Likewise, our recognition of the centrality of gender to questions of state and identity formation raises the question of agency, that is, how particular girls and women respond to, appropriate, or reject the social discourses and values that shape their education. By treating women as the subjects, rather than merely the objects, of schooling, these essays reveal how schools can act simultaneously as both barrier to and gateway for the development of Chinese women.

Interpreting women's educational experiences requires embracing such contraries. On the one hand, Paul Bailey concludes that, given the meager provisions for and tiny number of females studying in China's first state-supported schools, women's education was not a significant feature of the state-building process in the early twentieth century. On the other hand, the civilizing discourse used to justify such schools—that girls' education would bring virtue to the household and strength to the nation—also promoted environments like Zhili First Women's Normal School, whose teachers, Sarah Coles McElroy suggests, inevitably inspired transformed perceptions of gender among China's elites and the redefinition of women's public role in Chinese society.

Striking parallels exist between the educational purposes of Zhili and the sense of entitlement and social service reconstructed across a century by the alumni of the missionary institution, the Shanghai McTyeire School for Girls, described by Heidi Ross. Both schools embodied the dual aim of cultivating virtuous housewives and high-minded citizens, and it appears that both schools' graduates appropriated this aim for their own purposes, even as those purposes were sometimes sidelined by the interests of "national salvation."

The nationalist and missionary refrain that Chinese women were victims in need of educational uplift is echoed in Mette Hansen's case study of minority education policies for socialist nation building. Hansen's portrait of the (unpredictable) power of schools to reproduce gendered identities and minority stereotypes indicates that the lessons of state schooling have significantly different meaning for boys and girls of minority backgrounds. The complicity of such schools in the exoticization of minority girls for profit, however, also underscores the contradictory outcomes of girls' schooling in China as state funding and control has been devolved to local communities. While minority school representations of gender and ethnic stereotypes alienate parents and pupils from the state curriculum, the private school initiative for rural girls described in Ross's study assists female students to construct a space for resisting debilitating representations of rural girls as poor and backward.

Ping-Chun Hsiung's examination of women's studies programs in Chinese universities likewise shows how reform era policies have unintentionally enabled women to construct "autonomous spaces within an otherwise authoritarian apparatus." Yet, as women's studies programs provide the means to channel "individual dissent into collective endeavor," their sustainability and legitimacy also depend upon the extraordinary political dexterity of their leaders. Like their early-twentieth-century foremothers, advocates of women's studies secure their programs by reimagining institutional resources and maintaining delicate relationships with state agencies like the All China Women's Federation (ACWF). Hsiung's sympathetic depiction of the ACWF's contradictory mandate to promote CCP policies and represent the interests of women, brings us full circle to the most salient theme in this section, the efforts by women in education and society, on the margins throughout the twentieth century, to claim "new ground whenever and wherever possible."

Taken together, our essays indicate that neither the public-private nor the school-society relationship should be conceptualized as composed primarily of "separate and opposing forces." The voices of women transcribed in our studies provide an eloquent testimony to the multiple meanings that *tradition, family,* and *nation* have had for women and how these meanings have served as reference points, during different periods of the twentieth century, for the purposes of women's schooling, for the construction of personal identity and social duty, and, ultimately, for the transformation of gender relations. In doing so, our section provides fascinating clues to the applicability and usefulness of concepts such as agency and civil society to understanding social changes in twentieth-century China as well as how gender, social class, and ethnicity intersect to shape women's relationships to schooling.

Active Citizen or Efficient Housewife? The Debate over Women's Education in Early-Twentieth-Century China

Paul Bailey

Educational reform was a crucial aspect of the state-building process that began during the last decade of the Qing dynasty. Officials, scholars, and educators after 1900 insisted on the need for a national school system that would train a disciplined and hardworking people who would contribute to national unity and prosperity. As far as the dynasty and its officials were concerned, a national school system, by promoting the virtues of loyalty and obedience, would also consolidate the foundations of dynastic rule. Educators and gentry reformers, on the other hand, preferred to highlight the contributions a national school system would make in divesting the lower classes of their "backward" customs and "superstitious" outlook (so graphically illustrated, in the eyes of the gentry elite, by the Boxer Uprising in 1899–1900) as well as equipping them with the skills necessary for China to compete economically on the international stage.[1]

Yet when regulations for a national school system were drawn up in 1904 no formal provision was made for the education of girls. Zhang Zhidong, the governor-general of Hunan and Hubei and one of the key architects of the 1904 school system, argued that girls had always been educated in the home and that strict segregation of the sexes had always been respected. "It is not appropriate," he insisted, "to allow young girls to enter school in large groups and to wander about the streets." It was even more inappropriate, Zhang continued, "to let girls read western books and study foreign customs, which will gradually cause them to act independently and have contempt for their [future] parents-in-law."[2] The establishment of formal education for girls would be a disaster, in Zhang's view, and he concluded: "Therefore, girls can only be educated within the family and receive instruction from the mother or from the nurse to enable them to have a basic grasp of literacy and be conversant with necessary family affairs and with the appropriate tasks befitting a woman."[3]

With the abolition of the civil service examinations in 1905 (the training for which in official and private academies had constituted one of the most important aspects of traditional education) the new school system, incorporating a wider curriculum than instruction in the Confucian classics, assumed increasing importance, especially as reformers and educators underlined the connection between the wealth and strength of Western countries and Japan and the commitment of those countries to nationwide education. The Qing government finally sanctioned female education in 1907, but even then cautious attitudes prevailed. Allowance was only made for separate primary schools and lower normal schools (to train primary schoolteachers). In the preamble to the school regulations the Board of Education (*xuebu*), which had been created in 1905, noted that education for girls was necessary to perfect "women's virtue" (*nüde*), which consisted of steadfast chastity (*zhengjing*), obedience (*shunliang*), compassion (*cishu*), and proper conduct (*duanqian*). The inculcation of such virtues, the Board of Education explained, would enable girls in the future to assist their husbands (*xiangfu*) and correct their sons (*xunzi*). At the same time, it was made clear that girls' schools were not to be exposed to "heterodox theories promoting unrestrained freedom" (*fangzong ziyou zhi pishuo*). These "subversive" theories, according to the Board of Education, included the advocacy of free-choice marriage; not distinguishing clearly between the male and female spheres; and the sanctioning of women's membership in political associations and participation in public meetings.[4]

Since girls were different from boys, the Board of Education declared, their future lives would follow a different trajectory. The curriculum for normal schools therefore placed much emphasis on the teaching of household affairs (*jiashi*) and household management (*jiazheng*), which required a frugal and hardworking attitude, a meticulous sense of organization, and a love of cleanliness and hygiene. Finally, the Board of Education (evidently oblivious to the actual experiences of most peasant women) insisted that girls were to be taught skills (such as embroidery, sericulture, sewing, and handicrafts) that would eliminate their "parasitic dependence" (*zuoshi*) and allow them to improve the family livelihood.[5]

Of course, even before the government sanctioned women's education in 1907 a number of private girls' schools had been opened (especially in Shanghai), where more formal, provincially funded institutions such as the Beiyang

Women's Normal School (established in early 1906) had made an appearance.[6] Gentry and local officials before 1907 were also in the process of establishing a wide variety of half-day literacy and vocational schools for girls, many of which (as in the case of boys' schools) were housed in ancestral halls, former Confucian academies (*shuyuan*), and expropriated Buddhist monasteries.[7] The Board of Education, in fact, referred to this phenomenon as justification for issuing the 1907 regulations, noting that the time had now come to "regulate" women's education and bring it under some form of coordinated control. Furthermore, in 1912, following the overthrow of the Qing dynasty and the creation of a republic, a new education system provided for the establishment of secondary schools for girls and sanctioned coeducation at the primary level.[8] In 1919 higher-level education for women was finally sanctioned with the founding of Beijing Women's Higher Normal School and the allowing of women to enroll in Beijing University.[9]

Yet in terms of numbers of schools and school enrollment the progress of women's education during the early years of the republic remained pitifully slow. The number of female students increased from 1,853 (0.21 percent of the school-age population) in 1907 to 141,130 (4.81 percent of the school-age population) in 1912–13. By 1922–23 the total had reached 417,820 (6.32 percent of the school-age population).[10] At the primary level the number of girls increased from 130,808 in 1912–13 to only 164,719 in 1916–17 (the number of boys at primary school increased from 2,662,825 to 3,678,736 in the same period).[11] By 1922 primary school enrollment for girls totaled 403,742 (6.19 percent of the total). Interestingly, the proportion of girls at secondary school was slightly higher, although absolute numbers did not increase significantly—from 10,066 in 1912 (9.77 percent of the total) to 11,824 in 1922 (6.46 percent of the total).[12] Also, whereas the number of schools for boys increased from 84,883 (2,792,257 students) in 1912 to 117,658 (3,801,730 students) in 1916, the number of schools for girls rose from 2,389 (141,130 students) to only 3,461 (172,724 students) during the same period.[13]

Figures for school enrollment in the individual provinces are even more striking. In the metropolitan province of Zhili, for example, whereas school enrollment for boys in 1916 (totaling 506,997) averaged 32.84 percent of the male school-age population, for girls (totaling 12,834) it was 1.24 percent of the female school-age population. Of the 119 districts in the province only 59 registered female enrollment in schools above 1 percent of the school-age population (the highest being 8.73 percent). Thirty-five districts, on the other hand, registered male enrollment in schools above 40 percent of the school-age population.[14] In Sichuan province there were 13,469 lower primary schools for boys (415,778 students) in 1916 but only 363 for girls (20,239 students). At the higher primary level there were 764 schools for boys (41,911 students) and 72 for girls (2,367 students).[15] Even in Beijing girls were considerably disadvantaged. At the end of 1916 the Beijing Education Bureau issued figures for lower and higher primary school enrollment during the year 1915–16. Whereas there was a total of 204 lower primary schools for boys (18,971 students), there were only 23 such schools for girls (2,452 students). A similar disparity existed at the higher primary level, with 50 schools for boys (3,644 students) and only 13 for girls (254 students).[16]

It would seem, then, that women's education was not a significant feature of China's state-building process in the early twentieth century.[17] Yet, although educational opportunities for girls grew only slowly (especially when compared with those for boys) during this period, considerable debate nevertheless took place over the merits, nature, and role of women's education, which was to have relevance beyond the early twentieth century. In contrast to pioneering new work on gender discourse in the seventeenth and eighteenth centuries, however, which had implications for the significance and meaning of women's education,[18] there has been surprisingly little discussion of this early-twentieth-century debate.[19]

To a great extent the parameters of this debate were set in the 1890s with the reform proposals of Zheng Guanying (1842–1923) and Liang Qichao (1873–1929). Zheng, a comprador and manager of modern enterprises, was one of the first reformers to advocate women's education but for the specific purpose of training "virtuous women, virtuous wives and virtuous mothers" (*xiannü, xianqi, xianmu*).[20] As will be discussed later, Zheng would be the first of many who attributed social and moral malaise to women's "backwardness." The lack of education among women was even worse than among men, he declared, claiming that they spent their days idly gossiping with older women, engaging in superstitious practices and frittering away the savings earned by their husbands. For Zheng women's lack of education meant that men could not rely on "assistance from within the household" (*neizhu*). Although women need not be as highly educated or learned as men, he argued, an education that would make them morally upright, literate, numerate, and competent in "handling everyday matters" (such as embroidery, cooking, and household budgeting) would relieve husbands of undue anxiety and bring virtue to the household.[21]

Liang Qichao also emphasized the "worthy mother and good wife" (*xianmu liangqi*) ideal to justify the implementation of women's education, but he also highlighted two additional benefits. First, Liang suggested that educated women would be morally and physically equipped to bear fitter sons and to oversee their upbringing as future citizens of the country, and, second, he declared that education would provide women with a profession or trade (*zhiye*) so that they would cease being parasitic consumers (*fenlizhe*) and become producers (*shenglizhe*). This would both lighten the burden of responsibility placed upon husbands and revive the country's economic fortunes.[22] The idea that education would make women less dependent on men by providing them with the means for their own economic livelihood was also to recur throughout the early years of the twentieth century, but it was riddled with ambiguity: when Liang referred to women learning a trade, it was not entirely clear whether he envisaged women as independent actors in society competing professionally with men or as skilled handicraft workers in the home contributing to family harmony and prosperity.

After 1900 the debate was joined by the general periodical press, specialist journals on education, and an emerging women's press—journals to which women contributed and which were sometimes edited by women themselves.[23] School texts and readers for girls also began to appear several years before the Qing government issued regulations on primary and lower normal schools for women in 1907, providing an intriguing glimpse of how educators perceived the scope and purpose of women's education. Discussion often revolved around whether there were innate gender differences that might determine the kind of education provided, to what extent women's education might or might not subvert the political and social order, and, finally, what exactly were to be the duties and contributions of the female citizen.

Although during the last years of the dynasty the periodical press, especially journals published by overseas Chinese students in Japan, frequently emphasized the importance of women's education in order to "forge citizens" and train "the mothers of the nation" (*guomin zhi mu*),[24] it was often justified in terms of dealing with the baneful influence of women within the home. Not only were women ignorant of, and uninterested in, public affairs, but they also wasted time and money on personal adornment and superstitious Buddhist devotions. As a consequence, they were a bad influence on sons, a constant source of anxiety for husbands, and inefficient managers of the household. Women, in effect, served as a convenient scapegoat for all the perceived ills affecting Chinese society. Even the most radical publication on women's rights that appeared before 1911, *Nüjie zhong* for example (Warning Bell for Women), written by Jin Songcen (1874–1947), was underpinned by these assumptions.[25]

On the one hand, Jin advocated equality between men and women, insisting that women had rights to education and free-choice marriage, to own property, to interact and move freely in society, and to manage a business. He also saw no reason why women should not (in the future) be involved in politics and government.²⁶ Jin's principal aim, however, was to mobilize women for the political struggle against the dynasty.²⁷ He ascribed to women a hidden power to move and inspire people (*ganren zhi moli*) because of their serene and compassionate outlook. This, according to Jin, would make them especially suitable as primary schoolteachers and as agitators among the people. Since women occupied the lowest rungs of society, Jin declared, they would have a natural empathy for the laboring classes (*laodong shehui zhi ren*) and, like the female Narodniks in Russia, would be able to move people to tears and sow hatred of autocracy among young and old alike.²⁸

On the other hand, like many of his contemporaries, Jin blamed women for China's plight. Although he rejected the argument that there were fundamental differences between the sexes in their mental and physical capacities and in their emotional and psychological profiles, Jin in effect subscribed to such a view when he declared, as a matter of course, that women were overly dependent, submissive, superstitious, narcissistic, and incompetent in household affairs.²⁹ In the final analysis women's moral failings (not men's) were at the core of China's problem; Jin's educational aims for women therefore focused on the training of pure (*chunjie*), chaste (*jianzhen*), and bold (*jilie*) revolutionaries. In the process women would become fully developed and autonomous individuals with "appropriate" male-like natures.³⁰ Nevertheless, Jin still rejected the idea of coeducation (except at the lower primary level), since he deemed it inappropriate for older boys and girls to study together.³¹

There were exceptions to this negative view of women's character and behavior.³² A 1903 article in *Nüxue bao* (Journal of Women's Education) noted that because Chinese women had been the most oppressed in the world their liberation struggle would be more heroic than any that had taken place in the West. Furthermore, the author maintained, twentieth-century Chinese women would achieve more than their sisters in the West because of three unique characteristics they possessed, characteristics that also made them superior to Chinese men as well. First, Chinese women had resoluteness and perseverance (*jianzhi xin*), tried and tested by their continuing devotion to parents despite oppression within the home. This devotion, in fact, once transferred from parents to country would make Chinese women more unshakeable patriots than their male counterparts. Second, they had kind and compassionate natures (*ciai xin*), which endowed them with a natural sense of justice and commitment to helping the less well-off. Unlike men, women in government would therefore place more emphasis on equality and human solidarity. Third, women had an acute sense of vengeance (*baofu xin*) and a more seething hatred (*chouhen xin*) of oppression. Unlike Chinese men, who were always quite willing to accept the status quo as long as it did not affect their selfish interests, women would therefore be more dependable and stead-fast anti-Manchu revolutionaries. Once Chinese women availed themselves of the opportunity for education, the author concluded, there was no limit to what they could achieve.[33]

Much more common, however, was the view expressed during the same year in another student journal. Although China's weakness, the author admit-ted, was partly due to men's selfish and unpatriotic attitudes, the most serious cause for concern was the behavior and outlook of women. Not only were they ignorant and petty minded, but they were quite happy to be treated as playthings and ornaments. Chinese women were a far cry from their counter-parts in the West, the author claimed, who were morally impeachable, far-sighted, independent, and devoted to the public welfare.[34]

An appropriate education for women, therefore, was often discussed in terms of benefiting husbands, the household, and, ultimately, society. The principal of a girls' school opened in Beijing in 1906 noted that because of women's "dependent natures" (*yilai xing*) men ruined themselves economi-cally; an education that provided skills to enhance the family income was the answer.[35] Others were concerned that women's education provide instruction in household skills. Jiang Weiqiao, a prominent educator and compiler of school textbooks, expressed alarm in 1910 that girls in modern schools were getting above their station. On returning home, they were not only incapable of cooking and sewing, but they also disdained performing such chores. No wonder, he lamented, that lower-class families were reluctant to send their daughters to school. Jiang suggested that modern schools for girls pay more attention to the teaching of traditional domestic skills such as embroidery, weaving, and flower making, especially as the number of professions for women would always be limited. In any case, he concluded, such skills ac-corded more appropriately with girls' natures.[36] Jiang had evidently under-gone a change in attitude, since three years previously he had compiled a collection of songs for girls schools, one of which urged girls to enroll in modern schools in order to acquire a knowledge of physics, chemistry, mathe-matics, and foreign languages.[37]

The importance of household management (*jiazheng*), which was to be increasingly emphasized during the early years of the republic, began to be mentioned at this time in discussions of women's education. One 1905 article noted that an uneducated woman's inability to look after the house-hold properly, which affected family harmony and well-being, would dam-age her *son's* chances of attending school. There was thus, in the author's view, a direct link between women's education and the improvement of social mores (*shehui fengqi*).[38] Significantly, an article explaining the causes of poverty listed as the most important a man's inability to "acquire a virtuous wife" (*bu de xianqi*), defined as someone who would be an efficient household manager.[39]

Even when women's education was not discussed in terms of improving domestic skills, the assumption was always that educated women would provide the required assistance for husbands and thereby gain men's approval. Thus, Jiang Kanghu, an educational advisor to Governor-General Yuan Shikai and founder of China's first socialist party in 1912, insisted in 1910 that women's education involved more than mere instruction in cooking and embroidery. The *xianmu liangqi* ideal entailed more than just aspiring to be a good housewife and mother, Jiang declared, because, if a wife was not acquainted with national affairs, how could she be expected to assist her husband and encourage him to "achieve great things in the world" (*wei haojie*)?[40]

Even Qiu Jin, who joined the anti-Qing revolutionary movement while studying in Japan and founded a women's journal, *Zhongguo nübao* (Chinese Women's Magazine), in 1907 to promote women's emancipation, demonstrated a similar ambiguity in her thinking. As with many others, she painted a dismal (and monolithic) picture of Chinese women in the first issue of her journal:

> While our 200 million male compatriots have already advanced, our 200 million female compatriots are still mired in the utter darkness of the eighteen layers of hell. They cannot even envisage a way of climbing up one layer, with their feet bound so small, their combed hair glossy and inlaid with flowers, their bodies wrapped in silks and satins, and their white-powdered faces smeared with rouge. They pass their entire lives knowing only how to depend on men . . . They are meek, subservient and fawning . . . They live the life of obsequious servility.[41]

Although Qiu Jin then emphasized the potential of education in allowing women to gain qualifications and acquire a trade, the two benefits she suggested would accrue from such a situation were prosperity for the family and the gaining of men's respect.

School textbooks published before 1911 reflected many of these assumptions and ambiguities concerning the role and purpose of women's education. The introduction to a 1905 text bemoaned the fact that Chinese women spent their time either gambling or burning incense, concerned only with personal adornment and doting (*chongai*) on their husbands to impress relatives and neighbors. No wonder that men were apathetic and the country as a whole was in such a sorry plight![42] Women who have not attended school, one lesson claimed, were more useless than animals and insects.[43] Although the text insisted that girls had the same patriotic duty as boys to become involved in national affairs and protect the country,[44] many of the individual lessons reinforced the idea that women's principal role was to manage the household effectively, which was considered an indispensable feature of women's special talents.[45] In fact, the onus was very much on women to ensure family harmony and prosperity.[46] Such prosperity would come about not by women engaging in their usual superstitious devotions to Buddhist deities but by their dextrous handling of, and contribution to, the family budget. They would then no longer be looked down on by men or insulted by their in-laws.[47] Also, whereas the eighteenth-century official and educator Chen Hongmou (1696–1771) had stressed the importance of women's management of the *jia* (nuclear household) as a prerequisite for the survival of the *zong* (patriarchal lineage), both the periodical press and school textbooks in the early twentieth century linked successful (individual) household management directly with the health of the nation and the state.[48]

School texts also contained a bewildering array of contradictory images and messages. Pictures of girls lifting weights or riding bicycles[49] were juxtaposed with those portraying dutiful daughters sweeping and cleaning the family home.[50] In contrast to a common portrayal of women as meek, submissive, and tenderhearted, some school texts noted that education would temper their "naturally" fierce (*xionghan*), scheming, and envious natures.[51] A teaching manual published in 1908 insisted that women should take pleasure from being obedient to husbands and parents (instead of seeking solace from "useless" religious devotion) and consisted of lessons detailing how to arrange household furniture and keep the house clean; on the other hand, girls were urged to think of their country, a commitment that was seen as more important than being married or not.[52]

It might be noted that the negative views of women's character and behavior that pervaded the periodical press were accompanied by increasing discussion of innate gender differences. Many of the articles dealing with this issue, in fact, were translated from the Japanese. One such article, published in 1911, noted that boys were more active and imaginative than girls, who were more emotional and flighty. Girls, moreover, were more affected by feelings of jealousy (*jidu xin*) and suspicion (*caiji xin*). Whereas boys were naturally independent and therefore had the potential to work successfully in society, girls were born to serve and please and hence were more suited to working in the home.[53] A Japanese teaching manual for normal schools translated into Chinese in 1905 expressed similar views; it was perfectly natural, the manual noted, for boys eventually to immerse themselves in public activities and for girls to occupy themselves with household affairs. Education, therefore, helped to complete and perfect their natural inclinations.⁵⁴

Nevertheless, there was a constant fear during the last years of the dynasty (especially among government authorities) that women's education had the potential to subvert the social order and unleash moral anarchy. An article in Liang Qichao's *Xinmin congbao* (New People's Miscellany) in 1904 warned that if girls were provided with too much of an advanced education they would begin to look down on boys and might even rebel against their destiny of becoming mothers.⁵⁵ The Beijing Education Bureau in 1907 insisted that a collection of songs for girls' schools published by the Wenming Book Company be revised because the songs contained references to free marriage (*ziyou jiehun*) and criticized the practice of matchmaking.⁵⁶ Authorities also feared that private schools for girls were attracting the wrong kind of students; many of the students of one such school in Changsha (Hunan province) in 1909 were apparently local prostitutes who spent most of their free time "recklessly engaged in lewd activities" (*sixing yinluan*) and exerting a bad influence on the daughters of good families.⁵⁷ A women's journal in 1904 feared that female students would fall prey to men peddling ideas of free love and that promiscuity would abound; furthermore, it wondered, what about those "girls of dubious character" (*fei anfen nüzi*)? It was assumed they would use the pretext of leaving home and attending school to indulge their illicit sexual desires (*jianli zhi si*).⁵⁸ Educated women might also cause family tragedy; a Beijing journal in 1907 blamed women's education for the suicide of a mother-in-law, apparently because of frequent insubordination and abuse from an educated daughter-in-law.⁵⁹ On the eve of the 1911 Revolution a contributor to *Dongfang zazhi* (Eastern Miscellany) complained that women were using the opportunity to gain an education to break ties with the family; if women led independent lives and were economically self-sufficient, they would no longer desire to get married.⁶⁰

The debate over women's education during the last decade of the Qing was therefore fraught with ambiguity and contradiction. The insistence on equal educational rights for women coexisted with assumptions of innate gender differences that strictly determined (and limited) the content and purpose of women's education. While women were exhorted to become more concerned with public affairs and to strive for economic independence, it was also assumed that women should be trained to become efficient and organized housewives. Also, while education for women was seen as a crucial panacea for national revival, fears were likewise expressed that such an education might very well undermine the gender and family order.

Conservative disquiet about the potentially subversive effects of women's education was reinforced in the wake of the 1911 Revolution. During the revolution itself women had organized military battalions and mobile Red Cross teams and shortly afterward created political associations lobbying for voting rights.[61] The Women's Public Lecture Association (Nüzi xuanjiang hui), founded in March 1912, declared that the establishment of a republic after just a few months was an event unparalleled in world history and that it was therefore even more urgent that women be granted equal political and educational rights to enable them to assume their legitimate role as republican citizens.[62]

Such demands were fiercely contested. The insistence on equal political rights was perceived as a threat to the "natural" gender division of labor. The basis of a healthy state, one author declared, was sound families; if women were involved in politics, the family would disintegrate and society would begin to crumble. In any event, he continued, men's natures equipped them for politics and government because they thought more of the long term, while women were more adept at running a family because they always thought of more immediate needs.[63] The scuffles that took place in early 1912 at the National Assembly in Nanjing as a result of suffragettes demanding that equal political rights be enshrined in the new constitution only confirmed conservative fears of "boisterous" and "unrestrained" women. The suffragettes were condemned for their lack of decorum and respect, and their actions were cited as proof of women's unfitness for government.[64]

At a time when social customs and attitudes (at least in the cities) were undergoing change, some observers were alarmed at the growing visibility and independence of female students reflected in the phenomenon of young boys and girls walking around together in public and in the "outrageous" dress styles female students adopted such as scarlet stockings and trousers that did not go below the knees.[65] Harking back to Zhang Zhidong's warning in 1904, educators in the early republic feared that the growing numbers of independent-minded and freedom-loving female students would usher in sexual anarchy.[66] Significantly, educators (both male and female) also warned that new fads in schoolgirl dress posed a threat to the nation's reproductive future. Thus, a supervisor at Shanghai Women's Normal School in 1915 noted the prevalence among students of tight-fitting undergarments that tended to "flatten" the breasts. Having finally recognized the dangers of footbinding, she declared, Chinese women were now paradoxically binding their breasts in the vain quest for beauty. Such restrictions on natural development, she concluded, would ultimately impair their reproductive role and lead to the weakening of the race.[67]

Not surprisingly, the new republican education system of 1912, which sanctioned (separate) secondary education for girls,[68] stressed the inculcation of traditional virtues such as chastity, purity, and gentleness (*zhenshu*) in girls' schools (while also, somewhat paradoxically, encouraging the "spirit of independence") and incorporated the teaching of domestic skills (*jiashi ke*) in the secondary school curriculum.[69] The republican government also cracked down on women's public activities in much the same way as the new Meiji government in Japan after 1868.[70] Thus, public order regulations issued in March 1914 forbade women, along with soldiers, monks, and primary school-teachers, from joining political associations.[71] Throughout the early years of the republic educational authorities paid careful attention to the "appropriate" reading material for female students. The Education Ministry established the Popular Education Research Association (Tongsu jiaoyu yanjiu hui) with the express purpose of classifying educational and other published material; any books that were deemed "inferior" were banned.[72] Significantly, one of the books classified as "superior" for educational purposes in 1918 was on the improvement of household management. It included an anecdote of a Chinese Christian woman who was inspired by the spotlessly clean and orderly house of a Western missionary; on her return home she set her own house in order (*zhijia zhixu*), which entailed not only tidying up and rearranging the furniture in an orderly way but also forcing her husband to stop smoking opium and to seek a job.[73]

Perhaps the most significant aspect of this conservative backlash, however, was the official campaign to encourage virtuous behavior among women. Official regulations issued in 1914 recommended that women deserving of commendation (*baoyang*) might include those who had demonstrated chastity and uprightness (*jielie zhencao*), had been involved in charitable work for the poor and needy, and had set an example for hard work and thriftiness (*qinjian*).[74] In fact, one year earlier, in 1913, the Internal Affairs Ministry had insisted that the need for "chaste" women (*lienü jiefu*) was as relevant as ever, while the Beijing parliament declared that the encouragement of chaste and filial behavior among women was crucially urgent to restore social order and end the current malaise of moral anarchy.[75] The 1914 regulations were revised and reissued in 1917, with commendation to be awarded to women who had exhibited outstanding filial and virtuous behavior, heroic chastity, harmonious interaction with in-laws and relatives, and skill in arts and crafts (*yishu*).[76] The official journal of the Internal Affairs Ministry regularly published lists of chaste widows and "heroic women" who had committed suicide on the death of their husbands or after being raped.[77] One novel classified as superior (*shangdeng*) for educational purposes by the Education Ministry in 1918 concerned a "female martyr" who had committed suicide after she lost her husband and children during the revolution.[78]

While official authorities in the early republic called for the revival of women's traditional virtues, educators and women's journals (many of whose contributors were women themselves) promoted what might be called the "professionalization" of household management. A journal for women students in 1912 dismissed the idea that a woman's household duties prevented her from participating in politics. After all, it noted, housework was a profession (*zhiye*) like any other, and, since having a profession did not prevent men from being involved in political affairs, the same situation applied to women.[79] As he had done before, Jiang Weiqiao continued to insist that domestic science was the most important subject in girls schools, but now he buttressed his argument by claiming that expertise in household affairs was considered a professional vocation in the West.[80] Many women's journals, such as *Funü zazhi* (Ladies' Magazine),[81] included columns devoted to "household management," while specialist journals on the family home also appeared at this time.[82] Others published articles on how to keep gardens and courtyards tidy, how to look after pets, and how to maintain household appliances in good working order.[83] Articles from Western middle-class women's magazines were also translated, such as the one reporting on a nationwide competition in the United States to discover the wife who had most successfully furthered her husband's career through frugal housekeeping.[84] In fact, a woman's personal hygiene and deportment within the family home became a matter of public discourse at this time. Articles advised women to rise early, to clean their teeth and wash their faces properly, to refrain from smoking, and to exercise before breakfast.[85]

Underpinning this refrain highlighting the "model" housewife was a continuing dissatisfaction with the direction in which women's education was perceived to be traveling as well as with the behavior of female students themselves. The principal of a girls' lower primary school in Sichuan, for example, was at pains to point out in 1915 that her school emphasized instruction in "practical" knowledge such as bookkeeping (*buji*) so that it would not become the object of criticism and slander.[86] Writers complained that girls sought education merely for status and image and that they indulged in "extravagance and showiness" (*shechi huali*) instead of being seriously committed to the learning of domestic skills.[87] One journal noted that female students were behaving as if they had just been released from prison, acting with reckless abandon, and breaking every convention and taboo; they were advised to "regulate" their behavior and be less frivolous, on the one hand, and more moderate in their opinions, on the other.[88] Female students were accused of being irascible, aggressive, and egotistical; they might be able to discuss international affairs, one commentator admitted, but they possessed no household skills.[89] Some blamed moral laxity and social decay entirely on women who had received a modern education; such an education was not meant to bring about a decadent "Paris-style" society or to be used as the foundation for women's rights but, rather, to train wise mothers and virtuous wives and to promote the ideals of faithfulness and compliance (*zhenshun*).[90] Even a radical journal like *Xin qingnian* (New Youth) could espouse such views. A 1917 article maintained that, if education could consolidate women's traditional virtues of compliance and service (*fucong*), Chinese women would become the best in the world.[91]

Unfortunately, a teacher in a Shanghai women's school lamented, the promotion of equal rights had gone too far. Calm-natured and patient Chinese women had been stirred up by such ideas to engage in fruitless and confrontational competition with men. An education that perfected women's natural abilities and prepared them to respect their duties in marriage and the home was required.[92] Even in the West, one journal observed, more cautious and sensible attitudes were beginning to prevail, yet in China people were perversely demanding *more* equality.[93] There was no need for an advanced education for women, another journal claimed; otherwise, they would simply become a "wasted resource" (*feiwu*)—unable to manage the household competently and thereby contribute usefully to society.[94] Existing girls' schools were described as "manufacturing plants for high level wastrels" (*gaodeng youmin zhi zhuangzao chang*) because either girls from poor backgrounds could not afford to attend or, even if they did, ran the risk of picking up bad habits like disdaining domestic work.[95] It is clear that for many educators women were to be "reformed" through education solely in the interest of preserving family and social order. Thus, an educational official speaking in 1916 to graduates of a normal school in Henan called on his audience to campaign against women's continued adherence to superstitious beliefs, footbinding, a short-term and selfish outlook, and decadent extravagance. At the same time, however, he condemned "fashionable" theories of individualism, female suffrage, and sexual equality; what was required was the promotion of "women's virtues" (*nüde*) such as obedience and chastity so that women would fulfill their ordained role as stabilizing influences in the family and society.[96] It was no coincidence either that in the early years of the republic articles began to appear on the thought of the Swedish feminist Ellen Key, who argued that marriage and the family were the central focus of a woman's life and that work outside the home made women sterile or incapable of bringing up children.[97]

Notwithstanding the outrage expressed by some educators at the increasing public visibility of schoolgirls and the perceived superficiality of women's education, the early years of the republic witnessed a growing, almost unspoken tendency for women actively to seek knowledge outside the home. Thus, the education inspector of Fujian province noted in 1913 that the weekly talks given by the popular science lecture association (Tongsu kexue jiangyan hui) in the provincial capital regularly attracted an audience of eight to nine hundred people that included both men and women.[98] A 1919 official report on the public library in the provincial capital of Shaanxi, which listed the occupational background of its readers, included a separate category for women; on average a total of 116 women apparently visited the library each month between June 1918 and August 1919.[99]

Intriguingly, too, the very same journals that preached the virtues of diligent domesticity presented quite different images of women's lives. Thus, while some articles in the *Funü shibao* (Ladies' Times) called for an education that would "forge mothers of the nation" (*zhuzao guomin mu*), others referred enthusiastically to a new world trend of active women driving trains, flying planes, and engaging in competitive sports.[100] There was at this time considerable interest in the phenomenon of female aviators (*nü feixingjia*). In 1914 *Nuzi shijie* (Women's World) published an account of the adventures of an American aviatrix, while in 1917 *Funü zazhi* (Ladies Magazine) reported on the flight from Japan to Shanghai of another American female aviator, Katherine Stinson, quoting her as saying that women were potentially better flyers than men because they did not dissipate themselves with smoking and drinking.[101] In another article (with the English title "The Bride of Danger") the French-woman Marie Marvingt was described as the world's first great female athlete (*da yundong jia*) with her feats of derring-do such as climbing mountains and flying in air balloons.[102] It might also be noted that women's journals at this time regularly reported (with approval) on the holding of athletic meets among schoolgirls; one such event in Shanghai in 1915 brought together over 250 girls from various schools to take part in calisthenics, military-style marches, and obstacle races. Such energy, the report noted, was an inspiration for all women in "old-fashioned families."[103]

Furthermore, the perceived innate features of women's character that were cited as justification for limiting the role of women to that of diligent household manager might be seen by some as a positive advantage in the public sphere. Thus, a 1922 article in *Xin funü* (New Woman) argued that women's gentle and meek natures (*roushun*) would equip them to be more tactful and polite than men working in telephone exchanges and post offices. They would also be superior accountants (because they were more meticulous), railway employees (because they would avoid conflict with passengers), lawyers (because they had better memories and could express themselves more clearly), and train or bus drivers (because their patience and forbearance would prevent accidents).[104]

Nevertheless, school readers for girls throughout the early republican period continued to emphasize the importance of dutiful obedience to parents, husbands, and in-laws as well as to assume that a woman's role was primarily to maintain a frugal, hygienic, and well-organized household. One series of readers also attributed an almost proselytizing role to efficient housewives, with lessons showing one young woman reproaching her neighbor for keeping an "unhygienic" household or women enthusiastically seeking instruction from a model household manager.[105] Needless to say, the well-organized housewife had to be spotlessly clean herself. As one lesson noted: "An unkempt and dishevelled appearance is harmful to health and one's bearing. Therefore, one's hair must be constantly combed and the face constantly washed. Efforts should be made to keep clean and tidy."[106] In fact, the running of a smooth household was sometimes described in military terms; a lesson from one ethics reader, entitled "Honouring the Military" (*shangwu*), advised women to cultivate a forceful and martial outlook in the home.[107] (A 1918 article in the country's foremost educational journal explicitly compared women's naturally ordained and self-sacrificing role as household manager with men's duty to protect the country through military service.)[108]

Although some ethics readers insisted that girls adopt a "competitive spirit" in life, they also pointed out that girls had to be obliging and compliant (*wanshun*) as well as faithful and chaste (*shoujie*).[109] Again, while lessons declared that everyone should have a profession, it was made clear that the appropriate occupations for women were nursing, primary school teaching, embroidery, and sericulture.[110] In the final analysis women were to be faithful helpmates for their husbands. A lesson on the significance of marriage in one lower primary school reader that was in use throughout the 1920s and 1930s encapsulated all the features of women's perceived ideal role and character:

> Xu Sheng was fairly young and did nothing. His wife, Lu Rong, often tried to persuade him to study. Every time he behaved badly she would bring him to his senses with her tears. Lu Rong's father, knowing the situation, became very angry and offered to find her another husband. She replied that the way (*dao*) of marriage was never to separate and remarry. Xu Sheng was moved by this and began to exert himself in study. Finally, he made something of himself.[111]

Just as elite anxieties during the eighteenth century in the wake of expanding social mobility (and the consequent blurring of status boundaries) were often manifested in particular attention to the appropriate moral instruction for women (that would maintain gender hierarchies and boundaries),[112] so the national crisis in the early twentieth century likewise focused attention on women. Their perceived "failings" and character flaws symbolized for officials and educators alike the degeneration of the country. Only an education that would transform women into frugal, hygienic, and persevering household managers demonstrating loyalty to husbands and sensitivity to family harmony would guarantee social and moral order and hence national survival. It might also be noted that the consternation and anxieties felt by officials and educators during the early years of the republic when confronted with the practice of women's education and which led to the ever more strident championing of traditional women's virtues as well as more entrenched assumptions about appropriate gender behavior and roles were to have a relevance beyond the 1910s. In many ways echoes of this early-twentieth-century discourse can be detected in the patriarchal practices and attitudes within the early CCP, in the ambivalence toward politically active and "unfeminine" women felt by male Guomindang leaders in the late 1920s, and even in the recent debate during the 1980s over sexuality and gender roles, which has resurrected stereotypes of the "feminine" in reaction against the androgynization of the Cultural Revolution period.[113]

NOTES

1. Paul Bailey, *Reform the People: Changing Attitudes towards Popular Education in Early Twentieth Century China* (Vancouver: University of British Columbia Press, 1990), chaps. 1–2.

2. Taga Akigoro, comp., *Kindai Chūgoku kyōiku shi shiryo* (Materials on the history of education in modern China) (Tokyo: Nihon gakujutsu shinkokai, 1972), 1:311.

3. Zhang Zhidong et. al., *Zouding xuetang zhangcheng* (Memorials determining school regulations) (1904; reprint, Taibei: Jindai Zhongguo shiliao congkan, 1972), 492–93.

4. The 1907 regulations for girls' primary and lower normal schools are printed in Li Youning and Zhang Yufa, eds., *Jindai Zhongguo nüquan yundong shiliao* (Source materials on the women's rights movement in modern China) (Taibei: Zhuanji wenxueshe, 1975) (hereafter cited as *Shiliao*), 2:974–89; and in Shu Xincheng, comp., *Zhongguo jindai jiaoyushi ziliao* (Materials on modern Chinese educational history) (Beijing: Renmin jiaoyu chubanshe, 1962), 3:800–819. See also Chen Qingzhi, *Zhongguo jiaoyushi* (Chinese educational history) (Shanghai: Shangwu yinshuguan, 1936), 612–14.

5. An indication of the importance attached to these skills, referred to as *nügong* (women's work), can be seen in the number of hours prescribed for courses in the

higher primary school curriculum. In the first two years *nügong* was to be taught for five hours per week (out of a total of thirty hours). In the third and fourth years it was to occupy six hours per week (compared to two hours each for history, geography, and science).

6. The Beiyang Women's Normal School, founded in 1906 and later known as Zhili First Women's Normal School, is the subject of Sarah Coles McElroy's essay in this volume.

7. See the reports in *Dongfang zazhi* (Eastern miscellany) from 1904 onward. Many of these reports are reprinted in *Shiliao* 2:1052–85. The Board of Education also proposed in 1907 that Buddhist convents (*niguan*) be converted into girls' schools in which the novices would be the students and the head of the convent the principal. Such a "converted" school, the Board of Education noted, would attract more funds through religious donations. See *Beijing nübao* (Beijing women's daily), no. 585 (20 April 1907). In fact, Buddhist nuns sometimes took the initiative themselves. In Huzhou a group of younger nuns wishing to return to the secular world suggested using the convent as an elementary school. *Beijing nübao*, no. 597 (1 May 1907).

8. Coeducation at the primary level during the early years of the republic was evidently not put into practice. Educational statistics from this period list separate boys' and girls' schools for both lower and higher primary levels.

9. Beijing Women's Higher Normal originated as a lower normal school in 1908. Significantly, it was the only higher-level educational institution for women supported by the central government during the 1920s. In 1931 it was merged with Beijing Normal University. For a study of this school, see Yen-Chu Sun, "Chinese National Higher Education for Women in the Context of Social Reform, 1919–1929: A Case Study" (Ph.D. diss., New York University, 1985). In 1920, 9 women enrolled at Beijing University, aged between nineteen and twenty-eight. Six registered to study philosophy, 2 to study English, and 1 to study Chinese. *Jiefang huabao* (Liberation pictorial), no. 1 (May 1920): *xinwen* 2–4. By 1922 there were 665 female students enrolled in government and private universities (excluding missionary institutions), representing 2.1 percent of the university population. See Zhonghua quanguo funü lianhehui, comp., *Zhongguo funü yundong shi* (A history of the Chinese women's movement) (Beijing: Chunqiu chubanshe, 1989), 95–96.

10. Zhonghua jiaoyu gaijin she, comp., *Zhongguo jiaoyu tongji gailan* (General overview of China's educational statistics) (Shanghai: 1923), 5.

11. Huang Yanpei, "Zhongguo ershiwu nianjian quanguo jiaoyu tongji de zong jiancha" (General survey of China's educational statistics in the last twenty-five years), *Renwen* (Humanities) 4, no. 5 (15 June 1933): 19–20. By 1945 the total number of girls in primary school had reached 5,583,342 (25.57 percent of the total). Colin Mackerras, "Education in the Guomindang Period, 1928–1949," in David Pong and Edmund Fung, eds., *Ideal and Reality: Social and Political Change in Modern China, 1860–1949* (Lanham, Md.: University Press of America, 1985), 170–73.

12. The proportion of girls in lower vocational schools was also higher, totaling 8.58 percent in 1923. Zhonghua jiaoyu gaijinshe, comp., *Zhongguo jiaoyu tongji gailan*, 53.

13. Huang Yanpei, *Zhongguo jiaoyu shiyao* (A summary of China's educational history) (Shanghai: Shangwu yinshuguan, 1930), 139–40. Distinguishing between primary

and secondary levels, the number of primary schools for boys increased from 84,035 in 1912–13 to 116,740 in 1916–17 and those for girls from 2,283 to 3,363 in the same period; the number of secondary schools for boys increased from 722 to 834, while those for girls decreased from 105 to 98. Huang Yanpei, "Zhongguo ershiwu nianjian jiaoyu tongji de zong jiancha," 13–17, 18–20.

14. *Jiaoyu gongbao* (Educational bulletin) 3, no. 3 (April 1916): *jizai,* 21–37.

15. Sheng Shaorao, "Zhenxing Sichuan nüzi jiaoyu de qianyan" (Some simple words on how to promote women's education in Sichuan), in Zhonghua quanguo funü lianhehui, comp., *Wusi shiqi funü wenti wenxuan* (Selected writings on the woman question during the May fourth period) (Beijing: Sanlian shudian, 1981), 288–89.

16. *Jiaoyu gongbao* (December 1916): *linshi zengkan,* 10. This special issue of the *Jiaoyu gongbao* is reprinted in Taga Akigoro, comp., *Kindai Chugoku kyōiku shi shiryo,* 2:316–78.

17. Indeed, a recent work on educational reform in the twentieth century hardly mentions the subject at all, other than to note the sanctioning of primary and secondary schooling for girls in 1907 and 1912 and the low enrollment rate of girls in modern schools. Suzanne Pepper, *Radicalism and Education Reform in Twentieth Century China* (Cambridge: Cambridge University Press, 1996), 60, 61, 76. In contrast, Sarah Coles McElroy emphasizes the role of women's education in promoting social change in the early twentieth century. See her essay in this volume and her Ph.D. dissertation, "Transforming China through Education: Yan Xiu, Zhang Boling, and the Effort to Build a New School System, 1901–1927" (Yale University, 1996), 74–91, 129–40, 182–96, 223–33.

18. See, for example, Dorothy Ko, "Pursuing Talent and Virtue: Education and Women's Culture in Seventeenth and Eighteenth Century China," *Late Imperial China* 13, no. 1 (June 1992): 9–39; Dorothy Ko, *Teachers of the Inner Chambers: Women and Culture in Seventeenth Century China* (Stanford: Stanford University Press, 1994), chap. 4; Susan Mann, "Fuxue [Women's Learning] by Zhang Xuecheng, China's First History of Women's Culture," *Late Imperial China* 13, no. 1 (June 1992): 40–62; Susan Mann, "Learned Women in the Eighteenth Century," in Christina Gilmartin, Gail Hershatter, Lisa Rofel, and Tyrene White, eds., *Engendering China: Women, Culture and the State* (Cambridge, Mass.: Harvard University Press, 1994), 27–64; Susan Mann, "The Education of Daughters in the Mid-Qing Period," in Benjamin Elman and Alexander Woodside, eds., *Education and Society in Late Imperial China, 1600–1900* (Berkeley: University of California Press, 1994), 19–49; William Rowe, "Women and the Family in Mid-Qing Social Thought: The Case of Chen Hongmou," *Late Imperial China* 13, no. 2 (December 1992): 1–41. For a useful overview of English-language studies on Chinese women during the period 1500–1800, see Paul Ropp, "Women in Late Imperial China: A Review of Recent English-Language Scholarship," *Women's History Review* 3, no. 3 (1994): 347–83.

19. For previous discussions, see Charlotte Beahan, "The Women's Movement and Nationalism in Late Ch'ing China" (Ph.D. diss., Columbia University, 1976), 321–62; Sally Borthwick, *Education and Social Change: The Beginnings of the Modern Era* (Stanford: Stanford University Press, 1983), 114–18; Sally Borthwick, "Changing Concepts of the Role of Women from the Late Qing to the May Fourth Period," in David Pong and

Edmund Fung, eds., *Ideal and Reality: Social and Political Change in Modern China, 1860–1949* (Lanham: University Press of America, 1985), 63–91. For discussion in Chinese, see Zhou Hanguang, "Qingmo de nüzi jiaoyu" (Women's education in the late Qing), *Zhongguo lishi xuehui shixue jikan* (Collected papers of the Institute for Chinese History), no. 18 (July 1987): 241–69; Liao Xiuzhen, "Qingmo nüxue zai xuezhishang de yanjin ji nüzi xiaoxue jiaoyu de fazhan" (The evolution of women's education within the school system in the late Qing and the development of primary education for girls), in Li Youning and Zhang Yufa, eds., *Zhongguo funü shilun wenji* (Collection of historical essays on Chinese women) (Taibei: Shangwu yinshuguan, 1988), 2:203–55; Zhonghua quanguo funü lianhehui, comp., *Zhongguo funü yundong shi*, 33–39; Liu Jucai, *Zhongguo jindai funü yundong shi* (A history of the modern Chinese women's movement) (Liaoning: Zhongguo funü chubanshe, 1989), 211–49; and Huang Yanli, "Zhongguo funü jiaoyu zhi jinxi" (Chinese women's education yesterday and today), in Bao Jialin, ed., *Zhongguo funü shilunji xuji* (Supplementary volume of collected historical essays on Chinese women) (Taibei: Daoxiang chubanshe, 1991), 259–85.

20. Zheng Guanying, "Nüjiao" (On women's education), in *Zheng Guanying ji* (Collected works of Zheng Guanying) (Shanghai: Renmin chubanshe, 1982), 1:287–90. Zheng also called for the abolition of footbinding; this in itself was not new, since male reformers in the late eighteenth and early nineteenth centuries had also condemned the practice as well as the male double standards involved in insistence upon widow chastity while sanctioning concubinage. See Paul Ropp, "The Seeds of Change: Reflections on the Condition of Women in the Early and Mid-Ch'ing," *Signs* 2, no. 1 (Autumn 1976): 5–23. What *was* new was Zheng's reference to Western ridicule as a reason for abolishing the practice.

21. Zheng noted that one consequence of women's illiteracy was the inconvenience caused husbands who were away from the home. Since women were unable to read letters from their husbands, Zheng argued, they had to ask relatives or neighbors to do so, thus compromising the family's privacy.

22. *Shiliao* 1:549–56. Like Liang, another writer was to group women among the ranks of consumers, which included redundant officials, servants, monks, bandits, teachers, and "profligate sons of the rich." *Dongfang zazhi*, 1, no. 6 (1904): *sheshuo*, 115–20.

23. For a useful introduction to the women's press from 1902 to 1989, see Tian Jingkun and Zheng Shaoyan, eds., *Zhongguo jinxiandai funü baokan tonglan* (General overview of the Chinese women's periodical press in modern and contemporary China) (Beijing: Haiyang chubanshe, 1990). I am grateful to Professor Xu Huiqi of the Chinese Academy of Social Sciences for giving me a copy of this work. Information on women's journals published during the last years of the Qing and early years of the republic can also be found in Zhongguo shehui kexueyuan jindaishi yanjiusuo, comp., *Xinhai geming shiqi qikan jieshao* (An introduction to periodicals published around the time of the 1911 Revolution) (Beijing: Renmin chubanshe, 1982, 1983, 1986, 1987), 1:461–73; 2:446–58; 3:75–78, 402–10, 504–10; 4:67–71, 333–40, 563–65, 680–93; 5:150–58, 302–9, 351–61. For an analysis in English, see Charlotte Beahan, "Feminism and Nationalism in the Chinese Women's Press, 1902–1911," *Modern China* 1, no. 4 (October 1975): 379–415.

24. Qing Ru, "Lun nüxue" (On women's education), *Zhongguo xin nüjie zazhi* (New

world of Chinese women), no. 2 (1907) (reprinted in *Shiliao*, 556–61), is a typical example of this view linking women's education with the prosperity of the family, protection of the country, and survival of the race.

25. Jin Songcen, who used the pseudonym *Ai ziyou* (Lover of freedom), was a member of Sun Yat-sen's Revive China Society (*Xingzhong hui*) who set up a branch association in his home district of Wujiang (Jiangsu province) as well as founding a girls' school. *Nüjie zhong* was published in Shanghai in 1903 under the auspices of the Shanghai Patriotic Girls' School established by Cai Yuanpei. The preface referred to the book as the "American Liberty Bell" (*meilijian zhi ziyou zhong*). For analyses of the text, see Liu Jucai, *Zhongguo jindai funü yundong shi*, 153–65; and Louise Edwards, "Chin Sung-ts'en's 'A Tocsin for Women': The Dextrous Merger of Radicalism and Conservatism in Feminism of the Early Twentieth Century," *Jindai Zhongguo funüshi yanjiu* (Research studies on modern Chinese women's history), no. 2 (June 1994): 117–40. Although Edwards notes that the text had been presumed lost for many years until its recent discovery by Professor Li You-ning, I came across a copy in the library of the Modern History Research Institute of the Chinese Academy of Social Sciences in Beijing during the winter of 1995.

26. Jin Songcen, *Nüjie zhong* (Shanghai: Datong shuju, 1903), 51–52, 67. Jin argued that women could be members of parliament and even president, although he also noted that women's preoccupation with education would leave them little time for politics in the foreseeable future (57).

27. As Louise Edwards points out ("Chin Sung-ts'en's 'A Tocsin for Women,' " 122), Jin's advocacy of women's rights was instrumental to the principal aim of overthrowing the Qing dynasty.

28. Jin Songcen, *Nüjie zhong*, 29–30. Jin translates the populism of the Narodniks as *qushen zhuyi* (lit: "to forfeit oneself-ism").

29. Ibid., 9–10, 15–16, 17–20.

30. Jin Songcen, *Nüjie zhong*, 45. Jin's phrase is *juyou nanxing zhi ren* (lit: "a person having a male-like nature"). It might also be noted, however, that Jin's proposed curriculum for women's normal schools was considerably broader than that prescribed by the Qing government in 1907. It included the teaching of Chinese and foreign history and geography, mathematics, physics, chemistry, English, psychology, law, economics, and physical education. Household management (*jiazheng*) would be included in the teaching of ethics (*lunli*). See *Nüjie zhong*, 39–40. In contrast to Jin's assumption that women should be more like men, a fascinating article in 1907 presented a radical alternative view. Anticipating feminist arguments later in the century, it noted that women were always being judged by the standards set by men and were only considered autonomous moral beings once they spoke and acted as men. Yet this would mean women behaving immorally (e.g., engaging in wars), whereas, in fact, women's behavior and outlook were more in tune with "natural morality" (*tianli*). Women, the article concluded, deserved freedom on their own merits and for its own sake. See "Nan'nü pingdeng de zhenli" (True principles concerning gender equality), *Beijing nübao*, no. 592 (27 April 1907).

31. Other prominent educators such as Luo Zhenyu and Lu Feigui were equally opposed to coeducation. See Luo's comments in *Dongfang zazhi* 3, no. 9 (1906): *jiaoyu,*

186, and Lu Feigui's article on the subject in *Jiaoyu zazhi* [Educational review] 2, no. 11 (1911); *zhuzhang*, 57. Lu argued that after twelve to thirteen years of age sexual feelings would develop among children, and this would damage health and morality if there were coeducation.

32. See, for example, an article in *Dongfang zazhi* 1, no. 8 (1904): *shiye*, 109–12, which noted that Chinese women's resilience and perseverance gave them an advantage over their Western counterparts; and *Jinghua xinbao* (Beijing vernacular journal), nos. 236–37 (June 1906), which claimed that Chinese women's innate aesthetic sense would make them superior to male workers in manufacturing industry.

33. "Zhongguo nüzi zhi qiantu" (The future path of Chinese women), *Nüxue bao* (Journal of women's studies), no. 4 (1903), reprinted in *Shiliao*, 1:393–96. The author styled herself "a woman from south of Hunan and Hubei" (*chunan nüzi*). Very few female writers focused on women's oppression of other women. A notable exception was He Zhen, a prominent member of the Chinese anarchist group in Japan during the early years of the twentieth century. See her article "Lun Zhongguo nüzi suoshou zhi candu" (On the cruel poison women have to take), *Tianyi bao* (Journal of natural justice), no. 15 (1907), reprinted in *Shiliao*, 1:39–43. See also Peter Zarrow, "He Zhen and Anarcho-Feminism in China," *Journal of Asian Studies* 47, no. 4 (November 1988): 796–813.

34. Hu Bin, "Lun Zhongguo zhi shuairuo nüzi bude ci qi zui" (Why women cannot escape the blame for China's weakness), *Jiangsu*, no. 3 (1903), reprinted in *Shiliao*, 1:403.

35. *Shiliao*, 2:1111. The school was opened in the buildings of the Sichuan *huiguan* (native place association). Another article referred to women as a "wasted resource" (*feiwu*) because of their nonparticipation in economic production. *Beijing nübao*, no. 583 (18 April 1907).

36. Jiang Weiqiao, "Nüzi jiaoyu" (Women's education), reprinted in *Shiliao*, 1: 645–46.

37. "Quanxue" (Exhortation to study), in Jiang Weiqiao, comp., *Nüzi xin changge* (New songs for girls) (Shanghai: n.p., 1907).

38. "Lun nüxue suoyi xingguo" (Why women's education will revive the country), *Dongfang zazhi* 2, no. 11 (1905): *jiaoyu*, 254–56. See also *Dongfang zazhi* 3, no. 13 (1906): *jiaoyu*, 241. Articles translated from the Japanese at this time also referred to *jiazheng* (household management) as the most important part of the curriculum for girls' schools. See, for example, *Nü bao* (Women's journal) 1, no. 1 (1909): *jiating*, 63–70.

39. *Jiaoyu zazhi* 3, no. 8 (1911): *mingzhu*, 22. The other reasons included the influence of bad customs, deception by others, a lack of economic know-how, not adapting to the times, and being lazy and superstitious.

40. *Shiliao*, 2:1214.

41. Ibid., 1:433–34. Another article in a women's journal drew a similarly bleak picture, pointing out that girls were oppressed within the home, physically weak, and intellectually stunted, easily stirred up by women's gossip, dominated by mothers-in-law, and prey to temptations offered by promiscuous Buddhist monks. Ya Te, "Lun zhuzao guomin mu" (Forging mothers of the nation), *Nüzi shijie* (Women's world), no. 7 (1904): *lunshuo*, 1–7.

42. Fang Liusheng, comp., *Nüzi guowen duben* (Chinese reader for female students) (Shanghai: Shangwu yinshuguan, 1905). The preface also included detailed instructions on how to unbound feet using a liquid solution of vinegar and salty water.

43. Ibid., lesson 21, 5a–b.

44. Ibid., lesson 7, 2a.

45. Ibid., lesson 27, 6b–7a.

46. Ibid., lesson 41, 10b.

47. Ibid., lesson 56, 15a; lesson 58, 15b; lesson 59, 16a; lesson 62, 16b–17a. As another lesson noted (63, 17a), the solution to poverty "does not lie in the temple of Guanyin but in the classroom."

48. On Chen Hongmou's ideas on the household role of women, see Rowe, "Women and the Family in Mid-Qing Social Thought," 10–12.

49. Physical education for girls was frequently cited as a requirement for national strength. Western women, who were described as "immortals" (*xianshen*), with their healthy bodies and love of the outdoors, were often contrasted with listless and emaciated Chinese women, with their small breasts and deformed feet. See "Nüzi jianyi de tiyu" (Simple ways to carry out physical education amongst girls), *Nüzi shijie*, no. 10 (1904): *jiaoyu*, 1–8.

50. *Zuixin nüzi xiushen jiaokeshu* (Latest ethics textbook for girls) (Shanghai: Chunxueshe, 1906), 3b, 8b, 9b. There is an intriguing parallel between the ambivalence some Chinese educators may have felt at the prospect of physically active women exercising autonomy in the public sphere and that demonstrated by Western missionaries. While the latter promoted physical education among boys and girls in their schools specifically to undermine what they perceived as outmoded Chinese gender conventions and to expand social space for Chinese girls and women, their continued adherence to the notions of separate sex roles and feminine propriety prompted an uneasiness with the uninhibited Chinese response. As early as 1899, the principal of the Methodist McTyeire Girls School, Laura Haygood, was expressing disquiet at the "thought of Chinese women on bicycles," which would give them "a distorted vision" of "the proprieties of life." Gail Graham, "Exercising Control: Sports and Physical Education in American Protestant Mission Schools in China, 1880–1930," *Signs: Journal of Women in Culture and Society* 20, no. 1 (1994): 44–45. The McTyeire Girls School is the subject of Heidi Ross's essay in this volume.

51. *Zuixin nüzi xiushen jiaokeshu,* 17a. Other articles in the periodical press maintained that women had wicked natures (*e gen xing*), demonstrated by the "fact" that they were invariably at the center of any crime. "Lun she nüfan xiyisuo" (On the establishment of training institutes for female criminals), *Shuntian shibao* (1906), reprinted in *Shiliao,* 1:709–12. The discourse on gender and crime during the late Qing period and early republic is a subject that I hope to explore later.

52. *Chudeng xiaoxue nüzi guowen jiaoshouben* (Teaching manual for girls' lower primary schools) (Shanghai: Zhongguo tushu gongsi, 1908), lesson 21, 42–43; lesson 29, 58–60; lesson 32, 65–67; lesson 33, 67–68.

53. *Jiaoyu zazhi,* 2, no. 12 (1911): *jiaoshou guanli,* 147–52.

54. *Nüzi jiaoyuxue jiaokeshu* (Textbook on female education) (Tokyo: 1905), 33–34.

55. "Jiaoyu mudi lun" (On the aims of education), *Xinmin congbao* (New people's miscellany) 13, no. 67 (1904): *jiaoyu,* 1–19.

56. *Beijing nübao,* no. 581 (16 April 1907). Even France, the Education Bureau noted, which was the most enthusiastic champion of freedom, had strict conventions on seeking parental permission for marriage. The central Board of Education was also alarmed at the activities of female students returning from Japan. In 1909 it instructed the governor of Jiangxi to close down a public lecture association promoting free marriage (*ziyou jiehun yanshuo hui*) that had been opened in the provincial capital by a number of returned female students. *Shiliao,* 2:950.

57. *Shiliao,* 2:1195. In Guangzhou the education bureau expressed alarm that women and girls from the "lower classes" (*xialiu funü*) were infiltrating schools as teachers and students. *Shiliao,* 2:1135.

58. "Nüquan shuo" (On women's rights), *Nüzi shijie,* no. 5 (1904): *sheshuo,* 1–5.

59. *Beijing nübao,* no. 591 (26 April 1907). As always, however, contradictory images abounded. In the same issue a story pointed to the dangers of women *not* receiving a modern education, the benefits of which included the elimination of their "superstitious" and "primitive" beliefs. The journal reported the case of a mother who had killed her son in order to use his heart for medicine to cure her paramour's illness. It is interesting to note, nevertheless, that this particular journal often commented on the adverse effects of what it saw as an "expansion of women's rights" (*nüquan pengzhang*) such as wives assaulting their husbands (no. 586, 21 April 1907) or women arguing with men on the street (no. 591, 26 April 1907).

60. Qian Zhixiu, "Nüzi zhiye wenti" (The question of women's professions), *Dongfang zazhi* 8, no. 9 (1911): 4–7.

61. Kazuko Ono, *Chinese Women in a Century of Revolution, 1850–1950* (Stanford: Stanford University Press, 1989), chap. 4.

62. *Da gong bao* (Impartial daily), 3 March 1912. One women's journal argued that, if women were granted equal political rights, they would be able to bring their innate sense of meticulousness and steadfastness to the processes of government, social solidarity would be strengthened, and (in an interesting reversal of the usual formula) they would be compelled to seek economic independence in order to take advantage of such rights. See Chong Laigao, "Nüquan yu guojia zhi guanxi" (The relationship between women's rights and the state), *Shenzhou nübao* (Chinese women's daily), no. 1 (1912): *lunshuo,* 5–13. Some advocated radical strategies to bring about political equality. Thus, an open letter addressed to suffragettes in 1913 championed the principle of "no husband-ism" (*wufu zhuyi*). Women should seek divorce, refuse to get married, or go abroad in order to cut all links with men back home; the latter would then fear for the disappearance of the race and cave in to women's demands. *Da gong bao,* 4 January 1913, *zalu.*

63. "Nüzi canzheng lun" (On women's suffrage), *Da gong bao,* 27 and 28 March 1912.

64. "Lun nüzi yaoqiu canzheng quan zhi guaixiang" (On the odd phenomenon of women demanding political rights), *Da gong bao,* 30 March 1912. The suffragettes apparently broke windows, kicked guards to the ground, and grabbed assembly members by their jackets. "Disruptive" behavior by suffragettes in the West was also

frequently alluded to, although some women's journals preferred to highlight the disruptions of suffragette meetings caused by male rowdies. See *Shenzhou nübao,* no. 1 (1912): *jishi,* 89, for a report on a Hyde Park meeting in London that ended in chaos because of the loutish behavior of male onlookers.

65. See *Dagong bao,* 18 May and 15 June 1913; and *Jiaoyu zazhi* 5, no. 4 (1913): *jishi,* 30. Foreign observers also commented on the general indiscipline among young people in the wake of the revolution; it was as if, one noted, all restraints had been lifted, resulting in a joyful "hysteria" among young men and women. J. Rodes, *Scènes de la vie revolutionnaire en Chine, 1911–1914* (Paris: 1917), 66–67. For a useful discussion of changes in social customs (e.g., hairstyles, fashion, terms of address), see Hu Shengwu and Cheng Weikun, "Minchu shehui fengshang de yanbian" (The evolution of social customs in the early republic), *Jindaishi yanjiu* (Research into modern history) 34, no. 4 (July 1986): 136–62.

66. *Da gong bao,* 18 May 1913. *dailun.* If schools did not employ experts to provide scientific instruction on sexual matters, the newspaper warned, society would ultimately drown in a "sea of unrestrained promiscuity" (*aihe niehai*). For an analysis of the discourse on sexuality and the emerging "medicalization" of gender difference, see Frank Dikötter, *Sex, Culture and Modernity in China: Medical Science and the Construction of Sexual Identities in the Early Republican Period* (Honolulu: University of Hawaii Press, 1995).

67. Shen Weizhen, "Lun xiao banbi yu nüzi tiyu" (On sleeveless undergarments and girls' physical education), *Funü zazhi* 1, no. 1 (January 1915): *jiazheng,* 1–2. Other fashions condemned by women's journals included the wearing of gold-rimmed spectacles (even if the wearers were not shortsighted) and high-heeled leather shoes. See Piao Ping, "Lixiang zhi nüxuesheng" (The ideal female student), *Funü zazhi* 1, no. 3 (March 1915): *lunshuo,* 1–5. For an intriguing discussion of the debate concerning women's fashion (particularly the *qipao,* or *cheongsam*) and how this was linked to changing representations of the nation, see Antonia Finnane, "What Should Women Wear? A National Problem," *Modern China* 22, no. 2 (April 1996): 99–131.

68. Prejudice against girls studying beyond the primary level continued well after 1912, however. For example, the reform-minded warlord of Shanxi, Yan Xishan, was quite willing in the 1920s to encourage peasant girls to attend vocational schools in order to learn spinning and weaving skills, but he did not sanction formal secondary education for girls until 1925. Donald Gillin, *Warlord: Yen His-shan in Shansi Province, 1911–1949* (Princeton: Princeton University Press, 1967), 34–35.

69. Shu Xincheng, comp., *Zhongguo jindai jiaoyushi ziliao,* 2:456, 527. Although in 1918 the Education Ministry sanctioned the teaching of vocational courses (such as business studies) in girls' secondary schools, it still insisted that domestic science was the most important subject in the curriculum. *Zhonghua jiaoyujie* (Chinese educational world) 5, no. 2 (January 1918): *baogao,* 2.

70. For a discussion of the changing state discourse on gender in Japan after 1868, see Sharon Sievers, *Flowers in Salt: The Beginnings of Feminist Consciousness in Modern Japan* (Stanford: Stanford University Press, 1983), 11–13, 22–23, 50–60, 107, 111–13; Sharon Nolte and Sally Hastings, "The Meiji State's Policy toward Women, 1890–1910," in Gail Lee Bernstein, ed., *Recreating Japanese Women, 1600–1945* (Berkeley:

University of California Press, 1991), 151–74; Sheldon Garon, "Women's Groups and the Japanese State: Contending Approaches to Political Integration, 1890–1945," *Journal of Japanese Studies* 19, no. 1 (Winter 1993): 10–15.

71. *Zhengfu gongbao* (Government gazette) 23, no. 653 (12 March 1914): *mingling,* 59, 60. Associations with the aim of "disrupting political order" or "jeopardizing good customs" were not permitted.

72. Not that such attempts were always successful. The association complained in 1917 that books banned in Beijing were often widely published in other places such as Shanghai. Zhongguo di er lishi dang'an guan (National Second Historical Archives of China), *Jiaoyubu* (Ministry of Education), 57–101.

73. Ibid., *Jiaoyubu,* 57–104. Books that were deemed unsuitable included *Nüxuesheng mimi riji* (The secret diary of a female student) and *Seyu shijie* (The world of sex). Even the eighteenth-century vernacular novel *Honglou meng* (Dream of the red chamber) was placed on the banned list. See *Anhui jiaoyu yuekan* (Anhui educational monthly), no. 14 (1919): *gongwen,* 56. Books on the lives of female students were often classified with those on pornography or family scandals as the epitome of salacious reading material.

74. *Zhengfu gongbao* 23, no. 662 (12 March 1914): *mingling,* 170–71. See also Zhongguo di er lishi dang'an guan, *Neiwubu* (Ministry of Internal Affairs), 00–1620. Whether living or dead, a woman's son, grandson, or relative could petition the local magistrate for condemnation. All cases were to be submitted to the *Neiwubu* for verification and approval. An inscribed medal in gold or silver would then be issued.

75. Zhongguo di er lishi dangan guan, *Neiwubu,* 00–1620.

76. *Zhengfu gongbao* 67, no. 664 (21 November 1917): *mingling,* 170–72. Tang Hualong, the internal affairs minister, defined *chaste widows* as those over fifty years of age who had remained "loyal" for over thirty years, those who had died before the age of fifty but who had remained "chaste widows" for at least ten years, and those who remained "chaste" after the death of their fiancé. "Heroic women" (*liefu lienü*) referred to those who committed suicide after being raped or after losing a husband. Ibid., 67:673 (30 November 1917): *gongwen,* 569–70. A "commendation fee" of six Chinese dollars was payable in advance.

77. See, for example, *Neiwu gongbao* (Official gazette of the Internal Affairs Ministry), no. 23 (August 1915), 2–4, for a list of seventy-eight chaste widows (still living) and twenty-three who had recently died; and 5–6 for a list of twenty five widows who had committed suicide upon their husbands' deaths or after suffering rape. See also Zhongguo di er lishi dang'an guan, *Neiwubu,* 00–5023 for reports on chaste widows and filial daughters. Interestingly, one daughter in Zhili province in 1916 apparently committed suicide after the death of her mother; it was supposed to be the death of a husband that prompted such action.

78. *Jiaoyu gongbao* 5, no. 2 (January 1918): *baogao,* 2.

79. "Lun nüzi yingyou canzheng quan" (Women should have political rights), *Nüxuesheng zazhi* (Journal of the female student), no. 3 (1912): *lunshuo,* 11–12. Significantly, the journal also contrasted the expertise of Western housewives (with their knowledge of budgeting, hygiene, etc.) with the incompetence and backwardness of their Chinese counterparts. When young, the journal noted, Chinese women fritter

away money on adornment, and when they are older they waste it on religious devotions, a phenomenon the journal referred to as *shaonian yang yingjiang laonian yang heshang* (when young, women subsidize the silversmith; when old, they subsidize monks). See "Lun woguo furen buneng zhijia zhi hai" (The harm caused by Chinese women not knowing how to manage the household), *Nüxuesheng zazhi*, no. 2 (1911): *sheshuo*, 1–2.

80. Jiang Weiqiao, "Lun nüxuexiao zhi jiashi shixi" (On the concrete practice of domestic science in girls schools), *Jiaoyu zazhi* 9, no. 6 (1917): 105–11.

81. *Funü zazhi* began publication in 1915 and ran until 1931. See J. Nivard, "Women and the Women's Press: The Case of the Ladies' Journal [*Funü zazhi*], 1915–1931," *Republican China* 10, no. 1b (November 1984); 37–55. Circulation of this journal was considerably higher than other women's journals of the time.

82. See, for example, *Jiating zazhi* (Family magazine), which began publication in 1915. The first issue included an article on the "proper" way to organize room furniture.

83. *Zhongguo funüjie* (World of Chinese women) 1, no. 5 (May 1915).

84. "Meiguo yibai xianqi zhi zishu" (The personal accounts of one hundred virtuous American wives), *Zhongguo funüjie* 1, no. 8 (August 1915); 1, no. 9 (September 1915); 1, no. 12 (December 1915); 2, no. 1 (January 1916). Chinese women studying in the United States after the turn of the century, many of whom were products of a missionary education back home in China, also subscribed to the claim that an extensive training in homemaking should form the core of women's education. One of these students, Hu Binxia (who studied at Wellesley College from 1907 to 1913), went on to become editor-in-chief of *Funü zazhi* from 1916 to 1919. As a recent article points out, the belief that the domestic sphere was the legitimate domain for women was held by both Western female missionaries in China and teaching circles in the United States, where home economics gained status as an academic discipline in colleges during the early twentieth century. Weili Ye, " 'Nü Liuxuesheng': The Story of American-Educated Chinese Women, 1880s–1920s," *Modern China* 20, no. 3 (July 1994): 325–26.

85. *Zhonghua funüjie* 1, no. 10 (October 1915); 1, no. 11 (November 1915); 1, no 12 (December 1915); 2, no. 1 (January 1916). Proscriptions against women smoking clashed with the image of the "patriotic" Chinese woman enjoying a Chinese-produced cigarette in advertisements put out by the Nanyang Company. See *Xin funü* (New woman) 3, no. 5 (1 September 1920).

86. Chen Yiqin, "Yu zhi xuexiao shenghuo" (Our school life), *Funü zazhi* 1, no. 11 (November 1915): *tongxin*, 1–3.

87. De Zheng, "Lun Zhongguo nüzi shenghuo zhi zhuangkuang" (The situation of Chinese women's lives), *Nüzi zazhi* (Women's magazine) 1, no. 1 (January 1915), *shelun*.

88. "Jinggao nüxuesheng" (A polite warning for female students), *Zhonghua funüjie* 1, no. 7 (July 1915). Girls, it was suggested, should engage in respectable social activities with boys (as in the West) and stop advocating "gender revolution" (*nan'nü geming*). No doubt, educators had in mind the protests and strikes carried out by female students, such as the one at No. 2 Provincial Women's Normal School in Jinan in 1915. After students were disciplined for arguing with the administration, more than sixty went on strike and marched on the offices of the local police bureau condemning the

arbitrary behavior of the school principal. *Zhonghua funüjie* 1, no. 11 (November 1915), *tebie jishi.*

89. Piao Ping, "Lixiang zhi nüxuesheng," *Funü zazhi,* 1, no. 3 (March 1915): *lunshuo,* 1–5; Xia Zhen, "Yu zhi zhonggao yu nüxuesheng" (My sincere advice to female students), *Funü zazhi* 1, no. 4 (April 1915): *lunshuo,* 4–5.

90. Wang Zhanglu, "Fu de" (On women's virtue), *Zhonghua funüjie* 1, no. 1 (January 1915); Li Foru, "Nüjie zhenyan" (Exhortation to women), *Zhonghua funüjie* 1, no. 10 (October 1915). Women's customs and behavior in France were often portrayed as the epitome of extravagance and debauchery; the breakup of families, increasing rates of divorce, and a declining birthrate were assumed to be the result.

91. Yu Tiansui, "Yu zhi nüzi jiaoyu guan" (My views on women's education), *Funü zazhi* 1, no. 1 (January 1915): *lunshuo,* 1–3.

92. Ibid.

93. Wu Chongmin, "Nannü ziyou pingdeng zhi zhenjie" (A true explication of male-female equality), *Zhonghua funüjie* 1, no. 1 (January 1915). This contrast between a conservative West and a radical China is an intriguing inversion of the usual view adopted by Chinese radical intellectuals at the height of the New Culture Movement and May Fourth Movement (1915–21). It may also be no coincidence that one women's journal at this time bewailed the interest shown in foreign models of "female heroism" rather than taking pride in Chinese heroines of the past. See the article on Qin Liangyu (A Ming loyalist who participated in military resistance against the Qing) in *Nüzi zazhi* 1, no. 1 (January 1915), *chuanji.*

94. Nan Hua, "Nüzi jiaoyu zhi yanjiu" (Research into female education), *Nüzi zazhi* 1, no. 1 (January 1915). *shelun.* Note the different connotation of *feiwu* compared with that before 1911 (see n. 35), when it implied women's nonparticipation in economic production.

95. Yan Lin, "Nüxiao qinlao jiaoyu zhi shishi fangfa" (Methods to carry out women's education emphasizing diligent work), *Funü zazhi* 3, no. 4 (April 1917): 7–10.

96. Shi Baoan, "Henan nüzi shifan xuexiao biye xunci" (Address to graduates of the Henan Women's Normal School), *Funü zazhi* 2, no. 1 (January 1916); *jishumen,* 1–10. The moral health of society was not the only responsibility imposed upon women. Another article blamed women for the fact that China ranked very low in the international hygiene stakes. The filthy and excrement-covered streets to be found throughout China, the article lamented, was a direct result of women's sloppy inattention to hygiene within the household. Lin Xia, "Hezhe wei wu funü jinhou wushiwunian nei zhi zhiwu" (What should be women's task in our country over the next fifty-five years?), *Funü zazhi* 2, no. 6 (June 1916): *sheshuo,* 1–5.

97. Ellen Key, "The Woman Movement" (1912), in Sheila Jeffreys, ed., *The Sexuality Debates* (London: Routledge and Kegan Paul, 1987), 575. Excerpts from Ellen Key's *The Century of the Child* (1900) had already been translated in *Jiaoyu shijie* (Educational world), 127 (1906): *xueli,* 1–19. Excerpts from her other work, *Love and Marriage,* were translated in *Funü zazhi* 6, no. 3 (March 1920): *mingzhu,* 1–12. See also "Ailunkai nüshi zhuan" (A biography of Ellen Key), *Jiaoyu zazhi* 6, no. 7 (1914): *shizhuan,* 29–34.

98. Taga Akigoro, comp., *Kindai Chūgoku kyōiku shi shiryo,* 2:309.

99. *Jiaoyu gongbao* 6, no. 10 (October 1919): *baogao,* 1–12. The other categories of

library visitors were politicians and officials (an average of 162 per month), students (which may have included women, an average of 362 per month), soldiers (an average of 1,125 per month), and artisans/workers/merchants (an average of 178 per month).

100. "Shijie nüzi zhi xin yicai" (The extraordinary new splendor of women in the world), *Funü shibao* 9 (February 1913): 5–8.

101. "Mei nüshi Hai Na zhi feixing ji" (An account of the flying exploits of the American Woman, Hanna), *Nüzi shijie*, no. 1 (December 1914): *biji*, 1–7. The name given was Hanna Rion [Ver] Beck; *Funü zazhi* 3, no. 3 (March 1917): *yuxing*, 20. The name of the American aviatrix flying into Shanghai was given as Shi Di Sheng, a reference to Katherine Stinson. An article in *Shuntian shibao* (Beijing times), 2 March 1917, reporting her stay and public talks on flying in Shanghai renders her name as Shi Tian Sun. Reports on other feats of Western female aviators can be found in *Zhonghua funüjie* 1, no. 3 (March 1915); and *Jiefang huabao*, no. 2 (June 1920). For a discussion of the significance of these early solo flights for women's empowerment, see Sian Reynolds, "High Flyers: Women Aviators in Pre-War France," *History Today* 39, no. 4 (1989): 36–41. Katherine Stinson had begun exhibition flying in 1913 and was the first woman to carry the U.S. mail by air, in September of that year. She toured Japan and China, where no woman had flown before, during the first half of 1917. Twenty-five thousand people apparently watched her first performance in Tokyo; in Beijing she flew in front of the Temple of Agriculture. J. Lomax, *Women of the Air* (John Murray: London, 1986), 29–33.

102. "Weixian zhi xinfu" (The bride of danger), *Nüzi shijie*, no. 3 (March 1915): *yizhu*, 1–10. On Marie Marvingt, see S. Reynolds, *France between the Wars: Gender and Politics* (London: Routledge and Kegan Paul, 1986).

103. *Funü zazhi* 1, no. 7 (July 1915): *jitzai*, 1–2.

104. Zhi Jie, "Guanyu nüzi zhiye wenti de shangque" (On the question of women's professions), *Xin funü* (New ladies journal) 1, no. 1 (December 1922): 5–11. Another writer in 1920 took for granted the innate gentleness and serenity (*jingmo*) of women but argued that this would stand them in good stead for higher study and research. Guo Miaoran, "Nüzi jiaoyu de sange shiqi" (The three stages of women's education), in *Wusi shiqi funü wenti wenxuan*, 276–83.

105. *Nüzi guowen jiaoke shu* (Chinese readers for girls' lower primary schools) (Shanghai: Zhonghua shuju, 1914–16), 8 vols. See vol. 4 (lesson 28), vol. 7 (lessons 43, 44). These readers were reprinted for the eighth time in 1921. See also Leon Wieger, *Chine Moderne*, vol. 9: *Moralisme* (Hienhsien: 1920), 80–104, 216–46, for translations of primary school readers for girls published by the Commercial Press in Shanghai. One example reported in the contemporary press of what a "vigilant housewife" might do may not have been welcomed by husbands. A woman from Chapei in Shanghai reported her husband to the police for smoking opium in the family home, leading to his imprisonment for a month. *Shen pao*, 7 September 1915.

106. *Nüzi guowen jiaokeshu*, vol. 5 (lesson 31). See also *Nüzi xiushen jiaoshou shu* (Teaching manual for ethics in girls' higher primary schools) (Shanghai: Zhonghua shuju, 1915), 3 vols. Vol. 1 (lesson 9) and vol. 2 (lesson 30) advised girls to wash clothes and clean dishes often as well as to bathe constantly. By the 1920s specialized textbooks on women's fitness and appearance began to be published, emphasizing the impor-tance of regular facial features, clean and white teeth, well-developed breasts, and

smooth skin devoid of body hair. See Chen Yongsheng, *Nüzi meirong yundong fa* (Ways for women to exercise for a beautiful appearance) (Shanghai: 1924). Chen was a physical education instructor at several women's normal schools.

107. *Nüxzi xiushen jiaokeshu* (Ethical reader for girls higher primary schools) (Shanghai: Zhonghua shuju, 1914), vol. 3 (lesson 21).

108. Tian Min, "Jinhou nüzi jiaoyu zhi fangzhen" (The direction of women's education in the future), *Jiaoyu zazhi* 10, no. 8 (August 1918): *yanlun*, 107–10.

109. *Nüzi xiushen jiaoshou shu* (Teaching manual for ethics in girls' lower primary schools) (Shanghai: Zhonghua shuju, 1915–1916), vol. 2 (lesson 13), vol. 7 (lessons 7, 15).

110. Ibid., vol. 8 (lesson 2).

111. Leon Wieger, *Chine Moderne*, vol. 9: *Moralisme*, 92.

112. Susan Mann, "Grooming a Daughter for Marriage: Brides and Wives in the Mid-Ch'ing Period," in Rubie Watson and Patricia Ebrey, eds., *Marriage and Inequality in Chinese Society* (Berkeley: University of California Press, 1991), 206.

113. On patriarchal attitudes and practices within the early CCP, see Christina Gilmartin, *Engendering the Chinese Revolution: Radical Women, Communist Politics, and Mass Movements in the 1920s* (Berkeley: University of California Press, 1995), chaps. 1–4; for Guomindang hostility toward politically active women in the late 1920s and 1930s and the promotion of more "feminine" virtues, see Norma Diamond, "Women under Kuomintang Rule: Variations on the Feminine Mystique," *Modern China* 1, no. 1 (January 1975): 3–45; and Elisabeth Croll, *Feminism and Socialism in China* (London: Routledge and Kegan Paul, 1978), chap. 6; on the 1980s discourse on sexuality and appropriate gender roles, see Emily Honig and Gail Hershatter, *Personal Voices: Chinese Women in the 1980s* (Stanford: Stanford University Press, 1988), chaps. 1–2.

Forging a New Role for Women: Zhili First Women's Normal School and the Growth of Women's Education in China, 1901–21

Sarah Coles McElroy

In 1901 the Qing government promulgated an ambitious reform program known as the "New Policies," which among other measures called for the establishment of a Western-style school system. In the ensuing months officials and gentry at the local level failed to implement the government's proposal immediately, some hesitating to commit their resources to the new institutions and others opposing any move that might threaten the existing civil service examination system. After some initial trepidation, however, many members of the elite who believed in the importance of reform began to establish new primary schools for boys, their efforts proving especially successful in regions where provincial leaders supported institutional change.[1]

Founding schools for girls, however, was a much more challenging endeavor. The Qing government did not sanction schooling for girls until 1907; many of the elite, because of their belief in traditional social roles, resisted sending girls to school. Some reformers, however, believed that promoting women's education was essential to reinvigorating the Chinese nation and, as a result, began to establish schools for girls. The new institutions that appeared during the last decade of the Qing dynasty were not the first formal schools for girls to exist in China, since Western missionaries had set up girls' schools during the nineteenth century. But the Chinese elite had taken few steps to develop women's schooling in previous decades. One of the few Chinese experiments undertaken in the 1890s—a girls' school founded by Liang Qichao and several colleagues in Shanghai—survived for only a year. The Chinese reformers who opened schools for women after 1901 thus brought into being a new branch of education in China. As a result of their efforts, girls' primary and normal schools began providing elite women with new educational and career opportunities.[2]

While the reformers who introduced women's schooling believed in improving women's educational level, most of them failed to support equal schooling for women and men. Over the late Qing and early Republic, their attitudes toward women's schooling shifted little, many emphasizing the differences between boys and girls, some hesitantly supporting and others opposing coeducation, and most failing to promote secondary and tertiary schooling for women.[3] Throughout the first two decades of the century, the number of women being educated remained very low, and only in the early 1920s did women gain access to higher education. Nevertheless, the appearance and modest growth of women's education during these years led to social change.

Founded in Tianjin in 1906, Zhili First Women's Normal School (Zhili diyi nüzi shifan xuexiao) was one of the earliest women's teacher training schools to be established. The goal of the school's founder was to provide teachers for the new girls' primary schools, a number of which had appeared after 1901 despite the Qing government's failure to approve women's schooling up to that point. The students at the school, meanwhile, not only gained academic and professional training, but during the early Republican years many also developed a new understanding of their role within Chinese society. In the late 1910s students at the school protested in the streets against social inequality and national humiliation—a dramatic phenomenon since a few years earlier elite women had rarely been seen in public. The developments at Zhili First Women's Normal School vividly illustrate that, despite educational reformers' hesitant attitudes and the small numbers of women's schools overall, education for women in the early twentieth century significantly affected women's lives and helped to transform Chinese society.

The Introduction of Education for Women, 1901–1904

During the first few years after the Qing government promulgated the New Policies, a lively debate arose in the newly emerging press about women's schooling. According to the prevailing view found in journals and newspapers, women should be educated so that they would provide better instruction for their children than mothers in earlier generations; some writers argued that education should also train women for the workforce. Despite their varying opinions on the role of women in society, all who participated in the debate agreed that the ultimate purpose of educating women was to revitalize the Chinese nation.

In 1904 the Qing government issued a set of regulations for the new school system, which decreed that women's education be confined to the home. The regulations acknowledged the importance of improving education within the family in order to develop children's abilities: "If all the women in the country lack education, then mothers cannot provide good education, children's bodies cannot be strong, and [children] cannot have excellent temperaments and habits. The education of young children is equal to a sacred task; it is truly the primary foundation of education for the people." As a result of this outlook, the authors of the regulations called for provincial educational authorities to publish suitable reading materials for women. Yet Zhang Zhidong and the other officials who composed the rules believed that women should not attend schools outside the home, a practice that they believed would expose women to too many Western customs.[4]

Writers for the press, in contrast, commonly argued that formal schooling for women must be set up if Western-style education were to be a success in China. In one article a teacher provided an illustration of how the lack of schooling for women could impede the education of their sons: "I have a student who is over 10 years old . . . I told him that the earth is round . . . he said, my mother did not say that . . . my mother, nurse, and female servant all said that the earth is square and flat." In this author's view a boy surrounded by ignorant women in his early years is much harder to teach when he enters school: "The failure to promote women's education is the greatest possible obstacle to the progress of the new education."[5]

For some writers the purpose of women's education was not only to improve the educational level of the younger generation but also to prepare women for work outside the home. In a widely known 1897 article entitled "On Women's Education," Liang Qichao argued that women should be educated so that they could provide for the well-being of their children, increase production, and help to strengthen the nation. In his view confining a large part of the population to the home was a waste of human resources, and women should be taught skills that would enable them to contribute to China's economic advancement.[6] An author writing a few years later urging the establishment of women's schools similarly argued: "If women's education is promoted, then each person can earn a living; this is the raw material for advancing the country's power and the reason that Europe, America, and Japan could become wealthy and powerful."[7]

Finally, some contemporary writers argued that women should be educated so that they could throw off the shackles of the past and gain full equality with men. Lü Bicheng, a woman who wrote for the Tianjin newspaper *Dagong bao,* believed, like others, that women's education would contribute to China's self-strengthening: "As regards the way of strengthening the country, its ultimate source lies in promoting education, and women's education is the root of the root and the source of the source. If the roots are not solid then the branches will not flourish; if the source is not pure, then the flow will be muddy."[8] But Lü Bicheng also promoted women's education for the sake of liberating women from traditional constraints. In an article entitled "On the Purpose of Promoting Women's Education" Lü Bicheng detailed the cruel conditions of women's lives and called for women to seek out education as a way to escape their oppression:

> My 200 million comrades with dying hearts filled with grief, people of whom it can truly be said that your bodies are alive but your hearts dead, I only hope that from this point forward each one will be awakened from her deep dream and her spirit aroused and will pursue learning and do away with all obstructions to enlightenment.[9]

Because of their conviction that educating women would help to strengthen the Chinese nation, reformers soon began to establish primary schools for girls. Since the Qing government had not yet approved women's schooling and no national regulations existed to guide reformers, each school reflected the vision of its founders.

The first Chinese-run schools for women appeared in Shanghai.[10] The Shanghai Attending to Fundamentals Women's Academy (Wuben nüshu), the first such school to be established, opened in the fall of 1902, its stated aim being to "cultivate virtuous wives and good mothers."[11] Yet, despite the school's emphasis on traditional women's roles, some of the students became involved in patriotic activities, several students, for example, giving public speeches in support of the Anti-American Boycott, a protest against the anti-Chinese exclusion laws and the mistreatment of Chinese in the United States that reached its height in the summer of 1905.[12]

Later in the fall of 1902 Cai Yuanpei and other members of the Chinese Educational Society[13] founded the Patriotic Women's School (Aiguo nüxue).[14] In striking contrast to the director of the Attending to Fundamentals Women's Academy, the founders of the Patriotic Women's School sought to involve women in political affairs. The stated purpose of the school was to increase women's mental, moral, and physical strength and, true to the school's name, to develop the students' patriotic spirit.[15] During his term as director Cai

Yuanpei encouraged the women to participate in the growing revolutionary movement. In addition to studying the history of revolution in the West, the students received training in bomb making and assassination. It was remarkable that one of the first Chinese-run women's schools to exist perpetrated such violent activities.[16]

In contrast to Shanghai and the lower Yangzi region, the North appeared to be barren territory for promoting women's education during the early reform period. Northerners had a reputation for conservatism, and indeed many of the elite opposed radical departures from tradition such as sending women to school. Even Tianjin, a treaty port, was considered to be much more conservative than Shanghai, its counterpart in the lower Yangzi region:

> In contemporary trends, commercial ports are the trendsetters. Among the ports that lead the way, Shanghai is the dominant one . . . Tianjin is the most advanced place in the North and there are many migrants from the South there too, but none of the women from Tianjin imitate the Shanghai style, much less their kind of education. From this one can see that northern customs are simplistic and unenlightened.

According to the author of this statement, after women's schools opened up in Shanghai, women's schooling spread to other areas in the Lower Yangzi region, but in the North educated men continued to refer to women's education and women's rights as "the wild words of the new party" and "the heretical views of the western religion."[17]

Despite the hostile climate, women's schooling appeared in Tianjin not long after the promulgation of the New Policies. In 1903 a group of Tianjin gentry drew up a plan to promote women's education, recommending the immediate creation of four schools for women in the homes of wealthy gentry,[18] and the following year the young female journalist Lü Bicheng founded the Beiyang Women's Public School.[19] While not so advanced as Shanghai, Tianjin became a center of women's education, inspiring a province-wide movement to expand schooling for women.[20]

The Early Growth of Women's Education, 1905–11

After the abolition of the civil service examinations in 1905, Western-style education gained greater acceptance among the Chinese elite and expanded more rapidly than in the previous few years. Not only did reformers aim to increase the number of new schools for men, but some also strove to build on the steps taken since 1901 and improve women's schooling. The acute shortage of female teachers, however, posed an obstacle to their efforts. Some educators chose to hire men to teach in women's schools,[21] a less than ideal solution since boys' schools also lacked a sufficient number of teachers. Some reformers therefore began to open up women's teacher training schools.

The Founding of Beiyang Women's Normal School

Beiyang Women's Normal School, later known as Zhili First Women's Normal School, was founded in early 1906, the first women's teacher training school to appear in Zhili province.[22] Fu Zengxiang,[23] a protégé of Yuan Shikai, who later served as Zhili's commissioner of education, founded the school with Yuan Shikai's encouragement and financial support.

Prior to opening the school, Fu Zengxiang traveled to Shanghai to seek out students, placing an advertisement for the school in a Shanghai newspaper. After testing the students who came for the entrance examination, Fu returned to Tianjin with a contingent of young women.[24] In all likelihood Fu traveled south to look for students because he could not find enough qualified applicants in the Tianjin area. Since Tianjin had only a handful of girls' primary schools, few women had received the basic education necessary to enter normal school. In the first year of the school's operation, students from Zhejiang and Jiangsu numbered sixty to Zhili's ten, and the southern students continued to outnumber the northern students until 1911, several years after Fu's departure as the school's director.[25] As a result, Fu was criticized for using northern funds to educate outsiders.[26]

Despite Fu Zengxiang's recruitment of "outsiders," Beiyang Women's Normal School attracted much interest and support in Tianjin. Many of Tianjin's important educational figures attended the school's opening ceremony. The head of Zhili's Bureau of Educational Affairs gave the opening speech, and several female teachers, including Lu Bicheng, also addressed the assembly.[27]

The purpose of Beiyang Women's Normal School, as outlined in the school regulations, was to train higher and lower primary schoolteachers in order to facilitate the growth of primary schooling for girls. Initially, the school would offer a short-term course; then, after seeing through the first class of graduates, school officials would establish a complete course of studies. The sense of urgency is apparent.[28]

Even though Fu Zengxiang was committed to training female teachers as quickly as possible, he believed in holding women to traditional standards of behavior. Good character was an entrance requirement for the school, the regulations stating that those with "a disreputable family background" or "an impure character" would not be accepted. According to the regulations, the school would emphasize the female virtues (*fude*)—in the traditional culture such virtues included chastity, thrift, and obedience to parents, parents-in-law, and husband—and seek to mold the future teachers' behavior so that they would be models for the younger generation. In addition, students would be warned not to talk about "radical and excessively modern doctrines and opinions."[29] As far as the founder and administrators of the school were concerned, Beiyang Women's Normal School would not produce a group of hotheaded radicals but a set of teachers committed to traditional principles.

Although he held to traditional views on women's behavior, Fu Zeng-xiang believed in providing excellent academic training. The school thus offered a comprehensive curriculum that would prepare the women to teach a full range of courses in the girls' primary schools. The short-term course would be divided into two divisions—one offering a concentration in the humanities and the other in the sciences—the students in each taking a set of required courses and several electives. The required courses for the humanities division consisted of moral cultivation (*xiushen*), education, Chinese language, history, geography, home economics, and calisthenics. The electives included calligraphy, drawing, handicrafts, and music. The sciences division offered mathematics and science instead of history and geography and made drawing a required subject. Even though the short-term course would last just one and a half years, the students were to receive a thorough training in each discipline. The education class, for example, would cover educational history, applied psychology, introduction to logic, educational principles, teaching methods, child care, administrative methods, and teaching practice in a primary school set up for the purpose as an affiliated institution. In addition to gaining a good academic training, the students were required to study home economics, a subject peculiar to a women's normal school, so that, once qualified as teachers, they would be able to teach household skills to the girls in their charge. The course covered such topics as housekeeping, hygiene, and family finances and bookkeeping. These future teachers were expected to train capable mothers and household managers as well as to give girls a foundation in the basic academic disciplines.[30]

Commentators in the local press described the opening of Beiyang Women's Normal School as a noteworthy event: "Beiyang Women's Normal School is a starting point in the development of women's education in China. In fact, there has not been a great undertaking like this for 4000 years; it is recruiting talent from a number of provinces."[31] The exaggerated description of the school's significance reminds us that the founding of a women's normal school was a dramatic innovation—no precedent for women's teacher training schools existed in traditional China (but women's normal schools were appearing in other parts of the country). The school song also conveyed a sense of mission:

> For more than 4000 years women have lived in darkness.... Many scholars assemble like a cloud south of Beijing [in Tianjin].... One person can arouse the consciousness of one hundred people; teaching should always be respected. Extensively nurturing the spread of civilization is the responsibility of our disciples.[32]

A northern newspaper, the *Shuntian Times,* provided coverage of the school's first graduation, held in early 1908. Once again it was an important ceremonial occasion, drawing together many of Tianjin's educators to celebrate the achievements of one of Tianjin's new schools. As principal of the school, Fu Zengxiang was the first to address the assembly, exhorting the students to have a strong sense of responsibility and encouraging them to live out four ideals in their lives: dedication to learning, concern for the public welfare, perseverance, and renewed esteem for the traditional Chinese female virtues. As this speech and the school regulations indicated, Fu Zengxiang did not see the training of female teachers as an assault on traditional principles. On the contrary, he expected his students to serve as virtuous role models for the next generation.[33] Yet, by training women for a role outside the home, Fu Zengxiang and other founders of normal schools were initiating an important change in the social status of women. While their teaching opportunities were still limited (since they could only teach at girls' primary schools and kindergartens), women could now acquire an independent professional position within Chinese society.

*The Board of Education's Regulations and the Development of
Women's Education*

As Fu Zengxiang established and built up Beiyang Women's Normal School, the newly created Board of Education (founded in late 1905) began to devise a set of regulations on women's education. In 1907 it issued regulations on women's primary and normal schools, recognizing women's schooling for the first time as a legitimate component of the new educational system. By this action the Board of Education sought to control the developments in women's schooling that had already occurred but declined to open up higher levels of education to women.

The main goal of the regulations was "to extend knowledge and to preserve the rites," making use of foreign models only if they accorded with Chinese customs. According to the board, the government regulations were necessary to ensure that the women's schools already in existence did not adversely influence society. The board firmly upheld traditional standards of behavior for women, seeking to prevent the spread of such Western norms as young men and women choosing their own marriage partners. All women's schools were expected to adhere to the new regulations—including, for example, the prohibition on employing male teachers—and, if they transgressed the rules, educational and local officials were to discipline them.

Influenced by the three goals of men's schooling—moral (*de*), intellectual (*zhi*), and physical (*ti*) development—the regulations described the purpose of primary education for girls as "cultivating women's morality and conduct and essential knowledge and skills and paying attention to physical development." The goal of women's normal schools, according to the regulations, was to train elementary schoolteachers and to improve education in the home.[34]

Although the regulations gave legitimacy to reformers' efforts to expand women's schooling, they offered no solutions to the problems facing these reformers. The crippling lack of teachers, for example, continued to hinder the growth of women's schools. A report on the development of education in Zhili province noted that most of the female teachers being employed in the schools were not qualified to teach; as a result, the new girls' primary schools had low academic standards. The only solution, the report concluded, was to use male teachers, an explicit rejection of one of the board's regulations.[35]

The author of an article in a women's journal offered a more far-ranging criticism of the central government's regulations on women's education: "The reason that the Board of Education firmly decided on regulations for women's schools is that it desired to ban women's education." For this author each one of the provisions in the regulations was "a ban on women's schooling in disguise." The rule that women's schools should only use female teachers especially aroused this author's indignation:

> The female world . . . lacks talent; as education is first opening up, it has to borrow talent from the male world. These regulations prohibit the use of male teachers . . . female teachers are rare and you cannot get many of them . . . if there are no teachers then there will be no students; if there are no students then there will be no future teachers. How then can there be schools?[36]

The lack of female teachers, and of teachers in general for those reform-ers willing to ignore the regulations and employ male teachers in women's schools, was not the only problem holding back the growth of women's education. The general scarcity of resources also posed a serious obstacle to the founding of new women's schools. As a result, some reformers began to consider overcoming the gap between women's and men's schooling by edu-cating boys and girls together.

For some educators, coeducation was the most efficient way to expand learning opportunities for women. In one author's view the resources for setting up separate girls' schools simply did not exist: "Are [villages and towns] going to multiply their expenses and set up a separate school for girls in order to comply with the Board's regulations? No! If they adhere to the Board's regulations, it will only result in women's not receiving the same education as men." Recognizing the benefits of separate schooling, this author nevertheless believed that boys and girls under the age of ten are not signifi-cantly different; the establishment of coeducational primary schools would therefore not be harmful to society and would in fact help China to achieve universal education. Recent developments in Japan supported his view: "Ja-pan is a country that developed later [than the West]. According to the statistics for 1900 (Meiji 32), 87 percent of school-age boys and 60 percent of school-age girls were attending school. In 1905 (Meiji 37), 97 percent of school-age boys and 92 percent of school-age girls were attending school . . . the reason that they could attain this is that boys and girls do not go to separate schools."[37]

Lu Feikui, a well-known educator who often published articles in the press, made a similar argument in the *Educational Review*. While he believed that separate schooling was preferable to coeducation, he felt that current circumstances necessitated some degree of it: "If a poor out-of-the-way place has already reluctantly set up a [boys'] primary school, it cannot possibly set up a girls' school as well. . . . If co-education is not allowed, it is no different than not allowing girls to be educated; this is the reason that we must have co-education." Despite his preference for separate schooling, Lufei identified some possible advantages of boys and girls studying together: "Boys' and girls' characters are not the same; one can avail oneself of this to bring them into agreement. Boys will be influenced by girls and become gentle; girls will be influenced by boys and can be expected to become active."[38]

While some educators saw coeducation as a necessary alternative to separate schooling, boys and girls were not commonly educated together before 1911. It is hard to determine the extent of coeducation in these years;

since it was officially proscribed, educators may not have wanted to advertise their experiments in coeducation. By all accounts coeducation in primary schools was not often seen before the Republican period.

The number of girls' primary schools, however, did increase after 1905, despite the many difficulties reformers encountered. Late in 1906 an article on education in Zhili singled out the growth of women's education as one of the three most important changes of the past year. Whereas the year before very few places outside Tianjin boast women's schools, by the end of 1906 thirty or forty places reported having opened schools for girls.[39] In Zhili as a whole, between 1905 and 1906, the number of women's schools jumped from 13 to 78, with the number of students rising from 203 to 1,803. In 1906 Zhili educated more female students than any other province in the empire (Jiangsu came next with 853 students). Nationwide, the number of female students in 1906 rose to almost 7,000 students from just under 2,000 in 1905. Even though women's schooling began to grow more rapidly after 1905, the tiny number of female students attests to the gradual development of new-style schooling for women compared to that for men: in 1907 about 77 men's schools existed for every women's school.[40] Nevertheless, between 1905 and 1911 reformers laid the groundwork for the future growth of women's education by promoting coeducation, setting up new primary schools for girls, and providing the first normal school training for women. The appearance of the first few women's teacher training schools, of which Beiyang Women's Normal School was a prominent example, revealed that some reformers were willing to depart from long-held cultural assumptions about male and female roles—which decreed that elite women pass their days within the walls of their own homes— without seeking to alter dramatically women's standing within society.

The Gradual Expansion of Women's Education, 1912–18

After the downfall of the Qing empire in 1911, the new government set up a Ministry of Education, headed by former revolutionary Cai Yuanpei, and issued new school regulations.[41] Despite the political and institutional changes of the early Republic, the expansion of Western-style education progressed much as it had in the late Qing, with prominent members of local society playing the greatest role in expanding Western-style schooling. For the most part members of the elite espoused the same opinions and goals as in the previous decade, most still believing, for example, that schooling for women would benefit the nation but not seeking to offer women the same educational opportunities as men. As a result, the number of women's schools grew modestly during the early Republic. Nevertheless, many of the existing schools, such as Beiyang Women's Normal School, introduced women to new experiences and ideas that changed their perspective on their role in Chinese society.

Changes at Zhili Women's Normal School

Since its founding in 1906, Beiyang Women's Normal School, now known as Zhili Women's Normal School, had graduated several groups of students. The first set of seventy-eight students had completed the short-term teacher training course, and one-fourth of them had then entered the full-length course. In 1912 fifty students completed the entire course, and another group of students graduated from a short-term course. In a short period, therefore, the school sent over one hundred female teachers out to work in the new girls' primary schools.[42] By 1915 the students at Zhili First Women's Normal School numbered just over two hundred, more than half of them coming from Zhili. In the late Qing, because of Fu Zengxiang's recruitment efforts in the lower Yangzi region, the students from Jiangsu and Zhejiang had outnumbered the students from Zhili, but after 1911 the proportions changed, and Zhili students dominated the student body. Even so, students came from several different provinces to study at the school. The teachers hailed from nine provinces and two foreign countries.[43]

In 1915, when Zhang Boling, the president of the well-known Nankai Middle School in Tianjin, briefly served as the interim president of Zhili Women's Normal School, Ma Qianli, a teacher at Nankai Middle School, joined the administration as dean and greatly influenced the school's development, overseeing academic and physical improvements (including the introduction of electric lighting to all the school's classrooms, offices, and dormitories). In the academic sphere Ma Qianli broadened the school's curriculum, offering lectures on moral cultivation, for example, that often focused on national and international affairs and aimed to develop the students' social consciousness.[44]

In 1916 the school introduced extracurricular activities, which would take place for an hour or two after class every day.[45] Ma Qianli promoted the development of extracurricular athletics and also helped to develop the custom of holding an athletics meet on the school's anniversary every year. On the occasion of its tenth anniversary, in 1916, Zhili Women's Normal School held its first large-scale public anniversary celebration, which, as a result of Ma Qianli's influence, featured the students' athletic abilities. Because members of local society watched the students compete in such events as running, long jump, and javelin and discus, the anniversary celebration spread the message that physical education was an important aspect of women's schooling.[46]

The students at Zhili Women's Normal School not only had the opportunity to participate in after-school sports but could also create their own extracurricular organizations. The fourth-year students, for example, formed their own student government, an organization that, in the words of the alumni magazine, "molds students' ability to accomplish things and develops good habits."[47] A lecture society, founded in 1916, gave the students the opportunity to encounter a variety of new ideas. The guest lecturers included local educators and nationally recognized figures who spoke about issues related to education and women's rights.[48]

Two lectures, in particular, deepened the students' understanding of the woman's position within Chinese society. In 1916 Tao Menghe, a friend of Hu Shi who was associated with the New Youth group, lectured on the treatment of women through the centuries. "Whether or not a country is civilized depends on women's position [in that society]," declared Tao at the outset. He went on to describe attitudes toward women in various countries across the course of history. Turning to the contemporary West, Tao noted with approval that thirteen U.S. states had now given women the right to vote. In his conclusion Tao identified three stages of development in the treatment of women: the barbarous, the half-civilized, and the civilized. In the final, civilized stage women would enjoy equal rights with men, complete protection under the law, and freedom of marriage. Believing that China was at the beginning of the third stage, Tao urged the young women at Zhili Women's Normal School to make education more widely available to other young women and to help realize the civilized stage of development in China.[49]

In 1918 Cai Yuanpei, now president of Beijing University, also addressed the students. Cai's lecture focused on liberty, equality, and fraternity (*ziyou, pingdeng, boai*), ideals that he had discovered as a student in France. Noting that the Chinese had only a superficial understanding of these principles and that many traditional scholars opposed them, Cai discussed each one in relation to women's lives. Liberty, according to Cai, meant freedom of thought and gave rise to all the great advances in the various fields of inquiry. Women, he argued, should be able to exercise freedom of thought and contribute to the advancement of knowledge. Madame Curie had turned the scientific world upside down with her discovery of uranium. How could one then say, as many Chinese educators at the time were arguing, that women should only attend to household affairs and not pursue other occupations? In Cai's view women should be able to gain a higher education and take up the occupation of their choice. Inequality within society, for Cai Yuanpei, resulted from a lack of equal educational opportunity. In present-day China women were clearly the victims of educational inequality, so Cai again called for the opening of higher education to women. Fraternity, Cai believed, was lacking in China, as evidenced in the provincial and other rivalries that divided the nation. But he maintained that women had a special aptitude for practicing fraternity and should use this ability to benefit Chinese society. After demonstrating to the female students how the three principles applied to their lives, Cai recommended that upon graduation they enroll at the Beijing Kongde Women's School (Kongde nüxue)[50] to prepare for studies in France, where they could acquire "the true spirit of liberty, equality, and fraternity."[51]

As a result of their opportunity to participate in extracurricular sports, found their own organizations, and attend lectures on improving the status of Chinese women, the students at Zhili Women's Normal School could not help but grow confident in their abilities and develop a new vision of the role they could play in Chinese society. Cai Yuanpei's challenge to the students in 1918 to pursue higher education and the career of their choice certainly contrasted with Fu Zengxiang's 1908 admonition to abide by the traditional female virtues. Over the course of a few years the school had developed from an institution offering primary schoolteacher training to a place that not only trained future teachers but also challenged women to realize their full potential and struggle for women's rights.

The Limited Growth of Women's Schooling

During the years that students at Zhili Women's Normal School developed their skills and discovered new ideas, many reformers failed to expand women's educational opportunities. The Ministry of Education adopted a moderate position on women's schooling, introducing coeducation at the lower elementary level in 1912 but also decreeing that women be taught "chastity and purity."[52] In the summer of 1914 the minister of education gave a speech emphasizing that women's education should aim to create "virtuous wives and good mothers." Subsequently, the ministry issued five regulations for women's schools, which included a prohibition on women cutting their hair and a prohibition on free marriage.[53]

Among the educated elite a spectrum of opinions existed on the woman's position in society. The well-known educator Lu Feikui identified the two ends of the spectrum as the radical party and the ultraconservative party. In the radicals' view women could do whatever men could do—for example, they could work as politicians, military personnel, and engineers—so their education should be equal to men's. The conservatives, according to Lu

Feikui, still adhered to the traditional saying "Women without talent are virtuous" and thus recommended that women just learn a few characters for the purpose of managing family affairs. Lu Feikui himself, along with many other reformers, took a middle position. In his view schooling should prepare women for their future roles as wives and mothers; women could pursue some occupations but were not capable of everything that men could do.[54]

Like Lu Feikui, a writer for the *Educational Review* also drew attention to the importance of women's domestic responsibilities. Women's work in the home, he maintained, gave them the power to help shape the nature of Chinese society: "a country's national character, customs, and practices all result from women's nurture." Those who called for women's independence had misunderstood the true significance of household affairs, taking them to be "the trivial things done by maidservants." In fact, this author argued, managing a household not only entailed overseeing household hygiene and economics but, above all, was focused on "the education of children." This essay firmly reiterated the argument of the late Qing that women had to be educated so that they could teach their own children and help strengthen the nation.[55]

Even writers who supported equal educational opportunities for women drew attention to the differences between the sexes. An article in the radical journal *New Youth,* for example, argued that women should be able to attend university and earn the same degrees as men but maintained that "there are many kinds of education, some appropriate to men and not to women and vice versa." The author believed that women were suited to the arts, while men had an aptitude for science.[56]

Since only a few educators believed in equal educational opportunities for women and men and advocated opening higher education up to women, during the 1910s the expansion of women's education occurred primarily at the elementary school level. By 1915 there were 180,000 students in girls' schools, up from 15,000 in 1907, this jump being almost entirely an increase in primary school students.[57] The number of normal school students gradually grew, but the number of female middle school students remained very low— only just over 700 in the academic year 1916–17. Thus, most women who attended school (still a tiny fraction of women as a whole) could only receive an elementary education.[58]

Despite the continued small numbers, the opportunities for women to be exposed to new ideas, as at Zhili Women's Normal School, meant that some women had rising expectations. Before the end of the decade some of the female students educated in the previous few years would act on the challenges they had heard and become the first group of women to influence the nation's social and political development.

Female Student Activism and Changes in Women's Education, 1919–21

Following the outbreak in 1919 of political demonstrations against the imperialist powers and the weak central government, the struggle for educational equality took an important step forward. The school and university students involved in the protests committed themselves not only to fighting for China's national rights but also to achieving greater equality within Chinese society. Indignant at the sharply different treatment of men and women, the students sought to set women free from their bonds and increase their educational opportunities.

Zhili First Women's Normal School Students' Involvement in the May Fourth Movement

From 1919 onward female students for the first time played a significant role in a protest movement. Most of the women who became involved in the demonstrations of these years had graduated from or were currently students at the women's schools established since 1901. Female students in Tianjin actively participated in the political protests, the students at Zhili Women's Normal School (which in 1916 had changed its name to Zhili First Women's Normal School)[59] providing leadership for other young women in the city.

As soon as students in Tianjin gained word of the demonstrations and student arrests in Beijing on 4 May, students at Zhili First Women's Normal School began to hold planning meetings to determine how they could contribute to the student movement. Within a few days they decided to form a women's patriotic organization and took several important preparatory steps: they cabled the Beijing government asking that it refuse to sign the Versailles Treaty and release the arrested students; contacted the school's graduates and students in Tianjin's women's middle schools in order to create a women's organization; met with students in all the men's schools of the middle school level and above so as to adopt a common course of action; and propagated a boycott of Japanese goods and a promotion of Chinese products. Over the next few weeks students at the school engaged in dramatic actions to spread the message of patriotism—for example, writing slogans in blood, such as "Boycott Japanese goods," and posting them in the school corridors. After several weeks of organizing, on 25 May Zhili First Women's Normal School students led the founding meeting, attended by over six hundred female students, of the Tianjin Association of Patriotic

Women Comrades (Tianjin nüjie aiguo tongzhi hui), the first such women's organization of its kind to be established in China.[60]

The regulations for the Tianjin Association of Patriotic Women Comrades stated that the organization's primary purpose was the promotion of Chinese products and the awakening of patriotism among women.[61] Over the next few months female students in Tianjin threw themselves into the work of promoting nationalist sentiment. The lecture corps of the association, led by Zhli First Women's Normal School student Deng Yingchao (future wife of Zhou Enlai), sent groups of women out to city lecture halls and into the streets (a radical change, for just a few years before elite women had rarely been seen outside the walls of their own homes) to admonish city residents to resist Japan and help save the Chinese nation. During one such afternoon of lecturing, more than sixty female students went out in teams and lectured over the course of four hours to an estimated audience of one thousand. According to a newspaper report, many of those who listened to the students were very moved by their words.[62]

In the fall of 1919 the most active members of the Tianjin Association of Patriotic Women Comrades and the prominent members of its male counterpart, the Tianjin United Students Association (Tianjin xuesheng lianhe hui) joined forces to found the Awakening Society (Juewu she). All ten of the founding female members (there were also ten founding male members) had graduated from or were currently students at Zhili First Women's Normal School. The Awakening Society's goal was to reform Chinese thought and society; attaining equality between men and women was an important part of its agenda. A few months after its founding, the society helped to forge a merger of the female and male student associations in Tianjin, creating a new organization in which men and women worked together on an equal basis.[63]

As a result of their commitment to the protest movement, students at Zhli First Women's Normal School soon came into conflict with the school administrators. According to Deng Yingchao, students often returned late in the day from giving speeches or attending meetings to find that the school would not serve them the evening meal. The struggle between the students and the school authorities came to a head in May 1920. The students intended to participate in meetings and demonstrations on 7 May, as they had the year before, to remember the day in 1915 when the Chinese government had agreed to the humiliating Twenty-one Demands made by the Japanese government and to protest Japan's ongoing aggression toward China. As a result, student representatives met with school authorities to request that they declare a school holiday on 7 May. When the administrators declined to do so, the several hundred students at the school decided to stay away from class anyway. According to Deng Yingchao, "It seemed as if the hearts of several hundred people had been linked up into a chain, and not one person went into the classroom." The students spent the day giving speeches on the city streets condemning Japanese imperialism and calling for the revocation of the Twenty-one Demands. Furious at the students' defiance, the school authorities posted an announcement stating that all students had been expelled. Accordingly, the students moved out of the school and stayed with their families or friends or in inns. But twelve days later, with the support of public opinion and their own families and with the help of mediators, the students won the battle with school administrators and returned to school. As their struggle to participate in the demonstrations and willingness to risk cutting short their own education revealed, the students espoused goals very different from the ones Fu Zengxiang had hoped to inculcate in his students. The young women studying at Zhili First Women's Normal School in the late 1910s committed themselves not to developing female virtues but to awakening the Chinese populace, with the goal of strengthening the Chinese nation.[64]

Several years later in an address to Zhili First Women's Normal School students and teachers, Deng Yingchao spoke proudly about the students' accomplishments during the demonstrations of 1919 and 1920: "At that time the Normal School students' spirit of courage, struggle and sacrifice . . . were heard of far and near; there were none who did not admire them." In her eyes "the spirit that the Chinese people had always lacked, especially the spirit that women had lacked, could be found among the Women's Normal School students." Even though she was speaking about her own and her classmates' achievements, Deng Yingchao rightly drew attention to their "spirit." As a result of their education, their ties with other young women, and their contacts with male students, the students at Zhili First Women's Normal School developed the confidence to hold their own opinions, to defy traditional authority figures, and to fight for their beliefs. The ramifications for society could be significant. In Deng Yingchao's words: "as for the rare . . . spirit of the Women's Normal School students, if it could continue to progressively develop, in Tianjin student circles, in Chinese women's circles, and, in the future when they go into society to be teachers, in children's circles . . . how many beautiful fruits will appear!"[65]

The Opening of Higher Education to Women

Around the country the May Fourth Movement led to greater support for improving women's educational opportunities. At its fifth annual meeting in October 1919, the National Federation of Education Associations made a significant proposal for improving women's education, recommending the elimination of the chief difference between men's and women's schooling and the realization of coeducation at each level of the school system. According to this proposal, lower primary schools should be completely coeducational; higher primary and middle schools should either be coeducational or hold separate classes in the same school, depending on local circumstances and the number of students; normal and higher normal schools should be coeducational, with the exception of some special classes, such as home economics classes for women; and universities should be completely coeducational. Only industrial schools and extension schools should maintain their single-sex status. Such schools were devoted to vocational preparation, and in this area, the federation's proposal maintained, men and women should receive different instruction.[66]

As the federation's proposal indicated, many educators now not only supported the spread of coeducation but also believed in opening higher education to women so that they could enjoy the same educational opportunities as men. One author questioned bluntly: "Why is it that men can receive higher education and there are no institutions in which women can receive higher education?"[67] A writer for one of the new student journals argued that women's education must be improved from the top downward. According to this author, opening higher education to women would have three major advantages: giving women equal educational opportunity; immediately improving women's position within society and showing them that they are not inferior to men; and training female leaders who would then teach and guide their fellow women.[68]

As a result of student activists' efforts and the support of sympathetic educators, less than a year after the May Fourth demonstrations began women gained admittance to several universities. At Beijing University (Beida) well-known professors, including Hu Shi and Tao Menghe, supported women's request for admission. Hu Shi recommended three steps for making higher education accessible to women: universities should hire female professors, either Chinese or foreign; women should be allowed to audit classes; and the women's middle school curriculum should be overhauled so that it would prepare women for university. The last of these steps could not be immediately realized. But at the beginning of the spring term in February 1920, nine women entered Beida to audit classes. This small cohort of pioneers came from the ranks of the privileged women who had the academic qualifications to be able to attend university. Even among the women with the necessary background, many were held back by familial and societal pressures from pursuing higher education. As one of the women attending Beida postulated, some women did not gain their family's approval; others perhaps had supportive families but were afraid to enter a primarily male institution.[69]

Despite the obstacles holding women back from entering university, other universities soon followed Beida's lead. According to one report, by 1922 there were 665 women receiving higher education in Chinese institutions (the figure does not include missionary-run colleges and universities). About a third of these women were attending Beijing Women's Higher Normal School; eleven women were studying at Beida and twenty-three at Nankai University.[70] While the number of female students entering university remained very small, women had now gained a significant new educational opportunity, if they could first acquire the academic background necessary for attending university.

The growth of secondary schooling for women, however, was very slow. In many places a college or university was opened to women without a middle school first being established, so it was hard for women to prepare for university admittance. According to one observer, only after several universities opened their doors to women did educators begin to take the problem of secondary schooling for women seriously and start establishing women's middle schools or accepting women into men's middle schools.[71] Figures from a 1923 report indicate how few women's middle schools existed. In that year there were only twenty-five women's middle schools in the country with a total of 3,249 students, compared to over 100,000 male students in middle schools.[72] Thus, women's secondary schools still needed to be developed if women were to enjoy full access to education, from the primary to the tertiary level.

Conclusion

In the late Qing, educational reformers were inspired largely by nationalist motivations to set up the first women's primary schools, followed by normal schools to train teachers for the new institutions. Many of those who founded women's schools, such as Fu Zengxiang, did not anticipate the consequences that would flow from the development of women's education. Their goal was to train better mothers who would help strengthen the nation, without compromising the practice of the traditional female virtues. Within several years, however, many women who studied at the new schools rejected the traditional social code and began to struggle for greater social equality.

In less than twenty years, the educational opportunities available to elite women changed dramatically (peasant and worker families would rarely have had the means or inclination to send their daughters to school, if perchance a girls' school existed in their village or neighborhood). Prior to 1901 a young woman from an elite family who wished to attend school could only go to a missionary institution since no long-standing Chinese-run schools for women existed. By 1911 a privileged woman would more readily be able to receive an education at a Chinese-run school and could potentially go on to a normal school for further training. Ten years later, partly as a result of women's own efforts, a few women with the right educational background could attend university. Although only a small number of women could take advantage of such opportunities, many of the women who attended the new schools gained inspiration from their experience of studying and forming organizations together with other women. Their exposure to new ideas about women's rights and roles also motivated them to work for social change. As the experience of Zhili First Women's Normal School students reveals, in the late 1910s elite women who may have been confined to their family courtyards just a few years earlier took to the streets to spread their views and created associations to fight for their rights. In the space of one generation Western-style education helped some privileged women develop the courage to speak for themselves and gave them the desire to forge a new position for all women in Chinese society.

NOTES

1. For informative analyses of various aspects of the late Qing educational reforms, see Marianne Bastid, *Educational Reform in Early Twentieth-Century China,* tran. Paul Bailey (Ann Arbor: Center for Chinese Studies, University of Michigan, 1986); Sally Borthwick, *Education and Social Change in China: The Beginnings of the Modern Era* (Stanford: Hoover Institution Press, 1983); and Paul Bailey, *Reform the People: Changing Attitudes toward Popular Education in Early 20th-Century China* (Edinburgh: Edinburgh University Press, 1990).

2. Very little has been written in English on the appearance and growth of women's schooling in China. Chinese overviews of women's education in the early twentieth century include: Huang Xinxian, *Zhongguo jin xiandai nüzi jiaoyu* (Women's education in China during the modern and contemporary eras) (Fuzhou: 1992); Liao Xiuzhen, *Qingmo de nüzi jiaoyu* (Women's education in the late Qing) (Taibei: 1980); Liao Xiuzhen, "Qingmo nüxue zai xuezhi shang de yanjin ji nüzi xiaoxue jiaoyu de fazhan" (The evolution of women's education within the educational system and the development of women's elementary education in the late Qing), in Li Youning and Zhang Yufa, eds., *Zhongguo funü shi lunwen ji* (Collected essays on the history of Chinese women) (Taibei: Shangwu yinshuguan 1988); and Lu Yanzhen, *Zhongguo jindai nüzi jiaoyu shi, 1895–1945* (History of women's education in modern China) (Taibei: Wenshizhe chubanshe, 1989).

3. For a detailed analysis of attitudes toward women's education, see Paul Bailey's essay in this volume.

4. "Mengyangyuan ji jiating jiaoyufa" (The method of kindergarten and home education), *Zouding xuetang zhangcheng* 3.

5. "Xing nüxue yiyong yinbiaozi shuo" (When establishing women's schools we should use phonetic transcriptions), *Dagong bao,* 21 September 1902.

6. Zheng Shixing, *Liang Qichao jiaoyu sixiang* (Liang Qichao's educational thought) (Taibei: Zhongyang wenwu gongying she, 1980), 97.

7. "Lun nüxue buke zaihuan" (The founding of women's schools cannot be further delayed), *Zhili jiaoyu zazhi* 13 (29 September 1905): 22–24. Originally appeared in *Shi bao* (Eastern times).

8. Lü Bicheng, "Lun shanghai yishe nüxuebao ji nüxue diaochahui" (Shanghai should found a journal of women's education and a women's education study society), *Zhili jiaoyu zazhi* 12 (13 September 1905): 31–33. Originally appeared in *Shi bao.*

9. Lü Bicheng, "Lun tichang nüxue zhi zongzhi" (On the purpose of promoting women's education), *Dongfang zazhi* 1, no. 5 (1904): 108–11. Originally appeared in *Dagong bao,* 6 April 1904. A young woman writing for *Women's World* also advocated women's education for the sake of achieving equality with men: "If we do not advocate women's education, then the day of equality will never come. Wash away 3,000 years of evil customs, awaken 200 million from their long dream, uproot the spirit of dependence, arouse a spirit of independence!" See "Yu chang pingdeng xian xing nüxue lun" (If you want to introduce equality, you must first establish women's schooling), *Nüzi shijie,* 16 February 1904, reprinted in Zhonghua quanguo funü lianhe hui funü yundong lishi yanjiu shi, ed., *Zhongguo jindai funü yundong lishi ziliao, 1840–1918* (Historical materials on the modern Chinese women's movement) (Beijing: Zhongguo funü chubanshe, 1991), 300–301.

10. According to one set of statistics, by the end of 1903 the number of Chinese-run women's schools had reached seventeen, and five of them were in Shanghai. Huang Xinxian, *Zhongguo jin xiandai nüzi jiaoyu,* 29.

11. There is considerable disagreement in the secondary sources about when the Attending to Fundamentals Women's Academy was actually founded and whether or not it preceded the Patriotic Women's School. Some sources claim that the school was founded in 1898, but most authors believe that it was the first women's school to appear after the introduction of the New Policies. The latter group does not agree, however, on whether the school was founded in 1901 or 1902. I think the confusion stems from the fact that the founder first set up a school in his own home and then in the fall of 1902, when the school moved to a new address, changed the name to Wuben nüshu. See Chen Xuexun, ed., *Zhongguo jindai jiaoyu dashi ji* (Chronicle of events in modern Chinese education) (Shanghai: Shanghai jiaoyu chubanshe, 1981), 120–21. I have given the latter date as the founding date. For a discussion of the disagreement over dates, see Liao Xiuzhen, "The Evolution of Women's Education within the Educational System and the Development of Women's Elementary Education in the Late Qing," 246 n. 45. Also see Zhang Jianren and Zhang Jianmin, "Zhongguo jindai nüzi jiaoyu fazhan shuping" (A review of the development of women's education in modern China), *Hebei shifan daxue xuebao* 3 (1989): 70.

12. Chen Xuexun, ed., *Zhongguo jindai jiaoyu dashi ji*, 148.

13. The Chinese Educational Society was founded by Cai Yuanpei and several other intellectuals in 1902 for the purpose of improving teaching methods and textbooks, but it later became an organization for promoting revolution. See William Duiker, *Ts'ai Yuan-p'ei, Educator of Modern China* (University Park: Pennsylvania State University Press, 1977), 9.

14. Again, there is disagreement over the school's founding date. Liao Xiuzhen believes that the school was launched in the winter of 1901 and fully established sometime between the founding of the Chinese Educational Society in the spring of 1902 and the founding of the Patriotic Study Society in the late fall. See Liao Xiuzhen, "The Evolution of Women's Education within the Educational System and the Development of Women's Elementary Education in the Late Qing," 246 n. 46. I have followed the date given in Chen Xuexun, ed., *Zhongguo jindai jiaoyu dashi ji*, 123. An article from the *Journal of Women's Education* also supports this date. See "Ji Shanghai Aiguo nüxue xiao" (A record of Shanghai's Patriotic Women's School), *Nüxue bao* 4 (1903), reprinted in Li Youning and Zhang Yufa, eds., *Jindai Zhongguo nüquan yundong shiliao, 1842–1911* (Materials on the modern Chinese women's rights movement) (Taibei: Zhuanji wenxue chabanshe, 1975), 1007.

15. "Aiguo nüxue xiao zhangcheng" (Regulations for the Patriotic Women's School), *Jingzhong ribao* (Alarm bell daily), 1 August 1904, reprinted in Zhonghua quanguo funü lianhe hui funü yundong lishi yanjiu shi, ed., *Zhongguo jindai funü yundong lishi ziliao*, 320.

16. Huang Xinxian, *Zhongguo jin xiandai nüzi jiaoyu*, 27.

17. "Tianjin ni xing nüxue yi" (Tianjin's tentative decision to open women's schools), *Dagong bao*, 1 July 1902.

18. "Tianjin shiban nüxuetang zhangcheng" (Tianjin's provisional regulations for women's schools), *Dagong bao*, 28 May 1903.

19. "Tianjin nüxuetang chuangban jianzhang" (A Tianjin women's school sets up simple regulations), *Dagong bao*, 12 October 1904.

20. Statistics from 1907 show that Zhili had a greater number of women's schools and female students than any other province. See Li Youning and Zhang Yufa, eds., *Jindai Zhongguo nüquan yundong shiliao*, vol. 2, 1165–66. Also see 1908 Board of Education statistics reproduced in Liao Xiuzhen, "The Development of Women's Education in the Educational System and the Growth of Female Elementary Education in the Late Qing," 224–27.

21. Han Tiyun, "Nüxuetang jiaoyuan zhi wenti" (The problem of teachers in women's schools), *Zhili jiaoyu zazhi*, 14 (October 1906): 1–4.

22. "Zhili ge shu nüxuetang jiaoyuan xuesheng yilanbiao" (A chart of the teachers and students in women's schools in every district of Zhili), *Zhili jiaoyu zazhi* 17 (1907): 71–76.

23. Fu Zengxiang, a *jinshi* degree holder of 1898, in the last decade of the Qing worked for Yuan Shikai as a promoter of modern education, serving as commissioner of education for Zhili from 1908 until 1911. In addition to founding the Beiyang Women's Normal School, Fu also founded a women's normal school in Beijing. Since

Fu set up the first two women's normal schools in the north, all of the early women's normal school graduates in Tianjin and Beijing were, as described by one of his students, "children of Fu." See Shen Yiyun, *Yiyun huiyi* (*Zhuaji wenxue congkan,* 11) (Taibei: Zhuanji wenxue chubanshe, 1980), 1:41. According to a historian of women's education, between 1904 and 1911 only fifteen women's normal schools were established nationwide, so Fu made a significant contribution to the overall trend. See Huang Xinxian, *Zhongguo jin xiandai nüzi jiaoyu,* 43. Fu became minister of education in 1917 but resigned after the outbreak of student demonstrations in May 1919. In the early 1920s, after preparing a report on the foreign and domestic loans that had been made to the central government, Fu withdrew from public life and devoted himself to book collecting, becoming a noted bibliophile. See Howard Boorman, ed., *Biographical Dictionary of Republican China* (New York: Columbia University Press, 1971), 2:46–47; and *Minguo renwu xiao zhuan* (Biographical sketches of Republican personages) (Taibei: Zhuanji wenxue chubanshe, 1980), 3:240–42.

24. Shen Yiyu, *Yiyun huiyi,* 1:38–40.

25. Bar graph in *Zhili diyi nüzi shifan xuexiao xiaoyou hui huibao* (Alumni report of Zhili First Women's Normal School) (1915, vol. 1), page following nine pages of charts showing the teachers' length of service at the school.

26. Shen Yiyun, *Yiyun huiyi,* 41.

27. "Beiyang Nüshifan Xuetang kaixiao jisheng" (A record of the opening of Beiyang Women's Normal School), *Zhili jiaoyu zazhi* 9 (22 June 1906): 1–2. Also see *Da gong bao,* 14 July 1906.

28. "Beiyang Nüzi Shifan Xuetang zhangcheng" (The regulations for Beiyang Women's Normal School), *Dongfang zazhi* 3, no. 9 (1906): 225.

29. Ibid., 227 and 225–26.

30. Ibid., 226.

31. Han Tiyun, "Nüxuetang jiaoyuan zhi wenti" (The problem of teachers in women's schools), *Zhili jiaoyu zazhi* 14 (2 October 1906): 1–4.

32. *Zhili diyi nüzi shifan xuexiao xiaoyou hui huibao* 1 (1915), *Xiaoge* (School song).

33. "Beiyang Nüshifan Xuetang kaixiao jisheng," *Shuntian shibao,* GX34.1.12 (13 February 1908), reprinted in Li Youning and Zhang Yufa, eds., *Jindai Zhongguo nüquan yundong shiliao,* 1166–68. Also see *Dagong bao,* 10 February 1908.

34. "Xuebu zou xiangyi nüzi shifan xuetang ji nüzi xiaoxuetang zhangcheng zhe" (Memorial of the Board of Education making a detailed proposal regarding regulations for women's normal schools and women's elementary schools), *Dongfang zazhi* 4, no. 4 (1907), reprinted in Li Youning and Zhang Yufa, eds., *Jindai Zhongguo nüquan yundong shiliao,* 975–89. Having sanctioned women's education, in 1970, the Qing government for the first time sponsored three women to study abroad; the three studied at Wellesley College. See Weili Ye, " 'Nü Liuxuesheng': The Story of American-Educated Chinese Women, 1880s–1920s," *Modern China* 20, no. 3 (July 1994): 325.

35. "Xuebu zou pai diaocha Zhili xuewuyuan baogaoshu" (A report of the officials commissioned by the Board of Education to investigate Zhili's educational affairs), *Dongfang zazhi* 4, no. 11 (1907): 285–86.

36. Ru Jin, "Lun Xuebu yanding nüxue zhangcheng" (The Board of Education

firmly decides on the regulations for women's education), *Shenzhou nübao* 1, no. 1 (1907), reprinted in Zhonghua quanguo funü lianhe hui funü yundong lishi yanjiu shi, ed., *Zhongguo jindai funü yundong lishi ziliao*, 308–9.

37. Shen Yi, "Lun nüzi zhi putong jiaoyu" (A discussion of women's elementary education), *Jiaoyu zazhi* 1, no. 6 (1909): 73–74.

38. Lu Feikui, "Nan nü gongxue wenti" (The problem of coeducation), *Jiaoyu zazhi* 2, no. 11 (1910): 5–6.

39. Han Tiyun, "Lun Zhili xuewu jinbu zhi cidi bin zhu qi fada zhi qiantu" (A discussion of the order of progress in Zhili's educational affairs and a celebration of the prospects for their development), *Zhili jiaoyu zazhi* 22 (28 January 1907): 1–4.

40. Liao Xiuzhen, "The Evolution of Women's Education within the Educational System and the Development of Women's Elementary Education in the Late Qing," 224–29.

41. For a discussion of changes in the educational system after 1912, see Paul Bailey, *Reform the People*, 134–67.

42. "Benxiao yange shilue" (A brief history of the development of this school), *Zhili diyi nüzi shifan xuexiao xiaoyou hui huibao* 1 (April 1916): 1–2.

43. Chart on the origins of teachers and chart on the number of students, in *Zhili diyi nüzi shifan xuexiao xiaoyou hui huibao* 1 (April 1916).

44. Ma Cuiguan, "Xianfu Ma Qinli xiansheng wei zhenxing zhonghua zhandou de yisheng" (My late father Mr. Ma Qianli's life of struggle to rejuvenate China), in Ma Cuiguan, ed., *Ershi shiji chu Tianjin aiguo jiaoyu jia Ma Qianli xiansheng dansheng bai zhounian jinian, 1885–1985* (Commemoration of the one hundredth anniversary of the birthday of the early-twentieth-century Tianjin patriotic educator Ma Qianli) (Tianjin: 1985), 15 17.

45. "Benxiao dashi ji" (A record of important events at this school), *Zhili diyi nüzi shifan xuexiao xiaoyou hui huibao* 2 (December 1916): 1.

46. Ma Cuiguan, "My late father Mr. Ma Qianli's life of struggle to rejuvenate China," 16.

47. "Benxiao dashi ji," *Zhili diyi nüzi shifan xuexiao xiaoyou hui huibao* 5 (December 1918): 3–4.

48. Ibid., 4 (December 1917): 1.

49. "Tao xiansheng Yuhe jiangyan nüzi diwei zhi bianqian" (Mr. Tao Menghe lectures on the changes in women's position), *Zhili diyi nüzi shifan xuexiao xiaoyou hui huibao* 2 (December 1916): 1 and 5.

50. The name was a Chinese transliteration of Comte.

51. "Cai Jiemin xiansheng yanshuo ziyou pingdeng boai" (Mr. Cai Jiemin's [Yuan-pei] speech on liberty, equality, and fraternity), *Zhili diyi nüzi shifan xuexiao xiaoyou hui huibao* 5 (December 1918): 1–5.

52. Paul Bailey, *Reform the People*, 154.

53. Chen Xuexun, ed., *Zhongguo jindai jiaoyu dashi ji*, 256 and 282.

54. Lu Feikui, "Nüzi jiaoyu wenti" (The problem of women's education) (1913), in Lu Feikui, *Jiaoyu wencun*, pt. 4, 24.

55. Tian Min, "Jinhou nüzi jiaoyu zhi fangzhen" (The guiding policy for women's education from today forward), *Jiaoyu zazhi* 10, no. 8 (1918): 107.

56. Liang Hualan, "Nüzi jiaoyu" (Women's education), *Xin qingnian* 3, no. 1 (1917): 1.

57. Zhao Zhangzheng, "Minguo chuchuang nüzi jiaoyu" (The founding of the Republic and women's education), *Minguo dangan* 1 (1992): 74.

58. Huang Xinxian, *Zhongguo jin xiandai nüzi jiaoyu*, 105 and 108.

59. *Hebei sheng li nüzi shifan xueyuan sishier zhounian xiaoqing tekan* (Special issue on the forty-second anniversary of the founding of the Hebei Provincial Women's Normal College) (22 April 1948): 1.

60. Liang Jisheng (under pseudonym Dian Bing), "Deng Yingchao, Liu Qingyang, Guo Longzhen—Wusi shiqi de sanwei nü shifansheng" (Deng Yingchao, Liu Qingyang, and Guo Longzhen—Three women's normal school students in the May Fourth period), in Wang Liyun and Song Jiange, eds., *Shifan qunying guangyao zhonghua* (Xi'an: 1992) (An honorable gathering of China's teacher-training heroes), 3:107. Also see Li Yunhua, "Jianshu Wusi shiqi tianjin de funü jiefang yundong" (A simple account of the women's liberation movement in Tianjin during the May Fourth period), *Lishi jiaoxue* 7 (1988): 16.

61. *Da gong bao*, 24–26 May 1919, reprinted in Zhonggong Tianjin shiwei dangshi ziliao zhengji weiyuan hui and Tianjin shi funü lianhe hui, eds. *Deng Yingchao yu Tianjin zaoqi funü yundong* (Deng Yingchao and the early Tianjin women's movement) (Beijing: Zhongguo funü chubanshe, 1987), 6–8.

62. *Yishi bao*, 2 September 1919, reprinted in Zhonggong Tianjin shiwei dangshi ziliao zhengji weiyuan hui and Tianjin shi funü lianhe hui, eds., *Deng Yingchao yu Tianjin zaoqi funü yundong*, 30.

63. Liang Jisheng, "Deng Yingchao, Liu Qingyang, and Guo Longzhen—Three women's normal school students in the May Fourth period," 112–13.

64. Deng Yingchao, "Liangge shi wo nanwang de wuqi—bin gao nüshifan de shisheng" (Two May Sevenths that are difficult for me to forget—A complete recounting to the women's normal school teachers and students), *Nü Xing*, 15 May 1923, reprinted in Dong Zhenxiu, ed., *Qingnian Deng Yingchao de daolu* (Deng Yingchao's path in youth) (Tianjin: 1992), 6–8.

65. Ibid., 6 and 9.

66. "Diwuci quanguo jiaoyuhui lianhe huiyi juean" (The fifth resolution of the National Federation of Education Associations), *Jiaoyu zazhi* 11, no. 11 (1919): 50.

67. Jia Fengzhen, "Jinhou wuguo jiaoyu shang yingxing gexin zhi dian" (The aspects of Chinese education that should be reformed from today forward), *Jiaoyu zazhi* 11, no. 12 (1919): 8.

68. Zhou Binglin, "Kaifang daxue yu funü jiefang" (The opening up of the universities and the liberation of women), *Shaonian Zhongguo* 1, no. 4 (October 1919), reprinted in Zhonghua quanguo funü lianhe hui funü yundong lishi yanjiu shi, ed., *Wusi shiqi funü wenti wenxuan* (Selected works on the women's problem during the May Fourth period) (Beijing: Shenghuo, dushu, xinzhi sanlian shudian, 1981), 257–58.

69. Xu Yanzhi, "Beijing Daxue nannü gongxiao ji" (A record of coeducation at Beijing University), *Shaonian shijie* 1, no. 7 (1920), reprinted in Zhonghua quanguo funü lianhe hui funü yundong lishi yanjiu shi, ed., *Wusi shiqi funü wenti wenxuan*, 267–68 and 270.

70. Chen Dongyuan, *Zhongguo funü shenghuo shi* (History of the life of Chinese

women) (Zhongguo wenhua shi congshu, pt. 2) (Shanghai: Shangwu yinshuguan, 1937), 389–91.

71. Liao Shicheng, "Sanshiwu nian lai Zhongguo zhi zhongxue jiaoyu" (Middle school education in China over the last thirty-five years), in Cai Yuanpei, et al., *Wanqing sanshiwu nian lai zhi Zongguo jiaoyu (1897–1931)* (Chinese education in the final thirty-five years of the Qing dynasty) (1931: reprint, Hong Kong: 1969), 45.

72. Yu Qingtang, "Sanshiwu nian lai zhongguo zhi nüzi jiaoyu" (Women's education in China over the last thirty-five years), in Cai Yuanpei et al., *Wanqing sanshiwu nian lai zhi Zhongguo jiaoyu*, 190.

Historical Memory, Community Service, Hope: Reclaiming the Social Purposes of Education for the Shanghai McTyeire Schools for Girls

Heidi Ross

Prologue: October 30, 1995

Ten guests assemble around a banquet table in Nanchang, Jiangxi province, to celebrate the inauguration of the "Yu Cai Xue Zheng Project Hope for Girls." (Yucai Xue Zheng xiwang gongcheng). The project provides a high school education to forty-two girls who have come to the capital from fifteen of the province's poorest counties. Guests one through three, alumni of the Shanghai McTyeire School for Girls (Zhongxi nüxiao), occupy positions of honor. Each left China decades ago and built a financially successful life in Hong Kong, Australia, and the United States, respectively. Guests four and five are farmers who have traveled two days to reach this gathering. The men are semiliterate, from villages with annual per capita incomes of less than U.S. $100. Their daughters' educations are being fully funded by McTyeirean alumni. Guests six and seven are the principal and vice principal of McTyeire's successor institution, the Shanghai Number Three Girls' School (Shanghai shisan nüzi zhongxue), institutional consultant to the project. Guest eight is an energetic thirty-seven-year-old who paid her way through college by styling the hair of her mother's friends. After saving a sizable nest egg as a fashion designer in Shenzhen, she returned home in 1991 to found Yu Cai Private Secondary School (Yucai sili zhongxue). Guest number nine, the personal maid of guest number one, is a highly educated woman from the Philippines, struggling to put three children through college. I am guest number ten.

As the evening wears on, we realize how fascinating and contingent this meeting is. We have so little in common, come from opposite ends of the Earth. What else but fate, wonders one of the fathers, could have brought us together? The occasion has different meanings for each of us. McTyeireans have come to reclaim a legacy, to extend a community of sisterhood to girls who would otherwise be unable to pursue a high school education. Fathers have come with gratitude, on behalf of a far-flung collection of poor parents with great expectations for their daughters. Number Three School administrators have come to honor a request made by influential donors and to profile their school's national reputation. I have come to document a lesson in girls' schooling at the boundaries. A decade ago Chinese leaders, like their counterparts worldwide, had little to say about girls' education. Now Chinese economists declare that girls' schooling is the "highest return investment" the nation can make. I look at the two fathers sitting to my left. Their daughters are the magic bullets of Chinese development.

Introduction: Re-membering McTyeire's Legacy of Community Service

> "Community is an idea that becomes reality because we believe in it, not vice versa."
>
> —Stevan Harrell

This essay on the power of memory and narrative to create individual and community identity is part of a larger history of the McTyeire School for Girls, Republican China's most prestigious girls' secondary school.[1] Southern Methodist missionaries founded McTyeire in 1892 to provide a Christian education to Chinese daughters of "the well-to-do classes." McTyeire lost its religious affiliation in 1952, was consolidated with St. Mary's School for Girls,[2] and was renamed the Shanghai Number Three Girls' School (hereafter referred to as Number Three). Number Three was designated a center for research on female development (*jiaoyu keyan xianjin xuexiao*) in 1982. As China's only all-female key school, Number Three has become a national model for public and private girls' schools founded by educators and parents eager to provide appropriate educational opportunities for their daughters.

The development rhetoric in contemporary China that anchors the nation's economic well-being in girls' education is the latest version of a century-long discourse, well documented in this volume by Paul Bailey and

Sarah McElroy, that has identified Chinese women as both the solution to and scapegoat for the ills of the nation. Belief in the critical role of women in China's civilizing project likewise provided the justification for McTyeire's establishment, by Young J. Allen, the superintendent of the China Mission of the Methodist Episcopal Church South (MECS), and Bishop Holland N. McTyeire, founder of Vanderbilt University and McTyeire's namesake. Allen coordinated the MECS Women's Missionary Society in China and came, after two decades of work in Shanghai, to equate the elevation of Chinese women with the salvation of China: "the degrading systems of the East are based mainly on the condition of woman; and experience has demonstrated that if we could make any permanent impress on society, she must receive more attention." Believing that female missionaries "alone can reach the source of evil," Allen persuaded Laura Askew Haygood to travel to China to become the school's first principal.

Haygood was a graduate of the Wesleyan Female College in Macon, Georgia, and one of the cofounders of the MECS Home Mission Society. Shortly after agreeing to Allen's request, Haygood revealed in a letter to a friend her distaste for the "costly superficiality" of women's education in antebellum America. Sounding a lament strikingly similar to Chinese activists' criticisms of education limited to the cultivation of good wives and wise mothers, she wrote: "Why have we not told her that to grace her home, to make it bright and beautiful and good, is indeed womanly and wise, but for most of us need not, ought not, *must not* absorb all of love and time and mind? Why have we not made her feel that for her as truly as for her brother there is need of earnest, honest, thorough work, because the world has need of her? Do we not too often in our schools shut our girls *out* from the real world with its real needs, and shut them *in* to the narrow ways of self and selfish aims?"[3]

Embracing a vision of schooling that supported both virtue and talent, self-sacrifice, and self-enhancement, Haygood struggled against a severe shortage of funds and the stifling "authority of the dead" that she called Chinese traditional views on women to open McTyeire in March 1892, five years before the establishment of Shanghai's first locally funded and operated girls' school.[4] The school's inauguration was widely publicized and attended by Nie Qiqiu, Shanghai's *daotai* (Imperial Commissioner) from 1890 to 1894, and the vice-consul-general of the United States.[5] The school's Chinese name, translated as the Chinese-Western Girls' Academy, was chosen to remind wealthy treaty port parents of Young J. Allen's successful Anglo-Chinese school for boys. Haygood's trying efforts to find religious and educational purpose in Shanghai convinced her that she must not only educate Chinese girls with Christian sensibilities but also create an institution that was both school and waystation for female missionaries newly arrived in China. The McTyeire Home and School would provide a touchstone of familiarity to disoriented newcomers, a female community of solace, affection, and domestic good cheer for unmarried, professional women.

The conception of McTyeire as a protective yet dynamic combination of domestic empire and Chinese Mandarin garden was evidently shared by Haygood's successor, Helen Richardson, who gave it shape in McTyeire's logo, still emblazoned on Number Three sweatshirts as a sun radiating the words of the school's motto, "Live, love, grow." McTyeire's educational aims reflected both the accomplishments wealthy Chinese families desired in their daughters and the moral character and refined breeding that constituted the mission school's "gospel of gentility": (1) to offer students a firm grounding in Chinese and English through a liberal arts education; (2) to offer a series of elective classes in Western music; (3) to build a wholesome educational environment that would cultivate young Chinese women of high moral character and mental habits; and (4) to provide students with a fundamental knowledge of Christianity.[6]

I have traced in previous writing how tensions between Christian and national service, necessarily embodied in McTyeire's educational mission, magnified the (unpredictable) influences missionary educators had in promoting their students' social and political agency.[7] Generations of McTyeireans found inspiration for social service by balancing in different ways competing claims of Christian faith, nationalist loyalty, and socialist ideals. McTyeireans who had graduated prior to the May Fourth era felt inspired by and helped promote the imagined community created by the meeting of McTyeire's two cultures of female gentility, that of missionaries and that of upper-class, treaty port Chinese. In contrast, efforts by later generations of missionaries to assist students "to serve her home, her community, her nation and the world"[8] were interpreted by students in ways that threatened the mission enterprise. Embraced by its earliest pupils for the social alternatives it offered them, McTyeire was perceived by their daughters as both barrier and gateway to personal and social transformation.

In this essay I draw primarily upon life history narratives of alumni to portray McTyeire as an institution created and sustained by an enabling, if fractious, bond of women who have reimagined their individual and collective pasts in order to improve the present.[9] These narratives reveal that girls rarely accepted unaltered the roles dominant state and religious discourses held out for them. Yet, in contrast to the experience of Fuzhou Anglo-Chinese College students, discussed in a previous section of this volume, for whom the nation served as the primary point of reference for identity construction, McTyeireans sought and realized identity through a personal, even spiritual, definition of service.[10] McTyeirean narratives raise the possibility that the meaning of nationalist consciousness may have been quite different for male and female mission school students. In addition, they underscore the insistence with which McTyeireans have continued to create a coherent identity from discontinuous lived experiences and to extend and reinterpret for others the particular kind of Chinese identity they claim as their social legacy.

Class of 1920, China's first female lawyer. I wanted to enter law school, because I always complained about the laws against women in China. So I said I'm going to fight. When I grow up I'm going to be a lawyer and fight for the rights of women. But women of my time were so low, so below men, the law school wouldn't take any women. So I taught mathematics at McTyeire, the hardest subject at my old alma mater. And I waited, until I heard that law school was open for women. I waited nine years for the law school to open the door. Soochow University Law School. The Comparative Law School of China. I wanted to fight to show them how women can pass by men and be above men. When the law school opened the door I said to myself, "I am going to show you boys that I have bigger brains than you have." And when they posted my grades they were all shocked. How could this girl get A, A, A, A, A? Where does she get that? No one could find me after school. I hid myself in one of the pavilions. Nobody went to the pavilion. And I was there hiding myself to study. And I said to myself, "I'm going to beat you all, because you think men are superior to women. I'm going to show you women are superior to you."

Missionary educator, 1928–50. By the time I got there we had daughters of McTyeire graduates in school. You had among the faculty not only graduates of the best colleges in the United States and China, but they were born and bred McTyeire people. McTyeire was a wonderful place where young women were trained to be both confident and have a deep sense of responsibility. Their husbands had at least one thing in common. All were proud of their wives. . . . It was *zhongxi*, not *xizhong*. McTyeire was never a school run by foreigners for Chinese; it was always a cooperative venture in which American and Chinese worked together with mutual love and respect. McTyeire lives on in the lives of her daughters; women of strength and faith; women who have dared to make their school motto central in their living.

Class of 1933. The school was liberal in its approach to education. That encouraged an independence of spirit. We did things for ourselves, and had our own opinions. We could always manage the hardships better than our husbands. McTyeire girls gave their families face. Even though we were privileged, the school taught us to look beyond wealth and material values. We looked for deeper qualities. McTyeire-assisted students understand the importance of hard work. These women were in some sense the strength behind their husbands. We were able to do it all: mothers, educated, devoted and elegant wives, powerful businesswomen. Because we did not live on a mundane plane. The school was for our elevation.

Class of 1936. As a fifth-grader I was already a boarding student at McTyeire. We were homesick, but we were not allowed to go home, only every two weeks. At that time I must have been ten or eleven years old. Those were very happy times. Oh, it was actually an ivory tower. The campus was very beautiful. We were confined in it. Only every two weeks were we allowed to go home. And the campus was so very beautiful—forsythia, daffodils, peach blossoms, a lily pond, a little bridge, a little island, and the dragon wall and wisteria. And we took walks. We lay down on the lawn on warmer days, sang, played, talked. So it was a very happy life. Later on, when I became an adult, I looked back and thought what an isolated kind of life, when China was in a great turmoil. Warlords were fighting, Japanese were encroaching. And then they took over, and then the Nationalists and the communists were having all kinds of civil war. Suppression of the bandits, as Chiang Kai-shek called it. We knew nothing about those things. We were very isolated. Well, we were the privileged ones. We lived in the international concession, so we were protected by colonialism. So the bombing didn't bother us. We heard of refugees, of course, people who lived close to the Chinese territories, who fled to the international concession to take shelter. But we never really directly experienced bombing. Or, like the massacre in Nanking; those things were very remote. I don't know. It is a very sad case that we, somehow, got the kind of perception or the kind of attitude of looking down on Chinese culture. They didn't intentionally do this, but they always talked about beautiful, bright America, and we imagined it must be so good. At the same time China was herself in a very bad state. Were McTyeire girls really different? Well, we were cultured. I don't know how we learned it. We learned to be polite. We came from better families, some very wealthy. First of all, good family background, and then Westernized, and modernized in a way, and courteous. You learned how to dress, pay attention to your appearance. The school gave us a kind of intellectual property.

1947. The drive to be excellent, the kind of built-in standards. I think these were formed at McTyeire. You know, the Christian doctrine is to help people. Like when you work, you bring the Christian doctrine to your working life, to your daily living. Unlike Taoism and Buddhism. Buddhism is very passive, trains you to be tolerant of imperfection. Saying you come in and out of this life. You are here to suffer, to tolerate pain and suffering. I don't think Christianity is that at all. When you have such a good life you accept all this. You have a responsibility of returning part of it to the society or to the community, in addition to passing it on to your children. I mean the training, education, a code of ethics. That's right. You should do that with your children. But I also feel you have to extend beyond the immediate family. If you want to become part of the community, you have to put some investment into that community. Perhaps not for you but at least for your children, the next generation. Now, you can't just take and keep. That's not the kind of person I want to be.

McTyeirean narratives of privilege, community responsibility, and service are evoked by alumni regardless of age, political orientation, or religious conviction. McTyeire, in the words of a graduate of the class of 1941, "connoted cooperative living," and recollecting that lived experience prompts alumni to interpret McTyeire's pedagogical goal of *tongcai*, the capacity to understand and embody both Chinese and American cultures, in ways that minimize disagreements over whether missionaries were a source for positive social transformation. In contrast, in-house histories, particularly those written in the 1970s, condemn McTyeire's recreation of an upper-class American school on Chinese soil. In the more formulaic of these accounts missionary teachers subtly impelled students to view their own nation as dark, while McTyeire, breathtaking in its beauty, mandated religious training and replicated the patterns of bourgeois domesticity in home economic classes. Music (and its accompanying refinement of a Western aesthetic sensibility) was emphasized precisely because it was such an immediate and emotionally gripping tool of cultural hegemony.

The private and public lives of alumni belie the harshness of such portraits, although not their assertion regarding the powerful cultural claims McTyeire made on its students. The school's pastoral beauty, elaborate rituals, and generational ties between mothers and daughters forged strong bonds between students and their alma mater. Privileged and cosmopolitan backgrounds, coupled with unparalleled English fluency, set McTyeire students apart, made them feel special, different, entitled "McTyeire girls." "You can spot them a mile away," joked their appreciative husbands. Yet a commitment to service was also internalized by McTyeire's pupils, who were told, over and over again, that the privilege of being a McTyeire girl carried with it heavy social responsibilities.

The ambiguous image of this strong yet self-sacrificing and graceful woman, described by a graduate as "beauty and regimen and order and service and courtesy, the will to survive, to take responsibility for one's own and others' well-being," is not so different from current expectations for Number Three students. Associated with the McTyeire mystique of republican China and sheltered within the relative comfort and privilege of Number Three's walls, the girls have a reputation swiftly summed up by a Shanghai college student. "Why, those Number Three girls—don't you know? Either they're the first to get married in college, or they're pushy and loud, hard. They either like boys too much, or they're too much like boys." Despite such stereotypes, understanding that McTyeire's symbolic universe confers upon their school financial and social prestige, Number Three administrators have effectively appropriated it. In fact, remarkable similarities characterize the intentions of missionaries, who called their schools "nurseries for engendering principles," and of Chinese teachers, who describe Number Three as a "cradle of female talent."[11]

My conclusions regarding historical continuity recall Carolyn Heilbrun's reminder that stories told by (and about) women are rarely "truthful."[12] Indeed, McTyeirean school annuals and biographical accounts are laced with romanticism and nostalgia, depicting a three-, four-, or five-generation family of women sustained by "this wonderful school, its idyllic campus with spacious green lawn and weeping willow trees, the golden days I spent there, and the text of the school song that had inspired me to live up to the expectations laid down for the young girls who studied there."

> Class of 1946. It was so lovely, all these girls came marching in in violet *qipao*, and it was so gorgeous. And we were saying they look like orchids, two by two. There were twin sisters and they looked absolutely gorgeous. When they walked by I was just stunned. We were all stunned, all the little ones from Primary Number One and Primary Number Two. We were all in the auditorium, but sitting downstairs, as they went onto the stage to receive their diplomas. It was such a thrill. It was very exciting. They had a senior play and they sold tickets, and the little ones could buy the tickets.

We went by bus, and it was the greatest thrill. Now we looked forward to going there next year. The play was *Vanity Fair*. But when it came to my class play we had a play like a Broadway show. We invited a famous actor to come and be our director and we were so excited. This was a historical play. I was one of the main characters. I played the queen mother, the concubine queen mother. Oh, our young days were so full of nice things. They are good, good memories.

Such idealized portraits have allowed McTyeireans to remain connected across glaring political and religious differences—and diaspora. Far from seeing themselves as "the debris of history," mobility is constructed by emigrated alumni as a form of (often painful) challenge to create a network enabling them to act in concert—and usually in advance of the Chinese state. Consequently, I interpret narratives of McTyeirean harmony not as female "biographical disability" but as a method of inscribing practical power in the present. In her 1995 presidential address to the Association of Asian Studies Barbara Metcalf reflected that, after two centuries of a history of difference that benefited colonialists and nationalists, many of us yearn for (and write) a "history of connections, of mobility across space."[13] I believe this effort "to draw wide boundaries around human experience" likewise motivates McTyeireans. Their insistence on community is not, primarily, a safe, utilitarian discourse but, rather, a way of envisioning life as creative improvisation.

In *Composing a Life* Mary Catherine Bateson writes that the "process of improvisation that goes into composing a life is compounded in the process of remembering a life. . . . Yet it is this second process, composing a life through memory as well as through day-to-day choices, that seems to me most essential to creative living."[14] I have found no better description for the lives of McTyeireans and no better way to explain the hold on their consciousness and their actions of the narrative of community responsibility and service. McTyeireans have crafted their lives in the midst of unimaginably disruptive social change. Many graduates were made refugees of war, torn from families, children, material support. Still, they managed to regard the improvisation such disruption entailed not as a last resort but as a way of creating new life possibilities.

One of McTyeire's most successful lessons may have been its ability to offer students a stable environment in which to develop the strength to live life creatively in the face of great uncertainty. A member of the class of 1947 suggested: "What McTyeire gave us was confidence—not just good academic training. It was that everyone was appreciated and cherished for whatever their individual skills and strengths. Everyone was made to feel they belonged, were valued. Perhaps we were protected, naive, but we had the strength to survive suffering. Many left China with only one day to pack. Looking for jobs, working long hours, sacrificing. But somehow they not only survived, they were successful."

Such testimonies, of course, evoke an institution uncomfortably, unbelievably larger than life. When a graduate of the class of 1939 forgot her purse after an interview session, a classmate remarked that a common McTyeire trait was absentmindedness—an inattention to the small and inconsequential. Narratives confirm her suggestion that graduates were forced, despite their reputation for being pampered, to focus on the large matters of life. McTyeire was an institution that placed its female teachers and students in positions of unusual responsibility and independence, and most McTyeireans describe a school that "called out of themselves a better self." Christian women reconstruct their accounts of McTyeire and, through those accounts, of their lives, with varying forms of service to god and the nation at their centers. Chinese nationalist and socialist women tell stories that locate personal strength and independence in patriotism, revolution, and family. McTyeire's "larger than life" narratives still come in handy for Number Three. No public occasion passes when its pupils are not reminded how they are linked in a long line of prestigious women, including "Auntie" Song Qingling, McTyeire's most famous student.

Through the work of telling and retelling such stories, McTyeireans create a coherent identity that might be summarized as a recognition of self-worth, of privilege, and of the need to contribute to community. It was this recognition that gave rise to and provides the backdrop for the Yu Cai Xue Zheng Project Hope for Girls, named in memory of McTyeire and Number Three's late honorary principal. The negotiations that preceded the establishment of the project illustrate how the financial and institutional goals of Number Three administrators, the civic values of Yu Cai's energetic principal, and the personal search for self-definition and community of alumni living in China and abroad conjoin to define the relationship between education and social responsibility. These negotiations also suggest how tensions between education as a public and a private good animate the market narrative of Chinese schooling.

The Yu Cai Xue Zheng Project Hope for Girls

> "Lives do not serve as models; only stories do that."
> —Mary Catherine Bateson, *Peripheral Visions*

Xue Zheng. Any one individual's abilities have limits, just as the contributions one person can make for one's country during one's lifetime are small in the scheme of things. Nevertheless, through the power of education one can nurture a thousand able individuals, whose combined force can contribute greatly to the goodness of the nation.

In Memorium: "Our beloved Principal Xue Zheng passed away on May 21, 1995, at the age of ninety-four. All her life she dedicated herself to the education of teenage girls. Spanning a relationship of sixty-three years with our school, she held first McTyeire then Number Three together through the most tumultuous political upheavals of our times. With the strong support of McTyeire alumni abroad, she and her administrators succeeded in restoring our school to be the premier girls' high school in China."

The conviction held by Honorary Principal Xue Zheng about the power of education now provides the epitaph for the Yu Cai project. It appears prominently in each project description and on the cover of the inauguration brochure. It also figures heavily in the eulogies of Xue Zheng students and colleagues, compiled upon her death. Her photograph adorns the cover of this informal biography, eyes forward, head cocked upward, urging the onlooker to do better, strive harder. The brief histories of Xue Zheng's life are sentimental, emotional, comforting. Born in 1901, "when ignorant women were thought virtuous," Xue Zheng dressed as a boy in order to be tutored. "She defied her parents' wishes to study medicine, choosing education instead. She believed there was a limit to how many patients one doctor could heal, whereas educators could train thousands of able people, who together could make untold contributions." "She traveled to America twice to study for advanced degrees, and in 1949, just months shy of finishing her doctorate, she abandoned her work to return to liberated China." "Education was to her a personal duty, a vehicle for contributing to the nation. McTyeire was her home."

A colleague trying to understand why Xue Zheng remained loyal to the Communist Party after suffering during the Cultural Revolution (all the brutal details of which are left politely unrecorded) recounts that Xue once told her: "I often visited a friend's house, and was always greeted warmly. Then one day I arrived only to be spurned. I knew these weren't the true feelings of the friends I knew. They had been replaced by strangers." A former student, curious about Xue's faith in Christianity when she was a young woman, remembers that Xue explained: "Before liberation I became a Christian for salvation. But Christianity did not save me—or others. After liberation, the party did save people, I wanted to join." Xue Zheng was never so sure nor so simple in interviews several years before her death. Nevertheless, the eulogies, in recording only Xue Zheng's sacrifice and dedication and none of her pain, underscore how "lives do not serve as models; only stories do that."

> I went to school at Yenching, when Dr. Stuart was the president. He was really good. We had two students per room. Beijing is so different. Most of us were educated as very aggressive and challenging. You know we were educated to be very independent; most of us are devoted to our career. I never finished my doctorate. I had my dissertation outline, but it was liberation. Everyone was so excited, everyone was eager to come back. My advisor, Dr. French, implored me, "Goodness! Stay six more months and finish your doctorate!" Afterward, I did regret it. I couldn't buy a ticket by plane or by boat, and I waited and waited, so I didn't get to Shanghai until the middle of April. I could have stayed and come back in June. But coming back early had one good outcome. If I had stayed, during the Cultural Revolution I would have been criticized even more violently. We don't want to remember the Gang of Four. We want to forget them.

> My times [at McTyeire] were all troubles. [In] 1937 the war started. The best time was coming back, after the war. We moved out from school for two years. After the war we came back. Came back to the school campus, and this was a time of great cooperation to get the school back in shape. The foreign teachers in the U.S. came back one at a time. That was a really good period. After liberation was also a good time. The student body really grew. The Cultural Revolution was terrible, really terrible, but after that things got better. The male students were quite lovable when they were there. But when the girl students are with their male peers they don't dare do anything. They are timid. For instance, one of the parents came to me and said that he is very happy that his second daughter is in a girls' school, because the first daughter went to a co-ed school, and in biology class when they were dissecting frogs the boys worked, the girls merely watched. But his second daughter, she never stands on the sidelines.

In 1979, at the age of seventy-eight, Xue Zheng visited the United States and Hong Kong at the request of alumni. These alumni now mark her journey as the beginning of their efforts to reclaim McTyeire's legacy. Six years later Xue Zheng joined the Chinese Communist Party. At the age of ninety-one she began to contribute to China's Project Hope program, founded in 1989 by the

Chinese Communist Youth League (through the China Youth Development Foundation), by supporting the education of ten impoverished girls.

School reports suggest that Xue's example inspired alumni to organize their efforts on behalf of Jiangxi's rural girls. The reality, however, is that causality did not flow so neatly. Conversations about funding poor female students through an "adopt-a-student project" began in 1992, as preparations were being made for McTyeire's centennial anniversary celebration. After explaining to me the difficult attempts to explain to Number Three administrators that it was time international alumni began to fund projects for those truly in need, one alumni quoted Han Suyin to me, sighing, "Ah well, if one is going to be a bridge, one should be prepared to get stepped on."

The same year He Jing, Yu Cai's principal, made provincial and national headlines by establishing Jiangxi province's first private, not-for-profit, full-time secondary school. With the financial and professional assistance of a former high school teacher, He Jing raised 100,000 yuan as the seed capital for the school and, after sustained negotiation with the provincial education bureau, succeeded in founding the Yu Cai Private School. The school opened its doors to two hundred boys and girls, who enrolled in nursing, accounting, or general academic tracks and lived in a dormitory building leased from Jiangxi Normal College's attached secondary school. The school struggled through its first two years, relying on very young and retired teachers and inadequate funds derived from a per-semester tuition that ranged from 240 to 270 yuan. After paying 30,000 yuan each semester for leased buildings, in addition to teachers' salaries and capital improvements, Yu Cai's two-year costs of 655,000 yuan greatly exceeded its 290,000 yuan income.[15] He Jing spent much of her time fund-raising, dispelling rumors that the school was "just for rich people," and attempting to recruit new students.

Yu Cai's connection with McTyeirean alumni is a story of luck, timing, and ingenuity. He Jing read in a local paper that a group of Jiangxi high school principals would be traveling to Shanghai on a field trip for secondary school administrators. Hoping to participate herself, she contacted one of the organizers, who was so impressed that an unknown, young, female, private school principal would make the request that he accepted her proposal on the spot. The organizer was the principal of Number Three.

During her visit to Shanghai, He Jing charmed Number Three administrators with her energy and entrepreneurial drive. They had just received a request from McTyeirean alumni asking for assistance in identifying a rural school worthy of financial support. One of the conditions was that the school in question must have a female principal.

The next year Number Three administrators and teachers traveled to Nanchang three times to evaluate Yu Cai's teaching staff, curriculum, facilities, and financial status, and in October 1994 Number Three's vice principal traveled to San Francisco to report these findings to McTyeirean alumni. Meanwhile, alumni associations in Hong Kong and the United States began seeking sponsors "to help reverse the tragic trend of high illiteracy among Chinese women in impoverished villages, to promote McTyeire's legacy of Live, Love, and Grow beyond the Number Three Girls' School to those young girls struggling for their high school education." Specifically, alumni were asked to fund, at an annual per pupil cost of U.S. $300, the tuition, room and board, and book fees of forty girls, who would study together for three years in a special academic preparatory homeroom class at Yu Cai.[16] Sponsorship could be secured through contributions on behalf of individuals, families, or clusters of classmates. The only requirement was that sponsors must maintain personal contact with their wards in the form of photographs and letters of encouragement.

Approval of the project came rapidly from the Jiangxi Education Bureau, because of Number Three's reputation and because such partnerships had become an increasingly popular method throughout China for linking urban and rural schools, teachers, and students for mutual financial, pedagogical, and social support. In April 1995 the bureau contacted township education bureaus for lists of potential candidates. Yu Cai administrators were responsible for a preliminary ranking of these candidates, but Number Three faculty made the final selection of scholarship recipients, primarily to spare Yu Cai from political pressures and conflicts of interest. Admission criteria included an essay in which candidates were to demonstrate their sincerity and originality, a solid academic record, documentation of low income, and teacher recommendations regarding extracurricular talents and leadership abilities.

The primary recruitment region for students consisted of eleven counties, in Fuzhou, Ganzhou, Ji'an, and Shangrao prefectures, with annual household incomes ranging in 1992 from 647 to 1,725 yuan.[17] Annual per capita incomes of the girls' families ranged from an extremely low 100 to 800 yuan.[18] While many of these families have incomes higher than tens of millions of the 60 to 70 million people officially classified as poor by the Chinese government, they would certainly be included in the 350 million rural residents currently described as impoverished in recent World Bank reports. These families, without nonagricultural incomes or remittances from relatives working in cities, struggle to make ends meet in the face of declining agricultural infrastructure and, as yet, few village and township enterprises.

In addition to meeting the economic criteria outlined here, the students, who ranged in age from fourteen to seventeen, had all graduated from junior high school; had recommendations attesting to their independence, verbal skills, good foundation in English, good health (with the exception of two disabled students); and had a high combined score on the high school entrance examination. In her introductory essay one of the students reported that she had secretly registered for her first year at primary school at age nine in order to force her father to let her attend school. Two students came from families with five children, and one student's father was illiterate. None of the forty-two girls were able to continue their education, because their families could not afford the fees associated with attendance at their nearest public high schools.

The adopt-a-student plan was nearing fruition, with forty-two three-year scholarships secured by a total of eighty alumni, when Xue Zheng passed away. The project's primary supporter, a McTyeire graduate of the class of 1947, had just returned from China after turning over U.S. $12,000 to finance the scholarships for the 1995–96 academic year. She asked in an alumni newsletter for her schoolmates' "concurrence to rename the project, Xue Zheng Project Hope." "Rather than an elaborate memorial service and eulogies," she concluded, "this title is the most fitting tribute to our principal."

> September 20, 1995. Dear McTyeirean Grannies, greetings! All of us from the Yu Cai Senior Middle School Group send to you our most sincere welcome. Indeed, we are so grateful to you for giving us this opportunity to attend school. Some of us expected to find a job after we graduated from junior secondary school, to take on a bit of responsibility in support of our families. Some of us hoped to attend a secondary technical school, the sooner the better to find employment to earn money for our families. But, when we heard the news that Yu Cai had accepted us, all of us were wild with joy at this once in a lifetime opportunity. From the time we entered Yu Cai's gate, cherishing the excitement, we have felt from the depths of our hearts a profound sense of mission. Our mission is to come here to study to build our families, our villages, our hometowns. This is the hope that you have supporting us. This is also the hope of our families and villages and relatives who have sent us here. We are newcomers and have had to struggle hard. Yet we have already adjusted to our school life, and the school has organized exceptional teachers to work with us. Thus, we certainly will work hard, and in the future, with our accomplishments, we will return to our families to develop the economy of our families and villages. In fact, these accomplishments will represent our heartfelt thanks for your assistance. Indeed, already we are benefitting

from our well-rounded education, morally, intellectually, physical, aesthetically, and in our labor. We hold strict expectations for ourselves so that we may become successors to and builders of the next century.

At the end of October 1995 a ten-member delegation of McTyeire alumni, Number Three administrators, and friends attended ceremonies marking the inauguration of the Yu Cai Project. The event, accompanied by a schoolwide assembly featuring speeches and musical performances, was widely reported in provincial and national media, with sentimental articles and (patronizing) images of fathers, not knowing what to say, bowing to alumni, thankful that their daughters, "covered in dust from the countryside but with high hopes," could receive an education.

In striking contrast to Xue Zheng's strict but familial administrative style, He Jing noted in her opening address three keys to her "management strategy," "seeking survival through competition; seeking quality through effective administration; striving to run a first-class school." Yu Cai's students, all of whom are required to board on the school campus, wear simple uniforms made of cotton camouflage material. Asked if this military look was primarily for economy, He Jing shook her head and said that the school uniforms were designed to embody concretely values for students (students "of a lesser quality," she reminds me, "than you would find in key schools like Number Three") that are associated in North America with tough, working-class schools—"discipline, frugality, clear expectations, unbending regulations." On the surface the school's buildings, even by China's spartan standards, look like barracks. But inside this no-nonsense setting, He Jing explains, Yu Cai's pedagogy is "flexible and open. Because, unlike the 42 'McTyeire girls,' most students have come to Yu Cai for a second chance. Their high school entrance examination scores sometimes fall below the cut-off point for gaining entrance into regular public high schools. The students need encouragement—to discuss questions among themselves, to form close mentoring relationships with teachers and with each other."

He Jing guides her school with an eclectic mix of progressive and traditional views on schooling that take "moral education as a center for well-rounded students." "We believe that private schools look after the moral development and discipline of students more than their public school counterparts. We want students to know how to be good, valuable citizens, to be of use. Yes, we demand that students not leave the school grounds on their own. We regulate their healthy environments. But I also want to expand their horizons, take them on field trips, provide them outside lectures by teachers from Shanghai."

These experiences, she believes, are particularly important for her "McTyeire girls, who have so many expectations placed upon them." Their three-year curriculum, designed to follow State Education Commission guidelines for general academic high schools, includes three kinds of classes: "core" courses in mathematics, chemistry, physics, Chinese, politics, and English; "supplemental" courses in history, biology, physical education, and geography; and "electives" in computer science, music, calligraphy, art, and fashion design. He Jing is especially proud of these elective classes, which she presents to parents and the community as signposts of the school's educational mission, material resources, openness to reform in teaching methods, and quality of teacher preparation.

In reflecting on the students' academic progress, He Jing lists the girls' strengths and shortcomings in ways that mirror, almost identically, Number Three (and general Chinese) descriptions of how high school girls differ from, and begin to fall short of, their male peers.[19] The McTyeire girls "are compliant, exhibit excellent conduct and discipline. They are highly motivated to learn, love their school and classmates, respect their teachers and parents, and are grateful for the life-saving support from their donors. They are diligent, frugal, and willing to work hard. They appreciate the care and understanding of their principal and teachers. They also have a tremendous interest in learning English. However, they also have trouble overcoming homesickness. They lack self-confidence and are overly sensitive to criticism. They lack exposure to the outside world, are caught in the details of their daily lives that they cannot always put into perspective."

In the eyes of supportive parents Yu Cai provides a new possibility of future access for their daughters to both academic and technical training, the latter becoming more popular in many rural communities, where families believe that technical skills (rather than the slim hope of college) will "provide the single leap that takes the student over the rural gate."[20] The girls' villages do not have the expanding commercial economies that open up options after graduation, however, and parents also express anxiety about their daughters' futures, particularly that they might lose their daughters to jobs in Nanchang.

Despite such concerns, He Jing has been successful in convincing parents, and Number Three, of the efficacy of Yu Cai's training for its students' future options. Yu Cai's first class of students graduated in 1995. Although they had entry examination scores well below those of the average Nanchang regular high school student, 51 percent matriculated, upon graduation, to junior colleges and tertiary technical schools. In addition, 74 percent of the junior high school students that entered Yu Cai during its first year of operation were accepted by key high schools and senior secondary technical schools.

He Jing discusses these enviable results in the context of McTyeire's legacy, and its alumni's generosity, in publicity about her school's academic programs. In school speeches and written reports she notes that three of the forty-four outstanding women included in a volume on Chinese female doctorates, published as part of a series commemorating the Fourth World Conference on Women, were McTyeireans. Prospective students could easily interpret such remarks as if it were Yu Cai's heritage being discussed. Following an enthusiastic account of Yu Cai's history and its illustrious foreign donors, school brochures present a description of Yu Cai's school pin, "shaped like Jiangxi's borders, the white background signifying students growing up in purity and representing the sincere hope of the Jiangxi people for educating talent. A flower opens in the middle of this white field, sprouting green leaves and stem forming a *Y* (standing for the *y* in Yu Cai), with a red blossom (shaped like the *c* in Yu Cai)." "The young plant stands erect," He Jing points out, "like a celebrating figure, an educated youth contributing to China."

The Yu Cai-Number Three Partnership: A Study in Educational Prosperity and Disparity

> That individuals have value, that they are given a choice, that society rewards excellence and hard work, these are compelling messages. But China's educational reform process is also a case study in how efficiency is achieved at the expense of equity and how excellence is attained with the creation of disparity.
>   —Kai-ming Cheng, "A Decade's Reform in China's Education, Social Consequences and Implications for Research"

The development of the Yu Cai–Number Three partnership and the changing narrative of service upon which it has been justified parallels changing school policies in China's reform era that embody a contest between expansion and diversification, reflecting the contradictory goal, evident in Chinese educational policy since 1949, of balancing equality of educational opportunity with advanced training for economic development.[21] This contest was reinforced by two reforms in secondary education in the mid-1980s. The first reform redefined basic schooling by extending compulsory education from six to nine years. The second reform was diversification at the senior high school level. Insufficient vocational schooling, a legacy of Cultural Revolution policies to extend a common education to all students, was identified as the "weakest link" in Chinese education. In particular, the "underdevelopment" of vocational training was blamed for education's failure to provide employment options for youths. By 1990 China had come close to meeting its goal of vocationalizing half of its senior secondary schools. Expanding employment opportunities in cities like Shanghai made vocationalization efforts so successful that 60 percent of senior secondary pupils were enrolled in vocational programs, a trend that has continued, arguably making China's vocational education system the most comprehensive in the world.[22]

Coupled with expansion and diversification was the implementation of a "school responsibility system" in which increased autonomy and experimentation were overwhelmed by the quest for economic efficiency. The model of the efficient secondary school became popularized as state educational funding failed to keep up with teacher salaries and material costs. Although Chinese educators resisted equating educational quality with output measures, the qualitative dimensions of teaching and learning were preempted by economic concerns. Financing formulas designed to encourage schools to initiate profit-making schemes became remarkably widespread. By the early 1990s school-run enterprises engaged three-quarters of China's primary and secondary school students.

The simultaneous effort to increase access to and track secondary education benefited elite key schools like Number Three and, coupled with market reforms, laid the groundwork for the official approval of private schools like Yu Cai. Unfortunately, invigorated teaching and leadership in, and parental commitment to, China's most privileged schools were accompanied by shortfalls in educational provision for less prosperous regions of China, where only 3.8 percent of the population had attained a senior secondary school education by 1990—a proportion identical to the number of urban Chinese who had attained a college education. In fact, from 1982 to 1990 the average amount of schooling for Chinese citizens, currently between seven and eight years, increased on average by only three months.[23] This was not only a result of low government expenditures on education (a very low 2.5 percent of GDP between the period from 1952 to the present) but also the result of declining public confidence in the relationship between formal schooling and social mobility. It is also probably a result of educational decentralization, which has meant that "the central government has lost its influence in guiding and supervising education at and below the provincial level."[24]

As China pursues the course of educational diversification, which involves greater commitment to vocational training that has direct business linkages, and continued devolution of school funding and authority, schools become localized, commercially driven, highly competitive, and anxious institutions. In 1993 local governments contributed 87 percent of the total governmental expenditure on education. In 1995 the contribution to total educational expenditures in China on the part of the central government was a mere 11 percent. The fact of the matter is that this mobilization of local resources (which has been so controversial that nearly half of China's provinces at one point called for a reversal of educational devolution) has had the effect of making schools much more community than state institutions. As economic conditions in China's communities become more diverse, so do their schools.[25]

The widening gap between China's haves and have-nots, between Number Three students and their Yu Cai sisters, is indicative of a pattern that influences not just the provision of education but all basic services. Disparities in access to schooling, as in health care, are fueled by fiscal and management decentralization, escalating costs in the form of user fees, and the lack of governmental mechanisms for redirecting funds to those who need them most. While China's educational services are not as severely strained as basic health provision (90 percent of cooperative medical services collapsed in the 1980s), an individual school's finances nevertheless are determined largely by the wealth of the local community.

The Yu Cai project is a clear example of how prosperity and increasing pluralism in Chinese education is, paradoxically, creating disparity. Unfortunately, even if they had the inclination, state leaders, who, through policy and by default, have handed over financial and managerial educational responsibilities to local governments, are in no position to implement compensatory programs for the poor. Instead, schools are increasingly shaped by the concerns and resources of specific communities, which are, in turn, motivated by local, often unstable market forces. This situation raises a key normative question that has animated any number of conversations among Number Three and Yu Cai educators and their McTyeirean supporters: "How can education respond to the market economy without entering the market?"[26]

Private School Alternatives

Private schools like Yu Cai have emerged as the new symbol of education's exchange value. Lack of seats in secondary schools, lack of state funding, irrelevance of the public school curriculum to (particularly rural) students' lives and employment opportunities, rigidity and control in the public sector that inhibit reform, and restricted entrance to quality education were among the reasons for the rise of private schools in large numbers in the 1990s. As parents, business leaders, and citizens see clearly that relying on the government will not solve the shortage of educational funding and resources, private education has become a major force in educational reform, as Chan and Mok discuss in a previous section in this volume.

This process, already begun in the early 1980s, was recognized and legitimized by the state in 1987, with the publication of the document "Provisional Regulation on the Establishment of Schools by Societal Forces," which contained concrete provisions for the establishment and management of nongovernmental schools. By 1993, a year after He Jing founded Yu Cai, the "Outline of Chinese Educational Reform and Development" confirmed that "the state adopts a policy of active encouragement, vigorous support, correct guidance and enhanced management of schools established according to law by social organizations and individual citizens."[27]

Nationally, the expansion of private schooling has been breathtaking. By the end of 1993 there were roughly twenty thousand nongovernmental schools of different types (including kindergartens) across the country. Approximately seven hundred of these institutions were secondary schools (enrolling a total of 130,000 students). By 1995 private schools absorbed as many as 4 percent of all students in China.[28]

Yu Cai differs dramatically from the "elite" urban private schools that have featured so dramatically in international reports on Chinese school privatization. These schools' high tuition and fees (10,000–20,000 yuan annually) represent, primarily, demands for quality education by wealthy parents whose children have failed to enter prestigious key schools or high-quality technical high schools. Elite private schools are often boarding schools that offer comfortable living arrangements, small class size, English language and computer competency, extracurricular activities, and generous custodial provisions to attract and accommodate busy professional and divorced parents. They hire qualified contract teachers with high salaries and seek to develop a "whole dragon" system of schooling that provides a route to social mobility (from primary school through college) entirely outside the state-run educational system. They define their management and educational responsibilities with the vocabulary of performance and competition—with the student conceived as an independent client. In contrast, schools such as Yu Cai are designed mainly for students who fail to pass the examination to enter senior high school. Students enroll in these schools in the hope of having a second chance at social mobility. Because the schools can charge only the very low fees that the families they serve can afford, their programs suffer from inadequate teaching equipment and personnel.

The quality and intentions of private schools vary tremendously, with the crassest sort of proprietary schools being well represented. The Yu Cai School and the Xue Zheng Project it supports remind us, however, that in China private schools are more than just entrepreneurial responses to changing economic and political forces in Chinese society. At their best, and Yu Cai does not yet have the resources to rank in that category, private schools, more than their public school counterparts, provide sites of innovation in: (1) approaches to teaching; (2) recognition of students' rights; (3) development of artistic technique and creativity; and (4) a depoliticized curriculum (a depoliticized humanism). Private schools have the potential for letting talented educators, freed from the constraints of the state teaching outline, put their educational philosophies into practice and make full use of the untapped talents of veteran teachers who have had to retire from the public school system by age fifty or fifty-five.

Likewise, private schools are not uniformly contributing to increasing levels of educational inequality, precisely because they fill educational gaps left by a state unable or unwilling to provide sufficient schooling for increasing (and increasingly diverse) educational demands by the public. Chinese schools, once tightly linked to national interests, have been gradually reshaped to reflect a combination of interests derived from powerful social groups and "market" forces. In other words, social groups like the McTyeire alumni and individuals like He Jing have usurped social functions of education previously monopolized by the state.

The Rise of Girls' Schooling

Due to the saliency of gender issues in economic development, Chinese officials have embraced female education and joined international efforts, such as the signing of the 1990 World Conference on Education for All Declaration, that "target" female education as an urgent priority. China's Program for the Development of Chinese Women (1995–2000), as well as its Goals 2000 plan to eradicate illiteracy and universalize nine years of schooling by the end of the decade, identify girls' education as the linchpin of development. Yet, as the State Education Commission encourages public agencies, nongovernmental organizations, and private citizens to promote girls' education, girls and women, particularly those living in China's poorest regions, continue to pay a high educational price for market socialism. As families pick up an increasing percentage of the costs of schooling, as communities struggle to keep schools funded, and as girls leave school to work at home or in local enterprises, female literacy rates and school attainment in

China's villages and towns stagnate. Girls between the ages of six and fourteen constituted two-thirds of the ten million students who dropped out of Chinese schools in 1996. Evaluated in the context of the social disruptions of the last decade, such figures explain why "gender has exploded as an arena for the expression of popular discontent, conflicts with state power, and deeply felt longings for prosperity."[29]

The reappearance of all-girls' schools and classes in China reflects most distinctively the increasing plurality of Chinese school experiences.[30] Girls' schools serving exceptionally diverse constituencies have appeared in cities as well as in the countryside, in developed as well as in underdeveloped areas of the country. Offering public, private, academic, and vocational options for girls from advantaged and poor and "minority" families, the missions and curricula of girls' schools vary dramatically, even when they train girls for identical labor markets, and raise intriguing questions regarding how class and gender intersect to make schools gateways or barriers to the full participation of girls in Chinese society.

A private vocational girls school in Beijing, for example, requires that all its pupils study martial arts, wrestling, driving, computer literacy, and English—for the purpose of "opening as many routes of employment to young women as possible." The school admits girls who have been screened out by the senior high school entrance examination. The formal and informal curricula are explicitly planned to help girls become confident in their abilities and be more employable in Beijing's competitive job market—while also providing them the option of heading toward higher education. In contrast, a public vocational all-girls' school, also in Beijing, describes its approach to girls' education as cultivating the "special characteristics of Eastern women." Its senior secondary school pupils study cosmetology, fashion, and tourism—making beds and pouring drinks with grace and deliberation. The students are trained for popular (and very gender-stereotyped) jobs in the rising service and foreign trade sector in the country.[31]

Coupled with renewed and strong essentialism in gender roles, these contrasting approaches to girls' education underscore how relatively high educational levels and gender awareness are not necessarily linked, nor are schools always viewed, even by educators who think daily about what it means to teach girls, as dynamically gendered institutions. Nor surprisingly, trends documented by researchers that indicate how all but the highest-scoring female students in Chinese secondary schools adjust downward their educational and professional expectations[32] are rarely discussed by teachers, while such trends often are viewed by female students as simply "the way things are."[33]

Conclusion: McTyeire's Narrative of Public Service

A second group of forty-two girls, the Yu Cai Xue Zheng class of 2000, began studying at Yu Cai in September 1997. According to He Jing, they will continue the McTyeirean legacy, as the class of 1998 begins its last year of schooling. McTyeirean alumni who have supported both groups of girls report unexpected emotions, remembering anew the potential of education to transform identity. They do not call their philanthropy a form of intervention. Yet, as Yu Cai girls see themselves, for the first time, not just desirous of but deserving of a high school education, they rewrite their own identities, aligning their expectations with those of a very successful group of "grannies" and "aunties."

> Class of 1951, "Engineering Hope across the Pacific." My first thought—what a wonderfully altruistic project to allow me to exercise my social responsibility. When it came down to having to write a check, I wondered: my money could be siphoned by bureaucratic corruption in China. Nonetheless, I sent the check. This project was just like all other charities—save the environment, save the endangered animals, save the children—only a financial commitment. Then I was to have to write to the student—what could I say? I could still speak but to have to write with the aid of a dictionary—really! But if you make a trip like I did, you will find that you had made the best buy with your dollars. Each student's life touched me deeply: each family history was framed in an unshakable tradition of feminine devaluation and fierce struggle to survive rural poverty. To the students, the sponsors were real generous people that changed the course of their lives. We were not just anonymous charity dollars. We opened the doors of high school education for them. They wanted to communicate their gratitude to us individually. They studied hard even though their village schooling rendered them uncompetitive with urban students. They did not want to fail themselves, their parents, their village, but, most of all, their sponsors. Parents who wanted their daughters to escape the hardships they endured now believed that perhaps their offspring could finally break out to find another livelihood. If and when you make a trip to Nanchang, you will experience firsthand that you have taken part in making a difference through engineering hope for someone, possibly like you once were—but for the grace of God.

Becoming a part of McTyeire and Number Three's history has given Yu Cai's McTyeire girls a powerful narrative with which to replace their previous designations as poor rural girls in need of welfare, even salvation. In this sense, through the Yu Cai project, McTyeirean donors have indeed re-inscribed their own life stories and, in handing them over, have given these girls a powerful story to live by. The story is illustrated to help the girls place themselves historically, often by a photograph of Auntie Song Qingling, when she was a McTyeire girl, jauntily posed, one knee raised, mischievous. Students are also shown pictures of the green sweep of McTyeire / Number Three's lawn, its stained-glass windows and science laboratories. There are exemplary teachers and students, eminent guest speakers, actresses, and dancers. And there are the donors themselves, those scattered "peaches and plums" who have enriched the world with their achievements. Above all, these pictures and their accompanying narrative give the girls a vocabulary of control and of identity.

This may not be such a small legacy. China's changing economy, the redefinition of schooling as a personal investment, and the withdrawal of the state from private affairs and public services have rendered people's understanding of their relationships to culture, the state, and the economy increasingly complex and open to public scrutiny.[34] The separation of political from economic power as well as the depoliticization of daily life have been credited with simultaneously "enlarging the space for popular initiative" and accelerating "the public hunger for autonomous and protected social lives."[35] This mixed message about the possibility for Chinese citizens to reappropriate the public sphere in a way that is meaningful to their everyday lives provides a clue for evaluating the social significance of the legacy of public service passed from McTyeireans to the girls they sponsor.

Certainly, neither He Jing nor Number Three advisors nor McTyeireans have seen their experiment as any expression of democracy or harbinger of civil society. The Yu Cai Project, for them, is intended to transform individual lives, not social or political structures. Nevertheless, the rich associational life that swirls around the project and the attempts by so many McTyeirean, Number Three, and Yu Cai individuals to mobilize resources for joint purposes might be interpreted as a form of negotiated participation that is neither economic nor political but cultural, "granting different groups the right to have their own stories told in the space reserved for public discourse, a space that has traditionally been restricted."[36] From this perspective, in reclaiming the social purposes of education that they were taught to admire and serve, McTyeirean women have helped create what Ping-Chun Hsiung in this volume calls "autonomous spaces" or what Ningsha Zhong and Ruth Hayhoe refer to in this volume as a "space for practical action." The ideal of community service that their project embodies has helped Yu Cai, and its students, find a public voice, a way to be "political," a way "to take one's place in whatever discourse is essential to action and the right to have one's part matter."[37]

NOTES

1. I am deeply grateful to countless members of the McTyeire, Number Three, and Yu Cai communities who have made this study possible. In particular, I wish to thank Chen Jingyu, Number Three's librarian; Rosalyn Koo, graduate of the McTyeire class of 1947; He Jing, the principal of Yu Cai; the late Xue Zheng, McTyeire's honorary principal; Jean Craig, McTyeire's last surviving missionary educator; and the fine staff at the United Methodist Church's Global Ministries Commission on Archives and History, for their support and generosity. Colgate University, the Spencer Foundation, the National Endowment for the Humanities, and the History of Christianity in China Project have funded various portions of this study. Finally, I wish to thank Daniel Bays, Judith Liu, and Ruth Hayhoe for their thoughtful comments on various drafts of my work. All undocumented quotations are based on the author's personal interviews.

2. St. Mary's was an Episcopalian school informally affiliated with St. John's University. Its grounds were taken over by the Shanghai Textile Engineering Institute in 1952.

3. Oswald E. and Anna Muse Brown, *Life and Letters of Laura Askew Haygood* (Nashville: Publishing House of the Methodist Episcopal Church South, 1904), 92–94.

4. Sarah Coles McElroy's discussion in this volume of the founding of the first Chinese-run schools for females in Shanghai illustrates how the diverse interests of nation building, revolution, and desire to maintain social stability intersected in the curricula designed for girls and women.

5. Nie's daughter was one of seven girls in McTyeire's first class. Enrollment expanded to twenty-nine in 1897. These students' fathers included three officials, the manager of the imperial telegraph, an editor of a Shanghai newspaper, and five Episcopalian and Methodist ministers. By 1903 the school had ninety-nine pupils, thirty of whom were Christians.

6. See Jane Hunter, *The Gospel of Gentility: American Women Missionaries at the Turn-of-the-Century China* (New Haven: Yale University Press, 1984).

7. See Heidi Ross, "Cradle of Female Talent: The McTyeire Home and School, 1892–1937," in Daniel H. Bays, ed., *Christianity in China* (Stanford: Stanford University Press, 1996), 209–27.

8. Ida Belle Lewis, *The Education of Girls in China* (New York: Teachers College, Columbia University, 1919), 89.

9. Life history interviews with nearly seventy-five alumni have been conducted between the years of 1989 and 1996. Many of these are recorded in Heidi Ross, *Telling Women's Lives* (San Francisco: McTyeire Alumnae Association, 1993).

10. See the essay by Ryan Dunch in this volume.

11. See Jane Hunter, *Gospel of Gentility;* and Zilong Chen, "Nuzi rencai de yaolan" (Cradle of female talent), *Renmin Ribao,* 13 August 1987, 1.

12. Carolyn Heilbrun, *Writing a Woman's Life* (New York: Ballantine, 1988).

13. Barbara D. Metcalf, "Presidential Address: Too Little and Too Much: Reflections on Muslims in the History of India," *Journal of Asian Studies* 4, no. 54 (November 1995): 951–967.

14. Mary Catherine Bateson, *Composing a Life* (New York: Plume, 1990), 34.

15. Costs for the school's first four semesters included: building leases at thirty thousand yuan per semester; teacher salaries (30 percent of the budget); teaching equipment purchases (19 percent of the budget); construction and improvement of the school grounds (10 percent of the budget); recruitment of new students and advertising (8 percent of the budget); utilities (8 percent of the budget); school bus (7 percent of the budget); travel and promotion (6 percent of the budget); classroom and dormitory furnishings and maintenance (5 percent of the budget); reserve funds (5 percent of the budget); scholarships (3 percent of the budget); and teacher benefits (2 percent of the budget). The significant debts incurred in the school's first two years of operation was made up by 300,000 yuan in individual investments and a 65,000 yuan loan.

16. These costs are far greater than the government's estimated cost, 300 yuan each year, for keeping a girl who lives at home in school. The U.S. $300 (about 2,940 yuan at the time) was divided and used as follows: 38 percent tuition, 10 percent books and supplies, 14 percent dormitory facilities, 4 percent schools uniforms, and 34 percent food. The annual cost for each participant has since risen to U.S. $350, and, for the second class of students beginning their studies in 1997, alumnae are raising between U.S. $500–1,000 per year for each pupil.

17. The average annual per capita income for Jiangxi village families was 1,537.36 yuan in 1995.

18. Jiangxi province, located in eastern China, is categorized as belonging economically to China's "developing central" region (as is Inner Mongolia, Heilongjiang, Jilin, Shanxi, Henan, Hubei, Anhui, and Hunan). Of China's twenty-nine provinces and municipalities, Jiangxi ranked twenty-fifth in 1982 and twenty-third in 1993 in composite average years of schooling—7.3 and 7.6 years, respectively. In 1995, 43.78 percent of Jiangxi's junior high school graduates continued on to some form of high school training (slightly lower than the national average).

19. For a discussion of conceptions of how gender influences learning, see Heidi Ross, "Growing Up in a Chinese Secondary School for Girls," *Journal of Women and Gender Studies* 4, no. 1 (1993): 111–36.

20. Stanley Rosen, "The Impact of Economic Reform on Chinese Education: Markets and the Growth of Differentiation" (paper presented at the Conference on Social Consequences of Chinese Economic Reform, John K. Fairbank Center, Harvard University, May 1997).

21. Heidi Ross, "The Crisis in Chinese Secondary Schooling," in Irving Epstein, ed., *Chinese Education: Problems, Policies, and Prospects* (New York: Garland Press, 1991), 66–108. The field research upon which conclusions regarding current trends in Chinese schooling are based was conducted between 1995 and 1997 with support from Colgate University and the Spencer Foundation.

22. The figure in Shanghai is now closer to 70 percent and a topic of great debate.

23. X. B. Simon Zhao and Christopher S. P. Tong, "Spatial Disparity in China's

Educational Development: An Assessment from the Perspective of Economic Growth," *China Information* 11, no. 4 (1997): 14–40.

24. Ibid., 20.

25. See Cheng Kai-ming, "A Decade's Reform."

26. Lynn Paine, "Progress and Problems in China's Educational Reform," in William A. Joseph, ed., *China Briefing, 1994* (Boulder: Westview Press: 1994), 113–41.

27. Zhu Kaixuan, "Guanyu minban xuexiao de yixie wenti" (Problems associated with private schools) (address to the Chinese People's Political Consultative Conference, Beijing, 1994), 5.

28. Julia Kwong, "Introduction," *Chinese Education and Society* 29, no. 5 (1996): 3–5.

29. Christina Gilmarten et al., eds., *Engineering China* (Cambridge: Harvard University Press, 1994), 3.

30. In interviews conducted at three girls' schools in 1996, I was told there were over one hundred all-girl schools and colleges in China.

31. General information regarding particular private and girls' schools were obtained as a result of fieldwork conducted in eighteen schools in 1995–97.

32. Ibid.

33. Ross, "Growing Up."

34. Deborah Davis and Steven Harrell, eds., *Chinese Families in the Post-Mao Era* (Berkeley: University of California Press, 1993).

35. Martin K. Whyte, "Urban China: A Civil Society in the Making?" in Arthur L. Rosenbaum, ed., *State and Society in China: The Consequence of Reform* (Boulder: Westview, 1992), 88.

36. Walter Feinberg, *Japan and the Pursuit of a New American Identity* (New York: Routledge, 1993), 168.

37. Heilbrun, *Writing a Woman's Life*, 18.

Ethnic Minority Girls on Chinese School Benches: Gender Perspectives on Minority Education

Mette Halskov Hansen

This essay looks at how Chinese school education may influence minority students' gender and ethnic identities by changing their attitudes toward religion, their roles as men and women, and their expectations of life.[1] I argue that for many women belonging to ethnic minorities in China, participation in school education offers the opportunity to find jobs outside their villages and thereby enhance their status in Chinese society, while at the same time it instills in them feelings of cultural inadequacy. As a result, many of these women express contradictory feelings of, on the one hand, having gained pride as women through their (successful) participation in the state education system and, on the other hand, of having developed feelings of inferiority based on their ethnic affiliation.

This essay introduces a subject—Chinese education of ethnic minority girls and women—that has so far received little attention in the existing scholarly literature, both Chinese and Western, on women, education, or ethnic minorities in China. To be sure, Chinese scholars (and officials) have long shown an abiding concern with the development of school education among the peoples officially recognized as national minorities (*shaoshu minzu*). Numerous books, articles, and statistical compendiums are published every year describing the continuous development of "minority education" (*minzu jiaoyu*). These sources mostly demonstrate the low existing level of education among the national minorities and suggest ways for improving the condition of schools and education in minority areas. The Chinese state regards low levels of education among national minorities as an obstacle to modernization as well as being inconsistent with the official ideology of equality among the country's constituent nationalities and therefore also a potential source of ethnic conflict. Developing education among the minorities and paying attention to their own demands and needs for special educational measures is considered crucial to achieving the "unity of the nationalities" (*minzu tuanjie*) and is therefore accorded ideological (though not necessarily corresponding economic) priority.[2] Yet the specific question of providing educational opportunities to women belonging to ethnic minorities is rarely given special consideration in scholarly and political publications in China. While it is often noted that women belonging to national minorities have the highest illiteracy rates in China, Chinese discussions of minority education seldom discuss the issue in a local context or seek to analyze in depth the reasons behind this phenomenon.

This essay seeks to shed light on how minority women experience the Chinese educational system through a discussion of the ways in which gender perceptions were presented and discussed by female minority students during recent fieldwork in the province of Yunnan. Research was carried out in two locations in Yunnan: the Tai Autonomous Prefecture of Sipsong Panna and the Naxi Autonomous County of Lijiang. There are certain similarities between the political status and educational situation of women and national minorities as social groups in China: women and minorities alike have constitutionally guaranteed rights to equality, with the Han nationality and men, respectively, and, generally speaking, both groups also have a lower educational level than their male and Han counterparts. Some scholars have even drawn attention to the parallel between the construction of the very category of *shaoshu minzu* (national minorities) as a central element in the official nation-building project and ideology of ethnic equality and the category of *funü* (women) in the official ideology of gender equality.[3] Stevan Harrell suggests that, "in both cases, there is an objectification of a category that is peripheral (or, perhaps, in the linguistic sense, simply marked) with respect to the normal category of the civilizers, who are, in the first instance, male, and in the second, Han."[4] Others have pointed out that the academic and professional role models presented in contemporary school texts invariably tend to be male.[5] We may add that they are also all Han.

The few textbook stories that do portray ethnic minorities tend to confirm an image of poor, childlike, grateful people in need of help. Thus, for example, one contemporary primary school text contains a story about the poor Miao village in which the only Han Chinese family serves as a model by offering unselfish help to their poor, isolated Miao neighbor.[6] The feminization and eroticization of minorities in China (forcefully demonstrated by several scholars)[7] also has an increasingly significant commercial side that both enforces and reproduces stereotypes of "minority women," especially in minority areas that are popular among tourists, such as the Sipsong Panna region discussed here. As I shall attempt to show, such exoticized and eroticized representations of minorities and minority women often become part of these women's early school experience and therefore play a significant role in the transformation of their gender and ethnic identities as they prepare to make their way in Chinese society.

Minority Females' Participation in School Education

Official Chinese statistics reveal that, in spite of the CCP's egalitarian ideology of equality between men and women, women in China, on the whole, lag behind men in their level of education and constitute a minority in occupations that confer political power, social status, and high income.[8] Chinese social scientists have frequently attempted to explain this continued gender inequality in education in terms of the persistent negative influence of traditional conceptions of gender roles, justified by and partly derived from Confucian ideology. Surveys have shown, for example, that families have an important say in whether or not girls continue in school and that, in cases in which families must choose, most rural families prefer to educate sons. Educating a son is considered a better investment since he will remain in the family, while daughters eventually marry out.[9] In addition, Stanley Rosen and other scholars have argued that the modernization policy adopted in the 1980s has had certain negative effects on women's prospects for achieving equality of opportunity in education and therefore also in other spheres of social life.[10] For instance, in areas where households have access to employment opportunities, such as in local industries, it is often the male members of the household who take up wage labor, while the female household members are left to carry out domestic work, raise livestock, and cultivate the fields. Child labor is an important reason behind the lower level of school attendance among girls compared to boys.[11]

Not surprisingly, educational levels are lowest among rural girls and women. Likewise, as in many other countries, the rate of female participation is lowest at the higher levels of education. In 1994, 32 percent of females over fifteen years of age were illiterate, and women made up 70 percent of all illiterates in China.[12] In addition, one recent Chinese survey has shown that 83 percent of the more than 2.7 million children receiving no schooling in 1987 were girls and that 80 percent of the 2 million new illiterates each year are females.[13] At the same time, official statistics on female educational levels are rarely presented in relation to women's official ethnic status. It is indisputable, however, that minority women as a whole have the highest illiteracy rates. There are also huge discrepancies in the level of educational attainment among the fifty-six officially recognized nationalities as well as among men and women belonging to different nationalities. Nonetheless, according to official statistics, the fifty-five officially recognized national minorities tend to have fewer students and graduates at all levels of education than the majority nationality, the Han. Statistics from Yunnan show that its residents have among the lowest educational level of all provinces. Yet the provincial capital of Kunming and its surrounding areas, all of which are inhabited mostly by Han Chinese, have a much higher average level of education than the border and mountainous regions of the province, which are mostly inhabited by national minorities. Does this mean, then, that minorities have a lower educational level than the Han in Yunnan, or does it first of all confirm the profound differences between education in rural and urban areas, regardless of ethnic affiliation?

There is no easy answer to this question, and only local studies of the educational environment of men and women of different ethnic groups may reveal when, how, and why some ethnic minorities have lower attendance and completion rates than others. Many of the problems involved in popularizing education among women are in fact similar in rural Han and minority areas. In addition, however, it may also be significant that many ethnic minorities had no tradition of Chinese education, even among boys, before it was introduced in the 1950s, while, for some, Chinese education continues to be regarded as a foreign, imposed institution incompatible with their own ways of living and of perceiving the world.[14]

A second problem encountered when evaluating Chinese statistics on minority educational levels relates to the fact that all people in China have been classified in terms of fifty-six officially recognized nationalities (*minzu*). Educational statistics based on these official groupings may be highly misleading, however, since people classified as members of the same nationality may very well live far apart from one another, have no interaction, speak mutually unintelligible languages, and have different religious traditions and different histories of adopting or not adopting Chinese education.[15] Official statistics obliterate these potentially significant differences by lumping all the members of an officially recognized nationality into one group. Thus, accurate information on, for instance, an ethnic group like the Nuosu (classified as Yizu) or the Tai (Lue) (classified as Daizu) can only be obtained by means of local studies of the areas in which they actually live.[16]

Only scattered statistics are available on the educational participation of minority females in Yunnan. Educational departments within the local county governments I visited kept statistics that divided students and graduates into different nationalities and recorded the total number of girls and boys in school. But, since the two sets of figures are not interpolated, it is impossible to determine the relative participation rates of different nationalities within the same locality. The situation is further complicated by the fact that in some localities specific ethnic groups are singled out for preferential admission criteria. For these reasons the most reliable information we have on the local educational participation of national minorities comes from localities in which a single nationality predominates. In the following sections I first briefly describe the main features of female education in the two minority-populated areas of Lijiang and Sipsong Panna and then proceed to a detailed examination of the relationship between school education and gender perceptions in the two localities.

Lijiang

The majority of the population in Lijiang prefecture belong to the Naxi nationality, who constituted 58.4 percent of Lijiang's population in 1994. The Naxi have a long history of Confucian education and have often been singled out in popular and scholarly publications in China for their success in Chinese education, whether modern or Confucian.[17] Confucian education among the Naxi was directed exclusively almost toward boys; very few Naxi girls participated. This male bias continued with the introduction of modern education. My interviews with Naxi who had attended school or had been teachers under the early years of the Communist regime in the 1950s and early 1960s revealed that Lijiang's schools continued to be dominated by boys during this period and that it was common for classes of fifty students to contain only two or three girl pupils.

In national statistics the Naxi figure prominently as one of the few national minorities with a high percentage of students and graduates at all levels of education. This overall picture of success, however, masks significant problems and weaknesses in Naxi education. From my fieldwork in Naxi villages (and as recognized by the local Naxi government) even among such a small nationality as the Naxi (277,250 people in 1990) there are considerable discrepancies between urban and rural Naxi, with rural Naxi having by far the highest dropout rates. Moreover, while official publications on Naxi education in Lijiang rarely discuss the issue of female educational participation, Naxi education in Lijiang continues to be marked by a stark gender inequality that resembles that of rural Han Chinese areas. According to one source, Naxi made up 19.6 percent of all illiterates and half-literates in Yunnan in 1990, while Han accounted for 23.6 percent. In Lijiang prefecture 26 percent of the population was illiterate or half-literate in 1990, compared to only 16 percent in Kunming. When gender differences are taken into account, 64 percent of Lijiang women over twelve years of age were illiterate or half-literate, compared to 34 percent of men (1982 figures).[18] When we consider only the Naxi population of Lijiang, 38 percent of persons over twelve years of age were illiterate or half-literate in 1982, or nearly 23 percent of Naxi men and over 52 percent of Naxi women. The statistics suggest, and fieldwork confirmed, that the Naxi on the whole have a relatively high participation rate in all levels of education; it is also clear, however, that there is a clear tendency among Naxi to favor the education of boys over girls. In one Lijiang secondary school 74.5 percent of all graduates between 1985 and 1991 were male. In another lower secondary school in which nearly all students were Naxi (191 out of 204) 62 percent of students were boys, and only 38 percent were girls. All but two of the fourteen teachers (all Naxi) in this school were men, a pattern replicated in the county as a whole, where 72 percent of all teachers are men.[19]

Thus, the general situation of the Naxi is a high level of Chinese education with a gender bias in favor of males. The other ethnic minorities present in Lijiang, such as the Lisu, Miao, Premi, and others, have much lower levels of Chinese education than the Naxi; their dropout rates are higher, their illiteracy rates are higher, and their schools are often in dire condition. In Yunnan as a whole, the Lisu nationality had a female illiteracy and half-literacy rate of over 85 percent in 1982 (57.6 percent among males), while among the Miao the rate was even higher, at nearly 91 percent of females and 57 percent of males.[20]

Sipsong Panna

National statistics on the participation of members of the Dai nationality in Chinese education are not very helpful for understanding the educational level of the Tai people (an ethnic group officially considered to be part of the Dai nationality) living in the prefecture of Sipsong Panna. This is because the Tai in Sipsong Panna (284,639 people in 1990) make up only 25 percent of all people in China classified as Dai. National statistics on the Dai nationality portray a much higher level of participation in Chinese education than is the case among the Tai in Sipsong Panna.

Interestingly, whereas the Naxi have a relatively high participation rate but a clear gender bias in favor of males, the Tai in Sipsong Panna have a comparatively poor participation rate overall, including high dropout rates and relatively few students at the level of senior secondary and tertiary education, but less gender bias and therefore a comparatively high degree of female participation in Chinese education. Many Tai school dropouts are boys rather than girls, a phenomenon that is partly explained by the Tai's long-established custom of sending boys between the age of seven and fifteen to local Theravada Buddhist monasteries as novices to receive full-time religious training. This does not mean that most Tai girls remain in school, yet it presents the interesting case of an ethnic group whose proportion of girls enrolled in basic education is as high as that of boys and who also tend to have more girls continuing into higher levels of education than boys. I shall return to this later.

In the whole of Sipsong Panna prefecture over 89 percent of school-age children were enrolled in primary school in 1990. Among those enrolled, 55 percent completed five years of schooling, of which more than 88 percent actually graduated from primary school. Fully 76 percent of primary school students belonged to national minorities, compared to only 58 percent of students in lower secondary school and 31.7 percent in higher secondary school.[21] In 1995 there were a total of 4,356 registered Buddhist novices (all boys, most of them Tai) in Sipsong Panna. Among the school-age novices over 67 percent were also enrolled in school. These figures are only partly revealing, however, for we do not know the total number of school-age Tai boys nor the percentage of school-age Tai boys and girls attending school. My interviews in village schools showed that many boys, and especially novices, were enrolled in school without actually attending on a regular basis, and many dropped out after a few years.

Concerning illiteracy rates, the official figure for the Sipsong Panna population as a whole in 1990 was 25.75 percent illiterate or half-literate. One researcher reported that about half of the illiterates in Sipsong Panna in 1990 were Tai (who made up about one-third of the total population) and that 68 percent of all illiterates in the prefecture were women.[22] During interviews I conducted in Sipsong Panna villages many women told me that they had been recorded by the census takers as being literate simply for having participated in a few months of literacy training (mostly in Tai and Chinese) at some time in their lives, even though they were not able to read and write today.

In the early 1980s, when the official policy toward religious expression became more relaxed, the Tai began to rebuild their Buddhist temples. Consequently, some local officials expressed concern that some schools practically became "girls' schools" as many Tai boys left to become Buddhist novices. A number of new measures were then introduced, with varying degrees of success, to convince parents to send their sons to the Chinese schools.[23] Such so-called girls' schools no longer exist, but teachers in most village primary schools still complain about male novices who enroll but rarely turn up, do not do their homework, or drop out after a few years. A few statistics from the southern county of Mengla in Sipsong Panna show that the proportion of girls in school is indeed higher than in most other rural areas of Yunnan. The figures include all primary and regular secondary students in Mengla and are therefore not limited to Tai students. Since my fieldwork and local school statistics both show that other local ethnic groups such as the Akha tend to favor boys over girls in schooling, it is conceivable that the actual proportion of Tai girls to Tai boys is even higher than the following figures suggest (see tables 1 and 2).[24]

Educational patterns among the other minority ethnic groups in Sipsong Panna resemble to a large extent that of the rural areas of Lijiang: poverty is often a major reason for very low school attendance rates, and there is a tendency, among the Akha for instance, to favor education of sons when there is no possibility of providing for the education of all children. The Blang (and the few Kammu) are the only Theravada Buddhists in the area apart from the Tai, but most of them live under very poor conditions, and boys and girls alike have low levels of education. I visited several Blang villages that had temples with novices (who often could not read or write and had no monks to train them) and where the authorities had recently closed down the local primary school for lack of students.[25] In addition to the problem of convincing students to remain in school in these poor areas, it is also difficult for local education

TABLE 1.   Female Students in All Primary Schools in Mengla County, 1988

	Grade 1	Grade 2	Grade 3	Grade 4	Grade 5	Grade 6
Number of Students	3,572	3,147	2,590	2,340	2,294	1,775
Female Students	1,596	1,508	1,245	1,061	1,092	835
Percentage of Female Population	44.68	47.92	48.07	45.34	47.60	47.04

TABLE 2.   Female Students in Lower and Higher Secondary Schools in Mengla County, 1988

Grade of Lower and Higher Secondary Schools	1	2	3	4	5	6
Number of Students	1,050	710	631	203	177	141
Number of Female Students	503	313	291	105	92	71
Percent of Female Students	47.90	44.08	46.12	51.72	51.98	50.35

departments to find teachers who are willing to stay in these villages. They are poorly paid, face a harsh existence, and do not speak the local language; consequently, many of them look for a transfer as quickly as possible.

Daughters in School? Parental Attitudes

Campaigns for improving school attendance and graduation rates have mostly been directed toward parents. In the 1950s, when the Communist Party began its attempts to popularize Chinese state education in Sipsong Panna, work teams held large meetings for parents, trying to convince them to send their children to school; they organized literacy classes for grown-ups, and teachers went to the private homes of parents and argued for sending children to school. Later on, in the 1980s, parents in some Tai townships had to pay a deposit when a child started school and would lose it if the child dropped out. To a lesser degree, campaigns were directed toward monks, who were encouraged to let their novices go to school. Today Tai parents are widely criticized by local teachers and administrators for not paying sufficient attention to their children's education, that is, Chinese state-run school education. They are frequently reproached for being indifferent to whether or not their sons drop out and become novices and for readily agreeing when young Tai girls want to leave school and marry early. In the critical words of one educational cadre:

> The Aini [Akha] are best at studying, the Tai are the worst. They refuse to change their habits and they marry early. Even when they do not marry early, they do not want to study. The Tai are not interested in studying and it is the same with the Blang. Most of those who continue are Aini. They are better in enduring hard times, and their marriage customs are like those of us Han Chinese, that is, they do not marry so early. They have more contacts with us Han Chinese. Every year two hundred new students start here, but the majority of them have to be Tai according to our rules. That is because the Tai make up the principal ethnic group here. But anyway, there is always a majority of Aini students here because so many Tai drop out. When other minorities drop out of school it is because their family is poor and cannot afford to keep them in school. The Tai stop because of their customs. Their boys first learn Tai script in the temples and then when they go to school their Chinese is very bad, they do not understand teachers and they quickly drop out. We actually do not want all those Tai students here, but we have to take them.[26]

Unlike the Tai boys, Tai girls do not become novices and therefore participation in state schooling is their only opportunity for formal education. While most rural Tai parents I interviewed were concerned that at least one son should become a novice for some time, they were rather indifferent about whether or not their children would attend the local Chinese school. If the children themselves wanted to attend they would agree to it, and, if not, parents often took the view that they had no way of forcing their children to attend school. Interestingly, however, those parents who only had daughters tended to be more positive toward school education than parents with sons. This was especially true of parents who did not require their daughters' help in the household; such parents frequently expressed a desire for their daughters to attend school at least for the first six years, yet they rarely expressed specific expectations of them with regard to their academic performance or their chances of continuing in the education system. Participation in the state-run school system appeared to hold no symbolic value to the Tai beyond the practical value attached to basic literacy skills.

The government's difficulty in persuading Tai boys to remain in school has often been explained in terms of parents' preference for Buddhist-novice education, which conflicts with the state school system. It has been much more difficult, however, for researchers and teachers to identify a "logical" explanation for why many Tai girls leave school before the state's ideal minimum of nine years. Indeed, Chinese researchers disagree over whether state education among Tai girls has been a success: is it laudable that as many Tai girls as boys attend basic schooling, or is it lamentable that Tai females, like Tai males, have a higher-than-average dropout rate and that relatively few continue on to higher education? Some researchers have stressed that it is easier for the Chinese authorities to convince the Tai to send their daughters to school because the Tai, unlike the Han and the Naxi, have no tradition of preferring sons over daughters. The main reasons often identified for the absence of a strong male bias among the Tai are that Tai marriages are not arranged and are matrilocal; that is, husbands reside with the wife's family after marriage before forming their own household after a few years.[27] Others have argued, however, that an important reason for the low level of female education among Tai and Tibetans alike is that Buddhism only supports the education of boys and that parents are therefore not inclined to send girls to school.[28]

Both of these explanations focus on internal cultural characteristics that are supposed to explain a specific ethnic group's low participation in state education. According to such explanations, failed attempts to spread and popularize state education among a given ethnic minority are first of all due to the minority's inherited cultural traits, which are incompatible with the modern Chinese society and therefore need to be changed. In fact, this view of the cultural deficiencies of the Tai (and many other ethnic minorities) finds expression not only among many researchers and cadres at higher administrative levels but also at the local level among teachers and leaders who criticize parents for transmitting and encouraging values that are regarded as obstructing the goals of the state education system. Thus, Tai parents are criticized for, among other things, letting their sons becomes novices and monks, for supporting their daughters' early marriages, and for being indifferent to the school education of both sons and daughters. This view (in addition to mere economic calculation) also lies behind the recent heavy promotion of boarding school education among national minorities, since boarding school is regarded as a convenient and effective means of breaking the cultural influence of parents and other villagers upon children while at the same time ensuring that the children engage in schoolwork rather than domestic work.

Tai students' own perceptions of what their parents expected from them in school were largely consistent with what parents themselves expressed in interviews. Few felt strong expectations from their parents with regard to school performance. When parents were asked to mention specific things they desired for their children's future, only those with substantial Chinese education themselves (i.e., beyond lower secondary school) cited Chinese education or a job that was necessarily related to school education. By contrast, Akha parents' expectations of children who had managed to continue beyond primary and, especially, lower secondary school were higher than those of Tai parents. Discussions among Tai and Akha students of this phenomenon often revolved around the fact that Akha students, unlike Tai students, felt heavy family pressure to perform well in school in order to secure a job "outside the village." The most common perception of parental expectations among both Tai and Akha students was that parents wanted their child to become a "medical worker so that he or she could help the parents when they grew old." Akha students additionally said that, if nothing else, their parents wanted them "to escape the hard labor in the village" by finding outside work.

The Akha, Blang, Akhe, Phusa, Lahu, and other minorities living higher up in the mountains of Sipsong Panna generally have lower levels of education than those living at lower elevations, and in many villages only around 10 percent of school-age children manage to complete primary school. Several upland villages I visited had never produced a single primary school graduate. Yet rural Akha who continue to lower secondary school are often celebrated in their villages. *Success,* of course, is a relative term, and the highest expectation of most parents was for a child to gain admission to a specialized secondary school, which, unlike regular higher secondary education, guaranteed a job after graduation. Akha students in lower primary schools and in the Teachers' Training School, whom I interviewed, all expressed concern that their families had to suffer economically because they were in school and that, therefore, it was important they made up for this sacrifice by succeeding in the quest for a job outside the village. In addition, many female Akha students also mentioned that, due to poverty, most families in their villages preferred to focus on a son's education. Girls married early, moved to their husband's family, performed domestic work, and were not expected to leave the village. Female Akha students often faced the dilemma of being celebrated in the village and at the same time shunned by other village girls, who regarded them as alien after spending years at distant boarding schools.[29]

The most sudden and radical changes in female educational participation occurred during the Cultural Revolution, when communes took over the responsibility for organizing all school education and parents had nothing to gain economically from keeping their children at home to work in the fields. Children were expected to attend school, and they often did, mainly learning to read selected texts by Chairman Mao and working part-time in the fields. Today, however, there is a very clear difference between Naxi parents in the city of Lijiang who allow all their children to participate in compulsory education and those in the rural areas who still tend to favor sons when poverty forces them to choose between educating a son or daughter. Indeed, parents from different ethnic groups (Naxi, Nuosu, Miao, Tuoluo'en, Lisu, and Premi) in the poorest rural areas of Lijiang often shared a similar attitude toward their children's education: schooling is an onerous financial investment that also deprives the family of precious labor power. Fewer rural parents than urban ones believed—though many expressed the hope—that school education would lead to economic prosperity and a job outside the village.

Most parents said that they wished to invest in the education of at least one son and that it would be better to educate a son rather than a daughter because at least he would remain in the family. Very often, however, parents did not argue rationally for or against this view but simply took it for granted that sending a son rather than a daughter to school was the normal and acceptable way to behave. Many teachers in rural districts of Lijiang also complained that it was difficult to convince parents to let their daughters remain in school. My interviews suggested that many rural Naxi parents would be happy to see their daughters as well as their sons receive an education but that, when economic conditions forced them to choose one over the other, they would, without further rational consideration, express a male preference for the reasons mentioned earlier and because this was how their own parents and grandparents would have chosen.[30]

Historically, Confucian education was regarded by the Lijiang Naxi as a main route for sons to acquire enhanced social status for themselves and their families. Today many parents in rural Lijiang allow their daughters to receive a primary education but tend only to support sons continuing on to secondary education. As is the case in Sipsong Panna, participation in Chinese school education does not guarantee the rural Naxi in Lijiang an improved economic position or a nonagricultural job, but, unlike in Sipsong Panna, Chinese school education does confer social status and is considered a main road to knowledge and wisdom. Although most parents in the city of Lijiang want their daughters to complete nine years of compulsory education, male preference was reflected in the fact that several interviewees warned their daughters of the difficulties of finding a marriage partner if they were to obtain a higher education (or a better job). Such warnings appear to have an impact on young Naxi female students and graduates, who often expressed the view that the social price of succeeding in the education system was too high to make the effort worthwhile. Even so, I found that cultural explanations of the Naxi tendency to favor boys over girls in education were often less important than the economic constraints faced by families. It was my firm impression that more rural Naxi families in Lijiang would happily allow their daughters to attend school for longer if only they found they could afford it.

At the same time, many female minority students have found that in recent years it has become easier for them to obtain certain kinds of jobs precisely because they belong to an ethnic minority, are female, and have attended school for a few years. The tourist industry in Sipsong Panna, which is dominated by Han Chinese entrepreneurs, is presently booming, and there is a high demand for minority women who can speak enough Chinese to serve the increasing number of (predominantly male) tourists who visit the region from other parts of China. In Lijiang, for example, parents are often encouraged by the local government to send their daughters to school for longer periods of time precisely in order to meet this burgeoning demand for educated minority women in the tourism industry. Indeed, as we shall see, the state school system is complicitous in more ways than one in the current ongoing attempt to reproduce officially sanctioned representations of minority culture for popular consumption by mainly Han audiences.

How Schools Represent Minority Women

In minority areas the school, and the educational arena in general, often comes to play its own special role in representing minorities and minority women especially—one that reflects a mixture of official state representations transmitted via schoolbooks, popular Han Chinese exoticized representations, and representations produced and communicated by local minority elite members themselves. A recent example of representations of minority women is found in a new series of educational publications about women in Yunnan. Each nationality has its own booklet composed of a mixture of color pictures and brief texts about women. The front covers of the booklets all show pictures of women wearing traditional costumes, except for the booklet on the Han Chinese, titled "In Pursuit of Beauty," which shows three young, beautiful Han Chinese women wearing highly fashionable Western clothes.[31]

In recent years Sipsong Panna has become an attractive tourist spot for Han Chinese from all over China, and it has also become an important center for foreign trade since the opening of the borders with neighboring Southeast Asian states. In the imagination of many Han Chinese, the Tai people, and especially Tai women, have long been wrapped in an aura of mysticism, beauty, gentleness, and liberal sexual behavior, as is evident from numerous Chinese popular and pseudoscientific publications, TV series, and postcards. In the publication series mentioned earlier the booklet about the Tai shows a boat full of Tai women rowing while in traditional Tai dress and is entitled "Women Bathed in Holy Water."[32] Tourists come to Sipsong Panna to look at Tai women, to be served by Tai women, and to feel the "gentle atmosphere" of the Tai people. This gives rise to the curious situation in which other minority women and even Han women dress up as Tai when it is convenient for business. In addition, selected Tai villages have been transformed into living ethnographic museums, where tourists can pay to see a "real" Tai house from the inside while being served tea by a beautiful Tai girl.

The exotic representation and perception of the Tai and, especially, Tai women has become good business in Sipsong Panna. Today local schools are also engaged in the business of representing Tai women for the benefit of the tourist trade. State support for education is insufficient to ensure that schools in many minority areas have the same equipment, physical standard, and quality of teachers as schools in the more prosperous regions of China. Schools, however, have the potential to generate their own earnings and are encouraged by government to do so. The most common means of raising school income across China is still to grow and sell agricultural products from fields attached to the schools. Another means, increasingly common in minority and tourist areas, is to try to attract investment and/or aid from central units in China or from foreign sources. Some minority boarding schools appear to have been successful in the latter. In return, the schools provide contingents of colorfully dressed minority students to sing and perform at parties and other social occasions attended by important guests.

Students are sometimes requested by local school authorities to participate in such events, and, whereas several students in tertiary education complained that they were not paid for their performances (nor for simply wearing their "ethnic costumes" on certain occasions), most secondary school students appeared to take it for granted that they were required to perform on occasion for elite audiences made up mostly of middle-aged Han Chinese men in important social positions. It is true that at their own private parties the students of different ethnic groups often enjoyed performing and dancing for one another. Yet, by staging on command a public performance of minority students who "like to sing and dance," the schools actively participate in the commodification of minority women and serve to confirm and reinforce an exoticized image of minority peoples.

I observed strong discrepancies in the attitudes to these kind of performances among Tai and Akha students. Whereas Tai students normally wore clothes that resembled the traditional Tai-style dress both in and outside school, Akha girls would never think of putting on a traditional village costume and felt very embarrassed when they were required to do so by the school. For both Akha and Tai students alike, the Tai costume was associated with brightness, color, beauty, femininity, dancing, easygoing life, and gentleness, while traditional Akha dress was associated with darkness, a harsh life, poverty, and backwardness. Often Akha girls would tell me that they were jealous of the Tai dress and wished they could also wear it but that their skin color betrayed them as Akha. Many Akha students tended to dislike darker skin, which is associated with the non-Tai ethnic groups from the mountains, and they often brought this up when asked what they considered were the differences between Akha and Tai. They felt that their "backwardness" became too obvious when exposed to an influential audience representing modernity and money and when performing side by side with what they considered to be the more refined dancing, singing, and costumes of Tai girls.

In 1992 one boarding school for minority nationalities set up a special "tourism course." The course was open to students who had not passed the examination for higher secondary school and consisted of one year of training in preparation for work in the local tourist industry, mainly as tourist guides and as service personnel in hotels. The course included classes on "travel psychology" (*luyou xinlixue*), "behavioral norms" (*xingwei guifan*), "etiquette" (*liyi*), and "minority dance" (*minzu wudao*). This represents another example of how schools make use of the local tourist industry in order to generate school

income, while at the same time they participate in the construction and confir-
mation of stereotypical representations of minorities, especially minority
women. These representations invariably establish a contrast, implicit or explicit, between "traditional" minority people and the "modern" Han.

Female Students' Conception of Gender Roles

I have elsewhere argued that during their school education, and especially
through the boarding school experience, many ethnic minority students are
forced to reconsider the significance and relevance of the cultural values and
beliefs with which they have grown up and that this sometimes results in
shame and disregard for what has come to be considered as "backward"
customs.[33] Both male and female students appear to have been equally affected by the cultural repression they experience in school. At the same time,
however, it was also clear that changing notions of the value of one's cultural
and religious customs and beliefs were closely connected to changing concepts of gender roles and relations and that individual responses to state
education were far from being gender neutral. For instance, the salience of
learning (in school) that divination was a backward and "superstitious" habit
was experienced differently by Akha girls and boys. Similarly, the consequences of reverting to the old Tai script rather than using the new Tai script
while in school were different for Tai girls and boys. And the Naxi's often-
praised ability to learn from other nationalities and to succeed in Chinese
education had different implications for Naxi female and male students. Thus,
to understand ethnic responses to the state project of promoting a unified,
standardized state education system, we need also to look specifically at the
different political implications of this project for men and women.

One example of a political act that has so far only been understood from
an ethnic perspective, without paying attention to its gender-specific relevance, is the recent return to the old Tai script in Sipsong Panna. When the
Communist Party in the early 1950s decided to create new Roman scripts for a
select number of ethnic groups, it also decided to revise, simplify, and standardize some of the scripts that already existed. The Tai script used in Sipsong
Panna was one such script selected for simplification by a joint effort of Tai
and Chinese scholars. The new simplified script was supposed to ensure
standardization and make it easier for Tai to learn to read and write. It was
also expected to facilitate a gradual transition to Chinese and to break the
traditionally close relationship between the Tai script and Theravada Buddhism. The new, simplified script was decreed to be the only Tai script used in

schools, local newspapers, and other local publications, a situation that lasted from the late 1950s to the Cultural Revolution and again from 1978 until the late 1980s. During these periods only boys who were appointed as Buddhist novices in the temples were allowed to study the traditional Tai script. Tai girls who attended school during these periods learned only the new script, as did Tai women who participated in adult literacy classes.

In 1986 the local Sipsong Panna government, which was dominated by Tai, decided that the new script was to be replaced by the traditional one. They defended this change on grounds that the traditional script was still taught in the region's monasteries and that it constituted an indisputable part of the Tai cultural heritage as well as being the medium for traditional Tai texts. Some problems were mentioned in this regard; for instance, that report-ers at the local television station and newspaper were accustomed to the new script and would find it difficult to learn the old one. One group that was most directly affected by the decision yet was not even mentioned, however, were women who had learned the new script in school and who had no knowledge of the traditional script. Several female interviewees who had learned the new script told me that, with this new policy, their knowledge of written Tai was rendered largely useless.

Nonetheless, the ethnic, historical, and symbolic significance of the old Tai script was so strong that most female students and graduates welcomed the change. Many recalled having been told stories by their grandparents about how the Tai script had come into being and why it was important to the Tai and distinguished them from the other ethnic groups in the area. Al-though Tai women were not part of the formal learning culture in the villages, they nonetheless played an important role in transmitting the symbolic value of the Tai language to their children. Many argued strenuously in favor of the cultural advantages of returning to the traditional script, despite the fact that they themselves were practically disadvantaged by the move.

Then, in 1996, the local government decided to revert back to the new script. The result, at the time of this writing, has been that the teaching of the Tai script has been called off for nearly a year in most schools while textbooks are being revised. At the same time, the few schools experimenting with expanded bilingual Tai-Chinese education, using the old Tai script, have had to cancel their programs. Although it is difficult to know what the conse-quences of this latest decision will be, it will certainly add to the confusing relationship between the two scripts and to the division between monastery and school.

Concerning the question of the status of the Tai spoken and written language in schools, Tai female students were on the whole less engaged in the issue than males. In contrast with Tai males, they never had to choose between school or monastery, secular or Buddhist education, Chinese or Tai language. Had it had not been for the school, they would probably not have learned to read and write much anyway, they told me. Perhaps that was also why they tended to be less outspoken than male students against the suppression of religion in education and the lack of Tai language instruction beyond the primary level. If a female Tai wanted to leave the village, learn to read and write, or find a job outside of agriculture or local trade, the school system was one of the means available for achieving these aims. Therefore, those women with ambitions to continue in the school system (and they were relatively few among those I interviewed) attempted to adapt as best they could to existing realities, while those with little ambition to continue their education tended to keep a low profile and often dropped out after scoring poorly on an exam.

Another realm of school education in which gender differences acquire significance has to do with instilled notions of cultural backwardness and modernity. In school students learn that "superstitious activities" are "leftovers" from more "primitive stages of human society," while religion, on the other hand, only develops in more advanced forms of society. According to this official view, both will ultimately melt away in the socialist society, where there is no need to "escape from the real life." This understanding has clear implications for students' concepts of their own religious upbringing. It also has special implications for female students when their sex, in addition to their ethnic identity, both come to represent backwardness, superstition, and primitive behavior. Emily Chao has shown that in the Naxi elite's creation of "*dongba* culture" (*dongba wenhua*) as a signifier of Naxi identity and representation, the ritual priest, or *dongba*, has been granted an identity as male, learned, and literary, in contrast to his historical contemporary, the *sanba*, who is represented as female, backward, and illiterate.[34]

Unlike the *dongba*, the *sanba* have rarely been objects of scholarly research, nor have they achieved prominent symbolic value in the modern process of Naxi identification and of establishing the Naxi as an ethnic group in China. To the degree that Naxi students learn anything about Lijiang history and the history of the Naxi and other ethnic groups in the area, it is most likely to be related to the male *dongba* culture, which has been officially promoted as proof that the Naxi had early on developed their own script (and were therefore more culturally advanced than other nonliterate ethnic groups). In this way *dongba* activities and all that is connected to them changed during the course of one decade in the 1980s from being considered elements of superstition to evidence of advanced culture. Evening and day courses were set up for men and women who wished to study *dongba* culture.

The emphasis on *dongba* culture may have had a profound impact on Naxi students' and intellectuals' sense of ethnic pride and self-confidence, but for Naxi female students this privileging of the *dongba* as "the Naxi's own traditional intellectuals" also serves to confirm that literacy, development, and education are first of all identified with males. The perception is reinforced by the fact that the well-educated personages in Naxi history as well as today tend to be exclusively male. In Chinese publications Naxi are frequently characterized as an ethnic group that "loves learning." Naxi female students, whom I interviewed, often repeated this characterization—even though their own mothers were mostly illiterate and their own first priority with regard to a future husband was that he should have more education than themselves. Many also raised the complaint (often heard from Han Chinese women as well) that it was nearly impossible for a woman to marry after the age of thirty if she possessed a higher education or had a well-paid job in a private company.

Thus, while the more or less direct alteration of the content of education in Lijiang brought about by Naxi intellectuals and individual Naxi teachers in recent years has probably strengthened the ethnic identity of many Naxi students and helped to eradicate their feelings of belonging to a backward minority, this change has left unchallenged—and perhaps even reinforced—traditional concepts of Naxi men as bearers of civilization, education, and development and of Naxi women as representatives of tradition and family life.[35] New tales about Naxi heroes and famous Naxi people, and of the *dongba* heritage and *dongba* culture, may in the future become an increasingly significant, though often unofficial, part of school education. But the role models and bearers of this celebrated Naxi literary tradition are so far still predominantly men.

Discussions I held among Tai and Akha students about so-called superstitious practices in Akha villages highlighted how the female gender was often connected in students' minds to notions of superstition and backwardness. Through discussions among students about Akha female shamanism, it became clear that most students accepted a view that the superstition practiced in Akha villages confirmed a kind of backwardness that was first of all female in nature. In addition, most illiterate Akha were female. One discussion among Tai and Akha students in which the Akha students reluctantly talked about the female shamans in their village ended on the following note.

Tai student: "This dancing [by the Akha female shaman] is really terrifying."
Akha student: "I know. My father already does not believe in it anymore.

My mother always wants to call the *nipha* when we are sick, but my
father says it is superstition.

Akha student: "Yes, my father says the same. Women are much more
superstitious than men. Men are more open (*kaifang*) . . . I don't know
why."

One of the most striking observations during interviews with female
secondary students belonging to different ethnic groups in Sipsong Panna was
how attitudes toward religion, novices, and expectations of future life changed
with the age of the students. Obviously, a twelve-year-old Tai girl in her first
year of lower secondary school would reflect differently on her own life and
have a less analytical attitude toward her own cultural background than a
twenty-year-old student in her last year of specialized secondary school. Yet,
apart from this obvious maturation, there also seemed to be a growing resentment and stigmatization of what Tai students themselves regarded as the most
significant features of their previous village life: Buddhist religious beliefs and
practices, belief in spirits, the custom of sending boys to monasteries, speaking
the Tai language, and engaging in agricultural work. I believe this change was
connected to the school's undisguised promotion of a notion of development
and modernization that was inextricably bound up with atheism, the learning
of Chinese, and the study of "modern" subjects, which takes place only in
state-run schools. Tai girls in lower secondary schools tended to be very
outspoken and assertive in their statements concerning boys and men becoming novices or monks. Most argued that men behaved better if they had been
novices and that they were also more learned; often there was simply no doubt
in their minds that it took a period of novice-hood to make a man. As a result,
many did not find it necessary or relevant to argue why their future husband
should possess some Buddhist training. By contrast, female students at the
uppermost level of senior secondary school and those in tertiary education
were often more critical of the male novice experience. Their main argument
often paralleled that of the school—namely, that becoming a novice prevented one from receiving a good school education. And, since the girls were
educated in Chinese schools themselves, they also wanted husbands or boy-
friends with similar training.

During their time in boarding school Tai minority girls were prevented
from participating in the religious activities of their villages. They were also
taught that religion obstructs modernization, and at the same time they
gained a growing awareness that only through participation in Chinese school
education could they expect to attain desirable positions in government,
administration, and teaching. And, not least, through the deliberate omission

of Tai language, history, and culture in the curriculum, they internalized the school's message that these aspects of their heritage and identity were "useless" and incompatible with "development" and "modernization"—concepts that I never found formally discussed in schools but which were taken for granted as positive and commonly celebrated goals of the development of society. Most of these students appeared to have an abstract perception of the "Han Chinese" as the most "advanced" nationality, a notion that was transmitted to them directly through the school system. A common argument put forward by older Tai students against boys becoming Buddhist novices was that: "the Han are more developed than us so it would be a waste of time for a boy to go to a monastery—it would be better for him to learn Han Chinese from the Han in a Han school (*Hanzu xuexiao*)."[36] This argument was expressed by Tai female and male students alike, but I found that Tai female students in general were less critical of the messages transmitted by the school and more critical of the religious practices of their families.

One reason why school education may have a stronger and different impact on Tai girls and young women than on Tai males is that the school represents one of the only means available to Tai girls of becoming literate, of receiving an education, of finding a job, and of perhaps moving upward in society. They find possibilities in the state education system that they would not find elsewhere. In any case they do not have the choice of becoming novices, and many would not have learned to read and write Tai in the first place; as a result, Tai female students may find it easier than Tai males to accept the boarding school's pressure for assimilation and its demand that they reject a large degree of the cultural patterns and customs they were brought up with. Thus, the attitudes and responses of Tai female students at higher levels of education and among graduates toward the form and content of state education are frequently marked by a conflicting relationship between the loss of ethnic self-confidence as Tai and the gaining of self-confidence as female students who are praised in the school system for succeeding against the odds of being both Tai and woman.

It may be the case that, as an increasing number of Tai girls receive Chinese education and because they are more likely than boys to continue in the education system, the position of women in Tai society will gradually improve as these women gain influential positions in the various state organs and institutions that demand modern education and knowledge of the Chinese language. One Chinese researcher has argued that the change has already affected Tai women's position in the local Tai community because there are an increasing number of Tai women working in the administration and because they have become important in local trade.[37]

Conclusion

Studies on the Chinese education system have so far largely ignored education among the non-Han peoples, who live mainly in the vast border regions of the People's Republic. To the limited degree that scholars outside of China have concerned themselves with the policies and practice of Chinese education among non-Han minorities, they have mostly done so as part of more general studies of ethnic minorities in the People's Republic or of national policy toward minorities.[38] There are, however, a number of issues that call for a more integrated approach to the study of education in China as a whole and the study of education among ethnic minorities. One of those issues concerns the different ways in which boys and girls, men and women, conceive of, are influenced by, and respond to the content and form of standardized Chinese education as promoted by the state school system. For ethnic minority students of both sexes, the encounter with the state education system is often a powerful experience that to differing extents impacts upon students' ethnic self-perceptions; their perceptions of the Han; and their perceptions of the Chinese state, government, and nation. In short, the school often plays a crucial role in the ongoing process of ethnic identification.

The Chinese state has encountered numerous difficulties in its attempts to establish and popularize Chinese education among the different ethnic minorities, and many of these minorities have in turn responded to this project with passive or active resistance or simply indifference. Others, of course, have either had long experience in adopting and adapting various forms of Chinese education or have found social, political, or economic advantages in participating in, and eventually modifying, the form and content of local schools. In either case the deep significance of the concept, ideology, and policy of minority education (*minzu jiaoyu*) has ensured that Chinese and foreign researchers and government workers alike have first of all studied and treated "minorities" as such, rather than paying attention to the profound discrepancies between minority men and women in terms of their relation to education, concepts of education, and responses to the state education system.

This essay has attempted to show not only that, for important historical, cultural, economic, and political reasons, different ethnic groups have responded differently to the form and content of Chinese state education but also that the state education system is experienced differently by women and men within the same ethnic group. Processes of ethnic and gender identification are closely related—perhaps even interdependent. In the course of confrontation with an education system based on the Chinese language and suffused with notions of modernization, atheism, and nationalism that serve to transmit an eroticized, exoticized, and feminized image of non-Han peoples, the salience of the complex interconnectedness of ethnic and gender identities stands out.

One of the messages transmitted via the education system that clearly had an impact on female minority students' perception of women and of their own ethnic group concerns the backwardness of superstitious activity, which the school often presents as being directly connected to the popularity of female shamans and sorcerers as well as to traditional minority female costumes, illiteracy, and early marriage. In the case of the Akha, for example, all students were aware that their ethnic group was associated with backwardness, but, in addition, female Akha students were very conscious of the fact that this backwardness was mainly associated with things and practices connected to females. Naxi female students also faced the fact that education was until recently (and still is in some areas) mainly a male project and that a family's status was connected to the successful participation of its male members in Chinese education. Unlike the Akha, however, the Naxi belong to an ethnic group that is celebrated in China for its openness toward what is often described as "more developed nationalities" (notably the Han) and which has managed to establish itself as a well-known and influential national minority in China. The fact that most contemporary Naxi intellectuals are men, that those in former times who succeeded in Confucian education were men, and that even the Naxi's "own intellectuals," the *dongba,* were men apparently did not diminish Naxi female students' pride in their ethnic affiliation.

Regarding traditional, and to a certain extent contemporary, attitudes toward boys' and girls' education, the Naxi have much in common with the rural Han. A comparative approach incorporating Han women and men's perceptions of and responses to the messages of national unity, modernization, and concepts of development (*fazhan*) and backwardness (*luohou*), as transmitted in the national school system, would do much to increase our knowledge of how, why, and under what circumstances ethnic and gender identities, respectively, gain salience and what role school education plays in this process. The comparisons that have been made in this essay concerning the impact of state education on gender perceptions among different ethnic minorities suggest that, although ethnic identity clearly has different meanings and implications for female and male students, there are situations in which feelings of common ethnic identity acquire greater salience than gender-specific differences. Those situations are likely to occur when members of an ethnic minority are forced to reconsider the cultural values they have grown up with, such as often happens when minority students encounter a school system based on different values, language, history, and attitudes toward spiritual life than those learned within the family and village. When such confrontations are strongly felt, as in the case of the Tai students, whose cultural values, religion, and history are very distant from those of the central parts of China, a sense of common ethnic identity and the collective memory of one's past seem to become more important to the actors than gender-based differences.

NOTES

1. I am grateful for the valuable comments on earlier drafts of this essay raised by several participants at the Toronto conference on Education and Society in Twentieth-Century China (September 1997), especially Feng Xu. I also wish to thank Koen Wellens for his comments and the Danish Council for Development Research for financial support for the research and fieldwork upon which this essay is based.

2. As shown by Ping-Chun Hsiung in this volume, there is also a general inconsistency between the Chinese government's ideological and financial support for education.

3. See Tani Barlow, "Politics and Protocols of *Funü*: (Un)making National Women," in Christina K. Gilmartin et al., eds., *Engendering China: Women, Culture, and the State* (Cambridge, Mass.: Harvard University Press, 1994), 339–50, concerning efforts to construct the category of *funü*; also Stevan Harrell, "Introduction: Civilizing Projects and the Reaction to Them," in Stevan Harrell, ed., *Cultural Encounters on China's Ethnic Frontiers* (Seattle and London: University of Washington Press, 1995), 3–37, concerning the relation of ethnicity and gender.

4. Ibid., 12.

5. See, for example, Nan Ning, "Xingbie qishi" (Sexual discrimination: heaving a sigh about education), in *Zhongguo funü* (Chinese women) 2 (February 1989): 4–5.

6. *Yuwen* (Language), no. 5, primary school (Beijing: Renmin jiaoyu chubanshe, 1994), 114–17.

7. See especially Dru C. Gladney, "Representing Nationality in China: Refiguring Majority/Minority Identities," *Journal of Asian Studies* 1 (February 1994): 92–123; and Louise Schein, "Gender and Internal Orientalism in China," *Modern China* 23, no. 1 (January 1997): 69–98; Norma Diamond, "The Miao and Poison: Interactions on China's Southwest Frontier," *Ethnology* 27, no. 1 (1988): 1–25; Norma Diamond, "Defining the Miao: Ming, Qing and Contemporary Views," in Stevan Harrell, ed., *Cultural Encounters on China's Ethnic Frontiers*, 92–117.

8. See, for instance, Beverly Hooper, "China's Modernization: Are Young Women Going to Lose Out?" *Modern China* 10, no. 3 (1984): 317–43; "Gender and Education," in Irving Epstein, ed., *Chinese Education: Problems, Policies and Prospects* (New York: Garland Press, 1991).

9. See the surveys referred to in Stanley Rosen, "Women, Education and Modernisation," in Ruth Hayhoe, ed., *Education and Modernisation: The Chinese Experience* (Oxford: Pergamon Press, 1992), 271–72.

10. Ibid.; Hooper, "China's Modernization: Are Young Women Going to Lose Out?"; and "Gender and Education."

11. Elisabeth Croll, *Changing Identities of Chinese Women* (London and New Jersey: Hong Kong University Press, 1995).

12. "The Report of the People's Republic of China on the Implementation of the Nairobi Forward-Looking Strategies for the Advancement of Women, Beijing, China, 1994," reprinted in ibid., 133–35.

13. Rosen, "Women, Education and Modernisation," 260.

14. I have previously elaborated on this argument in Mette H. Hansen, *Lessons in Being Chinese: Minority State Education and Ethnic Identity in Southwest China* (Seattle: University of Washington Press, 1998).

15. The validity of the Chinese classification of nationalities has been widely discussed in China during the last decade. Recent Chinese scholarship confirms that the classification was a construction that was only ideologically, not practically, based on Stalin's criteria for an ethnic group. Obviously, many Chinese researchers are aware of this, but political circumstances sometimes make it impossible for them to acknowledge it in their writings. Scholars both in and outside China are currently debating whether a reclassification would be useful.

16. This is also true with respect to the Muslim Huizu, who are normally regarded as one of the nationalities with a high level of education. At all levels from senior secondary school, Muslim Hui produce more graduates per one thousand population than do the Han. Gladney's fieldwork among the Muslim Hui showed, however, that in some localities most Hui attended public school and studied the Koran in private, while in other areas school attendance was low and on the decrease. Thus, in one Han Chinese county the enrollment rate in 1982 was 93.9 percent, and 79 percent among girls; while in the adjacent all-Muslim county the enrollment rate was only 23.9 percent, with barely 9 percent of girls enrolled and only 2.9 percent of girls enrolled actually graduating. See Dru C. Gladney, *Muslim Chinese: Ethnic Nationalism in the People's Republic* (Cambridge, Mass.: Harvard University Press, 1991), 125.

17. Concerning the Naxi, see for instance Emily Chao, "Hegemony, Agency, and Representing the Past: The Invention of Dongba Culture among the Naxi of Southwest China," in Melissa Brown, ed., *Negotiating Ethnicities in China and Taiwan* (Berkeley: University of California Press, 1996), 208–40; Charles McKhann, "The Naxi and the Nationalities Question," in Stevan Harrell, ed., *Cultural Encounters on China's Ethnic Frontiers,* 39–63; Sidney D. White, "Fame and Sacrifice: The Gendered Construction of Naxi Identities," *Modern China* 23, no. 3 (July 1997): 298–327. Concerning education among the Naxi, see Hansen, *Lessons in Being Chinese;* and Mette H. Hansen, "Fostering 'Love of Learning': Naxi Responses to Ethnic Images in Chinese State Education," in Kjeld-Erik Broedsgaard and David Strand, eds., *Reconstructing Twentieth Century China: Social Control, Civil Society and National Identity* (Oxford: Oxford University Press, 1997).

18. Yang Chonglong, *Yunnan jiaoyu wenti yanjiu* (Research on Yunnan's educational problems) (Kunming: Yunnan jiaoyu chubanshe, 1995), 304; and *Minzu gongzuo* (Nationalities work) 4 (1985): 52–53.

19. Based on the author's interviews with headmaster and administration.

20. Yunnan Province Education Commission, ed., *Yunnan jiaoyu sishi nian, 1949–1989* (Forty years of education in Yunnan) (Kunming: Yunnan daxue chubanshe, n.d.), 120.

21. Sipsong Panna Education Department, *Xishuangbanna Zhou minzu jiaoyu qing-kuang* (The condition of minority education in Sipsong Panna prefecture) (MS, 1991), 1. See also Mette H. Hansen, "Teaching Backwardness or Equality? Chinese State Education among the Tai in Sipsong Panna," in Gerard Postiglione and Regie Stites, eds., *Education of National Minorities in China* (New York: Garland Press, 1998).

22. Yang Chonglong, *Yunnan jiaoyu wenti yanjiu* (Research on Yunnan's educational problems), 302; and Yang Shide, "Xishuangbanna Zhou jichu jiaoyu yu minzu suzhi de tantao" (An inquiry into the basic education and the quality of the nationalities in Sipsong Panna), in Yan Sanlong et al., eds., *Xishuangbanna minzu jiaoyu* (Minority education in Sipsong Panna) (Kunming: Yunnan minzu chubanshe, 1992), 10.

23. For further detail, see Hansen, "Teaching Backwardness or Equality."

24. Wang Xihong et al., eds., *Zhongguo bianjing minzu jiaoyu* (Education of China's minorities living in border areas) (Beijing: Zhongyang minzu xueyuan chubanshe, 1990), 271.

25. In such cases the township governments would normally attempt to restart the school again after a few years.

26. Interview with a leading administrative cadre at a nationalities school in Sipsong Panna.

27. Wang Xihong et al., eds., *Zhongguo bianjing minzu jiaoyu,* 271.

28. Sun Ruoqiong et al., eds., *Zhongguo shaoshu minzu jiaoyuxue gailun* (An introduction to the education of China's national minorities) (Beijing: Zhongguo laodong chubanshe, 1990), 267.

29. While many of their villages were not remote in terms of actual physical distance, they were only accessible on foot, which involved walking for a whole day, while even the cost of the bus ticket to the nearest village on the roadside was a financial burden to many families. As a consequence, many students in boarding schools (almost all non-Han) only visited their families during summer holiday and sometimes during the local Water Splashing Festival.

30. This might possibly, and gradually, be influenced by the state policy of population control, which has only been strictly enforced in the area since 1991. According to this policy, parents living in the city of Lijiang may have only one child, whereas rural families may have two children regardless of nationality.

31. Zhang Ning and Liu Wenxiao, *In Pursuit of Beauty: The Han* (Kunming: Yunnan jiaoyu chubanshe, 1995).

32. Zheng Xiaoyun and Yu Tao, *Women Bathed in Holy Water: The Dais* (Kunming: Yunnan jiaoyu chubanshe, 1995).

33. Hansen, *Lessons in Being Chinese.*

34. Chao, "Hegemony, Agency, and Re-presenting the Past," 218–19.

35. See also White, "Fame and Sacrifice."

36. Interview with a twenty-one-year-old Tai student.

37. Zheng Xiaoyun, "Dangdai Xishuangbanna Daizu shehui wenhua bianyi yanjiu"

(Research on current changes in the culture and society of the Dai Nationality in Sipsong Panna), in *Shehuixue yanjiu* (Sociological research), no. 1 (1991).

38. In addition to the articles and books already mentioned, other publications have also focused on the ways in which minority education is practiced in local areas. See, for instance, Wurlig Borchiged, "The Impact of Urban Ethnic Education on Modern Mongolian Ethnicity, 1949–1966," in Harrell, *Cultural Encounters on China's Ethnic Frontiers,* 278–301; and Chae-jin Lee, *China's Korean Minority: The Politics of Ethnic Education* (Boulder: Westview Press, 1986).

The Women's Studies Movement in China in the 1980s and 1990s

Ping-Chun Hsiung

This essay analyzes the interplay of structures and actors centered around the women's studies movement that has recently developed in the context of China's sociopolitical changes in the 1980s and 1990s. The movement entails the establishment of women's studies program in universities, restructuring of the All China Women's Federation (ACWF) (*Quanguo funü lianhe hui*) and emergence of service-oriented women's organizations. My discussion derives from, and seeks to contribute to, recent scholarship concerning women's subjectivity in the Third World, the relationship between local activism and global feminism, and the emergence of civil society in China. The first set of empirical questions my analysis intends to answer are: How did a group of female professionals and intellectuals who claimed not to have experienced discrimination come to recognize, and then fight against, gender inequalities in contemporary China? What can the movement tell us about Chinese women intellectuals and activists and their relationship with the state? What can the recently evolved exchange and dialogue between local and international feminist activism tell us about the relationship between local and global feminism?

Throughout my analysis I weave together personal efforts and structural conditions to capture both the personal and institutional aspects of the women's studies movement. To present and analyze women's actions and activities, I draw on their reflections and narratives. These narratives bring to light individual and collective dimensions of the engendered self as it has been created in and revealed by the subject's relationship to the broader historical, sociopolitical context of the postrevolutionary era. They are a rich source for exploring and recovering the contextual meanings of the women's studies movement as it is experienced by the women involved. I have emphasized the women's personal discourse in order to bring out certain features that have long been overlooked in the portrayal of Chinese women: their agency and practical shrewdness. The effort echoes recent scholarship that is critical of the representation of Third World women by First World feminists.[1]

The development of the women's studies movement in China sheds light on issues surrounding the recent debate about the emergence of civil society in China. In the context of the relationship between the state and society, this debate has focused on the organizational foundation of opposition and nonconformity and the possible transformation of the state's hegemonic control. Some analysts maintain, however, that the Chinese socialist state is not as omnipresent and suffocating as many have claimed. Although the communist state possesses oppressive, iron-fisted power to strike down any overt challenges, its giant bureaucratic system is fragmented and ineffective in most of its routine operations. Such a system therefore leaves enough room for individual, clandestine negotiation and manipulation.[2] While corruption and embezzlement are scandalous aspects of such manipulation, studies of recent changes in the economic, intellectual, and social spheres attest to the existence, and even expansion, of autonomous spaces within an otherwise authoritarian apparatus.

The development of a women's studies movement in China presents a unique case. On the one hand, the movement's objective—gender equality and women's liberation—has always been part of the CCP's rhetorical agenda. The movement, therefore, does not necessarily threaten the official status quo. Yet women intellectuals and professionals involved in the movement have called the state's position into question, sought alternative routes to address women's issues, and explored theoretical inquiry into women's emancipation beyond the orthodox Marxist theory of women. Their action and activism entail creating new spaces both *inside* and *outside* the official dominant sphere. In order to capture these particular nuances, my analysis does not conceptualize the nation-state and women's studies movement as two separate and opposing forces. Instead, I propose to examine the emergence of the women's studies movement as a series of sociopolitical events embedded in the structural framework of the nation-state. Accordingly, the second set of research questions I propose to address includes: What political, social, and financial resources have women in the women's studies movement mobilized to realize their aims? In what ways has the nation-state been supportive of and/or an impediment to women's initiatives? Under what conditions, and through what mechanisms, has the nation-state exerted its disciplinary power?

In the following sections I first examine the political meaning of being a woman in postrevolutionary China. The analysis sketches personal journeys of those women intellectuals and professionals who were later to take part in the women's studies movement. This is followed by an analysis of changes within the All China Women's Federation and the emergence of service-oriented women's organizations. My analysis of women's studies programs in Chinese universities and of the recent exchanges and dialogue between women activists in China and those in other countries highlights certain unique features of the women's studies movement in China. In the conclusion I reflect upon a series of events surrounding the movement.

The Personal Journey

Women born after 1949 grew up in a period when eliminating gender inequalities was officially advocated and upheld. Gender equality during that period, however, had particular attributes. On the one hand, the Chinese Communist Party (CCP) proclaimed that the proletarian revolution had created objective conditions for women's emancipation. It was therefore the responsibility of each woman to be self-liberated. The official script demanded that women leave the confines of domesticity to enter the public sphere and join their male counterparts in revolutionary causes. Within this cultural and political climate many women strove to become men's equals by becoming *identical* to men. As women intellectuals recall their adolescence/girlhood, quite a few of them use the term *jia xiaozi* (phony/disguised boy) to characterize themselves. Young girls either consciously or unconsciously emulated the behavioral traits of their male peers. A woman physics professor once revealed, for example:

> When I grew up, I never wanted to be with the girls. They were too emotional. I felt there was nothing I wanted to learn from them. I always hung around with the guys. I liked to argue with them. I learned to think logically and rationally this way. Being like a girl was just not my taste. They are too soft.[3]

To earn respect women often imposed stern measures on themselves to transcend gender differences. During the Cultural Revolution many young women either volunteered or at least demonstrated their willingness to go to the most poverty-stricken rural areas to be reeducated. Once they got there, they took pride in bearing the same level of physical hardship as their male counterparts. The following self-portraits are typical of the time:

> As a young woman born into an intellectual bourgeois family, I felt I needed to relate to workers and peasants; as a woman who was growing up during the era of equality of men and women, I needed to fit into the standards created for men. When I took part in voluntary labor, in spite of my menses, I stood with boy students in the water above my knees, scooping up sludge from the river or transplanting rice seedlings in water. . . . [In Tibet] I lived in a tent with holes on all sides, used my hand to eat the half-cooked mutton with the herdsman, and rode horses to keep sheep and cattle within bounds. I fell off my horse once and suffered a moderate cerebral concussion, but I did not stop my work. At the time I did everything with great enthusiasm and did not feel tired. Illness did not deter me. I only thought that the dream that women would live like men had come to pass at last in my generation.[4]

> When I was sent to the countryside, I vowed to be as strong as a man. Even though I had never done any physical work before (before then, I had even never done any housework chores), I made myself carry out the most strenuous work that men did in the field. In the winter, I carried buckets of water weighing a hundred and fifty kilograms on my shoulder. Countless times, I fell. Countless times, I rolled down the hills with the buckets. My clothes were all wet and my shoulders were bleeding. But I never shed even a drop of tears.[5]

Abiding by Marxist doctrine, the iron woman was an icon of the post-revolutionary era. The term *daomeile* (being out of luck or having an unlucky break) was used among girls to refer to menstruation,[6] and other feminine attributes were rejected and looked down upon. Women intellectuals and professionals who have become leading figures in the contemporary women's studies movement claim that they never experienced discrimination:

> I was born in 1951 and I am now the editor-in-chief of *Farming Women Know It All.* I was a soldier for fourteen years. I was once a leader in the military's propaganda section. I simply went from the world of men to the world of women. I felt no sense of inequality or being discriminated against in that men's world because I was the leader of male soldiers.[7]

Their successful careers give them an unusual sense of self-confidence. They are convinced that women bear no traits innately inferior to those of their male counterparts. Some even attribute their success to their defeminized style and traits:

> I was in the army for 24 years. I didn't work for Fulian [All China Women's Federation]. Therefore, I once joked that I went from a place where there was no women's restroom to one where there are no men's. When I was a soldier, I looked down on women. I felt that they have the collective shortcomings of all human beings. I was once proud of the ways in which I was different from other women. Others attributed my success to the fact that men did not treat me like a woman, they treated me either as a colleague or a competitor. I was a bit proud of this viewpoint because [I thought] at least I did not have all the negative attributes of being a woman. At that time, I took pride in not identifying myself with my gender group.[8]

For many women, coming to see that being men's equal at work does not necessarily lead to women's liberation has been painful. Li Xiaojiang, one of the leading figures in the women's studies movement, reveals that she had excelled over many of her male colleagues at work before she found herself trapped in the domestic sphere:

> Getting married and then giving birth to a child almost completely changed my life and psychological world. They challenged the kind of independence I had valued the most.... Overwhelmed by baby's crying and endless housework, I painfully realized that I was ready to surrender my aspiration for a rewarding career to everyday survival. I fell into a trap, a trap that has buried many women before me.... I was surrounded by obstacles: husband and child, housework and relatives. [Endless demands] took up all my time and energy. They prevented me from doing what I had really wanted to do and from going to wherever I had wanted to go.... [Finally] I had to admit to myself that after years of study, I had known nothing about women.[9]

Liang Jun, a lecturer-turned-feminist, talks about being trapped by domestic responsibilities and professional demands:

> I was no longer the person I had been earlier. From the modern heroine, I had turned into a professional person and a housewife, whose life was confined to working at the office and doing housework at home. All day

long I was in a desperate hurry and felt exhausted. Gradually, the brave pledge to compete with men was abandoned as an illusion. I came to believe that a marital relationship could not remain balanced. ". . . so long as you are successful in your achievements, I am willing to do everything for you," I said to my husband. If I delayed doing housework because of official business, I would feel ashamed and guilty. But in my innermost self, I wished to develop myself. I shouldered the heavy load of work and life, unable to bear it, and yet unwilling to abandon it. Day and night I was worried, depressed, and resentful.[10]

These narratives bring out the contradiction at the heart of the CCP's program of women's liberation. On the one hand, it brought up a generation of successful professional and intellectual women whose achievement shatters the conventional, stereotypical notion of women's inborn inferiority. Yet their public involvement does not relieve those women of their domestic duties and the associated sense of entrapment. There exists a conflict between professional success and personal dissent that inspires them to ask why women's lives are so trying and demeaning and why, in a supposedly gender-equal society, women are still so overburdened and suppressed. As they look around, they come to realize that the effort to achieve gender equality through being men's equal has made women of their generation deny and suppress their own femaleness. The following excerpt describes a woman intellectual's journey to be reconnected with her gender group. It explains clearly the political context within which a misogynous identity was constructed.

When I began to identify myself with women (females), something incredible was found: women refused to be identified as females. This is the first womanly problem that emerged in my confrontation with Chinese women. Putting myself in their shoes, I was like that for a very long time. In the past, I was willing to be anything but female. "It is said that a real materialist fears nothing." However, what Chinese women fear most is being identified as females. "Female" is like a historical trap, and resembles the old era. In a society where "men and women are identical," no one would be so foolish and debased to turn back to look for females. To identify with "female" is especially hard for women intellectuals who have all had the *jia xiaozi* [phony/disguised guy] experience like me. It is more painful than experiencing a rebirth.[11]

An engendered female identity calls for a recognition of the "differences" between men and women. It entails a female-centered subjectivity that sets women free from the male-centered imposition implied in the CCP's approach to women's liberation:

> I am the first beneficiary of being identified with the female: I felt an unprecedented spiritual liberation and relaxation. The society has given us women the gift of "being men's equal," in exchange, we women have lost our identity as females. We therefore never found ourselves truly relaxed. In addition to the strain of double roles, the psychological burden has been exhausting. Whether in family or society, we have to keep in mind "his" criteria all the time. We cannot find anywhere or anytime to show our true self as females. The worst part was that we could turn to nobody for support because every woman is trying to prove the legend of "men and women are identical/equal." No one is willing to interrupt "women's liberation" with "female's personal issues."[12]

To break the code of silence, public lectures and writings have called for women's collective consciousness as well as for individual woman's "self-discovery, self-recognition and self-development." Ideologically speaking, the development of a subjective consciousness of femaleness among Chinese women challenges the Marxist insistence that women's liberalization is to be realized through class struggle. At the same time, a quest to satisfy women's independent needs and solve women's problems simultaneously undermines the CCP's official, hegemonic domination over women's issues.[13] The establishment of women's studies programs at the university level is an effort to transform individual dissent into collective endeavor. Before discussing the foundation and functioning of women's studies programs in Chinese universities, however, I shall deal with another major development in the institutional growth of the Chinese women's studies movement: the transformation of the All China Women's Federation in the face of myriad difficulties women have experienced in the era of reform.

Institutional Aspects of the Women's Studies Movement

Challenges That Confront the All China Women's Federation

The ACWF is a national mass organization with a dual mandate: (1) to follow the directives of the Chinese Communist Party; and (2) to represent the interests of Chinese women. The ACWF was originally founded in 1949 as a "united front organization of democratic women of all social strata and professions" to coordinate and give direction to women's work throughout China.[14] It was banned during the Cultural Revolution, and reinstated in 1978. Immediately after its reestablishment, there was an attempt to articulate a separate identity for the ACWF. High-level officials of the federation called for an examination of the paradox that the ACWF functioned both as a representative of women's interests and as a bureaucracy closely linked with the CCP leadership. Luo Qiong, then the vice chair of the ACWF's executive committee, proclaimed specifically that the Party should redefine its relationship with the mass organization. According to her, "the appropriate and effective way of the Party's leadership is to cultivate a lively, co-operative spirit with the mass organization. Most important, it ought to ensure a complete realization of the organization's own initiative and creativity."[15] Thus, the ACWF should function as an active, autonomous, and self-motivating agent. To do so, Luo urged the federation to adopt a bottom-up approach in order to incorporate the concerns of ordinary women into the core of its agenda. Local offices are encouraged not only to explore independent, financial resources but also to set their own priorities on women's work in accordance with the local situation.[16]

The call for internal, organizational restructuring runs parallel to external, societal challenges on the reform era. The ACWF not only is expected to handle practical matters such as female prostitution and the trafficking of women. The fact that a disproportionate number of women are being laid off from state enterprises and that discrimination against female graduates in job placement continues have also compelled the ACWF to raise a more fundamental question: Has the proletarian revolution really eliminated gender inequalities? As a mass organization representing women's interests, the ACWF is further troubled by controversial issues such as the one-child policy and spousal abuse. To meet these and other challenges, the ACWF has begun to establish its own research offices to conduct research, identify problems, formulate solutions, and recommend policies. Researchers and administrative staffs of the ACWF now debate issues that were once in forbidden territory. Thus, ACWF discussions are not limited to the resurgence of prostitution, arranged marriage, or discriminatory hiring and lay-off practices. Instead, some have openly questioned the applicability and usefulness of Marxism in analyzing and understanding women's situation. Others have come to denounce the claim of gender equality in socialist China.[17]

Although ACWF is an official organization, there is no consensus on various women's issues. Some ACWF officials attribute current problems that women encounter to their backwardness. Others talk about a resurgence of feudal practices and ideology. Still others believe that current problems have to do with state policies, which allow the market economy to become the sole driving force of the social order. These diverse explanations of women's problems lead to different proposals for solutions. For example, Guan Tao, the deputy director of the ACWF, argues that the working environment will become less discriminatory against women as modernization in technology and production abolishes jobs that require physical strength, and she maintains that developments in the service industry will eventually make housework less demanding for women. Gao Xiaoxian, the director of ACWF's research institute in Shaanxi province, believes that ACWF, as a well-established institution, should take on the responsibility of addressing some of the structural constraints women face—patriarchal norms and practices, high illiteracy especially among rural women, and capitalist exploitation of factory girls in coastal cities. In contrast, Li Xiaojiang, a leading figure in women's studies, argues for the dismissal of ACWF. According to Li, it is time for Chinese women to stop being passive victims by developing an autonomous, collective consciousness. Women should no longer expect the government/system or men to define and solve problems for them.

As a whole, these diverse voices represent the effort of intellectuals to challenge official propositions on women's liberation. The state and the ACWF are no longer the sole hegemonic entity in presenting and representing the Chinese woman. A pluralistic landscape has given rise to multiple, and sometimes conflicting, positions. Moreover, internal forces and external pressure have worked to push the ACWF to function less as an organization taking orders from the state and more in the domain of representing women's interests. Various projects and local initiatives have convened under the umbrella of the ACWF. As I will show later, a rigid notion of the ACWF as nothing but a political apparatus of the CCP state fails to capture adequately the dynamism within the federation, nor does it acknowledge intraorganizational ties and linkage that the federation has formed with other women's groups in recent years. Besides, many innovative professionals in the ACWF grew up in the Cultural Revolution era. They belong to the same cohort as those active intellectuals in academia. Personal ties and shared visions have brought them together to work on various new initiatives and projects.[18] Thus, women's activism in contemporary China is built as much upon personal ties as on an institutional base. The institutional boundary and oppositional position between the state and NGOs projected in the NGO model of Western feminist activism does not fit. The relationship between the ACWF and women's studies programs in universities presents a good example.

Establishment of Women's Studies Programs in Universities

Although the ACWF is often portrayed as a dogmatic state apparatus, scholars in the women's studies movement initially drew heavily upon its extensive structure and nationwide networks. In 1985, for example, a course entitled "women and household management" was introduced to a class of professional and government employees at the Henan Women's Cadres School, a school under the ACWF administration. The course covered topics such as what a woman is expected to do in the domestic sphere, how and why the demands of the home have exhausted many women physically and entrapped them psychologically, and how to combat gender-specific norms and practices.[19] Liang Jun, one of the students in that class, picked up the thread and went on to spread the message. Again, relying upon the ACWF arrangements and networks, Liang traveled across the country to reach women at local women cadre schools and in the trade unions, student groups, and in professional associations such as the Women Technical Workers' Association, the Women Cadres' Association, the Women's Teachers' Association, and the Women Medical Workers' Association. In the name of "women's education" her lectures covered topics like "women's self-realization, the dual roles of professional women, [and] the consciousness of female students."[20]

Along with allowing speakers who dealt with controversial topics to use its structures, the ACWF has permitted its official journals to serve as forums for scholars from the women's studies movement to articulate their analysis, put forth their vision, and advocate their cause.[21] Many scholars acknowledge the indispensable, ongoing support for their research and activism that they receive from ACWF staff.[22]

Most important, when scholars in the university attempt to institutionalize their endeavor on campus, they often call upon the ACWF to give their effort legitimacy and political clout. The director and research staff of ACWF's local branches are often invited to sit on the advisory committee of the program. As a deputy director of one women's studies program revealed:

We made it impossible for our President to turn down our proposal [to set up the program] because Madame xxx [director of the provincial ACWF] had been invited to be the head of our advisory committee. Besides, the President was further persuaded that it is true that in the long run, the program is going to make it easier for us to make noises on campus. However, if he did not approve the program at the outset, he would have been in hot water right away.[23]

When scholars of the women's studies program at Peking University described how they got their program set up, they mentioned the ample support and enthusiasm they had received from the national headquarters of the ACWF. The vice chancellor of the university even called the ACWF the program's "natal family," an organization that the program can always turn to.[24] The ACWF's critical role in the inauguration of women's studies programs in the universities can be summed up by the following opening remark made at an international conference organized by the women's studies program at Zhengzhou University. The conference put the program and its affiliated scholars under painstaking scrutiny because it was held several months after the 1989 Tiananmen event:

> I want to express my appreciation to directors and colleagues at the Women's Federation in Henan province, women's cadres school, and *Women's Lives* magazine (a magazine put out by the Women's Federation). Over the last years, we have supported each other in our effort to advance research on women's issues both at the provincial and national level. My special gratitude goes to comrade Yang Biru, the director of the Women's Federation in Henan, for her help and trust. Without such trust, support, and her unselfish, invaluable political backing, we would not have been able to convene this conference.[25]

Such evidence attests to the critical role played by the ACWF in giving birth to the women's studies movement. As a mass organization for women, the ACWF supplied invaluable political capital that the movement badly needed. I therefore disagree with the position held by many scholars that portrays the ACWF as nothing but an ideological state apparatus.[26] This view not only mistakenly treats the ACWF, an organization with thousands of branches and nearly a hundred thousand full-time working staff, as a homogeneous group and thus discourages a closer examination of the ever-changing micro-politics within the federation. It also fails to recognize the ongoing, intraorganizational relationship between the ACWF and many nongovernmental organizations that have emerged recently.

More generally, I believe that, in order to understand the institutional basis of the women's studies movement, we should ask what strategies have been adopted to take advantage of the progressively relaxing political climate in the reform era and also how and what resources in the preexisting system have been converted for the new initiatives.

Scholars involved in the establishment of China's first women's studies programs repeatedly emphasize that their programs were allowed to begin on condition that they ask for "no office, no budget, and no administrative staff."[27] In order to undertake new initiatives, all the program required was a legitimate status, symbolized by an official seal. Getting an official seal was rather easy in the reform era. For example, Funü Xuehui (Women's Society), the forerunner of the women's studies program at Zhengzhou University, acquired its official seal, and hence legitimate status, by affiliating itself with an already registered, official research institute. Once it had obtained its legal status, the association coordinated a new course to be taught at the Henan's Women's Cadre School. It also organized a national conference on women's issues and helped to publish a series of books on women. These activities laid a solid foundation for the women's studies program to be established at Zhengzhou University.

Not asking for additional financial and administrative support was a strategic move on the part of women scholars. It did not imply that resources were not needed to work on new initiatives. Li Xiaojiang, the director of the women's studies program at Zhengzhou University, explains how a "public sphere" was created within the old socialist system:

> In the old [existing socialist] system, everyone occupies a position to get paid. But the system itself allows no room for new initiatives. Even though we had virtually nothing to begin with, [the reason] our organization [program] could survive and develop was mainly because we were parasitical to the old system. I always tell people that we take a two-route approach (*liangtiaotui zoulu*). As individuals, we all belong to the old socialist system. We have our secured "iron rice bowl." As an organization, however, we are outside of the system, and hence don't bear all the encumbrances of the old system. Because we are part of the system, we are able to turn our supposedly supernumerary positions to work on new initiatives. Best of all, we never have to worry about not having a "rice bowl."[28]

This testimony demonstrates that at the institutional level there has been a parasitical relationship between the women's studies movement and the existing system. Although many of the programs came to exist with no additional administrative cost, human and financial resources in the existing system were appropriated and diverted to the new initiatives. The strategic move implied in the maneuver speaks loudly of women's agency and dexterity.

At the institutional level the establishment of women's studies centers at the universities means that the ACWF no longer has a monopoly as a representative of women's interests and voices. As a result, ideas and activities that do not completely conform with the official, orthodox approach can now germinate. Some scholars are beginning to search for answers about women's subordination outside the Marxist framework. Their research and publications intend to trace the historical roots of women's subordination. At the same time, they want to create a knowledge that is not male centered. Furthermore, the formal status of various centers gives scholars and activists legitimacy to offer new courses, conduct research, and organize conferences on women's issues. The centers also function as magnets in helping researchers and activists to make contacts and conduct collaborative work nationally and internationally.[29]

Emergence of Women's Organizations Outside the Universities

If the establishment of women's studies program resulted from scholars' calls for change within the academic sphere, the women's organizations outside of the universities have been set up in response to mounting social problems in society at large. Scholars who are dissatisfied with abstract, theoretical, academic exercises address these problems by taking an action-oriented approach. The Jinglun Family Center set up by sociologist Chen Yiyun, for example, provides a wide range of counseling services to individuals with family and marital problems. It also offers training programs to social workers. Chen's crusade began in the 1980s, when her inquiry into marriage and family issues brought her into personal contact with victims of divorce, domestic violence, and sexual harassment. She also learned that rapid social changes have created many problems in people's family and married lives. The narratives of her clients made her realize that sociological knowledge built upon conventional survey questionnaires fails to capture accurately the complicated problems her interviewees encountered in their real lives. Moreover, academic research becomes relevant to the struggling individual only if it is applied to action-oriented programs. Chen Yiyun and her colleagues at the center have given numerous lectures and counseling sessions on marriage and family nationwide. The Women's Hotline is another service-oriented organization in Beijing. As the first of its kind in China, it provides call-in counseling to distressed individuals. Set up by Wang Xingjuan, a retiree from the ACWF in 1992, the service has received an estimated thirty-thousand phone calls since that time.

Several aspects of these new organizations deserve further discussion. First, rapid social changes followed by economic reform have affected, and sometimes challenged, norms and values that used to regulate family lives and marital relationships. Individual men and women troubled by these new changes are in desperate search for answers. Knowledge and services dispensed by existing academic establishments, including the educational system and mass organizations such as the ACWF, have failed to meet the new demand. Organizations such as the Jinglung and Maple Leaves Centers arise to fill the vacuum by providing public lectures, personal counseling, and television and radio programs that cover personal matters ranging from marital relationships and sexual orientation to extramarital affairs. Although the issues covered are of interest to men and women, the centers' services particularly benefit women, who have suffered most from the negative consequences of recent reforms.

Second, the applied nature of the various programs goes beyond rigidly defined academic/scholarly boundaries. As a result, the intellectuals and professionals devoted to the work have taken up their mission as a personal crusade. They rarely receive recognition, support, or funding from the institutions to which they are formally affiliated, despite the fact that hundreds and thousands of Chinese have benefited from such programs.[30] Besides, they often have to draw upon their personal resources to make the shift. Family living rooms are used for counseling purposes. Other family members are called upon to handle hundreds of letters pouring in weekly. The devotion and commitment resemble the fulfillment of an intellectual's social responsibilities that is advocated in Confucius' teaching. The effort to bridge the gap between abstract, theoretical knowledge construction and applied community service has added an important dimension to the women's studies movement in China.

Third, the notion of nongovernmental organization (NGO) is still new in contemporary China. The CCP-led state continues to be suspicious of the NGOs' objectives, activities, and influence. Restrictive government rules and regulations have not been conducive to their grassroots initiatives. The state's inclination to be obstructive is most evident in its handling of events surrounding the 1995 United Nation's World Conference on Women and its accompanying Non-Governmental Organization Forum.

International Exchanges

In the early 1980s Chinese scholars and activists came into contact with international feminism mainly through translation of such classic works as Simone de Beavoir's *The Second Sex, The Feminine Mystique* (Germaine Greer), and Carolyn Heilbrun's *In a Different Voice.* During this period only a few Chinese scholars visited the West. Portrayal of Chinese women was predominantly done by Western sinologists with minimum consultation and collaboration with the Chinese counterparts. An international conference held at

Harvard University in 1992 marked the beginning of a new era. At that conference Chinese women scholars engaged in public debates on the nature, historical path, and future prospects of women's liberation in China.[31] From then on, indigenous perspectives gained a more prominent place in the international arena. International exchange reached its height in preparations for the United Nation's Fourth World Conference on Women in the summer of 1995.

An estimated thirty-five to forty thousand women from around the world, including five thousand Chinese women, attended the conference and its Non-Governmental Organization Forum. Preparation was under way years before 1995: an unprecedented number of Chinese women had participated in regional conferences abroad, organized international or national conferences at home, and engaged in dialogue with international women's groups. Although Chinese women's voices were excluded from debates concerning women's issues in China, the conference and the NGO forum did give Chinese women a chance to tell the world what they had being doing at home. Most important, the occasion brought them in direct contact with international feminism and feminist activism. These exposures and exchanges have been a mixed blessing for the women's studies movement in China.[32]

At the institutional level many women faculty who wanted to set up women's studies programs at their universities used the upcoming women's conference as justification for their cause. Quite a few of them managed to get their programs registered and approved before the conference. There was also an increase in intra-institutional collaboration. Initiatives involving scholars and activists at universities, the ACWF, official trade unions, and other women's organizations were funded in celebration of China's hosting of the conference.

Many academic journals had special issues on women, and an unprecedented number of books on women were published. These included case studies, collections of articles on specific subjects, translations of English publications, and introductions to the international women's movement. An encyclopedia, statistical data, and historical documents on Chinese women were also compiled. Two projects are particularly useful in facilitating international exchanges. An *English-Chinese Lexicon of Women and Law* explains terms such as *feminism, gender,* and *NGO* by referring to their historical, political, and/or cultural context in the West. The Chinese-English entries include current expressions that reflect Chinese women's economic, political, and social position and status. As a whole, the *Lexicon* serves as a constant reminder and useful tool for those involved in international, cross-cultural dialogue.[33] In a book entitled *A Review of Western Feminist Research* scholars affiliated to the Chinese Society for Women's Studies in the United States provide a critical analysis of feminist scholarship in various academic disciplines and fields in the United States. The society's members are Chinese students and scholars from overseas who seek to encourage the study of Chinese women; the book is the product of their long-term commitment to their sisters in the homeland.[34]

The unprecedented enthusiasm and activism among women and women's groups were marred by a perceived sense of threat on the part of the CCP's top leaders in early 1995. The fear that international women's groups might stage protests and demonstrations during the conference displaced their original intention to raise China's international profile by hosting the event. The site of the NGO forum was moved away from Beijing and was accompanied by tighter control over women's research and activism. Activities associated with the conference and the Chinese delegates themselves were closely scrutinized. The desire of CCP officials to publicize the regime's accomplishments with regard to women's liberation made them condemn any discussion or research that focused on the problems of Chinese women as counter to the national interest. The greatest irony came when the women's studies program at Zhengzhou University, the first women's studies program in China, was shut down prior to the conference on the pretext of its "involvement in the bourgeois feminist movement" and its director prevented from attending the forum.[35] To weather the freezing political climate, women scholars and activists put their heads down and kept their voices low. "Just keep a low profile and wait for the paranoia to pass," many said.[36]

The most positive aspect of the international exchange has been the cross-fertilization between global and local feminist activism. On the one hand, the global/local contact helps to nourish more relaxed attitudes toward Western terms such as *feminism* and *feminist movement* that used to have a negative connotation in China. Foreign visits and international exchange have also made Chinese activists aware of issues they had once overlooked. Discussion and research on domestic violence and sexual harassment have flourished. Furthermore, Chinese activists find that many problems they have encountered are identical to those being acted on by international women's groups abroad. This new understanding encourages Chinese activists and scholars to press for further changes and improvements at home. This commonality and a sense of sisterhood have also made it easier for Chinese activists and scholars to raise and discuss their problems at the international platform: doing so is no longer perceived as an act of washing one's dirty linen in public.

In sharp contrast to this sense of global sisterhood is Chinese women activist and scholar's parallel effort at asserting their autonomy vis-à-vis the international women's groups, on the one hand, and the CCP-led state, on the other. Stepping into the international arena, Chinese women come to witness and experience the dominating power of First World women. After long being spoken for and/or about by their domineering sisters of the First World, Chinese women are gradually learning how to make their voices heard in the international arena. At least to some Chinese activists and scholars Western feminism offers no solutions for Chinese women's liberation. Concerted efforts must be made to formulate a feminism and a feminist activism that incorporate China's cultural, historical, and sociopolitical characteristics.

When abroad, Chinese activists and scholars witness daring actions and diverse initiatives organized by various women's groups. They also come to appreciate a women's movement that has its roots in popular, local activism, rather than in a state-orchestrated course of action dominated by the CCP. Many scholars and activists begin to get involved in projects and initiatives that go beyond the official territory. Most significantly, earlier calls to revise and renegotiate women's relationship with the CCP-led state now find a broader sociopolitical constituency. A multitude of lively, diverse voices are gradually weakening the CCP's monolithic, hegemonic position. The chilly climate and tightening control inflicted by the CCP signals the powerful impact that Chinese, and international, women's movements are perceived to possess. Although the silencing measures willed by the CCP-led state continue to be a potential threat, the conference has been referred to as "a historic turning point" for the women's movement in China because activities leading up to it have made the pluralist approach toward women's issues an irreversible trend.[37]

Conclusion and Discussion

China's women's studies movement has emerged as a result of the efforts by intellectual and professional women to address unresolved issues embedded in the CCP's approach to gender equality. It is also a response to the negative consequences for women of the state's economic reform. In recent years exchanges and dialogue with international women's groups have enriched the movement and introduced Chinese women scholars and activists to new challenges.

Institutionalization of the women's studies movement has meant a conversion of human and financial resources within the higher educational system that has led to changes in the curriculum and, more generally, to a transformation of the landscape of knowledge. As a whole, the alternately volatile and relaxed political atmosphere of the reform era has been critical for the development of the Chinese women's studies movement. The ACWF has, in turn, supported and oppressed women's initiatives. The paradoxical nature of the CCP-led state presents a great challenge to scholars in the China field in which the oppressive nature of the CCP state is predominantly featured. Women activists in China, on the other hand, continue to keep their wits about the local and national politics and take new ground whenever and wherever possible.

The conviction and activism of intellectual and professional women constitute the main driving forces of the women's studies movement in China. Within an ever-changing political climate, they seize the opportunities for innovation. Strategically, they take advantage of cracks in the existing system and make their way into new territory. The women's studies movement in China testifies to Chinese women's vision, agency, and determination, which have seldom been sufficiently recognized and acknowledged.

NOTES

1. Chandra T. Mohanty, "Under Western Eyes: Feminist Scholarship and Colonial Discourses," in *Third World Women and the Politics of Feminism,* ed. Chandra T. Mohanty et al. (Bloomington: Indiana University Press, 1991), 51–80; Aihwa Ong, "Colonialism and Modernity: Feminist Re-Presentations of Women in Non-Western Societies," *Inscriptions* 3, no. 4 (1988): 79–93; Gayatri C. Spivak, *The Other Worlds: Essays in Cultural Politics* (New York: Methuen, 1987).

2. Vivienne Shue, *The Search of the State: Sketches of the Chinese Body Politic* (Stanford: Stanford University Press, 1988); Y-L. Liu, "Reform from Below: The Private Economy and Local Politics in the Rural Industrialization of Wenzhou," *China Quarterly* 130 (1992): 293–322.

3. Author's personal communication.

4. Jun Liang, "A Serious Mission," in *Changing Lives: Life Stories of Asian Pioneers in Women's Studies,* ed. Committee on Women's Studies in Asia (New York: The Feminist Press, 1995), 125–26.

5. Li Xiaojiang, "Preface," *Zouxiang nüren* (Towards the femininity of women) (Hong Kong: Association for the Advancement of Feminism, 1993), 3.

6. To this day many women in China still refer to menstruation as being *daomeile.* For example, one would tell a friend that she has a headache because "*wo kuaiyao daomeile*" (I'm having my menstruation soon).

7. Xie Lihua, in "Xiantan shuo shao zhiyi: Zhongwai funü gongzuo lüetan" (Dialogue One: chatting on women's work) in *Nüxing de fanxiang: Yiqun ceng canyu '95 funü dahui guoji choubei huiyi de Zhongguo nüxing de xinsheng jieji* (Reflection and resonance: stories of Chinese women involved in international preparatory activities

for the 1995 NGO Forum on Women), ed. Wong Yuen Ling (Beijing: Ford Foundation, 1995), 214.

8. Liu Bohong, in ibid., 224.

9. Li Xiaojiang, *Zouxiang nüren*, 4–5.

10. Jun Liang, "A Serious Mission," 126–27.

11. Li Xiaojiang, "Creating A Public Sphere: A Self-Portrait in Women's Studies Movement in China," *Asian Journal of Women's Studies* 2 (1996): 83.

12. Ibid., 84.

13. Li, *Zouxiang nüren*, 19–20.

14. *Zhongguo funü yundong wenxian ziliao huibian* (A collection of documents on the Chinese women's movement) (Beijing: Zhongguo funü chubanshe, 1988).

15. Luo Qiang, "Fulian shi guangda funü de zhongyao daibiaozhe" (The ACWF is the representative of the mass women) (speech presented to the Women's Federation in Xingjiang Autonomous Region, September 19, 1979), in *Zhongguo funü yundong wenxian ziliao huibian*, 497.

16. Kang Keqing, "Fenfa ziqiang kaichuang funü yundong xingjumian" (Striving ahead for a new era in the women's movement) (report presented to the Fifth National Women's Congress, September 2, 1983), in *Zhungguo funü yundong wenxian ziliao huibian*, 845–58.

17. Tan Sheng, "Shehui zhuanxing yu Zhongguo funü jiuye" (Social change and Chinese women's employment), in *Zhongguo funü yu fazhan* (Chinese women and development), ed. Du Fangqin et al. (Zhengzhou: Henan renmin chubanshe, 1993), 380–82.

18. Zheng Wang, "Maoism, Feminism, and the UN Conference on Women: Women's Studies Research in Contemporary China," *Journal of Women's History* 8, no. 4 (1997): 126–51.

19. Li Xiaojiang, "Creating a Public Sphere," 84–85.

20. Jun Liang, "A Serious Mission," 132.

21. Li Xiaojiang, *Gonggong kongjian de chuangzao—funü yanjiu yundong: Yili gean de ziwo fenxi* (Creating a public sphere women's studies movement: a case in self-analysis) (unpublished monograph, 1995), 12.

22. Many international scholars also record that they have had to rely on the ACWF staff and networks for their field research in China. See Hill Gates, "Cultural Support for Birth Limitation among Urban Capital-Owning Women," in Deborah Davis and Stevan Harrel, eds., *Chinese Families in the Post-Mao Era* (Berkeley: University of California Press, 1993), 251–76; Ellen Judd, *Gender and Power in Rural North China* (Stanford: Stanford University Press, 1994); and Margery Wolf, *Revolution Postponed: Women in Contemporary China* (Stanford: Stanford University Press, 1985).

23. Author's personal communication.

24. *Funü yanjiu dongtai* (Events of women's studies), Research Center on Women's Issues in China and Foreign Countries, Beijing University, no. 1 (1993): 6.

25. Li Xiaojiang, *Zouxiang nüren*, 69. In Li Xiaojiang, *Nüjie da huishi* (A remarkable women's rendezvous), Li provides a rather metaphorical description of the tremendous pressure intended to prevent the conference from being convened. Her remarks on the political maneuver are most telling. She emphasized that, "under such a

political climate, one has to be courageous to call for a conference. However, it takes artful dexterity to actually make the conference a reality. We have plenty of courage. We are in no shortage of dexterous sense either."

26. Kay A. Johnson, *Women, the Family, and Peasant Revolution in China* (Chicago: University of Chicago Press, 1983); Judith Stacey, *Patriarchy and Socialist Revolution in China* (Berkeley: University of California Press, 1983); Wolf, *Revolution Postponed.*

27. Tao Jie, "Women's Studies in China," *Women's Studies Quarterly,* nos. 1–2 (1996): 358; Fangqin Du, *Faxian funü de lishi* (The discovery of women's history) (Tianjin: Shehui chubanshe, 1996); Li, "Creating a Public Sphere," 73.

28. Li, *Gonggong kongjian de chuangzao,* 13.

29. Tao, "Women's Studies in China," 358.

30. For example, for many years, Chen Yiyun could not get a promotion from her research institute, nor was she given research funding. According to Chen: "In the somber hall of academia, even printed words are ranked hierarchically. My books and articles are written for the general public. They are seen [by my colleagues] as trivial and non-scholarly. Besides, because there are very few women in research institutions, it is very difficult to receive funding for research projects on and conducted by women." *Zhongguo funü bao* (1994).

31. Christina Gilmartin et al., *Engendering China: Women, Culture, and the State* (Cambridge, Mass.: Harvard University Press, 1994).

32. In an unpublished 1996 essay entitled "The Making of Chinese Women's Gender and National Identities: An Analysis of the Political Discourse Surrounding the 1995 World Conference on Women in Beijing" Ping-chun Hsiung and Renita Yuk-lin Wong examine the discursive politics that surrounded the conference and NGO forum and its implications.

33. Sharon K. Hom and Chunying Xin, *English-Chinese Lexicon of Women and Law* (Beijing: United Nations Educational, Scientific and Cultural Organization and China Translation and Publishing Corporation, 1995).

34. Zhou Jiangqiang, ed., *Xifang nüxing zhuyi yanjiu pingjie* (A review of Western feminist research) (Beijing: Sanlian shudian, 1995.)

35. Li Xiaojiang, *Wo wei shenmo bu canjia 95 shifuhui* (Why I refused to attend the '95 Women's Conference) (unpublished open letter, 1996).

36. Wang, "Maoism, Feminism, and the UN Conference on Women," 197. The political tide turned once again after the conference was concluded without major incidents and embarrassment. Celebrations were held by various offices of the ACWF, and individual delegates were congratulated for their contributions. The women's studies program headed by Li Xiaojiang was relocated to Henan University in 1996.

37. Ibid.; Li, *Wo shenmo bu canjia 95 shifuhui.*

Glossary

Aichi Daigaku　愛知大學
Aiguo nüxue　愛國女學
Anhui shifan daxue fushu zhongxue　安徽師範大學附屬中學
Arao Sei　荒尾 精

Bai Yongda　白永達
baihua　白話
Bailu dong　白鹿洞
banlao qu　半老區
baofu xin　報復心
baoyang　褒揚
bense jiaohui　本色教會
bense yundong　本色運動
bu de xianqi　不得賢妻
buji　簿記

Cai Yuanpei　蔡元培
caiji xin　猜忌心
Cangqian　倉前
Chan, David K. K.　陳建強
Chen Hengting　陳衡庭
Chen Heqing　陳河清
Chen Lin　陳霖
Chen Nengguang (Bintai)　陳能 (丙台)
Chen Yiling　陳義令
Chen Zhilin (Zhiting)　陳之麟 (芷汀)
Chen Zhimei　陳之美
Chen Zizhan　陳子展

chongai　寵愛
Chongqing　重慶
Chongqing gongye guanli xueyuan　重慶工業管理學院
Chongqing shifan xueyuan　重慶師範學院
chouhen xin　仇恨心
Chuanjiao bainian jinian huiyi　傳教百年紀念會議
chudeng shiye xuetang　初等實業學堂
chudeng xiao xuetang　初等小學堂
chuji shifan xuetang　初級師範學堂
Chūka Gakuseibu　中華學生部
chunjie　純潔
Chunqiu　春秋
ciai xin　慈愛心
cishu　慈淑
Cui Dan　崔丹
Cuiwen Zhongxue　粹文中學
cun tianli, mie renyu　存天理, 滅人欲
cun xue　村學
cun zhang　村長

Dagong bao　大公報
Dai Jitao　戴季陶
daigaku　大學
daishimei　大使命
Daizu　傣族
danghua jiaoyu　黨化教育

451

dangyi　黨義

danzi　單字

dao　道

daomei le　倒霉了

daoxue　道學

daxue　大學

daxue ling　大學令

daxuetang　大學堂

daxue yuan　大學院

daxue yubeike　大學預備科

dayundongjia　大運動家

de　德

Deng Ken　鄧墾

Deng Xiaoping　鄧小平

Deng Yingchao　鄧穎超

deyu　德育

dianshi　殿試

Ding Gang　丁鋼

Dong Zhongshu　董仲舒

dongba wenhua　東巴文化

Dongbei daxue　東北大學

Dongbei jiaotong daxue　東北交通大學

Dongfang zazhi　東方雜誌

Dongwu　東吳

doufu　豆腐

duanqian　端謙

duo qudao　多渠道

er nai shi zhi guang　爾乃世之光

fa Kong Meng　法孔孟

fan yu qing　反欲情

fangzong ziyou zhi pishuo　放從自由之
　　僻說

Fanzhen nüzi xiaoxue　范真女子小學

faren　法人

fazhan　發展

fazhan guyou wenhua　發展固有文化

fei anfen nüzi　非安分女子

feiwu　廢物

Feng Yong　馮庸

fengshui　風水

Fengtian　奉天

fen jiaoxi　分教習

fenke daxue　分科大學

fenlizhe　分利者

fu　府

fu jiaoshou　副教授

fu jiaoxi　副教習

Fu Zengxiang　傅增湘

fucong　服從

fude　婦德

funü　婦女

Funü shibao　婦女時報

Funü xuehui　婦女學會

Funü zazhi　婦女雜誌

ganren zhi moli　感人之魔力

gaodeng shifan xuexiao　高等師範學校

gaodeng shiye xuetang　高等實業學堂

gaodeng xue　高等學

gaodeng xuetang　高等學堂

gaodeng youmin chuangzao chang　高等
　　游民創造廠

gaozhuang　告狀

Gendai Chūgoku Gakubu　現代中國學部

gexing　個性

Gong si li daxue guicheng 公私立大學規程

gongban 公辦

gongfen 工分

gongmin xunlian 公民訓練

gongnong jiaoyu 工農教育

gongshi 貢士

Goto Ryuzaburo 後藤 隆三郎

Goto Shimpei 後藤 新平

guanhua 官話

guanxi 關係

Guoli Beiping shifan daxue 國立北平師範大學

guomin 國民

guomin xuexiao 國民學校

guomin zhi mu 國民之母

guoyu 國語

guozi jian 國子監

guozi xue 國子學

Han Wudi 漢武帝

hanzu xuexiao 漢族學校

Haerbin gongye daxue 哈爾濱工業大學

He Jing 何靜

He Zengming 賀增明

Hebei shengli yixueyuan 河北省立醫學院

Hsiung Ping-Chun 熊秉純

Hu Jun 胡峻

Hu Shi 胡適

Huang Yanpei 黃炎培

Huaxi 華西

Huazhong 華中

huishi 會試

Huiwen nüxiao 匯文女校

Hunan zixiu daxue 湖南自修大學

Ide Saburo 井手 三郎

Imai Hideo 今井 秀雄

jia 家

jia xiaozi 假小子

jiang hui 講會

Jiang Jieshi 蔣介石

Jiang Menglin 蔣夢麟

Jiang Weiqiao 蔣維喬

Jiang Zemin 江澤民

jianli zhi si 姦利之私

jianzhen 堅貞

jianzhi xin 堅執心

jiao 教

jiao an 教案

jiaohui xuexiao 教會學校

jiaoshou 教授

jiaoshou zhixiao 教授治校

jiaoyan shi 教研室

jiaoyan zu 教研組

jiaoyu jiuguo 教育救國

jiaoyu keyan xianjin xuexiao 教育科研先進學校

jiaoyu wanneng 教育萬能

jiashi 家事

jiashi ke 家事課

jiazheng 家政

jiazhong shiye xuexiao 甲種實業學校

jidu xin 忌妒心

jielie zhencao 節烈貞操

jigong xuexiao 技工學校

jilie 激烈

Jilin 吉林

Jilin daxue 吉林大學

Jilin falü zhuanke xuexiao 吉林法律專科學校

Jin Songcen 金松岑

Jinjiang shuyuan 錦江書院

Jinling 金陵

Jinling daxue 金陵大學

Jingxing bao 警醒報

Jingxing she 警醒社

jingxue ke daxue 經學科大學

jingxue yuan 經學院

jinja 神社

jinshi 進士

jinshi ke 進士科

Juewu she 覺悟社

juren 舉人

kaifang 開放

Kanaya Kazuhide 金谷 一秀

Kang Youwei 康有為

Kazan kai 霞山會

keji fuli 克己復禮

kejiao xingguo 科教興國

keyou kewu 可有可無

kiken shiso 危險思想

kokka teki kannen 國家的觀念

Kongzi (Confucius) 孔子

Kongde nüxue 孔德女學

Konoe Atsumaro 近藤 篤麿

koutou 叩頭

Koyūkai 滬友會

Kui Jun 奎俊

Laozi 老子

laodongke 勞動課

laodong shehui zhi ren 勞動社會之人

Lee Jong Auk 李鍾玉

Li Chenggan 李承干

Li Lanqing 李嵐清

Liji 禮記

lixue 理學

li, yi, lian, chi 禮, 義, 廉, 恥

Liang Qichao 梁啟超

Liang Shuming 梁漱冥

liangtiaotui zoulu 兩條腿走路

lianxi shiji 聯繫實際

lienü jiefu 烈女節婦

Lijiang 麗江

lijiao gangling 立教綱領

Lijiazhuang 李家莊

Lim Kei Chul 林啟哲

Lin Handa 林漢達

Lin Sen 林森

Lingnan 嶺南

Liu Kunyi 劉坤一

Liu Menggeng 劉夢庚

Liu Shuzhen 劉樹真

liyi 禮儀

Lü Bicheng 呂碧城

Lu Feikui 陸費逵

Lu Xun 魯迅

lunli 倫理

lunli xue 倫理學

luohou 落後

Lüshun 旅順

Lüshun gongke daxue 旅順工科大學

Lüshun gongke xuetang　旅順工科學

lüyou xinli xue　旅游心理學

Ma Qianli　馬千里
Ma Xiangbo　馬相伯
Ma Xulun　馬敍倫
mantou　饅頭
Manzhou yike daxue　滿州醫科大學
Manzhouli (Manchuria)　滿州里
Mao Zedong　毛澤東
Matsuo Shunichi　松尾　俊市
Meiji　明治
Minagawa Toyoji　皆川　豊治
minban　民辦
Minban jiaoyu tiandi　民辦教育天地
mingyi　名義
Minnan jiuhuohui　閩南救火會
minquan　民權
minxin　民心
minzhong jiaoyu　民眾教育
minzu　民族
minzu jiaoyu　民族教育
minzu tuanjie　民族團結
minzu wudao　民族舞蹈
Mo Zi　墨子
Mok Ka-Ho　莫家豪

Nagai Sen　長井　洗
Nan Manzhou yixuetang　南滿州醫學堂
Nanjing daxue　南京大學
Nanjing tongwen shuyuan　南京同文書院
Naxi　納西
neizhu　內助
Nezu Hajime　根津　一

Nisshin Bōeki Kenkyujo　日清貿易研究所
nongmin jiaoyu　農民教育
nongmin yeyu jiaoyu yiban yi shizi xuewenhua weizhu　農民業餘教育一般以識字學文化為主
nongye jishu xuexiao　農業技術學校
nü feixing jia　女飛行家
nüde　女德
Nüjie zhong　女界鍾
Nüxue bao　女學報
nüzi shifan xuetang　女子師範學堂
Nüzi shijie　女子世界
nüzi xiao xuetang　女子小學堂
Nüzi xuanjiang hui　女子宣講會

Ōsaki Toraji　大崎　虎二
Ōtsuka Yutaka　大塚　豐
Ōuchi Chozo　大內　暢三
Ozawa Toyokichi　小沢　豐吉

Pei Chao　裴潮
peiyang wuchan jieji jieban ren　培養無產階級接班人
pingmin jiaoyu　平民教育
pinmin jiaoyu　貧民教育
putong hua　普通話

Qian Junrui　錢君瑞
Qiaonan gongyi she　橋南公益社
qigong　氣功
Qilu　齊魯
qinai　親愛
Qinding xuetang zhangcheng　欽定學堂章程

qing 情

qinjian 勤儉

qinlue zhengce 侵略政策

Qiu Jin 秋瑾

Qiu Linshu 邱麟書

Quanguo funü lianhe hui 全國婦女聯合會

quyi 曲藝

ren zhi fa, zai ai ren, buzai ai wo 仁之法,在愛人, 不在愛我

rencai 人才

renge hua 人格化

renquan 人權

roushun 柔順

Saito Kazuo 齋藤 和雄

sanji banxue, liangji guanli 三級辦學, 兩級管理

sanmin zhuyi 三民主義

sanzi aiguo yundong 三字愛國運動

Sanzi Jing 三字經

saomang dui 掃盲隊

Sato Tsueyoshi 佐藤 恆義

Sei-A Hyōshō no tō 靖亞表紹 ９塔

Sei-A Jinja 靖亞神社

senmon gakkō 專門學校

Shandong 山東

shang ziran, zhan gexing 尚自然展個性

shangdeng 上等

shangwu 尚武

Shanghai shisan nüzi zhongxue 上海市三女子中學

shaoshu minzu 少數民族

shashen chengren 殺身成仁

shechi huali 奢侈華麗

shehui fengqi 社會風氣

shehui jiaoyu/shakai kyoiku 社會教育

shehui liliang 社會力量

shehui zhuyi jianshe 社會主義建設

Sheng Yuehan 聖約翰

shenglizhe 生利者

shengren 聖人

shifan xuexiao 師範學校

shifu 師傅

Shigu 石鼓

Shina tsu 支那通

Shinto 神道

shishi 志士

Shishi xinbao 時事新報

shishi zhengzhi jiaoyu 時事政治教育

shiye buxi putong xuetang 實業補習普通學堂

shiye buxi xuexiao 實業補習學校

shōmuka 商務科

shoujie 守節

shunliang 順良

shuxue 書學

shuyuan 書院

Shuowen jiezi 說文解字

Sichuan lianhe daxue 四川聯合大學

Sili Feng Yong daxue 私立馮庸大學

simen xue 四門學

Sipsong Panna (Xishuangbanna) 西雙版納

sishu 私塾

sishu xiansheng 私塾先生

sixing yinluan 肆行淫亂

Song Qingling　宋慶齡
Song Xiaolian　宋小廉
suan xue　算學
Sun Zhongshan (Yixian)　孫中山 (逸仙)
Suzuki Masao　鈴木 正雄

tai xue　太學
Takanarita　高成田
Takeuchi Yoshimi　竹內 好
Tao Xingzhi　陶行知
tecai　特才
ti　體
tian ren he yi　天人合一
tiancai　天才
Tianjin nüjie aiguo tongzhi hui　天津女界愛國同志會
Tianjin xuesheng lianhe hui　天津學生聯合會
tigao minzu suzhi　提高民族素質
Tiyu hui　體育會
Tō-A Dōbun Shoin　東亞同文書院
Tō-A Dōbunkai　東亞同文會
Tō-A no keirin　東亞 經綸
Tokugawa　德川
Tokyo Dōbun Shoin　東京同文書院
tongcai　通才
Tongmeng hui　同盟會
tongru yuan　通儒院
tongsu　通俗
Tongsu kexue jiangyan hui　通俗科學講研會
tongsu liyi　通俗禮儀
Tongsu yanjiu hui　通俗研究會
tuanti xunlian　團體訓練

tuomang　脫盲

Umezaki Kakuichi　梅崎 覺一

Wan Shuyong　萬樹庸
Wang Anshi　王安石
Wang Guowei　王國維
Wang Yongjiang　王永江
Wang Yuqing　王宇清
Wang Zhaofan　汪兆璠
wanshun　婉順
wei haojie　為豪杰
weisheng yuan　衛生員
wen　文
Wen Yidou　聞一多
wenhua shuiping he zhengzhi shuiping　文化水平和政治水平
wenmang　文盲
Wuben nüshu　務本女塾
wuwei　無為

xian　縣
xiangfu　相夫
xiangshi　鄉試
Xiangya　湘雅
xianjun　先軍
xianmu　賢母
xianmu liangqi　賢母良妻
xiannü　賢女
xianqi　賢妻
xianshi shenghuo ren　現實生活人
Xiao Jing　孝經
xiao xuetang　小學堂
xiaoti　孝悌

xiaoxue 小學
xiaozhang 校長
Xiaozhuang 曉莊
Xiehe 協合
xin 心
Xin funü 新婦女
Xin qingnian 新青年
Xinan lianhe daxue 西南聯合大學
Xinan Zhen 新安鎮
xing 性
xing xiangjin ye, xi xiangyuan ye 性相近
也, 習相遠也
Xingdong 興東
xingwei guifan 行為規範
xingxue yaozhi 興學要旨
Xinmin 新民
Xinmin congbao 新民叢報
xionghan 凶悍
xiuji 修己
xiushen 修身
xue 學
Xue Fenshi 薛芬士
xue yi zhi yong 學以致用
Xuebu 學部
xuezhang 學長
Xun Zi 荀子
xunci 訓詞
xunzi 訓子

Yan Yangchu 晏陽初
Yanjing 燕京
Yao Shun Yu Tang Wen Wu Zhou Gong
堯舜禹湯文武周公
yi 意

yilai xing 依賴性
Yin Xuecun 殷雪村
yincai shijiao 因才施教
Yingtian fu 應天府
yishi 醫士
yishu 藝術
yitu xuetang 藝徒學堂
yizhong shiye xuexiao 乙種實業學校
Yizu 彝族
yongci 永慈
youji shifan xuetang 優級師範學堂
youji xiqi 游擊習氣
youjiao wulei 有教無類
youjin jiyuan 由近及遠
youti youyong 有體有用
youzhi shishang 有志士商
yu 欲
Yu Jiaju 余家菊
yu you zhongda zhengzhi renwu 遇有重
大政治任務
yuan 元
Yuan Shikai 袁世凱
Yuan Zheng 袁征
yucai 育才
Yucai sili zhongxue 育才私立中學
Yucai Xue Zheng xiwang gongcheng 育
才薛正希望工程
Yuelu 岳麓
yuke 預科
Yun Daiying 惲代英

zafei 雜費
zeren 責任
zeren zhi 責任制

Zhang Boling　張伯苓

Zhang Heling　張鶴齡

Zhang Henjia　張亨佳

Zhang Juzheng　張居正

Zhang Xueliang　張學良

Zhang Zhidong　張之洞

Zhao Houda　趙厚達

Zhao Jingxin　趙景信

Zhao Ziyang　趙紫陽

Zhejiang　浙江

zhen　鎮

Zheng Guanying　鄭觀應

zheng jiaoxi　正教習

Zheng Xian　鄭錫安

zhenggui　正規

zhengjiao heyi　政教合一

zhengjing　正經

zhenshu　貞淑

zhenshun　貞順

zhi　智

zhihui bu　指揮部

zhijia zhixu　治家秩序

Zhijiang　之江

Zhili　直隸

Zhili diyi nüzi shifan xuexiao　直隸第一
　女子師範學校

zhisheng xianshi　至聖先師

zhiye　職業

Zhong Ningsha　仲寧莎

zhong xuetang　中學堂

zhong xuexiao　中學校

zhongdeng shiye xuetang　中等實業學堂

zhongdeng xue　中等學

Zhongguo hua　中國化

Zhongguo nübao　中國女報

Zhongguo zhi mingyun　中國之命運

Zhonghua jidujiao xiejin hui　中華基督教
　協進會

*zhongjun, zunkong, shanggong, shangwu,
　shangshi*　忠君, 尊孔, 尚公, 尚武, 尚實

Zhongxi nüxiao　中西女校

Zhongxi xuetang　中西學堂

zhongzhuan　中專

zhou　州

Zhou Enlai　周恩來

zhu jiaoshou　助教授

Zhu Xi　朱熹

Zhuangzi　莊子

zhuanmen xuexiao　專門學校

zhujiao　助教

zhushou　助手

zhuzao guomin mu　鑄造國民母

zichuan　自傳

zidong　自動

zifei sheng　自費生

zijue　自覺

zili　自立

ziyang　自養

ziyou jiehun　自由結婚

ziyou, pingdeng, boai　自由, 平等, 博愛

zizhi　自治

zizhiquan　自治權

zizhuquan　自主權

zong　宗

Zouping　鄒平

Zunjing shuyuan　尊經書院

Zuo Yaoxian　左耀先

zuoshi　坐食

Bibliography

Abe, Hiroshi, ed. *Nit-Chū kyōiku Bunka Kōryū to Masatsu* (Sino-Japanese educational and cultural exchanges and conflicts). Tokyo: Daiichi Shobō Publisher, 1983.

Alitto, Guy S. *The Last Confucian: Liang Shu-ming and the Chinese Dilemma of Modernity.* 2d ed. Berkeley: University of California Press, 1986.

Ames, Roger, trans. and comm. *Sun Tzu: the Master of Warfare.* New York: Ballantine Books, 1993.

Anderson, Benedict. *Imagined Communities: Reflections on the Origin and Spread of Nationalism. Rev. ed.* New York: Verso, 1991.

Anglo-Chinese College after Twenty-two Months of War: Chinas Reconstruction through Armed Resistance. Foochow: Christian Herald Industrial Mission Press, 1939.

Arnove, Robert F., and Harvey J. Graff, eds. *National Literacy Campaigns: Historical and Comparative Perspectives.* New York: Plenum Press, 1987.

Ayers, William. *Chang Chih-tung and Educational Reform in China.* Cambridge: Harvard University Press, 1971.

Bailey, Paul. *Reform the People: Changing Attitudes towards Popular Education in Early 20th Century China.* Vancouver: University of British Columbia Press; Edinburgh: Edinburgh University Press, 1990.

Bao, Jialin, ed. *Zhongguo funü shilunji xuji* (Supplementary volume of collected historical essays on Chinese women). Taibei: Daoxiang chubanshe, 1991.

Bastid, Marianne. *Educational Reform in Early 20th-Century China.* Trans. Paul Bailey. Ann Arbor: Center for Chinese Studies, University of Michigan, 1988.

Bateson, Mary Catherine. *Composing a Life.* New York: Plume, 1990.

Bays, Daniel H., ed. *Christianity in China: From the Eighteenth Century to the Present,* Stanford: Stanford University Press, 1996.

Beahan, Charlotte. "The Women's Movement and Nationalism in Late Ch'ing China." Ph.D. diss. Columbia University, 1976.

Becker, Howard S. *The Outsiders: Studies in the Sociology of Deviance.* New York: Free Press, 1973.

Bernstein, G. Lee, ed. *Recreating Japanese Women, 1600–1945.* Berkeley: University of California Press, 1991.

Berstecher, Dieter, ed. *Education and Rural Development: Issues for Planning and Research.* Paris: Unesco, International Institute for Educational Planning, 1985.

Bim-Bud, B. M. "Antropologicheskiye osnovanija teorii i praktiki obrazovanija" (The anthropological basis for educational theory and practice). *Pedagogy,* no. 5 (1994).

Bing, Sang. *Wanqing xuetang yu shehui biange* (Schools and social change in the late Qing). Shanghai: Xuelin chubanshe, 1995.

Blonsky, P. P. *Izbranije pedagogicheskije i psikhologicheskije sochineniya* (Selected pedagogical and psychological works). Moscow: Pedagogika, 1979.

Bodalev, A. A., et al. "Kontseptsija vospitanija uchascchejsia molodiozhi" (The concept of bringing up youth at schools). *Pedagogy,* nos. 3–4 (1992).

Boli, John. *New Citizens for a New Society: The Institutional Origins of Mass Schooling in Sweden.* Oxford: Pergamon Press, 1989.

Bondarevskaya, E. V., et al. "Teorija i praktika lichnostno-orientirovannogo obrazovanija" (Theory and practice of individual-oriented pedagogy). *Pedagogy,* no. 5 (1996).

Boorman, Howard L., and Richard C. Howard, eds. *Biographical Dictionary of Republican China.* New York: Columbia University Press, 1971.

Borthwick, Sally. *Education and Social Change in China: The Beginnings of the Modern Era.* Stanford: Hoover Institution Press, 1983.

Brook, T., and B. Michael Frolic, eds. *China and Civil Society.* New York: M. E. Sharpe, 1997.

Burgess, John S. *The Guilds of Peking.* New York: Columbia University Press, 1928.

Bush, Richard C., Jr. *Religion in Communist China.* Nashville: Abingdon Press, 1970.

Cai Yuanpei meixue wenxuan (Cai Yuanpei's selected works on aesthetics). Beijing: Beijing Daxue chubanshe, 1983.

Cai Yuanpei xuanji (Selected works of Cai Yuanpei). Beijing: Zhonghua shuju, 1984.

Cai, Yuanpei, et al. *Wanqing sanshiwu nian lai zhi Zhongguo jiaoyu, 1897–1931* (Chinese education in the late Qing and over the last thirty-five years). 1931. Reprint. Hong Kong: 1969.

Caldarola, Carlo. *Christianity: The Japanese Way.* Leiden: E. J. Brill, 1979.

Chan, C., and N. Chow. *More Welfare after Economic Reform? Welfare Development in the People's Republic of China.* Hong Kong: Center of Urban Planning and Environmental Management, University of Hong Kong, 1992.

Chang, Geun Hwang. "Political and Social Factors in the Establishment of Buddhism and Christianity in Korea: Social Change and Acculturation by the Acceptance of Foreign Religions in Korea." Master's thesis, University of Georgia, 1992.

Chao, Emily. "Hegemony, Agency, and Re-presenting the Past: The Invention of Dongba Culture among the Naxi of Southwest China." In Melissa Brown, ed., *Negotiating Ethnicities in China and Taiwan,* 208–40. Berkeley: University of California Press, 1996.

Chauncey, Helen R. *Schoolhouse Politicians: Locality and State during the Chinese Republic.* Honolulu: University of Hawaii Press, 1992.

Chen, Baochen, et al., comp. *Dezong jinghuangdi shilu.* Beijing: Zhonghua shuju, 1987.

Chen, C. C., in collaboration with Fredericia M. Bunge. *Medicine in Rural China: A*

Personal Account. Berkeley, Los Angeles, and London: University of California Press, 1989.

Chen, Dongyuan. *Zhongguo funu shenghuo shi* (A history of women's life in China). *Zhongguo wenhua shi congshu,* pt. 2, Shanghai: Shangwu yinshuguan, 1937.

Chen, Duxiu. "Xiandai xiyang jiaoyu" (Western education in modern times). *Chen Duxiu wenzhang xuan* (Chen Duxiu's selected papers). Beijing: Sanlian shudian, 1984.

Chen, Jingpan, ed. *Zhongguo jin xiandai jiaoyujia zhuan* (Biographies of modern and contemporary Chinese educators). Beijing: Beijing Shifan Daxue chubanshe, 1987.

Chen, Qingzhi. *Zhongguo jiaoyushi* (A history of Chinese education). 1936. Reprint. Taibei: Taiwan shangxu yinshuguan, 1963.

Chen, Qitian. *Zuijin sanshinian Zhngguo jiaoyu shi* (History of Chinese education in the last thirty years). 1930. Reprint. Taipei: Wenxing shudian, 1962.

Chen, Theodore Hsi-en. *Chinese Education since 1949: Academic and Revolutionary Models.* New York: Pergamon Press, 1981.

Chen, Xuexun, ed. *Zhongguo jindai jiaoyu dashi ji* (A record of the major events in modern Chinese education). Shanghai: Shanghai jiaoyu chubanshe, 1981.

Chen, Yongsheng. *Nüzi meirong yundong fa* (Ways for women to exercise for a beautiful appearance). Shanghai: 1924.

Cheng, Chung-ying. "A Theory of Confucian Selfhood: Self-Cultivation and Free Will in Confucian Philosophy." In M. L. Titarenko et al., eds., *Kitaiskaya philosophia i sovremennaya tsivilizatsiya* (Chinese philosophy and modern civilization), Moscow: Vostochnaya literatura, 1997.

Cheng, J., and S. MacPherson, eds. *Development in Southern China: A Report on the Pearl River Delta Including the Special Economic Zone.* Hong Kong: Longman, 1995.

Cheng, Joseph Y. S., and Maurice Brosseau, eds. *China Review 1993.* Hong Kong: Chinese University Press, 1993.

Chiang, Yung-chen. "Social Engineering and the Social Sciences in China, 1898–1949." Ph.D. diss., Harvard University, 1986.

China National Institute of Educational Research. *A Study of NGO-Sponsored and Private Higher Education in China.* Beijing: UNESCO, 1995.

Chinaeva, M. I. "Problemi perestroiki shkoli" (Problems of school reform). *Pedagogy,* nos. 7–8 (1992).

Chinese Communist Party Central Committee. *Program for Reform and Development of China's Education.* Beijing: Chinese Communist Party Central Committee, 1993.

Chongqing gongye guanli xueyuan: xiaoshi, 1940–95 (Chongqing industrial management institute: a brief history, 1940–95). Chongqing: Chongqing gongye guanli xueyuan, 1995.

Chongqing shifan xueyuan xiaoshi (A history of Chongqing Teacher's College). Chongqing: Chongqing shifan xueyuan, 1995.

Chow, Tse-tsung. *The May Fourth Movement: Intellectual Revolution in Modern China.* 1960. Reprint. Stanford: Stanford University Press, 1967.

Clark, Donald N. *Christianity in Modern Korea.* Lanham, Md.: University Press of America, 1986.

Cohen, Paul A. "Christian Missions and Their Impact to 1900." In John K. Fairbank, ed., *The Cambridge History of China, vol. 10: Late Ch'ing, 1800–1911*, pt. 1. Cambridge: Cambridge University Press, 1978.

—————. *China and Christianity: The Missionary Movement and the Growth of Chinese Antiforeignism, 1860–1870*. Cambridge, Mass.: Harvard University Press, 1963.

Committee on Women's Studies in Asia. *Changing Lives: Life Stories of Asian Pioneers in Women's Studies*. New York: The Feminist Press, 1995.

Creative Group. "Chuangzaoxing siwei yu gexing jiaoxue moshide shiyan yanjiu" (Experiments in creative thinking and the personality-teaching mode). *Jiaoyu yanjiu*, no. 2 (1993).

Croll, Elisabeth. *Feminism and Socialism in China*. London: Routledge and Kegan Paul, 1978.

—————. *Changing Identities of Chinese Women*. London and New Jersey: Hong Kong University Press, 1995.

Dai, Ruqian, and Shiqi Wan. " 'Fahui techang' bing bu dengyu 'fazhan gexing' " ("Tapping talents" is not equal to "personality development"). *Jiaoyu yanjiu yu shiyan*, no. 3 (1990).

—————. "Gexing fazhan yu jiaoyu gaige shiyan" (Personality development and educational reform experiments). *Jiaoyu yanjiu*, no. 7 (1989).

Daigaku Kyojushoku no Shiteki Hensen to Syoruikei ni kansuru Kenkyu (Study on the historical development of professorship and its typology). Tokyo: National Institute for Educational Research of Japan, 1989.

Davis, Deborah, and Steven Harrell, eds. *Chinese Families in the Post-Mao Era*. Berkeley: University of California Press, 1993.

de Bary, W. Theodore, and John W. Chaffee, eds. *Neo-Confucian Education: The Formative Stage*. Berkeley: University of California Press, 1989.

Dikötter, F. *Sex, Culture and Modernity in China: Medical Science and the Construction of Sexual Identities in the Early Republican Period*. Honolulu: Hawaii University Press, 1995.

Ding, Shouhe, ed. *Xinhai geming shiqi qikan jieshao* (An introduction to periodicals of the 1911 Revolution period). Beijing: Renmin chubanshe, 1983.

Ding, Zhenglin. "Jiaoyu gaige yu gexing fazhan" (Educational reform and personality development). *Huadong Shifan Daxue xuebao, jiaoyu kexueban* (The journal of East China Normal University, pedagogical issue), no. 3 (1989).

Dong, Baoliang. *Cong Hubei kan Zhongguo jiaoyu jindaihua* (Study on the modernization of education in China from the case of Hubei province). Guangzhou: Guangdong Jiaoyu chubanshe, 1996.

Dong, Ding, ed. *Xuefu jiwen: sili yanjing daxue* (The records of universities: private Yanjing University). Taibei: Nanjing chuban youxian gongsi, 1982.

Dong, Zhenxiu, ed. *Qingnian Deng Yingchao de daolu* (The route followed by the young Deng Yingchao). Tianjin: 1992.

Du, Fangqin. *Faxian funü de lishi* (The discovery of women's history). Tianjin: Shehui chubanshe, 1996.

Du, Fangqin, et al., eds. *Zhongguo funü yu fazhan* (Chinese women and development). Zhengzhou: Henan renmin chubanshe, 1993.

Duiker, William. *Ts'ai Yuan-p'ei, Educator of Modern China*. University Park: Pennsylvania State University Press, 1977.

Dunch, Ryan. "Piety, Patriotism, Progress: Chinese Protestants in Fuzhou Society and the Making of a Modern China, 1857–1927." Ph.D. diss., Yale University, 1996.

Eaton, Richard M. "Comparative History as World History: Religious Conversion in Modern India." *Journal of World History* 8, no. 2 (Fall 1997); 271.

Egan, Susan Chan. *A Latterday Confucian: Reminiscences of William Hung, 1893–1980*. Cambridge: Council on East Asian Studies, Harvard University, 1987.

Eisenstadt, N. *Modernization: Protest and Change*. New York: Prentice-Hall, 1966.

Eklof, Ben. *Russian Peasant Schools: Officialdom, Village Culture, and Popular Pedagogy, 1861–1914*. Berkeley: University of California Press, 1986.

Elman, Benjamin A., and Alexander Woodside, eds. *Education and Society in Late Imperial China, 1600–1900*, Berkeley: University of California Press, 1994.

Elvin, Mark, and G. William Skinner, eds. *The Chinese City between Two Worlds*, Stanford: Stanford University Press, 1974.

Epstein, Irving, ed. *Chinese Education: Problems, Policies and Prospects*. New York: Garland Press, 1991.

Esherick, Joseph W. *Reform and Revolution in China: The 1911 Revolution in Hunan and Hubei*. Berkeley: University of California Press, 1976.

Expert Group. "Cujin chuzhongsheng gexing zuiyou fazhande shiyan tansuo" (An experiment in making the students in junior middle schools develop the best personalities). *Jiaoyu yanjiu*, no. 1 (1994).

Fairbank, John King. *China: A New History*. Cambridge, Mass.: Belknap Press of Harvard University, 1992.

Falkenheim, Victor C., ed. *Citizens and Groups in Contemporary China*. Ann Arbor: Centre for Chinese Studies, 1987.

Feinberg, Walter. *Japan and the Pursuit of a New American Identity*. New York: Routledge, 1993.

Fenn, William Purvance. *Christian Higher Education in Changing China, 1890–1950*. Grand Rapids, Mich.: W. B. Eerdmans, 1976.

Fitzpatrick, Sheila. *Education and Social Mobility in the Soviet Union, 1921–1934*. Cambridge: Cambridge University Press, 1979.

Ford, Eddy Lucius. *The History of the Educational Work of the Methodist Episcopal Church in China: A Study of Its Development and Present Trends*. Foochow: Christian Herald Mission Press, 1938.

Freyn, Hubert. *Chinese Education in the War*. Shanghai: Kelly and Walsh, 1940.

Fu, Songtao. "Xianshi shenghuo ren shi jiaoyuxuede loji qidian" (Human beings in real life is the logical starting point of pedagogy). *Jiaoyu yanjiu*, no. 6 (1996).

Fujian sheng jiaoyu tongji (Educational statistics for Fujian province). Fuzhou: Fujian jiaoyuting, 1931.

Gaimusho johobu, Information Division, Ministry of Foreign Affairs, Japan. *Kaitei gendai Shina jimmeikan* (Revised biographical dictionary of contemporary China). Tokyo: n.p., 1928.

Gao, Pingshu. *Cai Yuanpei nianpu* (A chronicle of Cai Yuanpei's life). Beijing: Zhonghua shuju, 1980.

———, comp. *Cai Yuanpei quanji.* Beijing: Zhonghua shuju, 1984.

———, ed. *Cai Yuanpei jiaoyu lunzhu xuan* (Cai Yuanpei's selected works on education). Beijing: Renmin jiaoyu chubanshe, 1991.

Gao, Qi, ed. *Zhongguo xiandai jiaoyu shi* (History of modern Chinese education). Beijing: Beijing Shifan Daxue chubanshe, 1985.

Gazman, Oleg S. "From Authoritarian Education to the Pedagogic of Freedom." *New Educational Values* (Moscow: Innovator), no. 2 (1995).

Genetinsky, V. I. "Individualnost kak predmet pedagogicheskoi antropologii" (Individuality as a subject of pedagogical anthropology). *Sovetskaya Pedagogika* (Soviet pedagogy), no. 9 (1991).

Gilbert, Alan D. *Religion and Society in Industrial England: Church, Chapel and Social Change, 1740–1914.* London and New York: Longman, 1976.

Gilbuch, J. Z. "Idei differentsiirovannogo obucheniya v nashei pedagogike" (Individual-oriented ideas in our pedagogy). *Pedagogy,* no. 5 (1994).

Gilley, Sheridan, and W. J. Sheils, eds. *A History of Religion in Britain: Practice and Belief from Pre-Roman Times to the Present.* Oxford and Cambridge, Mass.: Blackwell, 1994.

Gillin, D. *Warlord: Yen Hsi-shan in Shansi Province, 1911–1949.* Princeton: Princeton University Press, 1967.

Gilmartin, Christina. *Engendering the Chinese Revolution: Radical Women, Communist Politics and Mass Movements in the 1920s.* Berkeley: University of California Press, 1995.

Gilmartin, Christina K., et al., eds. *Engendering China: Women, Culture and the State.* Cambridge, Mass.: Harvard University Press, 1994.

Gladney, Dru C. *Muslim Chinese: Ethnic Nationalism in the People's Republic.* Cambridge: Harvard University Press, 1991.

———. "Representing Nationality in China: Refiguring Majority/Minority Identities." *Journal of Asian Studies,* no. 1 (February 1994): 92–123.

Gorshkova, V. V. *Problema Subyecta v Pedagogike* (The problem of a subject in pedagogy). Leningrad: Rossijski gosudarstvenni pedagogicheskii Universitet, 1991.

Graff, Harvey J., ed. *Literacy and Social Development in the West: A Reader.* Cambridge and New York: Cambridge University Press, 1981.

Gu, Hua. *A Small Town Called Hibiscus.* Trans. Gladys Yang. Beijing: Panda Books, 1983.

Gu, Mingyuan. "Jiaoyu kexue ying cong 'Wusi' jingshen zhong xiqu shenmo yingyang" (What kind of nourishment should educational science absorb from the spirit of the May 4th Movement?). *Jiaoyu yanjiu,* no. 6 (1989).

———, ed. *Zhongguo jiaoyu daxi* (The encyclopedic series of Chinese education). Wuhan: Hubei jiaoyu chubanshe, 1994.

Guandong jiaoyu yuekan she, comp. *Zhongyang ji Guangdongshen xianxing jiaoyu fagui* (Current national and Guangdong provincial regulations on education). Guangzhou: Guangdong jiaoyu yuekanshe, 1949.

Guangdong Yearbook Editorial Committee. *Guangdong Yearbook 1994.* Guangdong: Guangdong Yearbook Press, 1994.

Guojia jiaowei bangongting. *Zhongguo jiaoyu gaige he fazhan wenxian xuanbian* (Selected documents on Chinese education reform and development). Beijing: Renmin jiaoyu chubanshe, 1993.

Guo, Qijia. *Zhongguo jiaoyu sixing shi* (The history of Chinese pedagogical ideas). Beijing: Jiaoyu kexue chubanshe, 1987.

Guo, Sheng, et al., eds. *Xin zhongguo jiaoyu sishi nian* (The past forty years of education in new China). Fuzhou: Fujian jiaoyu chubanshe, 1989.

Guojia jiaowei chengren jiaoyusi. *Zhongguo gaodeng hanshou jiaoyu, dashiji, wenxian, ziliao* (Chinese higher-distance education). Beijing: Renmin daxue chubanshe, 1994.

Haerbin Gongye Daxue jianshi (Brief history of Haerbin Institute of Technology). Haerbin: Haerbin gongxueyuan chubanshe, 1985.

Hansen, Mette H. "Fostering 'Love of Learning': Naxi Responses to Ethnic Images in Chinese State Education." In Kjeld-Erik Broedsgaard and David Strand, eds., *Reconstructing Twentieth Century China: Social Control, Civil Society and National Identity*. Oxford: Oxford University Press, 1998.

———. *Lessons in Being Chinese: Minority State Education and Ethnic Identity in Southwest China*. Seattle: University of Washington Press, 1998.

———. "Teaching Backwardness or Equality? Chinese State Education among the Tai in Sipsong Panna." In Gerard Postiglione and Regie Stites, eds., *Education of National Minorities in China*. New York: Garland Press, 1998.

Harrell, Stevan, ed. *Cultural Encounters on China's Ethnic Frontiers*. Seattle and London: University of Washington Press, 1995.

Hayford, Charles W. *To The People: James Yen and Village China*. New York: Columbia University Press, 1990.

Hayhoe, Ruth. *China's Universities, 1895–1995: A Century of Cultural Conflict*. New York and London: Garland Press, 1996.

———. *China's Universities and the Open Door*. Armonk, N.Y.: M. E. Sharpe, 1989.

———, ed. *Education and Modernisation: The Chinese Experience*. Oxford: Pergamon Press, 1992.

Hayhoe, Ruth, and Marianne Bastid, eds. *China's Education and the Industrialized World: Studies in Cultural Transfer*. Armonk, N.Y.: M. E. Sharpe, 1987.

Hayhoe, Ruth, and Julia Pan, eds. *East-West Dialogue in Knowledge and Higher Education*. New York: M. E. Sharpe, 1996.

He, Xiaoxia, and Jinghuan Shi. *Jiaohui xuexiao yu Zhongguo jindaihua* (Christian schools and modernization of education in China). Guangzhou: Guangdong Jiaoyu chubanshe, 1996.

Hobsbawm, E. J. *Nations and Nationalism since 1780: Programme, Myth, Reality*, 2d ed. Cambridge, New York, and Melbourne: Cambridge University Press, 1992.

Hobsbawm, Eric, and Terence Ranger, eds. *The Invention of Tradition*. Cambridge: Cambridge University Press, 1983.

Holm, David. *Art and Ideology in Revolutionary China*. Oxford: Clarendon University Press, 1991.

Holtom, D. C. *Modern Japan and Shinto Nationalism: A Study of Present-Day Trends in Japanese Religions*. Chicago: University of Chicago Press, 1943.

Hom, Sharon K., and Chunying Xin. *English-Chinese Lexicon of Women and Law*.

Beijing: United Nations Educational, Scientific and Cultural Organization and China Translation and Publishing Corporation, 1995.

Honig, E., and G. Hershatter. *Personal Voices: Chinese Women in the 1980s*. Stanford: Stanford University Press, 1988.

Hu, Shi. *Hu Shi xuanji* (Selected works of Hu Shi). Taibei: Wenxing shudian, 1966.

Hu, Zhongpin. "Ren shi jiaoyude chufadian" (Human beings, the starting point of education). *Jiaoyu yanjiu*, no. 8 (1989).

Huang, Ji. *Jiaoyu zhexue* (Philosophy of education). Beijing: 1985.

Huang, Jiajing, et al., eds. *Gaige Dacao Zhong de Zhuliang Sanjiaozhou Jiaoyu* (Education in the Pearl River delta amid tides of reform). Guangdong: Gaodeng Jiaoyu Chubanshe, 1993.

Huang, Xinxian. *Zhongguo jin xiandai nüzi jiaoyu* (Modern and recent women's education in China). Fuzhou: 1992.

Huang, Yanpei. *Zhongguo jiaoyu shiyao* (A summary of China's educational history). Shanghai: Shangwu yinshuguan, 1930.

Hunt, Lynn. *Politics, Culture and Class in the French Revolution*. Berkeley: University of California Press, 1984.

Hunter, Jane. *The Gospel of Gentility: American Women Missionaries at the Turn-of-the-Century China*. New Haven: Yale University Press, 1984.

Ichisada, Miyazaki. *China's Examination Hell: The Civil Service Examinations of Imperial China*. Trans. Conrad Schirokauer. New York: Weatherhill, 1971.

Ishii, Akira. *Chū-So Kankeishi no Kenkyu, 1945–1950* (A study on the history of Sino-Soviet relations, 1945–1950). Tokyo: Tokyo University Press, 1990.

―――, ed. *The Chinese and the Japanese: Essays in Political and Cultural Interactions*. Princeton: Princeton University Press, 1980.

Israel, John. *Student Nationalism in China, 1927–1937*. Stanford: Stanford University Press, 1966.

Jeffreys, S., ed. *The Sexuality Debates*. London: Routledge and Kegan Paul, 1987.

Jiang, Niandong, et al., eds. *Wei Manzhouguo shi* (History of pseudo Manchukuo). Changchun: Jilin renmin chubanshe, 1980.

Jiaowu jiao'an dang (1860–1911) (The Zongli Yamen archives on Christian affairs and on cases and disputes involving missionaries and converts [1860–1911]). Ser. 1–7. Taibei: Institute of Modern History, Academia Sinica, 1974–81.

Jiaoyu bu canshishi, comp. *Jiaoyu faling* (Educational regulations). Shanghai: Zhonghua shuju, 1947.

Jiaoyu bu jiaoyu nianjian bianzuan weiyuanhui. *Dierci Zhongguo jiaoyu nianjian* (Second China education year book). Shanghai: Shangwu yinshu guan, 1948.

Jiaoyu bu. *Diyici Zhongguo jiaoyu nianjian* (First China Education Yearbook). Shanghai: Kaiming Shudian, 1934.

Jiaoyu bu, comp. *Jiaoyu fagui huibian* (Collection of educational regulations). Beijing: 1919.

Jin, Guantao, and Qingfeng Liu. *Kaifang zhong de bianqian* (Changes since the adoption of open-door policies). Hong Kong: Chinese University Press, 1993.

Jin, Songcen. *Nüjie zhong*. Shanghai: Datong shuju, 1903.

Jin, Xibin. *Cong cihou dao chaoqian: 20 shiji renli ziben xueshuo, jiaoyu jingjixue* (From lagging to leading: the human resources capital theories in the twentieth century, educational economics). Jinan: Shandong jiaoyu chubanshe, 1995.

Jin, Zhongming. "Gexing jiaoyu yu rende quanmian fazhan" (Personality education and individual all-round development). *Jiaoyu yanjiu*, no. 7 (1989).

Jinyang xuekan bianji bu, comp. *Zhongguo xiandai shehui kexuejia zhuanlue*, vol. 2 (Biographical sketches of contemporary Chinese social scientists), Taiyuan: Shanxi renmin chubanshe, 1983. 10 vols.

Johnson, David, Andrew J. Nathan, and Evelyn S. Rawski, eds. *Popular Culture in Late Imperial China*. Berkeley: University of California Press, 1985.

Johnson, Kay A. *Women, the Family and Peasant Revolution in China*. Chicago: University of Chicago Press, 1983.

Judd, Ellen. *Gender and Power in Rural North China*. Stanford: Stanford University Press, 1994.

Kapterev, P. F. "Istorija Russkoj Pedagogiki" (A history of Russian pedagogy). *Pedagogy*, no. 5 (1994).

Keenan, Barry. *The Dewey Experiment in China: Educational Reform and Political Power in the Early Republic*. Cambridge, Mass.: Harvard University Press, 1977.

Kinkley, Jeffrey C., ed. *After Mao: Chinese Literature and Society*. Cambridge, Mass.: Council on East Asian Studies, Harvard University, 1985.

Klein, Donald W., and Ann B. Clark, eds. *Biographical dictionary of Chinese communism, 1921–1965*. 2 vols. Cambridge, Mass.: Harvard University Press, 1971.

Ko, Dorothy, *Teachers of the Inner Chambers: Women and Culture in Seventeenth Century China*. Stanford: Stanford University Press, 1994.

Kuang, Pinghe. " 'Xin siwei' tuidong xiade Sulian jiaoyu gaige" (The Soviet Union's educational reform is promoted by the "new thinking") *Jiaoyu yanjiu*, no. 6 (1989).

Kulnevich, S. V. *Pedagogica lichnosti* (Pedagogics of personality). Rostov na Donu: Rostovskii Pedagogicheskii Universitet, 1995.

Kuo, Ping-wen. *The Chinese System of Public Education*. 1915. Reprint. New York: AMS Press, 1972.

Lacy, Walter N. *A Hundred Years of Chinese Methodism*. Nashville: Abingdon-Cokesbury Press, 1948.

Lambert, Tony. *The Resurrection of the Chinese Church*. London: Hodder and Stoughton, 1991.

Lao zhaopian (Old photographs). Jinan: Shandong huabao chubanshe, 1997.

Latourette, Kenneth Scott. *A History of Christian Missions in China*. 1929. Reprint. Taibei: Cheng-wen, 1973.

League of Nations Mission of Educational Experts. *The Reorganization of Education in China*. Paris: League of Nations Institute of Intellectual Cooperation, 1932.

Le Grand, J., and W. Bartlett, eds. *Quasi-Marketization and Social Policy*. London: Macmillan, 1993.

Le Grand, J., and R. Robinson, eds. *Privatization and the Welfare State*. London: George Allen and Unwin, 1985.

Lee, Chae-jin. *China's Korean Minority: The Politics of Ethnic Education*. Boulder: Westview Press, 1986.

Levine, Kenneth. *The Social Context of Literacy.* London: Routledge and Kegan Paul, 1986.

Levy, Marion J., Jr. *Modernization: Latecomers and Survivors.* New York: Basic Books, 1972.

Lewis, Ida Belle. *The Education of Girls in China.* New York: Teachers College, Columbia University, 1919.

Li, Qingmin. "Shiying yu chaoyue: deyu dui xiandaihua shehuide yingda" (Adaptation and transcendence: the response of moral education to modern society). *Jiaoyu yanjiu,* no. 8 (1989).

Li, Xiaojiang. *Zouxing nüren* (Towards the femininity of women). Hong Kong: Association for the Advancement of Feminism, 1993.

Li, Xisuo. *Jindai Zhongguo de liuxuesheng* (Modern China's oversea students). Beijing: Renmin chubanshe, 1987.

Li, Youning, and Yufa Zhang, eds. *Zhongguo funü shilun wenji* (Collection of historical essays on Chinese women). Taibei: Shangwu yinshuguan, 1988.

———. *Jindai Zhongguo nüquan yundong shiliao* (Source materials on the women's rights movement in modern China). Taibei: Zhuanji wenxue chubanshe, 1975.

Li, Zehou. *Zhongguo xiandai sixiangshi lun* (On the history of modern Chinese thought). Hefei: Anhui wenyi chubanshe, 1994.

Liang, Qichao. *Yinbingshi heji* (Complete works from the Ice-Drinker's Studio). Beijing: Zhonghua shuju, 1989.

Liao, Xiuzhen. *Qingmo de nüzi jiaoyu* (Women's education in the late Qing). Taibei: 1980.

Lieberthal, Kenneth, et al. *Perspectives on China: Four Anniversaries.* Armonk, N.Y.: M. E. Sharpe, 1991.

Lin, Bih-jaw, and Li-min Fan, eds. *Education in Mainland China.* Taibei: Institute of International Relations, National Chengchi University, 1990.

Link, Perry. *Evening Chats in Beijing: Probing China's Predicament.* New York: W. W. Norton, 1992.

Liu, Dehua, et al., eds. *Zhongguo jiaoyu guanlishi* (A history of Chinese educational administration). Jinan: Shandong jiaoyu chubanshe, 1990.

Liu, Fonian, et al., eds. *Zhongguo jiaoyu de weilai* (The future of Chinese education). Hefei: Anhui jiaoyu chubanshe, 1995.

Liu, Gang. "Jiaoyu zhexuezhong you quan rende lilun yanjiu jinzhan he cunzaide wenti" (Some problems and prospects in the human being theory in the philosophy of education in analysis and perspectives in Chinese pedagogy after the third plenum of the CCP). Beijing: 1988.

Liu, Jinzao. *Qingchao xu wenxian tongkao.* Shanghai: Shangwu yinshuguan, 1935.

Liu, Jucai. *Zhongguo jindai funü yundong shi* (A history of the modern Chinese women's movement). Liaoning: Zhongguo funü chubanshe, 1989.

Liu, Qi. "Gexing, qunxing, shehui" (Individuality, masses, society). *Huadong Shifan Daxue xuebao: Jiaoyu kexueban* (The journal of East China Normal University, pedagogical issue), no. 2 (1989).

Liu, Yifan. *Zhongguo dangdai gaodeng jiaoyu shilue* (A brief history of the Chinese contemporary higher education). Wuhan: Huazhong ligong daxue, 1991.

Liu, Zizheng. *Huang Naishang yu Xin Fuzhou* (Huang Naishang and the new Fuzhou). Singapore: Nanyang xuehui, 1979.

Löfstedt, Jan-Ingvar. *Practice and Work in Chinese Education: Why, How and How Much.* Stockholm: University of Stockholm, Center for Pacific Asia Studies, Working Paper no. 5, 1987.

Lomax, J. *Women of the Air.* London: John Murray, 1986.

Lu Xun zawen xuan (Selected essays of Lu Xun). Shanghai: Shanghai Renmin chubanshe, 1973.

Lu, Yanzhen. *Zhongguo jindai nüzi jiaoyu shi, 1895–1945* (A history of women's education in China in modern times). Taibei: Wenshizhe chubanshe, 1989.

Lu, Yongling. "Standing between Two Worlds: Ma's Xiangbo's Educational Thoughts and Practice." In Ruth Hayhoe and Yongling Lu, eds. *Ma Xiangbo and the Mind of Modern China, 1840–1939.* Armonk, N.Y.: M. E. Sharpe, 1996.

Lutz, Jessie G. *China and the Christian Colleges, 1850–1950.* Ithaca: Cornell University Press, 1971.

———. *Chinese Politics and Christian Missions: The Anti-Christian Movements of 1920–1928.* Notre Dame, Ind.: Cross-Cultural Publications, 1988.

Lutz, Jessie G., and Rolland Ray Lutz. *Hakka Chinese Confront Protestant Christianity, 1850–1900: With the Autobiographies of Eight Hakka Christians, and Commentary.* Armonk, N.Y.: M. E. Sharpe, 1998.

Ma, Cuiguan, ed. *Ershi shiji chu Tianjin aiguo jiaoyu jia Ma Qianli xiansheng dansheng bai zhounian jinian, 1885–1985* (A hundredth-birthday commemoration of the early-twentieth-century patriotic Tianjin educator Mr. Ma Qianli). Tianjin: 1985.

MacFarquhar, Roderick. *The Hundred Flowers Campaign and the Chinese Intellectuals.* New York: Octagon Books, 1974.

MacPherson, S., and Joseph Y. S. Cheng, eds. *The Economic and Social Developments in South China.* London: Edward Elgar, 1996.

Madancy, Joyce Ann. "Ambitious Interlude: The Anti-Opium Campaign in China's Fujian Province, 1906–1917." Ph.D. diss., University of Michigan, 1996.

Matunin, B. G. "Lichnost ili individualnost?" (Personality or individuality?) *Pedagogica,* no. 3 (1993).

Maximova, G. J. *Vzaimosvijaz tvorcheskikh idei i opita S. T. Shatskogo s kontseptsijami i praktikoi zarubezhnoi pedagogiki* (The interrelationships of S. T. Shatski's creative ideas and experience with the experience of foreign education). Moscow: Academy of Pedagogical Sciences, 1991.

McElroy, Sarah Coles. "Transforming China through Education: Yan Xiu, Zhang Boling, and the Effort to Build a New School System, 1901–1927." Ph.D. diss., Yale University, 1996.

Meng, Wangjin. "Zhongguo chuantong wenhua beijingxia de guomin xinli yu jiaoyu" (People's psychology and education under Chinese traditional culture). *Jiaoyu yanjiu,* no. 2 (1992).

Meskill, John. *Academies in Ming China: A Historical Essay.* Tucson: Association for Asian Studies by the University of Arizona, 1982.

Miao, Chester S., and Frank W. Price. *Religion and Character in Christian Middle*

Schools: A Study of Religious Education in Christian Private Middle Schools of China. Shanghai: China Christian Educational Association, 1929.

Moffet, Samuel Hugh. *A History of Christianity in Asia,* vol. 1: *Beginnings to 1500.* San Francisco: HarperCollins, 1992.

Mohanty, Chandra T., et al., eds. *Third World Women and the Politics of Feminism.* Bloomington: Indiana University Press, 1991.

Neville, Robert C. "Some Confucian-Christian Comparisons." In M. L. Titarenko et al., eds., *Kitaiskaya philosophia i sovremennaya tsivilizatsiya* (Chinese philosophy and modern civilization). Moscow: Vostochnaya literatura, 1997.

Nüzi xiushen jiaokeshu (Ethical reader for girls higher primary schools). Shanghai: Zhongua shuju, 1914.

Nüzi xiushen jiaoshou shu (Teaching manual for ethics in girls lower primary schools). Shanghai: Zhonghua shuju, 1915–16.

Nylan, M. "Confucian Piety and Individualism in Han China." *Journal of the American Oriental Society* 116, no. 1 (1996).

Ono, K. *Chinese Women in a Century of Revolution, 1850–1950.* Stanford: Stanford University Press, 1989.

Oswald, E., and Anna Muse Brown. *Life and Letters of Laura Askew Haygood.* Nashville: Publishing House of the Methodist Episcopal Church South, 1904.

Peake, Cyrus H. *Nationalism and Education in Modern China.* New York: Columbia University Press, 1932.

Pepper, Suzanne. *Radicalism and Education Reform in Twentieth-Century China: The Search for an Ideal Development Model.* Cambridge: Cambridge University Press, 1996.

Peterson, Glen. *The Power of Words: Literacy and Revolution in South China, 1949–1995.* Vancouver: University of British Columbia Press, 1997.

Physical Training College of Chengdu, ed. *Zhongguo jindai tiyu shi ziliao.* Chengdu: Sichuan jiaoyu chubanshe, 1988.

Pong, D., and E. Fung, eds. *Ideal and Reality: Social and Political Change in Modern China, 1860–1949.* Lanham, Md.: University Press of America, 1985.

Postiglione, Gerard, and Regie Stites, eds. *Education of National Minorities in China.* New York: Garland Press, 1998.

Prianikova, V. G. "Antropologo-gumanisticheskoje napravlenije v otechestvennoi pedagogike" (The anthropological-humanistic trend in our country's pedagogy). *Pedagogy,* no. 2 (1995).

Price, Ronald F. "Convergence or Copying: China and the Soviet Union." In Ruth Hayhoe and Marianne Bastid, eds., *China's Education and the Industrialized World.* Armonk, N.Y.: M. E. Sharpe, 1987.

Propaganda Team. "Dangqian zhongxuesheng rensheng jiazhi quxiangde tedian yu jiaoyude sikao" (Life-value choice and the education of middle school students). *Jiaoyu yanjiu,* no. 3 (1993).

Qian, Manqian, and Linxiang Jin. *Zhongguo jindai xuezhi bijiao yanjiu* (The comparative studies of school systems in China in modern times). Guangzhou: Guangdong Jiaoyu chubanshe, 1996.

Qiu, Daogen, ed. *Kangjian zhong de Fujian sili xuexiao* (Fujian private schools during reconstruction through resistance). Fuzhou: n.p., 1940.

Qu, Xingui, and Liangyan Tang, eds. *Zhongguo jindai jiaoyushi ziliao huibian, xuezhi yanbian* (A collection of historical materials of Chinese education in modern times—evolution of the school system). Shanghai: Jiaoyu chubanshe, 1991.

Rashdall, Hastings. *The Universities of Europe in the Middle Ages.* Oxford: Clarendon Press, 1895.

Rawski, Evelyn Sakakida. *Education and Popular Literacy in Ch'ing China.* Ann Arbor: University of Michigan Press, 1979.

Revijakina, V. I. "Opit differentsiatsii obuchenija v shkolje 20-kh godov" (The experience of educational differentiation in schools during the 1920s). *Pedagogy,* no. 11 (1991).

Reynolds, Douglas R. *China, 1898–1912: The Xinzheng Revolution and Japan.* Cambridge, Mass.: Council on East Asian Studies, Harvard University, 1993.

———. "Chinese Area Studies in Prewar China: Japan's Tō-a Dōbun Shoin in Shanghai, 1900–1945." *Journal of Asian Studies* 45, no. 5 (November 1986): 945–70.

———. "Japanese Buddhist Mission Work in China and the Challenge of Christianity, 1868–1915." Paper presented at the 1989 Symposium, History of Christianity in China Project, University of Kansas, Lawrence, June 18–23, 1989.

———. "Training Young China Hands: Tō-A Dōbun Shoin and Its Precursors, 1886–1945." In Peter Duus, Ramon H. Myers, and Mark R. Peattie, eds., *The Japanese Informal Empire in China, 1895–1937.* Princeton: Princeton University Press, 1989.

———, ed. and trans. *China, 1895–1912: State-Sponsored Reforms and China's Late-Qing Revolution: Selected Essays from Zhongguo Jindai Shi* (Modern Chinese history, 1840–1919), double issue of *Chinese Studies in History* (Spring–Summer 1995).

Reynolds, S. *France between the Wars: Gender and Politics.* London: Routledge and Kegan Paul, 1986.

Rezvitski, I. M. *Lichnost, Individualnost, Obshchestvo* (Personality, individuality, society). Moscow: Politizdat, 1984.

Richard, Timothy. *Forty-Five Years in China.* New York: Frederick A. Stokes Co., 1916.

Rosenbaum, Arthur L., ed. *State and Society in China: The Consequence of Reform.* Boulder: Westview, 1992.

Ross, Heidi. *Telling Women's Lives.* San Francisco: McTyeire Alumnae Association, 1993.

Rozman, Gilbert, ed. *The Modernization of China.* New York: Free Press, 1981.

Rubinstein, Murray A. *The Protestant Community on Modern Taiwan: Mission, Seminary, and Church,* Armonk, N.Y.: M. E. Sharpe, 1991.

Saito, Kazuo. *Watashi no Jinsei Kaiko* (My life reminiscences). Mr. Kazuo Saito's Posthumous Manuscripts Publishing Association, 1989.

Schein, Louise. "Gender and Internal Orientalism in China." *Modern China* 23, no. 1 (January 1997): 69–98.

Schirokauer, Conrad. *A Brief History of Chinese and Japanese Civilizations,* 2d ed. San Diego: Harcourt Brace Jovanovich, 1989.

Schoenhals, Michael. *Doing Things with Words in Chinese Politics: Five Studies.* Berkeley: Institute of East Asian Studies, University of California, 1992.

Schwarcz, Vera. *The Chinese Enlightenment: Intellectuals and the Legacy of the May Fourth Movement of 1919.* Berkeley: University of California Press, 1986.

Schwartz, Benjamin. *In Search of Wealth and Power: Yen Fu and the West.* Cambridge, Mass.: Harvard University Press, 1964.

Scott, James C. *Weapons of the Weak: Everyday Forms of Peasant Resistance.* New Haven: Yale University Press, 1985.

Seeberg, Vilma. *Literacy in China: The Effects of the National Development Context and Policy on Literacy Levels, 1949–1979.* Bochum: Brockmeyer, 1990.

Shatsklii, S. T. *Izbranije pedagogicheskije sochinenija* (Selected pedagogical works). Moscow: Pedagogica, 1980.

Shen, Yiyun. *Yiyun huiyi* (Yiyun's reminiscences). *Zhuanji wenxue congkan* 11, vol. 1, Taibei: Zhuanji wenxue chubanshe, 1980.

Sheng, Langxi. *Zhongguo shuyuan zhidu* (The system of Chinese traditional academies). Shanghai: Zhonghua shuju, 1934.

Shi, Jinghuan. *Jidujiao jiaoyu yu zhishifengzi* (Christian education and Chinese intellectuals). Fuzhou: Fujian jiaoyu chubanshe, 1996.

Shishi wenti yanjiuhui, ed. *Kangzhan zhong de Zhongguo wenhua jiaoyu* (Chinese culture and education in the war of resistance). Beijing: Zhongguo xiandaishi ziliao bianji weiyuanhui, 1957.

Shively, Donald H., ed. *Tradition and Modernization in Japanese Culture.* Princeton: Princeton University Press, 1971.

Shiyi jie sanzhong quanhui yilai zhongyao jiaoyu wenxian (Important education documents since the third plenary of the eleventh congress of the Communist Party). Beijing: Jiaoyu kexue chubanshe, 1992.

Showa Jinmei Jiten (Who's who of the Showa era), vol. 4: *Section of overseas territories.* Tokyo: Nihon Tosho Center, 1987.

Shu, Xincheng, comp. *Zhongguo jindai jiaoyu shi ziliao* (Historical materials on modern Chinese education). Beijing: Renmin jiaoyu chubanshe, 1961.

———, ed. *Jindai zhongguo jiaoyu shiliao* (Historical materials on modern Chinese education). Shanghai: Zhonghua shuju, 1928.

———, ed. *Xiandai zhongguo jiaoyu shi ziliao* (Historical materials on contemporary Chinese education). Beijing: Renmin jiaoyu chubanshe, 1962.

Shubinsky, V. S. "Chelovek kak tsel vospitanija" (The human being as the goal of education). *Pedagogy*, nos. 3–4 (1992).

Shue, Vivienne. *The Reach of the State: Sketches of the Chinese Body Politic.* Stanford: Stanford University Press, 1988.

Sichuan daxue jianjie (Sichuan Union University brochure). Chengdu: Sichuan Union University, 1995.

Sichuan daxue xiao bangongshi. *Sichuan daxue nianjian* (Sichuan university yearbook). Chengdu: Sichuan daxue chubanshe, 1994.

Sichuan daxue xiaoshi bianxiezu. *Sichuan daxue shigao* (A history of Sichuan University). Chengdu: Sichuan daxue chubanshe, 1985.

Sichuan gaodeng jiaoyu he zhongdeng jiaoyu nianjian (The yearbook of Sichuan higher education and secondary education). Chengdu: Sichuan jiaoyu chubanshe, 1988.

Sievers, S. *Flowers in Salt: The Beginnings of Feminist Consciousness in Modern Japan.* Stanford: Stanford University Press, 1983.

Sites, C. M. Lacey, ed. *Educational Institutions of the Methodist Episcopal Church in China*. Shanghai: Methodist Publishing House, 1907.

Sites, S. Moore, and Nathan Sites. *An Epic of the East*. New York: Fleming H. Revell and Co., 1912.

Smith, Arthur H. *VIllage Life in China: A Study of Sociology*. New York: Fleming H. Revell Co., 1898.

Song, Ong Siang. *One Hundred Years of History of the Chinese in Singapore*. 1967. Reprint. Singapore: Oxford University Press, 1984.

Special Committee on Survey and Occupation, China Continuation Committee. *The Christian Occupation of China: A General Survey of the Numerical Strength and Geographical Distribution of the Christian Forces in China*. Shanghai: China Continuation Committee, 1922.

Spence, Jonathan D. *God's Chinese Son: The Heavenly Kingdom of Hong Xiuquan*. New York: W. W. Norton, 1996.

Spivak, Gayatri C. *The Other Worlds: Essays in Cultural Politics*. New York: Methuen, 1987.

Stacey, Judith. *Patriarch and Socialist Revolution in China*. Berkeley: University of California Press, 1983.

State Education Commission, ed. *Xin de lichengbei: quanguo jiaoyu gongzuo huiyi wenjian huibian* (A new milestone: a collection of documents of the national educational conference). Beijing: Jiaoyu kexue chubanshe, 1994.

State Education Commission and Shanghai Institute for Human Resources Development. *Zhongguo jiaoyu jingfei fazhan baogao, 1996* (Annual development report on China's educational finance 1996). Beijing: Educational Science Press, 1997.

State Education Commission Policies and Law Department. *Law and Regulation on Basic Education of the People's Republic of China*. Beijing: Beijing Normal University, 1993.

Stauffer, Milton T., ed. *The Christian Occupation of China*. Shanghai: China Continuation Committee, 1922.

———, ed. *Zhonghua guizhu*. Trans. Cai Yongchun. Beijing: 1985.

Stevenson, H. W., and J. Stingler. *The Learning Gap: Why Our Schools Are Failing and What We Can Learn from Japanese and Chinese Education*. New York: Summit Books, 1992.

Street, Brian V. *Literacy in Theory and Practice*. Cambridge and New York: Cambridge University Press, 1984.

Sun, Ruoqiong, et al., eds. *Zhongguo shaoshu minzu jiao yuxue gailun* (An introduction to the education of China's national minorities). Beijing: Zhongguo laodong chubanshe, 1990.

Sun, Xining. "Rende jiazhi, jiaoyu jiazhi, deyu jiazhi" (The value of human beings, the value of education, the value of moral education). *Jiaoyu yanjiu*, nos. 5–6 (1989).

Sun, Xining, et al. "Rende zhutixing neihan yu rende zhutixing jiaoyu" (On the meaning of human beings' subject nature and subject education). *Jiaoyu yanjiu*, no. 10 (1995).

Sun, Yen-Chu. "Chinese National Higher Education for Women in the Context of Social Reform, 1919–1929: A Case Study." Ph.D. diss., New York University, 1985.

Taga, Akigoro, comp. *Kindai Chūgoku kyōiku shi shiryo* (Materials on the history of education in modern China). Tokyo: Nihon gakujutsu shinkokai, 1972.

Tahara, Teijiro, comp. *Shinmatsu minsho Chūgoku kanshin jimmeiroku* (Biographies of Chinese officials and gentry of the late Qing and early Republic). Dalian: Chūgoku kenkyūkai, 1918.

Tan, Bian. *Wan qing de baihuawen yundong* (The vernacular language movement in the late Qing dynasty). Wuhan: Hubei renmin chubanshe, 1966.

Tao Xingzhi jiaoyu wenxuan (Selected educational works of Tao Xingzhi). Beijing: Jiaoyu kexue chubanshe, 1981.

Tao Xingzhi wenji (Collected works of Tao Xingzhi). Nanjing: Jiangsu jiaoyu chubanshe, 1991.

Thøgersen, Stig. *Secondary Education in China after Mao: Reform and Social Conflict.* Aarhus: Aarhus University Press, 1990.

Tian, Bing. "Guanyu cujin ertong gexing quanmian hexie fazhande tansuo" (Explorations in promoting all-round harmonious development in children's personality). *Jiaoyu yanjiu,* no. 3 (1994).

Tian, Jingkun, and Shaoyan Zheng, eds. *Zhongguo jinxiandai funü baokan tonglan* (General overview of the Chinese women's periodical press in modern and contemporary China). Beijing: Haiyang chubanshe, 1990.

Tian, Zhengping. *Liuxuesheng yu Zhongguo jiaoyu jindaihua* (Returned students and the modernization of education in China). Guangzhou: Guangdong jiaoyu chubanshe, 1996.

Tu, Wei-ming, ed. *China in Transformation.* Cambridge, Mass.: Harvard University Press, 1994.

Unit 1. "Individualizatsija i differentsiatsija obuchenija" (Individualization and differentiation in educational process). Moscow: 1990.

United Group. "Xiaoxuesheng zhutixing fazhan shiyan yu zhibiao tixide dianli cepin yanjiu" (A joint study of the experiment in developing primary students' subjectivity and the establishment of an indicator system). *Jiaoyu yanjiu,* no. 12 (1994).

Vendrovskaya, R. B. *Shkola 20-kh godov: pojiski i rezultati* (School in the 1920s: explorations and results). Moscow: International Pedagogical Academy, 1993.

Wang, Daojun, and Wenan Guo. "Guanyu zhuti jiaoyu sixiangde sikao" (On subjectivity in education). *Jiaoyu yanjiu,* no. 11 (1992).

Wang, Donghua. "Guanyu rende fazhan yinsu ji qi jiegou yu gongneng yanjiu" (Research on the factors affecting a human being's development, composition and functions). *Henan Jiaoyu Xueyuan xuebao* (Journal of Henan Pedagogical Institute), no. 2 (1989).

Wang, Jianjun. *Zhongguo jindai jiaokeshu fazhan yanjiu* (Study on the development of modern textbooks in China). Guangzhou: Guangdong Jiaoyu chubanshe, 1996.

Wang, Liyun, and Jiange Song, eds. *Shifan qunying, guangyao zhonghua* (A large number of brilliant minds in teacher training, brilliant light of the Chinese Republic). Vol. 3. Xi'an: 1992.

Wang, Wenjun, et al., eds. *Nankai daxue xiaoshi ziliaoxuan* (Selected materials of the history of Nankai university). Tianjin: Nankai daxue chubanshe, 1989.

Wang, Xihong, et al., eds. *Zhongguo bianjing minzu jiao yu* (Education of China's minorities living in border areas). Beijing: Zhongyang minzu xueyuan chubanshe, 1990.

Wang, Zhenqian, Qing Qiu, and Kefu Jiang, eds. *Dongbei Daxue shigao* (Manuscript of history of Northeastern University). Changchun: Dongbei Shifan Daxue chubanshe, 1988.

Wang, Zhixin. *Zhongguo jidujiao shigang* (Historical outline of the Christianity in China). Shanghai: Shanghai: N.p., 1930.

Wasserstrom, Jeffrey N. *Student Protests in Twentieth-Century China: The View from Shanghai.* Stanford: Stanford University Press, 1991.

Watson, R., and P. Ebrey, eds. *Marriage and Inequality in Chinese Society.* Berkeley: University of California Press, 1991.

Watt, John. *Individualism and Educational Theory.* London: Kluwer, 1989.

White, Sydney D. "Fame and Sacrifice: The Gendered Construction of Naxi Identities." *Modern China* 23, no. 3 (July 1997): 298–327.

Whyte, Bob. *Unfinished Encounter: China and Christianity.* Harrisburg, Pa.: Morehouse Publishing, 1988.

Wolf, Margery. *Revolution Postponed: Women in Contemporary China.* Stanford: Stanford University Press, 1985.

Wong, L., and S. MacPherson, eds. *Social Change and Social Policy in Contemporary China.* Averbury: Aldershot, 1995.

Wright, Arthur F. *Buddhism in Chinese History.* Stanford: Stanford University Press, 1959.

Wright, Mary Clabaugh, ed. *China in Revolution: The First Phase, 1900–1913.* New Haven: Yale University Press, 1968.

Wu, Lien-teh. *The Plague Fighter: The Autobiography of a Modern Chinese Physician Wu Lien-teh.* Cambridge: University of Cambridge Press, 1959.

Wu, Qiang, ed. *Dongbei lunxian shisi nian jiaoyu shiliao, di 1 ji* (Materials on educational history during fourteen years of occupation in the Northeast Region, no. 1). Changchun: Jilin jiaoyu chubanshe, 1989.

Wu, Yanyin, et al. *Zuijin sanshiwunian zhi Zhongguo jiaoyu* (Chinese education in the last thirty-five years). Shanghai: Shangwu yishuguan, 1931.

Wusi shiqi de shetuan (The social organizations during the period of the May Fourth Movement). Beijing: Sanlian shudian, 1979.

Xiao, Di, ed. *Jiachui xiansong zai chuncheng* (Teaching and studying in Kunming). Kunming: Yunnan renmin chubanshe, 1986.

Xiong, Mingan. *Zhongguo Gaodeng jiaoyushi* (A history of Chinese higher education). Chongqing: Chongqing chubanshe, 1983.

Xu, Youchun, et al., eds. *Minguo renwu da cidian* (Dictionary of Republican biography). Shijiazhuang: Hebei renmin chubanshe, 1991.

Xuan, Haoping, ed. *Dazhong yuwen lunzhan* (The debate over the popular language and literature). Shanghai: Qizhi shuju, 1935.

Yamamoto, Sumiko. *Chūgoku Kirisutokyo shi kenkyu: Purotesutanto no "dochakuka" o choshin to shite* (Studies on the history of Christianity in China: with special reference to the "indigenization" of Protestant Churches in the first half of the twentieth century). Tokyo: Tokyo Daigaku Shuppankai, 1972.

Yanan Shishi wenti yanjiuhui, ed. *Riben diguo zhuyu zai Zhongguo lunxianqu* (Japanese imperialism in occupied territories of China). Shanghai: Shanghai renmin chubanshe, 1958.

Yang, Chonglong. *Yunnan jiaoyu wenti yanjiu* (Research on Yunnan's educational problems). Kunming: Yunnan jiaoyu chubanshe, 1995.

Yang, Deguang, and Xinghuo Jin, eds. *Zhongguo gaodeng jiaoyu gaige de shijian yu fazhan qushi* (The practice and development trends of the higher education reform in China). Shanghai: Tongji daxue chubanshe, 1990.

Yang, Dennis Tao. "Education and Off-Farm Work." *Economic Development and Cultural Change* 45, no. 3 (April 1997): 613–32.

Yang, Martin C. *A Chinese Village: Taitou, Shandong Province.* London: Kegan Paul, 1947.

Ye, Lan. "Shidai jingshen yu xin jiaoyu lixiangde goujian" (The moral symbol of a new era and the construction of a new educational ideal). *Jiaoyu yanjiu,* no. 10 (1994).

Yeh, Wen-hsin. *The Alienated Academy: Culture and Politics in Republican China, 1919–1937.* Cambridge: Harvard University Press, 1990.

Yi Tao wei shi, xian shen jiaoyu (Learn from Tao, dedicate your life to education). Nanjing: Nanjingshi jiaoyu xuehui, 1990.

Yip, Ka-che. *Health and National Reconstruction in Nationalist China: The Development of Modern Health Services, 1928–1937.* Ann Arbor: Association for Asian Studies, Monograph and Occasional Paper Series no. 50, 1995.

———. *Religion, Nationalism, and Chinese Students: The Anti-Christian Movement of 1922–1927.* Bellingham: Western Washington University Press, 1980.

Yoshimi, Takeuchi. *Nippon to Ajia: Takeuchi Yoshimi hyoronsho daisankan* (Japan and Asia, vol. 3: Collected essays of Takeuchi Yoshimi). Tokyo: Chikuma Shobō, 1966.

Yuan, Zheng. *Zhonghua wenhua tongzhi: xuexiao zhi* (Comprehensive annals on Chinese culture: the school gazetteer). Shanghai: Shanghai renmin chubanshe, 1997.

Zakon Rossiiskoy Federatsii ob obpazovanii (Russian Federation law on education). Moscow: Novaya shkola Press, 1992.

Zhang, Bin. *Cong Zhejiang kan Zhongguo jiaoyu jindaihua* (Study on the modernization of education in China from the case of Zheijiang province). Guangzhou: Guangdong Jiaoyu chubanshe, 1996.

Zhang, Jian, ed. *Zhongguo jiaoyu de fangzhen yu zhengce yanjiu* (Research on political line and policies in Chiense education). Beijing: Zhongguo jiaoyu chubanshe, 1992.

Zhang, Li, and Jiantang Liu. *Zhongguo jiao'an shi* (A History of Anti-Christian incidents in China). Chengdu: Sichuan Sheng Shehui Kexueyuan Chubanshe, 1987.

Zhang, Ling. "Jiaoyu mudi ziwo shixian shi qiantan" (An elementary investigation of self-realization theory as an educational goal). *Jiaoyu lilun yu shixian* 9, no. 2 (1989).

Zhang, Longhua, et al., eds. *Zhongguo yuwen jiaoyu shigang* (An outline of the history of language and literature education in China). Changsha: Hunan shifan daxue chubanshe, 1991.

Zhang, Lu, ed. *Zhang Zonglin xiangcun jiaoyu lunji* (Zhang Zonglin's selected works on rural education). Changsha: Hunan jiaoyu chubanshe, 1987.

Zhang, Tongshan. "Luelun ren shi zhuti yu ketide tongyi" (A discussion on the unity of a human being as a subject and an object). *Jiaoyu yanjiu,* no. 2 (1990).

Zhang, Wusheng. "Jiaoyu yu rende fazhande jige wenti" (Several issues concerning the relation of education to the development of human beings). *Jiaoyu yanjiu,* no. 11 (1989).

Zhang, Xianwen, et al. *Zhonghua Minguo shigang* (An outline history of the Republic of China). Zhengzhou: Henan renmin chubanshe, 1985.

Zhang, Zhidong, et al. *Zouding xuetang zhangcheng* (Memorials determining school regulations). 1904. Reprint. Taibei: Jindai Zhongguo shiliao congkan, 723–24, 1972.

Zhao, Erxun, et al. *Qingshi gao* (Draft history of the Qing dynasty). Beijing: Zhonghua shuju, 1976.

Zhao, Hongchun. *Jindai zhongxiyi lunzheng shi* (History of the modern controversy between Western and Chinese medicine). Shijiazhuan: 1982.

Zheng, Lansun (Zuyin), et al., eds. *Fujian xinhai guangfu shiliao* (Historical materials on the Xinhai Revolution in Fujian). Liancheng, Fujian: Jianguo chubanshe, 1940.

Zheng, Xiaoyun. "Dangdai Xishuangbanna Daizu shehui wenhua bianyi yanjiu" (Research on the changes of the culture and society of the Dai nationality in present Sipsong Panna). *Shehuixue yanjiu* (Sociological research), no. 1.

Zhili di yi nuzi shifan xuexiao xiaoyou hui huibao (Journal of the Alumni Association of Zhili First Women's Normal School). (1915–17).

Zhonggong Tianjin shi weidang shi ziliao zhengji weiyuanhui and Tianjin shi funü lianhe hui, eds. *Deng Yingchao yu Tianjin zaoqi funü yundong* (Deng Yingchao and Tianjin's early women's movement). Beijing: Zhongguo funü chubanshe, 1987.

Zhonggong zhnogyang bangong ting, ed. *Zhongguo nongcun de shehui zhuyi gaochao: xuanben* (Socialist high tide in China's villages: selections). Beijing: Renmin chubanshe, 1956.

Zhongguo dier lishi dangan guan, comp. *Zhonghua Minguo shi dangan ziliao huibian* (Collection of archival materials on republican Chinese history), vol. 2. Nanjing: Jiangsu renmin chubanshe, 1981.

Zhongguo funü yundong wenxian ziliao huibian (A collection of documents on the Chinese women's movement. Beijing: Zhongguo funü chubanshe, 1988.

Zhongguo jiaoyu gaige he fazhan wenxian xuanbian (The selected documents of the reform and development of China's education). Beijing: Renmin jiaoyu chubanshe, 1993.

Zhongguo jiaoyu nianjian bianji bu, ed. *Zhongguo jiaoyu nianjian, 1949–1984* (Chinese educational yearbook, 1949–1989). Beijing: Zhongguo dabaike quanshu chubanshe, 1984.

Zhongguo shehui kexueyuan jindaishi yanjiusuo, comp. *Xinhai geming shiqi qikan jieshao* (An introduction to periodicals published around the time of the 1911 Revolution). Beijing: Renmin chubanshe, 1982, 1983, 1986, 1987.

Zhongguo tongji nianjian 1993 (Statistical yearbook of China, 1993). Beijing: Zhongguo tongji chubanshe, 1993.

Zhonghua jiaoyu gaijin she, comp. *Zhongguo jiaoyu tongji gailan* (General overview of China's educational statistics). Shanghai: 1923.

Zhonghua quanguo funü lianhe hui funü yundong lishi yanjiu shi, ed. *Zhongguo jindai funü yundong lishi ziliao, 1840–1918* (Materials on the history of the women's movement in modern China). Beijing: Zhongguo funü chubanshe, 1991.

Zhonghua quanguo funü lianhehui, comp. *Wusi shiqi funü wenti wenxuan* (Selected writings on the woman question during the May Fourth period). Beijing: Sanlian shudian, 1981.

Zhonghua quanguo funü lianhehui, comp. *Zhonguo funü yundong shi* (A history of the Chinese women's movement). Beijing: Chunqiu chubanshe, 1989.

Zhonghua renmin gongheguo jiaoyubu gongnong jiaoyusi, ed. *Gongnong jiaoyu wenxian huibian, nongmin jiaoyu* (Compendium of documents on worker-peasant education, peasant education). Beijing: N.p., 1979.

Zhou, Guping. *Jindai xifang jiaoyu lilun zai Zhongguo de chuanbo* (The spread of Western educational theories in China in modern times). Guangzhou: Guangdong Jiaoyu chubanshe, 1996.

Zhou, Haobo. "Shilun jiaoyu guochengzhong de ertong zhutixing" (On the subject nature of children in the process of education). *Jiaoyu yanjiu*, no. 6 (1989).

Zhou, Jiangqiang, ed., *Xifang nüxing zhuyi yanjiu pingjie* (An analytical Introduction of Western feminisms). Beijing: Sanlian shudian, 1995.

Zhu, Shoupeng, comp. *Guangxuchao donghualu* (East Gate chronicle of the Emperor Guangxu's reign). Beijing: Zhonghua shuju, 1958.

Zhu, Xiaoman. "Qinggan jiaoyude yishi jiqi teshu jizhi" (The sense and mechanism of emotional education). *Jiaoyu yanjiu*, no. 7 (1993).

Zhu, Youxian, et al., eds. *Zhongguo jindai xuezhi shiliao* (Historical materials on the modern Chinese educational system). Shanghai: Huadong shifan daxue chubanshe, 1985.

Zhu, Zhimin. "Jin xiandai zhongguode jiaoyu yu 'Wusi' " (Modern education in China and the May Fourth Movement). *Jiaoyu yanjiu*, no. 6 (1989).

"Zouping xian jiaoyuzhi" bianzuan lingdao xiaozu, ed. *Zouping xian jiaoyuzhi* (Zouping county education gazetteer). Jinan: Shandong sheng chuban zongshe, 1990.

Contributors

Paul Bailey is Reader in East Asian History, University of Edinburgh.

Nina Y. Borevskaya is Leading Researcher, Institute of the Far East, Russian Academy of Sciences, Moscow.

David K. K. Chan is Associate Professor, Department of Applied Social Studies, City University of Hong Kong.

Dan Cui has a Ph.D. degree from the London School of Economics and is currently affiliated with the Joint Centre on Asia Pacific Studies, University of Toronto, and York University.

Ryan Dunch is Assistant Professor, Department of History and Classics, University of Alberta.

Gang Ding is Professor and Dean of the Faculty of Educational Science and Technology, East China Normal University.

Mette Halskov Hansen is Associate Professor, Department of East European and Oriental Languages, University of Oslo.

Ruth Hayhoe is Director, Hong Kong Institute of Education, formerly Professor at the Ontario Institute for Studies in Education, University of Toronto.

Ping-Chun Hsiung is Associate Professor, Department of Sociology, University of Toronto.

Sarah Coles McElroy earned her Ph.D. degree at Yale University and has recently taught at Yale University, Boston College, and Smith College.

Ka-Ho Mok is Associate Professor, Department of Public and Social Administration, City University of Hong Kong.

Yutaka Otsuka is Professor in the Graduate School of International Development, Nagoya University.

Glen Peterson is Associate Professor, Department of History, University of British Columbia.

Douglas R. Reynolds is Professor of Chinese and Japanese History, Georgia State University in Atlanta.

Heidi Ross is Associate Professor of Education and Director of Asia Studies, Colgate University.

Stig Thøgersen is Associate Professor of Chinese Language and Society, Department of East Asian Studies, University of Aarhus.

Zheng Yuan is Professor, Department of Education, South China Normal University.

Ningsha Zhong received her Ph.D. degree at the Ontario Institute for Studies in Education, University of Toronto, and is currently affiliated with University of Toronto.

Index